The Art
of
the Essay

The Art of the Essay

Second Edition

edited by Leslie Fiedler

STATE UNIVERSITY OF NEW YORK AT BUFFALO

Thomas Y. Crowell Company
New York   Established 1834

Designed by Barbara Kohn Isaac

Manufactured in the United States of America

Preface to the Second Edition

The ambitions of this collection remain pretty much the same this second time around, though the total size of it has shrunk a little. It still begins with the prototype of the essay in Montaigne and ends with examples of current modes; but a few particularly long-winded selections of first excellence (including Hawthorne's witty and winning, "The Custom House") have been cut, along with some more recent pieces which simply do not hold up on re-examination. These excisions have made room for a larger representation of quite contemporary writing, especially by those authors who have come to seem, over the last decade or so, prophets and sages, whether to the young or the mass media, or both: for instance, Norman O. Brown, Buckminster Fuller, Marshall McLuhan, and Charles Olson.

I have also re-edited rather drastically the section on Mass Culture, which was a pioneering effort ten years ago but has now become a standard feature in all similar collections. Nonetheless, it remains a subject of great interest, not only in itself, but also as a source of continuing good writing in the field of the essay. And so I have dropped and added to suit new directions and new tastes, especially my own, without, however, cutting down the total number of pages or the proportionate bulk of the section in the whole volume.

Nothing is more vain, I know, than pursuing fashion; but nothing more delightful either—as long as one retains that modicum of detachment and irony so essential to all pursuits, and not least to the making of anthologies.

L.F.

BUFFALO, N.Y., 1969

Preface to the First Edition

This is intended to be more than another book of readings for the introductory composition course, though there is nothing in it which a freshman could not read with (one hopes) profit and enjoyment. It is also, and especially, a collection of essays aimed at making clear what the essay at its best *is*. Though not historically exhaustive, it covers the whole field from Montaigne to the present, and is arranged to illustrate the shifting uses of the form without ever losing sight of its essential function of exploring the self. Such a collection seems capable of providing the beginning writer with pertinent models at every stage, and offers new possibilities to the teacher interested in using readings as more than occasions for classroom bull-sessions. The selections from the classic essay are balanced by a wide representation of contemporary work, much of it bearing on the field of mass culture where the student is most at home. At no point has a desire to be representative been allowed to dictate the reprinting of essays which do not meet the highest standards for style and theme. Only the *living* essay, whatever the date of its composition, has been included.

Although this anthology is not intended as a full demonstration of all the uses of prose, our definition of the essay, for reasons made apparent elsewhere, is extremely broad: it includes letters; sections carved out of longer prose works; at least one selection that would ordinarily be classified as a short story; and, indeed, one selection that was not formally written out at all and is an *ex tempore* radio talk. Exercise questions make the student aware of such departures from the usual essay form and require comment on them.

The exercise questions—about six for each selection, nearly all of them requiring an essay type of answer—are designed for several purposes. Just as a good many of the essays have been selected because they are natural foils to one another, so many of the questions ask the student to make comparisons among various essays. Some questions try to help the student understand the logic of the essay. Still others try to get him to see the basic assumptions and values of the author. Finally, and perhaps most importantly: a number of questions introduce the student to the rudiments of *literary* analysis—they require him to pay attention to such things as the author's tone, organization of his material, and rhetorical devices (for example, the kinds of metaphors that are used). The various types of questions allow the teacher a good deal of flexibility and enable him to concentrate on what his students need most.

L.F.

Missoula, Montana 1958

Contents

Part IV The Discovery of High Culture   345

The Art of the Essay

Part One

The
Discovery of the Self

The essay begins, as we have had occasion to remark, with the discovery of the self. At the start of the modern period, somewhere, that is to say, between the full flowering of the Renaissance and the eruption of the French Revolution, a tendency develops to replace at the highest levels of art such older *objective* forms as epic and tragedy with the more *subjective* ones, lyric, autobiography, novel and essay. As the middle classes succeed in taking over from the aristocracy culturally as well as politically and economically, inwardness and personality (what is called in fiction "character") become the chief concerns of literature; the interest of thinking and reading men shifts from what is representative in a given person, what he stands for in terms of a class, to what is peculiar in him: to his individuality rather than his humanity. Though verse persists, of course, prose more and more becomes the favored instrument for exploring the newly defined self.

Michel de Montaigne is usually credited with the invention of the tentative, exploratory form we call the essay, whose essential subject is always the self, though the avowed occasion of each of his pieces (declared in the titles) may be variously Riches, Pride, War, Love, etc. Certainly, it was Montaigne who perfected first an urbane, ironical, skeptical point of view, which excludes no reader; a meditative, wide-ranging, versatile style; a moderate, self-deprecatory tone; a gentle-

1

manly show of knowledgeability capable of quotation and allusion without pedantry. The feel of his work is something midway between that of an overheard conversation of a man with himself and of the confidence of one friend to another in a world where a code of courtesy protects us from embarrassing revelations and tedious insistence upon a point. From him in a direct line descend all essayists who remain essentially autobiographers, all explorers of the self, who seek clues to that self directly in their own lives and the trivial details of their daily routines. It is with this kind of essay, in its various developments, that the first part of this book is concerned.

Although Montaigne finds one fascinating emulator in Jean Jacques Rousseau, elsewhere in Europe after his time the essay appears on the verge of losing forever the intimacy and directness which are its *raison d'être*. It achieves a success which comes close to killing the form; for with the invention of the magazine in the eighteenth century, the essay seems for a while on the verge of becoming the favorite reading matter of those who read at all. It is difficult for us now to turn with real pleasure to the work of the first generations of professional literary journalists: the elegant and playful or the formal and didactic essays of the age of Addison and Steele and Dr. Johnson; though, indeed, they remained until only yesterday (still, I suppose, remain in some quarters) required reading for bored and hostile high-school students. Some of the essayists of the eighteenth century were men of talent, some even of genius; but so concerned were they to "instruct and delight," according to the best critical principles of the time, that they lost the secret of directly revealing the self, and became merely fashionable, the prey of changing modes in style and diction. In such circumstances, the autobiographical essay, the very essence of the genre, tends to disappear under a flood of instructive and witty pieces on dueling, novel-reading and the nature of the fancy. Meanwhile, the speaking voice, the conversational tone is lost everywhere beneath the long, carefully balanced periods and the embroidery of classical allusions.

There are no examples from the first period of the triumph of the magazine included in this collection; but the interested reader may find it fruitful to look at the essays of, say, James Boswell, printed in his magazine *The Hypochondriack,* pieces on such subjects as love and drinking (on which he spoke with special authority), and to compare them with the candid and spontaneous record of his journals. They provide a contrast, typical of the age, between a private response to experience, sensitive and alive, and a public formalization of that response, essentially cold and dead, however witty. In the nineteenth century, the situation grew, on the whole, even worse, as a growing gentility imposed tighter and tighter restrictions, and wit itself turned into whimsy and downright cuteness. By and large, it is in the letters and diaries of the period, where less artificial constraint comes between the writer and his self, that we must seek a continuing tradition of the essay, driven underground but not extinguished completely; and the interested reader, if still interested, can find examples in, say, the correspondence of Byron.

It is, at any rate, to the letter and the journal that the better essayists of our own century turn to learn their trade and find their tone, to establish an unbroken link with the founders of the form. From Addison and Steele, they can derive nothing; there is more life even in the characteristic patterns of malicious, feminine gossip, of the sort which provides a lively model for Gertrude Stein's pretended autobiography of her companion, Alice B. Toklas. The cultured literary spite with which (in the name of Miss Toklas) Miss Stein dissects Ernest Hemingway gives us finally a real glimpse into Miss Stein herself (whether her account is true to its avowed subject doesn't matter; it is true to her), her Paris ménage, the world of artists and writers which she inhabited and in part helped form.

At any rate, the possibilities are enormous, once the misleading goals of genteel reticence and high finish are renounced. They range from the almost naked confession of Fitzgerald's meditation on his own crackup, which seems more a cry of anguish than a work of art, to the almost fictional organization of Dylan Thomas's piece, which seems well on the way to becoming a short story. Quite similar materials can be treated in quite different ways; childhood, for instance, being rendered by Thomas in terms of pathos and humor, and turned into near-melodrama by Graham Greene in "Revolver in the Cupboard." The essay reveals, not only by the facts it alludes to, but by its rhythms, its metaphors, its very language, which are also aspects of the self, sometimes more truly the self, it would seem, than remembered details of a life. It is not uncharacteristic of our age that humor and melodrama, pathos and irony, still held together in a writer like Rousseau, are apt to fall apart—into, say, Perelman and Graham Greene, with, doubtless, a loss on both sides. Occasionally, however, a writer like James Baldwin will manage to put the dissociated elements of a whole view of the self back together again. It is this ability to see ironically *around* the self as well as pathetically *into* the self which keeps Baldwin from the fault of self-pity, and which prevents him from turning his account into a stereotype of the Difficulties of the Negro Abroad.

These essays contain not only revelations of the self, but of the society in which the self is defined: In Stein, a view of expatriate society nourished by the transatlantic prosperity of the years after World War I; in Fitzgerald, a glimpse of the same society fallen from ebullience to melancholy after the Depression had brought its bright, young men home; in Baldwin, a sense of the post-World War II West, confronting a basic shift in the relations of white and colored peoples. Yet in each of these essays, the writer reaches for a particular rather than a typical self, for an inwardness not explicable in social terms alone.

The reader will find present in these essays, if not everywhere at least frequently enough, one common conviction beneath all the differences of form and tone and theme; and this common conviction he may find a useful guide in beginning his own writing in the essay. It is the belief that the essential clue to the self lies not so much in the society outside the man as in the child within him. The Wordsworthian notion that the child is father to the man, strengthened by the teaching of Freud about the importance of infantile desires and delusions, moves many at least of these essayists, whose typical motion is back through time: from more recent events to the last recapturable moment of the past. Like Thomas remembering a childhood visit, Graham Greene recalling a first vision of violence and evil, they search for those deep experiences which give a pattern and significance to what follows. The clue to the self seems to them what Greene calls in the title of his collection of essays "The Lost Childhood," the lost, original, selfhood; and the search for the self becomes the search for the child one was, and in some disconcertingly essential way, still is.

1. Of Presumption

MICHEL DE MONTAIGNE

Michel Eyquem de Montaigne (1533–1592) invented the form as well as the name of the essay. One to whom skepticism seemed the only civilized way of regarding the world, and to whom the self was the only ultimately rewarding subject, he has so completely written himself down in three volumes of essays that it seems impertinent for anyone else to try to describe his life. In a time of brutal religious and national struggles, he maintained a sweet detachment and equanimity, a gentle irony in regard to himself and his world that makes him the model for all succeeding essayists to whom the form seems a vital aspect of civilized living.

But to come to my own particular case, I think it would be very difficult to find a man who has a smaller opinion than I have of myself.

I regard myself as a very ordinary person, except in this respect, that I do regard myself in that light. I plead guilty to the meanest and commonest defects; I neither disclaim nor excuse them. The only value that I set upon myself is that I know my own value.

If I have any vainglory, it is superficially poured upon me, through the treachery of my nature, and has not so much body that my judgement can perceive it; I am sprinkled but not dyed with it.

For indeed, with regard to intellectual achievements of any kind, I never produced anything that filled me with satisfaction. And the approval of others does not repay me. My taste is delicate and hard to please, and especially with regard to my own work. I continually repudiate myself, and feel myself at all times fluctuating and bending by reason of my weakness. I have nothing of my own that satisfies my judgement. My sight is clear and normal enough, but when at work it becomes blurred.

This I experience most evidently in the case of poetry. I am extremely

SOURCE: E. J. Trenchmann, ed., *The Essays of Michel de Montaigne* (London: Oxford University Press, 1927), pp. 80–113. Reprinted by permission.

fond of it, and I can form a pretty good judgement of others' work; but when I try to set my hand to it I am indeed but a child, and the result is something I cannot tolerate. We may play the fool in anything else, but not in poetry:

> For Gods and men and booksellers refuse
> To countenance a mediocre Muse. (Horace.)

Would to Heaven that these lines were inscribed over the doors of all our printers' shops, to forbid the entrance of so many versifiers!

> None more conceited than a sorry poet. (Martial.)

Why are not our people like this? Dionysius the father valued nothing of his so highly as his poetry. At the season of the Olympian games, with chariots surpassing all others in magnificence, he also sent poets and musicians to present his verses, together with tents and pavilions royally gilt and tapestried. When they began to recite his lines, the charm and excellence of the delivery at first attracted the attention of the people; but after considering the inanity of the composition, they first showed disdain, then, becoming more and more exasperated, they soon fell into a fury and angrily rushed his tents and tore them all in pieces. And when his chariots failed to make a show in the races, and the vessel which carried back his people missed the coast of Sicily and was driven before the gale and dashed against the rocks at Tarentum, they took it for a certain sign that the gods, like themselves, were incensed against the badness of his poem. And even the sailors who escaped from the shipwreck backed up the opinion of the people, with which also the oracle that predicted his death seemed in some sort to agree.

This was to the effect 'that Dionysius should be near his end when he had vanquished those who were better than himself'. These he interpreted to be the Carthaginians, whose forces were greater than his own. Being at war with them he often dodged the victory, or qualified it, in order not to incur the fate intended by that oracle. But he misunderstood it; for the God was thinking of the occasion when, by favour and injustice, he gained the advantage at Athens over the tragic poets who were better than he, and in competition with whom he had his play, called 'The Leneians',[1] acted. He died immediately after this victory, partly in consequence of the excessive joy he felt at his success.

[1] Not quite accurate. The play had another name, but was acted at the Leneian games. As to Dionysius's death, it was not the excessive joy, but the deep potations with which he celebrated his victory, that brought it on.

What I find tolerable in my own work is not so really and in itself, but by comparison with other and worse things which I observe to be well received. I envy the happiness of those who are able to rejoice and find a satisfaction in their productions; for that is an easy way of indulging oneself, since the source of our pleasure is in ourselves, especially if we are strong in our self-conceit.

I know a poet against whom everybody, the strong and the weak, in the crowd and in the chamber, against whom heaven and earth cry out that he is no poet. For all that he will not abate a jot of the measure to which he has cut himself; ever beginning again, ever persisting, ever reconsidering, he is all the stronger and more stubborn in his good opinion of himself for being the only one who holds it.

My works are so far from pleasing me that, as often as I peruse them, so often do they annoy me:

> When I re-read I blush at what I've written;
> For many things I see when even I,
> Being judge, account but fit to be erased. (Ovid.)

I have always an idea in my mind, a sort of blurred picture, which shows me, as in a dream, a better form than that I have framed; but I cannot grasp it and turn it to account. And yet that idea is but on a middle plane. From this I conclude that the productions of those great and fertile minds of the past are very far beyond the utmost stretch of my imagination and desire. Their writings not only satisfy me to the full, but they excite my astonished and rapturous admiration. I see and appreciate their beauty, if not so far as they are capable of being appreciated, at least so far that I cannot possibly aspire to equal them.

Whatever I take in hand, I owe a sacrifice to the Graces, as Plutarch says of some one, to conciliate their favour:

> If anything should please that I indite,
> Into men's minds if it infuse delight,
> I owe it to the charming Graces. (Poet unknown.)

But they always leave me in the lurch. All that I write is rude; it lacks grace and beauty. I am unable to make the most of things. My style adds nothing to the matter.[2] Therefore I need a strong matter, with plenty of

---

[2] A commentator points out that Montaigne here seems to flatly contradict what he said in another place: 'Do not look to the matter, but to the shape that I give it. My humour is to regard the form more than the substance.'

grip, and one that shines by its own light. When I take up a popular theme and one of a more sprightly nature, I do so in obedience to my own instinct, as I do not affect a solemn and gloomy wisdom, like the world in general; to enliven myself, not my style, which is rather suited to a grave and austere subject (at least if I may call that a style which is a way of speaking without form or rule, a popular jargon, proceeding without definitions, without divisions, without conclusions, hazy, like that of Amafanius and Rabirius).[3]

I can neither please, nor delight, nor tickle. The best story in the world becomes dull and dry by my handling. I can only speak in real earnest and am entirely without that facility which I observe in many of my friends of entertaining any chance people and keeping a whole company amused, or of holding the attention of a prince with all kinds of small talk, without boring him. Those people never run short of matter, by reason of their gift in laying hold of the first that comes to hand, and adapting it to the humour and capacity of those they are talking with.

Princes are not very fond of serious talk; nor am I of telling stories. The first and most obvious arguments which are usually the most readily accepted, I am unable to hit upon; a poor preacher for the gentry! When once I start a subject I am apt to exhaust it.

Cicero thinks that in philosophical treatises the most difficult part is the exordium. If that be so, I confine myself to the conclusion.

And yet we must tune the string to every kind of note; and the sharpest is that which comes least often into play. It needs at least as much perfection to develop an empty theme as to sustain a weighty one. At times one needs to handle a matter superficially, at other times to dig deeply into it. I know well that most people keep to that lower stage, being unable to see beneath the outer rind. But I also know that the greatest masters, both Xenophon and Plato, often unbend and employ that lower and popular manner of speaking and treating of matters, enhancing them however with the charm that never fails them.

Now in my style there is no ease and polish; it is harsh and disdainful, disposed to be free and unrestrained. And as such it flatters my inclination, if not my judgement. But I am very sensible of the fact that I sometimes allow myself to go too far, and that by endeavoring to avoid art and affectation, I drop into them on another side:

---

[3] Two men mentioned by Cicero. The former was one of the earlier Roman writers of the Epicurean school. Of the latter nothing is known.

I grow obscure in trying to be brief. (Horace.)

Plato says that length and brevity are not qualities that either take from or give value to style.

I could not, though I tried, attain to that even, smooth and correct style of other writers. And, although the concise and rhythmic style of Sallust best suits my humour, yet I find Caesar both greater and less easy to copy. And if my inclination prompts me rather to imitate the style of Seneca, I have yet a higher estimation of that of Plutarch.

As in doing, so also in speaking, I simply follow my natural bent; which is perhaps the reason why I am better at speaking than at writing. Movement and action put life into words, especially with those who, like me, move briskly and become heated. Demeanour, face, voice, attitude, and the gown may set off a speech, which in itself is mere twaddle. Messala complains, in Tacitus, of some tight garments or other worn in his time, and of the arrangement of the benches from which the orators had to speak, and which impaired their eloquence.

My French is corrupt, both in pronunciation and in other respects, through the barbarism of my native place. I have never known a man of the hither provinces [4] whose native speech did not show a very perceptible twang, and offend purely French ears. Not however that I am very expert in my Périgord patois, for I can speak it no better than I can German. Nor do I much care; for (like the other dialects around me, going from district to district, those of Poitou, Saintonge, Angoumois, Limoges, and Auvergne) it is a languid, drawling, long-winded language.

There is certainly above us, towards the mountains, a Gascon dialect which I consider singularly fine, blunt, concise, expressive, and indeed a more virile and soldier-like language than any I know; as sinewy, forcible, and direct as the French is graceful, neat, and fluent.

As for Latin, which was given me for my mother-tongue, I have, through want of practice, lost the ready use of it in speaking; nay, in writing too, though at one time I could be called a master-hand at it. There you may see how much I fall short in that direction.

Beauty is a highly commendable quality in human intercourse. It is the first means of winning the favour of other people, and no man is so barbarous and surly as not to feel the attraction of it in some degree. The body has a great part in our being, and holds an eminent place in it;

[4] i.e., south of the Charente, the boundary of the Languedoc.

hence its structure and composition are well worthy of consideration.

They are to blame who would disunite our two principal parts and keep them apart. They should on the contrary be coupled and joined together. We should bid the soul, not to stand aside and entertain herself alone, not to despise and forsake the body (nor can she do so, except by some pretence and hypocrisy), but to become allied with him, to embrace him, cherish him, assist him, control him, advise him, correct him and bring him back when he goes astray; in short marry him and become his spouse, that they may not appear to be pulling in different and opposite directions, but to live together in unity and harmony.

Christians have a particular instruction concerning this bond. For they know that the divine justice embraces this union and fellowship of body and soul, to the extent of making the body capable of everlasting rewards; and that God looks at the actions of the whole man, and wills that he shall receive, as one whole, his punishment or his wage, according to his deserts.

The Peripatetic school, of all sects the most sociable, makes this the sole care of Wisdom, to provide for and procure the common good of these two associated parts. And they point out that the other sects, through not giving sufficient consideration to this admixture, took sides, one for the body, another for the soul, with equal error on both sides; and that they lost sight of their subject, which is Man, and their guide, which they generally admit to be Nature.

It is probable that the first of human distinctions, and the first consideration which gave to some men a pre-eminence over others, was the advantage of beauty:

> They portioned out their flocks and fields
> And gave to each according to his beauty,
> Or strength or sense. For beauty was prized,
> And strength was valued. (Lucretius.)

Well, I am a little below the middle height. This is not only an ugly defect, but it is also a disadvantage, especially in those who are in office and command. For the authority given by a fine presence and bodily dignity is lacking. C. Marius was unwilling to enlist soldiers under six feet.

The Courtier [5] is quite right when, in the gentleman he is training, he

---

[5] *The Courtier;* see vol. i., p. 286.

prefers a moderate stature rather than any other; and objects to anything unusual that would make him too noticeable. But if he fails to be of the right middle height, I should prefer, in a military man, that he should exceed it.

Little men, says Aristotle, are very pretty, but not handsome; and as a great soul connotes greatness, so a big and tall body connotes beauty. The Ethiopians and the Indians, he says, when they elected their kings or magistrates, had regard to the beauty and lofty stature of the candidates. They were right. For the sight of a tall and handsome leader marching at the head of his army inspires his followers with respect and his enemies with terror:

> Himself too Turnus, of surpassing mould.
> Amid the foremost moving, arms in hand,
> By a whole head o'ertops them. (Virgil.)

Our great, divine, and heavenly King, about whom everything should be carefully, religiously, and reverently remarked, did not despise bodily advantages: *thou art fairer than the children of men* (Psalms). And Plato desires beauty, as well as temperance and courage, in the guardians of his Republic.

It is very humiliating, if you are standing among your servants, to be addressed with the question, 'Where is your master?' and to receive only the fag-end of a salute made to your secretary or your barber. As happened to poor Philopoemen.[6] Being the first of his company to arrive at a house where he was expected, his hostess, who did not know him and received him rather coldly, made use of him to help her maids draw water and stir the fire against Philopoemen's coming. When the gentlemen of his suite appeared, and caught him busily engaged in this pleasant occupation (for he had not failed to obey the lady's orders), they asked him what he was doing there. 'I am paying the penalty of my ugliness,' he replied.

Other kinds of beauty are for the women; beauty of stature is the only beauty of man. When a man is small, neither a broad and round forehead, nor clear and soft eyes, nor an average nose, nor small ears and mouth, nor white and regular teeth, nor a thick, smooth, auburn beard, nor curly hair, nor a properly rounded head, nor a fresh complexion,

---

[6] The 1580 edition has Phocion, with the remark, 'I can easily mistake a name, but not the substance.'

nor a pleasant face, nor an odourless body, nor a correct symmetry of limbs, will make him handsome.

As to myself, I have a sturdy, thick-set figure; my face is full without being fat; my disposition between the jovial and the melancholy, moderately warm and sanguine;

> My legs are stiff with bristles,
> And hair is on my chest. (Martial.)

I enjoyed a robust and vigorous health until I was well on in years, and was rarely troubled by illness.

Such I was, for I am not portraying myself now that I have entered the avenues of old age, being long past forty:

> And now by slow degrees
> Years break my strength, my vigorous growth destroy,
> And drag me downward to a dull decay. (Lucretius.)

Henceforth I shall be only half a man, and no longer myself. I escape and steal away from myself every day:

> Then too the years they rob us, as they run,
> Of all things we delight in, one by one. (Horace.)

Skill and agility I have never had; and yet I am the son of a very nimble father, who retained his sprightliness to an extreme old age. He could scarcely find a man in his station of life to equal him in all bodily exercises; whilst I have hardly come across one who did not surpass me, except in running, at which I was middling good. Of music, either vocal, for which my voice is very ill-adapted, or instrumental, they could never teach me anything. In dancing, tennis, wrestling, I was never able to acquire more than a very slight and ordinary skill; in swimming, fencing, vaulting, and leaping, none at all.

My hands are so awkward, that I cannot even write legibly enough for myself; so that I prefer to re-write what I have scribbled rather than give myself the trouble of deciphering it.[7] And I can hardly read any better. I feel that I bore my listeners. Otherwise, a good scholar.[8] I can-

[7] On this point we can at least flatly contradict Montaigne. His handwriting, which is open to all the world to see, never gave anybody any trouble.

[8] A reminiscence of a well-known line of Marot, who, after enumerating all his vices and shortcomings, ends up with
Au demourant, le meilleur fils du monde,
'otherwise, the best son in the world.'

not fold a letter correctly, nor could I ever cut a pen, nor carve at table worth a rap, nor saddle and bridle a horse, nor properly carry a hawk and let it fly, nor speak with hound, hawk, or horse.

In short, my bodily and mental faculties are very much on a par. There is no briskness, only perfect strength and vigour. I can stand hard work, but only when it is voluntary, and as long as my desire prompts me,

> Where the zest and the sport
> Makes the labour seem light, and the long hours short. (Horace.)

Otherwise, unless I am allured by some pleasure, and have no guide except my free will and inclination, I am good for nothing. For I have arrived at that stage when, excepting health and life, there is nothing for which I would bite my nails and that I would purchase at the price of mental torment and constraint:

> For all the sands and all the golden wealth
> That shady Tagus rolls into the sea. (Juvenal.)

Extremely idle, extremely independent, both by nature and habit, I would as willingly lend my blood as my pains.

I have a soul that belongs wholly to itself and is accustomed to go its own way. Having had, to this hour, neither master nor governor forced upon me, I have gone ahead as far as I pleased, and at my own pace. This has made me slack and unfit in the service of others, and of no use to any but myself.

And, as far as I am concerned, there was no need to force my heavy, lazy, and do-nothing disposition. For, having enjoyed from my birth such a degree of fortune that I had reason to be satisfied with it [a reason, however, which a thousand others of my acquaintance would rather have used as a plank over which to pass in quest of fortune, worries, and anxieties]; and being endowed with as much sense as I felt I had occasion for, I have neither sought nor taken anything:

> Fair winds we may not have, nor swelling sails,
> Yet neither have we always adverse gales.
> In strength, in worth, in influence, powers of mind,
> In rank and fortune though I were behind
> The very foremost, many yet there be
> That in their turn come lagging after me. (Horace.)

A sufficiency was all I needed to make me content; that, however, if rightly considered, implies a well-ordered state of mind, equally difficult in every station of life, and, as we see by experience, more often found with want than with plenty. Since, as with our other passions, the hunger for wealth is perhaps whetted more by its enjoyment than by its scarcity, and the virtue of moderation is rarer than that of patience. And all I needed was to enjoy in tranquility the good things that God in his bounty placed in my hands.

I have never fancied any kind of tiresome labour. I have hardly ever [9] had any but my own affairs to manage; or, if I have, it has been on condition of managing them at my own times and in my own way, when they were committed to me by people who trusted me, who knew me and did not hustle me. For expert horsemen will get some service out of even a restive and broken-winded nag.

Even in childhood my training was relaxed and free, and I was not subjected to a rigorous discipline. All this has produced in me a sensitive disposition that is impatient of anxieties; to such a degree that I prefer any losses or irregularities that concern me to be kept from my knowledge. I put down under the heading of my expenses what it costs me to feed and maintain my negligence:

> Poor is the house wherein there's not a deal
> Which masters never miss, and varlets steal. (Horace.)

I prefer not to take count of what I have, that I may be the less sensible of what I lose. I pray those that live with me, if they are wanting in attachment to me and treat me accordingly, to cheat me with all outward decency. For want of sufficient fortitude to endure the troubles, misfortunes, and crosses that we are liable to, and being unable to keep up the strain of regulating and managing my affairs, I leave myself entirely in the hands of Fortune, and to the best of my power foster this notion in myself, 'to be prepared for the worst in all things, and to resolve to bear that worst meekly and patiently.' For that alone do I strive; that is the aim to which I direct all my thoughts.

In the face of a danger I do not so much consider how I shall escape it as how little it matters whether I escape it or not. Even though I should succumb, what would it matter? Not being able to control events, I con-

[9] The editions previous to that of 1588 had 'never', which was altered to 'hardly ever' after Montaigne had been Mayor of Bordeaux for four years.

trol myself; and I adapt myself to them, if they do not adapt themselves
to me. I am hardly cunning enough to dodge Fortune, to escape from her
or to compel her, and wisely to direct and incline matters to serve my
purpose. Still less have I the patience to suffer the hard and painful
anxiety needed to do so. And the most painful position for me is to be
kept in suspense in urgent affairs, and tossed between fear and hope.

Deliberation, even in the most indifferent things, is a trouble to me;
and my mind is more put to it to suffer the various shocks and shakes of
doubt and deliberation than to settle down and acquiesce in any course
whatever, after the die is cast. My sleep has been disturbed by few passions; but the slightest deliberation will disturb it. So too, having the
choice of ways, I generally avoid the steep and slippery hill-side, and
take the high road, however deep the mud, where I can sink no lower,
and feel secure. And I prefer a misfortune pure and simple, in which I
am no longer tormented and worried after feeling certain that it cannot
be mended; and which at the first push plunges me directly into
suffering:

The ills that plague me most are those half-known. (Seneca.)

When a thing has happened, I bear myself like a man; when it has to
be carried through, like a boy. The dread of falling throws me into a
greater fever than the fall itself. The game is not worth the candle. The
miser suffers more from his passion than the pauper, and the jealous
man than the cuckold. And it is often better to lose your vineyard than
to go to law about it. The lowest step is the firmest. There lies safety.
There you have need but of yourself. There it is grounded and rests
solely upon itself.

Is there not something philosophical in the attitude of a certain gentleman who was well-known? He married when he was well on in years,
having spent his youth in convivial company; moreover, great at telling
merry tales. Remembering how often he had had occasion to laugh at
others who 'wore the horns', he resolved to be safe and under cover, and
married a woman whom he picked up in a place where any man could
have what he needed for his money, and made a match of it with her.
'How d'ye do, Mistress Whore?'—'How d'ye do, Master Cuckold?'
And he was always ready to talk openly about his venture to anybody
who came to see him, and so took the wind out of the sails of any would-
be scandal-monger or tale-bearer, and the point off their sting.

With regard to ambition, which is neighbour, or rather daughter, to presumption, Fortune, to advance me, would have had to come and take me by the hand. For I could never have gone to any trouble for an uncertain hope, or submitted to all the difficulties which attend those who try to push themselves into favour at the beginning of their career:

> I will not purchase hope at any price. (Terence.)

I cling to what I see and have, and keep the harbour well in view:

> Into the sea one oar I plunge,
> And with the other rake the sands. (Propertius.)

And besides, we seldom advance very far unless we first risk what we have. And I am of opinion that if we have sufficient to keep up the state we are born and accustomed to, it is foolish to let it go in the uncertain hope of increasing it. The man to whom Fortune has denied a foothold and the means of settling down into a calm and peaceful life, may be excused if he risks what he has, since in any case necessity sends him out to seek a living:

> In evil we must take the boldest step. (Seneca.)

And I could more readily excuse a younger son for scattering his portion to the winds, than one who has the honor of his family in his keeping, and cannot become necessitous except by his own fault.

With the advice of my good friends in the past I have found the shorter and easier way of being rid of that ambition and sitting still:

> Who would not win the palm of victory
> Without the sweat and dust of the arena? (Horace.)

Besides, having a very sound judgement of my own powers, and knowing that I am not capable of great things, and remembering that saying of the late Chancellor Olivier that 'the French are like apes, climbing up a tree from branch to branch, and having reached the topmost bough, showing their backsides':

> 'Tis base to take a load one cannot bear,
> And, fainting 'neath it, bend the knee and yield. (Propertius.)

Even the irreproachable qualities I possess have been useless in this age. My easy-going ways would have been called slackness and weakness; my fidelity and conscientiousness would have been deemed scrupulous and squeamish, my frankness and independence troublesome, rash and inconsiderate.

Ill luck is of some good. It is not amiss to be born in a very depraved age; for, by comparison with others you may earn a cheap reputation for goodness. The man who in our days is only guilty of parricide and sacrilege is a good man, and an honourable:

> If now a friend do not deny a trust,
> If he restore a purse with all its rust,
> His faith is deemed prodigious, fit to be
> Enrolled in sacred books of Tuscany,
> Or celebrated by some sacrifice
> Of lambs with garlands decked. (Juvenal.)

And there never was a time and place when a ruler could expect a greater and more certain reward for goodness and justice. I shall be much mistaken if the first who makes it his business to push himself into favour and influence by that path, does not easily outstrip his fellows. Force and violence can do something, but not always everything.

We see tradesmen, village justices, artisans, holding their own with the nobles in valour and military knowledge. They give a good account of themselves both in public battles and in private combats; they fight, they defend cities in our wars. A Prince's special qualities are eclipsed in this crowd. Let him shine by his humanity, his truth, his loyalty, his moderation, and especially in his justice: marks rarely seen, unknown and banished. Only by the goodwill of the people can he carry out his functions; and no other qualities gain their affection as do those, being much more beneficial to them than the others. *There is nothing so popular as goodness* (Cicero).

By this standard [10] I should be as great and out of the common as I am dwarf-like and common by the standard of some of the past ages, when, if no other stronger qualities concurred, it was usual to find a man moderate in his revenge, slow to resent an insult, religiously scrupulous in keeping his word, neither double-faced nor cunning, nor accom-

[10] I.e., by comparing myself with my contemporaries.

modating his faith to others' wishes or to every occasion.[11] Rather would I allow a transaction to break its neck than twist my words in order to further it.

For, with regard to this new-fangled virtue of hypocrisy and dissimulation, which is now held in so great honour, I have a deadly hatred of it. Of all the vices I know of none that gives more evidence of a mean and craven spirit. It shows a cowardly and servile disposition to disguise ourselves and hide behind a mask, and not to dare to show ourselves as we are. By that means the men of our day train themselves to perfidy. Being accustomed to speak untruths, they make no scruple of breaking their word.

A generous heart should not belie its thoughts, but should be ready to show its inmost depths. It is either all good, or at least all human.

Aristotle regards it as the duty of a great soul to hate and love openly, to judge, to speak in all freedom, and, when the truth is in question, to pay attention to the approval or disapproval of others.

Apollonius said it was for slaves to lie, and for free men to speak truth.

That is the first and fundamental part of virtue. We must love her for herself. He who tells the truth because he is obliged to do so, and because it serves his turn, and who is not afraid of telling an untruth when it is of no importance to anybody, is not truthful enough.

My soul naturally abominates a lie, and hates even to think one. I feel an inward shame and pricking remorse if one happens to escape me, as sometimes it does, if the occasion is unexpected and I am taken unawares.

It is not always necessary to say everything; that would be foolishness. But what we say should be what we think; the contrary would be knavery. I do not know what advantage people expect who continually feign and dissemble, except it be not to be believed even when they speak the truth. That may deceive men once or twice, but to make a profession of secrecy, and to boast, as some of our rulers have done, 'that they would throw their shirt into the fire, if it were privy to their real intentions' (which was a saying of the ancient Metellus of Macedon); and 'that the man who cannot dissemble cannot rule',[12] is to warn

---

[11] By these words Montaigne originally intended to characterize himself. The earlier editions have: 'By this standard I should have been moderate in *my* revenge, &c.'

[12] A favourite saying of Louis XI. The other was also attributed to Charles VIII.

those who have to deal with them, that what they say is but lying and deceit. *The more artful and cunning a man is the more is he hated and suspected, when he loses his reputation for honesty* (Cicero).

A man would be very simple who allowed himself to be beguiled either by the looks or the words of one who relies upon never being the same outside and within, as Tiberius did. And I cannot see how such people can share in human transactions, as they never utter anything that can be accepted as current coin.

He who is disloyal to the truth is also disloyal to falsehood.

Those men of our time who, in drawing up the duties of a Prince,[13] considered only his advantage, without any regard for his good faith and conscience, might perhaps have been in the right, supposing the affairs of the Prince had been so disposed by Fortune that he could settle them once for all by a single breach of faith. But that is not the way things happen. He often has occasion to enter upon the same transaction. He has to draw up more than one peace, more than one treaty, in his life. The gain which allures him to the first breach of faith (and gain is almost always the end in view, as it is of every other kind of villainy; sacrilege, murder, rebellion, treachery, are all committed for profit of some kind or other), this first gain is followed by endless losses, and the Prince, after this example of his faithlessness, is barred from every opportunity of treating and negotiating.

When, during my boyhood, Solyman, of the Ottoman race, a race that is not over-scrupulous in the keeping of promises and pacts, after making a raid with his army on Otranto, was told that Mercurino de Gratinare and the inhabitants of Castro were kept prisoners after having surrendered the place, in contravention of the terms of capitulation, he sent word that they should be released; for, as he said, having some other great enterprises on hand in those parts, such a breach of faith, although it might appear to be a present gain, would in the future bring upon him a disrepute and distrust of infinite prejudice.

Now for my part, I would rather be a troublesome and indiscreet bore than a fawner and dissembler.

I allow that there may be a little touch of pride and obstinacy mixed with my integrity and candour, that takes no consideration of others. And methinks I tend to grow a little more outspoken where I should be less so, and that, where I should show the more respect, I become the

---

[13] Macchiavelli, author of *The Prince*, and his followers.

more heated in upholding my opinion. It may also be that, for want of tact, I let Nature have her own way. Using the same freedom of speech and demeanour with men in high position that I have used in my own house, I am sensible of how much it inclines to indiscretion and incivility. But, besides that I was born that way, I am not quick-witted enough to dodge a sudden question, and escape by some shift, or to invent a truth. Nor is my memory good enough to keep to a truth I have thus invented, and I certainly lack the assurance to stick to it.

Wherefore through feebleness I put on a bold face. I take refuge in candour and always say what I think, both by nature and design, leaving it to Fortune to guide the issue.

Aristippus said that the best fruit he had gathered from Philosophy was that he spoke freely and openly to every man.

The memory is a wonderfully serviceable implement, without which the judgement does its duty very laboriously; in me it is entirely wanting. If a matter is expounded to me, it must be done piece-meal. For it is not in my power to answer a proposition with several different heads. I cannot carry a message without noting it in my tablets. And if I have to make a long-winded speech of any importance, I am reduced to the poor and miserable necessity of getting by heart, word for word, what I have to say; otherwise I should have neither method nor assurance, being afraid of my memory playing me a trick. But with this expedient I find it no less difficult. It takes me three hours to learn three lines. And besides, in a composition of my own, the freedom and authority with which I change the order and alter a word, continually varying the matter, makes it the more difficult to keep it in mind.

Now, the more I distrust my memory the more muddled does she become; she serves me best by chance, and I have to woo her unconcernedly. For if I hustle her she is put out; when she once begins to totter, the more I sound her the more perplexed and entangled does she become. She waits upon me at her own time, not at mine.

The same defect I find in my memory I find also in several other parts. I shun all command, obligation, and constraint. What at other times I can do easily and naturally I am unable to do if I strictly and expressly command myself to do it. Even those parts of my body that have any particular freedom and authority over themselves sometimes refuse to obey me, if I intend them to do me a necessary service at a fixed time and place. They spurn such a compulsory and tyrannical order. They shrink through fear and spite, and become paralysed.

One day, being in a place where it is considered a barbarous piece of discourtesy not to pledge those who invite you to drink, although they allowed me every freedom, I tried to play the part of a good boon companion, out of respect to the ladies who were of the company, according to the custom of the country.[14] But there was compensation; for, as I was preparing, under threats, to force myself beyond my habit and inclination, my gullet became so stopped that I was unable to swallow a single drop, and was debarred from drinking even as much as I needed for my meal. And my thirst was fully quenched by the great amount of drink that my imagination had anticipated.

This effect is most apparent in those who have the most powerful and vivid imagination; yet it is natural, and there is no one who does not in some degree feel it. An eminent archer, who had been condemned to death, was offered the chance of saving his life if he would give a signal proof of his skill; he declined to attempt it, fearing lest the too great strain on his will might misdirect his aim, and that, instead of saving his life, he might also forfeit the reputation he had acquired in shooting with the bow.

A man whose thoughts are elsewhere will not fail, when he is walking, to take every time the same number and length of steps, within an inch; but if he gives his attention to measuring and counting them, he will find that what he did naturally and by chance he will not do so exactly by design.

My library, which is a handsome one among country libraries, is situated at one corner of my house.[15] If anything enters my head that I wish to look up or to write down there, I am obliged, for fear of its escaping me while merely crossing the courtyard, to communicate it to some other person. If, in speaking, I am so bold as to digress ever so little from the thread, I never fail to lose it; for which reason I force myself to be short, concise, and sparing of words. My servants I am obliged to call after the name of their occupation or their province,[16] for I have great difficulty in remembering names. I can tell indeed that it has three syl-

---

[14] Probably a reminiscence of his travels, which took him through part of Germany.

[15] More precisely, in a tower which forms an angle of the large courtyard, where it still stands.

[16] This, however, appears to have been a common practice. In the comedies of Molière and others we find such names of valets as Basque, Champagne, Picard, &c.

lables, that it has a harsh sound, that it begins or ends with such and such a letter. And if I should live long, I am not sure that I shall not forget my own name, as others have done.

Messala Corvinus was two years without a trace of memory, and the same is said of George of Trebizond. And in my own interest I often reflect what kind of a life was theirs, and whether without this faculty I shall have enough left to support me in easy circumstances. And, if I look closely into the matter, I fear that this privation, if complete, will be attended with the loss of all the functions of the mind. *It is certain that the memory is the only receptacle, not only of Philosophy, but of all that concerns the conduct of life, and of all the arts* (Cicero).

I'm full of cracks, and leak out every way. (Terence.)

More than once it has happened to me to forget the watchword which I had given out three hours before, or received from another; to forget where I had hidden my purse, whatever Cicero may say.[17] I help myself to lose what I have carefully locked up.

Memory is the receptacle and coffer of knowledge. Mine being so defective I have no great cause to complain if I know so little. I know in a general way the names of the arts, and of what they treat, but nothing more. I turn over the leaves of books; I do not study them. What I retain of them I no longer recognize as another's. Only my judgement has profited by the thoughts and ideas it has imbibed from them. The author, the place, the words and other circumstances, are immediately forgotten.

And I am so eminent in forgetfulness that I forget my own writings and compositions no less than the rest. At every turn people quote my Essays to me without my being aware of it. If any one would know where to find the lines and examples I have here accumulated, I should be at a great loss to tell him.[18] And yet I have begged them only at well-known and famous doors, not satisfied with their being rich unless they also came from rich and honourable hands. Authority and reason there co-operate with one another.

It will be no great wonder if my book follows the fortune of other

[17] 'I have never heard of any old man forgetting where he has hidden his treasure.' —Cicero, *Of Old Age*.

[18] Montaigne gave no references, and his editors, beginning with Mlle de Gournay, have no doubt had great trouble in identifying the twelve hundred and more quotations.

books, and if my memory loses its hold of what I write, as it does of what I read; of what I give as well as of what I receive.

Besides the defect of memory I have others which greatly contribute to my ignorance. My mind is slow and blunt; the least cloud will arrest its point, so that (for example) I never set it any problem, however easy, that it could unravel. Any idle subtlety will perplex me. Of games in which the intellect has its part, as chess, cards, draughts, and others, I have only the rudest idea.

My apprehension is slow and muddled; but what it once grasps it grasps thoroughly, and embraces very closely, very deeply and very comprehensively, for as long as it does grasp it. I have a long, sound and perfect sight, but it is soon tired by work and becomes dim; for which reason I cannot converse for any length of time with my book except with another's help.

The younger Pliny will tell those who have not experienced it how important [19] is this delay to those who are fond of reading.

No mind is so feeble and brute-like that it does not give plain evidence of some particular faculty; none is so deeply buried but that it will start up at one place or another. And how it comes to pass that a mind that is blind and asleep to all else is found to be clear, wide-awake, and excelling all others in one particular direction, is a question for the masters. But the best minds are those which are far-reaching, open and ready to embrace all things; if not educated, at least capable of education.

What I say is a condemnation of my own. For whether from weakness or indifference (and I am far from approving indifference to what lies at our feet, what we have in hand, what most nearly concerns the employment of our time), no mind is so absurdly ignorant as mine of many such ordinary things, of which it is a disgrace to be ignorant. I must relate a few examples.

I was born and bred in the country and among field-labourers; I have had the business of husbandry in my own hands ever since my predecessors in the possession of the property I enjoy left me to succeed to it. And yet I can add up neither with counters nor with a pen. Most of our

[19] Perhaps Montaigne intended to say 'vexatious' (*importun*), and had in mind an anecdote which Pliny tells of his uncle: 'I remember once, his reader having pronounced a word wrongly, somebody at the table made him repeat it; upon which my uncle asked him if he understood it? He acknowledged that he did: 'Why then, said he, would you make him go back again? We have lost, by this interruption, above ten lines': so covetous was this great man of time.

coins are unknown to me.[20] I cannot differentiate between one grain and another, either in the ground or in the barn, unless the difference be too glaring; and can scarcely distinguish between the cabbages and lettuces in my garden. I do not even know the names of the chief implements of husbandry, nor the rudest principles of agriculture, which the boys know. I know still less of the mechanical arts, of trade and merchandise, of the nature and diversity of fruits, wines, and foodstuffs, of training a hawk or physicking a horse or a hound. And, to complete my disgrace, only a month ago I was caught in ignorance of the fact that leaven is used in making bread, and of the meaning of allowing wine to ferment.

Somebody at Athens once conjectured an aptitude for mathematics in a man he saw cleverly arranging a load of brushwood and making it up into faggots. Truly in my case one could draw quite the opposite conclusion; for give me a whole kitchen-battery and you will see me starving.

From this outline of my confession you may imagine other things to my prejudice. But whatever I make myself out to be, provided it be such as I am, I attain my purpose. So I will not apologize for daring to put in writing such paltry and trivial details as these. The meanness of the subject [21] compels me to do it. You may condemn my purpose, but not my treatment of it. After all I see well enough, without being informed of the fact by another, how unimportant and worthless all this is, and how foolish my design. It is enough if my judgement is not put out, of which these are the essays:

> Be nosy, be all nose, till your nose appear
> So big that Atlas it refuse to bear;
> Though even against Latinus you inveigh,
> Against my trifles you no more can say
> Than I have said myself. Then to what end
> Should you to render tooth for tooth contend?
> You must have meat if you'd be full, my friend.
> Lose not your labour; but on those that so
> Admire themselves your deadliest venom throw.
> That these things nothing are full well I know.
>   (Martial.)

---

[20] It must be remembered that coinage was in Montaigne's time not so simple as it is now. Every important city appears to have had its own.

[21] Meaning himself, as stated in earlier editions.

I am not obliged to refrain from saying absurd things, provided I do not deceive myself and know them to be such. And to trip knowingly is so usual with me that I seldom trip any other way; I never trip by accident. It is a slight accusation to attribute my foolish actions to heedlessness, since I cannot deny that I usually attribute my vicious actions to the same.

One day at Bar-le-Duc I saw King Francis the Second being presented with a portrait which King René of Sicily had painted himself, and sent to him to recall him to his memory. Why should not every one be allowed, in like manner, to portray himself with his pen, as he did with his brush? I will not then omit also this scar, which is very unfit to be published: my want of resolution, a very serious drawback in transacting the business of the world. In dubious enterprises I am at a loss which side to take:

Nor yes nor no my inmost heart will say. (Petrarch.)

I can maintain an opinion, but I cannot choose one.

For in human affairs, to whatever side we lean, we are confronted by many probabilities which confirm our opinions (and the philosopher Chrysippus said that he wished to learn of Zeno and Cleanthes, his masters, only their doctrines, for, as to proofs and reasons, he could furnish enough himself); so, whichever way I turn, I can always provide myself with grounds and probabilities enough to keep me there. Hence I hold myself in suspense, with freedom to choose, until the occasion urges me. And then, to confess the truth, I most often throw the feather into the wind, as the saying goes, and commit myself to the mercy of Fortune. A very slight turn and circumstance will carry me along:

When the mind doubts and oscillates,
A pin will turn the scales. (Terence.)

The uncertainty of my judgement is so evenly balanced on most occasions, that I could readily decide it by a throw of the dice. And, when I ponder over our human disabilities, I note that even sacred history gives examples of that custom of leaving it to chance and Fortune to determine the choice in doubtful cases: *The lot fell upon Matthias* (Acts).

Human reason is a two-edged and dangerous sword. And even in the hand of Socrates, her most intimate and familiar friend, observe that it is a stick with many ends.

Thus I am fitted only for following and am easily carried away with the crowd. I have not sufficient confidence in my own strength to take upon me to command and lead; I am quite content to find my steps marked out by others. If I must run the risk of a doubtful choice, I prefer that it be under one who is more assured of his opinions, and espouses them more strongly, than I do mine, the ground and foundation of which I find to be very slippery.

And yet I am not too easily imposed upon, since I perceive a like weakness in the contrary opinions. *The mere habit of assenting seems to be dangerous and slippery* (Cicero). Especially in political matters there is a large field for hesitation and conflict:

> As scales correct and pressed by equal weights,
> Nor rise, nor dip, but keep an even poise. (Tibullus.)

Macchiavelli's reasons, for example, were sound enough for the subject they treated of, yet it was very easy to combat them; and they who did so made it no less easy to combat theirs. In that kind of argument there can never be wanting matter for answers, rejoinders, replications, triplications, quadruplications,[22] and that endless chain of disputes which our lawyers draw out to as great a length as they can in favour of law-suits:

> We lunge and parry, dodging in and out,
> Like Samnites at a tedious fencing-bout; (Horace.)

since the reasons have little other foundation than experience, and human actions and passions take on such an endless variety of forms.

A shrewd person of our days says that if, when our almanacs say cold, you say hot, and wet when they say dry, and always put the opposite of what they predict, you might lay a wager upon either event, without caring which side you take; except in cases that admit of no uncertainty, as if you promised extreme heat at Christmas, or the rigours of winter at Midsummer.

I should say the same about these political controversies; whatever part they set you to play, you will have as fair a prospect as your adversary, provided that you do not run counter to principles that are too solid and obvious. And yet, according to my way of thinking, in public

---

[22] *Dupliques, répliques, tripliques,* like their English equivalents, seem to be legal terms. Montaigne goes one better and adds a *quadruplique.*

matters no course of proceeding is so bad, provided it have age and continuity to recommend it, but that it is better than change and uncertainty. Our morals are extremely corrupt, and wonderfully incline to the worse. Many of our laws and customs are barbarous and monstrous; yet, by reason of the difficulty of improving our condition, and the danger of the whole State toppling to pieces, if I could put a spoke into our wheel and stop it at this point, I would do it with a light heart:

> No acts so foul and shameful could I tell
> But that far worse remain behind. (Juvenal.)

The worst thing I observe in our State is instability; our laws cannot, any more than our clothes, settle down to any fixed shape. It is very easy to condemn a government for its imperfection, for all mortal things are full of it. It is very easy to generate in a people a contempt for their ancient observances; no man ever attempted it without succeeding. But many have come to grief in their attempt to establish a better state of things in place of what they have destroyed.

I seldom consult my prudence in my conduct; I generally allow myself to follow the ordinary routine of the world. Happy are the people who do what they are commanded better than they who command, without troubling their heads about reasons; who allow themselves gently to roll according to the heavenly rolling. Obedience is never pure and simple in one who talks and argues.

In fine, to return to myself, the only quality for which I take some credit to myself is that in which no man ever thought himself deficient. My self-approbation is common and vulgar, and shared by all; for what man ever imagined he was lacking in Sense? That would be a self-contradictory proposition. It is a disease that never exists where it is seen; it is very strong and tenacious, but at the first glimmer the patient has of it it is seen through and dispersed, as a thick fog is dispersed by sunbeams.

To accuse oneself in this case would be to excuse, and to condemn oneself would be to absolve. There never was a streetporter or any silly woman who did not think they had enough sense for their needs. We are ready enough to acknowledge others to have the advantage over us in courage, bodily strength, experience, agility, beauty; but the advantage in judgement we yield to none. And we think we could have discovered the reasons which naturally occur to the mind of another, if we had adopted his point of view.

We quite readily admit the learning, style, and such other qualities as we see in the works of another, if he excels us therein; but regarding them as mere products of the understanding, each one of us thinks he could have discovered the same in himself. And he does not easily perceive the importance and difficulty of them, unless they be at an extreme and incomparable distance, and scarcely even then.

(And he who could very clearly discern the height of another's judgement would be able to raise his own to the same pitch.)

So it is a kind of exercise for which I must expect very little praise and commendation, and a kind of composition which promises little reputation.

And then, for whom do you write? The scholars, to whom it falls to sit in judgement on books, value them only for their learning, and will admit no procedure in the mind but along the lines of art and erudition. If you have mistaken one of the Scipios for the other, can you say anything worth saying? According to them, the man who is ignorant of Aristotle is at the same time ignorant of himself. Vulgar and commonplace minds, on the other hand, cannot discern the charm and power of a lofty and elegant style. Now, these two classes of people are in possession of the world. The third class by whom it is your lot to be judged, that of men of naturally strong and well-regulated intellect, is so small, that for that reason they have neither name nor position with us. It is time half wasted to aspire and endeavour to please them.

It is commonly said that the fairest portion of her favours that Nature has given us is that of Sense; for there is no man who is not contented with his share of it. Is not that reasonable? He who should see beyond would see beyond his sight.

I think my opinions are good and sound; but who does not think the same of his? One of the best proofs I have of this is the small estimation in which I hold myself. For if I had not been very sure of those opinions they might easily have been led astray by the singular affection I bear myself; as one who concentrates it almost all upon himself, and does not squander much of it on others. All the love that others distribute among an infinite number of friends and acquaintances, upon their glory and their grandeur, I dedicate entirely to the tranquility of my mind and to myself. If any escapes me in other directions, it is not really with my deliberate consent:

By instinct trained for self to thrive and live. (Lucretius.)

Well, I seem to be very bold in so persistently condemning my own littleness. It is indeed a subject on which I exercise my judgement as much as on any other. The world always looks over the way; I turn my eyes inwards. There I fix them and keep them fixed. Every one looks in front of him; I look within myself. I have no business but with myself, I continually reflect upon myself, examine and analyse myself. Other men, if they will but see it, always go abroad; they always go straight ahead:

No man attempts to dive into himself. (Persius.)

As for me, I revolve in myself.

This capacity which I have, whatever it may be worth, for sifting the truth, and my independence in not readily subjecting my belief, I owe chiefly to myself. For the most abiding and general ideas I have are those which, so to say, were born with me; they are natural and entirely my own. When I begat them, with a strong and bold, but rather hazy and imperfect begetting, they were crude and simple; I have since confirmed and established them with the authority of others, and the sound reasonings of those ancient writers with whom I found myself to agree. They strengthened my hold upon them, and enabled me more fully to possess and enjoy them.

Whilst all others seek to recommend themselves by an active and ready wit, I lay claim to steadiness; the satisfaction they seek in conspicuous and signal deeds, or in some particular talent, I find in the order, the consistency, and moderation of my opinions and conduct. *Now it is certain that, if anything in the world is becoming, it is a constant uniformity in our whole lives and particular actions; which it is impossible we should ever maintain so long as we run counter to our inclinations, and follow after those of other people* (Cicero).

Here then you see to what degree I am guilty of what I called the first kind of Presumption. Of the second, which consists in not having a sufficiently high opinion of others, I know not whether I can so fully exonerate myself; for, at whatever cost to myself, I am resolved to speak the truth.

Whether it be perhaps that my continual intercourse with the habits of mind of the ancient writers, and the picture I have formed of those richly-endowed minds of the past, have put me out of humour with others, and with myself; or that we do in truth live in an age which produces only very indifferent things, the fact remains that I see nothing worthy of great admiration. At the same time I know few men so intimately that I am qualified to pass judgement upon them; and those with whom my station in life brings me most frequently into contact are, for the most part, men who pay little attention to their mental culture, and to whom the greatest blessing is honour, and valour the greatest perfection.

Whatever I see that is fine in others I am very ready to praise and esteem. Nay, I often express more admiration than I feel, and that is the extent to which I allow myself to be untruthful. For I am unable to originate anything untrue. I willingly testify to the laudable qualities I see in my friends, and of a foot of merit I generally make a foot and a half. But attribute to them qualities they do not possess I cannot, nor can I openly defend their imperfections.

Even to my enemies I honestly concede the honour that is their due. My feelings may change, but not my judgement. I do not confuse my animosity with other circumstances that are foreign to it; and I am so jealous of the independence of my judgement that I can very hardly part with it for any passion whatever. I do myself more injury by lying than I do the man about whom I lie.

This laudable and generous custom has been observed in the Persian nation, that they speak of their deadly enemies, and at the same time wage war to the death with them, fairly and honourably, in so far as they deserve it by their valour.

I know men enough who have divers fine qualities, the one wit, the other courage, another skill, another conscience, another eloquence, one, one science, another, another. But as for a man great in all respects, combining all those fine qualities, or possessing one in so eminent a degree as to excite wonder or be comparable with those we honour in the past, it has not been my fortune to meet with him. The greatest I have known in the flesh, I mean for natural qualities of the soul, and of the best disposition, was Etienne de La Boëtie. His was a full mind indeed that appeared beautiful from every point of view, a soul of the old stamp, which would have produced great things if Fortune had so willed it. And he added greatly to his rich nature by learning and study.

But I know not how it is, and it is undoubtedly the case, that there is as much vanity and as little intelligence in those men who lay claim to the highest abilities, who meddle with literary pursuits and bookish occupations, as in any other class of people; whether it is that more is required and expected of them, and common defects are inexcusable in them, or, perhaps, because the conceit they have of their learning makes them bolder to show off and push themselves too far forward, the result being that they betray and give themselves away.

As an artist gives more evidence of his dullness when working upon a rich material that he has in hand, by applying and mixing it stupidly and against the rules of his work, than when using a baser material; and as we are more shocked by a fault in a statue of gold than in a plaster model: so do these men when they quote things which would be good in themselves and in their proper place; for they serve them up without discrimination, doing honour to their memory at the expense of their intelligence. They do honour to Cicero, to Galen, to Ulpian and Saint Jerome, and bring ridicule upon themselves.

I readily return to that subject of our absurd educational system; its aim has been to make us, not good and wise, but learned; and it has succeeded. It has not taught us to follow and embrace Virtue or Wisdom, but has impressed upon us their derivation and etymology. We can decline Virtue, if we cannot love it. If we do not know what Wisdom is by practice and experience, we know it by jargon and by heart. We are not content with knowing the origin of our neighbours, their kindred and their inter-marriages; we wish to be friends with them, to establish some intercourse and understanding with them. This education has taught us the definition, the divisions, and sub-divisions of Virtue, as we know the surnames and branches of a genealogical tree, without further caring to become familiar and intimate with her. It has selected, for our instruction, not those books which contain the soundest and truest opinions, but those which speak the best Greek and Latin; and with all those fine words has poured into our minds the most unprofitable ideas of the ancients.

A good education changes one's outlook and character, as in the case of Polemo. This dissipated young Greek, happening to hear Xenocrates lecture, was struck not only by the eloquence and learning of the professor, and carried home not only the knowledge of some noble matter, but a more substantial and palpable fruit, which was a sudden change and amendment of his former life. Who was ever affected in that way by our education?

> Say, will you act like Polemo
> On his conversion long ago?
> The signs discard of your disease,—
> Your mits, the swathings of your knees,
> Your mufflers too,—as he, 'tis said,

Slipped off the chaplets from his head
Which, flushed with revel, still he wore
When he was stricken to the core
By the undinner'd sage's lore. (Horace.)

To me the least contemptible class of people are those who, by reason of their simplicity, stand on the lowest rung; their relations with each other are better regulated. I generally find the morals and the language of the peasants more in accordance with the teachings of true Philosophy than those of our philosophers. *The common people are wiser, because they are as wise as they need be* (Lactantius).

In my opinion, the most remarkable men judging by outward appearance (for to judge them in my own way I should need more light thrown upon them) have been, for eminence in war and soldier-like qualities, the Duke of Guise,[23] who died at Orleans, and the late Marshal Strozzi; [23] for great ability and uncommon merit, Olivier and l'Hôpital, Chancellors of France. Poetry too I think has flourished in our century; we have an abundance of good craftsmen in that trade,[24] Daurat, Bèze, Buchanan, l'Hôpital, Montdoré, Turnebus. As to the French poets, I think they have raised their art to the highest pitch it will ever attain; and in those qualities in which Ronsard and Du Bellay excel, I do not think they fall far short of the perfection of ancient poetry. Adrianus Turnebus knew more, and knew better what he did know, than any man of his time, and long before his time.

The lives of the Duke of Alva, lately dead, and of our Constable de Montmorency were noble lives, and in several respects their fortunes were uncommonly alike. But the beauty and lustre of the latter's death, in the sight of Paris and of his King, and in their service, fighting against his nearest relations, at the head of an army victorious through his leadership, and coming so suddenly in an advanced old age, deserves, in my opinion, to rank among the noteworthy events of my time.

The same may be said of the constant goodness, the gentle manners and the scrupulous affability of Monsieur de la Nouë, who lived all his life surrounded by violent deeds of armed factions (a real school of treachery, inhumanity, and brigandage), a great and most experienced warrior.

(I have taken pleasure in proclaiming, in several places, the hopes I entertain of Marie de Gournay le Jars, my *fille d'alliance,* whom I truly

[23] François de Guise, 1519–63; Piero Strozzi, d. 1558.
[24] Montaigne means writers of Latin poetry.

love, with a more than paternal affection, and whom in my solitude and retreat I cherish as one of the best parts of my own being. She is now my chief concern in this world. If I may presage from her youth, her soul will be some day capable of the finest things, and amongst others, of the perfection of that very sacred friendship, to which, as far as my reading goes, none of her sex has yet been able to rise. Her sincerity and steadfast character are quite equal to it. Her affection for me is more than superabundant, and such in short that it leaves nothing to be desired. I could wish, however, that she were not so cruelly troubled by apprehensions of my end, since we first met when I was fifty-five years of age. Her appreciation, as a woman, and of this century, and so young, and alone in her district, of the first Essays, and the wonderful impetuosity of her love and desire to make my acquaintance, long before setting eyes on me, merely on the strength of her esteem, are circumstances well worthy of consideration.) [25]

Other virtues have been little, if at all, prized in this age; but valour is become common through Civil wars. And in this respect we have souls brave even to perfection, and so numerous that it is impossible to sift them out.

Those are all I have known hitherto who have shown any extraordinary and uncommon greatness.

2. The Crack-Up

F. SCOTT FITZGERALD

Francis Scott Fitzgerald (1896–1940), author of *The Great Gatsby* and *Tender Is the Night,* has become almost *the* symbol of the Jazz Age in America. All the wildly furious pursuit of pleasure that

SOURCE: F. Scott Fitzgerald, *The Crack-Up,* ed. Edmund Wilson (New York: New Directions, 1945), pp. 69–74. Copyright 1936 by Esquire, Inc. Copyright 1945 by New Directions. Reprinted by permission of New Directions Publishing Company.

[25] This passage does not appear in the 'Bordeaux Manuscript'; which omission, in the opinion of at least one commentator, casts some doubt upon its authenticity.

marked the era just after World War I is caught in his work, as is the underlying melancholy into which it collapsed with the prosperity that sustained it. A midwesterner who moved East and then on to Europe, a young man dazzled by wealth and success, Fitzgerald is a typical victim as well as the leading spokesman for an era. In the morning-after of the thirties, he looked back on his life and that of his times with horror and heartbreak. *The Crack-Up* (a collection of his occasional writings made by Edmund Wilson) is the record of that horror and heartbreak.

Of course all life is a process of breaking down, but the blows that do the dramatic side of the work—the big sudden blows that come, or seem to come, from outside—the ones you remember and blame things on and, in moments of weakness, tell your friends about, don't show their effect all at once. There is another sort of blow that comes from within—that you don't feel until it's too late to do anything about it, until you realize with finality that in some regard you will never be as good a man again. The first sort of breakage seems to happen quick—the second kind happens almost without your knowing it but is realized suddenly indeed.

Before I go on with this short history, let me make a general observation—the test of a first-rate intelligence is the ability to hold two opposed ideas in the mind at the same time, and still retain the ability to function. One should, for example, be able to see that things are hopeless and yet be determined to make them otherwise. This philosophy fitted on to my early adult life, when I saw the improbable, the implausible, often the "impossible," come true. Life was something you dominated if you were any good. Life yielded easily to intelligence and effort, or to what proportion could be mustered of both. It seemed a romantic business to be a successful literary man—you were not ever going to be as famous as a movie star but what note you had was probably longer-lived—you were never going to have the power of a man of strong political or religious convictions but you were certainly more independent. Of course within the practice of your trade you were forever unsatisfied—but I, for one, would not have chosen any other.

As the twenties passed, with my own twenties marching a little ahead of them, my two juvenile regrets—at not being big enough (or good enough) to play football in college, and at not getting overseas during the war—resolved themselves into childish waking dreams of imaginary heroism that were good enough to go to sleep on in restless nights. The big problems of life seemed to solve themselves, and if the business of fixing them was difficult, it made one too tired to think of more general problems.

Life, ten years ago, was largely a personal matter. I must hold in balance the sense of the futility of effort and the sense of the necessity to struggle; the conviction of the inevitability of failure and still the determination to "succeed"—and, more than these, the contradiction between the dead hand of the past and the high intentions of the future. If I could do this through the common ills—domestic, professional and personal—then the ego would continue as an arrow shot from nothingness with such force that only gravity would bring it to earth at last.

For seventeen years, with a year of deliberate loafing and resting out in the center—things went on like that, with a new chore only a nice prospect for the next day. I was living hard, too, but: "Up to forty-nine it'll be all right," I said. "I can count on that. For a man who's lived as I have, that's all you could ask."

—And then, ten years this side of forty-nine, I suddenly realized that I had prematurely cracked.

II

Now a man can crack in many ways—can crack in the head—in which case the power of decision is taken from you by others! or in the body, when one can but submit to the white hospital world; or in the nerves. William Seabrook in an unsympathetic book tells, with some pride and a movie ending, of how he became a public charge. What led to his alcoholism or was bound up with it, was a collapse of his nervous system. Though the present writer was not so entangled—having at the time not tasted so much as a glass of beer for six months—it was his nervous reflexes that were giving way—too much anger and too many tears.

Moreover, to go back to my thesis that life has a varying offensive, the realization of having cracked was not simultaneous with a blow, but with a reprieve.

Not long before, I had sat in the office of a great doctor and listened to a grave sentence. With what, in retrospect, seems some equanimity, I had gone on about my affairs in the city where I was then living, not caring much, not thinking how much had been left undone, or what would become of this and that responsibility, like people do in books; I was well insured and anyhow I had been only a mediocre caretaker of most of the things left in my hands, even of my talent.

But I had a strong sudden instinct that I must be alone. I didn't want to see any people at all. I had seen so many people all my life—I was an average mixer, but more than average in a tendency to identify myself, my ideas, my destiny, with those of all classes that I came in contact with. I was always saving or being saved—in a single morning I would go through the emotions ascribable to Wellington at Waterloo. I lived in a world of inscrutable hostiles and inalienable friends and supporters.

But now I wanted to be absolutely alone and so arranged a certain insulation from ordinary cares.

It was not an unhappy time. I went away and there were fewer people. I found I was good-and-tired. I could lie around and was glad to, sleeping or dozing sometimes twenty hours a day and in the intervals trying resolutely not to think—instead I made lists—made lists and tore them up, hundreds of lists: of cavalry leaders and football players and cities, and popular tunes and pitchers, and happy times, and hobbies and houses lived in and how many suits since I left the army and how many pairs of shoes (I didn't count the suit I bought in Sorrento that shrunk, nor the pumps and dress shirt and collar that I carried around for years and never wore, because the pumps got damp and grainy and the shirt and collar got yellow and starch-rotted). And lists of women I'd liked, and of the times I had let myself be snubbed by people who had not been my betters in character or ability.

—And then suddenly, surprisingly, I got better.

—And cracked like an old plate as soon as I heard the news.

That is the real end of this story. What was to be done about it will have to rest in what used to be called the "womb of time." Suffice it to say that after about an hour of solitary pillow-hugging, I began to realize that for two years my life had been drawing on resources that I did not possess, that I had been mortgaging myself physically and spiritually up to the hilt. What was the small gift of life given back in comparison to that?—when there had once been a pride of direction and a confidence in enduring independence.

I realized that in those two years, in order to preserve something—an inner hush maybe, maybe not—I had weaned myself from all the things I used to love—that every act of life from the morning toothbrush to the friend at dinner had become an effort. I saw that for a long time I had not liked people and things, but only followed the rickety old pretense of liking. I saw that even my love for those closest to me was become only an attempt to love, that my casual relations—with an editor, a tobacco seller, the child of a friend, were only what I remembered I *should* do, from other days. All in the same month I became bitter about such things as the sound of the radio, the advertisements in the magazines, the screech of tracks, the dead silence of the country—contemptuous at human softness, immediately (if secretively) quarrelsome toward hardness—hating the night when I couldn't sleep and hating the day because it went toward night. I slept on the heart side now because I knew that the sooner I could tire that out, even a little, the sooner would come that blessed hour of nightmare which, like a catharsis, would enable me to better meet the new day.

There were certain spots, certain faces I could look at. Like most Middle Westerners, I have never had any but the vaguest race prejudices—I always had a secret yen for the lovely Scandinavian blondes who sat on porches in St. Paul but hadn't emerged enough economically to be part of what was then society. They were too nice to be "chickens" and too quickly off the farmlands to seize a place in the sun, but I remember going round blocks to catch a single glimpse of shining hair—the bright shock of a girl I'd never know. This is urban, unpopular talk. It strays afield from the fact that in these latter days I couldn't stand the sight of Celts, English, Politicians, Strangers, Virginians, Negroes (light or dark), Hunting People, or retail clerks, and middlemen in general, all writers (I avoided writers very carefully because they can perpetuate trouble as no one else can)—and all the classes as classes and most of them as members of their class . . .

Trying to cling to something, I like doctors and girl children up to the age of about thirteen and well-brought-up boy children from about eight years old on. I could have peace and happiness with these few categories of people. I forgot to add that I liked old men—men over seventy, sometimes over sixty if their faces looked seasoned. I like Katharine Hepburn's face on the screen, no matter what was said about her pretentiousness, and Miriam Hopkins' face, and old friends if I only saw them once a year and could remember their ghosts.

All rather inhuman and undernourished, isn't it? Well, that, children, is the true sign of cracking up.

It is not a pretty picture. Inevitably it was carted here and there within its frame and exposed to various critics. One of them can only be described as a person whose life makes other people's lives seem like death—even this time when she was cast in the usually unappealing role of Job's comforter. In spite of the fact that this story is over, let me append our conversation as a sort of postscript:

"Instead of being so sorry for yourself, listen—" she said. (She always says "Listen," because she thinks while she talks—*really* thinks.) So she said: "Listen, Suppose this wasn't a crack in you—suppose it was a crack in the Grand Canyon."

"The crack's in me," I said heroically.

"Listen! The world only exists in your eyes—your conception of it. You can make it as big or as small as you want to. And you're trying to be a little puny individual. By God, if I ever cracked, I'd try to make the world crack with me. Listen! The world only exists through your apprehension of it, and so it's much better to say that it's not you that's cracked—it's the Grand Canyon."

"Baby et up all her Spinoza?"

"I don't know anything about Spinoza. I know—" She spoke, then, of old woes of her own, that seemed, in the telling, to have been more dolorous than mine, and how she had met them, over-ridden them, beaten them.

I felt a certain reaction to what she said, but I am a slow-thinking man, and it occurred to me simultaneously that of all natural forces, vitality is the incommunicable one. In days when juice came into one as an article without duty, one tried to distribute it—but always without success; to further mix metaphors, vitality never "takes." You have it or you haven't it, like health or brown eyes or honor or a baritone voice. I might have asked some of it from her, neatly wrapped and ready for home cooking and digestion, but I could never have got it—not if I'd waited around for a thousand hours with the tin cup of self-pity. I could walk from her door, holding myself very carefully like cracked crockery, and go away into the world of bitterness, where I was making a home with such materials as are found there—and quote to myself after I left her door:

"Ye are the salt of the earth. But if the salt hath lost its savour, wherewith shall it be salted?"
Matthew 5:13.

3. The Revolver in the Corner Cupboard

GRAHAM GREENE

Graham Greene (1904–   ), British playwright, novelist and script-writer, has been engaged in a life-long attempt to use the devices of the "thriller" and the chase story for the highest ends of literature. His most successful venture along these lines is his novel *The Power and the Glory* (1946), an account of a banned priest in the jungles of Mexico. In his restless search for new backgrounds, Greene has ranged through many countries, producing along the way travel books as well as fiction. Fundamentally a religious writer and a convinced convert to Catholicism, Greene has often dismayed his own co-religionists by portraying the difficulties of the religious life realistically rather than sentimentally. The essay included here is one of his several efforts to find in his earlier life the critical events that have shaped his maturity.

I can remember very clearly the afternoon I found the revolver in the brown deal corner cupboard in the bedroom which I shared with my elder brother. It was the early autumn of 1922. I was seventeen and terribly bored and in love with my sister's governess—one of those miserable, hopeless, romantic loves of adolescence that set in many minds the idea that love and despair are inextricable and that successful love hardly deserves the name. At that age one may fall irrevocably in love with failure, and success of any kind loses half its savour before it is experienced. Such a love is surrendered once and for all to the singer at the pavement's edge, the bankrupt, the old school friend who wants to touch you for a dollar. Perhaps in many so conditioned it is the love for God that mainly survives, because in his eyes they can imagine themselves remaining always drab, seedy, unsuccessful, and therefore worthy of notice.

The revolver was a small genteel object with six chambers like a tiny

SOURCE: Graham Greene, *The Lost Childhood* (New York: The Viking Press, 1951), pp. 67–70. Reprinted by permission.

egg stand, and there was a cardboard box of bullets. It has only recently occurred to me that they may have been blanks; I always assumed them to be live ammunition, and I never mentioned the discovery to my brother because I had realized the moment I saw the revolver the use I intended to make of it. (I don't to this day know why he possessed it; certainly he had no licence, and he was only three years older than myself. A large family is as departmental as a Ministry.)

My brother was away—probably climbing in the Lake District— and until he returned the revolver was to all intents mine. I knew what to do with it because I had been reading a book (the name Ossendowski comes to mind as the possible author) describing how the White Russian officers, condemned to inaction in South Russia at the tail-end of the counter-revolutionary war, used to invent hazards with which to escape boredom. One man would slip a charge into a revolver and turn the chambers at random, and his companion would put the revolver to his head and pull the trigger. The chance, of course, was six to one in favour of life.

How easily one forgets emotions. If I were dealing now with an imaginary character, I would feel it necessary for verisimilitude to make him hesitate, put the revolver back into the cupboard, return to it again after an interval, reluctantly and fearfully, when the burden of boredom became too great. But in fact I think there was no hesitation at all, for the next I can remember is crossing Berkhamsted Common, gashed here and there between the gorse bushes with the stray trenches of the first Great War, towards the Ashridge beeches. Perhaps before I had made the discovery boredom had already reached an intolerable depth.

I think the boredom was far deeper than the love. It had always been a feature of childhood: it would set in on the second day of the school holidays. The first day was all happiness, and, after the horrible confinement and publicity of school, seemed to consist of light, space and silence. But a prison conditions its inhabitants. I never wanted to return to it (and finally expressed my rebellion by the simple act of running away), but yet I was so conditioned that freedom bored me unutterably.

The psycho-analysis that followed my act of rebellion had fixed the boredom as hypo fixes the image on the negative. I emerged from those delightful months in London spent at my analyst's house—perhaps the happiest months of my life—correctly orientated, able to take a proper extrovert interest in my fellows (the jargon rises to the lips), but wrung dry. For years, it seems to me, I could take no aesthetic interest in any

visual thing at all: staring at a sight that others assured me was beautiful, I would feel nothing. I was fixed in my boredom. (Writing this I
come on a remark of Rilke: 'Psycho-analysis is too fundamental a help
for me, it helps you once and for all, it clears you up, and to find myself
finally cleared up one day might be even more helpless than this chaos.')

Now with the revolver in my pocket I was beginning to emerge. I had
stumbled on the perfect cure. I was going to escape in one way or another, and because escape was inseparably connected with the Common
in my mind, it was there that I went.

The wilderness of gorse, old trenches, abandoned butts was the un-
changing backcloth of most of the adventures of childhood. It was to the
Common I had decamped for my act of rebellion some years before,
with the intention, expressed in a letter left after breakfast on the heavy
black sideboard, that there I would stay, day and night, until either I
had starved or my parents had given in; when I pictured war it was always in terms of this Common, and myself leading a guerrilla campaign
in the ragged waste, for no one, I was persuaded, knew its paths so intimately (how humiliating that in my own domestic campaign I was am-
bused by my elder sister after a few hours).

Beyond the Common lay a wide grass ride known for some reason as
Cold Harbor to which I would occasionally with some fear take a horse,
and beyond this again stretched Ashridge Park; the smooth olive skin of
beech trees and the thick last year's quagmire of leaves, dark like old
pennies. Deliberately I chose my ground, I believe without any real fear
—perhaps because I was uncertain myself whether I was play-acting;
perhaps because so many acts which my elders would have regarded as
neurotic, but which I still consider to have been under the circumstances
highly reasonable, lay in the background of this more dangerous venture.

There had been, for example, perhaps five or six years before, the
disappointing morning in the dark room by the linen cupboard on the
eve of term when I had patiently drunk a quantity of hypo under the
impression that it was poisonous: on another occasion the blue glass
bottle of hay fever lotion which as it contained a small quantity of cocaine had probably been good for my mood: the bunch of deadly night-
shade that I had eaten with only a slight narcotic effect: the twenty
aspirins I had taken before swimming in the empty out-of-term school
baths (I can still remember the curious sensation of swimming through
wool): these acts may have removed all sense of strangeness as I slipped

a bullet into a chamber and, holding the revolver behind my back, spun the chambers round.

Had I romantic thoughts about the governess? Undoubtedly I must have had, but I think that at the most they simply eased the medicine down. Boredom, aridity, those were the main emotions. Unhappy love has, I suppose, sometimes driven boys to suicide, but this was not suicide, whatever a coroner's jury might have said of it: it was a gamble with six chances to one against an inquest. The romantic flavour—the autumn scene, the small heavy compact shape lying in the fingers— that perhaps was a tribute to adolescent love, but the discovery that it was possible to enjoy again the visible world by risking its total loss was one I was bound to make sooner or later.

I put the muzzle of the revolver in my right ear and pulled the trigger. There was a minute click, and looking down at the chamber I could see that the charge had moved into place. I was out by one. I remember an extraordinary sense of jubilation. It was as if a light had been turned on. My heart was knocking in its cage, and I felt that life contained an infinite number of possibilities. It was like a young man's first successful experience of sex—as if in that Ashridge glade one had passed a test of manhood. I went home and put the revolver back in the corner cupboard.

The odd thing about this experience was that it was repeated several times. At fairly long intervals I found myself craving for the drug. I took the revolver with me when I went up to Oxford and I would walk out from Headington towards Elsfield down what is now a wide arterial road, smooth and shiny like the walls of a public lavatory. Then it was a sodden unfrequented country lane. The revolver would be whipped behind my back, the chambers twisted, the muzzle quickly and surreptitiously inserted beneath the black and ugly winter tree, the trigger pulled.

Slowly the effect of the drug wore off—I lost the sense of jubilation, I began to gain from the experience only the crude kick of excitement. It was like the difference between love and lust. And as the quality of the experience deteriorated so my sense of responsibility grew and worried me. I wrote a very bad piece of free verse (free because it was easier in that way to express my meaning without literary equivocation) describing how, in order to give a fictitious sense of danger, I would 'press the trigger of a revolver I already know to be empty'. This piece of verse I would leave permanently on my desk, so that if I lost my gamble, there would be incontrovertible evidence of an accident, and my parents, I thought, would be less troubled than by an apparent suicide—or than by the rather bizarre truth.

But it was back at Berkhamsted that I paid a permanent farewell to the drug. As I took my fifth dose it occurred to me that I wasn't even excited: I was beginning to pull the trigger about as casually as I might take an aspirin tablet. I decided to give the revolver—which was six chambered—a sixth and last chance. Twirling the chambers round, I put the muzzle to my ear for the last time and heard the familiar empty click as the chambers revolved. I was through with the drug, and walking back over the Common, down the new road by the ruined castle, past the private entrance to the gritty old railway station—reserved for the use of Lord Brownlow—my mind was already busy on other plans. One campaign was over, but the war against boredom had got to go on.

I put the revolver back in the corner cupboard, and going downstairs I lied gently and convincingly to my parents that a friend had invited me to join him in Paris.

4. A Visit to Grandpa's

D Y L A N   T H O M A S

Dylan Thomas (1914–1953), a dramatic and romantic figure, came to play a role in our century much like Byron's in his. Thomas's lecture tours in the United States, his public readings of his own poetry and his public living of his disordered life, soon made him as much a legend as a poet. Difficult and involved as it often is, his poetry when read aloud carries an immediate emotional impact. Welsh in origin and living in Wales all his life, Thomas wrestled in verse and prose with the problems of his Welshness; and this essay represents one attempt to come to terms with his past and his people.

SOURCE: Dylan Thomas, *Portrait of the Artist as a Young Dog* (New York: New Directions, 1940), pp. 31–39. Copyright 1940 by New Directions Publishing Corporation. Reprinted by permission of New Directions Publishing Corporation, J. M. Dent & Sons Ltd., and the Trustees for the copyrights of the late Dylan Thomas.

In the middle of the night I woke from a dream full of whips and lariats as long as serpents, and runaway coaches on mountain passes, and wide, windy gallops over cactus fields, and I heard the old man in the next room crying, 'Gee-up!' and 'Whoa!' and trotting his tongue on the roof of his mouth.

It was the first time I had stayed in grandpa's house. The floorboards had squeaked like mice as I climbed into bed, and the mice between the walls had creaked like wood as though another visitor was walking on them. It was a mild summer night, but curtains had flapped and branches beaten against the window. I had pulled the sheets over my head, and soon was roaring and riding in a book.

'Whoa there, my beauties!' cried grandpa. His voice sounded very young and loud, and his tongue had powerful hooves, and he made his bedroom into a great meadow. I thought I would see if he was ill, or had set his bed-clothes on fire, for my mother had said that he lit his pipe under the blankets, and had warned me to run to his help if I smelt smoke in the night. I went on tiptoe through the darkness to his bed-room door, brushing against the furniture and upsetting a candlestick with a thump. When I saw there was a light in the room I felt frightened, and as I opened the door I heard grandpa shout, 'Gee-up!' as loudly as a bull with a megaphone.

He was sitting straight up in bed and rocking from side to side as though the bed were on a rough road; the knotted edges of the counter-pane were his reins; his invisible horses stood in a shadow beyond the bedside candle. Over a white flannel nightshirt he was wearing a red waistcoat with walnut-sized brass buttons. The over-filled bowl of his pipe smouldered among his whiskers like a little, burning hayrick on a stick. At the sight of me, his hands dropped from the reins and lay blue and quiet, the bed stopped still on a level road, he muffled his tongue into silence, and the horses drew softly up.

'Is there anything the matter, grandpa?' I asked, though the clothes were not on fire. His face in the candlelight looked like a ragged quilt pinned upright on the black air and patched all over with goat-beards.

He stared at me mildly. Then he blew down his pipe, scattering the sparks and making a high, wet dog-whistle of the stem, and shouted: 'Ask no questions.'

After a pause, he said slyly: 'Do you ever have nightmares, boy?'

I said: 'No.'

'Oh, yes, you do,' he said.

I said I was woken by a voice that was shouting to horses.

'What did I tell you?' he said. 'You eat too much. Who ever heard of horses in a bedroom?'

He fumbled under his pillow, brought out a small, tinkling bag, and carefully untied its strings. He put a sovereign in my hand, and said 'Buy a cake.' I thanked him and wished him good night.

As I closed my bedroom door, I heard his voice crying loudly and gaily, 'Gee-up!' and the rocking of the travelling bed.

In the morning I woke from a dream of fiery horses on a plain that was littered with furniture, and of large, cloudy men who rode six horses at a time and whipped them with burning bed-clothes. Grandpa was at breakfast, dressed in deep black. After breakfast he said, 'There was a terrible loud wind last night,' and sat in his arm-chair by the hearth to make clay balls for the fire. Later in the morning he took me for a walk, through Johnstown village and into the fields on the Llanstephan road.

A man with a whippet said, 'There's a nice morning, Mr. Thomas,' and when he had gone, leanly as his dog, into the short-treed green wood he should not have entered because of the notices, grandpa said: 'There, do you hear what he called you? Mister!'

We passed by small cottages, and all the men who leant on the gates congratulated grandpa on the fine morning. We passed through the wood full of pigeons, and their wings broke the branches as they rushed to the tops of the trees. Among the soft, contented voices and the loud, timid flying, grandpa said, like a man calling across a field: 'If you heard those old birds in the night, you'd wake me up and say there were horses in the trees.'

We walked back slowly, for he was tired, and the lean man stalked out of the forbidden wood with a rabbit held as gently over his arm as a girl's arm in a warm sleeve.

On the last day but one of my visit I was taken to Llanstephan in a governess cart pulled by a short, weak pony. Grandpa might have been driving a bison, so tightly he held the reins, so ferociously cracked the long whip, so blasphemously shouted warning to boys who played in the road, so stoutly stood with his gaitered legs apart and cursed the demon strength and wilfulness of his tottering pony.

'Look out, boy!' he cried when we came to each corner, and pulled and tugged and jerked and sweated and waved his whip like a rubber sword. And when the pony had crept miserably round each corner, grandpa turned to me with a sighing smile: 'We weathered that one, boy.'

When we came to Llanstephan village at the top of the hill, he left the cart by the 'Edwinsford Arms' and patted the pony's muzzle and gave it sugar, saying: 'You're a weak little pony, Jim, to pull big men like us.'

He had strong beer and I had lemonade, and he paid Mrs. Edwinsford with a sovereign out of the tinkling bag; she inquired after his health, and he said that Llangadock was better for the tubes. We went to look at the churchyard and the sea, and sat in the wood called the Sticks, and stood on the concert platform in the middle of the wood where visitors sang on midsummer nights and, year by year, the innocent of the village was elected mayor. Grandpa paused at the churchyard and pointed over the iron gate at the angelic headstones and the poor wooden crosses. 'There's no sense in lying there,' he said.

We journeyed back furiously: Jim was a bison again.

I woke late on my last morning, out of dreams where the Llanstephan sea carried bright sailing-boats as long as liners, and heavenly choirs in the Sticks, dressed in bards' robes and brass-buttoned waistcoats, sang in a strange Welsh to the departing sailors. Grandpa was not at breakfast; he rose early. I walked in the fields with a new sling, and shot at the Towy gulls and the rooks in the parsonage trees. A warm wind blew from the summer points of the weather; a morning mist climbed from the ground and floated among the trees and hid the noisy birds; in the mist and the wind my pebbles flew lightly up like hailstones in a world on its head. The morning passed without a bird falling.

I broke my sling and returned for the midday meal through the parson's orchard. Once, grandpa told me, the parson had bought three ducks at Carmarthen Fair and made a pond for them in the centre of the garden; but they waddled to the gutter under the crumbling doorsteps of the house, and swam and quacked there. When I reached the end of the orchard path, I looked through a hole in the hedge and saw that the parson had made a tunnel through the rockery that was between the gutter and the pond and had set up a notice in plain writing: 'This way to the pond.'

The ducks were still swimming under the steps.

Grandpa was not in the cottage. I went into the garden, but grandpa was not staring at the fruit-trees. I called across to a man who leant on a spade in the field beyond the garden hedge: 'Have you seen my grandpa this morning?'

He did not stop digging, and answered over his shoulder: 'I seen him in his fancy waistcoat.'

Griff, the barber, lived in the next cottage. I called to him through the open door: 'Mr. Griff, have you seen my grandpa?'

The barber came out in his shirtsleeves.

I said: 'He's wearing his best waistcoat.' I did not know if it was important, but grandpa wore his waistcoat only in the night.

'Has grandpa been to Llanstephan?' asked Mr. Griff anxiously.

'We went there yesterday in a little trap,' I said.

He hurried indoors and I heard him talking in Welsh, and he came out again with his white coat on, and he carried a striped and coloured walking-stick. He strode down the village street and I ran by his side.

When we stopped at the tailor's shop, he cried out, 'Dan!' and Dan Tailor stepped from his window where he sat like an Indian priest but wearing a derby hat. 'Dai Thomas has got his waistcoat on,' said Mr. Griff, 'and he's been to Llanstephan.'

As Dan Tailor searched for his overcoat, Mr. Griff was striding on. 'Will Evans,' he called outside the carpenter's shop, 'Dai Thomas has been to Llanstephan, and he's got his waistcoat on.'

'I'll tell Morgan now,' said the carpenter's wife out of the hammering, sawing darkness of the shop.

We called at the butcher's shop and Mr. Price's house, and Mr. Griff repeated his message like a town crier.

We gathered together in Johnstown square. Dan Tailor had his bicycle, Mr. Price his pony-trap. Mr. Griff, the butcher, Morgan Carpenter, and I climbed into the shaking trap, and we trotted off towards Carmarthen town. The tailor led the way, ringing his bell as though there were a fire or a robbery, and an old woman by the gate of a cottage at the end of the street ran inside like a pelted hen. Another woman waved a bright handkerchief.

'Where are we going?' I asked.

Grandpa's neighbours were as solemn as old men with black hats and jackets on the outskirts of a fair. Mr. Griff shook his head and mourned: 'I didn't expect this again from Dai Thomas.'

'Not after last time,' said Mr. Price sadly.

We trotted on, we crept up Constitution Hill, we rattled down into Lammas Street, and the tailor still rang his bell and a dog ran, squealing, in front of his wheels. As we clip-clopped over the cobbles that led down to the Tory bridge, I remembered grandpa's nightly noisy journeys that rocked the bed and shook the walls, and I saw his gay waist-coat in a vision and his patchwork head tufted and smiling in the candle-light. The tailor before us turned round on his saddle, his bicycle wobbled and skidded. 'I see Dai Thomas!' he cried.

The trap rattled on to the bridge, and I saw grandpa there; the buttons of his waistcoat shone in the sun, he wore his tight, black Sunday trousers and a tall, dusty hat I had seen in a cupboard in the attic, and he carried an ancient bag. He bowed to us. 'Good morning, Mr. Price,' he said, 'and Mr. Griff and Mr. Morgan and Mr. Evans.' To me, he said 'Good morning, boy.'

Mr. Griff pointed his coloured stick at him.

'And what do you think you are doing on Carmarthen bridge in the middle of the afternoon,' he said sternly, 'with your best waistcoat and your old hat?'

Grandpa did not answer, but inclined his face to the river wind, so that his beard was set dancing and wagging as though he talked, and watched the coracle men move, like turtles, on the shore.

Mr. Griff raised his stunted barber's pole. 'And where do you think you are going,' he said, 'with your old black bag?'

Grandpa said: 'I am going to Llangadock to be buried.' And he watched the coracle shells slip into the water lightly, and the gulls complain over the fish-filled water as bitterly as Mr. Price complained:

'But you aren't dead yet, Dai Thomas.'

For a moment grandpa reflected, then: 'There's no sense in lying dead in Llanstephan,' he said. 'The ground is comfy in Llangadock; you can twitch your legs without putting them in the sea.'

His neighbours moved close to him. They said: 'You aren't dead, Mr. Thomas.'

'How can you be buried, then?'

'Nobody's going to bury you in Llanstephan.'

'Come on home, Mr. Thomas.'

'There's strong beer for tea.'

'And cake.'

But grandpa stood firmly on the bridge, and clutched his bag to his side, and stared at the flowing river and the sky, like a prophet who has no doubt.

5. Stranger in the Village

JAMES BALDWIN

James Baldwin (1924–   ) is one of the most talented and original Negro writers in America. Though he has frequently lived abroad— once for a period of several years—his imaginative concern is chiefly with this country and its problems. Besides his essays, which are largely concerned with the difficulties of a black man in a white society, he has written two notable novels, *Giovanni's Room* (1956) and *Go Tell It on the Mountain* (1963), in both of which he attempts to get beyond the conventional Negro novel with its stereotyped themes and passions. More recently, he has been seen as a playwright, most impressively in *Blues for Mr. Charlie,* and has attempted a large-scale novel, *Another Country* (1962), more successful with the popular audience than with the critics.

From all available evidence no black man had ever set foot in this tiny Swiss village before I came. I was told before arriving that I would probably be a "sight" for the village; I took this to mean that people of my complexion were rarely seen in Switzerland, and also that city people are always something of a "sight" outside of the city. It did not occur to me—possibly because I am an American that there could be people anywhere who had never seen a Negro.

It is a fact which cannot be explained on the basis of the inaccessibility of the village. The village is very high, but it is only four hours from Milan and three hours from Lausanne. It is true that it is virtually unknown. Few people making plans for a holiday would elect to come here. On the other hand, the villagers are able, presumably, to come and go as they please—which they do: to another town at the foot of the mountain, with a population of approximately five thousand, the nearest place to see a movie or go to the bank. In the village there is no movie

SOURCE: James Baldwin, *Notes of a Native Son* (Boston: Beacon Press, 1953), pp. 159–75. Copyright 1953 by the Beacon Press; 1955 by James Baldwin. Reprinted by permission of the Beacon Press.

house, no bank, no library, no theater; very few radios, one jeep, one station wagon; and, at the moment, one typewriter, mine, an invention which the woman next door to me here had never seen. There are about six hundred people living here, all Catholic—I conclude this from the fact that the Catholic church is open all year round, whereas the Protestant chapel, set off on a hill a little removed from the village, is open only in the summertime when the tourists arrive. There are four or five hotels, all closed now, and four or five *bistros,* of which, however, only two do any business during the winter. These two do not do a great deal, for life in the village seems to end around nine or ten o'clock. There are a few stores, butcher, baker, *épicerie,* a hardware store, and a money-changer—who cannot change travelers' checks, but must send them down to the bank, an operation which takes two or three days. There is something called the *Ballet Haus,* closed in the winter and used for God knows what, certainly not ballet, during the summer. There seems to be only one schoolhouse in the village, and this for the quite young children; I suppose this to mean that their older brothers and sisters at some point descend from these mountains in order to complete their education—possibly, again, to the town just below. The landscape is absolutely forbidding, mountains towering on all four sides, ice and snow as far as the eye can reach. In this white wilderness, men and women and children move all day, carrying washing, wood, buckets of milk or water, sometimes skiing on Sunday afternoons. All week long boys and young men are to be seen shoveling snow off the rooftops, or dragging wood down from the forest in sleds.

The village's only real attraction, which explains the tourist season, is the hot spring water. A disquietingly high proportion of these tourists are cripples, or semi-cripples, who come year after year—from other parts of Switzerland, usually—to take the waters. This lends the village, at the height of the season, a rather terrifying air of sanctity, as though it were a lesser Lourdes. There is often something beautiful, there is always something awful, in the spectacle of a person who has lost one of his faculties, a faculty he never questioned until it was gone, and who struggles to recover it. Yet people remain people, on crutches or indeed on deathbeds; and wherever I passed, the first summer I was here, among the native villagers, or among the lame, a wind passed with me—of astonishment, curiosity, amusement, and outrage. That first summer I stayed two weeks and never intended to return. But I did return in the winter, to work; the village offers, obviously, no distractions whatever and has the further advantage of being extremely cheap. Now it is winter again, a year later, and I am here again. Everyone in the village knows my name, though they scarcely ever use it, knows that I come from America—though, this, apparently, they will never really believe: black men come from Africa—and everyone knows that I am the friend of the son of a woman who was born here, and that I am staying in their chalet. But I remain as much a stranger today as I was the first day I arrived, and the children shout *Neger! Neger!* as I walk along the streets.

It must be admitted that in the beginning I was far too shocked to have any real reaction. In so far as I reacted at all, I reacted by trying to be pleasant—it being a great part of the American Negro's education (long before he goes to school) that he must make people "like" him. This smile-and-the-world-smiles-with-you routine worked about as well in this situation as it had in the situation for which it was designed, which is to say that it did not work at all. No one, after all, can be liked whose human weight and complexity cannot be, or has not been, admitted. My smile was simply another unheard-of phenomenon which allowed them to see my teeth—they did not, really, see my smile and I began to think that, should I take to snarling, no one would notice any difference. All of the physical characteristics of the Negro which had caused me, in America, a very different and almost forgotten pain were nothing less than miraculous—or infernal—in the eyes of the village people. Some thought my hair was the color of tar, that it had the texture of wire, or the texture of cotton. It was jocularly suggested that I might let it all grow long and make myself a winter coat. If I sat in the sun for more than five minutes some daring creature was certain to come along and gingerly put his fingers on my hair, as though he were afraid of an electric shock, or put his hand on my hand, astonished that the color did not rub off. In all of this, in which it must be conceded there was yet no suggestion that I was human: I was simply a living wonder.

I knew that they did not mean to be unkind, and I know it now; it is necessary, nevertheless, for me to repeat this to myself each time that I walk out of the chalet. The children who shout *Neger!* have no way of knowing the echoes this sound raises in me. They are brimming with good humor and the more daring swell with pride when I stop to speak with them. Just the same, there are days when I cannot pause and smile, when I have no heart to play with them; when, indeed, I mutter sourly to myself, exactly as I muttered on the streets of a city these children have never seen, when I was no bigger than these children are now: *Your* mother was a *nigger*. Joyce is right about history being a nightmare—but it may be the nightmare from which no one *can* awaken. People are trapped in history and history is trapped in them.

II

There is a custom in the village—I am told it is repeated in many villages—of "buying" African natives for the purpose of converting them to Christianity. There stands in the church all year round a small box with a slot for money, decorated with a black figurine, and into this box the villagers drop their francs. During the *carnaval* which precedes Lent, two village children have their faces blackened—out of which bloodless darkness their blue eyes shine like ice—and fantastic horsehair wigs are placed on their blond heads; thus disguised, they solicit among the villagers for money for the missionaries in Africa. Between the box in the church and the blackened children, the village "bought" last year six or eight African natives. This was reported to me with pride by the wife of one of the *bistro* owners and I was careful to express astonishment and pleasure at the solicitude shown by the village for the souls of black folks. The *bistro* owner's wife beamed with a pleasure far more genuine than my own and seemed to feel that I might now breathe more easily concerning the souls of at least six of my kinsmen.

I tried not to think of these so lately baptized kinsmen, of the price they themselves would pay, and said nothing about my father, who having taken his own conversion too literally, never, at bottom, forgave the white world (which he described as heathen) for having saddled him with a Christ in whom, to judge at least from their treatment of him, they themselves no longer believed. I thought of white men arriving for the first time in an African village, strangers there, as I am a stranger here, and tried to imagine the astounded populace touching their hair and marveling at the color of their skin. But there is a great difference between being the first white man to be seen by Africans and being the first black man to be seen by whites. The white man takes the astonishment as tribute, for he arrives to conquer and to convert the natives, whose inferiority in relation to himself is not even to be questioned; whereas I, without a thought of conquest, find myself among a people whose culture controls me, has even, in a sense, created me, people who have cost me more in anguish and rage than they will ever know, who yet do not even know of my existence. The astonishment with which I might have greeted them, should they have stumbled into my African village a few hundred years ago, might have rejoiced their hearts. But the astonishment with which they greet me today can only poison mine.

And this is so despite everything I may do to feel differently, despite my friendly conversations with the *bistro* owner's wife, despite their three-year-old son who has at last become my friend, despite the *saluts* and *bonsoirs* which I exchange with people as I walk, despite the fact that I know that no individual can be taken to task for what history is doing, or has done. I say that the culture of these people controls me— but they can scarcely be held responsible for European culture. America comes out of Europe, but these people have never seen America, nor have most of them seen more of Europe than the hamlet at the foot of their mountain. Yet, they move with an authority which I shall never have, and they regard me, quite rightly, not only as a stranger in their village but as a suspect latecomer, bearing no credentials, to everything they have—however unconsciously—inherited.

For this village, even were it incomparably more remote and incredibly more primitive, is the West, the West onto which I have been so strangely grafted. These people cannot be, from the point of view of power, strangers anywhere in the world: they have made the modern world, in effect, even if they do not know it. The most illiterate among them is related, in a way that I am not, to Dante, Shakespeare, Michelangelo, Aeschylus, Da Vinci, Rembrandt, and Racine; the cathedral at Chartres says something to them which it cannot say to me, as indeed would New York's Empire State Building, should anyone here ever see it. Out of their hymns and dances come Beethoven and Bach. Go back a few centuries and they are in their full glory—but I am in Africa, watching the conquerors arrive.

The rage of the disesteemed is personally fruitless, but it is also absolutely inevitable; this rage, so generally discounted, so little understood even among the people whose daily bread it is, is one of the things that makes history. Rage can only with difficulty, and never entirely, be brought under the domination of the intelligence and is therefore not susceptible to any arguments whatever. This is a fact which ordinary representatives of the *Herrenvolk,* having never felt this rage and being unable to imagine it, quite fail to understand. Also, rage cannot be hidden, it can only be dissembled. This dissembling deludes the thoughtless, and strengthens rage, and adds to rage, contempt. There are, no doubt, as many ways of coping with the resulting complex of tensions as there are black men in the world, but no black man can hope ever to be entirely liberated from this internal warfare—rage, dissembling, and contempt having inevitably accompanied his first realization of the power of white men. What is crucial here is that, since white men represent in the black man's world so heavy a weight, white men have for black men a reality which is far from being reciprocal; and hence all black men have toward all white men an attitude which is designed, really, either to rob the white man of the jewel of his naïveté, or else to make it cost him dear.

The black man insists, by whatever means he finds at his disposal, that the white man cease to regard him as an exotic rarity and recognize him as a human being. This is a very charged and difficult moment, for there is a great deal of will power involved in the white man's naïveté. Most people are not naturally reflective any more than they are naturally malicious, and the white man prefers to keep the black man at a certain human remove because it is easier for him thus to preserve his simplicity and avoid being called to account for crimes committed by his forefathers, or his neighbors. He is inescapably aware, nevertheless, that he is in a better position in the world than black men are, nor can he quite put to death the suspicion that he is hated by black men therefore. He does not wish to be hated, neither does he wish to change places, at this point in his uneasiness he can scarcely avoid having recourse to those legends which white men have created about black men, the most usual effect of which is that the white man finds himself enmeshed, so to speak, in his own language which describes hell, as well as the attributes which lead one to hell, as being as black as night.

Every legend, moreover, contains its residuum of truth, and the root function of language is to control the universe by describing it. It is of quite considerable significance that black men remain, in the imagination, and in overwhelming numbers in fact, beyond the disciplines of salvation; and this despite the fact that the West has been "buying" African natives for centuries. There is, I should hazard, an instantaneous necessity to be divorced from this so visibly unsaved stranger, in whose heart, moreover, one cannot guess what dreams of vengeance are being nourished; and, at the same time, there are few things on earth more attractive than the idea of the unspeakable liberty which is allowed the unredeemed. When, beneath the black mask, a human being begins to make himself felt one cannot escape a certain awful wonder as to what kind of human being it is. What one's imagination makes of other people is dictated, of course, by the laws of one's own personality and it is one of the ironies of black-white relations that, by means of what the white man imagines the black man to be, the black man is enabled to know who the white man is.

I have said, for example, that I am as much a stranger in this village today as I was the first summer I arrived, but this is not quite true. The villagers wonder less about the texture of my hair than they did then, and wonder rather more about me. And the fact that their wonder now exists on another level is reflected in their attitudes and in their eyes. There are the children who make those delightful, hilarious, sometimes astonishingly grave overtures of friendship in the unpredictable fashion of children; other children, having been taught that the devil is a black man, scream in genuine anguish as I approach. Some of the older women never pass without a friendly greeting, never pass, indeed, if it seems that they will be able to engage me in conversation; other women look down or look away or rather contemptuously smirk. Some of the men drink with me and suggest that I learn how to ski—partly, I gather, because they cannot imagine what I would look like on skis—and want to know if I am married, and ask questions about my *métier*. But some of the men have accused *le sale nègre*—behind my back— of stealing wood and there is already in the eyes of some of them that peculiar, intent, paranoiac malevolence which one sometimes surprises in the eyes of American white men when, out walking with their Sunday girl, they see a Negro male approach.

There is a dreadful abyss between the streets of this village and the streets of the city in which I was born, between the children who shout *Neger!* today and those who shouted *Nigger!* yesterday—the abyss is experience, the American experience. The syllable hurled behind me today expresses, above all, wonder; I am a stranger here. But I am not a stranger in America and the same syllable riding on the American air expresses the war my presence has occasioned in the American soul.

III

For this village brings home to me this fact: that there was a day, and not really a very distant day, when Americans were scarcely Americans at all but discontented Europeans, facing a great unconquered continent and strolling, say, into a marketplace and seeing black men for the first time. The shock this spectacle afforded is suggested, surely, by the promptness with which they decided that these black men were not really men but cattle. It is true that the necessity on the part of the settlers of the New World of reconciling their moral assumptions with the fact—and the necessity—of slavery enhanced immensely the charm of this idea, and it is also true that this idea expresses, with a truly American bluntness, the attitude which to varying extents all masters have had toward all slaves.

But between all former slaves and slave-owners and the drama which begins for Americans over three hundred years ago at Jamestown, there are at least two differences to be observed. The American Negro slave could not suppose, for one thing, as slaves in past epochs had supposed and often done, that he would ever be able to wrest the power from his master's hands. This was a supposition which the modern era, which was to bring about such vast changes in the aims and dimensions of power, put to death; it only begins, in unprecedented fashion, and with dreadful implications, to be resurrected today. But even had this supposition persisted with undiminished force, the American Negro slave could not have used it to lend his condition dignity, for the reason that this supposition rests on another: that the slave in exile yet remains related to his past, has some means—if only in memory—of revering and sustaining the forms of his former life, is able, in short, to maintain his identity.

This was not the case with the American Negro slave. He is unique among the black men of the world in that his past was taken from him, almost literally, at one blow. One wonders what on earth the first slave found to say to the first dark child he bore. I am told that there are Haitians able to trace their ancestry back to African kings, but any American Negro wishing to go back so far will find his journey through time abruptly arrested by the signature on the bill of sale which served as the entrance paper for his ancestor. At the time—to say nothing of the circumstances—of the enslavement of the captive black man who was to become the American Negro, there was not the remotest possibility that he would ever take power from his master's hands. There was no reason to suppose that his situation would ever change, nor was there, shortly, anything to indicate that his situation had ever been different. It was his necessity, in the words of E. Franklin Frazier, to find a "motive for living under American culture or die." The identity of the American Negro comes out of this extreme situation, and the evolution of this identity was a source of the most intolerable anxiety in the minds and the lives of his masters.

For the history of the American Negro is unique also in this: that the question of his humanity, and of his rights therefore as a human being, became a burning one for several generations of Americans, so burning a question that it ultimately became one of those used to divide the nation. It is out of this argument that the venom of the epithet *Nigger!* is derived. It is an argument which Europe has never had, and hence Europe quite sincerely fails to understand how or why the argument arose in the first place, why its effects are so frequently disastrous and always so unpredictable, why it refuses until today to be entirely settled. Europe's black possessions remained—and do remain—in Europe's colonies, at which remove they represented no threat whatever to European identity. If they posed any problem at all for the European conscience, it was a problem which remained comfortingly abstract: in effect, the black man, *as a man,* did not exist for Europe. But in America, even as a slave, he was an inescapable part of the general social fabric and no American could escape having an attitude toward him. Americans attempt until today to make an abstraction of the Negro, but the very nature of these abstractions reveals the tremendous effects the presence of the Negro has had on the American character.

When one considers the history of the Negro in America it is of the greatest importance to recognize that the moral beliefs of a person, or a people, are never really as tenuous as life—which is not moral—very often causes them to appear; these create for them a frame of reference and a necessary hope, the hope being that when life has done its worst they will be enabled to rise above themselves and to triumph over life. Life would scarcely be bearable if this hope did not exist. Again, even when the worst has been said, to betray a belief is not by any means to have put oneself beyond its power; the betrayal of a belief is not the same thing as ceasing to believe. If this were not so there would be no moral standards in the world at all. Yet one must also recognize that morality is based on ideas and that all ideas are dangerous—dangerous because ideas can only lead to action and where the action leads no man can say. And dangerous in this respect: that confronted with the impossibility of remaining faithful to one's beliefs, and the equal impossibility of becoming free of them, one can be driven to the most inhuman excesses. The ideas on which American beliefs are based are not, though Americans often seem to think so, ideas which originated in

America. They came out of Europe. And the establishment of democracy on the American continent was scarcely as radical a break with the past as was the necessity, which Americans faced, of broadening this concept to include black men.

This was, literally, a hard necessity. It was impossible, for one thing, for Americans to abandon their beliefs, not only because these beliefs alone seemed able to justify the sacrifices they had endured and the blood that they had spilled, but also because these beliefs afforded them their only bulwark against a moral chaos as absolute as the physical chaos of the continent it was their destiny to conquer. But in the situation in which Americans found themselves, these beliefs threatened an idea which, whether or not one likes to think so, is the very warp and woof of the heritage of the West, the idea of white supremacy.

Americans have made themselves notorious by the shrillness and the brutality with which they have insisted on this idea, but they did not invent it; and it has escaped the world's notice that those very excesses of which Americans have been guilty imply a certain, unprecedented uneasiness over the idea's life and power, if not, indeed, the idea's validity. The idea of white supremacy rests simply on the fact that white men are the creators of civilization (the present civilization, which is the only one that matters; all previous civilizations are simply "contributions" to our own) and are therefore civilization's guardians and defenders. Thus it was impossible for Americans to accept the black man as one of themselves, for to do so was to jeopardize their status as white men. But not so to accept him was to deny his human reality, his human weight and complexity, and the strain of denying the overwhelmingly undeniable forced Americans into rationalizations so fantastic that they approached the pathological.

At the root of the American Negro problem is the necessity of the American white man to find a way of living with the Negro in order to be able to live with himself. And the history of this problem can be reduced to the means used by Americans—lynch law and law, segregation and legal acceptance, terrorization and concession—either to come to terms with this necessity, or to find a way around it, or (most usually) to find a way of doing both these things at once. The resulting spectacle, at once foolish and dreadful, led someone to make the quite accurate observation that "the Negro-in-America is a form of insanity which overtakes white men."

In this long battle, a battle by no means finished, the unforeseeable effects of which will be felt by many future generations, the white man's motive was the protection of his identity; the black man was motivated by the need to establish an identity. And despite the terrorization which the Negro in America endured and endures sporadically until today, despite the cruel and totally inescapable ambivalence of his status in his country, the battle for his identity has long ago been won. He is not a visitor to the West, but a citizen there, an American; as American as the Americans who despise him, the Americans who fear him, the Americans who love him—the Americans who became less than themselves, or rose to be greater than themselves by virtue of the fact that the challenge he represented was inescapable. He is perhaps the only black man in the world whose relationship to white men is more terrible, more subtle, and more meaningful than the relationship of bitter possessed to uncertain possessor. His survival depended, and his development depends, on his ability to turn his peculiar status in the Western world to his own advantage and, it may be, to the very great advantage of that world. It remains for him to fashion out of his experience that which will give him sustenance, and a voice.

The cathedral at Chartres, I have said, says something to the people of this village which it cannot say to me; but it is important to understand that this cathedral says something to me which it cannot say to them. Perhaps they are struck by the power of the spires, the glory of the windows; but they have known God, after all, longer than I have known him, and in a different way, and I am terrified by the slippery bottomless well to be found in the crypt, down which heretics were hurled to death, and by the obscene, inescapable gargoyles jutting out of the stone and seeming to say that God and the devil can never be divorced. I doubt that the villagers think of the devil when they face a cathedral because they have never been identified with the devil. But I must accept the status which myth, if nothing else, gives me in the West before I can hope to change the myth.

Yet, if the American Negro has arrived at his identity by virtue of the absoluteness of this estrangement from his past, American white men still nourish the illusion that there is some means of recovering the European innocence, of returning to a state in which black men do not exist. This is one of the greatest errors Americans can make. The identity they fought so hard to protect has, by virtue of that battle, undergone a change: Americans are as unlike any other white people in the world as it is possible to be. I do not think, for example, that it is too much to suggest that the American vision of the world—which allows so little reality, generally speaking, for any of the darker forces in human life, which tends until today to paint moral issues in glaring black and white—owes a great deal to the battle waged by Americans to maintain between themselves and black men a human separation which could not be bridged. It is only now beginning to be borne in on us—very faintly, it must be admitted, very slowly, and very much against our will—that this vision of the world is dangerously inaccurate; and perfectly useless. For it protects our moral high-mindedness at the terrible expense of weakening our grasp of reality. People who shut their eyes to reality simply invite their own destruction, and anyone who insists on remaining in a state of innocence long after that innocence is dead turns himself into a monster.

The time has come to realize that the inter-racial drama acted out on the American continent has not only created a new black man, it has created a new white man, too. No road whatever will lead Americans back to the simplicity of this European village where white men still have the luxury of looking on me as a stranger. I am not really a stranger any longer for any American alive. One of the things that distinguishes Americans from other people is that no other people has ever been so deeply involved in the lives of black men, and vice versa. This fact faced, with all its implications, it can be seen that the history of the American Negro problem is not merely shameful, it is also something of an achievement. For even when the worst has been said, it must also be added that the perpetual challenge posed by this problem was always, somehow, perpetually met. It is precisely this black-white experience which may prove of indispensable value to us in the world we face today. This world is white no longer, and it will never be white again.

6. *From* The Autobiography of Alice B. Toklas

GERTRUDE STEIN

Gertrude Stein (1874–1946) was a key figure among the American expatriates who flocked to Europe (especially Paris) in the period between World War I and the Great Depression. She herself had actually left her native America in 1903, after spending four years in Johns Hopkins Medical School; and she was an established figure when such writers as Hemingway left the United States for France. Her salon included not only writers, American and European, but many of the since famous French painters. She has the double distinction of having helped discover Picasso, Matisse *et al.* for an American public, and of having coined (or popularized) the phrase "the Lost Generation," by which the generation of Hemingway and Fitzgerald was pleased to call itself. She was a difficult woman, most of whose friendships ended in misunderstandings; but her malice and talent for gossip helped produce most of the best pages of *The Autobiography of Alice B. Toklas* (Miss Toklas was actually her secretary and life-long companion), from which the present selection comes. Miss Stein's experiments in prose and verse (novels, opera libretti, short stories, etc.) made her a well-known figure even to those who could not or would not read her difficult work. She became a great favorite of American G.I.'s after World War II, and was planning to return to the United States when she died.

The first thing that happened when we were back in Paris was Hemingway with a letter of introduction from Sherwood Anderson.

I remember very well the impression I had of Hemingway that first afternoon. He was an extraordinarily good-looking young man, twenty-three years old. It was not long after that that everybody was twenty-six. It became the period of being twenty-six. During the next two or

SOURCE: Gertrude Stein, *The Autobiography of Alice B. Toklas* (New York: Random House, Inc., 1933), pp. 212–20. Copyright 1933 and renewed 1961 by Alice B. Toklas. Reprinted by permission of Random House, Inc.

three years all the young men were twenty-six years old. It was the
right age apparently for that time and place. There were one or two
under twenty, for example George Lynes but they did not count as
Gertrude Stein carefully explained to them. If they were young men
they were twenty-six. Later on, much later on they were twenty-one
and twenty-two.

So Hemingway was twenty-three, rather foreign looking, with passionately interested, rather than interesting eyes. He sat in front of
Gertrude Stein and listened and looked.

They talked then, and more and more, a great deal together. He
asked her to come and spend an evening in their apartment and look at
his work. Hemingway had then and has always a very good instinct for
finding apartments in strange but pleasing localities and good femmes
de ménage and good food. This his first apartment was just off the
place du Tertre. We spent the evening there and he and Gertrude Stein
went over all the writing he had done up to that time. He had begun the
novel that it was inevitable he would begin and there were the little
poems afterwards printed by McAlmon in the Contact Edition. Gertrude Stein rather liked the poems, they were direct, Kiplingesque, but
the novel she found wanting. There is a great deal of description in
this, she said, and not particularly good description. Begin over again
and concentrate, she said.

Hemingway was at this time Paris correspondent for a canadian
newspaper. He was obliged there to express what he called the canadian viewpoint.

He and Gertrude Stein used to walk together and talk together a
great deal. One day she said to him, look here, you say you and your
wife have a little money between you. Is it enough to live on if you live
quietly. Yes, he said. Well, she said, then do it. If you keep on doing
newspaper work you will never see things, you will only see words and
that will not do, that is of course if you intend to be a writer. Hemingway said he undoubtedly intended to be a writer. He and his wife went
away on a trip and shortly after Hemingway turned up alone. He came
to the house about ten o'clock in the morning and he stayed, he stayed
for lunch, he stayed all afternoon, he stayed for dinner and he stayed
until about ten o'clock at night and then all of a sudden he announced
that his wife was enceinte and then with great bitterness, and I, I am
too young to be a father. We consoled him as best we could and sent
him on his way.

When they came back Hemingway said that he had made up his mind. They would go back to America and he would work hard for a year and with what he would earn and what they had they would settle down and he would give up newspaper work and make himself a writer. They went away and well within the prescribed year they came back with a new born baby. Newspaper work was over.

The first thing to do when they came back was as they thought to get the baby baptised. They wanted Gertrude Stein and myself to be god-mothers and an english war comrade of Hemingway was to be god-father. We were all born of different religions and most of us were not practising any, so it was rather difficult to know in what church the baby could be baptised. We spent a great deal of time that winter, all of us, discussing the matter. Finally it was decided that it should be baptised episcopalian and episcopalian it was. Just how it was managed with the assortment of god-parents I am sure I do not know, but it was baptised in the episcopalian chapel.

Writer or painter god-parents are notoriously unreliable. That is, there is certain before long to be a cooling of friendship. I know several cases of this, poor Paulot Picasso's god-parents have wandered out of sight and just as naturally it is a long time since any of us have seen or heard of our Hemingway god-child.

However in the beginning we were active god-parents, I particularly. I embroidered a little chair and I knitted a gay coloured garment for the god-child. In the meantime the god-child's father was very earnestly at work making himself a writer.

Gertrude Stein never corrects any detail of anybody's writing, she sticks strictly to general principles, the way of seeing what the writer chooses to see, and the relation between that vision and the way it gets down. When the vision is not complete the words are flat, it is very simple, there can be no mistake about it, so she insists. It was at this time that Hemingway began the short things that afterwards were printed in a volume called *In Our Time*.

One day Hemingway came in very excited about Ford Madox Ford and the Transatlantic. Ford Madox Ford had started the Transatlantic some months before. A good many years before, indeed before the war we had met Ford Madox Ford who was at that time Ford Madox Hueffer. He was married to Violet Hunt and Violet Hunt and Gertrude Stein were next to each other at the tea table and talked a great deal together. I was next to Ford Madox Hueffer and I liked him very much and I liked his stories of Mistral and Tarascon and I liked his having been followed about in that land of the french royalist, on account of his resemblance to the Bourbon claimant. I had never seen the Bourbon claimant but Ford at that time undoubtedly might have been a Bourbon.

We had heard that Ford was in Paris, but we had not happened to meet. Gertrude Stein had however seen copies of the Transatlantic and found it interesting but had thought nothing further about it.

Hemingway came in then very excited and said that Ford wanted something of Gertrude Stein's for the next number and he, Hemingway, wanted The Making of Americans to be run in it as a serial and he had to have the first fifty pages at once. Gertrude Stein was of course quite overcome with her excitement at this idea, but there was no copy of the manuscript except the one that we had had bound. That makes no difference, said Hemingway, I will copy it. And he and I between us did copy it and it was printed in the next number of the Transatlantic. So for the first time a piece of the monumental work which was the beginning, really the beginning of modern writing, was printed, and we were very happy. Later on when things were difficult between Gertrude Stein and Hemingway, she always remembered with gratitude that after all it was Hemingway who first caused to be printed a piece of The Making of Americans. She always says, yes sure I have a weakness for Hemingway. After all he was the first of the young men to knock on my door and he did make Ford print the first piece of The Making of Americans.

I myself have not so much confidence that Hemingway did do this. I have never known what the story is but I have always been certain that there was some other story behind it all. That is the way I feel about it.

Gertrude Stein and Sherwood Anderson are very funny on the subject of Hemingway. The last time that Sherwood was in Paris they often talked about him. Hemingway had been formed by the two of them and they were both a little proud and a little ashamed of the work of their minds. Hemingway had at one moment, when he had repudiated Sherwood Anderson and all his works, written him a letter in the name of american literature which he, Hemingway, in company with his contemporaries was about to save, telling Sherwood just what he, Hemingway thought about Sherwood's work, and, that thinking, was in no sense complimentary. When Sherwood came to Paris Hemingway naturally was afraid. Sherwood as naturally was not.

As I say he and Gertrude Stein were endlessly amusing on the subject. They admitted that Hemingway was yellow, he is, Gertrude Stein insisted, just like the flat-boat men on the Mississippi river as described by Mark Twain. But what a book, they both agreed, would be the real story of Hemingway, not those he writes but the confessions of the real Ernest Hemingway. It would be for another audience than the audience Hemingway now has but it would be very wonderful. And then they both agreed that they have a weakness for Hemingway because he is such a good pupil. He is a rotten pupil, I protested. You don't understand, they both said, it is so flattering to have a pupil who does it without understanding it, in other words, he takes training and anybody who takes training is a favourite pupil. They both admit it to be a weakness. Gertrude Stein added further, you see he is like Derain. You remember Monsieur de Tuille said, when I did not understand why Derain was having the success he was having that it was because he looks like a modern and he smells of the museums. And that is Hemingway, he looks like a modern and he smells of the museums. But what a story that of the real Hem, and one he should tell himself but alas he never will. After all, as he himself once murmured, there is the career, the career.

But to come back to the events that were happening.

Hemingway did it all. He copied the manuscript and corrected the proof. Correcting proofs is, as I said before, like dusting, you learn the values of the thing as no reading suffices to teach it to you. In correcting these proofs Hemingway learned a great deal and he admired all that he learned. It was at this time that he wrote to Gertrude Stein saying that it was she who had done the work in writing The Making of Americans and he and all his had but to devote their lives to seeing that it was published.

He had hopes of being able to accomplish this. Some one, I think by the name of Sterne, said that he could place it with a publisher. Gertrude Stein and Hemingway believed that he could, but soon Hemingway reported that Sterne had entered into his period of unreliability. That was the end of that.

In the meantime and sometime before this Mina Loy had brought McAlmon to the house and he came from time to time and he brought his wife and brought William Carlos Williams. And finally he wanted to print The Making of Americans in the Contact Edition and finally he did. I will come to that.

In the meantime McAlmon had printed the three poems and ten stories of Hemingway and William Bird had printed In Our Time and Hemingway was getting to be known. He was coming to know Dos Passos and Fitzgerald and Bromfield and George Antheil and everybody else and Harold Loeb was once more in Paris. Hemingway had become a writer. He was also a shadow-boxer, thanks to Sherwood, and he heard about bull-fighting from me. I have always loved spanish dancing and spanish bull-fighting and I loved to show the photographs of bull-fighters and bull-fighting. I also loved to show the photograph where Gertrude Stein and I were in the front row and had our picture taken there accidentally. In these days Hemingway was teaching some young chap how to box. The boy did not know how, but by accident he knocked Hemingway out. I believe this sometimes happens. At any rate in these days Hemingway although a sportsman was easily tired. He used to get quite worn out walking from his house to ours. But then he had been worn by the war. Even now he is, as Hélène says all men are, fragile. Recently a robust friend of his said to Gertrude Stein, Ernest is very fragile, whenever he does anything sporting something breaks, his arm, his leg, or his head.

In those early days Hemingway liked all his contemporaries except Cummings. He accused Cummings of having copied everything, not from anybody but from somebody. Gertrude Stein who had been much impressed by The Enormous Room said that Cummings did not copy, he was the natural heir of the New England tradition with its aridity and its sterility, but also with its individuality. They disagreed about this. They also disagreed about Sherwood Anderson. Gertrude Stein contended that Sherwood Anderson had a genius for using a sentence to convey a direct emotion, this was in the great american tradition, and that really except Sherwood there was no one in America who could write a clear and passionate sentence. Hemingway did not believe this, he did not like Sherwood's taste. Taste has nothing to do with sentences, contended Gertrude Stein. She also added that Fitzgerald was the only one of the younger writers who wrote naturally in sentences.

Gertrude Stein and Fitzgerald are very peculiar in their relation to each other. Gertrude Stein had been very much impressed by This Side of Paradise. She read it when it came out and before she knew any of the young american writers. She said of it that it was this book that really created for the public the new generation. She has never changed her opinion about this. She thinks this equally true of *The Great Gatsby*. She thinks Fitzgerald will be read when many of his well known contemporaries are forgotten. Fitzgerald always says that he thinks Gertrude Stein says these things just to annoy him by making him think that she means them, and he adds in his favourite way, and her doing it is the cruellest thing I ever heard. They always however have a very good time when they meet. And the last time they met they had a good time with themselves and Hemingway.

Then there was McAlmon. McAlmon had one quality that appealed to Gertrude Stein abundance, he could go on writing, but she complained that it was dull.

There was also Glenway Wescott but Glenway Wescott at no time interested Gertrude Stein. He has a certain syrup but it does not pour.

So then Hemingway's career was begun. For a little while we saw less of him and then he began to come again. He used to recount to Gertrude Stein the conversations that he afterwards used in The Sun Also Rises and they talked endlessly about the character of Harold Loeb. At this time Hemingway was preparing his volume of short stories to submit to publishers in America. One evening after we had not seen him for a while he turned up with Shipman. Shipman was an amusing boy who was to inherit a few thousand dollars when he came of age. He was not of age. He was to buy the Transatlantic Review when he came of age, so Hemingway said. He was to support a surrealist review when he came of age, André Masson said. He was to buy a house in the country when he came of age, Josette Gris said. As a matter of fact when he came of age nobody who had known him then seemed to know what he did do with his inheritance. Hemingway brought him with him to the house to talk about buying the Transatlantic and incidentally he brought the manuscript he intended sending to America. He handed it to Gertrude Stein. He had added to his stories a little story of meditations and in these he said that The Enormous Room was the greatest book he had ever read. It was then that Gertrude Stein said, Hemingway, remarks are not literature.

After this we did not see Hemingway for quite a while and then we went to see some one, just after The Making of Americans was printed and Hemingway who was there came up to Gertrude Stein and began to explain why he would not be able to write a review of the book. Just then a heavy hand fell on his shoulder and Ford Madox Ford said, young man it is I who wish to speak to Gertrude Stein. Ford then said to her, I wish to ask your permission to dedicate my new book to you. May I. Gertrude Stein and I were both awfully pleased and touched.

For some years after this Gertrude Stein and Hemingway did not meet. And then we heard that he was back in Paris and telling a number of people how much he wanted to see her. Don't you come home with Hemingway on your arm, I used to say when she went out for a walk. Sure enough one day she did come back bringing him with her.

They sat and talked a long time. Finally I heard her say, Hemingway, after all you are ninety percent Rotarian. Can't you, he said, make it eighty percent. No, said she regretfully, I can't. After all, as she always says, he did, and I may say, he does have moments of disinterestedness.

After that they met quite often. Gertrude Stein always says she likes to see him, he is so wonderful. And if he could only tell his own story. In their last conversation she accused him of having killed a great many of his rivals and put them under the sod. I never, said Hemingway, seriously killed anybody but one man and he was a bad man and, he deserved it, but if I killed anybody else I did it unknowingly, and so I am not responsible.

It was Ford who once said of Hemingway, he comes and sits at my feet and praises me. It makes me nervous. Hemingway also said once, I turn my flame which is a small one down and down and then suddenly there is a big explosion. If there were nothing but explosions my work would be so exciting nobody could bear it.

However, whatever I say, Gertrude Stein always says, yes I know but I have a weakness for Hemingway.

Part Two

The Discovery of Place

In his quest for a sense of the self, the essayist soon finds that he is tempted (even driven) beyond the self to what surrounds and forms that self, to the family and the community with their remembered history and their legends. The search for identity leads outward as well as inward, and the sensitive observer turns his eye on the place he knows best: the place from which he begins or the one in which he chooses to end, the place from which he has fled or the one to which he has come after his flight. The home place that the essayist evokes is not the town or the nation recorded by the social scientist; it is compounded not of statistics and summaries of documents, but of sights remembered and feelings relived. It is not the place of everyone, not a common place, but a unique, a peculiar experience.

It is no more the place proudly celebrated by the Chamber of Commerce than it is that coldly recorded by the historian or geographer. When the writer memorializes his home town, he is apt to bring more dismay than satisfaction to the boosters he has left behind or among whom he continues to live. Art comes often out of a quarrel with experience, and it is the writer's business to remember what the rest of us find it pleasanter to forget: the discrepancy between what we dream we are and what in fact we manage to be. At any rate, when a poet like Dante frankly describes his native Florence or a later novelist like James Joyce or William Faulkner in all honesty re-creates his own Dublin or Oxford, Mississippi, he is accused of ill-will and slander. To be sure, after the writer is safely dead, the vilified home town erects a statue to its glorious vilifier; but that makes little difference in the earlier stages of the game. The plight of the essayist is not dissimilar in this respect from that of the writer of fiction.

Henry Miller in his own peculiar, extravagant way, Nelson Algren in his self-consciously simple prose and Leslie Fiedler in his painful probing of the State in which he has chosen to live continue each in his own manner the tradition of Hawthorne: the tradition of seeing honestly and reporting vigorously the facts of a life in which the author is deeply implicated. Miller is far from subtle, it is true, and Algren no subtler, but Hollywood is not subtle either, any more than is Chicago; and the ironies of these accounts must have added to them the further ironies that California has become the home of Miller and that Algren has never been able to leave the city whose failures he records so mercilessly.

If the bitterness is undeniable in what Fiedler has to say of Montana or Powers of Saint Paul or John Peale Bishop of Princeton there is love, too; indeed, it is outraged love which most often prompts the family quarrels out of which such essays are made, and which keeps a writer crying of the place he cannot leave off exposing: "I don't hate it. I don't. I don't." It is not *necessary,* of course, to feel bitterness as well as love toward the home place or the city one seeks out as symbol (Kazin, for instance, treats with some tenderness his remembered New York; and Katherine Anne Porter describes with almost sentimental reverence St. Francisville and the South for which it stands); but irony at least must always be present. A famous American author once shocked a mild, inquiring lady by insisting that to write about a place well one must *hate* rather than love it—hate it, he hastened to add, "as a man hates his own wife"! There is some rhetorical exaggeration in this remark—but it is not without its share of truth. Some doubleness of feeling there must be, some ambivalence in the essayist's approach to the place he celebrates or deplores; otherwise he will produce only propaganda pro or con, advertising positive or negative, rather than the sensitive response which tells the truth at once about the thing described and the person describing it.

It is not only interesting but essential to notice that almost all the writers included in the first division of this section have spent considerable periods abroad (Miller nearly ten years in Paris and Greece, Miss Porter several years in Mexico, etc.) and that one at least of these authors was prepared to declare himself a permanent expatriate. Yet all returned at last to the America in quarreling with which they had best defined themselves. Such a removal and return is a way of finding a perspective, of establishing the doubleness we have referred to above.

To supplement such a selection of essays about our country, it would have been possible to choose a corresponding group of pieces by some of the same authors about the Other Place, the countries to which they variously fled from the home place they could never really leave. Miller and Bishop have written on France, Fiedler on Italy, Miss Porter on Mexico, etc. It seemed, however, somehow more desirable to establish a contrast by setting against our first group the reactions of visiting Europeans, who found in the United States a needed otherness, against which they proceeded to define themselves and the traditions in which they had been bred. Crèvecoeur, for instance, represents the kind of European who, having first come to our country to stay, for one reason or another returns home—and thus speaks with special intimacy (occasionally with special malice) of a world in which he could not quite manage to live.

The selection from Crèvecoeur seemed a natural point of departure, since it represents in almost pure form the dream of America and of the American as a truly New World and a radically new kind of man. It is important to realize from the start that the European visitor has come to examine a country which he has known (or about which at least he has created fantasies) in his imagination before he has known it in reality. America is a fact of literature as well as one of geography. Reflecting on this, the reader will be in a better position to understand why quite ordinary failings in our government or among our citizens have seemed especially shocking to foreign observers, and why such observers seem sometimes disturbed beyond what the facts they report justify.

All of the essayists included here are professional writers of one kind or another; indeed, most of them are novelists, and precisely because of their practice in creating illusions of reality, they possess a sharpness of vision and a skill at presentation which make their indictments, however sketchy the knowledge behind them and however obvious the bias, uncomfortably convincing. Whatever we may continue to think we are, we know after reading these pieces how we strike the eye of a condescending schoolmaster like Matthew Arnold, a shrill and ambivalent prophet like D. H. Lawrence, a gloomy, anti-middle-class

French intellectual like Jean Paul Sartre. If finally we are tempted to think that these essayists have given us portraits of themselves rather than of our world, we must remember that the former is the real function of the essay; and that, moreover, from so many disparate responses a picture of something different from any single one of them emerges.

As a kind of rebuttal, we have added the essays of Mary McCarthy and Jacques Barzun, pieces written with an awareness of precisely this sort of European criticism in mind. These are no naive defenses of America, but reasoned and wary responses created by minds themselves at first tempted to accept much of the European case. Miss McCarthy's apology for our culture begins in direct answer to the request of a visiting existentialist—a lady, to be sure, but one of the school of Sartre, pledged to the same sombre morality and plagued by the same inherited platitudes. In addition, it seemed good to close with a pair of *general* essays by Americans; since the Europeans we have selected move so quickly to the level of generalization, while most of our American authors have insisted upon the particulars of some limited scene. Perhaps this suggests a fundamental difference between ways of talking about life and culture in the old world and the new, or perhaps it reflects only a more incidental one between the method of the essayist at home and abroad. In any case, one approach supplements the other; and the two in contrast may help the reader in his own search for himself, the world in which he has grown up, and a way to write about both.

7. Soirée in Hollywood

HENRY MILLER

Henry Miller (1891–   ) is an eccentric though basically American type. Born in Brooklyn of émigré German parents, he learned to

SOURCE: Henry Miller, *The Air-Conditioned Nightmare* (New York: New Directions, 1945), pp. 247–58. Copyright 1945 by New Directions. Reprinted by permission of New Directions Publishing Corporation.

speak English late, but acquired early a toughness of mind and a sense of independence which led him to give up any attempt at a formal education and expatriate himself to Paris in 1930. There he first won fame for a series of extravagant, bawdy, comical-serious books, banned by the United States government but much admired by some critics. The war brought him back to the United States, which he observed with a detached and critical eye and reported on in *The Air-Conditioned Nightmare* (1945), from which we have excerpted a section on Hollywood. Despite his wry comments on that state, Miller has chosen to establish a home in California.

My first evening in Hollywood. It was so typical that I almost thought it had been arranged for me. It was by sheer chance, however, that I found myself rolling up to the home of a millionaire in a handsome black Packard. I had been invited to dinner by a perfect stranger. I didn't even know my host's name. Nor do I know it now.

The first thing which struck me, on being introduced all around, was that I was in the presence of wealthy people, people who were bored to death and who were all, including the octogenarians, already three sheets to the wind. The host and hostess seemed to take pleasure in acting as bartenders. It was hard to follow the conversation because everybody was talking at cross purposes. The important thing was to get an edge on before sitting down to the table. One old geezer who had recently recovered from a horrible automobile accident was having his fifth old-fashioned—he was proud of the fact, proud that he could swill it like a youngster even though he was still partially crippled. Every one thought he was a marvel.

There wasn't an attractive woman about, except the one who had brought me to the place. The men looked like business men, except for one or two who looked like aged strike-breakers. There was one fairly young couple, in their thirties, I should say. The husband was a typical go-getter, one of those ex-football players who go in for publicity or insurance or the stock market, some clean all-American pursuit in which you run no risk of soiling your hands. He was a graduate of some Eastern University and had the intelligence of a high-grade chimpanzee.

That was the set-up. When every one had been properly soused dinner was announced. We seated ourselves at a long table, elegantly decorated, with three or four glasses beside each plate. The ice was abundant, of course. The service began, a dozen flunkeys buzzing at your elbow like horse flies. There was a surfeit of everything; a poor man would have had sufficient with the hors d'oeuvres alone. As they ate, they became more discursive, more argumentative. An elderly thug in a tuxedo who had the complexion of a boiled lobster was railing against labor agitators. He had a religious strain, much to my amazement, but it was more like Torquemada's than Christ's. President Roosevelt's name almost gave him an apoplectic fit. Roosevelt, Bridges, Stalin, Hitler—they were all in the same class to him. That is to say, they were anathema. He had an extraordinary appetite which served, it seemed, to stimulate his adrenal glands. By the time he had reached the meat course he was talking about hanging being too good for some people. The hostess, meanwhile, who was seated at his elbow, was carrying on one of those delightful inconsequential conversations with the person opposite her. She had left some beautiful dachshunds in Biarritz, or was it Sierra Leone, and to believe her, she was greatly worried about them. In times like these, she was saying, people forget about animals. People can be so cruel, especially in time of war. Why, in Peking the servants had run away and left her with forty trunks to pack—it was outrageous. It was so good to be back in California. God's own country, she called it. She hoped the war wouldn't spread to America. Dear me, where was one to go now? You couldn't feel safe anywhere, except in the desert perhaps.

The ex-football player was talking to some one at the far end of the table in a loud voice. It happened to be an Englishwoman and he was insulting her roundly and openly for daring to arouse sympathy for the English in this country. "Why don't you go back to England?" he shouted at the top of his voice. "What are you doing here? You're a menace. We're not fighting to hold the British Empire together. You're a menace. You ought to be expelled from the country."

The woman was trying to say that she was not English but Canadian, but she couldn't make herself heard above the din. The octogenarian, who was now sampling the champagne, was talking about the automobile accident. Nobody was paying any attention to him. Automobile accidents were too common—every one at the table had been in a smash-up at one time or another. One doesn't make a point about such things unless one is feeble-minded.

The hostess was clapping her hands frantically—she wanted to tell us a little story about an experience she had had in Africa once, on one of her safaris.

"Oh, can that!" shouted the football player. "I want to find out why this great country of ours, in the most crucial moment . . ."

"Shut up!" screamed the hostess. "You're drunk."

"That makes no difference," came his booming voice. "I want to know if we're all hundred percent Americans—and if not why not. I suspect that we have some traitors in our midst," and because I hadn't been taking part in any of the conversation he gave me a fixed, drunken look which was intended to make me declare myself. All I could do was smile. That seemed to infuriate him. His eyes roved about the table challengingly and finally, sensing an antagonist worthy of his mettle, rested on the aged, Florida-baked strike-breaker. The latter was at that moment quietly talking to the person beside him about his good friend, Cardinal So-and-so. He, the Cardinal, was always very good to the poor, I heard him say. A very gentle hard-working man, but he would tolerate no nonsense from the dirty labor agitators who were stirring up revolution, fomenting class hatred, preaching anarchy. The more he talked about his holy eminence, the Cardinal, the more he foamed at the mouth. But his rage in no way affected his appetite. He was carnivorous, bibulous, querulous, cantankerous and poisonous as a snake. One could almost see the bile spreading through his varicose veins. He was a man who had spent millions of dollars of the public's money to help the needy, as he put it. What he meant was to prevent the poor from organizing and fighting for their rights. Had he not been dressed like a banker he would have passed for a hod carrier. When he grew angry he not only became flushed but his whole body quivered like guava. He became so intoxicated by his own venom that finally he overstepped the bounds and began denouncing President Roosevelt as a crook and a traitor, among other things. One of the guests, a woman, protested. That brought the football hero to his feet. He said that no man could insult the President of the United States in his presence. The whole table was soon in an uproar. The flunkey at my elbow had just filled the huge liquor glass with some marvelous cognac. I took a sip and sat back with a grin, wondering how it would all end. The louder the altercation the more peaceful I became. *How do you like your new boarding house, Mr. Smith?* I heard President McKinley saying to his secretary. Every night, Mr. Smith, the president's private secretary, used to visit Mr. McKinley at his home and read aloud to him the amusing letters which he had selected from the daily correspondence. The president, who was overburdened with affairs of state, used to listen silently from his big armchair by the fire: it was his sole recreation. At the end he would always ask *"How do you like your new boarding house, Mr. Smith?"* So worn out by his duties he was that he couldn't think of anything else to say at the close of these séances. Even after Mr. Smith had left his boarding house and taken a room at a hotel President McKinley continued to say *"How do you like your new boarding house, Mr. Smith?"* Then came the Exposition and Csolgosz, who had no idea what a simpleton the president was, assassinated him. There was something wretched and incongruous about murdering a man like McKinley. I remember the incident only because that same day the horse that my aunt was using for a buggy ride got the blind staggers and ran into a lamp post and when I was going to the hospital to see my aunt the extras were out already and young as I was I understood that a great tragedy had befallen the nation. At the same time I felt sorry for Csolgosz—that's the strange thing about the incident. I don't know why I felt sorry for him, except that in some vague way I realized that the punishment meted out to him would be greater than the crime merited. Even at that tender age I felt that punishment was criminal. I couldn't understand why people should be punished—I don't yet. I couldn't even understand why God had the right to punish us for our sins. And of course, as I later realized, God doesn't punish us—we punish ourselves.

Thoughts like these were floating through my head when suddenly I became aware that people were leaving the table. The meal wasn't over yet, but the guests were departing. Something had happened while I was reminiscing. Pre-civil war days, I thought to myself. Infantilism rampant again. And if Roosevelt is assassinated they will make another Lincoln of him. Only this time the slaves will still be slaves. Meanwhile I overhear some one saying what a wonderful president Melvyn Douglas would make. I prick up my ears. I wonder do they mean Melvyn Douglas, the movie star? Yes, that's who they mean. He has a great mind, the woman is saying. And character. And *savoir faire*. Thinks I to myself "and who will the vice-president be, may I ask? Shure and it's not Jimmy Cagney you're thinkin' of?" But the woman is not worried about the vice-presidency. She had been to a palmist the other day and learned some interesting things about herself. Her life line was broken. "Think of it," she said, "all these years and I never knew it was broken. What do you suppose is going to happen? Does it mean war? Or do you think it means an accident?"

The hostess was running about like a wet hen. Trying to rustle up

enough hands for a game of bridge. A desperate soul, surrounded by
the booty of a thousand battles. "I understand you're a writer," she
said, as she tried to carom from my corner of the room to the bar.
"Won't you have something to drink—a highball or something? Dear
me, I don't know what's come over everybody this evening. I do hate to
hear these political discussions. That young man is positively rude. Of
course I don't approve of insulting the President of the United States in
public but just the same he might have used a little more tact. After all,
Mr. So-and-so is an elderly man. He's entitled to some respect, don't
you think? Oh, there's So-and-so!" and she dashed off to greet a
cinema star who had just dropped in.

The old geezer who was still tottering about handed me a highball. I
tried to tell him that I didn't want any but he insisted that I take it
anyway. He wanted to have a word with me, he said, winking at me as
though he had something very confidential to impart.

"My name is Harrison," he said. "H-a-r-r-i-s-o-n," spelling it out as
if it were a difficult name to remember.

"Now what is your name, may I ask?"

"My name is Miller—M-i-l-l-e-r," I answered, spelling it out in
Morse for him.

"Miller! Why, that's a very easy name to remember. We had a drug-
gist on our block by that name. Of course. *Miller*. Yes, a very common
name."

"So it is," I said.

"And what are you doing out here, Mr. Miller? You're a stranger, I
take it?"

"Yes," I said, "I'm just a visitor."

"You're in business, are you?"

"No, hardly. I'm just visiting California."

"I see. Well, where do you come from—the Middle West?"

"No, from New York."

"From New York City? Or from up State?"

"From the city."

"And have you been here very long?"

"No, just a few hours."

"A few hours? My, my . . . well, that's interesting. Very interesting. And will you be staying long, Mr. Miller?"

"I don't know. It depends."

"I see. Depends on how you like it here, is that it?"

"Yes, exactly."

"Well, it's a grand part of the world, I can tell you that. No place like California, I always say. Of course, I'm not a native. But I've been out here almost thirty years now. Wonderful climate. And wonderful people, too."

"I suppose so," I said, just to string him along. I was curious to see how long the idiot would keep up his infernal nonsense.

"You're not in business, you say?"

"No, I'm not."

"On a vacation, is that it?"

"No, not precisely. I'm an ornithologist, you see."

"A what? Well, that's interesting."

"Very," I said, with great solemnity.

"Then you may be staying with us for a while, is that it?"

"That's hard to say. I may stay a week and I may stay a year. It all depends. Depends on what specimens I find."

"I see. Interesting work, no doubt."

"Very!"

"Have you ever been to California before, Mr. Miller?"

"Yes, twenty-five years ago."

"Well, well, is that so? *Twenty-five years ago!* And now you're back again."

"Yes, back again."

"Were you doing the same thing when you were here before?"

"You mean ornithology?"

"Yes, that's it."

"No, I was digging ditches then."

"Digging ditches? You mean you were—*digging ditches?"*

"Yes, that's it, Mr. Harrison. It was either dig ditches or starve to death."

"Well, I'm glad you don't have to dig ditches any more. It's not much fun—*digging ditches,* is it?"

"No, especially if the ground is hard. Or if your back is weak. Or vice versa. Or let's say your mother has just been put in the mad house and the alarm goes off too soon."

"I beg your pardon! *What did you say?"*

"If things are not just right, I said. You know what I mean—bunions, lumbago, scrofula. It's different now, of course. I have my birds and other pets. Mornings I used to watch the sun rise. Then I would saddle the jackasses—I had two and the other fellow had three. . . ."

"This was in California, Mr. Miller?"

"Yes, twenty-five years ago. I had just done a stretch in San Quentin. . . ."

"San Quentin?"

"Yes, attempted suicide. I was really gaga but that didn't make any difference to them. You see, when my father set the house afire one of the horses kicked me in the temple. I used to get fainting fits and then after a time I got homicidal spells and finally I became suicidal. Of course I didn't know that the revolver was loaded. I took a pot shot at my sister, just for fun, and luckily I missed her. I tried to explain it to the judge but he wouldn't listen to me. I never carry a revolver any more. If I have to defend myself I use a jack-knife. The best thing, of course, is to use your knee. . . ."

"Excuse me, Mr. Miller, I have to speak to Mrs. So-and-so a moment. Very interesting what you say. *Very interesting indeed.* We must talk some more. Excuse me just a moment. . . ."

I slipped out of the house unnoticed and started to walk towards the foot of the hill. The highballs, the red and the white wines, the champagne, the cognac were gurgling inside me like a sewer. I had no idea where I was, whose house I had been in or whom I had been introduced to. Perhaps the boiled thug was an ex-Governor of the State. Perhaps the hostess was an ex-movie star, a light that had gone out forever. I remembered that some one had whispered in my ear that So-and-so had made a fortune in the opium traffic in China. Lord Haw-Haw probably. The Englishwoman with the horse face may have been a prominent novelist—or just a charity worker. I thought of my friend Fred, now Private Alfred Perlès, No. 13802023 in the 137th Pioneer Corps or something like that. Fred would have sung the Lorelei at the dinner table or asked for a better brand of cognac or made grimaces at the hostess. Or he might have gone to the telephone and called up Gloria Swanson, pretending to be Aldous Huxley or Chatto & Windus of Wimbledon. Fred would never have permitted the dinner to become a fiasco. Everything else failing he would have slipped his silky paw in some one's bosom, saying as he always did—"The left one is better. Fish it out, won't you please?"

I think frequently of Fred in moving about the country. He was always so damned eager to see America. His picture of America was

something like Kafka's. It would be a pity to disillusion him. And yet
who can say? He might enjoy it hugely. He might not see anything but
what he chose to see. I remember my visit to his own Vienna. Certainly
it was not the Vienna I had dreamed of. And yet today, when I think of
Vienna, I see the Vienna of my dreams and not the one with bed bugs
and broken zithers and stinking drains.

I wobble down the canyon road. It's very Californian somehow. I
like the scrubby hills, the weeping trees, the desert coolness. I had expected more fragrance in the air.

The stars are out in full strength. Turning a bend in the road I catch
a glimpse of the city below. The illumination is more faërique than in
other American cities. The red seems to predominate. A few hours
ago, towards dusk, I had a glimpse of it from the bedroom window of
the woman on the hill. Looking at it through the mirror on her dressing
table it seemed even more magical. It was like looking into the future
from the narrow window of an oubliette. Imagine the Marquis de Sade
looking at the city of Paris through the bars of his cell in the Bastille.
Los Angeles gives one the feeling of the future more strongly than any
city I know of. A bad future, too, like something out of Fritz Lang's
feeble imagination. *Good-bye, Mr. Chips!*

Walking along one of the Neon-lit streets. A shop window with Nylon stockings. Nothing in the window but a glass leg filled with water
and a sea horse rising and falling like a feather sailing through heavy
air. Thus we see how Surrealism penetrates to every nook and corner
of the world. Dali meanwhile is in Bowling Green, Va., thinking up a
loaf of bread 30 feet high by 125 feet long, to be removed from the
oven stealthily while every one sleeps and placed very circumspectly in
the main square of a big city, say Chicago or San Francisco. Just a loaf
of bread, enormous of course. No raison d'être. No propaganda. And
tomorrow night two loaves of bread, placed simultaneously in two big
cities, say New York and New Orleans. Nobody knows who brought
them or why they are there. And the next night three loaves of bread
—one in Berlin or Bucharest this time. And so on, ad infinitum. Tremendous, no? Would push the war news off the front page. That's what
Dali thinks, at any rate. Very interesting. *Very interesting, indeed.*
Excuse me now, I have to talk to a lady over in the corner. . . .

Tomorrow I will discover Sunset Boulevard. Eurythmic dancing,
ball room dancing, tap dancing, artistic photography, ordinary photography, lousy photography, electro-fever treatment, internal douche

treatment, ultra-violet ray treatment, elocution lessons, psychic readings, institutes of religion, astrological demonstrations, hands read,
feet manicured, elbows massaged, faces lifted, warts removed, fat reduced, insteps raised, corsets fitted, busts vibrated, corns removed,
hair dyed, glasses fitted, soda jerked, hangovers cured, headaches
driven away, flatulence dissipated, business improved, limousines
rented, the future made clear, the war made comprehensible, octane
made higher and butane lower, drive in and get indigestion, flush the
kidneys, get a cheap car wash, stay awake pills and go to sleep pills,
Chinese herbs are very good for you and without a Coca-cola life is
unthinkable. From the car window it's like a strip teaser doing the St.
Vitus dance—a corny one.

8. Princeton

JOHN PEALE BISHOP

John Peale Bishop (1892–1944) was born in West Virginia of Virginian parents, but the chief influence on his life seems to have been
Princeton. Not even his temporary removal to France influenced him
more than his college days when he met F. Scott Fitzgerald and Edmund Wilson. At first quite overshadowed by these friends, Bishop
has been winning, in large part since his death, substantial acclaim as
an essayist, poet and writer of fiction. His novel *Act of Darkness*
(1935) continues slowly to build up a reputation as one of the most
considerable works of the thirties.

Princeton University was founded in 1746 as a Presbyterian college
and is now one of the most desired and desirable places in America in
which to loiter through four years of one's youth. This establishment
of a place whence good Calvinists should go forth—laymen if need
be, divines if possible—was, from the first, doomed to failure. Cal-

SOURCE: John Peale Bishop, *The Collected Essays of John Peale Bishop* (New
York: Charles Scribner's Sons, 1948), pp. 31-40.

vinism requires a clear and mountainous air; Princeton is set near slow streams, and the air is always either softly damp or suave with sunlight. Although the trustees desperately made Jonathan Edwards president of the college, he could do nothing against the indulgent climate. It is evident that the cause was early lost, for the younger Aaron Burr, the first graduate to rise to distinction, destroyed a village virgin at sixteen and shot Alexander Hamilton when a little more mature. I drag in these somewhat doubtful details because it is my conviction that the University of Princeton is what it is largely on account of its site. Had it been left to Elizabeth(town), New Jersey, and named, as was originally intended, for Governor Belcher, its history and character might be quite otherwise.

This quiet leafy New Jersey town, continuously troubled by the sound of bells, still keeps a sense of its past. In Nassau Hall the Continental Congress sat in threatened assembly, and behind the second hand furniture shops of Witherspoon Street are the graves of a half dozen Signers. All but the most indifferent students are aware that a barren acre of cornland to the east of the town is the battlefield of Princeton. It is the privilege of certain towns to mumble over their past. Edinburgh, for example, wears its age proudly and obviously; little of London, except to the bearers of Baedekers, seems older than the Crystal Palace or the Albert Memorial.

Princeton is older than the rocks upon which it sits, perhaps because it needs but four years to establish a precedent in antiquity, so that, since the middle of the eighteenth century, forty generations of youth, each with its stiff customs and cries of revolt, have passed through the town on their way to middle age and mediocrity.

Tom D'Invilliers, the poetic feeder to the epigrammatic hero of *This Side of Paradise,* was aware of this when, with Amory Blaine, he crossed the campus on their last night before leaving for the war: "What we leave is more than this one class; it's the whole heritage of youth. We're just one generation—we are breaking all the links that seemed to bind us to top-booted and high-socked generations. We've walked arm and arm with Burr and Light Horse Harry Lee through half these deep blue nights."

The campus accepts this tradition and attempts an air of even greater age by borrowing an architecture of Oxonian medievalism. It is the fashion just now among intellectuals to decry this imitation of the English collegiate Gothic. But the only endurable form of American architecture is the ferro-concrete skyscraper, which in such a village would be ridiculous. Colonial Georgian is American only by virtue of its early importation. Besides, it has already been used in its two adaptable forms at Harvard and the University of Virginia. No, I am unfortunately fond of the grave beauty of these towers and spires trembling upward, intricately labored and grey; of these grey quadrangles and deep slate roofs, at night hooding under dormer windows' solitary lights, the slate only less luminous and blue than the sky uplifted above it; of Seventy-Nine stately, in red brick, and Holder, enclosing with cloisters and arches a square of sunlight and sod. . . .

Here it is possible that the student should believe himself in a rich current of life. Here no dreamer in his ivory tower, no drunkard, driveling and about to pass out under the table, is farther removed from actuality than the sophomore sunning his white-flanneled legs in front of the soda shops on Nassau Street. The trains that pass three miles away, plying between New York and Philadelphia, loaded with bankers, clergymen, fertilizer agents, Italian immigrants and cigar drummers, are only so many swift blurs trailing a long foam of smoky cloud across a wash of summer green. Life outside exists—for weekends and eventually for more troublesome purposes—but there is no immediate reason to bother about it. After four years, the undergraduate becomes so studiously lackadaisical, so imperturbably serene, that a young Princeton alumnus looks little better to him than a bank president or a United States senator.

For during these four years he will have heard an affirmation of the older aristocratic tradition—such as it was—of the Middle States, that barbarous gentility, that insistence on honor and physical courage, which America as a whole scarcely preserved after the eighteenth century. He will have found life more nicely adjusted than he is likely to find it again in his youth, and he will have had leisure in which to adjust himself after the turbulence of adolescence. During these years he will, according to his measure, acquire a more gracious conduct: the puritan will be forced toward tolerance; the philistine will become less raucous. And some will find the pathetic beauty of the wisdom of dead men and come with the fervor of contemporary discovery upon the books of those who have written beautifully of themselves.

Cut off from the present, it is possible to stare with a wild surmise at the past. In New York and Chicago, Dr. Johnson must remain a rather shadowy corpulence, ghostily closeted in bookstores. In Princeton, his

too solid flesh becomes as substantial as Mr. Chesterton's. Even
Tiberius descends from the monstrous and tragic cloud in which
Tacitus has enveloped him and dwindles to a studious and able admin-
istrator quite as credible as, say, the Honorable Josephus Daniels.
Dante may be found at the end of a dreary term in Italian. And the
young Swinburne, flamboyant and incarnate, with tossing red hair and
wobbly knees, emerges from the Chancellor Green Library with the
1866 volume in his tiny hands.

The campus, already aloof, becomes the more circumscribed because of a lack of girls in Princeton. There are some few, but they are
hedged about or wear flat-heeled shoes or serve epigrams with cucum-
ber sandwiches or—but enough. Of course, every once in a while
some unwary student returns from vacation sad-eyed and engaged,
and, in my generation, there was likewise a society known as the
Grousing Club, from whose adventures Fitzgerald drew heavily in his
thesis on petting. But in ordinary times the ordinary student contents
himself as best he can with masculine society and regards proms and
houseparties as something of a nuisance.

Trenton is near by, but bad form. Except for a few undiscriminating
freshmen, who ride by trolley on Saturday nights to dance with rouged
but chaste shopgirls, the place does not exist. New York and Philadelphia are possible, both socially and by reason of the Pennsylvania
Railroad. One mournful professor recently told me that everyone
spent the weekend in Princeton except the students. Certainly these
absences are more frequent than before Prohibition, when the Saturday night drinking parties at the Nass afforded passable amusement.
Then, at least, weekends were not talked about, whether one went to
Philadelphia for the Assembly or to New York for more ribald amusement.

II

What shall be said of the Princeton social system and the upperclass
clubs, of which so many bitter and uninteresting things have been said
already? The clubs have been called undemocratic, as if a goosestep
method should be applied to choosing one's friends. They have been
assailed as snobbish, when many a poor but honest student has found
that neither poverty nor honesty could keep visitations of upperclassmen and election committees from his door. It has been said that they

accustom the undergraduate to a too luxurious manner of living. Even this is, I am afraid, a fiction, for, if the architecture is at times pretentious, the food is unfortunately simple and wholesome—and it is to be remembered that the clubs are, first and last, eating clubs.

No, the trouble with the clubs is that, once in them, they matter so little after having seemed to matter so much. During the first two years even quite sane students look upon these formidable buildings on Prospect Street as having the awesomeness of the College of Cardinals and as bearing the hereditary privileges of the stalls of the Knights of the Garter. The President of Ivy—the most ancient of the clubs—is regarded more enviously than the President of the University, the Captain of the football team, the Governor of the State or the Prince of Wales. But once the elections are over, it is difficult for even the election committees to maintain their fervor.

These elections are held in the spring term of sophomore year, usually the first week in March. Invitations are sent out to a limited number of sophomores, who move among their own class, sounding out their friends and desirable acquaintances. A day or so later the bicker begins, and committees of upperclassmen from each club are free to approach the sophomores. The campus takes on an air of Old Home Week in a faintly alcoholic Bedlam. Juniors and seniors harass and harangue the amorphous sections; names are brought up to be blackballed or passed. Eventually—no one ever knows quite how—the sections are formed and signed up. The delirium ends, and the sophomore starts self-consciously to cultivate these bosom friends of a week's standing or, in loneliness and it may be with heartburnings, broods over his failure to realize himself.

Many an arrival at this season has based his success on brilliantine and a gift for silence. For at times it seems as if nothing matters much but that a man bear an agreeable person and maintain with slightly mature modifications the standards of prep school. Any extreme in habiliment, pleasures or opinions is apt to be characterized as "running it out," and to "run it out" is to lose all chance of social distinction. Talking too loudly at Commons, an undue concern over the souls of unconverted Chinese, drinking more liquor than can be held quietly and steadily, dressing too dowdily or too flamboyantly, the display of more money than necessary for maintenance on a plane with one's peers—all these are "running it out" and wooing damnation. I knew one able youth who barely got into a club on the ninth ballot because his legs were bowed so that he walked like a sailor in a heavy gale. Another sank far below his hopes after boasting too loudly and complacently of his goings-on in New York. Still another failed altogether because he wore pale yellow shirts and was near-sighted.

These somewhat naïve standards may be violated on occasion by the politician or the big man, but to the mere individualist they will be applied with contempt and intolerance. There are certain activities— all of them extra-curriculum—which have a recognized social value, though what a man does counts rather less at Princeton than elsewhere, certainly less than at Yale. Most influential are those sports which play to large crowds—football, baseball, track and crew. Closet athletics, such as wrestling and the parallel bars, are almost a disadvantage.

Outside of athletics, the most powerful organization is the Triangle Club, an unwieldy and smart assemblage, which each year tours a dozen cities, presenting a musical comedy written, book and music, by the undergraduates on a lively but slightly antiquated model. The English Dramatic Association, with a record of Elizabethan Comedies, Molière and Shaw, is looked on askance, and the more recent Théâtre Intime regarded as a little queer.

Of the publications, the *Daily Princetonian* is received, journalism being, as readers of the *New York Times* know, a highly reputable pursuit. The *Nassau Literary Magazine* suffers from its pretentious title, although literature is admitted in the curriculum. The Philadelphia Society, which is only the Y.M.C.A. in a Brooks suit, is socially and politically powerful. There is more to be said on this subject, but this should be enough to give a hint of the undergraduate's mind at the midpoint of his career.

Yet I do not wish to cry down the clubs. They are pleasant enough places in which to loll over a second cigarette at breakfast, with the sun striping the cloth and the bell for your nine-ten class, which you are quite conscious you are cutting, ringing outside. And dinner is crowded but intimate, with amiable kidding from the professional jesters and all the amenities of youth save wine. After dinner, the idlers saunter toward the movies, and a few will, for an hour, lean across the fire or, in warmer weather, stare wistfully into the blue emptiness of evening, as if youth were immutable and time had stopped. If the judgments on which the elections are based are immature, it is that the sophomores are themselves immature, the average age being but nineteen. The periodical revolts are raised not, as the leaders suppose, against the clubs, but against the intolerance of the young and youth's contempt for all that do not walk after their own way, whether because of some austerity of soul or weak ankles.

Once the division into clubs is made, it is largely ignored. Many of the idols of sophomore year are discovered to have not only clay feet but clay heads as well. The Secretary of the Triangle Club fails to be elected president; the promising athlete becomes ineligible. And a new valuation begins, based more on the individual and less on powerful friends. In the meanwhile, the junior has probably discovered that Princeton is a university and gives himself somewhat belatedly to such education as may be had in the two years that remain.

For it is unfortunately true that the first two years are spent on studies so general and elementary that they might well have been completed in preparatory school. Despite the fact that the entrance requirements of Princeton are as high as those of any university in the country, the average boy at entrance is little better than literate.

This is not the place to go into the defects of our educational system, but it is idle to rail at the universities for their lack of accomplishment while the average American boy of eighteen remains so hopelessly untrained and uninformed. The sole pretense of the preparatory schools seems to be (1) that they prepare their charges for college entrance exams, which is true and the beginning of their inadequacy; and (2) that they build character, which means that they uphold a sweet and serious ideal deriving somewhat from Tennyson's death-mask of the Victorian Prince Consort and somewhat from the most unselfish of the Boy Scouts. But I don't know that anything can be done about it, so long as we keep up a pretense of universal education.

At the beginning of the junior year, the student is free to choose a department in which henceforth he concentrates his energies. History and Economics gather the fairest crowds, with English and the Romance languages holding those who hope for an easy two years or who believe that Princeton can best be appreciated by following beautiful letters. Science, mathematics, and the ancient languages keep only small and serious groups.

During these last two years the ends of education are directed toward upholding the humanities and establishing a more intimate relation between student and instructor. This last is done chiefly through the preceptorials, small and conversational groups, which supplement the more formal lectures. The aim of the faculty now becomes, in theory at least, the inculcation of that form of education so abhorred by H. G. Wells, for Princeton does not attempt to make good citizens, but to create a respect for ideas and to make the student aware how intolerably men have suffered that beauty and wisdom might have form. Education is conceived as being quite as useless as a drawing by Da Vinci, and as having nothing to do with training a man to vote intelligently for Democratic congressmen or to become a more earnest member of the Christian Endeavor Society. There is a certain amount of social service hocus-pocus extant on the campus, and occasionally revivalists appear with theatrical gestures and voices like Dunsany gods, but they do little harm and represent a compromise rather than an aim.

These things are goodly and well enough for the average undergraduate, but the exceptional boy will not come off so happily. If he does not flunk out—which he is more than likely to do through indifference or boredom—he will waste most of his time, unless he discovers a more intimate relation with the faculty than the classroom allows or contemptuously devotes himself to reading outside his courses.

III

My first view of the Princeton faculty was in the autumn of 1913. I had been herded along with some four hundred other freshmen into the seats of Marquand Chapel—a hideous brownstone building, recently burned, to the rich delight of all those who care more for Christian architecture than for Christian instruction. My legs were lost in bulky corduroy trousers; my somewhat skimpy shoulders were evident under a tight black jersey. A black skullcap (the sole remaining vestige of this once compulsory uniform) fidgeted between my knees.

An old man, rosy as a stained-glass prophet and only a little less severe, flapped by in a gown of black.

"That's St. Peter, the sexton," whispered an informed freshman.

The organ began—an orgulous roll—and the academic procession passed slowly down the aisle beside me: gowns of voluminous black, hooded with orange, sapphire and crimson; the pale robes of the Doctors of Oxford and Cambridge, the rich proud reds of the Academie Française: mortar boards and beef-eater caps of crushed velvet, brilliant or black.

Presently they were seated in semi-lunar tiers in the chancel, and a speech began, tactful with platitudes. But I did not hear it. I was intent on the aspect of these grave, serene and reverend scholars; philosophers grown old in the pursuit of Truth, mathematicians entranced by the dizzying splendor of numbers, humanists who dined nightly with Lucretius, Erasmus, Pico della Mirandola and Sir Thomas More. I came out of the chapel still dazed by the sight of these noble creatures and was told to run home by bawdy sophomores eager for horsing.

Have I given you, gentle and credulous reader, a true impression of the Princeton faculty? The question is obviously rhetorical. I have not. I have looked on many academic processions since that day and have never been able to see more than a number of bored elderly gents, tricked out in cotton wrappers, black with an occasional gaudy streamer or color, worn over their everyday Kuppenheimers.

But if the faculty is not, as I supposed in my credulous eagerness, a noble body of rapt scholars, neither is it exclusively composed of the kind of professors made famous by their own published platitudes and the satires of intelligent critics. Most of them are old boys with a weakness for pedantry. They play golf in knickerbockers and are not more than ordinarily absentminded. If they are in their craft disinclined to face facts, their conversation is more full of good sense than is the average businessman's of their years. They lead, indeed, a cloistered life, and many of them are as chaste as the very gargoyles on their scholastic cells. They are jealous of their privileges and regard a doctor's thesis as the only substitute for an initiatory vow in their cult. But they are not moralists using the arrows of Apollo to point a Sunday text. If they deplore the text of Petronius Arbiter, it is not because of the horrible decay of Roman morals, but because of the decadence of Neronian Latin and the mutilations of the manuscript.

There are, of course, this being America, moral enthusiasts and pallid respectabilities who deplore the vagabondage, the thyrsus-twirling and harlot-hunting of the poets they pore over, and who would be mightily disturbed "should their Catullus walk that way." I have not forgotten that lecture where an hour was spent trying to bring the late Percy Bysshe Shelley safely into the Anglican Church. But neither have I forgotten that the wisest of the English faculty are as anxious that the student escape the dominance of the Victorian tradition as Mr. Ezra Pound might be in their place.

For beyond the pedants and the prudes there are still a few wise and gracious individuals, who are more than pedagogues and—on occasión—less than scholars. They do not write moral essays for the *Atlantic Monthly* nor contribute to the Sunday edition of the *New York Times,* having little in common with the box-office hokum professor, that crabbed and senile androgyne who rushes weekly into print to uphold his little store of dogma and to deplore with recent sorrow the death of Elizabeth Browning and Thomas Carlyle. Neither are they erudite non-intelligences, chattering over marginalia, useless phantoms in a noisy and passionate world. They are, rather, quiet-mannered gentlemen, urbane and skeptical, content to uphold the dignity of the scholar in an age without dignity and crassly uneducated. Sometimes I feel that they are all that is permanent in Princeton, when I return and find that all the men who were young with me are gone. Much of the grave charm of the place is due them, and I had rather the elms of McCosh Walk were cut down and burned away than that a single one of them should move from his chair.

*   *   *   *   *   *

After four years at Princeton, what remains beyond a piece of black-printed parchment, waxed and tabbed with a colored string? What beyond the recollection of Sage Tower, misty and strange, standing like a gray alchemist over October's gold; of the days of the big games, with broad orange banners over the towers and the gay, opulent, easy-going crowds come down in motors or by train; of my own small room in Witherspoon with books, dingily red and brown, or with golden blazonries, and the portrait of Georg Gyze, wistfully serene; of rolling marbles down the declining floor to bump against a lecturer who had droned overlong; of examination rooms, intense, hot and cigarette-less? What beyond the recollection of torchlight processions, the "whoop 'er up" song and the gargoyles creeping out into the crimson glare; of drunken students drilling imaginary squads under midnight windows; of the mid-year prom and the gymnasium diaphanous in streamers of apple-green and pink; of arriving drunk at the Phi Beta Kappa dinner and passing out before the roast; of students leaving a little sorrowfully and without illusion for the war, after farewell parties which began on Perrier Jouet '93 and ended on Great Western; of Holder Court under a decrescent moon, softened by snow as by age, startled by the sudden sound of revelling footsteps under the arches?

What remains beyond these and other such recollections? Well, not much, to be frank: a few friends whom time has proved, men with whom I have shared many things and who are after my own kind; a few books I should not otherwise have read; a smattering of Italian and the ability to pronounce Middle English passably well. But it is enough. If I had a son who was an ordinarily healthy, not too intelligent youth I should certainly send him to Princeton. But if ever I find myself the father of an extraordinary youth I shall not send him to college at all. I shall lock him up in a library until he is old enough to go to Paris.

9. Audubon's Happy Land

KATHERINE ANNE PORTER

Katherine Anne Porter (1890–   ) is recognized almost universally as among the most distinguished living writers of short stories, well-known for her collections of shorter fiction, *Flowering Judas* (1930) and *Pale Horse, Pale Rider* (1939). In 1962 she crowned her career with a long-delayed and eagerly-awaited novel, *Ship of Fools.* Miss Porter, who was born in Texas and lived through her early years in Louisiana, has returned to that southern scene often in her fiction (as she has also portrayed her later home in Mexico), evoking re-membered places with the grace and precision she displays in the essay included in this collection.

The center of St. Francisville is ugly as only small towns trying fran-tically to provide gasoline and sandwiches to passing motorists can be, but its lane-like streets unfold almost at once into grace and goodness. On the day of our visit, the only sign of special festivity was a splendid old Negro, in top hat, frock coat with nosegay in buttonhole, a black cotton umbrella shading his venerable head, seated before the casually contrived small office where we bought our tickets for the Audubon pilgrimage and were joined by our guide. The old Negro rose, bowed, raised his hat at arm's length to make an angle of forty-five degrees more or less, playing his role in the ceremonies not only as a detail of

SOURCE: Katherine Anne Porter, *The Days Before* (New York: Harcourt, Brace & World, 1939), pp. 162–71. Copyright 1939 by Katherine Anne Porter; copyright renewed 1966 by Katherine Anne Porter. Reprinted by permission.

the scene, but as part also of its history. Our guide appeared in a few minutes, tying a flowered kerchief under her chin, *babushka* fashion as she came. She was dark and thin and soft-voiced, so typically Louisiana French that we thought she must be from New Orleans, or the Bayou Teche country. It turned out that she was from Idaho, lately married to a cousin of the Percys' at "Greenwood." No matter; she belonged also, by virtue of love and attachment, as well as appearance, to the scene and its history.

Saint Francis, who preached to the birds, and Audubon, who painted them as no one before or since, are both commemorated in this place. In 1779, the monks of Saint Francis founded the town and christened it. Spain ruled the territory then, though the brothers Le Moyne —Iberville and Bienville—had claimed it three-quarters of a century before for France. The Spanish government made a classical error with the classical result. It invited wealthy foreign investors to help settle the country, and the foreign investors ended by taking final possession. These particular foreigners bore such names as Ratliff, Barrow, Wade, Hamilton, Percy; they were all men of substance and of worldly mind, mostly from Virginia and the Carolinas, who obtained by Spanish grant splendid parcels of land of about twelve thousand acres each. These acres formed a subtropical jungle to the very banks of the Mississippi. A man could not, said an old woodsman, sink his hunting knife to the hilt in it anywhere.

The newcomers had on their side the strong arm of slave labor, and definite views on caste, property, morals, and manners. They pushed back the Louisiana jungle mile by mile, uncovered rich lands, and raised splendid crops. They built charming houses and filled them with furniture from France and England. Their silver and porcelain and linen were such as befitted their pride, which was high, and their tastes, which were delicate and expensive. Their daughters sang, danced, and played the harpsichord; their sons played the flute and fought duels; they collected libraries, they hunted and played chess, and spent the winter season in New Orleans. They traveled much in Europe, and brought back always more and more Old World plunder. Everywhere, with ceaseless, intensely personal concern, they thought, talked, and played politics.

In a few short years, these wealthy, nostalgic Americans were, in the phrase of the day, "groaning under the galling yoke of Spain." They foregathered evening after evening in one or another of their mansions and groaned; that is to say, discussed the matter with shrewdness, realism, and a keen eye to the possibilities. They called upon President Madison to lend a hand in taking this territory from Spain, which continued to hold it for some reason long after the Louisiana Purchase. "President Madison," says a local historian of that day, "remained deaf to their cries." The Feliciana planters then stopped crying, organized a small army, and marched on the Spanish capital, Baton Rouge. Harsh as it sounds in such a gentlemanly sort of argument, they caused the Spanish Commandant to be killed as proof of the seriousness of their intentions. They then declared for themselves the Independent Republic of West Florida, with St. Francisville as its capital. A certain Mr. Fulwar Skipwith was elected President. All was done in form, with a Constitution, a Body of Laws, and a flag designed for the occasion. The strategy was a brilliant success. President Madison sent friendly troops to annex the infant republic to the United States of America. This Graustarkian event took place in 1810.

The next year, a Roosevelt (Nicholas), partner in an Eastern steamship company, sent the first steamboat into the Mississippi, straight past St. Francisville and her sister town, Bayou Sara. The days of opulence and glory began in earnest, based solidly on land, money crops, and transportation, to flourish for just half a century.

It is quite finished as to opulence, and the glory is now a gentle aura, radiating not so much from the past as from the present, for St. Francisville lives with graceful competence on stored wealth that is not merely tangible. The legend has, in fact, magnified the opulence into something more than it really was, to the infinite damage of a particular truth: that wealth in the pre-War South was very modest by present standards, and it was not ostentatious, even then. The important thing to know about St. Francisville, as perhaps a typical survivor of that culture, is this: no one there tells you about steamboat wealth, or wears the air of poverty living on its memories, or (and this is the constant, rather tiresome accusation of busy, hasty observer) "yearns for the good old days."

The town's most treasured inhabitant was Audubon, and its happiest memory. This is no afterthought, based on his later reputation. And it is the more interesting when we consider what kind of reputation Audubon's was, almost to the end; nothing at all that a really materialistic society would take seriously. He was an artist, but not a fashionable one, never successful by any worldly standards; but the people of St. Francisville loved him, recognized him, took him to themselves when he was unknown and almost in despair. And now in every house, they will show you some small souvenir of him, some record that he was once a guest there. The Pirries, of New Orleans and Oakley, near St. Francisville, captured him in New Orleans at the moment when he was heading East, disheartened, and brought him to Oakley for the pleasant employment of teaching their young daughter, Miss Eliza, to dance and draw, of mornings. His afternoons, and some of his evenings, he spent in the Feliciana woods, and we know what he found there.

The Feliciana country is not a jungle now, nor has it been for a great while. The modest, occasional rises of earth, called hills, are covered with civilized little woods, fenced grazing-fields for fine cattle, thatches of sugar cane, of corn, and orchards. Both Felicianas, east and west, are so handsome and amiable you might mistake them for one, instead of twins. For fear they will be confounded in the stranger's eye, the boundaries are marked plainly along the highway. The difference was to me that West Feliciana was holding a spring festival in honor of Audubon, and I, a returned Southerner, in effect a tourist, went straight through East Feliciana, which had not invited visitors, to West Feliciana, which had.

You are to think of this landscape as an April garden, flowering with trees and shrubs of the elegant, difficult kind that live so securely in this climate: camellias, gardenias, crêpe myrtle, fine old-fashioned roses; with simpler things, honeysuckle, dogwood, wisteria, magnolia, bridal-wreath, oleander, redbud, leaving no fence or corner bare. The birds of St. Francis and of Audubon fill the air with their light singing and their undisturbed flight. The great, dark oaks spread their immense branches fronded with moss; the camphor and cedar trees add their graceful shapes and their dry, spicy odors; and yes, just as you have been told, perhaps too often, there are the white, pillared houses seated in dignity, glimpsed first at a distance through their park-like gardens.

The celebrated oak *allées* are there at "Live Oak," at "Waverly," at "Rosedown," perhaps the finest grove of all at "Highland"—the wide, shaded driveways from the gate to the great door, all so appropriately designed for the ritual events of life, a wedding or a funeral procession, the christening party, the evening walks of betrothed lovers. W. B. Yeats causes one of his characters to reflect, in face of a grove of ancient trees, "that a man who planted trees, knowing that no descendant nearer than his great-grandson could stand under their shade, had a noble and generous confidence." That kind of confidence created this landscape, now as famous, as banal, if you like, as the horse-chestnuts along the Champs Elysées, as the perfume gardens of Grasse, as the canals of Venice, as the lilies-of-the-valley in the forest of Saint-Cloud. It possesses, too, the appeal of those much-visited scenes, and shares their nature, which is to demand nothing by way of arranged tribute; each newcomer may discover it for himself; but this landscape shares its peculiar treasure only with such as know there is something more here than mere hungry human pride in mahogany staircases and silver doorknobs. The real spirit of the place planted those oaks, and keeps them standing.

The first thing that might strike you is the simplicity, the comparative smallness of even the largest houses (in plain figures, "Greenwood" is one hundred feet square; there is a veranda one hundred and ten feet long at "The Myrtles," a long, narrow house), compared not only to the grandeur of their legend, but to anything of corresponding fame you may have seen, such as the princely houses of Florence or the Spanish palaces in Mexico, or, as a last resort, the Fifth Avenue museums of the fantastically rich of two or three generations ago. Their importance is of another kind—that of the oldest New York houses, or the Patrizieren houses in Basel; with a quality nearly akin to the Amalienburg in the forest near Munich, quite the loveliest house I ever saw, or expect to see. These St. Francisville houses are examples of pure domestic architecture, somehow urban in style, graceful, and differing from city houses in this particular, that they sit in landscapes designed to show them off; they are meant to be observed from every point of view. No two of them are alike, but they were all built to be lived in, by people who had a completely aristocratic sense of the house as a dwelling-place.

They are ample and their subtle proportions give them stateliness not accounted for in terms of actual size. They are placed in relation to the south wind and the morning sun. Their ceilings are right for this kind of architecture, and this kind of architecture is right for a hot climate. Their fireplaces are beautiful, well placed, in harmony with the rooms, and meant for fine log fires in the brief winters. Their windows are many, tall and rightly spaced for light and air, as well as for the view outward. All of them, from "Live Oak," built in 1779, to "The

Myrtles," built in the 1840's have in common the beauty and stability of cypress, blue poplar, apparently indestructible brick made especially for the chimneys and foundations, old methods of mortising and pinning, hand-forged nails.

"Live Oak" stands on a green knoll, and, from the front door, one looks straight through the central room to the rolling meadow bordered with iris in profuse bloom. This house is really tired, worn down to the bare grain, the furniture just what might have been left from some remote disaster, but it is beautiful, a place to live in with its wide, double porches and outside staircase in the early style of the Spanish in Louisiana, its dark paneling, and its air of gentle remoteness.

"Waverly" is another sort of thing altogether, a bright place full of color, where the old furniture is set off with gaily flowered rugs, and the heavy old Louisiana four-poster beds—of a kind to be found nowhere else—are dressed sprucely in fresh curtains. The white pillars of "Waverly" are flat and slender, and the graceful fan-lights of the front door are repeated on the second floor, with an especially airy effect. The vestiges of the old boxwood maze are being coaxed back to life there, and gardenias grow in hedges, as they should.

At "The Myrtles," the flowery iron grille of the long veranda sets the Victorian tone; the long dining-room still wears, between the thin moldings, its French wallpaper from 1840—sepia-colored panels from floor to ceiling of game birds and flowers. The cypress floor is honey-colored, the Italian marble mantel-piece was that day banked with branches of white dogwood. All the rooms are long, full of the softest light lying upon the smooth surfaces of old fruitwood and mahogany. From the back veranda, an old-fashioned back yard, full of country living, lay in the solid shade of grape arbors and trees rounded like baskets of flowers. Chickens roamed and picked there; there was a wood-pile with a great iron wash-pot up-ended against it, near the charred spot where the fire is still built to heat the water.

At "Virginia," we saw George Washington's account-book, made, I believe, at Valley Forge, with all the detailed outlay of that troublesome episode. "Virginia" is by way of being an inn now—that is to say, if travelers happen along they will be put up in tall, canopied beds under fine old quilted coverlets. The large silver spoons in the dining-room came from an ancestor of the Fisher family—Baron de Würmser, who had them as a gift from Frederick the Great. Generous-sized ladles they are, too, paper-thin and flexible. Like so many old coin silver spoons, they appear to have been chewed, and they have been. A thin silver spoon was once considered the ideal object for an infant to cut his teeth upon. But there were dents in a de Würmser soup ladle which testified that some Fisher infant must have been a saber-toothed tiger. "Surely no teething child did that," I remarked. "No," said the hostess, a fleeting shade of severity on her brow. "It was thrown out with the dish-water once, and the pigs got it." Here is the French passport for a Fisher grandfather, dated 1836. It was then he brought back the splendid flowered wallpaper, even now fresh in its discreet colors, the hand-painted mauve linen window-shades on rollers, then so fashionable, replacing the outmoded Venetian blinds; the ornate, almost morbidly feminine drawing-room chairs and sofas.

At "Greenwood," the host was engaged with a group of oil prospectors for, beneath charming, fruitful surfaces, the Felicianas are suspected of containing the dark, the sinister new treasure more powerful than gold. If so, what will become of the oaks and the flourishing fields and the gentle cattle? What will become of these lovely houses? "They make syrup and breed cattle here," said our guide: "that keeps 'Greenwood' going very well. Some people (she named them) wanted Mr. Percy to make a dude ranch of this place, but he wouldn't hear of it."

We mentioned our premonitions about St. Francisville if oil should be discovered. Our guide spoke up with the quiet recklessness of faith. "It wouldn't do any harm," she said. "The Feliciana people have had what money can buy, and they have something money can't buy, and they know it. They have nothing to sell. Tourists come here from all over and offer them thousands of dollars for their little things, just little things they don't need and hardly ever look at, but they won't sell them."

"Greenwood" is the typical Southern mansion of too many songs, too many stories—with the extravagant height of massive, round pillar, the too-high ceiling, the gleaming sweep of central hall, all in the 1830 Greek, gilded somewhat, but lightly. There is bareness; space dwarfing the human stature and breathing a faint bleakness. Yet the gentle groves and small hills are framed with overwhelming effect between those columns; effect grandiose beyond what the measuring eye knows is actually there.

It seems now that the builders should have known that this house was the end, never the beginning. It is quite improbable that anyone should again build a house like "Greenwood" to live in. But there it is, with the huge beams of the gallery being replaced, oil prospectors roaming about, and the hostess sitting in her drawing-room with the green-and-gold chairs, the lace curtains fine as bride veils drifting a little; the young girls in jodhpurs are going out to ride. Here, as everywhere else, there were no radios or gramophones going, no telephones visible or ringing; and it seemed to me suddenly that this silence, the silence of a house in order, of people at home, the silence of leisure, is the most desirable of all things we have lost.

At "Highland," descendants in the fourth generation stand in the shade of the oaks planted, as the old House Book records, in January 1832. The house is older. It has its share of drum tables, fiddle-backed chairs, carved door-frames and wainscoting, but its real beauty lies in the fall of light into the ample square rooms, the rise of the stair tread, the energy and firmness of its structure. The paneled doors swing on their hand-forged hinges as they did the day they were hung there; the edge of the first doorstep—an immense log cypress square-hewn— is as sharp as though feet had not stepped back and forth over it for one hundred and forty years.

"Rosedown" is more formal, with its fish pool and eighteenth-century statuary set along the *allée,* and in a semicircle before the conventionally planted garden. The office still stands there, and the "slave bell" in its low wooden frame. The "slave bell" was the dinner-bell for the whole plantation. Above all, at "Rosedown," the Ancestors still rule, still lend their unquenchable life to a little world of fabulous old ladies and a strange overgrowth of knicknacks sprouting like small, harmless fungi on a tree-trunk. Their portraits—Sully seems to have been the preferred painter—smile at you, or turn their attentive heads toward one another; as handsome and as gallant and elegantly dressed a set of young men and women as you would be apt to find blood-kin under one roof. "My great-great-grandfather," said the old, old lady, smiling back again at the high-headed, smooth-cheeked young beau in the frilled shirt-bosom and deep blue, sloping-shouldered coat. His eyes are the same bright hazel as her own. This was the only house in which the past lay like a fine dust in the air.

Steamboats brought wealth and change to St. Francisville once, and oil may do it again. In that case, we are to suppose that new grand pianos would replace the old, square, black Steinways of 1840, as they had in turn replaced the harpsichords. There would be a great deal of shoring up, replacement, planting, pruning, and adding. There would be travel again, and humanistic education. The young people who went away cannot, alas, come back young, but the young there now would not have to go away.

And what else would happen to this place, so occupied, so self-sufficient, so reassuringly solid and breathing? St. Francisville is not a monument, nor a *décor,* nor a wailing-wall for mourners for the past. It is a living town, moving at its own pace in a familiar world. But it was comforting to take a last glance backward as we turned into the main highway, at Audubon's Happy Land, reflecting that, for the present, in the whole place, if you except the fruits of the earth and the picture postcards at "Rosedown," there was nothing, really nothing, for sale.

10. The Hustlers

NELSON ALGREN

Nelson Algren (1909–), though born in Detroit, moved quite early to Chicago, which has been the background of most of his novels since. Algren is a belated survivor of the school of "proletarian fiction" which flourished in the thirties; that is, he not only describes realistically sordid backgrounds and seedy lives, but develops through his stories certain political notions about the evils of wealth and the virtues of the underdog. His celebration of the inhabitants of skid-row reached its widest audience when his novel *The Man with the Golden Arm* (1947) was turned into a motion picture. The essay reprinted here is from a book of similar pieces called *Chicago: City on the Make* (1961).

To the east were the moving waters as far as eye could follow. To the west a sea of grass as far as wind might reach.

SOURCE: Nelson Algren, *Chicago: City on the Make* (Oakland, Calif.: Angel Island Publications, 1961), pp. 14–22. Copyright © 1961. Reprinted by permission of Russell & Volkenig, Inc., as agents for the author.

Waters restlessly, with every motion, slipping out of used colors for new. So that each fresh wind off the lake washed the prairie grasses with used seacolors: the prairie moved in the light like a secondhand sea.

Till between the waters and the wind came the marked-down derelicts with the dollar signs for eyes.

Looking for any prairie portage at all that hadn't yet built a jail.

Beside any old secondhand sea.

The portage's single hotel was a barracks, its streets were pig-wallows, and all the long summer night the Pottawattomies mourned beside that river: down in the barracks the horse-dealers and horse-stealers were making a night of it again. Whiskey-and-vermilion hustlers, painting the night vermilion.

In the Indian grass the Indians listened: they too had lived by night.

And heard, in the uproar in the hotel, the first sounds of a city that was to live by night after the wilderness had passed. A city that was to roll boulevards down out of pig-wallows and roll its dark river uphill.

That was to forge, out of steel and blood-red neon, its own peculiar wilderness.

Yankee and *voyageur,* the Irish and the Dutch, Indian traders and Indian agents, halfbreed and quarterbreed and no breed at all, in the final counting they were all of a single breed. They all had hustler's blood. And kept the old Sauganash in a hustler's uproar.

They hustled the land, they hustled the Indian, they hustled by night and they hustled by day. They hustled guns and furs and peltries, grog and the blood-red whiskey-dye; they hustled with dice or a deck or a derringer. And decided the Indians were wasting every good hustler's time.

Slept till noon and scolded the Indians for being lazy.

Paid the Pottawattomies off in cash in the cool of the Indian evening: and had the cash back to the dime by the break of the Indian dawn.

They'd do anything under the sun except work for a living, and we remember them reverently, with Balaban and Katz, under such sub-titles as "Founding Fathers," "Dauntless Pioneers" or "Far-Visioned Conquerors."

Meaning merely they were out to make a fast buck off whoever was standing nearest.

They never conquered as well as they hustled—their arithmetic was sharper than their hunting knives. They skinned the redskin down to his final feather, the forests down to the ultimate leaf of autumn, the farmer out of his last wormy kernel of Indian corn; and passed the rain-swept seasons between cheerfully skinning one another.

One such easy skinner listing his vocation lightly, in the city's first directory, as Generous Sport.

Mountain grog seller and river gambler, Generous Sport and border jackal, blackleg braggart and coonskin roisterer, Long Knives from Kentucky and hatchet-men from New York, bondsmen, brokers and bounty jumpers—right from the go it was a broker's town and the brokers run it yet.

It's still the easiest joint in the country in which to jump bond, as well as for staying out of jail altogether. The price commonly being whatever you have in your wallet. If the wallet is empty a fifty-cent cigar will usually do it.

Indeed, the city's very first jailbird got a pass from the city fathers. An antique stray named Harper was knocked down, under the local vagrancy laws, to George White, the Negro town crier, for a quarter. And legally led away by White at the end of a rusty chain.

When antislavery feeling forced the Negro to let the white escape, George wanted only his two bits back. And couldn't collect a dime. So each night scandalized the darkness by crying his loss instead of the hour. He never got his two bits back, but he made a hundred-dollar uproar over it. Every hour on the hour. All night long.

The joint is still in an uproar. Every hour on the hour. All night long.

When the Do-Gooders try to quiet it down they only add drums to the tumult. The village squares arrived too late for a firm toehold.

In 1835 they declared a "season of prayer" and wrested two outlaws right out of the devil's clutches—yet the devil seemed not to miss the pair at all. So they tossed two harder customers into the pokey.

And still nobody cared.

Then they fined a brothel-keeper twenty-five silver dollars, and the battle between the Pure-of-Heart and the Brokers' Breed was joined for keeps. The ceaseless, city-wide, century-long guerilla warfare between the Do-As-I-Sayers and the Live-and-Let-Livers was on. With the brokers breaking in front.

Broke in front and stayed in front despite being crowded to the rail on occasion.

Not that there's been any lack of honest men and women sweating out Jane Addams' hopes here—but they get only two outs to the inning while the hustlers are taking four. When Big Bill Thompson put in the fix for Capone he tied the town to the rackets for keeps.

So that when the reform mayor who followed him attempted to enforce the Prohibition laws, he wakened such warfare on the streets that the Do-Gooders themselves put Thompson back at the wheel, realizing that henceforward nobody but an outlaw could maintain a semblance of law and order on the common highway. Big Bill greeted his fellow citizens correctly then with a cheery, "Fellow hoodlums!"

The best any mayor can do with the city since is just to keep it in repair.

Yet the Do-Gooders still go doggedly forward, making the hustlers struggle for their gold week in and week out, year after year, once or twice a decade tossing an unholy fright into the boys. And since it's a ninth-inning town, the ball game never being over till the last man is out, it remains Jane Addams' town as well as Big Bill's. The ball game isn't over yet.

But it's a rigged ball game.

Once upon a time, when Thirty-fifth Street was the far Southside and North Avenue was the limit on the north, something called the Law-and-Order League shut the Sunday beer halls, and the Beer-on-Sunday Party won the subsequent elections in a walk. A horde of horrified Ohio spinsters thereupon counterattacking the halls by praying at the bar rails pleading with the drinkers to kneel beside them.

There is no record of anyone getting sawdust in his cuffs: this was 1873, and thousands who had come to rebuild the ruins of the great fire were carrying ragged banners crying BREAD OR BLOOD on the streets. Sunday was the one day of the week the working stiff who was still working had to himself. So he just dipped his kisser deeper into his stein, wiped his moustache tidily and ordered another. He knew he wasn't getting any eight-hour day by kneeling for it.

Indignantly then in their hundreds the women marched to City Hall to demand legal prohibition of Sunday beer—and got turned down there cold. Working stiffs and out-of-work stiffs alike booing them gently back to Ohio.

After times had picked up again a Reverend Gipsy Smith, dressed like midnight itself, led twelve thousand black-gowned and black-tied saviors, carrying flaring torches and half stepping in funeral-march tempo to the menacing *boom* of a single drum, up and down the midnight streets of the old Levee.

The piano rolls stopped on a single surprised chord, the little red lamps blinked out together, the big drum called "Come to Jesus or Else," and the saviors cried in one all-accusing voice, "Where is my wandering boy tonight?"

"He ain't in here, Reverend," some awe-struck sinner answered earnestly—and the little red lamps flickered with laughter, a piano roll lightly tinkled a jeer, and the revelry crashed like window-glass with one deep-purple roar.

And roared on all night long.

"We have struck a blow for Jesus," the reverend announced without changing his shirt.

"A church and a W.C.T.U. never growed a big town yet," Old Cap Streeter contradicted him flatly. "Hit's still a frontier town."

Where the gouging and the cunning and the no-holds-barred spirit of the Middle Border still holds as true as rent day.

For despite the Girl Scouts and the Boy Scouts, the missionary societies and the Bible institutes, the Legion of Decency and Lieutenant Fulmer, Preston Bradley and the Epworth League, Emile Coué and Dwight L. Moody, there's no true season for salvation here. Good times or hard, it's still an infidel's capital six days a week.

And with a driving vigor and a reckless energy unmatched in the memory of man. Where only yesterday the pungent odor of stewed dog trailed across the marshes, now the million-candled billboards weaving drunken lights in the river's depths, boast of Old Fitzgerald, Vat 69, White Horse and Four Roses. Where only yesterday the evening crow crossed only lonely tepee fires, now the slender arc lamps burn.

To reveal our backstreets to the indifferent stars.

11. The Open Street

ALFRED KAZIN

Alfred Kazin (1915–   ) is known chiefly as a critic, particularly of
American literature. An early book on our literature won him wide
acclaim and he is at present teaching in that area at Amherst. He has,
however, been working for years on a long book of reminiscences
based on his early experiences among immigrant Jews in Brooklyn
and New York, and on his later attempts to find a place for himself
in American society. The passage printed here is from *A Walker in
the City* (1951), the first published installment of this long work, to
which he has since added a second part called *Starting Out in the
Thirties* (1965).

Every time I go back to Brownsville it is as if I had never been away.
From the moment I step off the train at Rockaway Avenue and smell
the leak out of the men's room, then the pickles from the stand just
below the subway steps, an instant rage comes over me, mixed with
dread and some unexpected tenderness. It is over ten years since I left
to live in "the city"—everything just out of Brownsville was always
"the city." Actually I did not go very far; it was enough that I could
leave Brownsville. Yet as I walk those familiarly choked streets at
dusk and see the old women sitting in front of the tenements, past and
present become each other's faces; I am back where I began.

It is always the old women in their shapeless flowered housedresses
and ritual wigs I see first; they give Brownsville back to me. In their
soft dumpy bodies and the unbudging way they occupy the tenement
stoops, their hands blankly folded in each other as if they had been
sitting on these stoops from the beginning of time, I sense again the old
foreboding that all my life would be like this. *Urime Yidn. Alfred,
what do you want of us poor Jews?*

The early hopelessness burns at my face like fog the minute I get off the subway. I can smell it in the air as soon as I walk down Rockaway Avenue. It hangs over the Negro tenements in the shadows of the El-darkened street, the torn and flapping canvas sign still listing the boys who went to war, the stagnant wells of candy stores and pool parlors, the torches flaring at dusk over the vegetable stands and pushcarts, the neon-blazing fronts of liquor stores, the piles of *Halvah* and chocolate kisses in the windows of the candy stores next to the *News* and *Mirror,* the dusty old drugstores where urns of rose and pink and blue colored water still swing from chains, and where next door Mr. A's sign still tells anyone walking down Rockaway Avenue that he has pants to fit any color suit. It is in the faces of the kids, who before they are ten have learned that Brownsville is a nursery of tough guys, and walk with a springy caution, like boxers approaching the center of the ring. Even the Negroes who have moved into the earliest slums deserted by the Jews along Rockaway Avenue have been infected with the damp sadness of the place, and slouch along the railings of their wormy wooden houses like animals in a cage. The Jewish district drains out here, but eddies back again on the next street; *they* have no connection with it. A Gypsy who lives in one of the empty stores is being re-proached by a tipsy Negro in a sweater and new pearl-gray fedora who has paid her to tell his fortune. *You promis' me, didnja? Didnja promis', you lousy f . . . ?* His voice fills the street with the empty rattle of a wooden wheel turning over and over.

The smell of damp out of the rotten hallways accompanies me all the way to Blake Avenue. Everything seems so small here now, old, mashed-in, more rundown even than I remember it, but with a heart-breaking familiarity at each door that makes me wonder if I can take in anything new, so strongly do I feel in Brownsville that I am walking in my sleep. I keep bumping awake at harsh intervals, then fall back into my trance again. In the last crazy afternoon light the neons over the delicatessens bathe all their wares in a cosmetic smile, but strip the street of every personal shadow and concealment. The torches over the pushcarts hold in a single breath of yellow flame the acid smell of half-sour pickles and herrings floating in their briny barrels. There is a dry rattle of loose newspaper sheets around the cracked stretched skins of the "chiney" oranges. Through the kitchen windows along every ground floor I can already see the containers of milk, the fresh round poppy-seed evening rolls. Time for supper, time to go home. The sudden uprooting I always feel at dusk cries out in a crash of heavy wooden boxes; a dozen crates of old seltzer bottles come rattling up from the cellar on an iron roller. Seltzer is still the poor Jew's dinner wine, a mild luxury infinitely prized above the water out of the faucets; there can be few families in Brownsville that still do not take a case of it every week. It sparkles, it can be mixed with sweet jellies and syrups; besides, the water in Europe was often unclean.

In a laundry window off Dumont Avenue a printed poster with a Star of David at the head proclaims solidarity with *"our magnificent brothers in Palestine."* A fiery breath of victory has come to Brownsville at last! Another poster calls for a demonstration against evictions. It is signed by one of those many subsidiaries of the Communist Party that I could detect if it were wrapped in twenty layers of disguise. "WORKERS AND PEOPLE OF BROWNSVILLE. . . !" Looking at that long-endured word *Landlord,* I feel myself quickening to the old battle cries.

And now I go over the whole route. Brownsville is that road which every other road in my life has had to cross.

When I was a child I thought we lived at the end of the world. It was the eternity of the subway ride into the city that first gave me this idea. It took a long time getting to "New York"; it seemed longer getting back. Even the I.R.T. got tired by the time it came to us, and ran up into the open for a breath of air before it got locked into its terminus at New Lots. As the train left the tunnel to rattle along the elevated tracks, I felt I was being jostled on a camel past the last way stations in the desert. Oh that ride from New York! Light came only at Sutter Avenue. First across the many stations of the Gentiles to the East River. Then clear across Brooklyn, almost to the brink of the ocean all our fathers crossed. All those first stations in Brooklyn—Clark, Borough Hall, Hoyt, Nevins, the junction of the East and West Side express lines—told me only that I was on the last leg home, though there was always a stirring of my heart at Hoyt, where the grimy subway platform was suddenly enlivened by Abraham and Straus's windows of ladies' wear. Atlantic Avenue was vaguely exciting, a cross-roads, the Long Island railroad; I never saw a soul get in or out at Bergen Street; the Grand Army Plaza, with its great empty caverns smoky with dust and chewing-gum wrappers, meant Prospect Park and that stone path beside a meadow where as a child I ran off from my father one summer twilight just in time to see the lamplighter go up the path lighting from the end of his pole each gas mantle suddenly flaring within its corolla of pleated paper—then, that summer I first strayed off the block for myself, the steps leading up from the boathouse, the long stalks of grass wound between the steps thick with the dust and smell of summer—then, that great summer at sixteen, my discovery in the Brooklyn Museum of Albert Pinkham Ryder's cracked oily fishing boats drifting under the moon. Franklin Avenue was where the Jews began—but all middle-class Jews, *alrightniks,* making out "all right" in the New World, they were still Gentiles to me as they went out into the wide and tree-lined Eastern Parkway. For us the journey went on and on—past Nostrand, past Kingston, past Utica, and only then out into the open at Sutter, overlooking Lincoln Terrace Park, "Tickle-Her" Park, the zoo of our adolescence, through which no girl could pass on a summer evening without its being understood forever after that she was "in"; past the rickety "two-family" private houses built in the fever of Brownsville's last real-estate boom; and then into Brownsville itself—Saratoga, Rockaway, and home. For those who lived still beyond, in East New York, there was Junius, there was Pennsylvania, there was Van Siclen, and so at last into New Lots, where the city goes back to the marsh, and even the subway ends.

Yet it was not just the long pent-up subway ride that led me to think of Brownsville as the margin of the city, the last place, the car barns where they locked up the subway and the trolley cars at night. There were always raw patches of unused city land all around us filled with "monument works" where they cut and stored tombstones, as there were still on our street farmhouses and the remains of old cobbled driveways down which chickens came squealing into our punchball games—but most of it dead land, neither country nor city, with that look of prairie waste I have so often seen on my walks along the fringes of American cities near the freight yards. We were nearer the ocean than the city, but our front on the ocean was Canarsie—in those days the great refuse dump through which I made my first and grimmest walks into the city—a place so celebrated in New York vaudeville houses for its squalor that the very sound of the word was always good for a laugh. CAN-NARR-SIE! They fell into the aisles. But that was the way to the ocean we always took summer evenings—through silent streets of old broken houses whose smoky red Victorian fronts looked as if the paint had clotted like blood and had then been mixed with soot—past infinite weedy lots, the smell of freshly cut boards in the lumber yards, the junk yards, the marshland eating the pavement, the truck farms, the bungalows that had lost a window or a door as they tottered on their poles against the damp and the ocean winds. The place as I have it in my mind still reeks of the fires burning in the refuse dumps. Farms that had once been the outposts of settlers in Revolutionary days had crumbled and sunk like wet sand. Canarsie was where they opened the sluice gates to let the city's muck out into the ocean. But at the end was the roar of the Atlantic and the summer house where we stood outside watching through lattices the sports being served with great pitchers of beer foaming onto the red-checked tablecloths. Summer, my summer! Summer!

We were of the city, but somehow not in it. Whenever I went off on my favorite walk to Highland Park in the "American" district to the north, on the border of Queens, and climbed the hill to the old reservoir from which I could look straight across to the skyscrapers of Manhattan, I saw New York as a foreign city. There, brilliant and unreal, the city had its life, as Brownsville was ours. That the two were joined in me I never knew then—not even on those glorious summer nights of my last weeks in high school when, with what an ache, I would come back into Brownsville along Liberty Avenue, and, as soon as I could see blocks ahead of me the Labor Lyceum, the malted milk and Fatima signs over the candy stores, the old women in their housedresses sitting in front of the tenements like priestesses of an ancient cult, knew I was home.

We were the end of the line. We were the children of the immigrants who had camped at the city's back door, in New York's rawest, remotest, cheapest ghetto, enclosed on one side by the Canarsie flats and on the other by the hallowed middle-class districts that showed the way to New York. "New York" was what we put last on our address, but first in thinking of the others around us. *They* were New York, the Gentiles, America; we were Brownsville—*Brunzvil,* as the old folks said —the dust of the earth to all Jews with money, and notoriously a place that measured all success by our skill in getting away from it. So that when poor Jews left, *even* Negroes, as we said, found it easy to settle on the margins of Brownsville, and with the coming of spring, bands of Gypsies, who would rent empty stores, hang their rugs around them like a desert tent, and bring a dusty and faintly sinister air of carnival into our neighborhood.

They have built a housing project deep down the center of Brownsville, from Rockaway to Stone, cutting clean diagonal forms within the onlooking streets, and leaving at one end only the public school I attended as a boy. As I walked past those indistinguishable red prisms of city houses, I kept remembering what they had pulled down to make this *project*—and despite my pleasure in all this space and light in Brownsville, despite even my envious wonder what our own life would have been if *we* had lived, as soon all of New York's masses will live, just like everybody else, still, I could not quite believe that what I saw before me was real. Brownsville in that model quarter looks like an old crone who has had a plastic operation, and to my amazement I miss her old, sly, and withered face. I miss all those ratty little wooden tenements, born with the smell of damp in them, in which there grew up how many schoolteachers, city accountants, rabbis, cancer specialists, functionaries of the revolution, and strong-arm men for Murder, Inc.; I miss that affected squirt who always wore a paste diamond on his left pinky and one unforgotten day, taught me to say *children* for *kids;* I miss the sinister "Coney Island" dives where before, during, and after the school day we all anxiously gobbled down hot dogs soggy in sauerkraut and mustard, and I slid along the sawdust floor fighting to get back the violin the tough guys always stole from my locker for a joke; I miss the poisonous sweetness I used to breathe in from the carmels melting inside the paper cartons every time I passed the candy wholesaler's on my way back from school; I miss the liturgical refrain *Kosher-Bosher* lettered on the windows of the butcher shops; the ducks at Thanksgiving hanging down the doorways of the chicken store; the clouds of white dust that rose up behind the windows of the mattress factory. Above all I miss the fence to the junk yard where I would wait with my store of little red volumes, THE WORLD'S GREATEST SELECTED SHORT STORIES, given us gratis by the *Literary Digest,* hoping for a glimpse of a girl named Deborah. At eleven or twelve I was so agonizedly in love with her, not least because she had been named after a prophetess in Israel, that I would stand at the fence for hours, even creep through the junk yard to be near her windows, with those little red books always in my hand. At home I would recite to myself in triumph the great lines from Judges: *Desolate were the open towns in Israel, they were desolate, until that I arose, Deborah. . . .* But near her I was afraid, and always took along volumes of THE WORLD'S GREATEST SELECTED SHORT STORIES as a gift, to ease my way into her house. She had five sisters, and every one of them always seemed to be home whenever I called. They would look up at me standing in their kitchen with the books in my hand, and laugh. "Look, boychik," the eldest once said to me in a kindly way, "you don't have to *buy* your way in here every time with those damned books just to see Deborah! Come on your own!"

There is something uncanny now about seeing the old vistas rear up at each end of that housing project. Despite those fresh diagonal walks, with their trees and children's sandboxes and Negro faces calmly at home with the white, so many of the old tenements have been left undisturbed on every side of the project, the streets beyond are so obviously just as they were when I grew up in them, that it is as if they had been ripped out of their original pattern and then pasted back again behind the unbelievable miniatures of the future.

To make that housing project they have torn away the lumber yard; the wholesale drygoods store where my dressmaker mother bought the first shirts I ever wore that she did not make herself; how many poolrooms; and that to me sinister shed that was so long a garage, but before that, in the days of the silents, a movie house where every week, while peddlers went up and down the aisles hawking ice-cream bricks and orange squeeze, I feasted in my terror and joy on the "episodes." It was there one afternoon, between the damp coldness in the movie house and the covetous cries of the peddlers, that I was first seized by that bitter guilt I always felt in the movies whenever there was still daylight outside. As I saw Monte Blue being locked into an Iron Maiden, it suddenly came on me that the penalty for my delicious reveries might be just such a death—a death as lonely, as sickeningly remote from all human aid, as the one I saw my hero calmly prepare to face against the yellow shadows of deepest Asia. Though that long-forgotten movie house now comes back on me as a primitive, folksy place—every time the main door was opened to let in peddlers with fresh goods, a hostile mocking wave of daylight fell against the screen, and in the lip-reading silence of the movies I could hear the steady whir and clacking of the machine and the screech of the trolley cars on Rockaway Avenue—I instantly saw in that ominous patch of light the torture box of life-in-death, some reproach calling out the punishment for my sin.

A sin, perhaps, only of my own devising; the sin I recorded against all idle enjoyment, looking on for its own sake alone; but a sin. The daylight was for grimness and labor.

I see that they have also torn out that little clapboard Protestant church that stood so long near the corner of Blake Avenue. It was the only church I ever saw in our neighborhood—the others were the Russian Orthodox meeting-house in East New York, and the Catholic church on East New York Avenue that marked the boundary, as I used to think of it, between us and the Italians stretching down Rockaway and Saratoga to Fulton. That little clapboard church must have been the last of its kind surviving from the days when all that land was owned by Scottish farmers. I remember the hymns that rolled out of the church on Sunday mornings, and how we sniffed as we went by. All those earnest, faded-looking people in their carefully brushed and strangely old-fashioned clothes must have come down there from a long way off. I never saw any of them except on Sunday mornings— the women often surprisingly quite fat, if not so fat as ours, and look- ing rather timid in their severe dresses and great straw hats with clus- ters of artificial flowers and wax berries along the brim as they waited for each other on the steps after the service; the men very stiff in their long four-buttoned jackets. They did not belong with us at all; I could never entirely believe that they were really there. One afternoon on my way back from school my curiosity got the better of me despite all my fear of Gentiles, and I stealthily crept in, never having entered a church in my life before, to examine what I was sure would be an exotic and idolatrous horror. It was the plainest thing I had ever seen —not, of course, homey, lived-in, and smelling of sour wine, snuff, and old prayer books, like our little wooden synagogue on Chester Street, but so varnished-clean and empty and austere, like our school auditorium, and so severely reserved above the altar and in the set rows of wooden pews to the service of an enigmatic cult, that the chief impression it made on me, who expected all Christians to be as fantas- tic as albinos, was that these people were not, apparently, so com- pletely different from us as I had imagined.

12. St. Paul: Home of the Saints

J. F. POWERS

J. F. Powers (1917–   ) passed the early part of his life in Illinois, but has spent most of his later career in Minnesota, though he has also recently lived in Ireland. Among the places he knows best is St. Paul, to which the essay in this collection is devoted. It was originally part of a series of such pieces printed in *Partisan Review* under the general title of "Cross Country." Mr. Powers is best known for his witty and acute analyses in short story form of life among the Roman Catholic clergy. Such volumes as *The Prince of Darkness* (1947) have established him in some quarters as the funniest, profoundest and most original of American Catholic fictionists.

St. Paul is located at 45 degrees north latitude, about halfway between the equator and the north pole, or a little more than 6,000 miles from either. Its longitude is about 93 degrees west. Accordingly, St. Paul is also very nearly midway between the Prime Meridian and the International Date Line, and enjoys a very central position.—*St. Paul: Location-Development-Opportunities,* by F. C. Miller, Ph.D.

The author of the work cited would have wished it that way, I think, and this account would be better if Minneapolis, the sister city, were not mentioned at all or designated only by chaste asterisks. In Dr. Miller's pages the word Minneapolis (and a very silly word it is) is not to be seen save as it appears of necessity in the names of railroads whose main objective presumably was to come to St. Paul. For instance, in establishing the exact whereabouts of the University of Minnesota (not the College of Agriculture which *is* in St. Paul), Dr. Miller solves the problem very nicely by saying it "is within easy access."

Today this is one of the debatable points in Miller. If you look at a

SOURCE: *Partisan Review,* XVI (July, 1949), 714-21. Copyright 1949 by *Partisan Review*. Reprinted by permission of author and publisher.

map, the two cities appear to be joined as one, but if you live here you know this to be an illusion. The yellow streetcars discourage traveling from one city to the other. They are an expensive public service (reputedly in the hands of Eastern interests), take forever to arrive anywhere (recently one got lost going to Minneapolis), hide away in their barns at dusk, and there are no pullman accommodations to be had for the trip. An express bus, also a tool of the interests, stops running at 8 P.M., but it is almost as elusive during the daytime and really acts as a teaser to make commuters content with the comparative stability and slow death of the rails. Even by private auto the trip from St. Paul to Minneapolis is long and winding, fraught with stops, starts, portages, and unless a native, one should take a guide. The fare by taxi is said to be $3.50. Some expected the invention of the aeroplane, later the helicopter, to solve the transportation problem, to bring us together in other ways too, but it never worked out.

The twin cities are anything but two of a kind. Only a stranger would reckon them so. To describe one city to its satisfaction is to malign the other. Minneapolis is still the Zenith of Sinclair Lewis, and proud of it. St. Paul, by comparison, is in part what a writer for the *Saturday Evening Post* called it, "slow and poky, and there are few extroverts around to disturb the calm." The last part is unfortunately too good to be true, but as might be expected the Chamber of Commerce braves fought the appraisal in bitter letters to the editor.

Both cities are doomed by climate and circumstance not to realize the bright promise of their beginnings. St. Paul lives in retirement and grows older gracefully. Minneapolis will very likely collapse all at once, like a noisy salesman from a heart attack. Doubtless St. Paul, the smaller twin (now), is more conscious of the war between the cities, having lost.

Minneapolis can assume a galling indifference to the struggle and get away with it, but the old meanness still crops out. On a street car in Minneapolis recently, I heard a passenger say as a colored woman rose to get off: "Look at that poor girl coming back from St. Paul," a reference to St. Paul's alleged dinginess and still no tribute to her industry. However, we find ways to get back. At Lexington Park, home of the St. Paul baseball club, the Saints, a good thing to say when a Minneapolis Miller flubs the ball a few feet is: "That woulda been a home run at Nicollet," a dig at Minneapolis' cracker-box ball park. (Alas, they are building a new one that will be bigger than ours!) When I first came to

St. Paul I heard the audience at a neighborhood theater boo when a selected short of the Minneapolis Aquatennial flashed on the screen. (I was puzzled then, but now I boo with them: I just can't get enough of this heady chauvinism.)

Minneapolis is a city on a plain. St. Paul rises from the river in a series of hills and valleys. On this Dr. Miller comments: "Some enthusiastic geographers have seriously proposed the substitution of the name of Terrace City." However, between Louis Galtier, the missionary priest who named the city after the disciple to whom his log chapel was dedicated, resenting the earlier Pig's Eye (after the proprietor of a small saloon), and Archbishop Ireland who built the Cathedral of St. Paul, the enthusiastic geographers have gotten nowhere with their proposal. The city remains Christian in name as it does Catholic in fact. Under the head of separation of church and state, it should be mentioned that the St. Paul clergy get passes to Lexington Park. On the other hand, Minneapolis has an FEPC law, but St. Paul, with half the city employees, has twice as many Negroes on the payroll.

The magnificent cathedral at the neck of Summit Avenue dominates the city and surrounding country. Warned by a succession of engineers that the lip of the hill would never support his dream, Archbishop Ireland insisted upon the site and searched until he found one who would agree with him. If he had not discovered his authority, it is probable, like a king, he would have created an acceptable one. And still he was a man of simple tastes, living in a cottage himself, and with Cardinal Gibbons an early defender of the Rights (and Knights) of Labor. He remains, historically, one of the few great American prelates to emerge from continuously poor crops. He was a strong temperance advocate who would have no part, however, in prohibition. He was an ultranationalist, too, who appears to have been absolutely sincere about it, and so it seems tolerable in retrospect, but the effects are still to be seen in the fact that St. Paul's two Catholic high schools for boys are both military academies. The majority of young Catholics go to the public schools of necessity (the military academies have scholastic and tuition requirements which serve as a brake to attendance). The present archbishop, however, is planning to build another high school. (St. Paul has had good luck with its archbishops. The present one is exceptional, no cold executive, a New Englander like the one before him, and he is said to think nothing of making the journey to Minneapolis by streetcar and to need protection from the various loonies who seek him out, finding no audience lower down.)

Dr. Miller writes: "What Man has done in St. Paul is scarcely less impressive than what Nature did in the dim past, since the site of St. Paul was raised above the ancient sea." No man has done more for St. Paul than James Jerome Hill, the empire builder. Here we sing of Jim —not Joe—Hill. His pages in the D.A.B. at the public library are thumbed and annotated—one feels that countless school children, and elders too, have gone to them seeking inspiration and guidance. His deeds and buildings and railroads live after him. (I had meant to do some exhaustive research on Mr. Hill, but the public library's copy of Josephson's *The Robber Barons,* in which Mr. Hill figures prominently, was in use, and the Hill Reference Library, which he endowed, does not list the book.) Mr. Hill was not a Catholic, but he paid for the St. Paul Seminary and contributed much to the building of the Cathedral—doubtless remembering that Archbishop Ireland had provided the immigrant settlers who in turn provided the revenue for Mr. Hill's railroads to the coast. Mr. Hill's grandson, serving his seventh term as a state representative, is said to be a small chip off the old block; it is a little late in the day, even here, to try to be more. The Hill mansion squats in stony gloom across from the Cathedral, is now owned by the Church (a gift), is used for educational purposes.

I have met only one native who knew F. Scott Fitzgerald here and when—and in his words: "He was a quiet neighborhood boy; you know he moved away." My informant was present at the party described in the story, "The Camel's Back," which Fitzgerald explains was written "with the express purpose of buying a platinum and diamond wrist watch which cost six hundred dollars." I thought my informant a little old to have known Fitzgerald as a contemporary until I realized he was about the vintage to have been one of the sad young men, and Fitzgerald himself, if living, would seem a little old to have known himself.

Some of the stories of the period are set in St. Paul, usually with no indication, sometimes under a thin disguise for no apparent reason. (There is much to be said for keeping one's friends and hometown out of it, but Fitzgerald did the kind of job that would only hold up in court.) Toledo in "The Camel's Back," not that it matters, is actually St. Paul. It would be hard to think of Toledo at all if it were not in the same baseball league with St. Paul, which, I submit, is how Fitzgerald managed to think of it. In his Notebooks, what there is of them in *The Crack-Up,* Summit Avenue, "our show street," becomes "Crest Avenue" and "A Museum of American Architectural Failures," which it certainly is, and James J. Hill, "our great man," goes as "R. R. Comerford," and Henry Hastings Sibley, "our first governor," as "Chelsea Arbuthnot." Fitzgerald notes somewhat despondently: "Arbuthnot was the first governor—and almost the last of Anglo-Saxon blood."

"The Ice Palace" is a story that still says something about St. Paul and more about Minnesota. Every year the local businessmen get together and put on a winter carnival with the usual floats and ceremonies. It happens in February, lasts ten days during which time we live merrily under a monarchy—this year under King Boreas XII who opened his reign with these words: "Let us unloose untapped laughter and make merry with good, clean fun. Yea, verily, let joy be unconfined." In private life the king works in a bank and the queen is a stenographer. A palace is erected from blocks of ice, and thereby hangs Fitzgerald's tale. In his time the palace was large enough for the principal character in the story to lose herself in, but this year (things are tough all over for royalty) it was more like a two-car garage. (I hate to think what might have happened to Summit Avenue itself if the Church hadn't discovered that the big houses make very good convents —more than ever the district deserves the name "Vatican City.")

In this story Harry Bellamy, the local boy, is a Yale man ("scratch a Yale man with both hands and you'll be lucky to find a coast-guard"), and like another Yale man, Tom Buchanan in *The Great Gatsby,* he fears for the future of the white race. Tom says: "Have you read *The Rise of the Colored Empires* by this man Goddard? . . . Well, it's a fine book, and everybody ought to read it. The idea is if we don't look out the white race will be—will be utterly submerged. It's all scientific stuff; it's been proved." And Harry says (of the half-submerged "damn Southerners"): "They're sort of—sort of degenerates—not at all like the old Southerners. They've lived so long down there with all the colored people that they've gotten lazy and shiftless."

"Can you feel the pep in the air?" Harry asks, but Sally Carrol Happer, who comes from the South, hates to think of there being snow on her grave and thinks some bitter thoughts about the society she finds in Minnesota, with Fitzgerald obviously on her side: ". . . the men seemed to do most of the talking while the girls sat in a haughty and expensive aloofness. . . . They just fade out when you look at them.

They're glorified domestics. Men are the center of every mixed group." It isn't that way now, and even then it must have been truer of Minnesota than of St. Paul and/or the Irish.

Obviously, given his name and antecedents, Fitzgerald longed to have been born where there was a history not just of settlers and Indians. "France was a land, England was a people, but America, having about it still that quality of the idea, was harder to utter—it was the graves at Shiloh and the tired, drawn, nervous faces of its great men, and the country boys dying in the Argonne for a phrase that was empty before their bodies withered. It was a willingness of the heart." In one story he says, "Warren was nineteen and rather pitying with those of his friends who hadn't gone East to college." If Fitzgerald himself was above "pitying" he was still too aware of going to Princeton, coming home for the holidays, a good part of the going because then he was "from" *somewhere,* so that one feels he was consciously fortunate— it's almost as though he just missed being sent to the state university. Where he lived on Summit Avenue was and is on the fringe—a building of the most impressive stone possible, but an apartment building nonetheless. Here, after running a half mile at its best, Summit Avenue seems to pause and relax before it begins again.

The Scandinavians who abound in Minnesota are described as "righteous, narrow, and cheerless, without infinite possibilities for great sorrow or joy." This, one feels, is a real complaint with Fitzgerald, and the situation remains critical today. Minnesota has still another Swedish governor, another honest man, another reformer. In the last election, alone among cities, St. Paul voted against him—not for sinful reasons entirely, but more out of boredom. St. Paul is now cleaner than Minneapolis, though once the haven of highranking public enemies who showed their gratitude by performing their duties elsewhere. Clean and dismal. It is impossible for an exiled horse-player to find a bookie, things have gone that far. The voice of the slot machine is no longer heard in the land. There is much betting, however, on football games—a very low-church form of gambling. Whenever more money is sought through taxation, the legislators think of liquor and cigarettes. (Recently, when they moved to slap another tax on these items, someone started up a terrible row by suggesting that coffee be taxed instead. Scandinavian coffee-drinkers were quickly interviewed by the papers and what they had to say made very sad reading indeed.)

Catholics predominate in St. Paul, Lutherans come next (they lead in Minneapolis), and the kind of hot-rod evangelism one sees down South is also popular, but the accepted religion is Athleticism. "Why, the best athletes in the world come from these States around here," Harry Bellamy says. "This is a man's country, I tell you. Look at John J. Fishburn!"—alias J. J. Comerford. The name most invoked is that of Bernie Bierman, coach-genius of the University football team, "the Golden Gophers." Mr. Bierman himself is known as "the Grey Eagle." There is a Bernie Bierman Hour on the radio during which Saturday's game is prayed over and incense offered to the days when Minnesota was great. Six of the seven Twin City stations carried every home game last year (the backsliding station played popular records, but one of the others re-broadcasted the game in the evening). It is a rare household that isn't headed by a hunter. Fly-tying is taught at an academy of art. The book page of the Sunday *Pioneer Press,* since the abdication of James Gray who used to do a daily review too, has been cut to one AP review, but the doings of duck and deer are watched closely, and there is a considerable body of criticism on these subjects. A *cause célèbre* concerns the pheasant and the fish. South Dakota has revoked hunting privileges for Minnesotans, and Minnesota threatens to retaliate by denying fishing licenses to South Dakotans. Both sides fear an "incident" in the cold war. Only one man is wise enough to arbitrate—Cedric Adams, the gifted columnist and newscaster, the friend of Arthur Godfrey and Bennett Cerf—but even he, like the Pope, is not trusted in all quarters. Meanwhile both sides claim to have the bomb.

In the war to come between New York and Chicago, in which there should be a P.R. Brigade, it is likely St. Paul would join whichever side Minneapolis didn't. This is not a certainty, of course, and one should not, as I do not, reckon entirely without the forces working for unity. Much might depend on what Boston did, with which St. Paul has faint affinities. ("When Boston was married to the locomotive, their first child was St. Paul, their second Portland."—Anon.) And if Minneapolis were attacked by Chicago, for plagiarism, say, it is safe to predict that St. Paul, seeing here a blow against Minnesota herself (*"L'E-toile du Nord über Alles"*) would close ranks with the old enemy.

It is true that this rivalry does not exist among the leisure classes of either city, at least not to the extent I've pictured it, but I have not spoken of this minority insulated as they are from the common concerns, from the simple loyalties and fears which they nevertheless arouse and prey upon as the need arises to market, as the local product, their beer, their war, their candidacy. They are welcome to the larger view and other refinements. Meanwhile, by way of envoi, I say with one citizen who wrote to the *St. Paul Pioneer Press*—"The only thing that marred my enjoyment of the recent carnival was the Minneapolis announcer on WTCN who described the last portion of the big Saturday parade as it marched through the (St. Paul) Auditorium. Twice during his description of the beauty and magnificence of the lovely girls and floats he said: 'Right here in the Minneapolis Auditorium.' If he had only said it once we might have excused it as a slip."

13. Montana: or The End of Jean Jacques Rousseau

LESLIE FIEDLER

Leslie Fiedler (1917–   ) first contributed his essay on Montana to the same series in which the Powers piece appeared, but had republished it in his collection *An End to Innocence* (1955). Mr. Fiedler was born and educated in the East, but lived in Montana from 1941 to 1964, with time off for extended stays elsewhere, including two years in Italy; he has since moved to Buffalo, New York. A writer of short stories and poems as well as an essayist, Mr. Fiedler became with the publication of the first edition of this volume a compiler of textbooks, too.

> *Hier oder nirgends ist Amerika.*
>
> Goethe

There is a sense, disturbing to good Montanans, in which Montana is a by-product of European letters, an invention of the Romantic move-

SOURCE: Leslie Fiedler, *An End to Innocence* (Boston: Beacon Press, 1955), pp. 131–41. Copyright 1955 by Beacon Press, Inc. Reprinted by permission of Beacon Press, Inc.

ment in literature. In 1743 a white man penetrated Montana for the
first time, but there was then simply nothing to *do* with it: nothing yet
to do economically in the first place, but also no way of assimilating
the land to the imagination. Before the secure establishment of the
categories of the *intéressant* and the "picturesque," how could one
have come to terms with the inhumanly virginal landscape: the
atrocious magnificence of the mountains, the illimitable brute fact of the
prairies? A new setting for hell, perhaps, but no background for any
human feeling discovered up to that point; even *Sturm und Drang* was
yet to come.

   And what of the Indians? The redskin had been part of daily life in
America and a display piece in Europe for a couple of hundred years,
but he had not yet made the leap from a fact of existence to one of
culture. *The Spirit of Christianity* of Chateaubriand and the expedition of Lewis and Clark that decisively opened Montana to the East
were almost exactly contemporary, and both had to await the turn of
the nineteenth century. Sacajawea, the Indian girl guide of Captain
Clark (the legendary Sacajawea, of course, shorn of such dissonant
realistic details as a husband, etc.), is as much a product of a new sensibility as Atala—and neither would have been possible without
Rousseau and the beautiful lie of the Noble Savage. By the time the
trapper had followed the explorer, and had been in turn followed by
the priest and the prospector, George Catlin in paint and James
Fenimore Cooper in the novel had fixed for the American imagination
the fictive Indian and the legend of the ennobling wilderness: the primitive as Utopia. Montana was psychologically possible.

   One knows generally that, behind the thin neo-Classical façade of
Virginia and Philadelphia and Boston, the mythical meanings of
America have traditionally been sustained by the Romantic sensibility
(the hero of the first American novel died a suicide, a copy of *Werther*
lying on the table beside him); that America had been unremittingly
dreamed from East to West as a testament to the original goodness of
man: from England and the Continent to the Atlantic seaboard; from
the Atlantic seaboard to the Midwest; from the Midwest to the Rocky
Mountains and the Pacific. And the margin where the Dream has encountered the resistance of fact, where the Noble Savage has confronted Original Sin (the edge of hysteria: of the twitching revivals,
ritual drunkenness, "shooting up the town," of the rape of nature and

the almost compulsive slaughter of beasts) we call simply: the Frontier.

Guilt and the Frontier are coupled from the first; but the inhabitants of a Primary Frontier, struggling for existence under marginal conditions, have neither the time nor energy to feel *consciously* the contradiction between their actuality and their dream. Survival is for them a sufficient victory. The contradiction remains largely unrealized, geographically sundered; for those who continue to dream the Dream are in their safe East (Cooper in Westchester or New York City), and those who live the fact have become total Westerners, deliberately cut off from history and myth, immune even to the implications of their own landscape. On into the second stage of the Frontier, it is dangerous for anyone who wants to *live* in a Western community to admire the scenery openly (it evokes the Dream); such sentiments are legitimate only for "dudes," that is to say, visitors and barnstorming politicians.

But the schoolmarm, pushing out before her the whore, symbol of the denial of romance, moves in from the East to marry the rancher or the mining engineer (a critical cultural event intuitively preserved as a convention of the Western movie); and the Dream and the fact confront each other openly. The schoolteacher brings with her the sentimentalized Frontier novel, and on all levels a demand begins to grow for some kind of art to nurture the myth, to turn a way of life into a culture. The legend is ready-made and waiting, and speedily finds forms in the pulps, the movies, the Western story, the fake cowboy song—manufactured at first by absentee dudes, but later ground out on the spot by cultural "compradors." The Secondary Frontier moves from naïveté to an elementary consciousness of history and discrepancy; on the one hand, it falsifies history, idealizing even the recent past into the image of the myth, while, on the other hand, it is driven to lay bare the failures of its founders to live up to the Rousseauistic ideal. The West is reinvented!

At the present moment, Montana is in some respects such a Secondary Frontier, torn between an idolatrous regard for its refurbished past (the naïve culture it holds up defiantly against the sophistication of the East, not realizing that the East *requires* of it precisely such a contemporary role), and a vague feeling of guilt at the confrontation of the legend of its past with the real history that keeps breaking through.

But in other respects, Montana has gone on to the next stage: the Tertiary or pseudo-Frontier, a past artificially contrived for commercial purposes, the Frontier as bread and butter.

In the last few years, Montana has seen an efflorescence of "Sheriff's Posses"; dude ranches; chamber of commerce rodeos, hiring professional riders; and large-scale "Pioneer Days," during which the bank clerk and the auto salesman grow beards and "go Western" to keep the tourist-crammed coaches of the Northern Pacific and the Great Northern rolling. The East has come to see its ancient dream in action—and they demand it on the line, available for the two-week vacationer. What the Easterner expects, the Montanan is prepared to give him, a sham mounted half in cynicism, half with the sense that this is, after all, what the West really means, merely made visible, vivid. There is, too, a good deal of "play" involved, a not wholly unsympathetic boyish pleasure in dressing up and pulling the leg of the outlander, which over-lays and to some degree mitigates the cruder motives of "going Western." But in Montana's larger cities and towns a new kind of entrepreneur has appeared: the Rodeo and Pioneer Days Manager, to whom the West is strictly business. There is scarcely a Montanan who does not at one remove or another share in the hoax and in the take; who has not, like the night-club Negro or the stage Irishman, become the pimp of his particularity, of the landscape and legend of his state.

Astonishingly ignorant of all this, I came from the East in 1941 to live in Montana, possessing only what might be called the standard Eastern equipment: the name of the state capital (mispronounced); dim memories of a rather absurd poem that had appeared, I believe, in *The Nation,* and that began: "Hot afternoons have been in Montana"; some information about Burton K. Wheeler; and the impression that Montana (or was it Idaho?) served Ernest Hemingway as a sort of alternative Green Hills of Africa. I had, in short, inherited a shabby remnant of the Romantic myth; and, trembling on an even more remote periphery of remembering, I was aware of visions of the Indian (out of Cooper and "The Vanishing American") and the Cowboy, looking very much like Tom Mix. I was prepared not to call cattle "cows," and resolutely to face down any student who came to argue about his grades armed with a six-shooter.

I was met unexpectedly by the Montana Face. What I had been expecting I do not clearly know; zest, I suppose, naïveté, a ruddy and straightforward kind of vigor—perhaps even honest brutality. What I found seemed, at first glance, reticent, sullen, weary—full of self-sufficient stupidity; a little later it appeared simply inarticulate, with all the dumb pathos of what cannot declare itself: a face developed not for sociability or feeling, but for facing into the weather. It said friendly things to be sure, and meant them; but it had no adequate physical expressions even for friendliness, and the muscles around the mouth and eyes were obviously unprepared to cope with the demands of any more complicated emotion. I felt a kind of innocence behind it, but an innocence difficult to distinguish from simple ignorance. In a way, there was something heartening in dealing with people who had never seen, for instance, a Negro or a Jew or a Servant, and were immune to all their bitter meanings; but the same people, I knew, had never seen an art museum or a ballet or even a movie in any language but their own, and the poverty of experience had left the possibilities of the human face in them incompletely realized.

"Healthy!" I was tempted to think contemptuously, missing the conventional stigmata of neurosis I had grown up thinking the inevitable concomitants of intelligence. It was true, certainly, that neither the uses nor the abuses of conversation, the intellectual play to which I was accustomed, flourished here; in that sense the faces didn't lie. They were conditioned by a mean, a parsimonious culture; but they were by no means mentally incurious—certainly not "healthy," rather pricked invisibly by insecurity and guilt. To believe anything else was to submit to a kind of parody of the Noble Savage, the Healthy Savage—stupidity as mental health. Indeed there was, in their very inadequacy at expressing their inwardness, the possibility of pathos at least—perhaps even tragedy. Such a face to stand at the focus of reality and myth, and in the midst of all the grandiloquence of the mountains! One reads behind it a challenge that demands a great, liberating art, a ritual of expression—and there is, of course, the movies.

The seediest moving-picture theater in town, I soon discovered, showed every Saturday the same kind of Western picture at which I had yelled and squirmed as a kid, clutching my box of jujubes; but in this context it was different. The children still eagerly attended, to be sure—but also the cowhands. In their run-over-at-the-heels boots and dirty jeans, they were apparently willing to invest a good part of their day off watching Gene and Roy, in carefully tailored togs, get the rustlers, save the ranch, and secure the Right; meanwhile making their own jobs, their everyday work into a symbol of the Natural Gentleman at home.

They *believed it all*—not only that the Good triumphs in the end, but that the authentic hero is the man who herds cattle. Unlike, for instance, the soldier at the war picture, they never snickered, but cheered at all the right places; and yet, going out from contemplating their idealized selves to get drunk or laid, they must somehow have felt the discrepancy, as failure or irony or God knows what. Certainly for the bystander watching the cowboy, a comic book under his arm, lounging beneath the bright poster of the latest Roy Rogers film, there is the sense of a joke on someone—and no one to laugh. It is nothing less than the total myth of the goodness of man in a state of nature that is at stake every Saturday after the show at the Rialto; and, though there is scarcely anyone who sees the issue clearly or as a whole, most Montanans are driven instinctively to try to close the gap.

The real cowpuncher begins to emulate his Hollywood version; and the run-of-the-mill professional rodeo rider, who has turned a community work-festival into paying entertainment, is an intermediary between life and the screen, the poor man's Gene Autry. A strange set of circumstances has preserved in the cowboy of the horse opera the Child of Nature, Natty Bumppo become Roy Rogers (the simple soul ennobled by intimacy with beasts and a virginal landscape), and has transformed his saga into the national myth. The boyhood of most living Americans does not go back, beyond the first movie cowpuncher, and these days the kid without a cowboy outfit is a second-class citizen anywhere in America. Uncle Sam still survives as our public symbol; but actually America has come to picture itself in chaps rather than striped pants. Since we are comparatively historyless and culturally dependent, our claim to moral supremacy rests upon a belief that a high civilization is at a maximum distance from goodness; the cowboy is more noble than the earl.

But, on the last frontiers of Montana, the noble lie of Rousseau is simply a lie; the face on the screen is debunked by the watcher. The tourist, of course, can always go to the better theaters, drink at the more elegant bars beside the local property owners, dressed up for Pioneer Days. The cowhands go to the shabby movie house off the main drag and do their drinking in their own dismal places. And when the resident Easterner or the visitor attempts to pursue the cowpuncher to his authentic dive, the owner gets rich, chases out the older whores, puts in neon lights and linoleum—which, I suppose, serves everybody right.

But the better-educated Montanan does not go to the Westerns. He discounts in advance the vulgar myth of the Cowboy, where the audience gives the fable the lie, and moves the Dream, the locus of innocence, back into a remoter past; the surviving Cowboy is surrendered for the irrecoverable Pioneer. It is the Frontiersman, the Guide who are proposed as symbols of original nobility: Jim Bridger or John Colter, who outran half a tribe of Indians, barefoot over brambles. But this means giving up to begin with the possibilities that the discovery of a New World had seemed to promise: a present past, a primitive *now,* America as a contemporary Golden Age.

When the point of irreconcilable conflict between fact and fiction had been reached earlier, the Dream had been projected westward toward a new Frontier—but Montana is a *last Frontier;* there is no more ultimate West. Here the myth of the Noble Woodsman can no longer be maintained in space (the dream of Rousseau reaches a cul-de-sac at the Lions Club luncheon in Two Dot, Montana); it retreats from geography into time, from a discoverable West into the realm of an irrecoverable past. But even the past is not really safe.

Under the compulsion to examine his past (and there have been recently several investigations, culminating in the Rockefeller Foundation-sponsored Montana Study), the contemporary Montanan, pledged to history though nostalgic for myth, becomes willy-nilly an iconoclast. Beside a John Colter he discovers a Henry Plummer, the sheriff who was for years secretly a bandit; and the lynch "justice" to which Plummer was brought seems to the modern point of view as ambiguous as his career. The figure of the Pioneer becomes ever more narrow, crude, brutal; his law is revealed as arbitrary force, his motive power as—greed. The Montanan poring over his past comes to seem like those dance-hall girls, of whom a local story tells, panning the ashes of a road agent who had been lynched and burned, for the gold it had been rumored he was carrying. Perhaps there had never been any gold in the first place. . . .

It is in his relations with the Indian that the Pioneer shows to worst advantage. The record of those relations is one of aggression and deceit and, more remotely, the smug assumption that anything goes with "Savages." There are honorable exceptions among the early missionaries, but it is hard for a Protestant culture to make a Jesuit its hero. For many years the famous painting of Custer's Last Stand hung in the state university, where the students were being taught facts that kept them from taking Custer for the innocent Victim, the symbolic figure of the white man betrayed by crafty redskins that he is elsewhere. In Montana it is difficult to see the slaughter at Little Big Horn as anything but the result of a tactical error in a long warfare with whose motives one can no longer sympathize.

Driving across Montana, the conscientious sightseer who slows up for the signs saying "Historic Point 1000 Feet" can read the roadside marker beside US 2 at Chinook, which memorializes "The usual fork-tongued methods of the white which had deprived these Indians of their hereditary lands," "One of the blackest records of our dealings with the Indians . . ." Or at Poplar he can learn how the Assiniboines "are now waiting passively for the fulfillment of treaties made with 'The Great White Father.' "

It is at first thoroughly disconcerting to discover such confessions of shame blessed by the state legislature and blazoned on the main roads where travelers are enjoined to stop and notice. What motives can underlie such declarations: The feeling that simple confession is enough for absolution? A compulsion to blurt out one's utmost indignity? A shallow show of regret that protects a basic indifference? It is not only the road markers that keep alive the memory of the repeated betrayals and acts of immoral appropriation that brought Montana into existence; there are books to document the story, and community pageants to present it in dramatic form. The recollection of a common guilt comes to be almost a patriotic duty.

What is primarily involved is, I think, an attempt to *identify* with the Indian. Notice in the sentences quoted from highway signs the use of Indian terminology, "fork-tongued," "Great White Father"—the attempt to get *inside* the Indian's predicament. If the Pioneer seems an ignoble figure beside the Indian, it is perhaps because he was, as a Noble Savage, not quite savage enough; as close as he was to nature, the White Pioneer, already corrupted by Europe and civilization, could not achieve the saving closeness. "Civilization," a road sign between Hysham and Forsyth ironically comments, "is a wonderful thing, according to some people." The corpse of Rousseau is still twitching.

At the beginnings of American literature, Cooper had suggested two avatars of primeval goodness: Pioneer and Indian, the alternative nobility of Natty Bumppo and Chingachgook; and the Montanan, struggling to hang on to the Romantic denial of Original Sin, turns to the latter, makes the injured Chief Joseph or Sitting Bull the Natural Gentleman in place of the deposed Frontiersman.

But the sentimentalized Indian will not stand up under scrutiny either. "The only good Indian is a dead Indian," the old folk saying asserts; and indeed the Montanan who is busy keeping the living Indian in the ghetto of the reservation cannot afford to believe too sincerely in his nobility. The cruelest aspect of social life in Montana is the exclusion of the Indian; deprived of his best land, forbidden access to the upper levels of white society, kept out of any job involving prestige, even in some churches confined to the back rows, but of course protected from whisky and comforted with hot lunches and free hospitals —the actual Indian is a constant reproach to the Montanan, who feels himself Nature's own democrat, and scorns the South for its treatment of the Negro, the East for its attitude toward the Jews. To justify the continuing exclusion of the Indian, the local white has evolved the theory that the redskin is *naturally* dirty, lazy, dishonest, incapable of assuming responsibility—a troublesome child; and this theory confronts dumbly any attempt at reasserting the myth of the Noble Savage.

The trick is, of course, to *keep* the Indian what he is, so that he may be pointed out, his present state held up as a justification for what has been done to him. And the trick works; the Indian acts as he is expected to; confirmed in indolence and filth, sustained by an occasional smuggled bout of drunkenness, he does not seem even to have clung to his original resentment, lapsing rather into apathy and a certain self-contempt. The only thing white civilization had brought to the Indian that might be judged a good was a new religion; but one hears tales now of the rise of dope-cults, of "Indian Christianity," in which Jesus and Mary and the drug *peyote* are equally adored. Once I traveled for two days with an Indian boy on his way to be inducted into the Army; and, when he opened the one paper satchel he carried, it contained: a single extra suit of long underwear and forty comic books—all the goods, material and spiritual, with which our culture had endowed him.

On the side of the whites, there is, I think, a constantly nagging though unconfessed sense of guilt, perhaps the chief terror that struggles to be registered on the baffled Montanan Face. It is a struggle much more difficult for the Montana "liberal" to deal with than those other conflicts between the desired and the actual to which he turns almost with relief: the fight with the Power Company or the Anaconda Copper Mining Company for the instruments of communication and the possibilities of freedom. The latter struggles tend to pre-empt the liberal's imagination, because on them he can take an unequivocal stand; but in respect to the Indian he is torn with inner feelings of guilt, the knowledge of his own complicity in perpetuating the stereotypes of prejudice and discrimination. In that relationship he cannot wholly dissociate himself from the oppressors; by his color, he is born into the camp of the Enemy.

There is, of course, no easy solution to the Indian problem; but so long as the Montanan fails to come to terms with the Indian, despised and outcast in his open-air ghettos, just so long will he be incapable of coming to terms with his own real past, of making the adjustment between myth and reality upon which a successful culture depends. When he admits that the Noble Savage is a lie; when he has learned that his state is where the myth comes to die (it is here, one is reminded, that the original of Huck Finn ended his days, a respected citizen), the Montanan may find the possibilities of tragedy and poetry for which so far he has searched his life in vain.

14. *From* Letters from an American Farmer

HECTOR ST. JEAN DE CRÈVECOEUR

Michel Guillaume Jean de Crèvecoeur (1735–1813) wrote under the pen-name of J. Hector St. John, a name honored by the citizens of St. Johnsbury, Vermont, whose town still preserves the memory of one of the first Europeans to celebrate the ideal of American character. Though he was born and died in France; though he wrote in French; though he fought with Montcalm against Wolfe and supported the Loyalists against the Revolutionists during our War for Independence, Crèvecoeur has come to seem an American writer.

SOURCE: Hector St. Jean de Crèvecoeur, *Letters from an American Farmer*, 1782, Letter II (London: J. M. Dent, 1926), pp. 157–90.

This selection is taken from his *Letters from an American Farmer* (1782), which he composed during his years as a settler in the United States on a frontier farm finally destroyed by Indians.

I wish I could be acquainted with the feelings and thoughts which must agitate the heart and present themselves to the mind of an enlightened Englishman, when he first lands on this continent. He must greatly rejoice, that he lived at a time to see this fair country discovered and settled; he must necessarily feel a share of national pride, when he views the chain of settlements which embellishes these extended shores. When he says to himself, this is the work of my countrymen, who, when convulsed by factions, afflicted by a variety of miseries and wants, restless and impatient, took refuge here. They brought along with them their national genius, to which they principally owe what liberty they enjoy, and what substance they possess. Here he sees the industry of his native country, displayed in a new manner, and traces in their works the embryos of all the arts, sciences, and ingenuity which flourish in Europe. Here he beholds fair cities, substantial villages, extensive fields, an immense country filled with decent houses, good roads, orchards, meadows, and bridges, where an hundred years ago all was wild, woody, and uncultivated!

What a train of pleasing ideas this fair spectacle must suggest! it is a prospect which must inspire a good citizen with the most heartfelt pleasure. The difficulty consists in the manner of viewing so extensive a scene. He is arrived on a new continent; a modern society offers itself to his contemplation, different from what he had hitherto seen. It is not composed, as in Europe, of great lords who possess every thing, and of a herd of people who have nothing. Here are no aristocratical families, no courts, no kings, no bishops, no ecclesiastical dominion, no invisible power giving to a few a very visible one; no great manufacturers employing thousands, no great refinements of luxury. The rich and the poor are not so far removed from each other as they are in Europe.

Some few towns excepted, we are all tillers of the earth, from Nova Scotia to West Florida. We are a people of cultivators, scattered over an immense territory, communicating with each other by means of good roads and navigable rivers, united by the silken bands of mild government, all respecting the laws without dreading their power, because they are equitable. We are all animated with the spirit of indus-

try, which is unfettered, and unrestrained, because each person works
for himself. If he travels through our rural districts, he views not the
hostile castle, and the haughty mansion, contrasted with the clay-built
hut and miserable cabin, where cattle and men help to keep each other
warm, and dwell in meanness, smoke, and indigence. A pleasing uniformity of decent competence appears throughout our habitations.
The meanest of our log-houses is a dry and comfortable habitation.
Lawyer or merchant are the fairest titles our towns afford; that of a
farmer is the only appellation of the rural inhabitants of our country.
It must take some time ere he can reconcile himself to our dictionary,
which is but short in words of dignity, and names of honour. There, on
a Sunday, he sees a congregation of respectable farmers and their
wives, all clad in neat homespun, well mounted, or riding in their own
humble waggons. There is not among them an esquire, saving the un-
lettered magistrate. There he sees a parson as simple as his flock, a
farmer who does not riot on the labour of others. We have no princes,
for whom we toil, starve, and bleed: we are the most perfect society
now existing in the world. Here man is free as he ought to be; nor is
this pleasing equality so transitory as many others are. Many ages will
not see the shores of our great lakes replenished with inland nations,
nor the unknown bounds of North America entirely peopled. Who can
tell how far it extends? Who can tell the millions of men whom it will
feed and contain? for no European foot has as yet travelled half the
extent of this mighty continent!

The next wish of this traveller will be to know whence came all
these people? they are a mixture of English, Scotch, Irish, Dutch, Germans, and Swedes. From this promiscuous breed, that race now called
Americans have arisen. The eastern provinces must indeed be excepted, as being the unmixed descendants of Englishmen. I have heard
many wish they had been more intermixed also: for my part, I am no
wisher; and think it much better as it has happened. They exhibit a
most conspicuous figure in this great and variegated picture; they too
enter for a great share in the pleasing perspective displayed in these
thirteen provinces. I know it is fashionable to reflect on them; but I
respect them for what they have done; for the accuracy and wisdom
with which they have settled their territory; for the decency of their
manners; for their early love of letters; their ancient college, the first in
this hemisphere; for their industry, which to me, who am but a farmer,
is the criterion of every thing. There never was a people, situated as

they are, who, with so ungrateful a soil, have done more in so short a time. Do you think that the monarchical ingredients which are more prevalent in other governments, have purged them from all foul stains? Their histories assert the contrary.

In this great American asylum, the poor of Europe have by some means met together, and in consequence of various causes; to what purpose should they ask one another, what countrymen they are? Alas, two thirds of them had no country. Can a wretch who wanders about, who works and starves, whose life is a continual scene of sore affliction of pinching penury; can that man call England or any other kingdom his country? A country that had no bread for him, whose fields procured him no harvest, who met with nothing but the frowns of the rich, the severity of the laws, with jails and punishments; who owned not a single foot of the extensive surface of this planet? No! urged by a variety of motives, here they came. Everything has tended to regenerate them; new laws, a new mode of living, a new social system; here they are become men: in Europe they were as so many useless plants, wanting vegetative mould, and refreshing showers; they withered, and were mowed down by want, hunger, and war: but now, by the power of transplantation, like all other plants, they have taken root and flourished! Formerly they were not numbered in any civil list of their country, except in those of the poor; here they rank as citizens. By what invisible power has this surprizing metamorphosis been performed? By that of the laws and that of their industry. The laws, the indulgent laws, protect them as they arrive, stamping on them the symbol of adoption; they receive ample rewards for their labours; these accumulated rewards procure them lands; those lands confer on them the title of freemen; and to that title every benefit is affixed which men can possibly require. This is the great operation daily performed by our laws. From whence proceed these laws? From our government. Whence that government? It is derived from the original genius and strong desire of the people, ratified and confirmed by government. This is the great chain which links us all, this is the picture which every province exhibits, Nova Scotia excepted. There the crown has done all; either there were no people who had genius, or it was not much attended to: the consequence is, that the province is very thinly inhabited indeed; the power of the crown, in conjunction with the musketos, has prevented men from settling there. Yet some part of it flourished once, and it contained a mild harmless set of people. But for the fault of a few leaders the whole were banished. The greatest political error the crown ever committed in America, was to cut off men from a country which wanted nothing but men!

What attachment can a poor European emigrant have for a country where he had nothing? The knowledge of the language, the love of a few kindred as poor as himself, were the only cords that tied him: his country is now that which gives him land, bread, protection, and consequence: *Ubi panis ibi patri,* is the motto of all emigrants. What then is the American, this new man? He is either an European, or the descendant of an European; hence that strange mixture of blood, which you will find in no other country. I could point out to you a man, whose grandfather was an Englishman, whose wife was Dutch, whose son married a French woman, and whose present four sons have now four wives of different nations. *He* is an American, who, leaving behind him all his ancient prejudices and manners, receives new ones from the new mode of life he has embraced, the new government he obeys, and the new rank he holds. He becomes an American by being received in the broad lap of our great *Alma Mater*.

Here individuals of all nations are melted into a new race of men, whose labours and posterity will one day cause great change in the world. Americans are the western pilgrims, who are carrying along with them that great mass of arts, sciences, vigour, and industry, which began long since in the east; they will finish the great circle. The Americans were once scattered all over Europe; here they are incorporated into one of the finest systems of population which has ever appeared, and which will hereafter become distinct by the power of the different climates they inhabit. The American ought, therefore, to love this country much better than that wherein either he or his forefathers were born. Here the rewards of his industry follow with equal steps the progress of his labour; his labour is founded on the basis of nature, *self-interest;* can it want a stronger allurement? Wives and children, who before in vain demanded of him a morsel of bread, now, fat and frolicsome, gladly help their father to clear those fields whence exuberant crops are to arise to feed and to clothe them all; without any part being claimed, either by a despotic prince, a rich abbot, or a mighty lord. Here religion demands but little of him; a small voluntary salary to the minister, and gratitude to God; can he refuse these? The American is a new man, who acts upon new principles; he must therefore entertain new ideas, and form new opinions. From involuntary idleness, servile dependence, penury, and useless labour, he has passed to toils of a very different nature, rewarded by ample subsistence.—This is an American. . . .

I wish I were able to trace all my ideas; if my ignorance prevents me from describing them properly, I hope I shall be able to delineate a few of the outlines, which are all I propose.

Those who live near the sea, feed more on fish than on flesh, and often encounter that boisterous element. This renders them more bold and enterprising; this leads them to neglect the confined occupations of the land. They see and converse with a variety of people; their intercourse with mankind becomes extensive. The sea inspires them with a love of traffic, a desire of transporting produce from one place to another; leads them to a variety of resources, which supply the place of labour. Those who inhabit the middle settlements, by far the most numerous, must be very different; the simple cultivation of the earth purifies them; but the indulgences of the government, the soft remonstrances of religion, the rank of independent free-holders, must necessarily inspire them with sentiments, very little known in Europe among people of the same class. What do I say? Europe has no such class of man; the early knowledge they require, the early bargains they make, give them a great degree of sagacity. As freemen, they will be litigious; pride and obstinacy are often the cause of law suits; the nature of our laws and governments may be another. As citizens, it is easy to imagine, that they will carefully read the newspapers, enter into every political disquisition, freely blame or censure governors and others. As farmers, they will be careful and anxious to get as much as they can, because what they get is their own. As northern men, they will love the cheerful cup. As Christians, religion curbs them not in their opinion; the general indulgence leaves every one to think for himself in spiritual matters; the laws inspect our actions; our thoughts are left to God. Industry, good living, selfishness, litigiousness, country politics, the pride of free men, religious indifference, are their characteristics. If you recede still farther from the sea, you will come into more modern settlements; they exhibit the same strong lineaments, in a ruder appearance. Religion seems to have still less influence, and their manners are less improved.

Now we arrive near the great woods, near the last inhabited districts; there men seem to be placed still farther beyond the reach of government, which in some measure leaves them to themselves. How can it pervade every corner? as they were driven there by misfortunes, necessity of beginnings, desire of acquiring large tracts of land, idleness, frequent want of economy, ancient debts; the reunion of such people does not afford a very pleasing spectacle. When discord, want of unity and friendship—when either drunkenness or idleness prevail in such remote districts—contention, inactivity, and wretchedness must ensue. There are not the same remedies to these evils as in a long established community. The few magistrates they have, are in general little better than the rest; they are often in a perfect state of war; that of man against man, sometimes decided by blows, sometimes by means of the law; that of man against every wild inhabitant of these venerable woods, of which they are come to dispossess them. There men appear to be no better than carnivorous animals when they can catch them; and when they are not able, they subsist on the grain.

He who would wish to see America in its proper light, and have a true idea of its feeble beginnings and barbarous rudiments, must visit our extended line of frontiers where the last settlers dwell, and where he may see the first labours of settlement, the mode of clearing the earth, in all their different appearances; where men are wholly left dependent on their native tempers, and on the spur of uncertain industry, which often fails, when not sanctified by the efficacy of a few moral rules. There, remote from the power of example, and check of shame, many families exhibit the most hideous parts of our society. They are a kind of forlorn hope, preceding by ten or twelve years the most respectable army of veterans which come after them. In that space, prosperity will polish some, vice and the law will drive off the rest, who uniting again with others like themselves will recede still farther; making room for more industrious people, who will finish their improvements, convert the log-house into a convenient habitation, and rejoicing that the first heavy labours are finished, will change in a few years that hitherto barbarous country into a fine, fertile, well regulated district.

Such is our progress, such is the march of the Europeans toward the interior parts of this continent. In all societies there are off-casts; this impure part serves as our precursors or pioneers; my father himself was one of that class; but he came upon honest principles, and was therefore one of the few who held fast; by good conduct and temperance, he transmitted to me his fair inheritance, when not above one in fourteen of his contemporaries had the same good fortune.

Forty years ago, this smiling country was thus inhabited; it is now purged, a general decency of manners prevails throughout; and such has been the fate of our best countries.

Exclusive of those general characteristics, each province has its own, founded on the government, climate, mode of husbandry, customs, and peculiarity of circumstances. Europeans submit insensibly to these great powers; and become in the course of a few generations, not only Americans in general, but either Pennsylvanians, Virginians, or provincials under some other name. Whoever traverses the continent, must easily observe those strong differences, which will grow more evident in time. The inhabitants of Canada, Massachusetts, the middle provinces, the southern ones will be as different as their climates; their only points of unity will be those of religion and language.

As I have endeavoured to shew you how Europeans become Americans; it may not be disagreeable to shew you likewise how the various Christian sects introduced, wear out, and how religious indifference becomes prevalent. When any considerable number of a particular sect happen to dwell contiguous to each other, they immediately erect a temple, and there worship the Divinity agreeably to their own peculiar ideas. Nobody disturbs them. If any new sect springs up in Europe, it may happen that many of its professors will come and settle in America. As they bring their zeal with them, they are at liberty to make proselytes if they can, and to build a meeting and to follow the dictates of their consciences; for neither the government nor any other power interferes. If they are peaceable subjects, and are industrious, what is it to their neighbours how and in what manner they think fit to address their prayers to the Supreme Being? But if the sectaries are not settled close together, if they are mixed with other denominations, their zeal will cool for want of fuel, and will be extinguished in a little time. Then the Americans become as to religion, what they are as to country, allied to all. In them the name of Englishman, Frenchman, and European is lost, and in like manner, the strict modes of Christianity as practised in Europe are lost also. . . .

Thus have I faintly and imperfectly endeavoured to trace our society from the sea to our woods! Yet you must not imagine that every person who moves back, acts upon the same principles, or falls into the same degeneracy. Many families carry with them all their decency of conduct, purity of morals, and respect of religion; but these are scarce, the power of example is sometimes irresistible. Even among these back-settlers, their depravity is greater or less, according to what nation or province they belong. Were I to adduce proofs of this, I might be accused of partiality. If there happens to be some rich intervals, some fertile bottoms, in those remote districts, the people will there prefer tilling the land to hunting, and will attach themselves to it; but even on these fertile spots you may plainly perceive the inhabitants to acquire a great degree of rusticity and selfishness.

It is in consequence of this straggling situation, and the astonishing power it has on manners, that the back-settlers of both the Carolinas, Virginia, and many other parts, have been long a set of lawless people; it has been even dangerous to travel among them. Government can do nothing in so extensive a country; better it should wink at these irregularities, than that it should use means inconsistent with its usual mildness. Time will efface those stains: in proportion as the great body of population approaches them they will reform, and become polished and subordinate. Whatever has been said of the four New England provinces, no such degeneracy of manners has ever tarnished their annals; their back-settlers have been kept within the bounds of decency, and government, by means of wise laws, and by the influence of religion. What a detestable idea such people must have given to natives of the Europeans! They trade with them, the worst of people are permitted to do that which none but persons of the best characters should be employed in. They get drunk with them, and often defraud the Indians. Their avarice, removed from the eyes of their superiors, knows no bounds; and aided by a little superiority of knowledge, these traders deceive them, and even sometimes shed blood. Hence those shocking violations, those sudden devastations which have so often stained our frontiers, when hundreds of innocent people have been sacrificed for the crimes of a few. It was in consequence of such behaviour, that the Indians took the hatchet against the Virginians in 1774. Thus are our first steps trod, thus are our first trees felled, in general, by the most vicious of our people; and thus the path is opened for the arrival of a second and better class, the true American freeholders; the most respectable set of people in this part of the world: respectable for their industry, their happy independence, the great share of freedom they possess, the good regulation of their families, and for extending the trade and dominion of our mother country.

Europe contains hardly any other distinctions but lords and tenants; this fair country alone is settled by freeholders, the possessors of the soil they cultivate, members of the government they obey, and the framers of their own laws, by means of their representatives. This is a thought which you have taught me to cherish; our distance from Europe, far from diminishing, rather adds to our usefulness and consequence as men and subjects. Had our forefathers remained there, they would only have crouded it, and perhaps prolonged those convulsions which had shook it so long. Every industrious European who transports himself here, may be compared to a sprout growing at the foot of a great tree; it enjoys and draws but a little portion of sap; wrench it from the parent roots, transplant it, and it will become a tree bearing fruit also. Colonists are therefore entitled to the consideration due to the most useful subjects; a hundred families barely existing in some parts of Scotland, will here in six years, cause an annual exportation of 10,000 bushels of wheat: 100 bushels being but a common quantity for an industrious family to sell, if they cultivate good land. It is here, then, that the idle may be employed, the useless become useful, and the poor become rich: but by riches I do not mean gold and silver; we have but little of those metals; I mean a better sort of wealth, cleared lands, cattle, good houses, good clothes, and an increase of people to enjoy them.

There is no wonder that this country has so many charms and presents to Europeans so many temptations to remain in it. A traveller in Europe becomes a stranger as soon as he quits his own kingdom; but it is otherwise here. We know, properly speaking, no strangers; this is every person's country; the variety of our soils, situations, climates, governments, and produce, hath something which must please every body. No sooner does an European arrive, no matter of what condition, than his eyes are opened upon the fair prospects; he hears his language spoke, he retraces many of his own country manners, he perpetually hears the names of families and towns with which he is acquainted; he sees happiness and prosperity in all places disseminated; he meets with hospitality, kindness, and plenty every where: he beholds hardly any poor, he seldom hears of punishments and executions; and he wonders at the elegance of our towns, those miracles of industry and freedom. He cannot admire enough our rural districts, our convenient roads, good taverns, and our many accommodations; he involuntarily loves a country where every thing is so lovely. When in England, he was a mere Englishman; here he stands on a larger portion of the globe, not less than its fourth part, and may see the productions of the north, in iron and naval stores; the provisions of Ireland, the grain of Egypt, the indigo, the rice of China. He does not find, as in Europe, a crowded society, where every place is over-stocked; he does not feel that perpetual collision of parties, that difficulty of beginning, that contention which oversets so many.

There is room for every body in America: has he any particular talent, or industry? he exerts it in order to procure a livelihood, and it succeeds. Is he a merchant? the avenues of trade are infinite; is he eminent in any respect? he will be employed and respected. Does he love a country life? pleasant farms present themselves; he may purchase what he wants, and thereby become an American farmer. Is he a labourer, sober and industrious; he need not go many miles, nor receive many informations before he will be hired, well fed at the table of his employer, and paid four or five times more than he can get in Europe. Does he want uncultivated lands? thousands of acres present themselves, which he may purchase cheap. Whatever be his talents or inclinations, if they are moderate, he may satisfy them. I do not mean, that every one who comes will grow rich in a little time; no, but he may procure an easy, decent maintenance, by his industry. Instead of starving, he will be fed; instead of being idle, he will have employment; and these are riches enough for such men as come over here. The rich stay in Europe; it is only the middling and poor that emigrate. Would you wish to travel in independent idleness, from north to south, you will find easy access, and most cheerful reception at every house; society without ostentation, good cheer without pride, and every decent diversion which the country affords, with little expense. It is no wonder that the European who has lived here a few years, is desirous to remain; Europe with all its pomp, is not to be compared to this continent, for men of middle stations or labourers.

An European, when he first arrives, seems limited in his intentions, as well as in his views; but he very suddenly alters his scale; two hundred miles formerly appeared a very great distance; it is now but a trifle; he no sooner breathes our air than he forms schemes, and embarks in designs he never would have thought of in his own country. There the plenitude of society confines many useful ideas, and often extinguishes the most laudable schemes which here ripen into maturity. Thus Europeans become Americans.

But how is this accomplished in that croud of low, indigent people, who flocks here every year from all parts of Europe? I will tell you; they no sooner arrive than they immediately feel the good effects of that plenty of provisions we possess: they fare on our best food, and are kindly entertained; their talents, character, and peculiar industry are immediately enquired into; they find countrymen every where disseminated, let them come from whatever part of Europe.

Let me select one as an epitome of the rest; he is hired, he goes to work, and works moderately; instead of being employed by a haughty person, he finds himself with his equal, placed at the substantial table of the farmer, or else at an inferior one as good; his wages are high, his bed is not like that bed of sorrow on which he used to lie: if he behaves with propriety, and is faithful, he is caressed, and becomes, as it were, a member of the family. He begins to feel the effects of a sort of resurrection; hitherto he had not lived, but simply vegetated; he now feels himself a man, because he is treated as such; the laws of his own country had overlooked him in his insignificancy; the laws of this cover him with their mantle. Judge what an alteration there must arise in the mind and thoughts of this man; he begins to forget his former servitude and dependence; his heart involuntarily swells and glows; this first swell inspires him with those new thoughts which constitute an American. What love can he entertain for a country where his existence was a burden to him! if he is a generous good man, the love of his new adoptive parent, will sink deep into his heart. He looks around, and sees many a prosperous person, who but a few years before was as poor as himself. This encourages him much; he begins to form some little scheme, the first, alas, he ever formed in his life. If he is wise, he thus spends two or three years, in which time he acquires knowledge, the use of tools, the modes of working the lands, felling trees, &c. This prepares the foundation of a good name, the most useful acquisition he can make. He is encouraged; he has gained friends; he is advised and directed; he feels bold; he purchases some land; he gives all the money he has brought over, as well as what he has earned, and trusts to the God of harvests for the discharge of the rest. His good name procures him credit; he is now possessed of the deed, conveying to him and his posterity the fee simple, and absolute property of two hundred acres of land, situated on such a river. What an epoch in this man's life! He is become a freeholder, from perhaps a German boor—he is now an American, a Pennsylvanian. He is naturalized; his name is enrolled with those of the other citizens of the province. Instead of being a vagrant, he has a place of residence; he is called the inhabitant of such a county, or of such a district, and for the first time in his life counts for something; for hitherto he had been a cypher. I only repeat what I have heard many say, and no wonder their hearts should glow, and be agitated with a multitude of feelings, not easy to describe. From nothing to start into being; from a servant to the rank of master; from being the slave of some despotic prince, to become a free man, invested with lands, to which every municipal blessing is annexed! What a change indeed! It is in consequence of that change, that he becomes an American.

This great metamorphosis has a double effect; it extinguishes all his European prejudices; he forgets that mechanism of subordination, that servility of disposition which poverty had taught him; and sometimes he is apt to forget it too much, often passing from one extreme to the other. If he is a good man, he forms schemes of future prosperity; he proposes to educate his children better than he has been educated himself; he thinks of future modes of conduct, feels an ardour to labour he never felt before. Pride steps in, and leads him to every thing that the laws do not forbid: he respects them; with a heart-felt gratitude he looks toward that government from whose wisdom all his new felicity is derived, and under whose wings and protection he now lives. These reflections constitute him the good man and the good subject.

Ye poor Europeans, ye, who sweat and work for the great—ye, who are obliged to give so many sheaves to the church, so many to your lords, so many to your government, and have hardly any left for yourselves—ye, who are held in less estimation than favourite hunters or useless lapdogs—ye, who only breathe the air of nature, because it cannot be withheld from you; it is here that ye can conceive the possibility of those feelings I have been describing; it is here the laws of naturalization invite every one to partake of our great labours and felicity, to till unrented, untaxed lands!

Many, corrupted beyond the power of amendment, have brought with them all their vices, and, disregarding the advantages held out to them, have gone on in their former career of iniquity, until they have been overtaken and punished by our laws. It is not every emigrant who succeeds; no, it is only the sober, the honest, and industrious: happy those, to whom this transition has served as a powerful spur to labour, to prosperity, and to the good establishment of children, born in the days of their poverty: and who had no other portion to expect, but the rags of their parents, had it not been for their happy emigration.

Others again, have been led astray by this enchanting scene; their new pride, instead of leading them to the fields, has kept them in idleness; the idea of possessing lands is all that satisfied them—though surrounded with fertility, they have mouldered away their time in inactivity, misinformed husbandry, and ineffectual endeavours. . . .

After a foreigner from any part of Europe is arrived, and become a citizen; let him devoutly listen to the voice of our great parent, which says to him, "Welcome to my shores, distressed European; bless the hour in which thou didst see my verdant fields, my fair navigable rivers, and my green mountains!—If thou wilt work, I have bread for thee; if thou wilt be honest, sober and industrious, I have greater rewards to confer on thee—ease and independence. I will give thee fields to feed and clothe thee; a comfortable fire-side to sit by, and tell thy children by what means thou hast prospered; and a decent bed to repose on. I shall endow thee, beside, with the immunities of a freeman. If thou wilt carefully educate thy children, teach them gratitude to God, and reverence to that government, that philanthropic government, which has collected here so many men and made them happy, I will also provide for thy progeny: and to every good man this ought to be the most holy, the most powerful, the most earnest wish he can possibly form, as well as the most consolatory prospect when he dies. Go thou, and work and till; thou shalt prosper, provided thou be just, grateful and industrious."

15. America Is Not Interesting

Matthew Arnold

Matthew Arnold (1822–1888), eminent poet, educator, and critic of literature and society, devoted most of his life to a battle against the two forces he felt most inimical to culture: the presumption of the scientists and the resistance to ideas and to beauty of the practical middle-class mind. He did not get to America until the latest years of

Source: Matthew Arnold, *Civilization in the United States: First and Last Impression of America* (Boston: Cupples and Hard, 1888), pp. 198–212.

his life (he visited in 1883 and again in 1886); but at any point he
would have found this essentially middle-class country too much under the influence of what he called "the philistines." One could hardly
have expected from him much more sympathy than is shown in *Civilization in the United States* (1888) from which this excerpt is taken.

But we must get nearer still to the heart of the question raised as to the
character and worth of American civilization. I have said how much
the word civilization really means—the humanization of man in society; his making progress there toward his true and full humanity. Partial and material achievement is always being put forward as civilization. We hear a nation called highly civilized by reason of its industry,
commerce, and wealth, or by reason of its liberty or equality, or by
reason of its numerous churches, schools, libraries, and newspapers.
But there is something in human nature, some instinct of growth, some
law of perfection, which rebels against this narrow account of the matter. And perhaps what human nature demands in civilization, over and
above all those obvious things which first occur to our thoughts—
what human nature, I say, demands in civilization, if it is to stand as a
high and satisfying civilization, is best described by the word *interesting.* Here is the extraordinary charm of the old Greek civilization; that
it is so *interesting.* Do not tell me only, says human nature, of the mag-
nitude of your institutions, your freedom, your equality; of the great
and growing number of your churches and schools, libraries and
newspapers; tell me also if your civilization—which is the grand
name you give to all this development—tell me if your civilization is
interesting.
     An American friend of mine, Professor Norton, has lately published
the early letters of Carlyle. If any one wants a good antidote to the
unpleasant effect left by Mr. Froude's *Life of Carlyle,* let him read
those letters. . . .
     Thomas Carlyle, the eldest son, a young man in wretched health and
worse spirits, was fighting his way in Edinburgh. One of his younger
brothers talked of emigrating. "The very best thing he could do!" we
should all say. Carlyle dissuades him. "You shall never," he writes,
"you shall never seriously meditate crossing the great Salt Pool to
plant yourself in the Yankee-land. That is a miserable fate for anyone,
at best; never dream of it. Could you banish yourself from all that is
interesting to your mind, forget the history, the glorious institutions,

the noble principles of old Scotland—that you might eat a better dinner, perhaps?"

There is our word launched—the word *interesting*. I am not saying that Carlyle's advice was good, or that young men should not emigrate. I do but take note, in the word *interesting,* of a requirement, a cry of aspiration, a cry not sounding in the imaginative Carlyle's own breast only, but sure of a response in his brother's breast also, and in human nature. . . .

Now the great sources of the *interesting* are distinction and beauty; that which is elevated, and that which is beautiful. Let us take the beautiful first, and consider how far it is present in American civilization. Evidently, that is the civilization's weak side. There is little to nourish and delight the sense of beauty there. In the long-settled states east of the Alleghanies the landscape in general is not interesting, the climate harsh and in extremes. The Americans are restless, eager to better themselves and to make fortunes; the inhabitant does not strike his roots lovingly down into the soil, as in rural England. In the valley of the Connecticut you will find farm after farm which the Yankee settler has abandoned in order to go West, leaving the farm to some new Irish immigrant. The charm of beauty which comes from ancientness and permanence of rural life the country could not yet have in a high degree, but it has it in an even less degree than might be expected. Then the Americans come originally, for the most part, from that great class in English society amongst whom the sense for conduct and business is much more strongly developed than the sense for beauty. If we in England were without the cathedrals, parish churches, and castles of the Catholic and Feudal Age, and without the houses of the Elizabethan age, but had only the towns and buildings which the rise of our middle class has created in the modern age, we should be in much the same case as the Americans. We should be living with much the same absence of training for the sense of beauty through the eye, from the aspect of outward things. The American cities have hardly anything to please a trained or a natural sense for beauty. They have buildings which cost a great deal of money and produce a certain effect—buildings, shall I say, such as our Midland Station of St. Pancras; but nothing such as Somerset House or Whitehall. One architect of genius they had—Richardson. I had the pleasure to know him; he is dead, alas! Much of his work was injured by the conditions under which he was obliged to execute it; I can recall but one building, and that of no great importance, where he seems to have had his own way, to be fully himself; but that is indeed excellent. In general, where the Americans succeed best in their architecture—in that art so indicative and educative of a people's sense for beauty—is in the fashion of their villa-cottages in wood. These are often original and at the same time very pleasing, but they are pretty and coquettish, not beautiful. Of the really beautiful in the other arts, and in literature, very little has been produced there as yet. I asked a German portrait painter, whom I found painting and prospering in America, how he liked the country. "How *can* an artist like it?" was his answer. The American artists live chiefly in Europe; all Americans of cultivation and wealth visit Europe more and more constantly. The mere nomenclature of the country acts upon a cultivated person like the incessant pricking of pins. What people in whom the sense for beauty and fitness was quick could have invented, or could tolerate, the hideous names ending in *ville,* the Briggsvilles, Higginsvilles, Jacksonvilles, rife from Maine to Florida; the jumble of unnatural and inappropriate names everywhere? On the line from Albany to Buffalo, you have, in one part, half the names in the classical dictionary to designate the stations; it is said that the folly is due to a surveyor who, when the country was laid out, happened to possess a classical dictionary; but a people with any artist-sense would have put down that surveyor. The Americans meekly retain his names; and, indeed, his strange Marcellus or Syracuse is perhaps not much worse than their congenital Briggsville.

So much as to beauty, and as to the provision, in the United States, for the sense of beauty. As to distinction, and the interest which human nature seeks from enjoying the effect made upon it by what is elevated, the case is much the same. There is very little to create such an effect, very much to thwart it. Goethe says somewhere that "the thrill of awe is the best thing humanity has." But, if there be discipline in which the Americans are wanting, it is the discipline of awe and respect. An austere and intense religion imposed on their Puritan founders the discipline of respect, and so provided for them the thrill of awe; but this religion is dying out. The Americans have produced plenty of men strong, shrewd, upright, able, effective; very few who are highly distinguished. Alexander Hamilton is indeed a man of rare distinction; Washington, though he has not the high mental distinction of Pericles or Caesar, has true distinction of style and character. But these men belong to the pre-American age. Lincoln's recent American biographers declare that Washington is but an Englishman, an English officer; the typical American, they say, is Abraham Lincoln. Now Lincoln is shrewd, sagacious, humorous, honest, courageous, firm; he is a man with qualities deserving the most sincere esteem and praise, but he has not distinction.

In truth, everything is against distinction in America, and against the sense of elevation to be gained through admiring and respecting it. The glorification of the "average man," who is quite a religion with statesmen and publicists there, is against it. The addiction to the "funny man," who is the national misfortune there, is against it. Above all, the newspapers are against it.

It is often said that every nation has the government it deserves. What is much more certain is that every nation has the newspapers it deserves. The newspaper is the direct product of the want felt; the supply answers closely and inevitably to the demand. I suppose no one knows what the American newspapers are, who has not been obliged, for some length of time, to read either those newspapers or none at all. Powerful and valuable contributions occur scattered about in them. But on the whole, and taking the total impression and effect made by them, I should say that if one were searching for the best means to efface and kill in a whole nation the discipline of respect, the feeling for what is elevated, one could not do better than take the American newspapers. The absence of truth and soberness in them, the poverty in serious interest, the personality and sensation-mongering, are beyond belief. There are a few newspapers which are in whole, or in part, exceptions. The *New York Nation,* a weekly paper, may be paralleled with the *Saturday Review* as it was in its old and good days; but the *New York Nation* is conducted by a foreigner, and has an extremely small sale. In general, the daily papers are such that when one returns home one is moved to admiration and thankfulness not only at the great London papers, like the *Times* or the *Standard,* but quite as much at the great provincial newspapers, too—papers like the *Leeds Mercury* and the *Yorkshire Post* in the north of England, like the *Scotsman* and the *Glasgow Herald* in Scotland. . . .

I once declared that in England the born lover of ideas and of light could not but feel that the sky over his head is of brass and iron. And so I say that, in America, he who craves for the *interesting* in civilization, he who requires from what surrounds him satisfaction for his sense of beauty, his sense for elevation, will feel the sky over his head to be of brass and iron. The human problem, then, is as yet solved in the United States most imperfectly; a great void exists in the civilization over there; a want of what is elevated and beautiful, of what is interesting.

The want is grave; it was probably, though he does not exactly bring it out, influencing Sir Lepel Griffin's feelings when he said that America is one of the last countries in which one would like to live. The want is such as to make any educated man feel that many countries, much less free and prosperous than the United States, are yet more truly civilized; have more which is interesting, have more to say to the soul; are countries, therefore, in which one would rather live.

The want is graver because it is so little recognized by the mass of Americans; nay, so loudly denied by them. If the community over there perceived the want and regretted it, sought for the right way of remedying it, and resolved that remedied it should be; if they said, or even if a number of leading spirits amongst them said: "Yes, we see what is wanting to our civilization, we see that the average man is a danger, we see that our newspapers are a scandal, that bondage to the common and ignoble is our snare; but under the circumstances our civilization could not well have been expected to begin differently. What you see are *beginnings,* they are crude, they are too predominantly material, they omit much, leave much to be desired—but they could not have been otherwise, they have been inevitable, and we will rise above them"; if the American frankly said this, one would not have a word to bring against it. One would *then* insist on no shortcoming, one would accept their admission that the human problem is at present quite insufficiently solved by them, and would press the matter no further. One would congratulate them on having solved the political problem and the social problem so successfully, and only remark, as I have said already, that in seeing clear and thinking straight on *our* political and social questions, we have great need to follow the example they set on theirs.

But now the Americans seem, in certain matters, to have agreed, as a people, to deceive themselves that they have what they have not, to cover the defects in their civilization by boasting, to fancy that they well and truly solve, not only the political and social problem, but the human problem too. One would say that they really do hope to find in tall talk and inflated sentiment a substitute for that real sense of elevation which human nature, as I have said, instinctively craves—and a

substitute which may do as well as the genuine article. The thrill of
awe, which Goethe pronounces to be the best thing humanity has, they
would fain create by proclaiming themselves at the top of their voices
to be "the greatest nation upon earth," by assuring one another, in the
language of their national historian, that "American democracy proceeds in its ascent as uniformly and majestically as the laws of being,
and is as certain as the decrees of eternity."

Or, again, far from admitting that their newspapers are a scandal,
they assure one another that their newspaper press is one of their most
signal distinctions. Far from admitting that in literature they have as
yet produced little that is important, they play at treating American
literature as if it were a great independent power; they reform the
spelling of the English language by the insight of their average man.
For every English writer they have an American writer to match; and
him good Americans read. The Western States are at this moment
being nourished and formed, we hear, on the novels of a native author
called Roe, instead of those of Scott and Dickens. Far from admitting
that their average man is a danger, and that his predominance has
brought about a plentiful lack of refinement, distinction, and beauty,
they declare in the words of my friend Colonel Higginson, a prominent
critic at Boston, that "Nature said, some years since: 'Thus far the
English is my best race, but we have had Englishmen enough; put in
one drop more of nervous fluid and make the American.' " And with
that drop a new range of promise opened on the human race, and a
lighter, finer, more highly organized type of mankind was born. Far
from admitting that the American accent, as the pressure of their
climate and of their average man has made it, is a thing to be striven
against, they assure one another that it is the right accent, the standard
English speech of the future. It reminds me of a thing in Smollet's
dinner-party of authors. Seated by "the philosopher who is writing a
most orthodox refutation of Bolingbroke, but in the meantime has just
been presented to the Grand Jury as a public nuisance for having blas-
phemed in an ale-house on the Lord's day"—seated by this philosopher is "the Scotchman who is giving lectures on the pronunciation of
the English language."

The worst of it is that all this tall talk and self-glorification meets
with hardly any rebuke from sane criticism over there. . . .

The new West promises to beat in the game of brag even the stout
champions I have been quoting. Those belong to the old Eastern

States; and the other day there was sent to me a California newspaper which calls all the Easterners "the unhappy denizens of a forbidding clime," and adds: "The time will surely come when all roads will lead to California. Here will be the home of art, science, literature, and profound knowledge."

Common-sense criticism, I repeat, of all this hollow stuff there is in America next to none. There are plenty of cultivated, judicious, delightful individuals there. They are our hope and America's hope; it is through their means that improvement must come. They know perfectly well how false and hollow the boastful stuff talked is; but they let storm of self-laudation rage, and say nothing. For political opponents and their doings there are in America hard words to be heard in abundance; for the real faults in American civilization, and for the foolish boasting which prolongs them, there is hardly a word of regret or blame, at least in public. Even in private, many of the most cultivated Americans shrink from the subject, are irritable and thin-skinned when it is canvassed. Public treatment of it, in a cool and sane spirit of criticism, there is none. In vain I might plead that I had set a good example of frankness, in confessing over here, that, so far from solving our problems successfully, we in England find ourselves with an upper class materialized, a middle class vulgarized, and a lower class brutalized. But it seems that nothing will embolden an American critic to say firmly and aloud to his countrymen and to his newspapers, that in America they do not solve the human problem successfully, and that with their present methods they never can. Consequently, the masses of the American people do really come to believe all they hear about their finer nervous organization, and the rightness of the American accent, and the importance of American literature; that is to say, they see things not as they are, but as they would like to see them be; they deceive themselves totally. And by such self-deception they shut against themselves the door to improvement, and do their best to make the reign of *das Gemeine* eternal. In what concerns the solving of the political and social problem they see clear and think straight; in what concerns the higher civilization they live in a fool's paradise. That it is which makes a famous French critic speak of "the hard unintelligence of the people of the United States"—of the very people who in general pass for being specially intelligent; and so, within certain limits, they are. But they have been so plied with nonsense and boasting that outside those limits, and where it is a question of things in which their civilization is weak, they seem, very many of them, as if in such things they had no power of perception whatever, no idea of a proper scale, no sense of the difference between good and bad. And at this rate they can never, after solving the political and social problem with success, go on to solve happily the human problem too, and thus at last make their civilization full and interesting.

To sum up, then. What really dissatisfies in American civilization is the want of the *interesting,* a want due chiefly to the want of those two great elements of the interesting, which are elevation and beauty. And the want of these elements is increased and prolonged by the Americans being assured that they have them when they have them not. And it seems to me that what the Americans now most urgently require is not so much a vast additional development of orthodox Protestantism, but rather a steady exhibition of cool and sane criticism by their men of light and leading over there.

16. The Spirit of Place

D. H. LAWRENCE

David Herbert Lawrence (1885–1930) was born in England of working-class parents, and educated on scholarships completely outside of English public school Oxford-Cambridge circles. He spent most of his adult life traveling in Europe, Australia and America, settling for a while in New Mexico but returning to Europe just in time to die. His fame as a novelist was in part a *succès de scandale* in the beginning (his complete *Lady Chatterley's Lover* was banned for a long time in the United States), but has continued to grow even after his death. One of his special skills, manifested in his novels and travel books alike, is an ability to evoke the very sight and feel of a place. The present essay comes from one of the most striking and unhackneyed books ever written on our life and literature, *Studies in Classic American Literature* (1923).

SOURCE: D. H. Lawrence, *Studies in Classic American Literature* (New York: Thomas Seltzer, Inc., 1923), pp. 1–12. Copyright 1923, 1951 by Frieda Lawrence. Reprinted by permission of The Viking Press, Inc.

Let us look at this American artist first. How did he ever get to America, to start with? Why isn't he a European still, like his father before him?

Now listen to me, don't listen to him. He'll tell you the lie you expect. Which is partly your fault for expecting it.

He didn't come in search of freedom of worship. England had more freedom of worship in the year 1700 than America had. Won by Englishmen who wanted freedom, and so stopped at home and fought for it. And got it. Freedom of worship? Read the history of New England during the first century of its existence.

Freedom anyhow? The land of the free! This the land of the free! Why, if I say anything that displeases them, the free mob will lynch me, and that's my freedom. Free? Why I have never been in any country where the individual has such an abject fear of his fellow countrymen. Because, as I say, they are free to lynch him the moment he shows he is not one of them.

No, no, if you're so fond of the truth about Queen Victoria, try a little about yourself.

Those Pilgrim Fathers and their successors never came here for freedom of worship. What did they set up when they got here? Freedom, would you call it?

They didn't come for freedom. Or if they did, they sadly went back on themselves.

All right then, what did they come for? For lots of reasons. Perhaps least of all in search of freedom of any sort: positive freedom, that is.

They came largely to get *away*—that most simple of motives. To get away. Away from what? In the long run, away from themselves. Away from everything. That's why most people have come to America, and still do come. To get away from everything they are and have been.

"Henceforth be masterless."

Which is all very well, but it isn't freedom. Rather the reverse. A hopeless sort of constraint. It is never freedom till you find something you really *positively want to be*. And people in America have always been shouting about the things they are *not*. Unless of course they are millionaires, made or in the making.

And after all there is a positive side to the movement. All that vast flood of human life that has flowed over the Atlantic in ships from Europe to America has not flowed over simply on a tide of revulsion from Europe and from the confinements of the European ways of life. This revulsion was, and still is, I believe, the prime motive in emigration. But there was some cause, even for the revulsion.

It seems as if at times man had a frenzy for getting away from any control of any sort. In Europe the old Christianity was the real master. The Church and the true aristocracy bore the responsibility for the working out of the Christian ideals: a little irregularly, maybe, but responsible nevertheless.

Mastery, kingship, fatherhood had their power destroyed at the time of the Renaissance.

And it was precisely at this moment that the great drift over the Atlantic started. What were men drifting away from? The old authority of Europe? Were they breaking the bonds of authority, and escaping to a new more absolute unrestrainedness? Maybe. But there was more to it.

Liberty is all very well, but men cannot live without masters. There is always a master. And men either live in glad obedience to the master they believe in, or they live in a frictional opposition to the master they wish to undermine. In America this frictional opposition has been the vital factor. It has given the Yankee his kick. Only the continual influx of more servile Europeans has provided America with an obedient labouring class. The true obedience never outlasting the first generation.

But there sits the old master, over in Europe. Like a parent. Somewhere deep in every American heart lies a rebellion against the old parenthood of Europe. Yet no American feels he has completely escaped its mastery. Hence the slow, smouldering patience of American opposition. The slow, smouldering, corrosive obedience to the old master Europe, the unwilling subject, the unremitting opposition.

Whatever else you are, be masterless.

> "Ca Ca Caliban
> Get a new master, be a new man."

Escaped slaves, we might say, people the republics of Liberia or Haiti. Liberia enough! Are we to look at America in the same way? A vast republic of escaped slaves. When you consider the hordes from eastern Europe, you might well say it: a vast republic of escaped slaves. But one dare not say this of the Pilgrim Fathers, and the great old body of idealist Americans, the modern Americans tortured with thought. A vast republic of escaped slaves. Look out, America! And a minority of earnest, self-tortured people.

The masterless.

> "Ca Ca Caliban
> Get a new master, be a new man."

What did the Pilgrim Fathers come for, then, when they came so gruesomely over the black sea? Oh, it was in a black spirit. A black revulsion from Europe, from the old authority of Europe, from kings and bishops and popes. And more. When you look into it, more. They were black, masterful men, they wanted something else. No kings, no bishops maybe. Even no God Almighty. But also, no more of this new "humanity" which followed the Renaissance. None of this new liberty which was to be so pretty in Europe. Something grimmer, by no means free-and-easy.

America has never been easy, and is not easy to-day. Americans have always been at a certain tension. Their liberty is a thing of sheer will, sheer tension: a liberty of THOU SHALT NOT. And it has been so from the first. The land of THOU SHALT NOT. Only the first commandment is: THOU SHALT NOT PRESUME TO BE A MASTER. Hence democracy.

"We are the masterless." That is what the American Eagle shrieks. It's a Hen-Eagle.

The Spaniards refused the post-Renaissance liberty of Europe. And the Spaniards filled most of America. The Yankees, too, refused, refused the post-Renaissance humanism of Europe. First and foremost, they hated masters. But under that, they hated the flowing ease of humour in Europe. At the bottom of the American soul was always a dark suspense, at the bottom of the Spanish-American soul the same. And this dark suspense hated and hates the old European spontaneity, watches it collapse with satisfaction.

Every continent has its own great spirit of place. Every people is polarized in some particular locality, which is home, the homeland. Different places on the face of the earth have different vital effluence, different vibration, different chemical exhalation, different polarity with different stars: call it what you like. But the spirit of place is a great reality. The Nile valley produced not only the corn, but the terrific religions of Egypt. China produces the Chinese, and will go on doing so. The Chinese in San Francisco will in time cease to be Chinese, for America is a great melting pot.

There was a tremendous polarity in Italy, in the city of Rome. And this seems to have died. For even places die. The Island of Great Britain had a wonderful terrestrial magnetism or polarity of its own, which made the British people. For the moment, this polarity seems to be breaking. Can England die? And what if England dies?

Men are less free than they imagine; ah, far less free. The freest are perhaps least free.

Men are free when they are in a living homeland, not when they are straying and breaking away. Men are free when they are obeying some deep, inward voice of religious belief. Obeying from within. Men are free when they belong to a living, organic, *believing* community, active in fulfilling some unfulfilled, perhaps unrealized purpose. Not when they are escaping to some wild west. The most unfree souls go west, and shout of freedom. Men are freest when they are most unconscious of freedom. The shout is a rattling of chains, always was.

Men are not free when they are doing just what they like. The moment you can do just what you like, there is nothing you care about doing. Men are only free when they are doing what the deepest self likes.

And there is getting down to the deepest self! It takes some diving.

Because the deepest self is way down, and the conscious self is an obstinate monkey. But of one thing we may be sure. If one wants to be free, one has to give up the illusion of doing what one likes, and seek what IT wishes done.

But before you can do what IT likes, you must first break the spell of the old mastery, the old IT.

Perhaps at the Renaissance, when kingship and fatherhood fell, Europe drifted into a very dangerous half-truth: of liberty and equality. Perhaps the men who went to America felt this, and so repudiated the old world altogether. Went one better than Europe. Liberty in America has meant so far the breaking away from *all* dominion. The true liberty will only begin when Americans discover IT, and proceed possibly to fulfill IT. IT being the deepest *whole* self of man, the self in its wholeness, not idealistic halfness.

That's why the Pilgrim Fathers came to America, then; and that's why we come. Driven by IT. We cannot see that invisible winds carry us, as they carry swarms of locusts, that invisible magnetism brings us as it brings the migrating birds to their unforeknown goal. But it is so. We are not the marvellous choosers and deciders we think we are. IT chooses for us, and decides for us. Unless of course we are just escaped slaves, vulgarly cocksure of our ready-made destiny. But if we are living people, in touch with the source, IT drives us and decides us. We are free only so long as we obey. When we run counter, and think we will do as we like, we just flee around like Orestes pursued by the Eumenides.

And still, when the great day begins, when Americans have at last discovered America and their own wholeness, still there will be the vast number of escaped slaves to reckon with, those who have no cocksure, ready-made destinies.

Which will win in America, the escaped slaves, or the new whole men?

The real American day hasn't begun yet. Or at least, not yet sunrise. So far it has been the false dawn. That is, in the progressive American consciousness there has been the one dominant desire, to do away with the old thing. Do away with masters, exalt the will of the people. The will of the people being nothing but a figment, the exalting doesn't count for much. So, in the name of the will of the people, get rid of masters. When you have got rid of masters, you are left with this mere phrase of the will of the people. Then you pause and bethink yourself, and try to recover your own wholeness.

So much for the conscious American motive, and for democracy over here. Democracy in America is just the tool with which the old mastery of Europe, the European spirit, is undermined. Europe destroyed, potentially, American democracy will evaporate. America will begin.

American consciousness has so far been a false dawn. The negative ideal of democracy. But underneath, and contrary to this open ideal, the first hints and revelations of IT. IT, the American whole soul.

You have got to pull the democratic and idealistic clothes off American utterance, and see what you can of the dusky body of IT underneath.

"Henceforth be masterless."

Henceforth be mastered.

17. American Cities

JEAN PAUL SARTRE

Jean Paul Sartre (1905–   ), French novelist, playwright, philosopher, psychologist, and editor, has probably done more than any other single person to make the word "existentialism" familiar to people with no professional interest in philosophy. "Existence precedes essence" is a phrase often offered as the key to this peculiarly modern way of understanding the world, a way derived in part from the Danish theologian Kierkegaard and the German philosophers Husserl and Heidegger, with the latter of whom Sartre studied before World War II. Though Sartre wrote essays and fiction before that war, he did not attract real attention until after he had entered the Resistance Movement against the Nazis. Since then, his bleak view of man's nature and destiny, his shifting political allegiance, even his personal life have commanded the attention of reading people all over the world. He has never collected the handful of essays he wrote on America during a wartime trip, but the piece included here appeared in a volume of translations of his works called *Literary and Philosophical Essays* (1955).

For the first few days I was lost. My eyes were not accustomed to the skyscrapers and they did not surprise me; they did not seem like man-made, man-inhabited constructions, but rather like rocks and hills, dead parts of the urban landscape one finds in cities built on a turbulent soil and which you pass without even noticing. At the same time, I was continually and vainly looking for something to catch my attention for a moment—a detail, a square, perhaps, or a public building. I did not yet know that these houses and streets should be seen in the mass.

In order to learn to live in these cities and to like them as Americans

SOURCE: Jean Paul Sartre, *Literary and Philosophical Essays* (London: S. G. Phillips, Inc., 1955). Copyright 1955 by S. G. Phillips, Inc. Reprinted by permission of publisher and Hutchinson Publishing Group Ltd.

do, I had to fly over the immense deserts of the west and south. Our European cities, submerged in human countrysides that have been worked over mile by mile, are continuous. And then we are vaguely aware that far away, across the sea, there is the desert, a myth. For the American, this myth is an everyday reality. We flew for hours between New Orleans and San Francisco, over an earth that was dry and red, clotted with verdigris bushes. Suddenly, a city, a little checkerboard flush with the ground, arose and then, again, the red earth, the Savannah, the twisted rocks of the Grand Canyon, and the snows of the Rocky Mountains.

After a few days of this diet, I came to understand that the American city was, originally, a camp in the desert. People from far away, attracted by a mine, a petroleum field or fertile land, arrived one fine day and settled as quickly as possible in a clearing, near a river. They built the vital parts of the town, the bank, the town hall, the church, and then hundreds of one-storey frame houses. The road, if there was one, served as a kind of spinal column to the town, and then streets were marked out like vertebrae, perpendicular to the road. It would be hard to count the American cities that have that kind of parting in the middle.

Nothing has changed since the time of the covered wagons; every year towns are founded in the United States, and they are founded according to the same methods.

Take Fontana, Tennessee, which is situated near one of the great T.V.A. dams. Twelve years ago there were pine-trees growing in the mountain's red soil. As soon as the construction of the dam began, the pines were felled and three towns—two white ones of 3000 and 5000 inhabitants each, and one Negro town—sprang from the soil. The workers live there with their families; four or five years ago, when work was in full swing, one birth was recorded each day. Half of the village looks like a pile-dwellers' community: the houses are of wood, with green roofs, and have been built on piles to avoid dampness. The other half is made of collapsible dwellings, "prefabricated houses." They too are of wood; they are constructed about 500 miles away and loaded onto trucks: a single team of men can set one up within four hours after its arrival. The smallest costs the employer two thousand dollars, and he rents them to his workers for nineteen dollars a month (thirty-one dollars if they are furnished). The interiors, with their mass-produced furniture, central heating, electric lamps, and refrigerators, remind one of ship cabins. Every square inch of these antiseptic little rooms has been utilized; the walls have clothes-presses and under the beds there are chests of drawers.

One leaves with a slightly depressed feeling, with the feeling of having seen the careful, small-scale reconstitution of a 1944 flat in the year 3000. The moment one steps outside one sees hundreds of houses, all alike, piled up, squashed against the earth, but retaining in their very form some sort of nomadic look. It looks like a caravan graveyard. The pile-dweller community and the caravan cemetery face one another. Between them a wide road climbs toward the pines. There you have a city, or rather the nucleus of an American city, with all its essential parts. Below is the Woolworth's, higher up the hospital, and at the top, a "mixed" church in which what might be called a minimum service — that is, one valid for all creeds — is conducted.

The striking thing is the lightness, the fragility of these buildings. The village has no weight, it seems barely to rest on the soil; it has not managed to leave a human imprint on the reddish earth and the dark forest; it is a temporary thing. And besides, it will soon take to the road; in two years the dam will be finished, the workers will leave, and the prefabricated houses will be taken down and sent to a Texas oil well or a Georgia cotton plantation, to reconstitute another Fontana, under other skies, with new inhabitants.

This roving village is no exception; in the United States, communities are born as they die — in a day. The Americans have no complaint to make; the main thing is to be able to carry their homes with them. These homes are the collections of objects, furnishings, photographs, and souvenirs belonging to them, that reflect their own image and constitute the inner, living landscape of their dwellings. These are their penates. Like Aeneas, they haul them about everywhere.

The "house" is the shell; it is abandoned on the slightest pretext.

We have workers' communities in France. But they are sedentary, and then they never become real cities; on the contrary, they are the artificial product of neighbouring cities. In America, just as any citizen can theoretically become President, so each Fontana can become Detroit or Minneapolis; all that is needed is a bit of luck. And conversely, Detroit and Minneapolis are Fontanas which have had luck. To take only one example: in 1905, Detroit had a population of 300,000. Its population is now 1,000,000.

The inhabitants of this city are perfectly aware of this luck; they like to recall in their books and films the time when their community was only an outpost. And that is why they pass so easily from city to outpost; they make no distinction between the two. Detroit and Minneapolis, Knoxville and Memphis were born temporary and have stayed that way. They will never, of course, take to the road again on the back of a truck. But they remain at the meeting point; they have never reached an internal temperature of solidification.

Things that would not constitute a change of situation for us are, for the American, occasions for real breaks with his past. There are many who, on going off to war, have sold their apartments and everything else, including their suits. What is the point of keeping something that will be outmoded upon their return? Soldiers' wives often reduce their scale of living and go to live more modestly in other neighbourhoods. Thus, sadness and faithfulness to the absent are marked by a removal.

The removals also indicate fluctuations in American fortunes.

It is customary, in the United States, for the fashionable neighbourhoods to slide from the centre to the outskirts of the city; after five years the centre of town is "polluted." If you walk about there, you come upon tumble-down houses that retain a pretentious look beneath their filth; you find a complicated kind of architecture, one-storey frame houses with entrances formed by peristyles supported by columns, gothic chalets, "colonial houses", etc. These were formerly aristocratic homes, now inhabited by the poor. Chicago's lurid Negro section contains some of these Greco-Roman temples; from the outside they still look well. But inside, twelve rat- and louse-plagued Negro families are crowded together in five or six rooms.

At the same time, changes are continually made within the same place. An apartment house is bought to be demolished, and a larger apartment house is built on the same plot. After five years, the new house is sold to a contractor who tears it down to build a third one. The result is that in the States a city is a moving landscape for its inhabitants, whereas our cities are our shells.

In France, one hears only from very old people what a forty-year-old American said to me in Chicago. "When I was young, this whole neighbourhood was taken up by a lake. But this part of the lake was filled in and built over." And a thirty-five-year-old lawyer who was showing me the Negro section said: "I was born here. Then it was a white section and, apart from servants, you would not have seen a Negro in the streets. Now the white people have left and 250,000 Negroes are crowded into their houses."

M. Verdier, the owner of the "City of Paris" department store in San Francisco, witnessed the earthquake and fire that destroyed three quarters of the city. At that time he was a young man; he remembers the disaster perfectly. He watched the reconstruction of the city which still had an Asiatic look around 1913, and then its rapid Americanization. Thus, he has superimposed memories of three San Franciscos.

We Europeans change within changeless cities, and our houses and neighbourhoods outlive us; American cities change faster than their inhabitants do, and it is the inhabitants who outlive the cities.

I am really visiting the United States in wartime; the vast life of the American city has suddenly become petrified; people hardly change their residence any more. But this stagnation is entirely temporary; the cities have been immobilized like the dancer on the film-screen who stays with his foot suspended in air when the film is stopped; one feels all about one the rising of the sap which will burst open the cities as soon as the war is ended.

First, there are immediate problems; Chicago's Negro section will have to be rebuilt, for instance. The government had begun this before Pearl Harbour. But the government-built apartment houses barely manage to shelter 7000 people. Now, there are 250,000 to be housed. Then the industrialists want to enlarge and transform their factories; the famous abattoirs of Chicago are going to be completely modernized.

Finally, the average American is obsessed by the image of the "modern house" which is considerably publicized and which will be, so we are told, a hundred times more comfortable than the present dwellings and whose construction in huge quantities certainly has its place in the plans for "industrial conversion" which are now springing up almost everywhere.

When the war is over, America will certainly be seized with a real construction fever. Today the American sees his city objectively; he does not dream of finding it ugly, but thinks it really old. If it were even older, like ours, he could find a social past, a tradition in it. We generally live in our grandfathers' houses. Our streets reflect the customs and ways of past centuries; they tend to filter the present; none of what goes on in the Rue Montorgueil or the Rue Pot-de-Fer is completely of the present. But the thirty-year-old American lives in a house that was built when he was twenty.

These houses that are too young to seem old seem merely outdated to them; they lag behind the other tools, the car that can be traded in every two years, the refrigerator or the wireless set. That is why they see their cities without vain sentimentality. They have grown slightly attached to them, as one becomes attached to one's car, but they consider them as instruments, rather than anything else, instruments to be exchanged for more convenient ones.

For us a city is, above all, a past; for them it is mainly a future; what they like in the city is everything it has not yet become and everything it can be.

What are the impressions of a European who arrives in an American city? First, he thinks he has been taken in. He has heard only about skyscrapers; New York and Chicago have been described to him as "upright cities." Now his first feeling is, on the contrary, that the average height of an American city is noticeably smaller than that of a French one. The immense majority of houses have only two storeys. Even in the very large cities, the five-storey apartment house is an exception.

Then he is struck by the lightness of the materials used. In the United States stone is less frequently used than in Europe. The skyscraper consists of a coating of concrete applied to a metal framework, and the other buildings are made of brick or wood. Even in the richest cities and the smartest sections, one often finds frame houses. New Orleans' lovely colonial houses are of wood; many of the pretty chalets belonging to the Hollywood stars and film-directors are made of wood; so are the "California style" cottages in San Francisco. Everywhere you find groups of frame houses crushed between two twenty-storeyed buildings.

The brick houses are the colour of dried blood, or, on the contrary, daubed and smeared with bright yellow, green or raw white.[1] In most of the cities, they are roofless cubes or rectangular parallelepipeds, with severely flat facades. All these houses, hastily constructed and made expressly to be hastily demolished, obviously bear a strange resemblance to Fontana's "prefabricated houses."

The lightness of these jerry-built houses, their loud colours alternating with the sombre red of the bricks, the extraordinary variety of their

---

[1] Kisling and Masson have often complained of the fact that the urban landscape of the United States is not very stimulating to painting. I believe this is partly due to the fact that the cities have already been painted. They do not have the hesitant colours of our own cities. What is one to do with these tones which already are art, or artifice at least? All one can do is leave them alone.

decorations which does not manage to conceal the uniformity of their patterns, all give one the feeling, when in the middle of the city, of walking through the suburbs of a watering town, like Trouville or Cabourg or La Baule. Only those ephemeral seaside chalets with their pretentious architectural style and their fragility can convey to those of my French readers who have never seen the States an idea of the American apartment house.

To complete the impression, I should also like to add that sometimes one also thinks of an exposition-city, but an obsolescent, dirty one, like those that ten years later, in some park, survive the celebration that occasioned them. For these shanties quickly grow dirty, particularly in industrial sections.

Chicago, blackened by its smoke clouded by the Lake Michigan fog, is a dark and gloomy red. Pittsburgh is more gloomy still. And there is nothing more immediately striking than the contrast between the formidable power, the inexhaustible abundance of what is called the "American Colossus" and the puny insignificance of those little houses that line the widest roads in the world. But on second thought, there is no clearer indication that America is not finished, that her ideas and plans, her social structure and her cities have only a strictly temporary reality.

These perfectly straight cities bear no trace of organization. Many of them have the rudimentary structure of a polypary. Los Angeles, in particular, is rather like a big earthworm that might be chopped into twenty pieces without being killed. If you go through this enormous urban cluster, probably the largest in the world, you come upon twenty juxtaposed cities, strictly identical, each with its poor section, its business streets, night-clubs and smart suburb, and you get the impression that a medium-sized urban centre has schizogenetically reproduced itself twenty times.[2]

In America, where the neighbourhoods are added on to each other as the region's prosperity attracts new immigrants, this juxtaposition is the rule. You pass without any transition from a poor street into an aristocratic avenue; a promenade lined with skyscrapers, museums and public monuments and adorned with lawns and trees, suddenly stops short above a smoky station; one frequently discovers at the feet

[2] To convey an idea of this city to the reader, I suggest that he try to imagine, not one Côte d'Azur city, but the entire region between Cannes and Menton.

of the largest buildings, along an aristocratic avenue, a "zone" of miserable little kitchen-gardens.

This is due to the fact that these cities that move at a rapid rate are not constructed in order to grow old, but move forward like modern armies, encircling the islands of resistance they are unable to destroy; the past does not manifest itself in them as it does in Europe, through public monuments, but through survivals. The wooden bridge in Chicago which spans a canal two steps away from the world's highest skyscrapers is a survival. The elevated railways, rolling noisily through the central streets of New York and Chicago, supported by great iron pillars and cross-girders, neatly touching the facades of houses on either side, are survivals. They are there simply because no one has taken the time to tear them down, and as a kind of indication of work to be done.

You find this disorder in each individual vista. Nowhere have I seen so many empty lots. Of course they do have a definite function; they are used as car parks. But they break the alignment of the street nonetheless sharply for all that. Suddenly it seems as if a bomb had fallen on three or four houses, reducing them to powder, and as if they had just been swept out: this is a "parking space," two hundred square metres of bare earth with its sole ornament, perhaps, a poster on a big hoarding. Suddenly the city seems unfinished, badly assembled; suddenly you rediscover the desert and the big empty site: noticeable at Fontana. I remember this Los Angeles landscape in the middle of the city, two modern apartment houses, two white cubes framing an empty lot with the ground torn up—a parking space. A few abandoned-looking cars were parked there. A palm tree grew like a weed between the cars. Down at the bottom there was a steep grassy hill, rather like the fortification mounds we use for garbage disposal. On top of the mound was a frame house, and a little below this a string stretched between two little trees, with multicoloured washing hanging out to dry. When one turned around the block of houses, the hill disappeared; its other side had been built up, covered with asphalt, streaked with tar roads, and pierced with a magnificent tunnel.

The most striking aspect of the American city is the vertical disorder. These brick shanties are of varying heights; I noted at random during a walk in Detroit the following successive proportions: one storey, two storeys, one storey, one storey, three storeys. You find the same proportions in Albuquerque or San Antonio, at the other end of

the country. In depth, above this irregular crenellation, you see apartment houses of all shapes and dimensions, long cases, thick thirty-
storeyed boxes with forty windows to a storey. As soon as there is a bit
of fog the colours fade away, and only volumes remain—every
variety of polyhedron. Between them, you have enormous empty
spaces, empty lots cut out in the sky.

In New York, and even in Chicago, the skyscraper is on home
ground, and imposes a new order upon the city. But everywhere else it
is out of place; the eye is unable to establish any unity between these
tall, gawky things and the little houses that run close to the ground; in
spite of itself it looks for that line so familiar in European cities, the
sky-line, and cannot find it. That is why the European feels at first as
though he were travelling through a rocky chaos that resembles a city
—something like Montpellier-le-Vieux—rather than a city.

But the European makes a mistake in visiting American cities as
one does Paris or Venice; they are not meant to be seen that way. The
streets here do not have the same meaning as our streets. In Europe, a
street is half-way between the path of communication and the sheltered "public place." It is on a footing with the cafés, as proved by the
use of the "terrasses" that spring up on the sidewalks of the cafés in
fine weather. Thus it changes its aspect more than a hundred times a
day, for the crowd that throngs the European street changes, and men
are its primary element. The American street is a piece of highway. It
sometimes stretches over many miles. It does not stimulate one to
walk. Ours are oblique and twisting, full of bends and secrets. The
American street is a straight line that gives itself away immediately. It
contains no mystery. You see the street straight through, from one
end to the other no matter what your location in it. And the distances
in American cities are too great to permit moving about on foot; in
most of them one gets about almost exclusively in cars, on buses and
by underground. Sometimes, while going from one appointment to another, I have been carried like a parcel from underground to escalator,
from escalator to elevator, from elevator to taxi, from taxi to bus and,
again, by metro and elevator, without walking a step.

In certain cities I noticed a real atrophy of the sidewalk. In Los Angeles, for example, on La Cienega, which is lined with bars, theatres,
restaurants, antique dealers and private residences, the sidewalks are
scarcely more than side-streets that lead customers and guests from
the roadway into the house. Lawns have been planted from the facades

to the roadway of this luxurious avenue. I followed a narrow path between the lawns for a long time without meeting a living soul, while to my right, cars streaked by on the road; all animation in the street had taken refuge on the high road.

New York and Chicago do not have neighbourhoods, but they do have a neighbourhood life; the American is not familiar with his city; once he is ten "blocks" away from his home, he is lost. This does not mean that there are no crowds in the business streets, but they are crowds that do not linger; people shop or emerge from the Underground to go to their offices.

I rarely saw an occasional Negro day-dreaming before a shop.

Yet one quickly begins to like American cities. Of course they all look alike. And when you arrive at Wichita, Saint Louis or Albuquerque, it is disappointing to realize that, hidden behind these magnificent and promising names, is the same standard checkboard city with the same red and green traffic lights and the same provincial look. But one gradually learns to tell them apart. Chicago, the noble, lurid city, red as the blood that trickles through its abattoirs, with its canals, the grey water of Lake Michigan and its streets crushed between clumsy and powerful buildings, in no way resembles San Francisco, city of air, salt and sea, built in the shape of an amphitheatre.

And then one finally comes to like their common element, that temporary look. Our beautiful closed cities, full as eggs, are a bit stifling. Our slanting, winding streets run head on against walls and houses; once you are inside the city, you can no longer see beyond. In America, these long, straight unobstructed streets carry one's glance, like canals, outside the city. You always see mountains or fields or the sea at the end of them, no matter where you may be.

Frail and temporary, formless and unfinished, they are haunted by the presence of the immense geographical space surrounding them. And precisely because their boulevards are highways, they always seem to be stopping places on the roads. They are not oppressive, they do not close you in; nothing in them is definitive, nothing is arrested. You feel, from your first glance, that your contact with these places is a temporary one; either you will leave them or they will change around you.

Let us beware of exaggerating; I have spent Sundays in the American provinces that were more depressing than Sundays anywhere else; I have seen those suburban "colonial style" inns where, at two dollars a head, middle-class families go to eat shrimp cocktails and turkey with cranberry sauce in silence while listening to the electric organ. One must not forget the heavy boredom that weighs over America.

But these slight cities, still so similar to Fontana and the outposts of the Far West, reveal the other side of the United States: their freedom. Here everyone is free—not to criticize or to reform their customs— but to flee them, to leave for the desert or another city. The cities are open, open to the world, and to the future. This is what gives them their adventurous look and, even in their ugliness and disorder, a touching beauty.

18. Innocents at Home

JACQUES BARZUN

Jacques Barzun (1907–   ), eminent educator and former Dean of Graduate Faculties at Columbia University, writes with a special authority deriving from his having been born in France. Too thoroughly naturalized to be included in the group of visiting Europeans (he was picked by *Time* magazine as perhaps the most typical among a group of American intellectuals), Mr. Barzun writes here what he himself calls "a declaration of love, spiced with a few harsh words."

The way to see America is from a lower berth about two in the morning. You've just left a station—it was the jerk of pulling out that woke you—and you raise the curtain a bit between thumb and forefinger to look out. You are in the middle of Kansas or Arizona, in the middle of the space where the freight cars spend the night and the men drink coffee out of cans. Then comes the signal tower, some bushes, a few shacks and—nothing. You see the last blue switch-light on the next track, and beyond is America—dark and grassy, or sandy, or rocky

SOURCE: Jacques Barzun, *God's Country and Mine* (Boston: Atlantic-Little, Brown and Co., 1954), pp. 3–24. Copyright 1954 by Jacques Barzun. Reprinted by permission of Atlantic-Little, Brown and Co.

—and no one there. Nothing but the irrational universe with you in the center trying to reason it out. It's only ten, fifteen minutes since you've left a thriving town but life has already been swallowed up in that ocean of matter which is and will remain as wild as it was made.

Come daylight, the fear vanishes but not the awe or the secret pleasure. It is a perpetual refreshment to the soul to see that the country is so large, so indifferent to the uses we have put it to, so like a piece of the earth's crust and unlike any map. No names on it, no lines, no walls with guns through them. It is good that in this place at least there is more of just plain territory per square mile than anywhere else in the civilized world. Europe is lovely but it looks like a poodle cut—the trees are numbered, the flat parts divided like a checkerboard, the rivers as slim and well-behaved as the mercury in a thermometer. The towns, like dead men's bones on the line of a caravan, huddle white and dry, crowded behind defenses that have crumbled. And everywhere the steeples point to remind you that you must look upward if you want space and serenity.

Here space is ubiquitous, even on the Atlantic Coast, which by the country's own scale is shriveled and thick with human beings. But even here we have space enough to swallow up the worst signs of our busy nonchalance, the car dumps. And even here we refuse to follow the ways of the citified: suburban street signs leave you in the lurch, and houses forget or conceal their separate numbers. Nearby the wilderness exists and has been kept: the Adirondacks are a paradise of woods and waterfalls and luxuriant vegetation—and yet it's only a small state preserve for city campers playing Indians with canoes and grocery-store pemmican. The sand dunes of Cape Cod are as accessible and linked with city life as any suburb, yet they stretch most of the time as empty as the desert, and they are moved by giant storms that feel like the last shaping flick of the Creator's thumb.

Starting from the greatest city in the world, almost invisible on a fair-sized map of the continent, one must push the wheels for three quarters of a day before reaching the midland seas that are the country's crown. By that point, too, one has traveled but a short distance away (as soil and spirit mark it) from America's European shore. Clock time has moved one hour back to wait for the sun, and the world perspective has somewhat changed. The doings of other men on the rim of the vast saucer in whose hollow one stands do begin to seem remote. The space on all sides dwarfs the subdivisions that are so real to the many millions beyond the seas. From America's rich gestating center south of the Great Lakes, one seems merely to overhear the world while one broods on the permanent functions of the earth. And yet that center is not central. Like the human heart, the Middle West is to one side of the median line. To really find the West there is still the Mississippi to ford, the long plains to cross, the Rockies to climb and five, six other chains to pass over, with deserts between, before going down into the last valley and reaching the country's Asiatic shore. The clocks have turned back twice again for the slow sun, and the traveler who has been drinking space is reeling.

The memory cannot hold all he has seen, for there is no common measure between the human senses and the unfolded spectacle. Quick variety—yes, we have nets fine enough to catch and retain that. But variety on a cosmic scale is beyond us. We can name the valleys, mountains, and gorges but we hardly know them. Anywhere in the world we hold our breath at moments of beauty and unexpectedness. But we cannot hold our breath for the hundred miles of endlessly renewed beauty in the Feather River Canyon. We probably give up and call it dull, but we only are hiding the truth from ourselves. Any stretch before us makes us stare and hold our breath again. Even the wastes and crags, the wreckage of the furnace days in those gray workshops of nature where it seems as if the fairer regions had been forged, are transcendently beautiful. The eighteen thousand square miles of the Great Basin in Oregon show nothing but dun palisades sloping backwards into flats of broken rocks—once the scene of unimaginable upheavals, now dedicated to carrying into the abyss, by means of its underground rivers, the broken particles of the split atom.

Magnificent, but is it art? Certainly not. Art follows rules based on our tiny comprehension. Art has to be comfortable for family men and women's clubs. None of America was made to *please*. It was made perhaps to satisfy a Worker in the Sublime, who knew that by heaping up triumphs on a grand scale he would successfully escape detection. Every region, every state, has its mystery, its defiance of probability —the colors of the Southwest, the virtuosity of desert life, the immense salt sea, the giant redwoods, the lake that won't freeze (though miles up in a crater) and that stays fresh (though without visible outlet) . . . When you think you've reached the end there is more—miles more—the source and the image of our abundance.

Only, in order to excuse so much exuberance of imagination, the

Workman buried a treasure somewhere in the middle of his plot, and toward this he enticed men by decorating with small restful shapes and sights, in familiar greens and browns, the coast nearest the supply of active men.

At the same time, the artificer kept the weather congenial to his own robust frame and violent fancy. The solemn scientificos who call any spot in the United States part of the Temperate Zone are kidding. A change of thirty degrees between sunup and sundown, repeated without warning of season fifty times a year; highs of 90° to 120° in summer, with natural steam provided free; lows of zero and less in winter, with snowfalls and blizzards and ice-storms—none of these can be called temperate except in the sense of tempering. If they don't kill, they give a steel-like elasticity to the constitution.

But although the country is fertile, almost tropical in vegetation and rich in minerals, its food is bland. Everything that grows here is large but not luscious. The juices are not concentrated—as if to discourage self-indulgence through the belly. And just as there are but few delicate, man-size landscapes, so there is a lack of concentrated drama in the mountains. We have nothing like the Alps. Our bareness is diffuse, it is diluted—once again—in space. Our overwhelming masses of mountain timber are unbroken by any grassy islands that might give the scale through man's taking his cattle there. Our pure rock and eternal snows are remote, instead of rising from the midst of our daily life.

True, we can show stunning contrasts. The evergreen slopes around Lake Tahoe make a beautiful discord with the watery mass fringed by pale flowers. But the presence of man is not felt, even when you see him there relaxing from the toil of getting his Reno divorce nearby. The place keeps aloof, untouchable. The drama, so familiar elsewhere, of man, master and victim of nature, is absent. Man here seems neither master nor victim but something which is at once more and less. He has not grown into and around the primal scene, but has either left it primitive or replaced it entirely by civilization. Maybe this is why he remains so innocent, his sense of struggle unembittered. The symbol of our relation to nature is the National Park, the State Reservation, where we go on purpose to see aboriginal America, and our amusement is to play at the hunting and fishing life with all the contraptions of technology at hand. Nature is not our context or background but solely our raw material and—for recreation—our plaything.

All this has a meaning that only those who live here can comprehend. Man on this continent does not "show" because he did not start
primitive with it. He came prepared. And yet the task of establishing
himself was so vast that the individual man who could typify the effort
did not count. The saga had to be lived so many times that the single
hero, the outstanding name, is lost in the mass. America was possessed
and civilized by the mass; it was a community enterprise from the
start, in which the leader leads and does not dominate. Even our discoverer bears a generic name: Cristobal Colón: The Colonizer. The
feats of conquest and settlement were as memorable as any in history
or legend, but being commanded wholesale by necessity they grew
commonplace. Who remembers the amazing life of Dr. Marcus Whitman, except schoolboys in Walla Walla? What of David Thompson,
John McLoughlin, Elijah White? John Jacob Astor lives in memory
not by his strenuous deeds, but by his descendants' leisure. We all
know Pike's Peak because of the jingle and the slogan, but who was
Pike? One in a million can tell you that this youthful hero's first name
was Zebulon, but whatever history says, tradition says no more.

True, it raises haunting visions to discover from a sign outside a gas
station at Murphy, North Carolina, that here De Soto and his men en-
camped in 1540. One can imagine the swampy ground sloping toward
the river—under the present concrete and asphalt that stretches to
the bridge. But for the ordinary traveler the reminiscence is barren. De
Soto is a car and so is La Salle. They do not live in our imagination, for
what they did many others did also, unknown soldiers of the conquest.
There is no disloyalty in recognizing that by the very essence of America's greatness there can be no *national* American history as there is
English or French history. What we have is state and county history
rich, varied, and of the utmost liveliness and reality; complete with
feuds, aristocrats, disasters, and leading roles. But on the greater scene
the telling incidents and towering figures are simply not there. They
may have existed but they have been dissolved away, not by time but
by space and numbers.

You will say with some justice that I exaggerate. Yes, in early days,
when America was still a colony of Europe, we can easily discern the
great men, the chief founding fathers, but they live in us as myths and
symbols rather than as flesh-and-blood people with distinct passions
and errors, or cruel egos and dreadful deaths. Washington, Franklin,
Hamilton, and Jefferson are wonderful legends—who will ever know

or believe all that Jefferson did?—but match these names with Alexander Borgia, Henry VIII, Luther, or Napoleon, and our heroes pale into unreality. For one thing, they have no wickedness to speak of. All we can muster as villains are Benedict Arnold and Aaron Burr—a pitiful showing of borderline cases. Lincoln alone is vivid because in spite of his amazing saintliness he embodies the meaning of what happened here. He signifies not one great man, or even Man, but mankind —anonymous, humble and irresistible like the sweep of the Father of Waters.

What happened here on this enormous expanse of intact wildness is that mankind got out from under and spread out. From under what? From under the lid—everybody, from under all the lids—kings, churches, aristocracies, landlords, the military caste, the burgher class, the lawyers, the lesser nobility, the petty bourgeoisie—the piles of subclasses on top of subclasses that formed the structure of old Europe. They left an old world to stretch their limbs and spread out flat, with only the sky above them. Their goal was space. When the Eastern end thickened into layers for a new social pyramid, the under-layers slid out again to the West.

At first, a good many of the upper orders came over too, but they rarely kept their hold. The Revolution put an end to the English and Tory ruling class. If some of them salvaged their goods they remained as well-to-do citizens and that is all. Who can name offhand anybody descended from a colonial governor or bishop or major general? The connection, if known, would scarcely affect one's behavior toward him or his place in the community. It would be just a curious fact, possibly as funny as the "fact" that Theodore Roosevelt, according to the chart in his old house, was descended from Richard the Lion-Hearted. It is true that some of our leading citizens take genealogies very gravely. It's a thriving industry to dig them out of churchyards with the aid of a vaulting imagination. But pedigree has seldom helped any American to get elected mayor or to sell insurance; the Fuller Brush man does not introduce himself as a Son of the War of 1812—ask any ten people what the Order of Cincinnati is. Americans may love getting together in costumed brotherhoods, but these impress the membership much more than the nation.

The same is true of the social cliques that keep their barriers high. Movement in and out of these groups is constant and their exclusivism is largely convivial—who goes to whose parties. It does not decide who runs corporations, schools, city government or anything else of importance. In fact, for all official and a good many unofficial posts, society manners and ways of speech are a handicap. Nor are the professions here encumbered by social pretensions as they still are abroad. Look at the names of our judges, doctors, scientists, men of letters, and university presidents. They do not have to be Cabot or Vanderhoof or Vere de Vere. They can be anything, pronounceable or not.

All of which says nothing against the proud inheritors of good old names. It only says something far more impressive for all the rest — which is that this country was peopled by underdogs, refugees, nobodies, and that it keeps on being run by them. The noble ancestors of the American people were, with negligible exceptions: starving peasants, poor mechanics, domestic servants, younger sons without prospects, unlucky youths who had to leave town in a hurry, adventurers and shady characters of all sorts — convicts too, for that matter — any kind of man or woman who for some reason found living in Europe intolerable. That also means, of course, men of faith and education who resented tyranny of one sort or another, like the original Puritans of 1620, the French Huguenots of 1685, the Liberal Germans of 1848 who wanted constitutional government, the Irish, driven by famine and hatred of England, and young nationals from all over who fled military service.

To say all this is nothing new. We know, the whole world knows, that the American people is in its origin a sampling of the peoples of Western Europe. America began by being the haven of the disinherited — the underside of Europe — and then two providential events took place. First, the Industrial Revolution broke out and destroyed the immemorial connection of wealth and power with land. Next, the search for new wealth from industry, mining, and railroads led the American capitalists of the nineteenth century to import labor from any and everywhere, of all colors and kinds, good or bad, literate or illiterate. In doing this they made the United States the testing ground of the possibility of mankind living together.

I harp on the idea of mankind because it is a sign of the future, not an exaggeration of the accomplished past. To begin with, we have here a complete Europe — Swedes cheek by jowl with Armenians, Hungarians with Poles, Germans with French, English with Italians, Jews with Christians, Orthodox Greek with Baptists, and so on ad infinitum. No one can say that all is love and kisses in this grand mixture. In many a town there are two sides of the railroad track and on one side the poorer group, very likely ethnic in character, is discriminated against. But at what a rate these distinctions disappear! In Europe a thousand years of war, pogroms and massacres settle nothing. Here two generations of common schooling, intermarriage, ward politics, and labor unions create social peace.

Now turn from Europe to the world. The greed of the planters brought over the ancestors of our 15 million Negroes; that of the rail-road builders brought the Chinese, by the tens of thousands, and the hundreds of thousands from Southern Europe, the Balkans, Greece, Asia Minor, and Russia. Not long after, at the end of our Spanish War, in came Puerto Ricans, Hawaiians, Filipinos, and Japanese. The Mexicans on our Southwestern border had long been drawn in for a similar exploitation. And the Indians we had always with us, from the days when we robbed them, killed them, and cheated them out of their ancestral lands.

That part by itself is not a pretty picture: we are only now and very slowly beginning to right a few of those wrongs. But the dark shadows are not all there is to see. We often overlook the real sweep of our democracy because we fail to add together what we know in fragments. We ignore the panorama and consider every item for our own ends or from our own tastes. We praise this and condemn that without noticing the connections and the meaning, and fail to see mankind all around us. We just read with curiosity the feature story that says Louisiana uses the Code Napoléon; that the Pennsylvania Dutch publish their own paper in their own inimitable English (this in a region they share with the descendants of their former persecutors); and that part of the ruling family of Tibet is now living in Baltimore. We never think that in loosing and mixing the masses we have all been civilized by the rubs and collisions—civilized not only from the top down, but from all parts interacting on one another, the humble teaching the proud in the literal way of the Gospels. It has proved a peculiar civilizing of the feelings for which there is as yet no name. But it is genuine and it is going on: the late war has for the hundredth time amplified our kaleidoscopic pattern of peoples, tongues, costumes, ideas, and religions.

All this has been, not automatic, but in the larger sense unplanned. How else could it have been, considering the steady dumping of the world's forgotten men—or surplus life—over here? The appearance of chaos is therefore true and important, though not in the way it is usually interpreted. We miss the central point if we think that great ideas like democracy become reality the way a blueprint becomes a car or a house, by an orderly arrangement of parts. Luck or Providence must intervene. And we must not expect the outcome to show perfect proportions frozen into place. History is movement, disarray as well as desirable direction. If the country had remained predominantly agricultural, the first comers would have taken all the land and kept down the rest of us as men had done elsewhere for seven thousand years. Once more a thin tough crust, with a deep-dish pie of human beings underneath. But every man's idea of escape to personal liberty, before or after he got here, combined with the needs of the industrial system to start an irresistible drive towards equalizing conditions. It is that drive, greater than any ideal of progress or party of resistance, that moves the world today, and we call it democracy.

This definition is no doubt incomplete. Every educated man who is a democrat at heart thinks first of the guarantees a true democracy gives to the individual—the vote, free speech, and free assembly. But most men outside the Western world are still largely indifferent to such rights. They want food, clothes, and shelter first and at all costs. Hence the dictatorships that trade on this desire by offering, say, a half-democracy, the democracy of rough equality. Here in America the thoughtful are properly concerned and most likely to dwell reproachfully on inequalities in wealth and opportunity, on injustices to unprotected persons and groups, on attempts to scoop up our individual rights and toss them to the winds of demagoguery. But while we resist being despoiled we must not lose faith in our combined industrial and emotional democracy. I call by that name our unpremeditated scheme which has an interest in pushing towards equality and fair treatment because that is the way we've learned to feel and because the scheme requires that we sell goods and keep our machinery going.

To those who decry this as "mere materialism" one need only ask when and where the world has seen a whole nation developing the habit, the tendency, of continually looking out for those who in one way or another are left out. We act abundantly on this strange motive, but let us be modest and call it but a tendency. If we had achieved the perfection of utopia and complete brotherhood, there would be nothing to talk about. Yet look at the subjects of unceasing agitation in our daily press: the rights of labor in bargaining, the fight for fair employment practices, for socialized medicine, against discrimination in Army and Navy, in colleges and hospitals, in restaurants, and places of public entertainment; in a word, the abolition of irrational privilege.

Millions, it is true, are against change. They condemn tyranny and act it out in their small, very small way. Inconsistency and resistance are to be expected. When one talks of mankind and its emergence on our soil, one must visualize men, not angels. But whatever the creature visualized one must not compare its behavior with an abstract ideal. One must compare it with the behavior of other men in the past. In the light of that contrast, it can be said that here in America, in spite of the vast problem of absorbing repeated injections of the world's peoples, the prevailing idea for a century has been, not the segregation or neutralization of these foreign bodies, but the abolition of differences, the equalizing of conditions. The reality in turn has taught the lesson that mankind is an inescapable fact. Instead of saying "Down with *them!* No, not *those!* Off with *their* heads!," we have not been afraid to take mankind out of hiding where we can look at it and deal with it as best we can, for the most part decently. There has been nothing like it since the wonderful hodge-podge of the late Roman Empire, and even there the common citizenship was theoretical and inoperative in far greater degree than it is with us.

One must immediately add that we have a thousand imperfections to blush for, heart-rending failures of justice manifested in lynchings, anti-Semitism, and racketeering; in cruelty to immigrants, to lunatics, to Indians, and to children. But before we rouse our energies to combat error we should from time to time restore our courage by taking in the whole scene, not in a detached but in a voluntarily calm spirit. The very things that upset us can be a source of strength, for aside from the effort to stem injustice and repress the oppressors, what is *the* most insistent theme of private mail and public press, of government posters and noncommercial ads, on radio and TV? Can it be denied that in a hundred different forms that theme is the fate of our fellow men? Floods break out along the Missouri or tornados in New England— the Red Cross is there and Federal and State aid pouring in. A polio epidemic—it's a rush of experts, nurses, and serum. The refugees, war brides, and homeless children from abroad, as well as our own minority groups, have not only spokesmen but disinterested outsiders who clamor ceaselessly into our ears that we help them bodily or fight for their rights: The native-born Japanese, cruelly displaced during the war, must be relocated. Farmers who have exhausted their soil must be allotted new lands and taught how to use them. We don't stop with the able-bodied. The blind, the paraplegics, the alcoholics, the insane, the sufferers from hookworm and deficiency diseases, those who lack dental care or eyeglasses, children without lunches—it's an endless round of reminders and requests. It's parental care for the unborn, vacations and play centers for the street boys, rehabilitation for victims of cerebral palsy or T.B., for the neurotic and sclerotic, cure for the venereal, employment for the ex-convicts, and occupational therapy for the jailed and the delinquent. You see business trucks carrying posters to say that the particular firm is ready to hire handicapped workers, and where these should apply for the names of other firms. Anyone who is hurt, anyone who feels or is inferior has a claim. One learns, for instance, by direct letter from a state senator, that there are half a million mentally retarded children in New York state alone. What is wanted is money for special schools, workshops, clinics, and camps, so that this one three-hundredth of the national population will not turn into so many unhappy derelicts but men and women like the rest of us.

This is at last moral philosophy in action. We are no longer allowed to say "Let the devil take the hindmost"; we say: "How can we bring these creatures into the fold?" No misfortune natural or acquired is any longer a bar to our sympathy or a sufficient cause for dismissal by the social conscience. We face all types of misery and misfitness and proclaim that they are equally entitled to our help, because mankind is what we aim to save. The first thing democracy has to be is inclusive. We worry about childhood, youth, the newly married, the middle-aged, the retired, the very old. We don't let God carry the burdens or the blame, *we* take them on. We don't let the kindly rich do a hand-to-mouth job of individual charity that perpetuates the evil, we try to organize the means to destroy it. No doubt the resources are inadequate and the services faulty, but the principle and the impulse are unheard-of in the only annals we have of the past, the annals of *in*humanity. There is an American Foundation for the Overseas Blind; we have yet to hear of a Foreign Foundation for the American Blind. But let us not grow self-righteous, let us rather acknowledge and thank God that there is in us a good honest selfish motive side by side with the kindly impulse, which otherwise would fester into pride of rectitude. The self-interest also shows that we have begun to estimate the waste, the loss in material output, the cost to us all, of prejudice and exclusion. That awareness is a lever to move the world.

It is clear that this amazing American spectacle has a meaning beyond our shores. Thinking about it leads us straight into the drama of Life *versus* Destruction which is being played out on our globe. What have we to offer the world beyond our despised but welcome dollars and our ability to organize the means of making more? I have purposely refrained from mentioning, as part of our way of life, on the one hand public housing, Federal credit for home building, unemployment and accident insurance, social security, and the like; and on the other hand the myriad enterprises for public education and entertainment —from the town libraries we owe to Andrew Carnegie to the free concerts and art exhibits springing up all over the land. Some of those things are traditional in the Old World; others are inevitable by-products of the factory system and the rise of labor to self-conscious power. But the groups and institutions most characteristic of our country, and the feelings and habits that go with them, represent something new—not an idea in the usual sense, a deed, a practice. Our moral significance, our contribution to Western culture, if you like, lies in this perpetual retesting and amplification of the noblest theories fathered by European philosophers. Our spirit is watered by three streams of thought, originally distinct but here mingled:

The eighteenth-century Enlightenment view of progress toward social reason, or what we Americans know as the Jeffersonian ideal;

The Romanticist view of man's diversity, inventiveness and love of risk by which society is forever kept in flux, forever changing;

And the native tradition of Deafness to Doctrine which permits our Federal system to subsist at the same time as it provides free room for carrying out the behests of our other two beliefs.

Is there then no role played by our religious inheritance? Many an American leader, from Lincoln to Eisenhower, has said that democracy is inconceivable without a religious basis, and it appears from a recent national survey that 99 per cent of the American people declared themselves religious believers. They are indeed, yet it is no less true that for the majority of Americans religion does not mean the Church militant—we are not a crusading people; nor does it mean the endless heart-searching of the mystic. It means the social gospel, the brotherhood of man interpreted in the most practical way.

Only thus has it been possible to survive as a polyglot nation of continental size: Diversity, Fraternity, Perfectibility. It is idle to report that for the last fifty years the eighteenth-century doctrine of the goodness and perfectibility of man has been given up by serious thinkers. (They are perhaps not serious enough.) It is idle to point out that the faith in initiative and the conduct of life by common reason has dropped away. Right here we see their daily and hourly application. Man is assumed to be good, for otherwise why bother about him? He is worthy of care regardless not only of his origin but of his defects. Insofar as we know how to cure them we perfect him. The perfectibility of man does not mean his transfiguration. It means his being given the means to be reasonably decent. He must have a job, or a treatment, or an artificial limb. His perfectibility may depend upon a set of false teeth, which will incline him toward proper digestion and self-respect as against the degradation of drink. We must not blink the fact that spirit and soul are entangled in humble matter—which is not the same as saying that spirit and soul do not exist or that they are "nothing but" a set of false teeth.

On all this the men of the eighteenth century could only speak out of a courageous faith, guessing at the brutishness of the creatures in the dark beneath their feet. A friend of liberty such as Edmund Burke could only call the common folk the "swinish multitude," and Hamilton was right if he said "Your people, sir, are a great beast." But we, swamped with a humanity made thus by the hands of others, have tackled the job of scraping it clean of filth and beastliness, of ignorance and superstition, and we have begun to see the thing succeed. We should not be misled by the clamor and the wailing. It is our success which is causing it. Everybody, from the youngest reactionary to the oldest happy pessimist, is judging by the self-same liberal ideal that he attacks. He finds things dreadfully bad because he has an exalted image of the good that his great-grandfather would have thought fantastic. Every protest implies that there is a standard of common right to appeal to, whereas before nothing short of slave revolts brought any change.

This does not mean that all is smooth and settled. But the complaints and heartaches do not mean that defeatism is the part of the wise. Mankind is perverse, to be sure, shortsighted, and it has a queer urge to devour itself like the snake in the fable. This self-destruction is what most sane men are forever trying to prevent, and they do it by assuaging intolerable evils. Let us bear in mind that it is not a hundred years since our brother the Negro began to be freed from our brother the Southerner. The advance is inadequate if we measure it by perfect freedom; it is enormous if we compare it with any other emancipation on record. And since Southerners themselves have taken the work in hand, the chances are good for orderly change—as order goes here on earth.

I mean by this a manageable dose of violence, bitterness, and folly. One must keep one's eye on probability and not go imagining the frictionless world of our dreams. The cry for "Order" is, on the face of it, always proper. It is a measure of our desire for decency. But how often does it spring from a really orderly set of feelings? Is it not frequently an expression of impatience, of ignorance of fact, of contempt for persons? It is too simple a view to proclaim that once upon a time there was Order, and now there is not, which is painful to all, so let us quickly return to the thirteenth century or the folds of the dress of Queen Anne. It is a pathetic mistake excusable only in youth to confuse the beautiful order of the paragraphs in Thomas Aquinas's book with the living, buzzing, fearsome society of his time. While he was writing, you could have witnessed—to take but one appalling occurrence—the Children's Crusade. You don't have to know more than its name to visualize the fate of these thirty thousand innocents who shortly disappeared off the face of Christendom by disease, starvation, and violent death—all of it at the hands of their own "orderly" fellow Christians. The luckiest were those sold into Mohammedan slavery.

And while this horror was going on with the blessing of the highest in church and state, the rest of Europe was seething as usual. The flourishing Provençal civilization was being destroyed in the wholesale massacre of heretics, while in England the fight leading to Magna Carta shows you on what terms rights were then obtained—at spear's point and only for barons at that. We are forced back to our original proposition: we are not inherently better men than our forefathers, but by dint of heeding the better men among us, and *doing something practical about it,* we have developed a truer because more exacting conception of mankind.

It is because we can no longer help talking about mankind, instead of merely Us and the people we approve, that our understanding of life cannot stay a family affair confined to these United States. We are extending it almost by reflex action to the rest of the globe. Through Point Four providing for the development of backward areas; through the Marshall Plan which, no matter what may be said about it, was the blood transfusion in the nick of time which saves the patient; through participation in a bewildering number of international organizations like the Children's Emergency Fund, as well as through private ventures for the medical, educational, dietary, and technological improvement of human life, we are carrying to every part of the world our own innocently shrewd form of the social gospel.

Once again I can imagine good judges of fact objecting to this description. I shall be told that we fail rather stupidly, that we are hated for everything we do abroad, every penny we spend mysteriously turning into a sign of our selfish, grasping nature. A year or so ago, all the clever "independent" minds I met in Europe kept telling me that American Imperialism was enslaving the world. The poor souls! They too are haunted by the mirage of a perfect Eden in which they would be prosperous, beloved, and thanked for deigning to be alive. So they resent having to take help, work for it, and readjust their habits to the pace of a productive century. It interferes even with their self-pity. They cannot see that American Imperialism (let them call it that if it makes them feel better) may be as clumsy, naive, and "materialistic" as they say and by that very fact preferable to any other form of meddling on record. It has no "line," no dogma, but works for results, generally to the benefit of those living where it works. The British and the French and the Belgians in the heart of Africa had for generations endured malaria like heroes, because you couldn't cover up all the water holes and empty barrels where the mosquitoes breed. The ruthless Americans came in and covered them up.

It is attention to practice and indifference to overarching beliefs that guarantees our innocence, but our critics are sodden with ideology and cannot take this in. None the less this nonsectarianism is one clear sign of superiority over Russia. Russia is a hundred years behind us in the mere fact of being bogged down in the party pamphlet of a couple of angry men; Russia's mental date is theirs: 1848. When one forgets for a moment all the bloodshed that has come from it, there is something profoundly comic about all the quibbling and confessing and excommunicating that has occupied the best Russian brains ever since they smuggled in Karl Marx.

To put it another way, the "Russian soul" has still not raised itself to the conception of mankind as such—what a former mayor of San Francisco elegantly called "the *tout ensemble* of the whole." Russia is still playing cops and robbers, hero and villain, believer and infidel, with all the deadly religious pride of the crusader. They kill you for their good. Whatever Communism was in the minds of its early prophets, from Saint Thomas More onward, it was not this; and Russia may yet go down in history as the nation that ruined an interesting idea.

There is no doubt a good reason why Russian Imperio-Communism is so rigid and self-righteous, and the reason points to a second ground of superiority in us. Starting a century late, with a people barely out of serfdom, Russia has had a gigantic job trying to catch up with the industrialized West. The habits of a new age are not acquired in a few years. The change was dreadful enough in England and France and Belgium in the 1800's, when three generations of men, women, and children were sacrificed to the machine above and below ground. Deliberate massacre and coercion in modern Russia correspond to this wrench from the soil to the factory, and express a furious will to succeed. That fact in itself should be a warning to all other peoples who think that American Imperialism means death-in-life. We are *not* desperate. By our standards and according to our lights, we *have* succeeded. Our motives are not those of the monomaniac, but the ordinary mixture of selfishness, generosity, and pride in demonstrated ability. We may brag of our know-how and toss around phrases about the American Way, but this is half-hearted official talk. The citizen, even the leading citizen, has local pride but no crusading faith. We could not turn federalism into imperialism if we tried. Our many faults include outbursts of brag and bounce, but we may justly claim the merit that in a world plagued by the petty, deadly self-conceit of tribe and clan we have no fanaticism in our souls, any more than any doctrine up our sleeves. The continuing guarantee of all this is that we are not a nation but a people.

We are many—our interests, groups, religions keep one another in check and accustom us to many-sidedness, to pluralism. Compare the ways of unity and of pluralism through the personalities they bring forth: Mrs. Franklin Roosevelt with her modest, lifelong giving of herself to multitudinous good causes that wholly ignore creed and color, power and factional politics; and the late Mrs. Eva Peron of Argentina, who by herself controlled her country's billion-dollar fund for good works. This sum was obviously not the fruit of her earnings, but part of the annual taxes paid by the common people—two days' pay from everybody. Yet Mrs. Peron, being a devout Catholic, which was her right, would certainly not have wasted a penny on a devout atheist, nor on a political opponent of her husband's, nor on people outside her country's borders. The whole tradition of centralized control and dominant faith goes with discrimination, personal power, and fabricated glory. There is a move to make Mrs. Peron a saint, but my devotions go to Mrs. Roosevelt.

The American Way, if it means any one thing more than another, means diversity, many powers, no concerted plan, no interest in putting over on anybody else the final strait jacket of a system so as to extort the miserable advantage of lip-service to catchwords. Not that there aren't some few million people among the hundred and fifty of our population who would like to do just what I deny. They may even succeed in their little corner—their family, office, shop, or village. The impulse is age-old and will not die in our generation. But on our soil it has a harder time thriving than in most places.

It is to our incredible land that we must come back for an explanation of the virtures that we have but dare not take personal credit for. We are openhanded, because we have had abundance and have spread it wide enough to overcome the meanness of man when hard pressed. Our first impulse is to help, because the memory of give-and-take, of mutual log-rolling in building the continent, is with us still. To this day the outsider who settles in almost any Western city is surprised to see a Welcome Wagon drive up to his new house and shower him with local goods. It is publicity for the tradesmen, to be sure, but it is none the less a gift in the old tradition—good will created in two senses, and quite innocently, without strings attached.

We are innocent because we have been—we still are—too busy to brood. We have not sought escape from evil by mental constructions of the kind that is easier to ram down others' throats than to make real. Innocence and success together have made us calm, not phlegmatic. The great American cultural trait is casualness. "Take it easy." It has its drawbacks but it is also a source of pleasure, as when one travels ten thousand miles across America, through crowded places or off the beaten track, and never once runs into hostile, suspicious, or servile behavior.

Finally, we have no preconceived antagonisms toward foreigners as such, because we are all foreigners to the place and to one another. Only the Indians have a right to be isolationist. We on the contrary are disposed to take the rest of the world as our responsibility because we still feel the tug of innumerable crisscrossing attachments to other lands. The school child in the heart of Ohio cheerfully puts her penny in the box for Greek Relief; there is a little Greek of the second generation in her class, or a Greek restaurant in town.

We are the world in epitome and so far we have not renounced our beginnings. Here again the size and inner diversity of our regions have helped us by preventing patriotism. I mean of course the exclusive love of a narrow corner of the earth, the feeling that away from it lie unbearable strangeness and dangerous enemies. Americans love their land and are as likely as anybody else to feel particular delight in some favorite spot. But they are also a people on the move. The buses, trains, planes, and hotels are perennially overflowing; the roads cannot carry us without constant widening and extension. We move our business and families and take our vacations in a dozen different places, with no thought that to be in Arkansas is to be in exile or that The Capital is heaven. We are explorers still, and in this century's wars have shown an adaptability to the remotest soils and cultures which is one of the highest forms of intelligence. Our European and pro-European critics are pitiably at fault when they keep wailing that "man needs roots." That is just what man does not need. Man is not a tree. If the analogy were true we would not be hitting our top branches against the roof of a cave. This is not to deny the profound disturbance which has come with the means of changing our abodes, speeding through space, juxtaposing ways of life. That is another great subject to be dealt with in its proper place. But for the moment the fact remains that equilibrium in motion is possible for man—we're in it.

Europe believes that man also needs a nation and the egotistical satisfactions that go with it. Well, America could form—and in a mild sense does form—five nations; the East, the Middle West, the South, the West Coast, and the Northwest. There is Texas, too, about which none dare speak but Texans. In passing from one to the other of these vast empires, one notices refreshing differences of accent and manner, of legend and local concern. The East has its eyes glued on Europe, the Far West on "the islands," on Japan, and on Australia. The Gulf thinks of Latin America, and the Northwest of Canada and our Alaskan march. Food and language reflect the different orientations. Even the currency offers surprising variations—the silver dollar beyond the Mississippi, the use of mills (one tenth of a cent) in St. Louis, the "tin" penny which oddly survives in the East. And despite all our standardization, the trademarks of ice cream, beer, and canned goods never stay the same for two hundred miles in any direction. We can thus be fervent regionalists if we like, we can be fire-eating jingoes about Texas or California, or some other part of the continent, without developing the sectionalism that kills—kills the heart within, first, and kills the neighbor next. We had one taste of that in the Civil War and once is enough.

Clearly it is the continent that has saved us. While it fed us, it put enough air and space between man and man to prevent the exasperation of hateful contacts. Blood has flowed but the land has mercifully soaked it up. We have no frontiers repeatedly marked in red, no plains and towns that are but graveyards for each successive generation. Canada and Mexico being also vast and adequate to their populations' needs, no pressure, no state of perpetual watchfulness has been the lot of Americans for a century past.

One's only sorrow is that in saying this one seems to be boasting about the gifts of Providence, and indirectly blaming Europe for being less favored. It is, alas, not boast or blame but self-justification. Europe and her many friends among us are the ones who boast of Europe's moral and cultural superiority, who make it a reproach that we do not come up to their standards and do not see the universe as they do. The relation is undoubtedly bitter for both. America is Europe's child, her Cinderella made to bloom by a kindly magic. The child's feelings—it is amply proved—are full of respect and admiration for the twice unjust parent. Still incredibly innocent, Cinderella is ever-ready to conciliate the anger that it can hardly understand: can it be true that in attempting to keep open house for all mankind, we have lost our birthright, squandered our intellectual heritage, so that Americanization is tantamount to barbarization?

Or is it possible that modern civilization is something new, incommensurable with the old, just like the character of the American adventure itself? One may want to give a just answer and yet feel that, whatever the answer, the time has come when America must no longer take scoldings with humility. And since it would be futile to transplant the European mind so as to make it see what is out there, beyond the Pullman window at 2 A.M., the American mind that is conscious of the blessings and the dangers at stake must try to redress the balance.

19. America the Beautiful

MARY MCCARTHY

Mary McCarthy (1912–   ) was born in Seattle, Washington. She first attracted attention with her drama criticism in the magazine *Partisan Review,* but is chiefly known for her cutting satirical novels and short stories of intellectual life, in which she spares neither her friends nor herself. Her autobiographical book *Memories of a Catholic Girlhood* (1957) seemed to show considerable mellowing and tenderness compared with her earlier works. But in *The Group* (1966), a best-selling novel later made into a movie, she returned to her earlier themes and tone, though somehow with diminished force and effectiveness. In the essay reprinted here, she writes of America not so much as a place she has experienced directly but as one *re*-seen back through the conventional criticism of expatriates and distinguished foreign visitors.

A visiting existentialist wanted recently to be taken to dinner at a really American place. This proposal, natural enough in a tourist, disclosed a situation thoroughly unnatural. Unless the visiting lady's object was suffering, there was no way of satisfying her demand. Sukiyaki joints, chop suey joints, Italian table d'hôte places, French provincial restaurants with the menu written on a slate, Irish chophouses, and Jewish delicatessens came abundantly to mind, but these were not what the lady wanted. Schrafft's or the Automat would have answered, yet to take her there would have been to turn oneself into a tourist and to present America as a spectacle, a New Yorker cartoon or a savage drawing in the New Masses. It was the beginning of an evening of humiliations. The visitor was lively and eager; her mind lay open and orderly, like a notebook ready for impressions. It was not long, however, before she shut it up with a snap. We had no recommendations to make to her. With movies, plays, current books, it was the same story as with the restaurants—*Open City, Les Enfants du Paradis,* Oscar Wilde, a reprint of Henry James were paté maison to this lady who wanted the definite flapjack. She did not believe us when we said that there were no good Hollywood movies, no good Broadway plays—only curios, she was merely confirmed in her impression that American intellectuals were "negative."

Yet the irritating thing was that we did not feel negative. We admired and liked our country; we preferred it to that imaginary America, land of the peaux rouges of Caldwell and Steinbeck, dumb paradise of violence and the detective story, which had excited the sensibilities of our visitor and of the up-to-date French literary world. But to found our preference, to locate it materially in some admirable object or institution, such as Chartres, say, or French café life, was for us, that night at any rate, an impossible undertaking. We heard ourselves saying that the real America was elsewhere, in the white frame houses and church spires of New England; yet we knew that we talked foolishly—we were not Granville Hicks and we looked ludicrous in his opinions. The Elevated, half a block away, interrupting us every time a train passed, gave us the lie on schedule, every eight minutes. But if the elm-shaded village green was a false or at least an insufficient address for the genius loci we honored, where then was it to be found? Surveyed from the vantage point of Europe, this large continent seemed suddenly deficient in objects of virtue. The Grand Canyon, Yellowstone Park, Jim Hill's mansion in St. Paul, Monticello, the blast furnaces of Pittsburgh, Mount Rainier, the yellow observatory at Amherst, the little-theatre movement in Cleveland, Ohio, a Greek revival house glimpsed from a car window in a lost river-town in New Jersey —these things were too small for the size of the country. Each of them, when pointed to, diminished in interest with the lady's perspective of distance. There was no sight that in itself seemed to justify her crossing of the Atlantic.

If she was interested in "conditions," that was a different matter. There are conditions everywhere; it takes no special genius to produce them. Yet would it be an act of hospitality to invite a visitor to a lynching? Unfortunately, nearly all the "sights" in America fall under the head of conditions. Hollywood, Reno, the share-croppers' homes in the South, the mining towns of Pennsylvania, Coney Island, the Chicago stockyards, Macy's, the Dodgers, Harlem, even Congress, the forum of our liberties, are spectacles rather than sights, to use the term in the colloquial sense of "Didn't he make a holy spectacle of himself?" An Englishman of almost any political opinion can show a visitor through the Houses of Parliament with a sense of pride or at least of indulgence toward his national foibles and traditions. The American, if he has a spark of national feeling, will be humiliated by the very prospect of a foreigner's visit to Congress—these, for the most part, illiterate hacks whose fancy vests are spotted with gravy, and whose speeches, hypocritical, unctuous and slovenly, are spotted also with the gravy of political patronage, these persons are a reflection on the democratic process rather than of it; they expose it in its underwear. In European legislation, we are told, a great deal of shady business goes on in private, behind the scenes. In America, it is just the opposite, anything good, presumably, is accomplished in camera, in the committee rooms.

It is so with all our institutions. For the visiting Europeans, a trip through the United States has, almost inevitably, the character of an exposé, and the American, on his side, is tempted by love of his country to lock the inquiring tourist in his hotel room and throw away the key. His contention that the visible and material America is not the real or the only one is more difficult to sustain than was the presumption of the "other" Germany behind the Nazi steel.

To some extent a citizen of any country will feel that the tourist's view of his homeland is a false one. The French will tell you that you have to go into their homes to see what the French people are really like. The intellectuals in the Left Bank cafés are not the real French intellectuals, etc., etc. In Italy, they complain that the tourist must not judge by the ristorantes; there one sees only black-market types. But in neither of these cases is the native really disturbed by the tourist's view of his country. If Versailles or Giotto's bell-tower in Florence do not tell the whole story, they are still not incongruous with it; you do not hear a Frenchman or an Italian object when these things are noticed by a visitor. With the American, the contradiction is more serious. He must, if he is to defend his country, repudiate its visible aspect almost entirely. He must say that its parade of phenomenology, its billboards, super-highways, even its skyscrapers, not only fail to represent the inner essence of his country but in fact contravene it. He may point, if he wishes, to certain beautiful objects, but here too he is in difficulties, for nearly everything that is beautiful and has not been produced by nature belongs to the 18th century, to a past with which he has very little connection, and which his ancestors, in many or most cases, had no part in building. Beacon Street and the Boston Common are very charming in the 18th-century manner, so are the sea captains' houses in the Massachusetts ports, and the ruined plantations of Louisiana, but an American from Brooklyn or the Middle West or the Pacific Coast finds the style of life embodied in them as foreign as Europe; indeed, the first sensation of a Westerner, coming upon Beacon Hill and the gold dome of the State House, is to feel that at last he has traveled "abroad." The American, if he is to speak the highest truth about his country, must refrain from pointing at all. The virtue of American civilization is that it is unmaterialistic.

This statement may strike a critic as whimsical or perverse. Everybody knows, it will be said, that America has the most materialistic civilization in the world, that Americans care only about money, they have no time or talent for living; look at radio, look at advertising, look at life insurance, look at the tired business man, at the Frigidaires and the Fords. In answer, the reader is invited first to look into his own heart and inquire whether he personally feels himself to be represented by these things, or whether he does not, on the contrary, feel them to be irrelevant to him, a necessary evil, part of the conditions of life. Other people, he will assume, care about them very much: the man down the street, the entire population of Detroit or Scarsdale, the back-country farmer, the urban poor or the rich. But he accepts these objects as imposed on him by a collective "otherness" of desire, an otherness he has not met directly but whose existence he infers from the number of automobiles, Frigidaires, or television sets he sees around him. Stepping into his new Buick convertible, he knows that he would gladly do without it, but imagines that to his neighbor, who is just backing his out of the driveway, this car is the motor of life. More often, however, the otherness is projected farther afield, onto a different class or social group, remote and alien. Thus the rich, who would like nothing better, they think, than for life to be a perpetual fishing trip with the trout grilled by a native guide, look patronizingly upon the whole apparatus of American civilization as a cheap Christmas present to the poor, and city people see the radio and the washing-machine as the farm-wife's solace.

It can be argued, of course, that the subjective view is prevaricating, possession of the Buick being nine-tenths of the social law. But who has ever met, outside of advertisements, a true parishioner of this church of Mammon? A man may take pride in a car, and a housewife in her new sink or wallpaper, but pleasure in new acquisitions is universal and eternal—an Italian man with a new gold tooth, a French bibliophile with a new edition, a woman with a new baby, a philosopher with a new thought, all these people are rejoicing in progress, in man's power to enlarge and improve. Before men showed off new cars, they showed off new horses; it is alleged against modern man that he did not make the car but his grandfather did not make the horse either. What is imputed to Americans is something quite different, an abject dependence on material possessions, an image of happiness as packaged by a manufacturer, content in a can. This view of American life is strongly urged by advertising agencies. We know the "other," of course, because we meet them every week in full force in the New Yorker or the Saturday Evening Post, those brightly colored families of dedicated consumers, waiting in unison on the porch for the dealer to deliver the new car, gobbling the new cereal ("Gee, Mom, is it good for you too?"), lining up to bank their pay-check, or fearfully anticipating the industrial accident and the insurance-check that will "compensate" for it. We meet them also, more troll-like underground, in the subway placards, in the ferociously complacent One-A-Day family, and we hear their courtiers sing to them on the radio of Ivory or Supersuds. The thing, however, that repels us in these advertisements is their naive falsity to life. Who are these advertising men kidding, besides the European tourist? Between the tired, sad, gentle faces of the strangers around us and these grinning Holy Families, there exists no possibility of even a wishful identification. We take a vitamin pill with the hope of feeling (possibly) a little less tired, but the superstition of buoyant health emblazoned in the bright, ugly pictures has no more power to move us than the blood of St. Januarius.

Familiarity has perhaps bred contempt in us Americans: until you have had a washing machine, you cannot imagine how little difference it will make to you. Europeans still believe that money brings happiness, witness the bought journalist, the bought politician, the bought general, the whole venality of European literary life, inconceivable in this country of the dollar. It is true that America produces and consumes more cars, soap, and bathtubs than any other nation, but we live among these objects rather than by them. Americans build skyscrapers; Le Corbusier worships them. Ehrenburg, our Soviet critic, fell in

love with the Check-O-Mat in American railway stations, writing
home paragraphs of song to this gadget—while deploring American
materialism. When an American heiress wants to buy a man, she at
once crosses the Atlantic. The only really materialistic people I have
ever met have been Europeans.

The strongest argument for the un-materialistic character of American life is the fact that we tolerate conditions that are, from a materialistic point of view, intolerable. What the foreigner finds most objec-
tionable in American life is its lack of basic comfort. No nation with
any sense of material well-being would endure the food we eat, the
cramped apartments we live in, the noise, the traffic, the crowded sub-
ways and buses. American life, in large cities, at any rate, is a perpetual assault on the senses and the nerves; it is out of asceticism, out of
unworldliness, precisely, that we bear it.

This republic was founded on an unworldly assumption, a denial of
"the facts of life." It is manifestly untrue that all men are created
equal; interpreted in worldly terms, this doctrine has resulted in a
pseudo-equality, that is, in standardization, in an equality of things
rather than of persons. The inalienable rights to life, liberty, and the
pursuit of happiness appear, in practice, to have become the inalienable right to a bathtub, a flush toilet, and a can of Spam. Left-wing
critics of America attribute this result to the intrusion of capitalism;
right-wing critics see it as the logical dead end of democracy. Capitalism has certainly played its part, mass production in itself demanding
large-scale distribution of uniform goods, till the consumer today is
the victim of the manufacturer who launches on him a regiment of
products for which he must make house-room in his soul. The buying
impulse, in its original force and purity, was not nearly so crass, however, or so meanly acquisitive as many radical critics suppose. The
purchase of a bathtub was the exercise of a spiritual right. The immigrant or the poor native American bought a bathtub, not because he
wanted to take a bath, but because he wanted to be in a position to do
so. This remains true in many fields today; possessions, when they are
desired, are not wanted for their own sakes but as tokens of an ideal
state of freedom, fraternity, and franchise. "Keeping up with the
Joneses" is a vulgarization of Jefferson's concept, but it too is a declaration of the rights of man, and decidedly unfeasible and visionary.
Where for a European, a fact is a fact, for us Americans, the real, if it
is relevant at all, is simply symbolic appearance. We are a nation of

twenty million bathrooms, with a humanist in every tub. One such humanist I used to hear of on Cape Cod had, on growing rich, installed two toilets side by side in his marble bathroom, on the model of the two-seater of his youth. He was a clear case of Americanism, hospitable, gregarious, and impractical, a theorist of perfection. Was his dream of the conquest of poverty a vulgar dream or a noble one, a material demand or a spiritual insistence? It is hard to think of him as a happy man, and in this too he is characteristically American, for the parity of the radio, the movies, and the washing machine has made Americans sad, reminding them of another parity of which these things were to be but emblems.

The American does not enjoy his possessions because sensory enjoyment was not his object, and he lives sparely and thinly among them, in the monastic discipline of Scarsdale or the barracks of Stuyvesant Town. Only among certain groups where franchise, socially speaking, has not been achieved, do pleasure and material splendor constitute a life-object and an occupation. Among the outcasts—Jews, Negroes, Catholics, and homosexuals—excluded from the communion of ascetics, the love of fabrics, gaudy show, and rich possessions still anachronistically flaunts itself. Once a norm has been reached, differing in the different classes, financial ambition itself seems to fade away. The self-made man finds, to his anger, his son uninterested in money; you have shirtsleeves to shirtsleeves in three generations. The great financial empires are a thing of the past. Recent immigrants—movie magnates and gangsters particularly—retain their acquisitiveness, but how long is it since anyone in the general public has murmured, wonderingly, "as rich as Rockefeller"?

If the dream of American fraternity had ended simply in this, the value of humanistic and egalitarian strivings would be seriously called into question. Jefferson, the Adamses, Franklin, Madison, would be in the position of Dostoevsky's Grand Inquisitor, who, desiring to make the Kingdom of God incarnate on earth, inaugurated the kingdom of the devil. If the nature of matter is such that the earthly paradise, once realized, becomes always the paradise of the earthly, and a spiritual conquest of matter becomes always an enslavement of spirit (conquered Gaul conquered Rome), then the atomic bomb is, as has been argued, the logical result of the Enlightenment, and the land of opportunity is, precisely, the land of death. This position, however, is a strictly materialist one, for it asserts the Fact of the bomb as the one

tremendous truth: subjective attitudes are irrelevant; it does not matter what we think or feel; possession again in this case is nine-tenths of
the law.

It must be admitted that there is a great similarity between the nation with its new bomb and the consumer with his new Buick. In both
cases, there is a disinclination to use the produce, stronger naturally in
the case of the bomb, but somebody has manufactured the thing, and
there seems to be no way not to use it, especially when everybody else
will be doing so. Here again the argument of the "others" is invoked to
justify our own procedures—if we had not invented the bomb, the
Germans would have; the Soviet Union will have it in a year, etc., etc.
This is keeping up with the Joneses indeed, our national propagandists
playing the role of the advertising men in persuading us of the "others'" intentions.

It seems likely at this moment that we will find no way of not using
the bomb, yet those who argue theoretically that this machine is the
true expression of our society leave us, in practice, with no means of
opposing it. We must differentiate ourselves from the bomb if we are
to avoid using it, and in private thought we do, distinguishing the
bomb sharply from our daily concerns and sentiments, feeling it as an
otherness that waits outside to descend on us, an otherness already destructive of normal life, since it prevents us from planning or hoping
by depriving us of a future. And this inner refusal of the bomb is also a
legacy of our past; it is a denial of the given, of the power of circumstances to shape us in their mold. Unfortunately, the whole asceticism
of our national character, our habit of living in but not through an environment, our alienation from objects, prepare us to endure the bomb
but not to confront it.

Passivity and not aggressiveness is the dominant trait of the American character. The movies, the radio, the super-highway have softened
us up for the atom bomb; we have lived with them without pleasure,
feeling them as a coercion on our natures, a coercion coming seemingly from nowhere and expressing nobody's will. The new coercion
finds us without the habit of protest; we are dissident but apart.

The very "negativeness," then, of American intellectuals is not a
mark of their separation from our society, but a true expression of its
separation from itself. We too are dissident but inactive. Intransigent
on paper, in "real life" we conform; yet we do not feel ourselves to be
dishonest, for to us the real life is rustling paper and the mental life is

flesh. And even in our mental life we are critical and rather unproductive; we leave it to the "others," the best-sellers, to create.

The fluctuating character of American life must, in part, have been responsible for this dissociated condition. Many an immigrant arrived in this country with the most materialistic expectations, hoping, not to escape from a world in which a man was the sum of his circumstances, but to become a new sum of circumstances himself. But this hope was self-defeating; the very ease with which new circumstances were acquired left insufficient time for a man to live into them: all along a great avenue in Minneapolis the huge chateaux were dark at night, save for a single light in each kitchen, where the family still sat, Swedish-style, about the stove. The pressure of democratic thought, moreover, forced a rising man often, unexpectedly, to recognize that he was not his position: a speeding ticket from a village constable could lay him low. Like the agitated United Nations delegates who got summonses on the Merritt Parkway, he might find the shock traumatic: a belief had been destroyed. The effect of these combined difficulties turned the new American into a nomad, who camped out in his circumstances, as it were, and was never assimilated to them. And, for the native American, the great waves of internal migration had the same result. The homelessness of the American, migrant in geography and on the map of finance, is the whole subject of the American realists of our period. European readers see in these writers only violence and brutality. They miss not only the pathos but the nomadic virtues associated with it, generosity, hospitality, equity, directness, politeness, simplicity of relations—traits which, together with a certain gentle timidity (as of unpracticed nomads), comprise the American character. Unobserved also is a peculiar nakedness, a look of being shorn of everything, that is very curiously American, corresponding to the spare wooden desolation of a frontier town and the bright thinness of the American light. The American character looks always as if it had just had a rather bad hair-cut, which gives it, in our eyes at any rate, a greater humanity than the European, which even among its beggars has an all too professional air.

The openness of the American situation creates the pity and the terror; status is no protection; life for the European is a career; for the American, it is a hazard. Slaves and women, said Aristotle, are not fit subjects for tragedy, but kings, rather, and noble men, men, that is, not defined by circumstances but outside them and seemingly impervious.

In America we have, subjectively speaking, no slaves and no women; the efforts of PM and the Stalinized playwrights to introduce, like the first step to servitude, a national psychology of the "little man" have been, so far, unrewarding. The little man is one who is embedded in status; things can be done for and to him generically by a central directive; his happiness flows from statistics. This conception mistakes the national passivity for abjection. Americans will not eat this humble pie; we are still nature's noblemen. Yet no tragedy results, though the protagonist is everywhere; dissociation takes the place of conflict, and the drama is mute.

This humanity, this plain and heroic accessibility, was what we would have liked to point out to the visiting Existentialist as our national glory. Modesty perhaps forbade and a lack of concrete examples —how could we point to ourselves? Had we done so, she would not have been interested. To a European, the humanity of an intellectual is of no particular moment; it is the barber pole that announces his profession and the hair oil dispensed inside. Europeans, moreover, have no curiosity about American intellectuals; we are insufficiently representative of the brute. Yet this anticipated and felt disparagement was not the whole cause of our reticence. We were silent for another reason: we were waiting to be discovered. Columbus, however, passed on, and this, very likely, was the true source of our humiliation. But this experience also was peculiarly American. We all expect to be found in the murk of otherness; it looks to us very easy since we know we are there. Time after time, the explorers have failed to see us. We have been patient, for the happy ending is our national belief. Now, however, that the future has been shut off from us, it is necessary for us to declare ourselves, at least for the record.

What it amounts to, in verity, is that we are the poor. This humanity we would claim for ourselves is the legacy, not only of the Enlightenment, but of the thousands and thousands of European peasants and poor townspeople who came here bringing their humanity and their sufferings with them. It is the absence of a stable upper class that is responsible for much of the vulgarity of the American scene. Should we blush before the visitor for this deficiency? The ugliness of American decoration, American entertainment, American literature—is not this the visible expression of the impoverishment of the European masses, a manifestation of all the backwardness, deprivation, and want that arrived here in boatloads from Europe? The immense popu-

larity of American movies abroad demonstrates that Europe is the unfinished negative of which America is the proof. The European
traveler, viewing with distaste a movie palace or a motorola, is only
looking into the terrible concavity of his continent of hunger inverted
startlingly into the convex. Our civilization, deformed as it is outwardly, is still an accomplishment; all this had to come to light.

America is indeed a revelation, though not quite the one that was
planned. Given a clean slate, man, it was hoped, would write the future. Instead, he has written his past. This past, inscribed on billboards, ball parks, dance halls, is not seemly, yet its objectification is a
kind of disburdenment. The past is at length outside. It does not disturb us as it does Europeans for our relation with it is both more distant and more familiar. We cannot hate it, for to hate it would be to
hate poverty, our eager ancestors, and ourselves.

If there were time, American civilization could be seen as a beginning, even a favorable one, for we have only to look around us to see
what a lot of sensibility a little ease will accrue. The children surpass
the fathers and Louis B. Mayer cannot be preserved intact in his
descendants. . . . Unfortunately, as things seem now, posterity is not
around the corner.

Part Three

The Discovery of Popular Culture

The essayist cannot consider for very long the relationship between the self and the society which forms it without coming to terms with *the ways in which most men become aware of that relationship.* It is not very often through the essay itself that ordinary people reach consciousness of themselves and their world; the essay is too sophisticated and abstract, too much a part of "high art" or "serious" literature.

The simplest way of achieving such self-consciousness (and this is the foundation of what we call "popular culture") is by *acting out.* Many of the activities in which we commonly engage, when we are not doing what we have to do to keep ourselves alive, are such an acting out: ritual or games or play, to use the conventional names. The child who "plays house," the adolescent who plays cards or baseball, city-dwellers on the beach or exurbanites at their parlor games—these are not merely amusing themselves: "exercising" or "relaxing" as we learn to say. They are demonstrating in action the values by which they live: fair play, competitiveness, quick thinking—sometimes, alas, malice or violence or the principle that what the referee doesn't see is o.k. for our side!

Many of our athletic rituals celebrate the beauty of violence, and this disturbs the good-hearted, high-minded observer; but violence is a fact of our lives and a shaping force in our dreams. Though bearbaiting has disappeared and cockfighting has been banned; though the bullfight never existed for most Americans, and the duel was always the sport of the chosen few, we manage to do quite well with the wrestling match, the prizefight, Sunday afternoon at the football stadium. Marquis of Queensberry Rules and shoulder pads make no difference, any more than the talk of sportsmanship or the fact of commercialization; the real point is the violence, the vicarious violence for all but the handful of actual players.

To be sure, styles in sports change; wrestling has almost disappeared from view, while boxing is in a decline, and baseball (never quite violent enough to begin with, except in the relationship of the audience to umpire) loses ground fast these days. This is, I suppose, pre-eminently the age of professional football, which looks good on color TV; and the words of Vince Lombardi to his Green Bay Packers are known to all readers of the sports pages, "You got to learn to live with pain."

Comparatively fewer and fewer members of the football audience, however, manage to make it to the stadium at all. Many hear the game instead over the car radio as they drive between town and town toward business or pleasure; while most, inert in the familiar darkness of their living rooms, follow it on television, as they sip the brand of beer urged on them during the time-outs. Sports become, slowly and relentlessly, no more or less real than other ritual occasions of violence, from the shoot out in a Western to the war in Vietnam: one more adjunct of radio, movies and TV—which in turn have become adjuncts of advertising, liveliest of the pop arts.

There are not just "three arts that beat as one," as some wag would have it, but four in fact—four beloved inventions of our age of gadgets and tinkering. It is well to remember that radio and movies and television, unlike advertising itself, were gadgets before they were fullfledged "popular arts," "media" before they were given a socially useful "message" by the sponsors and advertising agencies. They are for our harried age the equivalent of libraries and museums in a more leisurely and aristocratic one, the chief devices for the diffusion not really of another kind of culture (the name "mass culture" is in this respect misleading) but of commodities vestigially related to culture. The generalizing essays by Dwight Macdonald and Milton Klonsky concern themselves, with varying degrees of irony, with just these problems, and with the nature of the "Great Audience" for whom pop art exists.

It is this audience (especially that of TV, which grows at the expense of the others) which most worries some moralistic commentators, troubled because it is inert, because it reads pictures rather than words, because those pictures are aimed at the least mature among them, or in any case at what is least mature in all of them. Others, however, like Richard Hoggart and Marshall MacLuhan, waste no time deploring anything; but ask rather whether this new device has been transformed into a new form of expression, or if it remains only a means of transmitting pre-existing forms of popular culture like sports, Academy Award dinners, Miss America contests, presidential nominating conventions (including cops clubbing kids), and assassinations of public figures.

The movies and television considered in this light can be understood (never mind MacLuhan's famous mystification about "the medium is the message") as less direct ways of *acting out* on an even remoter level of vicariousness, that is, as "myth" rather than "ritual," our half-conscious need to know ourselves. If the essay by Warshow is one of the few written in the fifties which has meaning for us still, it is because he understands that to talk about the meaning, the social function of movies, requires talking about "myth," in his case talking about the meaning of the cowboy and the world in which we imagine him. Why after all *do* we sit contemplating that stereotypical figure in his stereotypical situations? Why do we *need* him? And why has he proved even more powerful than the commodities to whose ads he serves as a prelude? Why has he invaded the commercials themselves, making Marlboro Country his own?

With jazz, blues, rock, folk music, the world of pure sound that the radio has made its own (its only rival the jukebox), now that narrative in words has been surrendered to TV, the problem is somewhat more difficult. We are not accustomed to thinking of what pop music says; or realizing how, even without its lyrics—which have recently ceased to be banal without becoming primary—it also speaks, also creates a "myth." Leroi Jones, however, manages to give some sense of this order of meaning in jazz, especially as it reflects the aspirations of black Americans, and the conflict of black and white in the country they share.

And finally, when we approach those popular arts which still employ the printing press, the most ancient and by now honored of mass-production devices, we are likely to have difficulties of quite another sort. Though picture magazines, pulps, comic strips, comic books, detective novels and science fiction compete on the market with the kinds of magazines and books aimed at inclusion in libraries, even sometimes look like them, they are not to be confused with what used to be called "literature" or "belles-lettres." It is less confusing to think of them as primitive or reactionary forms of the kind whose highest development is film and television. Works of "literature" depend for their success primarily on form (organization, selection, subtlety of pattern, precision of diction and detail); popular art, on the other hand, lives chiefly by its *mythic* appeal, its ability to hit upon the pattern story and image which can transmit to everyone, simple or sophisticated, what they need to know, without making them aware that they are learning anything or, God forbid, improving themselves or enriching their lives.

Such sub-art should no more be condescended to in the name of criticism than should a dream. Like the latter, however, it can be profitably analyzed by those with a taste for analysis. And, indeed, to indulge a taste for it as a minor vice, unexamined and undefended, is another form of condescension. It is, however, quite possible to take pop art seriously, and end by hating it, even censoring or banning it; for it is only too easy to make a moral case against mass art, which panders to self-indulgence and a lust for violence and/or sex. But in the end, such condemnations seem irrelevant and unilluminating; once more, quite comparable to disapproving of a disturbing dream rather than attempting to discover what it means.

More to the point are such approaches as Auden's, discovering quite Christian significances in the detective story; or Jules Feiffer's, finding the real meaning of comic books by recalling what they had meant to his childhood; or Kingsley Amis's, discussing the social criticism implicit in science fiction, a subject on which scarcely anything of value had been written before his *New Maps of Hell*. The point is that Auden loves detective stories, Feiffer comic books, and Amis science fiction; and that without such affection, understanding is impossible —as Taylor Stoehr points out in his criticism of Stephen Marcus on pornography, which is also a form of pop fiction, though one difficult to talk about before the recent easing of censorship.

The reader is perhaps already aware that essays on mass culture do not always attain literary distinction. There is something about the subject itself which seems to debase attempts to encompass it. Certainly it is hard to describe in literary terms so non-literary a way of apprehending and presenting reality (or, if you please, fantasy); and the essayist fluctuates between sinking to the level of what he describes and being over-consciously "literary," or downright "cute."

The social scientist feels more at home in the field than the imaginative writer, for he has no special sense of style to embarrass him; and, after all, he is dealing with groups of people whose views he can represent statistically or turn to solemn platitudes in his most "scientific" jargon. It is precisely in the area of mass culture that one can watch the current struggle between the humane essayist trying to hang on to his traditional prerogative of describing men's behavior to themselves, and the scientific investigator asserting his claim to speak with greater accuracy and more authority—though to be sure with less grace.

There is, moreover, an almost irresistible temptation to moralize about the problems of the popular arts; too much seems at stake to pause over words or to polish sentences. The reader will notice how often the average commentator when he is not counting noses is blowing his top: violently objecting to violence or, for five cents a word, objecting to commercialism.

The novelists and poets (Agee and Auden, for instance) among our writers do considerably better on this score than the journalists and social scientists; they feel at least an obligation to write well of what is so ill composed. More interesting, though, are the somewhat younger writers represented (like Marcus, Amis, and especially Stoehr) who have grown up in a world finally committed to mass culture, with a comic book in hand and an ear full of recorded jazz. They come to maturity at a time when almost the first interest of the intellectual is in the popular arts, against which, indeed, he has to fight for life; when the would-be critic necessarily serves an apprenticeship in analyzing the movies or TV. Since the essay first came into its own, and Addison, for instance, felt the need to comment on the make-up and reading habits of young ladies, "popular culture" has been a standard subject of the genre; but this is the first generation of essayists as much at home with low culture as with high.

Out of their ranks came the moving spirits behind the two full-scale anthologies on popular culture which appeared in the mid-fifties (*The Scene Before You* [1955] and *Mass Culture: The Popular Arts in America* [1957]), both of which have provided several essays for this collection, and one of which was selected for mass distribution by a large book club. We have lived to see the criticism of mass culture in

the process of becoming itself mass culture! The work of these people,
though interesting, seems still indecisive, as if they remain unsure of
their real relationship to what they describe. But at least they began to
lay the groundwork for an approach to the popular arts which writers
like Amis and Jones and Feiffer have carried farther: an *essayistic* approach at once informed and lively, concerned with myth rather than
morality but pledged not to scientific analysis but to style.

20. A Theory of Mass Culture

DWIGHT MACDONALD

Dwight Macdonald (1906–   ) has recently written chiefly for journals like *Esquire* and *The New Yorker,* but edited between 1944 and
1949 an independent radical magazine called *Politics,* in which an
original version of this essay first appeared. Though his attention has
turned temporarily to other subjects, ranging from Henry Wallace to
the Ford Foundation, he has continued to be concerned with "popular culture" or "mass culture" as he himself has successively called it.

For about a century, Western culture has really been two cultures: the
traditional kind—let us call it "High Culture"—that is chronicled
in the textbooks, and a "Mass Culture" manufactured wholesale for
the market. In the old art forms, the artisans of Mass Culture have
long been at work: in the novel, the line stretches from Eugène Sue to
Lloyd C. Douglas; in music, from Offenbach to Tin-Pan Alley; in art
from the chromo to Maxfield Parrish and Norman Rockwell; in architecture, from Victorian Gothic to suburban Tudor. Mass Culture has
also developed new media of its own, into which the serious artist
rarely ventures: radio, the movies, comic books, detective stories, science fiction, television.

It is sometimes called "Popular Culture," but I think "Mass Cul-

SOURCE: Dwight Macdonald, "A Theory of Mass Culture," *Diogenes* (Summer,
1953), 1–17. Reprinted by permission of the author.

ture" a more accurate term, since its distinctive mark is that it is solely and directly an article for mass consumption, like chewing gum. A work of High Culture is occasionally popular, after all, though this is increasingly rare. Thus Dickens was even more popular than his contemporary, G. A. Henty, the difference being that he was an artist, communicating his individual vision to other individuals, while Henty was an impersonal manufacturer of an impersonal commodity for the masses.

The Nature of Mass Culture

The historical reasons for the growth of Mass Culture since the early 1800's are well known. Political democracy and popular education broke down the old upper-class monopoly of culture. Business enterprise found a profitable market in the cultural demands of the newly awakened masses, and the advance of technology made possible the cheap production of books, periodicals, pictures, music, and furniture, in sufficient quantities to satisfy this market. Modern technology also created new media such as the movies and television which are specially well adapted to mass manufacture and distribution.

The phenomenon is thus peculiar to modern times and differs radically from what was hitherto known as art or culture. It is true that Mass Culture began as, and to some extent still is, a parasitic, a cancerous growth on High Culture. As Clement Greenberg pointed out in "Avant-Garde and *Kitsch*" (*Partisan Review,* Fall, 1939): "The precondition of *kitsch* (a German term for 'Mass Culture') is the availability close at hand of a fully matured cultural tradition, whose discoveries, acquisitions, and perfected self-consciousness *kitsch* can take advantage of for its own ends." The connection, however, is not that of the leaf and the branch but rather that of the caterpillar and the leaf. *Kitsch* "mines" High Culture the way improvident frontiersmen mine the soil, extracting its riches and putting nothing back. Also, as *kitsch* develops, it begins to draw on its own past, and some of it evolves so far away from High Culture as to appear quite disconnected from it.

It is also true that Mass Culture is to some extent a continuation of the old Folk Art which until the Industrial Revolution was the culture of the common people, but here, too, the differences are more striking than the similarities. Folk Art grew from below. It was a spontaneous, autochthonous expression of the people, shaped by themselves, pretty

much without the benefit of High Culture, to suit their own needs.
Mass Culture is imposed from above. It is fabricated by technicians
hired by business; its audiences are passive consumers, their participation limited to the choice between buying and not buying. The Lords
of *kitsch,* in short, exploit the cultural needs of the masses in order to
make a profit and/or to maintain their class rule—in Communist
countries, only the second purpose obtains. (It is very different to *satisfy* popular tastes, as Robert Burns' poetry did, and to exploit them,
as Hollywood does.) Folk Art was the people's own institution, their
private little garden walled off from the great formal park of their
masters' High Culture. But Mass Culture breaks down the wall, inte-
grating the masses into a debased form of High Culture and thus becoming an instrument of political domination. If one had no other data
to go on, the nature of Mass Culture would reveal capitalism to be an
exploitive class society and not the harmonious commonwealth it is
sometimes alleged to be. The same goes even more strongly for Soviet
Communism and *its* special kind of Mass Culture.

Mass Culture: U.S.S.R.

"Everybody" knows that America is a land of Mass Culture, but it is
not so generally recognized that so is the Soviet Union. Certainly not
by the Communist leaders, one of whom has contemptuously observed
that the American people need not fear the peace-loving Soviet state
which has absolutely no desire to deprive them of their Coca-Cola and
comic books. Yet the fact is that the U.S.S.R. is even more a land of
Mass Culture than is the U.S.A. This is less easily recognizable because their Mass Culture is *in form* just the opposite of ours, being one
of propaganda and pedagogy rather than of entertainment. None the
less, it has the essential quality of Mass, as against High or Folk, Culture: it is manufactured for mass consumption by technicians employed by the ruling class and is not an expression of either the individual artist or the common people themselves. Like our own, it ex-
ploits rather than satisfies the cultural needs of the masses, though for
political rather than commercial reasons. Its quality is even lower: our
Supreme Court building is tasteless and pompous, but not to the lunatic degree of the proposed new Palace of the Soviets—a huge wedding cake of columns mounting up to an eighty-foot statue of Lenin;
Soviet movies are so much duller and cruder than our own that even

the American comrades shun them; the childish level of *serious* Soviet magazines devoted to matters of art or philosophy has to be read to be believed, and as for the popular press, it is as if Colonel McCormick ran every periodical in America.

Gresham's Law in Culture

The separation of Folk Art and High Culture in fairly watertight compartments corresponded to the sharp line once drawn between the common people and the aristocracy. The eruption of the masses onto the political stage has broken down this compartmentation, with disastrous cultural results. Whereas Folk Art had its own special quality, Mass Culture is at best a vulgarized reflection of High Culture. And whereas High Culture could formerly ignore the mob and seek to please only the *cognoscenti,* it must now compete with Mass Culture or be merged into it.

The problem is acute in the United States and not just because a prolific Mass Culture exists here. If there were a clearly defined cultural *élite,* then the masses could have their *kitsch* and the *élite* could have its High Culture, with everybody happy. But the boundary line is blurred. A statistically significant part of the population, I venture to guess, is chronically confronted with a choice between going to the movies or to a concert, between reading Tolstoy or a detective story, between looking at old masters or at a TV show; i.e., the pattern of their cultural lives is "open" to the point of being porous. Good art competes with *kitsch,* serious ideas compete with commercialized formulae—and the advantage lies all on one side. There seems to be a Gresham's Law in cultural as well as monetary circulation: bad stuff drives out the good, since it is more easily understood and enjoyed. It is this facility of access which at once sells *kitsch* on a wide market and also prevents it from achieving quality. Clement Greenberg writes that the special aesthetic quality of *kitsch* is that it "predigests art for the spectator and spares him effort, provides him with a shortcut to the pleasures of art that detours what is necessarily difficult in genuine art" because it includes the spectator's reactions in the work of art itself instead of forcing him to make his own responses. Thus "Eddie Guest and the Indian Love Lyrics are more 'poetic' than T. S. Eliot and Shakespeare." And so, too, our "collegiate Gothic" such as the Harkness Quadrangle at Yale is more picturesquely Gothic than

Chartres, and a pinup girl smoothly airbrushed by Petty is more sexy than a real naked woman.

When to this ease of consumption is added *kitsch's* ease of production because of its standardized nature, its prolific growth is easy to understand. It threatens High Culture by its sheer pervasiveness, its brutal, overwhelming *quantity*. The upper classes, who begin by using it to make money from the crude tastes of the masses and to dominate them politically, end by finding their own culture attacked and even threatened with destruction by the instrument they have thoughtlessly employed. (The same irony may be observed in modern politics, where most swords seem to have two edges; thus Nazism began as a tool of the big bourgeoisie and the army *Junkers* but ended by using *them* as *its* tools.)

Homogenized Culture

Like nineteenth-century capitalism, Mass Culture is a dynamic, revolutionary force, breaking down the old barriers of class, tradition, taste, and dissolving all cultural distinctions. It mixes and scrambles everything together, producing what might be called homogenized culture, after another American achievement, the homogenization process that distributes the globules of cream evenly throughout the milk instead of allowing them to float separately on top. It thus destroys all values, since value judgments imply discriminations. Mass Culture is very, very democratic: it absolutely refuses to discriminate against, or between, anything or anybody. All is grist to its mill, and all comes out finely ground indeed.

Consider *Life,* a typical homogenized mass-circulation magazine. It appears on the mahogany library tables of the rich, the glass end-tables of the middle-class and the oilcloth-covered kitchen tables of the poor. Its contents are as thoroughly homogenized as its circulation. The same issue will contain a serious exposition of atomic theory alongside a disquisition on Rita Hayworth's love life; photos of starving Korean children picking garbage from the ruins of Pusan and of sleek models wearing adhesive brassieres; an editorial hailing Bertrand Russell on his eightieth birthday ("A GREAT MIND IS STILL ANNOYING AND ADORNING OUR AGE") across from a full-page photo of a housewife arguing with an umpire at a baseball game ("MOM GETS THUMB"); a cover announcing in the same size type "A NEW FOREIGN POLICY, BY JOHN FOSTER DULLES" and "KERIMA: HER MARATHON KISS IS A MOVIE SENSATION"; nine color pages of Renoirs plus a memoir by his son, followed by a full-page picture of a roller-skating horse. The advertisements, of course, provide even more scope for the editor's homogenizing talents, as when a full-page photo of a ragged Bolivian peon grinningly drunk on coca leaves (which Mr. Luce's conscientious reporters tell us he chews to narcotize his chronic hunger pains) appears opposite an ad of a pretty, smiling, well-dressed American mother with her two pretty, smiling, well-dressed children (a boy and a girl, of course—children are always homogenized in American ads) looking raptly at a clown on a TV set ("RCA VICTOR BRINGS YOU A NEW KIND OF TELEVISION—SUPER SETS WITH 'PICTURE POWER' "). The peon would doubtless find the juxtaposition piquant if he could afford a copy of *Life,* which, fortunately for the Good Neighbor Policy, he cannot.

Academicism and Avantgardism

Until about 1930, High Culture tried to defend itself against the encroachments of Mass Culture in two opposite ways: Academicism, or an attempt to compete by imitation; and Avantgardism, or a withdrawal from competition.

Academicism is *kitsch* for the *élite:* spurious High Culture that is outwardly the real thing but actually as much a manufactured article as the cheaper cultural goods produced for the masses. It is recognized at the time for what it is only by the Avantgardists. A generation or two later, its real nature is understood by everyone and it quietly drops into the same oblivion as its franker sister-under-the-skin. Examples are painters such as Bougereau and Rosa Bonheur, critics such as Edmund Clarence Stedman and Edmund Gosse, the Beaux Arts school of architecture, composers such as the late Sir Edward Elgar, poets such as Stephen Phillips, and novelists such as Alphonse Daudet, Arnold Bennett, James Branch Cabell and Somerset Maugham.

The significance of the Avantgarde movement (by which I mean poets such as Rimbaud, novelists such as Joyce, composers such as Stravinsky, and painters such as Picasso) is that it simply refused to compete. Rejecting Academicism—and thus, at a second remove, also Mass Culture—it made a desperate attempt to fence off some area where the serious artist could still function. It created a new compartmentation of culture, on the basis of an intellectual rather than a social *élite*. The attempt was remarkably successful: to it we owe almost everything that is living in the art of the last fifty or so years. In fact, the High Culture of our times is pretty much identical with Avantgardism. The movement came at a time (1890–1930) when bourgeois values were being challenged both culturally and politically. (In this country, the cultural challenge did not come until World War I, so that our Avantgarde flourished only in the twenties.) In the thirties the two streams mingled briefly, after each had spent its real force, under the aegis of the Communists, only to sink together at the end of the decade into the sands of the wasteland we still live in. The rise of Nazism and the revelation in the Moscow Trials of the real nature of the new society in Russia inaugurated the present period, when men cling to the evils they know rather than risk possibly greater ones by pressing forward. Nor has the chronic state of war, hot or cold, that the world has been in since 1939 encouraged rebellion or experiment in either art or politics.

A Merger Has Been Arranged

In this new period, the competitors, as often happens in the business world, are merging. Mass Culture takes on the color of both varieties of the old High Culture, Academic and Avantgarde, while these latter are increasingly watered down with Mass elements. There is slowly emerging a tepid, flaccid Middlebrow Culture that threatens to engulf everything in its spreading ooze. Bauhaus modernism has at last trickled down, in a debased form of course, into our furniture, cafeterias, movie theatres, electric toasters, office buildings, drug stores, and railroad trains. Psychoanalysis is expounded sympathetically and superficially in popular magazines, and the psychoanalyst replaces the eccentric millionaire as the *deus ex machina* in many a movie. T. S. Eliot writes *The Cocktail Party* and it becomes a Broadway hit. (Though in some ways excellent, it is surely inferior to his *Murder in the Cathedral,* which in the unmerged thirties had to depend on WPA to get produced at all.)

The typical creator of *kitsch* today, at least in the old media, is an indeterminate specimen. There are no widely influential critics so completely terrible as, say, the late William Lyon Phelps was. Instead we have such gray creatures as Clifton Fadiman and Henry Seidel Canby. The artless numbers of an Eddie Guest are drowned out by the more sophisticated though equally commonplace strains of Benét's *John Brown's Body*. Maxfield Parrish yields to Rockwell Kent, Arthur Brisbane to Walter Lippmann, Theda Bara to Ingrid Bergman. We even have what might be called *l'avantgarde pompier* (or, in American, "phony Avantgardism"), as in the buildings of Raymond Hood and the later poetry of Archibald MacLeish, as there is also an academic Avantgardism in *belles lettres* so that now the "little" as well as the big magazines have their hack writers.

All this is not a raising of the level of Mass Culture, as might appear at first, but rather a corruption of High Culture. There is nothing more vulgar than sophisticated *kitsch*. Compare Conan Doyle's workmanlike and unpretentious Sherlock Holmes stories with the bogus "intellectuality" of Dorothy M. Sayers, who, like many contemporary detective-story writers, is a novelist *manquée* who ruins her stuff with literary attitudinizing. Or consider the relationship of Hollywood and Broadway. In the twenties, the two were sharply differentiated, movies being produced for the masses of the hinterland, theatre for an upper-class New York audience. The theatre was High Culture, mostly of the Academic variety (Theatre Guild) but with some spark of Avantgarde fire (the "little" or "experimental" theatre movement). The movies were definitely Mass Culture, mostly very bad but with some leaven of Avantgardism (Griffith, Stroheim) and Folk Art (Chaplin and other comedians). With the sound film, Broadway and Hollywood drew closer together. Plays are now produced mainly to sell the movie rights, with many being directly financed by the film companies. The merge has standardized the theatre to such an extent that even the early Theatre Guild seems vital in retrospect, while hardly a trace of the "experimental" theatre is left. And what have the movies gained? They are more sophisticated, the acting is subtler, the sets in better taste. But they too have become standardized: they are never as awful as they often were in the old days, but they are never as good either. They are better entertainment and worse art. The cinema of the twenties occasionally gave us the fresh charm of Folk Art or the imaginative intensity of Avantgardism. The coming of sound, and with it Broadway, degraded the camera to a recording instrument for an alien art form, the spoken play. The silent film had at least the *theoretical possibility,* even within the limits of Mass Culture, of being artistically significant. The sound film, within those limits, does not.

Division of Labor

The whole field could be approached from the standpoint of the division of labor. The more advanced technologically, the greater the division. Cf. the great Blackett-Semple-Hummert factory—the word is accurate—for the mass production of radio "soap operas." Or the fact that in Hollywood a composer for the movies is not *permitted* to make his own orchestrations any more than a director can do his own cutting. Or the "editorial formula" which every big-circulation magazine tailors its fiction and articles to fit, much as automobile parts are machined in Detroit. *Time* and *Newsweek* have carried specialization to its extreme: their writers don't even sign their work, which in fact is not properly theirs, since the gathering of data is done by a specialized corps of researchers and correspondents and the final article is often as much the result of the editor's blue-pencilling and rewriting as of the original author's efforts. The *"New Yorker* short story" is a definite genre—smooth, minor-key, casual, suggesting drama and sentiment without ever being crude enough to actually create it— which the editors have established by years of patient, skilful selection the same way a gardener develops a new kind of rose. They have, indeed, done their work all too well: would-be contributors now deluge them with lifeless imitations, and they have begun to beg writers not to follow the formula *quite* so closely.

Such art workers are as alienated from their brainwork as the industrial worker is from his handwork. The results are as bad qualitatively as they are impressive quantitatively. The only great films to come out of Hollywood, for example, were made before industrial elephantiasis had reduced the director to one of a number of technicians all operating at about the same level of authority. Our two greatest directors, Griffith and Stroheim, were artists, not specialists; they did everything themselves, dominated everything personally: the scenario, the actors, the camera work, and above all the cutting (or montage). Unity is essential in art; it cannot be achieved by a production line of specialists, however competent. There have been successful collective creations (Greek temples, Gothic churches, perhaps the *Iliad*) but their creators were part of a tradition which was strong enough to impose unity on their work. We have no such tradition today, and so art—as against *kitsch*—will result only when a single brain and sensibility is in full command. In the movies, only the director can even theoretically be in such a position; he was so in the pre-1930 cinema of this country, Germany, and the Soviet Union.

Griffith and Stroheim were both terrific egoists—crude, naïve, and not without charlatanry—who survived until the industry became highly enough organized to resist their vigorous personalities. By about 1925, both were outside looking in; the manufacture of commodities so costly to make and so profitable to sell was too serious a matter to be intrusted to artists.

"One word of advice, Von," Griffith said to Stroheim, who had been his assistant on *Intolerance,* when Stroheim came to him with the news that he had a chance to make a picture himself. "Make your pictures in your own way. Put your mark on them. Take a stand and stick to your guns. You'll make some enemies, but you'll make good pictures." Could that have been only thirty years ago?

Adultized Children and Infantile Adults

The homogenizing effects of *kitsch* also blur age lines. It would be interesting to know how many adults read the comics. We do know that comic books are by far the favorite reading matter of our soldiers and sailors, that some forty million comic books are sold a month, and that some seventy million people (most of whom must be adults, there just aren't that many kids) are estimated to read the newspaper comic strips every day. We also know that movie Westerns and radio and TV programs such as "The Lone Ranger" and "Captain Video" are by no means enjoyed only by children. On the other hand, children have access to such grown-up media as the movies, radio and TV. (Note that these newer arts are the ones which blur age lines because of the extremely modest demands they make on the audience's cultural equipment; thus there are many children's books but few children's movies.)

This merging of the child and grown-up audience means: (1) infantile regression of the latter, who, unable to cope with the strains and complexities of modern life, escape via *kitsch* (which in turn, confirms and enhances their infantilism); (2) "overstimulation" of the former, who grow up too fast. Or, as Max Horkheimer well puts it: "Development has ceased to exist. The child is grown up as soon as he can walk, and the grown-up in principle always remains the same." Also note (a) our cult of youth, which makes 18–22 the most admired and desired period of life, and (b) the sentimental worship of Mother ("Momism") as if we couldn't bear to grow up and be on our own. Peter Pan might be a better symbol of America than Uncle Sam.

Idols of Consumption

Too little attention has been paid to the connection of our Mass Culture with the historical evolution of American Society. In *Radio Research, 1942–43* (Paul F. Lazarsfeld, ed.), Leo Lowenthal compared the biographical articles in *Collier's* and *The Saturday Evening Post* for 1901 and 1940–41 and found that in the forty-year interval the proportion of articles about business and professional men and political leaders had declined while those about entertainers had gone up 50 per cent. Furthermore, the 1901 entertainers are mostly serious artists —opera singers, sculptors, pianists, etc.—while those of 1941 are *all* movie stars, baseball players, and such; and even the "serious" heroes in 1941 aren't so very serious after all: the businessmen and politicians are freaks, oddities, not the really powerful leaders as in 1901. The 1901 *Satevepost* heroes he calls "idols of production," those of today "idols of consumption."

Lowenthal notes that the modern *Satevepost* biographee is successful not because of his own personal abilities so much as because he "got the breaks." The whole competitive struggle is presented as a lottery in which a few winners, no more talented or energetic than any one else, drew the lucky tickets. The effect on the mass reader is at once consoling (it might have been me) and deadening to effort, ambition (there are no rules, so why struggle?). It is striking how closely this evolution parallels the country's economic development. Lowenthal observes that the "idols of production" maintained their dominance right through the twenties. The turning point was the 1929 depression when the problem became how to consume goods rather than how to produce them, and also when the arbitrariness and chaos of capitalism was forcefully brought home to the mass man. So he turned to "idols of consumption," or rather these were now offered him by the manufacturers of Mass Culture, and he accepted them. "They seem to lead to a dream world of the masses," observes Lowenthal, "who are no longer capable or willing to conceive of biographies primarily as a means of orientation and education. . . . He, the

American mass man, as reflected in his 'idols of consumption' appears no longer as a center of outwardly directed energies and actions on whose work and efficiency might depend mankind's progress. Instead of the 'givers' we are faced with the 'takers'. . . . They seem to stand for a phantasmagoria of world-wide social security—an attitude which asks for no more than to be served with the things needed for reproduction and recreation, an attitude which has lost every primary interest in how to invent, shape, or apply the tools leading to such purposes of mass satisfaction."

Sherlock Holmes to Mike Hammer

The role of science in Mass Culture has similarly changed from the rational and the purposive to the passive, accidental, even the catastrophic. Consider the evolution of the detective story, a genre which can be traced back to the memoirs of Vidocq, the master-detective of the Napoleonic era. Poe, who was peculiarly fascinated by scientific method, wrote the first and still best detective stories: *The Purloined Letter, The Gold Bug, The Mystery of Marie Roget, The Murders in the Rue Morgue.* Conan Doyle created the great folk hero, Sherlock Holmes, like Poe's Dupin a sage whose wizard's wand was scientific deduction (Poe's "ratiocination"). Such stories could only appeal to—in fact, only be comprehensible to—an audience accustomed to think in scientific terms: to survey the data, set up a hypothesis, test it by seeing whether it caught the murderer. The very idea of an art genre cast in the form of a problem to be solved by purely intellectual means could only have arisen in a scientific age. This kind of detective fiction, which might be called the "classic" style, is still widely practiced (well by Agatha Christie and John Dickson Carr, badly by the more popular Erle Stanley Gardner) but of late it has been overshadowed by the rank, noxious growth of works in the "sensational" style. This was inaugurated by Dashiell Hammett (whom André Gide was foolish enough to admire) and has recently been enormously stepped up in voltage by Mickey Spillane, whose six books to date have sold thirteen million copies. The sensationalists use what for the classicists was the point—the uncovering of the criminal —as a mere excuse for the minute description of scenes of bloodshed, brutality, lust, and alcoholism. The cool, astute, subtle Dupin-Holmes is replaced by the crude man of action whose prowess is measured not by intellectual mastery but by his capacity for liquor, women, and mayhem (he can "take it" as well as "dish it out"—Hammett's *The Glass Key* is largely a chronicle of the epic beatings absorbed by the hero before he finally staggers to the solution). Mike Hammer, Spillane's aptly named hero, is such a monumental blunderer that even Dr. Watson would have seen through him. According to Richard W. Johnston (*Life,* June 23, 1952), "Mike has one bizarre and memorable characteristic that sets him apart from all other fictional detectives: sheer incompetence. In the five Hammer cases, 48 people have been killed, and there is reason to believe that if Mike had kept out of the way, 34 of them—all innocent of the original crime—would have survived." A decade ago, the late George Orwell, apropos a "sensationalist" detective story of the time, *No Orchids for Miss Blandish,* showed how the brutalization of this genre mirrors the general degeneration in ethics from nineteenth-century standards. What he would have written had Mickey Spillane's works been then in existence I find it hard to imagine.

Frankenstein to Hiroshima

The real heirs of the "classic" detective story today, so far as the exploitation of science is concerned, are the writers of science fiction, where the marvels and horrors of the future must always be "scientifically possible"—just as Sherlock Holmes drew on no supernatural powers. This is the approach of the bourgeoisie, who think of science as their familiar instrument. The masses are less confident, more awed in their approach to science, and there are vast lower strata of science fiction where the marvellous is untrammeled by the limits of knowledge. To the masses, science is the modern *arcanum arcanorum,* at once the supreme mystery and the philosopher's stone that explains the mystery. The latter concept appears in comic strips such as "Superman" and in the charlatan-science exploited by "health fakers" and "nature fakers." Taken this way, science gives man mastery over his environment and is beneficent. But science itself is not understood, therefore not mastered, therefore terrifying because of its very power. Taken *this* way, as the supreme mystery, science becomes the stock in trade of the "horror" pulp magazines and comics and movies. It has got to the point, indeed, that if one sees a laboratory in a movie, one shudders, and the white coat of the scientist is as blood-chilling a sight as Count Dracula's black cloak. These "horror" films have apparently an indestructible popularity: *Frankenstein* is still shown, after twenty-one years, and the current revival of *King Kong* is expected to gross over 2 million dollars.

If the scientist's laboratory has acquired in Mass Culture a ghastly atmosphere, is this perhaps not one of those deep popular intuitions? From Frankenstein's laboratory to Maidenek and Hiroshima is not a long journey. Was there a popular suspicion, perhaps only half conscious, that the nineteenth-century trust in science, like the nineteenth-century trust in popular education, was mistaken, that science can as easily be used for antihuman as for prohuman ends, perhaps even more easily? For Mrs. Shelley's Frankenstein, the experimenter who brought disaster by pushing his science too far, is a scientific folk hero older than and still as famous as Mr. Doyle's successful and beneficent Sherlock Holmes.

The Problem of the Masses

Conservatives such as Ortega y Gasset and T. S. Eliot argue that since "the revolt of the masses" has led to the horrors of totalitarianism (and of California roadside architecture), the only hope is to rebuild the old class walls and bring the masses once more under aristocratic control. They think of the popular as synonymous with cheap and vulgar. Marxian radicals and liberals, on the other hand, see the masses as intrinsically healthy but as the dupes and victims of cultural exploitation by the Lords of *kitsch*—in the style of Rousseau's "noble savage" idea. If only the masses were offered good stuff instead of *kitsch*, how they would eat it up! How the level of Mass Culture would rise! Both these diagnoses seem to me fallacious: they assume that Mass Culture is (in the conservative view) or could be (in the liberal view) an expression of *people*, like Folk Art, whereas actually it is an expression of *masses*, a very different thing.

There are theoretical reasons why Mass Culture is not and can never be any good. I take it as axiomatic that culture can only be produced by and for human beings. But in so far as people are organized (more strictly, disorganized) as masses, they lose their human identity and quality. For the masses are in historical time what a crowd is in space: a large quantity of people unable to express themselves as human beings because they are related to one another neither as individuals nor as members of communities—indeed, they are not related *to each other* at all, but only to something distant, abstract, nonhuman: a football game, or bargain sale, in the case of a crowd, a system of industrial production, a party or a State in the case of the masses. The mass man is a solitary atom, uniform with and undifferentiated from thousands and millions of other atoms who go to make up "the lonely crowd," as David Riesman well calls American society. A folk or a people, however, is a community, i.e., a group of individuals linked to each other by common interests, work, traditions, values, and sentiments; something like a family, each of whose members has a special place and function as an individual while at the same time sharing the group's interests (family budget), sentiments (family quarrels), and culture (family jokes). The scale is small enough so that it "makes a difference" what the individual does, a first condition for human—as against mass—existence. He is at once more important as an individual than in mass society and at the same time more closely integrated into the community, his creativity nourished by a rich combination of individualism and communalism. (The great culture-bearing *élites* of the past have been communities of this kind.) In contrast, a mass society, like a crowd, is so undifferentiated and loosely structured that its atoms, in so far as human values go, tend to cohere only along the line of the least common denominator; its morality sinks to that of its most brutal and primitive members, its taste to that of the least sensitive and most ignorant. And in addition to everything else, the scale is simply too big, there are just *too many people.*

Yet this collective monstrosity, "the masses," "the public," is taken as a human norm by the scientific and artistic technicians of our Mass Culture. They at once degraded the public by treating it as an object, to be handled with the lack of ceremony and the objectivity of medical students dissecting a corpse, and at the same time flatter it, pander to its level of taste and ideas by taking these as the criterion of reality (in the case of questionnaire-sociologists and other "social scientists") or of art (in the case of the Lords of *kitsch*). When one hears a questionnaire-sociologist talk about how he will "set up" an investigation, one feels he regards people as a herd of dumb animals, as mere congeries of conditioned reflexes, his calculation being which reflex will be stimulated by which question. At the same time, of necessity, he sees the statistical majority as the great Reality, the secret of life he is trying to find out; like the *kitsch* Lords, he is wholly without values, willing to accept any idiocy if it is held by many people. The aristocrat and the democrat both criticize and argue with popular taste, the one with hostility, the other in friendship, for both attitudes proceed from a set of values. This is less degrading to the masses than the "objective" approach of Hollywood and the questionnaire-sociologists, just as it is less degrading to a man to be shouted at in anger than to be quietly assumed to be part of a machine. But the *plebs* have their dialectical revenge: complete indifference to their human *quality* means complete prostration before their statistical *quantity,* so that a movie magnate who cynically "gives the public what it wants"—i.e., assumes it wants trash—sweats with terror if box-office returns drop 10 per cent.

The Future of High Culture: Dark

The conservative proposal to save culture by restoring the old class lines has a more solid historical base than the Marxian hope for a new democratic, classless culture, for, with the possible (and important) exception of Periclean Athens, all the great cultures of the past were *élite* cultures. Politically, however, it is without meaning in a world dominated by the two great mass nations, U.S.A. and U.S.S.R. and becoming more industrialized, more massified all the time. The only practical thing along those lines would be to revive the *cultural élite* which the Avantgarde created. As I have already noted, the Avantgarde is now dying, partly from internal causes, partly suffocated by the competing Mass Culture, where it is not being absorbed into it. Of course this process has not reached 100 per cent, and doubtless never will unless the country goes either Fascist or Communist. There are still islands above the flood for those determined enough to reach them, and to stay on them: as Faulkner has shown, a writer can even use Hollywood instead of being used by it, if his purpose is firm enough. But the homogenization of High and Mass Culture has gone far and is going farther all the time, and there seems little reason to expect a revival of Avantgardism, that is, of a successful counter-movement to Mass Culture. Particularly not in this country, where the blurring of class lines, the absence of a stable cultural tradition, and the greater facilities for manufacturing and marketing *kitsch* all work in the other direction. The result is that our intelligentsia is remarkably small, weak, and disintegrated. One of the odd things about the American cultural scene is how many brainworkers there are and how few intellectuals, defining the former as specialists whose thinking is pretty much confined to their limited "fields" and the latter as persons who take all culture for their province. Not only are there few intellectuals, but they don't hang together, they have very little *esprit de corps,* very little sense of belonging to a community; they are so isolated from each other they don't even bother to quarrel—there hasn't been a really good fight among them since the Moscow Trials.

The Future of Mass Culture: Darker

If the conservative proposal to save our culture via the aristocratic Avantgarde seems historically unlikely, what of the democratic-liberal proposal? Is there a reasonable prospect of raising the level of Mass Culture? In his recent book, *The Great Audience,* Gilbert Seldes argues there is. He blames the present sad state of our Mass Culture on the stupidity of the Lords of *kitsch,* who underestimate the mental age of the public; the arrogance of the intellectuals, who make the same mistake and so snobbishly refuse to work for such mass media as radio, TV and movies; and the passivity of the public itself, which doesn't insist on better Mass Cultural products. This diagnosis seems to me superficial in that it blames everything on subjective, moral factors: stupidity, perversity, failure of will. My own feeling is that, as in the case of the alleged responsibility of the German (or Russian) people for the horrors of Nazism (or Soviet Communism), it is unjust to blame social groups for this result. Human beings have been caught up in the inexorable workings of a mechanism that forces them, with a pressure only heroes can resist (and one cannot *demand* that anybody be a hero, though one can *hope* for it), into its own pattern. I see Mass Culture as a reciprocating engine, and who is to say, once it has been set in motion, whether the stroke or the counterstroke is "responsible" for its continued action?

The Lords of *kitsch* sell culture to the masses. It is a debased, trivial culture that voids both the deep realities (sex, death, failure, tragedy) and also the simple, spontaneous pleasures, since the realities would be too real and the pleasures too *lively* to induce what Mr. Seldes calls "the mood of consent," i.e., a narcotized acceptance of Mass Culture and of the commodities it sells as a substitute for the unsettling and unpredictable (hence unsalable) joy, tragedy, wit, change, originality and beauty of real life. The masses, debauched by several generations of this sort of thing, in turn come to demand trivial and comfortable cultural products. Which came first, the chicken or the egg, the mass demand or its satisfaction (and further stimulation) is a question as academic as it is unanswerable. The engine is reciprocating and shows no signs of running down.

Indeed, far from Mass Culture getting better, we will be lucky if it doesn't get worse. When shall we see another popular humorist like Sholem Aleichem, whose books are still being translated from the Yiddish and for whose funeral in 1916 a hundred thousand inhabitants of the Bronx turned out? Or Finlay Peter Dunne, whose Mr. Dooley commented on the American scene with such wit that Henry Adams was a faithful reader and Henry James, on his famous return to his native land, wanted to meet only one American author, Dunne? Since Mass Culture is not an art form but a manufactured commodity, it tends always downward, toward cheapness—and so standardization—of production. Thus, T. W. Adorno has noted, in his brilliant essay "On Popular Music" (*Studies in Philosophy and Social Science,* New York, No. 1, 1941) that the chorus of every popular song *without* exception has the same number of bars, while Mr. Seldes remarks that Hollywood movies are cut in a uniformly rapid tempo, a shot rarely being held more than forty-five seconds, which gives them a standardized effect in contrast to the varied tempo of European film cutting. This sort of standardization means that what may have begun as something fresh and original is repeated until it becomes a nerveless routine —*vide* what happened to Fred Allen as a radio comedian. The only time Mass Culture is good is at the very beginning, before the "formula" has hardened, before the money boys and efficiency experts and audience-reaction analysts have moved in. Then for a while it may have the quality of real Folk Art. But the Folk artist today lacks the cultural roots and the intellectual toughness (both of which the Avantgarde artist has relatively more of) to resist for long the pressures of Mass Culture. His taste can be easily corrupted, his sense of his own special talent and limitations obscured, as in what happened to Disney between the gay, inventive early Mickey Mouse and Silly Symphony cartoons and the vulgar pretentiousness of *Fantasia* and heavy-handed sentimentality of *Snow White,* or to Westbrook Pegler who has regressed from an excellent sports writer, with a sure sense of form and a mastery of colloquial satire, into the rambling, coarse-grained, garrulous political pundit of today. Whatever virtues the Folk artist has, and they are many, staying power is not one of them. And staying power is the essential virtue of one who would hold his own against the spreading ooze of Mass Culture.

21. Movie Chronicle: The Westerner

ROBERT WARSHOW

Robert Warshow (1917–1955), whose untimely death cut off a developing interest in the movies and their meaning, explores in the essay reprinted here the archetypes in the Western, a mythic pattern which has passed from dime thrillers to pulp magazines to moving pictures to TV without seeming to lose its force.

> *They that have power to hurt and will do none,*
> *That do not do the thing they most do show,*
> *Who, moving others, are themselves as stone,*
> *Unmoved, cold, and to temptation slow;*
> *They rightly do inherit heaven's graces,*
> *And husband nature's riches from expense;*
> *They are the lords and owners of their faces,*
> *Others but stewards of their excellence.*
>
> [*Shakespeare, Sonnet* 94]

The two most successful creations of American movies are the gangster and the Westerner: men with guns. Guns as physical objects, and the postures associated with their use, form the visual and emotional center of both types of films. I suppose this reflects the importance of guns in the fantasy life of Americans; but that is a less illuminating point than it appears to be.

SOURCE: Robert Warshow, *The Immediate Experience* (New York: Doubleday & Company, Inc., 1962), pp. 135–54. Reprinted by permission of Paul Warshow.

The gangster movie, which no longer exists in its "classical" form, is a story of enterprise and success ending in precipitate failure. Success is conceived as an increasing power to work injury, it belongs to the city, and it is of course a form of evil (though the gangster's death, presented usually as "punishment," is perceived simply as defeat). The peculiarity of the gangster is his unceasing, nervous activity. The exact nature of his enterprises may remain vague, but his commitment to enterprise is always clear, and all the more clear because he operates outside the field of utility. He is without culture, without manners, without leisure, or at any rate his leisure is likely to be spent in debauchery so compulsively aggressive as to seem only another aspect of his "work." But he is graceful, moving like a dancer among the crowded dangers of the city.

Like other tycoons, the gangster is crude in conceiving his ends but by no means inarticulate; on the contrary, he is usually expansive and noisy (the introspective gangster is a fairly recent development), and can state definitely what he wants: to take over the North Side, to own a hundred suits, to be Number One. But new "frontiers" will present themselves infinitely, and by a rigid convention it is understood that as soon as he wishes to rest on his gains, he is on the way to destruction.

The gangster is lonely and melancholy, and can give the impression of a profound worldly wisdom. He appeals most to adolescents with their impatience and their feeling of being outsiders, but more generally he appeals to that side of all of us which refuses to believe in the "normal" possibilities of happiness and achievement; the gangster is the "no" to that great American "yes" which is stamped so big over our official culture and yet has so little to do with the way we really feel about our lives. But the gangster's loneliness and melancholy are not "authentic"; like everything else that belongs to him, they are not honestly come by: he is lonely and melancholy not because life ultimately demands such feelings but because he has put himself in a position where everybody wants to kill him and eventually somebody will. He is wide open and defenseless, incomplete because unable to accept any limits or come to terms with his own nature, fearful, loveless. And the story of his career is a nightmare inversion of the values of ambition and opportunity. From the window of Scarface's bullet-proof apartment can be seen an electric sign proclaiming: "The World Is Yours," and, if I remember, this sign is the last thing we see after Scarface lies dead in the street. In the end it is the gangster's weakness as much as his power and freedom that appeals to us; the world is not ours, but it is not his either, and in his death he "pays" for our fantasies, releasing us momentarily both from the concept of success, which he denies by caricaturing it, and from the need to succeed, which he shows to be dangerous.

The Western hero, by contrast, is a figure of repose. He resembles the gangster in being lonely and to some degree melancholy. But his melancholy comes from the "simple" recognition that life is unavoidably serious, not from the disproportions of his own temperament. And his loneliness is organic, not imposed on him by his situation but belonging to him intimately and testifying to his completeness. The gangster must reject others violently or draw them violently to him. The Westerner is not thus compelled to seek love; he is prepared to accept it, perhaps, but he never asks of it more than it can give, and we see him constantly in situations where love is at best an irrelevance. If there is a woman he loves, she is usually unable to understand his motives; she is against killing and being killed, and he finds it impossible to explain to her that there is no point in being "against" these things: they belong to his world.

Very often this woman is from the East and her failure to understand represents a clash of cultures. In the American mind, refinement, virtue, civilization, Christianity itself, are seen as feminine, and therefore women are often portrayed as possessing some kind of deeper wisdom, while the men, for all their apparent self-assurance, are fundamentally childish. But the West, lacking the graces of civilization, is the place "where men are men"; in Western movies, men have the deeper wisdom and the women are children. Those women in the Western movies who share the hero's understanding of life are prostitutes (or, as they are usually presented, barroom entertainers) —women, that is, who have come to understand in the most practical way how love can be an irrelevance, and therefore "fallen" women. The gangster, too, associates with prostitutes, but for him the important things about a prostitute are her passive availability and her costliness: she is part of his winnings. In Western movies, the important thing about a prostitute is her quasi-masculine independence: nobody owns her, nothing has to be explained to her, and she is not, like a virtuous woman, a "value" that demands to be protected. When the Westerner leaves the prostitute for a virtuous woman—for love— he is in fact forsaking a way of life, though the point of the choice is often obscured by having the prostitute killed by getting into the line of fire.

The Westerner is *par excellence* a man of leisure. Even when he wears the badge of a marshal or, more rarely, owns a ranch, he appears to be unemployed. We see him standing at a bar, or playing poker—a game which expresses perfectly his talent for remaining relaxed in the midst of tension—or perhaps camping out on the plains on some extraordinary errand. If he does own a ranch, it is in the background; we are not actually aware that he owns anything except his horse, his guns, and the one worn suit of clothing which is likely to remain unchanged all through the movie. It comes as a surprise to see him take money from his pocket or an extra shirt from his saddle-bags. As a rule we do not even know where he sleeps at night and don't think of asking. Yet it never occurs to us that he is a poor man; there is no poverty in Western movies, and really no wealth either: those great cattle domains and shipments of gold which figure so largely in the plots are moral and not material quantities, not the objects of contention but only its occasion. Possessions too are irrelevant.

Employment of some kind—usually unproductive—is always open to the Westerner, but when he accepts it, it is not because he needs to make a living, much less from any idea of "getting ahead." Where could he want to "get ahead" to? By the time we see him, he is already "there": he can ride a horse faultlessly, keep his countenance in the face of death, and draw his gun a little faster and shoot it a little straighter than anyone he is likely to meet. These are sharply defined acquirements, giving to the figure of the Westerner an apparent moral clarity which corresponds to the clarity of his physical image against his bare landscape; initially, at any rate, the Western movie presents itself as being without mystery, its whole universe comprehended in what we see on the screen.

Much of this apparent simplicity arises directly from those "cinematic" elements which have long been understood to give the Western theme its special appropriateness for the movies: the wide expanses of land, the free movement of men on horses. As guns constitute the visible moral center of the Western movie, suggesting continually the possibility of violence, so land and horses represent the movie's material basis, its sphere of action. But the land and the horses have also a moral significance: the physical freedom they represent belongs to the moral "openness" of the West—corresponding to the fact that guns are carried where they can be seen. (And, as we shall see, the character of land and horses changes as the Western film becomes more complex.)

The gangster's world is less open, and his arts not so easily identifiable as the Westerner's. Perhaps he too can keep his countenance, but the mask he wears is really no mask: its purpose is precisely to make evident the fact that he desperately wants to "get ahead" and will stop at nothing. Where the Westerner imposes himself by the appearance of unshakable control, the gangster's pre-eminence lies in the suggestion that he may at any moment lose control; his strength is not in being able to shoot faster or straighter than others, but in being more willing to shoot. "Do it first," says Scarface expounding his mode of operation, "and keep on doing it!" With the Westerner, it is a crucial point of honor *not* to "do it first"; his gun remains in its holster until the moment of combat.

There is no suggestion, however, that he draws the gun reluctantly. The Westerner could not fulfill himself if the moment did not finally come when he can shoot his enemy down. But because that moment is so thoroughly the expression of his being, it must be kept pure. He will not violate the accepted forms of combat though by doing so he could save a city. And he can wait. "When you call me that—smile!" the villain smiles weakly, soon he is laughing with horrible joviality, and the crisis is past. But it is allowed to pass because it must come again: sooner or later Trampas will "make his play," and the Virginian will be ready for him.

What does the Westerner fight for? We know he is on the side of justice and order, and of course it can be said he fights for these things. But such broad aims never correspond exactly to his real motives; they only offer him his opportunity. The Westerner himself, when an explanation is asked of him (usually by a woman), is likely to say that he does what he "has to do." If justice and order did not continually demand his protection, he would be without a calling. Indeed, we come upon him often in just that situation, as the reign of law settles over the West and he is forced to see that his day is over; those are the pictures which end with his death or with his departure for some more remote frontier. What he defends, at bottom, is the purity of his own image— in fact his honor. That is what makes him invulnerable. When the gangster is killed, his whole life is shown to have been a mistake, but the image the Westerner seeks to maintain can be presented as clearly in defeat as in victory: he fights not for advantage and not for the right, but to state what he is, and he must live in a world which permits that statement. The Westerner is the last gentleman, and the movies which over and over again tell his story are probably the last art form in which the concept of honor retains its strength.

Of course I do not mean to say that ideas of virtue and justice and courage have gone out of culture. Honor is more than these things: it is a style, concerned with harmonious appearances as much as with desirable consequences, and tending therefore toward the denial of life in favor of art. "Who hath it? he that died o' Wednesday." On the whole a world that leans to Falstaff's view is a more civilized and even, finally, a more graceful world. It is just the march of civilization that forces the Westerner to move on; and if we actually had to confront the question it might turn out that the woman who refuses to understand him is right as often as she is wrong. But we do not confront the question. Where the Westerner lives it is always about 1870—not the real 1870, either, or the real West—and he is killed or goes away when his position becomes problematical. The fact that he continues to hold our attention is evidence enough that, in his proper frame, he presents an image of personal nobility that is still real for us.

Clearly, this image easily becomes ridiculous: we need only look at William S. Hart or Tom Mix, who in the wooden absoluteness of their virtue represented little that an adult could take seriously; and doubtless such figures as Gene Autry or Roy Rogers are no better, though I confess I have seen none of their movies. Some film enthusiasts claim to find in the early, unsophisticated Westerns a "cinematic purity" that has since been lost; this idea is as valid, and finally as misleading, as T. S. Eliot's statement that *Everyman* is the only play in English that stays within the limitations of art. The truth is that the Westerner comes into the field of serious art only when his moral code, without ceasing to be compelling, is seen also to be imperfect. The Westerner at his best exhibits a moral ambiguity which darkens his image and saves him from absurdity; this ambiguity arises from the fact that, whatever his justifications, he is a killer of men.

In *The Virginian,* which is an archetypal Western movie as *Scarface* or *Little Caesar* are archetypal gangster movies, there is a lynching in which the hero (Gary Cooper), as leader of a posse, must supervise the hanging of his best friend for stealing cattle. With the growth of American "social consciousness," it is no longer possible to present a lynching in the movies unless the point is the illegality and injustice

of the lynching itself; *The Ox-Bow Incident,* made in 1943, explicitly
puts forward the newer point of view and can be regarded as a kind of
"anti-Western." But in 1929, when *The Virginian* was made, the
present inhibition about lynching was not yet in force; the justice, and
therefore the necessity, of the hanging is never questioned—except
by the schoolteacher from the East, whose refusal to understand serves
as usual to set forth more sharply the deeper seriousness of the West.
The Virginian is thus in a tragic dilemma where one moral absolute
conflicts with another and the choice of either must leave a moral
stain. If he had chosen to save his friend, he would have violated the
image of himself that he had made essential to his existence, and the
movie would have had to end with his death, for only by his death
could the image have been restored. Having chosen instead to sacrifice
his friend to the higher demands of the "code"—the only choice
worthy of him, as even the friend understands—he is none the less
stained by the killing, but what is needed now to set accounts straight
is not his death but the death of the villain Trampas, the leader of the
cattle thieves, who had escaped the posse and abandoned the Virginian's friend to his fate. Again the woman intervenes: Why must there
be *more* killing? If the hero really loved her, he would leave town, refusing Trampas's challenge. What good will it be if Trampas should
kill him? But the Virginian does once more what he "has to do," and in
avenging his friend's death wipes out the stain on his own honor. Yet
his victory cannot be complete: no death can be paid for and no stain
truly wiped out; the movie is still a tragedy, for though the hero escapes with his life, he has been forced to confront the ultimate limits of
his moral ideas.

This mature sense of limitation and unavoidable guilt is what gives
the Westerner a "right" to his melancholy. It is true that the gangster's
story is also a tragedy—in certain formal ways more clearly a tragedy
than the Westerner's—but it is a romantic tragedy, based on a hero
whose defeat springs with almost mechanical inevitability from the
outrageous presumption of his demands: the gangster is *bound* to go
on until he is killed. The Westerner is a more classical figure, self-
contained and limited to begin with, seeking not to extend his dominion but only to assert his personal value, and his tragedy lies in the fact
that even this circumscribed demand cannot be fully realized. Since
the Westerner is not a murderer but (most of the time) a man of virtue,
and since he is always prepared for defeat, he retains his inner invul-

nerability and his story need not end with his death (and usually does not); but what we finally respond to is not his victory but his defeat.

Up to a point, it is plain that the deeper seriousness of the good Western films comes from the introduction of a realism, both physical and psychological, that was missing with Tom Mix and William S. Hart. As lines of age have come into Gary Cooper's face since *The Virginian,* so the outlines of the Western movie in general have become less smooth, its background more drab. The sun still beats upon the town, but the camera is likely now to take advantage of this illumination to seek out more closely the shabbiness of buildings and furniture, the loose, worn hang of clothing, the wrinkles and dirt of the faces. Once it has been discovered that the true theme of the Western movie is not the freedom and expansiveness of frontier life, but its limitations, its material bareness, the pressures of obligation, then even the landscape itself ceases to be quite the arena of free movement it once was, but becomes instead a great empty waste, cutting down more often than it exaggerates the stature of the horseman who rides across it. We are more likely now to see the Westerner struggling against the obstacles of the physical world (as in the wonderful scenes on the desert and among the rocks in *The Last Posse*) than carelessly surmounting them. Even the horses, no longer the "friends" of man or the inspired chargers of knight-errantry, have lost much of the moral significance that once seemed to belong to them in their careering across the screen. It seems to me the horses grow tired and stumble more often than they did, and that we see them less frequently at the gallop.

In *The Gunfighter,* a remarkable film of a couple of years ago, the landscape has virtually disappeared. Most of the action takes place indoors, in a cheerless saloon where a tired "bad man" (Gregory Peck) contemplates the waste of his life, to be senselessly killed at the end by a vicious youngster setting off on the same futile path. The movie is done in cold, quiet tones of gray, and every object in it—faces, clothing, a table, the hero's heavy mustache—is given an air of uncompromising authenticity, suggesting those dim photographs of the nineteenth-century West in which Wyatt Earp, say, turns out to be a blank untidy figure posing awkwardly before some uninteresting building. This "authenticity," to be sure, is only aesthetic; the chief fact about nineteenth-century photographs, to my eyes at any rate, is how stonily they refuse to yield up the truth. But that limitation is just what is needed: by preserving some hint of the rigidity of archaic photography (only in tone and decor, never in composition), *The Gunfighter* can permit us to feel that we are looking at a more "real" West than the one the movies have accustomed us to—harder, duller, less "romantic"—and yet without forcing us outside the boundaries which give the Western movie its validity.

We come upon the hero of *The Gunfighter* at the end of a career in which he has never upheld justice and order, and has been at times, apparently, an actual criminal; in this case, it is clear that the hero has been wrong and the woman who has rejected his way of life has been right. He is thus without any of the larger justifications, and knows himself a ruined man. There can be no question of his "redeeming" himself in any socially constructive way. He is too much the victim of his own reputation to turn marshal as one of his old friends has done, and he is not offered the sentimental solution of a chance to give up his life for some good end; the whole point is that he exists outside the field of social value. Indeed, if we were once allowed to see him in the days of his "success," he might become a figure like the gangster, for his career has been aggressively "anti-social" and the practical problem he faces is the gangster's problem: there will always be somebody trying to kill him. Yet it is obviously absurd to speak of him as "anti-social," not only because we do not see him acting as a criminal, but more fundamentally because we do not see his milieu as a society. Of course it has its "social problems" and a kind of static history: civilization is always just at the point of driving out the old freedom; there are women and children to represent the possibility of a settled life; and there is the marshal, a bad man turned good, determined to keep at least his area of jurisdiction at peace. But these elements are not, in fact, a part of the film's "realism," even though they come out of the real history of the West; they belong to the conventions of the form, to that accepted framework which makes the film possible in the first place, and they exist not to provide a standard by which the gunfighter can be judged, but only to set him off. The true "civilization" of the Western movie is always embodied in an individual, good or bad is more a matter of personal bearing than of social consequences, and the conflict of good and bad is a duel between two men. Deeply troubled and obviously doomed, the gunfighter is the Western hero still, perhaps all the more because his value must express itself entirely in his own being—in his presence, the way he holds our eyes—and in contradiction to the facts. No matter what he has done, he *looks* right, and he remains invulnerable because, without acknowledging anyone else's right to judge him, he has judged his own failure and has already assimilated it, understanding—as no one else understands except the marshal and the barroom girl—that he can do nothing but play out the drama of the gun fight again and again until the time comes when it will be he who gets killed. What "redeems" him is that he no longer believes in this drama and nevertheless will continue to play his role perfectly: the pattern is all.

The proper function of realism in the Western movie can only be to deepen the lines of that pattern. It is an art form for connoisseurs where the spectator derives his pleasure from the appreciation of minor variations within the working out of a pre-established order. One does not want too much novelty: it comes as a shock, for instance, when the hero is made to operate without a gun, as has been done in several pictures (e.g., *Destry Rides Again*), and our uneasiness is allayed only when he is finally compelled to put his "pacifism" aside. If the hero can be shown to be troubled, complex, fallible, even eccentric, or the villain given some psychological taint or, better, some evocative physical mannerism, to shade the colors of his villainy, that is all to the good. Indeed, that kind of variation is absolutely necessary to keep the type from becoming sterile; we do not want to see the same movie over and over again, only the same form. But when the impulse toward realism is extended into a "reinterpretation" of the West as a developed society, drawing our eyes away from the hero if only to the extent of showing him as the one dominant figure in a complex social order, then the pattern is broken and the West itself begins to be uninteresting. If the "social problems" of the frontier are to be the movie's chief concern, there is no longer any point in re-examining these problems twenty times a year; they have been solved, and the people for whom they once were real are dead. Moreover, the hero himself, still the film's central figure, now tends to become its one unassimilable element, since he is the most "unreal."

The Ox-Bow Incident, by denying the convention of the lynching, presents us with a modern "social drama" and evokes a corresponding response, but in doing so it almost makes the Western setting irrelevant, a mere backdrop of beautiful scenery. (It is significant that *The Ox-Bow Incident* has no hero; a hero would have to stop the lynching or be killed in trying to stop it, and then the "problem" of lynching would no longer be central.) Even in *The Gunfighter* the women and children are a little too much in evidence, threatening constantly to become a real focus of concern instead of simply part of the given framework; and the young tough who kills the hero has too much the air of juvenile criminality: the hero himself could never have been like that, and the idea of a cycle being repeated therefore loses its sharpness. But the most striking example of the confusion created by a too conscientious "social realism" is in the celebrated *High Noon*.

In *High Noon* we find Gary Cooper still the upholder of order that he was in *The Virginian,* but twenty-four years older, stooped, slower moving, awkward, his face lined, the flesh sagging, a less beautiful and weaker figure, but with the suggestion of greater depth that belongs almost automatically to age. Like the hero of *The Gunfighter,* he no longer has to assert his character and is no longer interested in the drama of combat; it is hard to imagine that he might once have been so youthful as to say, "When you call me that—smile!" In fact, when we come upon him he is hanging up his guns and his marshal's badge in order to begin a new, peaceful life with his bride, who is a Quaker. But then the news comes that a man he had sent to prison has been pardoned and will get to town on the noon train; three friends of this man have come to wait for him at the station, and when the freed convict arrives the four of them will come to kill the marshal. He is thus trapped; the bride will object, the hero himself will waver much more than he would have done twenty-four years ago, but in the end he will play out the drama because it is what he "has to do." All this belongs to the established form (there is even the "fallen woman" who understands the marshal's position as his wife does not). Leaving aside the crudity of building up suspense by means of the clock, the actual Western drama of *High Noon* is well handled and forms a good companion piece to *The Virginian,* showing in both conception and technique the ways in which the Western movie has naturally developed.

But there is a second drama along with the first. As the marshal sets out to find deputies to help him deal with the four gunmen, we are taken through the various social strata of the town, each group in turn refusing its assistance out of cowardice, malice, irresponsibility, or venality. With this we are in the field of "social drama"—of a very low order, incidentally, altogether unconvincing and displaying a vulgar anti-populism that has marred some other movies of Stanley Kramer's. But the falsity of the "social drama" is less important than

the fact that it does not belong in the movie to begin with. The technical problem was to make it necessary for the marshal to face his enemies alone; to explain *why* the other townspeople are not at his side is
to raise a question which does not exist in the proper frame of the
Western movie, where the hero is "naturally" alone and it is only necessary to contrive the physical absence of those who might be his
allies, if any contrivance is needed at all. In addition, though the hero
of *High Noon* proves himself a better man than all around him the
actual effect of this contrast is to lessen his stature: he becomes only a
rejected man of virtue. In our final glimpse of him, as he rides away
through the town where he has spent most of his life without really
imposing himself on it, he is a pathetic rather than a tragic figure. And
his departure has another meaning as well; the "social drama" has no
place for him.

But there is also a different way of violating the Western form. This
is to yield entirely to its static quality as legend and to the "cinematic"
temptations of its landscape, the horses, the quiet men. John Ford's
famous *Stagecoach* (1938) had much of this unhappy preoccupation
with style, and the same director's *My Darling Clementine* (1946), a
soft and beautiful movie about Wyatt Earp, goes further along the
same path, offering indeed a superficial accuracy of historical reconstruction, but so loving in execution as to destroy the outlines of the
Western legend, assimilating it to the more sentimental legend of rural
America and making the hero a more dangerous Mr. Deeds. (*Powder
River,* a recent "routine" Western shamelessly copied from *My Darling Clementine,* is in most ways a better film; lacking the benefit of a
serious director, it is necessarily more concerned with drama than with
style.)

The highest expression of this aestheticizing tendency is in George
Stevens' *Shane,* where the legend of the West is virtually reduced to its
essentials and then fixed in the dreamy clarity of a fairy tale. There
never was so broad and bare and lovely a landscape as Stevens puts
before us, or so unimaginably comfortless a "town" as the little group
of buildings on the prairie to which the settlers must come for their
supplies and to buy a drink. The mere physical progress of the film,
following the style of *A Place in the Sun,* is so deliberately graceful
that everything seems to be happening at the bottom of a clear lake.
The hero (Alan Ladd) is hardly a man at all, but something like the
Spirit of the West, beautiful in fringed buckskins. He emerges myste-

riously from the plains, breathing sweetness and a melancholy which is no longer simply the Westerner's natural response to experience but has taken on spirituality; and when he has accomplished his mission, meeting and destroying in the black figure of Jack Palance a Spirit of Evil just as metaphysical as his own embodiment of virtue, he fades away again into the more distant West, a man whose "day is over," leaving behind the wondering little boy who might have imagined the whole story. The choice of Alan Ladd to play the leading role is alone an indication of this film's tendency. Actors like Gary Cooper or Gregory Peck are in themselves, as material objects, "realistic," seeming to bear in their bodies and their faces mortality, limitation, the knowledge of good and evil. Ladd is a more "aesthetic" object, with some of the "universality" of a piece of sculpture; his special quality is in his physical smoothness and serenity, unworldly and yet not innocent, but suggesting that no experience can really touch him. Stevens has tried to freeze the Western myth once and for all in the immobility of Alan Ladd's countenance. If *Shane* were "right," and fully successful, it might be possible to say there was no point in making any more Western movies; once the hero is apotheosized, variation and development are closed off.

Shane is not "right," but it is still true that the possibilities of fruitful variation in the Western movie are limited. The form can keep its freshness through endless repetitions only because of the special character of the film medium, where the physical difference between one object and another—above all, between one actor and another—is of such enormous importance, serving the function that is served by the variety of language in the perpetuation of literary types. In this sense, the "vocabulary" of films is much larger than that of literature and falls more readily into pleasing and significant arrangements. (That may explain why the middle levels of excellence are more easily reached in the movies than in literary forms, and perhaps also why the status of the movies as art is constantly being called into question.) But the advantage of this almost automatic particularity belongs to all films alike. Why does the Western movie especially have such a hold on our imagination?

Chiefly, I think, because it offers a serious orientation to the problem of violence such as can be found almost nowhere else in our culture. One of the well-known peculiarities of modern civilized opinion is its refusal to acknowledge the value of violence. This refusal is a virtue, but like many virtues it involves a certain willful blindness and it encourages hypocrisy. We train ourselves to be shocked or bored by cultural images of violence, and our very concept of heroism tends to be a passive one: we are less drawn to the brave young men who kill large numbers of our enemies than to the heroic prisoners who endure torture without capitulating. In art, though we may still be able to understand and participate in the values of the *Iliad,* a modern writer like Ernest Hemingway we find somewhat embarrassing; there is no doubt that he stirs us, but we cannot help recognizing also that he is a little childish. And in the criticism of popular culture, where the educated observer is usually under the illusion that he has nothing at stake, the presence of images of violence is often assumed to be in itself a sufficient ground for condemnation.

These attitudes, however, have not reduced the element of violence in our culture but, if anything, have helped to free it from moral control by letting it take on the aura of "emancipation." The celebration of acts of violence is left more and more to the irresponsible: on the higher cultural levels to writers like Céline, and lower down to Mickey Spillane or Horace McCoy, or to the comic books, television, and the movies. The gangster movie, with its numerous variations, belongs to this cultural "underground" which sets forth the attractions of violence in the face of all our higher social attitudes. It is a more "modern" genre than the Western, perhaps even more profound, because it confronts industrial society on its own ground—the city—and because, like much of our advanced art, it gains its effects by a gross insistence on its own narrow logic. But it is anti-social, resting on fantasies of irresponsible freedom. If we are brought finally to acquiesce in the denial of the fantasies, it is only because they have been shown to be dangerous, not because they have given way to a better vision of behavior.[1]

In war movies, to be sure, it is possible to present the uses of violence within a framework of responsibility. But there is the disadvantage that modern war is a co-operative enterprise; its violence is

[1] I am not concerned here with the actual social consequences of gangster movies, though I suspect they could not have been so pernicious as they were thought to be. Some of the compromises introduced to avoid the supposed bad effects of the old gangster movies may be, if anything, more dangerous, for the sadistic violence that once belonged only to the gangster is now commonly enlisted on the side of the law and thus goes undefeated, allowing us (if we wish) to find in the movies a sort of "confirmation" of our fantasies.

largely impersonal, and heroism belongs to the group more than to the individual. The hero of a war movie is most often simply a leader, and his superiority is likely to be expressed in a denial of the heroic: you are not supposed to be brave, you are supposed to get the job done and stay alive (this too, of course, is a kind of heroic posture, but a new— and "practical"—one). At its best, the war movie may represent a more civilized point of view than the Western, and if it were not continually marred by ideological sentimentality we might hope to find it developing into a higher form of drama. But it cannot supply the values we seek in the Western.

Those values are in the image of a single man who wears a gun on his thigh. The gun tells us that he lives in a world of violence, and even that he "believes in violence." But the drama is one of self-restraint: the moment of violence must come in its own time and according to its special laws, or else it is valueless. There is little cruelty in Western movies, and little sentimentality; our eyes are not focused on the sufferings of the defeated but on the deportment of the hero. Really, it is not violence at all which is the "point" of the Western movie, but a certain image of man, a style, which expresses itself most clearly in violence. Watch a child with his toy guns and you will see: what most interests him is not (as we so much fear) the fantasy of hurting others, but to work out how a man might look when he shoots or is shot. A hero is one who looks like a hero.

Whatever the limitations of such an idea in experience, it has always been valid in art, and has a special validity in an art where appearances are everything. The Western hero is necessarily an archaic figure; we do not really believe in him and would not have him step out of his rigidly conventionalized background. But his archaicism does not take away from his power; on the contrary, it adds to it by keeping him just a little beyond the reach of common sense and of absolutized emotion, the two usual impulses of our art. And he has, after all, his own kind of relevance. He is there to remind us of the possibility of style in an age which has put on itself the burden of pretending that style has no meaning, and, in the midst of our anxieties over the problem of violence, to suggest that even in killing or being killed we are not freed from the necessity of establishing satisfactory modes of behavior. Above all, the movies in which the Westerner plays out his role preserve for us the pleasure of a complete and self-contained drama —and one which still effortlessly crosses the boundaries which divide our culture—in a time when other, more consciously serious art forms are increasingly complex, uncertain, and ill-defined.

22. The Guilty Vicarage

W. H. AUDEN

W. H. Auden (1907–   ) approaches the detective story as one who has spent the larger part of his life reading in it. His understanding of its function and meaning is influenced not only by Aristotle (who, we are reminded, in writing about Greek tragedy was dealing with the "popular art" of his day) but by his own religious notions, derived in part from Kierkegaard. Auden is, of course, known chiefly as a poet, as one of the leading poets of the English-speaking world; but he is also a critic of real acuteness and remarkable originality.

A Confession

For me, as for many others, the reading of detective stories is an addiction like tobacco or alcohol. The symptoms of this are: Firstly, the intensity of the craving—if I have any work to do, I must be careful not to get hold of a detective story for, once I begin one, I cannot work or sleep till I have finished it. Secondly, its specificity—the story must conform to certain formulas (I find it very difficult, for example, to read one that is not set in rural England). And, thirdly, its immediacy. I forget the story as soon as I have finished it, and have no wish to read it again. If, as sometimes happens, I start reading one and find after a few pages that I have read it before, I cannot go on.

Such reactions convince me that, in my case at least, detective stories have nothing to do with works of art. It is possible, however, that an analysis of the detective story, i.e., of the kind of detective story I enjoy, may throw light, not only on its magical function, but also, by contrast, on the function of art.

SOURCE: *Harper's Magazine* (May, 1948), pp. 406–11. Reprinted by permission of Curtis Brown, Ltd.

Definition

The vulgar definition, "a Whodunit," is correct. The basic formula is this: a murder occurs; many are suspected; all but one suspect, who is the murderer, are eliminated; the murderer is arrested or dies.

This definition excludes:

(1) studies of murderers whose guilt is known, e.g., *Malice Afore-thought*. There are borderline cases in which the murderer is known and there are no false suspects, but the proof is lacking, e.g., many of the stories of Freeman Wills Crofts. Most of these are permissible.

(2) thrillers, spy stories, stories of master crooks, etc., when the identification of the criminal is subordinate to the defeat of his criminal designs.

The interest in the thriller is the ethical and eristic conflict between good and evil, between Us and Them. The interest in the study of a murderer is the observation, by the innocent many, of the sufferings of the guilty one. The interest in the detective story is the dialectic of innocence and guilt.

As in the Aristotelian description of tragedy, there is Concealment (the innocent seem guilty and the guilty seem innocent) and Manifestation (the real guilt is brought to consciousness). There is also peripeteia, in this case not a reversal of fortune but a double reversal from apparent guilt to innocence and from apparent innocence to guilt. The formula may be diagrammed as on page 235.

In Greek tragedy the audience knows the truth; the actors do not, but discover or bring to pass the inevitable. In modern, e.g., Elizabethan, tragedy the audience knows neither less nor more than the most knowing of the actors. In the detective story the audience does not know the truth at all; one of the actors—the murderer—does; and the detective, of his own free will, discovers and reveals what the murderer, of his own free will, tries to conceal.

Greek tragedy and the detective story have one characteristic in common, in which they both differ from modern tragedy, namely, the characters are not changed in or by their actions: in Greek tragedy because their actions are fated, in the detective story because the decisive event, the murder, has already occurred. Time and space therefore are simply the when and where of revealing either what has to happen or what has actually happened. In consequence, the detective story prob-

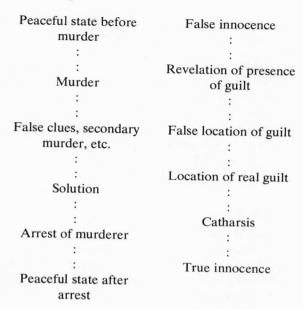

ably should, and usually does, obey the classical unities, whereas modern tragedy in which the characters develop with time can only do so by a technical tour de force; and the thriller, like the picaresque novel, even demands frequent changes of time and place.

Why Murder?

There are three classes of crime: (A) offenses against God and one's neighbor or neighbors; (B) offenses against God and society; (C) offenses against God. (All crimes, of course, are offenses against oneself.)

Murder is a member and the only member of Class B. The character common to all crimes in Class A is that it is possible, at least theoretically, either that restitution can be made to the injured party (e.g., stolen goods can be returned), or that the injured party can forgive the criminal (e.g., in the case of rape). Consequently, society as a whole is only indirectly involved; directly, its representatives (the police, etc.) act in the interests of the injured party.

Murder is unique in that it abolishes the party it injures, so that so-

ciety has to take the place of the victim and on his behalf demand restitution or grant forgiveness; it is the one crime in which society has a
direct interest.

Many detective stories begin with a death that appears to be suicide
and is later discovered to have been murder. Suicide is a crime belonging to Class C in which neither the criminal's neighbors nor society has
any interest, direct or indirect. As long as a death is believed to be suicide, even private curiosity is improper; as soon as it is proved to be
murder, public inquiry becomes a duty.

The detective story has five elements—the milieu, the victim, the
murderer, the suspects, the detectives.

The Milieu (Human)

The detective story requires:

(1) A closed society so that the possibility of an outside murderer
(and hence of the society being totally innocent) is excluded; and a
closely related society so that all its members are potentially suspect
(*cf.* the thriller, which requires an open society in which any stranger
may be a friend or enemy in disguise).

Such conditions are met by: (a) the group of blood relatives (the
Christmas dinner in the country house); (b) the closely knit geographical group (the old world village); (c) the occupational group (the theatrical company); (d) the group isolated by the neutral place (the Pullman car).

In this last type the concealment-manifestation formula applies not
only to the murder but also the relations between the members of the
group who first appear to be strangers to each other, but are later
found to be related.

(2) It must appear to be an innocent society in a state of grace, i.e.,
a society where there is no need of the law, no contradiction between
the aesthetic individual and the ethical universal, and where murder,
therefore, is the unheard-of act which precipitates a crisis (for it reveals that some member has fallen and is no longer in a state of grace).
The law becomes a reality and for a time all must live in its shadow, till
the fallen one is identified. With his arrest, innocence is restored, and
the law retires forever.

The characters in a detective story should, therefore, be eccentric
(aesthetically interesting individuals) and good (instinctively ethical)

—good, that is, either in appearance, later shown to be false, or in reality, first concealed by an appearance of bad.

It is a sound instinct that has made so many detective-story writers choose a college as a setting. The ruling passion of the ideal professor is the pursuit of knowledge for its own sake so that he is related to other human beings only indirectly through their common relation to the truth; and those passions, like lust and avarice and envy, which relate individuals directly and may lead to murder are, in his case, ideally excluded. If a murder occurs in a college, therefore, it is a sign that some colleague is not only a bad man but also a bad professor. Further, as the basic premise of academic life is that truth is universal and to be shared with all, the *gnosis* of a concrete crime and the *gnosis* of abstract ideas nicely parallel and parody each other.

(The even more ideal contradiction of a murder in a monastery is excluded by the fact that monks go regularly to confession and, while the murderer might well not confess his crime, the suspects who are innocent of murder but guilty of lesser sins cannot be supposed to conceal them without making the monastery absurd. Incidentally, is it an accident that the detective story has flourished most in predominantly Protestant countries?)

The detective-story writer is also wise to choose a society with an elaborate ritual and to describe this in detail. A ritual is a sign of harmony between the aesthetic and the ethical in which body and mind, individual will and general laws, are not in conflict. The murderer uses his knowledge of the ritual to commit the crime and can be caught only by someone who acquires an equal or superior familiarity with it.

The Milieu (Natural)

In the detective story, as in its mirror image, the Quest for the Grail, maps (the ritual of space) and timetables (the ritual of time) are desirable. Nature should reflect its human inhabitants, i.e., it should be the Great Good Place; for the more Eden-like it is, the greater the contradiction of murder. The country is preferable to the town, a well-to-do neighborhood (but not too well-to-do—or there will be a suspicion of ill-gotten gains) better than a slum. The corpse must shock not only because it is a corpse but also because, even for a corpse, it is shockingly out of place, as when a dog makes a mess on a drawing room carpet.

Mr. Raymond Chandler has written that he intends to take the body out of the vicarage garden and give murder back to those who are good at it. If he wishes to write detective stories, i.e., stories where the reader's principal interest is to learn who did it, he could not be more mistaken; for in a society of professional criminals, the only possible motives for desiring to identify the murderer are blackmail or revenge, which both apply to individuals, not to the group as a whole, and can equally well inspire murder. Actually, whatever he may say, I think Mr. Chandler is interested in writing, not detective stories, but serious studies of a criminal milieu, the Great Wrong Place, and his powerful but extremely depressing books should be read and judged, not as escape literature, but as works of art.

The Victim

The victim has to try to satisfy two contradictory requirements. He has to involve everyone in suspicion, which requires that he be a bad character; and he has to make everyone feel guilty, which requires that he be a good character. He cannot be a criminal because he could then be dealt with by the law and murder would be unnecessary. (Blackmail is the only exception.) The more general the temptation to murder he arouses, the better; e.g., the desire for freedom is a better motive than money alone or sex alone. On the whole, the best victim is the negative Father or Mother Image.

If there is more than one murder, the subsequent victims should be more innocent than the initial victim, i.e., the murderer should start with a real grievance and, as a consequence of righting it by illegitimate means, be forced to murder against his will where he has no grievance but his own guilt.

The Murderer

Murder is negative creation, and every murderer is therefore the rebel who claims the right to be omnipotent. His pathos is his refusal to suffer. The problem for the writer is to conceal his demonic pride from the other characters and from the reader, since, if a person has this pride, it tends to appear in everything he says and does. To surprise the reader when the identity of the murderer is revealed, yet at the same time to convince him that everything he has previously been told about the murderer is consistent with his being a murderer, is the test of a good detective story.

As to the murderer's end, of the three alternatives—execution, suicide, and madness—the first is preferable; for if he commits suicide he refuses to repent, and if he goes mad he cannot repent, but if he does not repent society cannot forgive. Execution on the other hand, is the act of atonement, by which the murderer is forgiven by society.

(*A suggestion for Mr. Chandler:* Among a group of efficient professional killers who murder for strictly professional reasons, there is one to whom, like Leopold and Loeb, murder is an *acte gratuite*. Presently murders begin to occur which have not been commissioned. The group is morally outraged and bewildered; it has to call in the police to detect the amateur murderer and rescue the professionals from a mutual suspicion which threatens to disrupt their organization and to injure their capacity to murder.)

The Suspects

The detective-story society is a society consisting of apparently innocent individuals, i.e., their aesthetic interest as individuals does not conflict with their ethical obligations to the universal. The murder is the act of disruption by which innocence is lost, and the individual and the law become opposed to each other. In the case of the murderer this opposition is completely real (till he is arrested and consents to be punished); in the case of the suspects it is mostly apparent.

But in order for the appearance to exist, there must be some element of reality; e.g., it is unsatisfactory if the suspicion is caused by chance or the murderer's malice alone. The suspects must be guilty of something, because, now that the aesthetic and the ethical are in opposition, if they are completely innocent (obedient to the ethical) they lose their aesthetic interest and the reader will ignore them.

For suspects, the principal causes of guilt are:

(1) the wish or even the intention to murder;

(2) crimes of Class A or vices of Class C (e.g., illicit amours) which the suspect is afraid or ashamed to reveal (see *Why Murder?*);

(3) a *hubris* of intellect which tries to solve the crime itself and despises the official police (assertion of the supremacy of the aesthetic

over the ethical). If great enough, this *hubris* leads to its subject getting murdered;

(4) a *hubris* of innocence which refuses to co-operate with the investigation;

(5) a lack of faith in another loved suspect, which leads its subject to hide or confuse clues.

The Detective

Completely satisfactory detectives are extremely rare. Indeed, I only know of three: Sherlock Holmes (Conan Doyle), Inspector French (Freeman Wills Crofts), and Father Brown (Chesterton).

The job of the detective is to restore the state of grace in which the aesthetic and the ethical are as one. Since the murderer who caused their disjunction is the aesthetically defiant individual, his opponent, the detective, must be either the official representative of the ethical or the exceptional individual who is himself in a state of grace. If he is the former, he is a professional; if he is the latter, he is an amateur. In either case, the detective must be the total stranger who cannot possibly be involved in the crime; this excludes the local police and should, I think, exclude the detective who is a friend of one of the suspects. The professional detective has the advantage that, since he is not an individual but a representative of the ethical, he does not need a motive for investigating the crime; but for the same reason he has the disadvantage of being unable to overlook the minor ethical violations of the suspects, and therefore it is harder for him to gain their confidence.

Most amateur detectives, on the other hand, are failures either because they are priggish supermen, like Lord Peter Wimsey and Philo Vance, who have no motive for being detectives except caprice, or because, like the detectives of the hard-boiled school, they are motivated by avarice or ambition and might just as well be murderers.

The amateur detective genius may have weaknesses to give him aesthetic interest, but they must not be of a kind which outrage ethics. The most satisfactory weaknesses are the solitary oral vices of eating and drinking or childish boasting. In his sexual life, the detective must be either celibate or happily married.

Between the amateur detective and the professional policeman stands the criminal lawyer whose *telos* is, not to discover who is guilty, but to prove that his client is innocent. His ethical justification is that human law is ethically imperfect, i.e., not an absolute manifestation of the universal and divine, and subject to chance aesthetic limitations, e.g., the intelligence or stupidity of individual policemen and juries (in consequence of which an innocent man may sometimes be judged guilty).

To correct this imperfection, the decision is arrived at through an aesthetic combat, i.e., the intellectual gifts of the defense versus those of the prosecution, just as in earlier days doubtful cases were solved by physical combat between the accused and the accuser.

The lawyer-detective (e.g., Joshua Clunk) is never quite satisfactory, therefore, because his interest in the truth or in all the innocent is subordinate to his interest in his client, whom he cannot desert, even if he should really be the guilty party, without ceasing to be a lawyer.

Sherlock Holmes

Holmes is the exceptional individual who is in a state of grace because he is a genius in whom scientific curiosity is raised to the status of a heroic passion. He is erudite but his knowledge is absolutely specialized (e.g., his ignorance of the Copernican system); he is in all matters outside his field as helpless as a child (e.g., his untidiness), and he pays the price for his scientific detachment (his neglect of feeling) by being the victim of melancholia which attacks him whenever he is unoccupied with a case (e.g., his violin playing and cocaine taking).

His motive for being a detective is, positively, a love of the neutral truth (he has no interest in the feelings of the guilty or the innocent), and, negatively, a need to escape from his own feelings of melancholy. His attitude toward people and his technique of observation and deduction are those of the chemist or physicist. If he chooses human beings rather than inanimate matter as his material, it is because investigating the inanimate is unheroically easy since it cannot tell lies, which human beings can and do, so that in dealing with them, observation must be twice as sharp and logic twice as rigorous.

Inspector French

His class and culture are the natural ones for a Scotland Yard inspector. (The old Oxonian Inspector is insufferable.) His motive is love of duty. Holmes detects for his own sake and shows the maximum indifference to all feelings except a negative fear of his own. French detects for the sake of the innocent members of society, and is indifferent only to his own feelings and those of the murderer. (He would much rather stay at home with his wife.) He is exceptional only in his exceptional love of duty which makes him take exceptional pains; he does only what all could do as well if they had the same patient industry (his checking of alibis for tiny flaws which careless hurry had missed). He outwits the murderer, partly because the latter is not quite so painstaking as he, and partly because the murderer must act alone, while he has the help of all the innocent people in the world who are doing their duty (e.g., the postmen, railway clerks, milkmen, etc., who become, accidentally, witnesses to the truth).

Father Brown

Like Holmes, an amateur; yet, like French, not an individual genius. His activities as a detective are an incidental part of his activities as a priest who cares for souls. His prime motive is compassion, of which the guilty are in greater need than the innocent, and he investigates murders, not for his own sake, nor even for the sake of the innocent, but for the sake of the murderer who can save his soul if he will confess and repent. He solves his cases, not by approaching them objectively like a scientist or a policeman, but by subjectively imagining himself to be the murderer, a process which is good not only for the murderer but for Father Brown himself because, as he says, "it gives a man his remorse beforehand."

Holmes and French can only help the murderer as teachers, i.e., they can teach him that murder will out and does not pay. More they cannot do since neither is tempted to murder; Holmes is too gifted, French too well trained in the habit of virtue. Father Brown can go further and help the murderer as an example, i.e., as a man who is also tempted to murder, but is able by faith to resist temptation.

The Reader

The most curious fact about the detective story is that it makes its greatest appeal precisely to those classes of people who are most immune to other forms of daydream literature. The typical detective story addict is a doctor or clergyman or scientist or artist, i.e., a fairly successful professional man with intellectual interests and well-read in his own field, who could never stomach the *Saturday Evening Post* or *True Confessions* or movie magazines or comics. If I ask myself why I cannot enjoy stories about strong silent men and lovely girls who make love in a beautiful landscape and come into millions of dollars, I cannot answer that I have no phantasies of being handsome and loved and rich, because of course I have (though my life is, perhaps, sufficiently fortunate to make me less envious in a naive way than some). No, I can only say that I am too conscious of the absurdity and evil of such wishes to enjoy seeing them reflected in print.

I can, to some degree, resist yielding to these or similar desires which tempt me, but I cannot prevent myself from having them to resist; and it is the fact that I have them which makes me feel guilty, so that instead of dreaming about indulging my desires, I dream about the removal of the guilt which I feel at their existence. This I still do, and must do, because guilt is a subjective feeling where any further step is only a reduplication—feeling guilty about my guilt. I suspect that the typical reader of detective stories is, like myself, a person who suffers from a sense of sin. From the point of view of ethics, desires and acts are good or bad, and I must choose the good and reject the bad, but the *I* which makes this choice is ethically neutral; it only becomes good or bad in its choice. To have a sense of sin means to feel guilty at there being an ethical choice to make, a guilt which, however "good" I may become, remains unchanged. As St. Paul says: "Except I had known the law, I had not known sin."

It is sometimes said that detective stories are read by respectable law-abiding citizens in order to gratify in phantasy the violent or murderous wishes they dare not, or are ashamed to, translate into action. This may be true for the reader of thrillers (which I rarely enjoy), but it is quite false for the reader of detective stories. On the contrary, the magical satisfaction the latter provide (which makes them escape literature not works of art) is the illusion of being dissociated from the murderer.

The magic formula is an innocence which is discovered to contain guilt; then a suspicion of being the guilty one; and finally a real innocence from which the guilty other has been expelled, a cure effected, not by me or my neighbors, but by the miraculous intervention of a genius from outside who removes guilt by giving knowledge of guilt.

(The detective story subscribes, in fact, to the Socratic daydream: "Sin is ignorance.")

If one thinks of a work of art which deals with murder, *Crime and Punishment* for example, its effect on the reader is to compel an identification with the murderer which he would prefer not to recognize. The identification of phantasy is always an attempt to avoid one's own suffering: the identification of art is a compelled sharing in the suffering of another. Kafka's *The Trial* is another instructive example of the difference between a work of art and the detective story. In the latter it is certain that a crime has been committed and, temporarily, uncertain to whom the guilt should be attached; as soon as this is known, the innocence of everyone else is certain. (Should it turn out that after all no crime has been committed, then all would be innocent.) In *The Trial,* on the other hand, it is the guilt that is certain and the crime that is uncertain; the aim of the hero's investigation is, not to prove his innocence (which would be impossible for he knows he is guilty), but to discover what, if anything, he has done to make himself guilty. K, the hero, is, in fact, a portrait of the kind of person who reads detective stories for escape.

The phantasy, then, which the detective story addict indulges is the phantasy of being restored to the Garden of Eden, to a state of innocence, where he may know love as love and not as the law. The driving force behind this daydream is the feeling of guilt, the cause of which is unknown to the dreamer. The phantasy of escape is the same, whether one explains the guilt in Christian, Freudian, or any other terms. One's way of trying to face the reality, on the other hand, will, of course, depend very much on one's creed.

23. *From* The Other Victorians

Steven Marcus

Steven Marcus (1928–   ), a professor of English literature at Columbia University who wrote earlier on Dickens, has recently published an impressive book on pornography in the nineteenth century, *The Other Victorians* (1966), the conclusion of which appears below.

Pornotopia

There is a passage in one of Max Weber's great essays on the methodology of the social sciences which is pertinent to our discussion. In it Weber is struggling to define with absolute rigor and clarity his difficult notion of the "ideal type." He is trying to demonstrate that this notion or analytical construct "has no connection at all with *value-judgments*," and that further "it has nothing to do with any type of perfection other than a purely *logical* one." To illustrate the distinction he has in mind, Weber states that "there are ideal types of brothels as well as of religions"; and he goes on to say that there are even "ideal types of those kinds of brothels which are technically 'expedient' from the point of view of police ethics as well as those of which the exact opposite" holds true. The writer or scholar who undertakes to discuss pornography has in effect made a contract to construct an ideal type of a brothel—and he has in addition contracted to maintain the distinctions that Weber established. This is not a simple task, as Weber himself was quick to recognize. On the one hand, he states, we must guard ourselves against such "crude misunderstandings . . . as the opinion that cultural significance should be attributed only to *valuable* phenomena. Prostitution is a *cultural* phenomenon just as much as religion or money." At the same time, and on the other hand, he continues, prostitution, religion, and money "are cultural phenomena *only* be-

SOURCE: Steven Marcus, *The Other Victorians* (New York: Basic Books, Inc., 1966), ch. 7, pp. 266–86. Copyright © 1964, 1965, 1966 by Steven Marcus, Basic Books, Inc., Publishers, New York. Reprinted by permission.

cause and *only* insofar as their existence and the form which they historically assume touch directly or indirectly on our cultural *interests* and arouse our striving for knowledge concerning problems brought into focus by the evaluative ideas which give *significance* to the fragment of reality analyzed by those concepts." Weber's strained and circling syntax attests to the difficulty of keeping these two fields of discourse distinct. Our interests and our values inevitably dictate our choice of subjects—the significance we attribute to any fragment of reality that we subject to analysis has its point of origin and reference in a realm external to the analysis itself. Nevertheless, in the course of analysis we must dissociate ourselves, as much as possible, from those very values that informed our choice of a subject to begin with. This is not altogether possible, in practice if not in logic—although I believe it to be logically impossible as well. Which is to say that in the social sciences, as much as in literary criticism, the problem of judgment remains central, unyielding, and full of impossible demands. That these demands are impossible in no way rules out the necessity that they be fulfilled.

Our difficulties seem to be further compounded if we examine another part of Weber's long definition-discussion of this heuristic idea or device. An ideal type, Weber remarks, is not "an average" of anything. It is formed rather by "the one-sided *accentuation* of one or more points of view and by the synthesis of a great many diffuse, discrete, more or less present and occasionally absent *concrete individual* phenomena, which are arranged according to those one-sidedly emphasized viewpoints into a unified *analytical* construct." In substance, he states, "this construct is like a *utopia* which has been arrived at by the analytical accentuation of certain elements of reality." And he goes on to add that "in its conceptual purity, this mental construct cannot be found empirically anywhere in reality. It is a *utopia.*" The writer who tries to take the next step beyond the analysis of specific works of a pornographic character, who extends his discussion in order to reach some synthetic or theoretical conclusions, is compelled to deal with utopia on two fronts. In summing up, sorting, and ordering the material he has already dealt with, he is employing the logical method of the ideal type—by abstraction, accentuation, suppression, emphasis, and rearrangement, he attains to a hypothetical or utopian conception of the material which earlier he had analytically dispersed. At the same time, however, in the instance of pornography that material itself inclines to take the form of a utopia. The literary genre that pornographic fantasies—particularly when they appear in the shape of pornographic fiction—tend most to resemble is the utopian fantasy. For our present purposes I call this fantasy pornotopia.

What is pornotopia?

Where, in the first place, does it exist? Or where, alternatively, does it take place? The word "utopia," of course, means "not place," or "not a place," or "no place." More than most utopias, pornography takes the injunction of its etymology literally—it may be said largely to exist at no place, and to take place in nowhere. The isolated castle on an inaccessible mountain top, the secluded country estate, set in the middle of a large park and surrounded by insurmountable walls, the mysterious town house in London or Paris, the carefully furnished and elaborately equipped set of apartments to be found in any city at all, the deserted cove at the seaside, or the solitary cottage atop the cliffs, the inside of a brothel rented for a day, a week, or a month, or the inside of a hotel room rented for a night—these are all the same place and are identically located. These places may be found in books; they may be read about in libraries or in studies; but their true existence is not the world, or even the world as it exists by special reference in literature. They truly exist behind our eyes, within our heads. To read a work of pornographic fiction is to rehearse the ineffably familiar; to locate that fantasy anywhere apart from the infinite, barren, yet plastic space that exists within our skulls is to deflect it from one of its chief purposes. A representative nineteenth-century novel begins, "In the town of X———, on a warm summer's day . . ." By the time we have finished with such a novel we have learned an astonishing number of things about that town and its weather, about its inhabitants, their families, how they go about making their livings, what their opinions may be upon a variety of topics, what they like and dislike, how they were born and how they die, what they leave behind and what they set up in store for the future. A representative pornographic novel may also begin with the town of X———and a summer's day, but it does not proceed from that point, as the novel does, by elaboration and extension. What typically happens is that after having presented the reader with some dozen concrete details—by way of a down payment on credibility, one assumes—the novel then leaves this deposit of particularities behind and proceeds by means of abstraction to its real business, which is after all largely irrelevant to considerations of place. In the century of national literatures, pornography produced a body of writing that was truly international in character. It is often impossible to tell whether a pornographic work of fiction is a translation or an original—one need only change the names, or the spelling of the names, of characters in order to conceal such a novel's origin. The *genius loci* of pornography speaks in the *lingua franca* of sex. One need not inquire very far to find sufficient reasons for pornography's indifference to place: in the kind of boundless, featureless freedom that most pornographic fantasies require for their action, such details are regarded as restrictions, limitations, distractions, or encumbrances.

Utopias commonly have some special relation to time, and pornotopia is no exception to this rule. Some utopias are set in a distant past, some are located in a distant future; almost all seem to be implicitly conceived as taking place at some special juncture in time, where time as we know it and some other kind of time intersect. Although utopias are often furnished with novel means of measuring and counting time —such as new kinds of clocks or calendars—it is sound to say that most of them are outside of time. So is pornotopia, although the special ways in which it represents its exemption need to be specified. To the question "What time is it in pornotopia?" one is tempted to answer, "It is always bedtime," for that is in a literal sense true. Sometimes a work of pornography, following the example of the novel, will establish an equivalence between time and the duration of a single life-span or personal history. In pornography, however, life or existence in time does not begin with birth; it begins with one's first sexual impulse or experience, and one is said to be born in pornotopia only after one has experienced his first erection or witnessed his first primal scene. Similarly, one is declared dead when, through either age or accident, one becomes impotent—which helps to explain why in pornotopia women are immortal, and why in pornographic novels there are so many old women, witches, and hags, and so few old men. In another sense, time in pornotopia is without duration; when the past is recalled, it is for the single purpose of arousing us in the present. And the effort of pornography in this regard is to achieve in consciousness the condition of the unconscious mind—a condition in which all things exist in a total, simultaneous present. Time, then, in pornotopia is sexual time; and its real unit of measurement is an internal one—the time it takes either for a sexual act to be represented or for an autoerotic act to be completed. (These last two distinctions depend upon whether one chooses to emphasize the author's or the reader's sense of time—in a considerable number of instances the two seem to coincide.)

On a larger scale, time in pornotopia is determined by the time it takes to run out a series of combinations. Given a limited number of variables—that is, persons of both sexes with their corresponding organs and appendages—and a limited number of juxtapositions into which these variables may be placed, time becomes a mathematical function and may be defined as however long it takes to represent or exhaust the predetermined number of units to be combined. This is why *The One Hundred and Twenty Days of Sodom* represents one kind of perfection in this genre. Pornography's mad genius, the Marquis de Sade, with psychotic rigidity and precision, and with psychotic logic, wrote his novel along strict arithmetical lines: so many of this and so many of these and those, doing this, that, and those to them in the following order or declension; to be succeeded on the following day, after all have changed hands or places by . . . et cetera, et cetera. Although it is commonly believed that Sade did not finish this novel, since large parts of it exist only in outline, such a conclusion is not acceptable. Having completed his outline, Sade had in effect written his novel—the rest is only filling in. The truth of this suggestion may be demonstrated by a reading of the novel: I can for myself find no essential difference between the filled-in parts and those that exist only in outline. Form and content are perfectly fused in the outline, and the filling-in or writing-out is largely a matter of adornment—a circumstance that both anticipates and points to certain distinctions which have to be made in considering pornography's relation to literature. It also serves to suggest that a pornographic novel might be written by a computer. If one feeds in the variables out will come the combinations. I have no doubt that one day this kind of literature will be produced, and I must confess to a sense of relief when I recognize that I will not be around to read it.

So much for the coordinates of space and time. We next may turn to the actual external world as it appears in pornotopia. How, for example, is nature represented? It is represented as follows. It is usually seen at eye-level. In the middle distance there looms a large irregular shape. On the horizon swell two immense snowy white hillocks; these are capped by great, pink, and as it were prehensile peaks or tips—as if the rosy-fingered dawn itself were playing just behind them. The landscape then undulates gently down to a broad, smooth, swelling plain, its soft rolling curves broken only in the lower center by a small volcanic crater or omphalos. Farther down, the scene narrows and changes in perspective. Off to the right and left jut two smooth snowy ridges. Between them, at their point of juncture, is a dark wood—we are now at the middle of our journey. This dark wood—sometimes it is called a thicket—is triangular in shape. It is also like a cedarn cover, and in its midst is a dark romantic chasm. In this chasm the wonders of nature abound. From its top there depends a large, pink stalactite, which changes shape, size, and color in accord with the movement of the tides below and within. Within the chasm—which is roughly pear-shaped—there are caverns measureless to man, grottoes, hermits' caves, underground streams—a whole internal and subterranean landscape. The climate is warm but wet. Thunderstorms are frequent in this region, as are tremors and quakings of the earth. The walls of the cavern often heave and contract in rhythmic violence, and when they do the salty streams that run through it double their flow. The whole place is dark yet visible. This is the center of the earth and the home of man.

The essential imagination of nature in pornotopia, then, is this immense, supine, female form. Sometimes this figure is represented in other positions and from other perspectives; sometimes other orifices are chosen for central emphasis. Whichever way it is regarded, however, this gigantic female shape is the principal external natural object in the world we are describing. Although I have in part composed this catalogue of features with a humorous intention, I should add that every image in it is taken from a work of pornography, and that all of these images are commonplaces—they really are the means through which writers of pornography conceive of the world. As for man in this setting he is really not part of nature. In the first place, he is actually not man. He is an enormous erect penis, to which there happens to be attached a human figure. Second, this organ is not a natural but a supernatural object. It is creator and destroyer, the source of all and the end of all being—it is literally omnipotent, and plays the role in pornotopia that gods and deities play elsewhere. It is the object of worship; and the nature that we have just finished describing exists—as does the universe in certain cosmogonies—for the sole purpose of confirming the existence of its creator. Finally, we should take notice of the gigantic size of these figures. This is not simply another aspect of their godlike characters; it suggests to us as well in what age of life the imagination of pornography has its grounds.

As for external nature as we ordinarily perceive it, that exists in pornotopia in an incidental yet interesting way. If a tree or a bush is represented as existing, the one purpose of its existence is as a place to copulate under or behind. If there is a stream, then the purpose of that stream is as a place in which to bathe before copulating. If a rainstorm comes up, then the purpose of that rainstorm is to drive one indoors in order to copulate. (When D. H. Lawrence dragged in a rainstorm in order to drive his lovers out of doors, he was doing something that no rightminded pornographer would ever dream of.) Nature, in other words, has no separate existence in pornotopia; it is not external to us, or "out there." There is no "out there" in pornography, which serves to indicate to us again in what phase of our mental existence this kind of thinking has its origins.

These attributes of nature in pornotopia are in turn connected with others, which have to do with the richness and inexhaustibility of life in this imaginary world—pornotopia is a pornocopia as well. Pornotopia is literally a world of grace abounding to the chief of sinners. All men in it are always and infinitely potent; all women fecundate with lust and flow inexhaustibly with sap or juice or both. Everyone is always ready for anything, and everyone is infinitely generous with his substance. It is always summertime in pornotopia, and it is a summertime of the emotions as well—no one is ever jealous, possessive, or really angry. All our aggressions are perfectly fused with our sexuality, and the only rage is the rage of lust, a happy fury indeed. Yet behind these representations of physiological abundance and sexual plenitude one senses an anxiety that points in the opposite direction. Pornotopia could in fact only have been imagined by persons who have suffered extreme deprivation, and I do not by this mean sexual deprivation in the genital sense alone. One gets the distinct impression, after reading a good deal of this literature, that it could only have been written by men who at some point in their lives had been starved. The insatiability depicted in it seems to me to be literal insatiability, and the orgies endlessly represented are the visions of permanently hungry men. The Marquis de Sade once again took the matter to its logical conclusion; when his orgies include the eating of excrement, and then finally move on to murder with the purpose of cannibalism, he was bringing to explicit statement the direction taken by almost all works of pornography. Inside of every pornographer there is an infant screaming for the breast from which he has been torn. Pornography represents an endless and infinitely repeated effort to recapture that breast, and the bliss it offered, as it often represents as well a revenge against the world—and the women in it—in which such cosmic injustice could occur.

Relations between human beings also take on a special appearance in pornotopia. It is in fact something of a misnomer to call these representations "relations between human beings." They are rather juxtapositions of human bodies, parts of bodies, limbs, and organs; they are depictions of positions and events, diagrammatic schema for sexual ballets—actually they are more like football plays than dances; they are at any rate as complicated as either. As an example of how such relations are represented, I will quote some passages from *The Romance of Lust*. This novel was published during the 1870's. It is in four volumes and runs to six hundred pages, every one of which is devoted to nothing other than the description of persons in sexual congress. This novel comes as close as anything I know to being a pure pornotopia in the sense that almost every human consideration apart from sexuality is excluded from it. The passages I quote were chosen almost at random.

We ran off two bouts in this delicious position, and then with more regulated passions rose to form more general combinations.

The Count had fucked the Egerton while we were engaged above the divine Frankland. Our first pose was suggested by the Egerton, who had been as yet less fucked than any. She had been also greatly taken with the glories of the Frankland's superb body, and especially struck with her extraordinary clitoris, and had taken the curious lech of wishing to have it in her bottomhole while riding St. George on my big prick. We all laughed at her odd choice, but agreed at once, especially the Frankland, whose greatest lech was to fuck very fair young women with her long and capable clitoris. A fairer creature than the lovely Egerton could not be found. The Frankland admitted that in her innermost heart she had longed thus to have the Egerton from the moment she had first seen her, and her delight and surprise at finding the dear Egerton had equally desired to possess her, fired her fierce lust with increased desire. I lay down, the Egerton straddled over, and feeling the delight of my huge prick when completely imbedded, she spent profusely with only two rebounds. Then sinking on my belly she presented her lovely arse to the lascivious embraces of the salacious Frankland. . . .

The Count next took the Benson in cunt while I blocked the rear aperture, and the Frankland once more enculed the Egerton, who dildoed herself in cunt at the same time; all of us running two courses. We then rose, purified, and refreshed. When our pricks were ready it was the Egerton who took me in front and the Count behind, and the Benson, who had grown lewd on the Frankland's clitoris, was sodomised by her and dildoed by herself. The Egerton still suffered a little in the double stretching, so that we ran but one exquisite bout, enabling us, whose powers began to fail, to be re-excited, and to finish with the double jouissance in the glorious body of the Frankland.

Before proceeding any further, I should like to direct attention to certain qualities in the prose of these passages. First, this prose manages to combine extreme fantasy with absolute cliché—as if the fantasy, however wild and excessive it may seem, had been gone through so many times that it had long since become incapable of being anything other than a weary and hopeless repetition of itself. Second, the whole representation takes place under the order of "regulated passions." That is to say everything in it—the movements and responses of the imaginary persons—is completely controlled, as things are in autoerotic fantasies but as they never are in the relations of human beings, and even, one might add, as they never are in the relations of human beings as these are represented in literature. Third, the relations between the persons in these passages are intricate and mechanical; the juxtaposition of organs and apertures is convoluted yet precise, and it is impossible to know the players without a score-card. In this connection, one should also note the tendency to abolish the distinction between the sexes: clitorises become penises, anuses are common to both sexes, and everyone is everything to everyone else. Yet this everything is confined strictly to the relations of organs, and what is going on may be described as organ grinding.

The Romance of Lust continues, after a short hiatus, as follows:

So to five women we thus had six men, and eventually a very handsome young priest, debauched by the others, joined our party, and we carried on the wildest and most extravagant orgies of every excess the most raging lust could devise. We made chains of pricks in arseholes, the women between with dildoes strapped round their waist, and shoved into the arseholes of the man before them, while his prick was into the arsehole of the woman in his front. . . .

Our second double couplings were, myself in my aunt's cunt, which incest stimulated uncle to a stand, and he took to his wife's arse while her nephew

incestuously fucked her cunt. The Count took to the delicious and most exciting tight cunt of the Dale, while her son shoved his prick into his mother's
arse, to her unspeakable satisfaction. Ellen and the Frankland amused themselves with tribadic extravagances.

This bout was long drawn out, and afforded inexpressible extasies to all
concerned. And after the wild cries and most bawdy oaths that instantly preceded the final extasy, the dead silence and long after enjoyments were drawn
out to a greater length than before. After which we all rose and purified, and
then took refreshments of wine and cake, while discussing our next arrangements of couples. . . .

I then took my aunt's arse while the lecherous Dale was underneath
gamahuching and dildoing her, and by putting the Dale close to the edge of
the bed, the Count stood between her legs, which were thrown over his
shoulders, and thus he fucked her, having taken a lech to fuck her cunt,
which was an exquisite one for fucking; her power of nip being nearly equal
to the Frankland, and only beaten by aunt's extraordinary power in that way.
We thus formed a group of four enchained in love's wildest sports together.

The Frankland was gamahuched by uncle while having Harry's prick in
her arse, Ellen acting postilion to Harry's arse while frigging herself with a
dildo.

The closing bout of the night was the Count into aunt's arse, my prick into
the Frankland's arse, Harry enjoying an old-fashioned fuck with his mother,
and Ellen under aunt to dildo and be gamahuched and dildoed by aunt. We
drew this bout out to an interminable length, and lay for nearly half-an-hour
in the annihilation of the delicious afterjoys. At last we rose, purified, and
then restoring our exhausted frames with champagne, embraced and sought
well earned sleep in our separate chambers.

The relations between persons set forth in such passages are in fact
combinations. They are outlines or blueprints, diagrams of directions
or vectors, and they must be read diagrammatically. They are, in other
words, sets of abstractions. Although the events and organs they refer
to are supposed to be concrete, one may observe how little concrete
detail, how few real particularities, these passages contain. Persons in
them are transformed into literal objects; these objects finally coalesce
into one object—oneself. The transactions represented in this writing
are difficult to follow because so little individuation has gone into
them. In a world whose organization is directed by the omnipotence of
thought, no such discriminations are necessary.

With this relentless circumscription of reality, with its tendency, on
the one hand, to exclude from itself everything that is not sexual and,
on the other, to include everything into itself by sexualizing all of real-

ity, pornography might appear to resemble poetry—at least some power analogous to metaphor appears to be always at work in it. This possibility brings us again to the question of the relation of pornography to literature. The subject is extremely complex, and I do not intend to deal with it systematically. I should like, however, to make a number of elementary distinctions.

Since it is written, printed, and read, and since it largely takes the form of fictional representations of human activities, pornography is of course, in a formal sense, literature. Furthermore, it is impossible to object theoretically to its purposes. There is, on the face of it, nothing illegitimate about a work whose purpose or intention is to arouse its readers sexually. If it is permissible for works of literature to move us to tears, to arouse our passions against injustice, to make us cringe with horror, and to purge us through pity and terror, then it is equally permissible—it lies within the orbit of literature's functions— for works of literature to excite us sexually. Two major works of literature may be adduced which undertake this project—part of the undertaking being, at least to my mind, a conscious intention on the author's part to move his readers sexually. *Madame Bovary* and the final section of *Ulysses* seem to me to have been written with such an intention. They also seem to me to have been successful in that intention. I will go one step further and assert that anyone who reads these works and is not sexually moved or aroused by Emma Bovary or Molly Bloom is not responding properly to literature, is not reading with the fullness and openness and attentiveness that literature demands.

Literature possesses, however, a multitude of intentions, but pornography possesses only one. This singleness of intention helps us to understand how it is that, in regard to pornography, the imponderable question of critical judgment has been solved. Given a work of literature whose unmistakable aim is to arouse its reader, and given a reader whose range of sexual responsiveness is not either altogether inhibited or aberrant, then a work of pornography is successful *per se* insofar as we are aroused by it. Keats's hope for literature in general has been ironically fulfilled: pornography proves itself upon our pulses, and elsewhere. Its success is physical, measurable, quantifiable; in it the common pursuit of true judgment comes to a dead halt. On this side, then, pornography falls into the same category as such simpler forms of literary utterance as propaganda and advertising. Its aim is to move us in the direction of action, and no doubt Plato, in *his* utopia, would have banned it along with poetry—which to his way of thinking exerted its influence in a similar way and toward similar ends. There remains an element of truth in this radical judgment.

Despite all this, we know as well that pornography is not literature. I have, at earlier and separate points in this work, tried to demonstrate how this negative circumstance operates, but it might be useful to bring several of these demonstrations together and quickly repeat and recapitulate them. First, there is the matter of form. Most works of literature have a beginning, a middle, and an end. Most works of pornography do not. A typical piece of pornographic fiction will usually have some kind of crude excuse for a beginning, but, having once begun, it goes on and on and ends nowhere. This impulse or compulsion to repeat, to repeat endlessly, is one of pornography's most striking qualities. A pornographic work of fiction characteristically develops by unremitting repetition and minute mechanical variation—the words that may describe this process are again, again, again, and more, more, more. We also observed that although pornography is obsessed with the idea of pleasure, of infinite pleasure, the idea of gratification, of an end to pleasure (pleasure being here an endless experience of retentiveness, without release) cannot develop. If form in art consists in the arousal in the reader of certain expectations and the fulfillment of those expectations, then in this context too pornography is resistant to form and opposed to art. For fulfillment implies completion, gratification, an end; and it is an end, a conclusion of any kind, that pornography most resists. The ideal pornographic novel, I should repeat, would go on forever; it would have no ending, just as in pornotopia there is ideally no such thing as time.

In terms of language, too, pornography stands in adverse relation to literature. Although a pornographic work of fiction is by necessity written, it might be more accurate to say that language for pornography is a prison from which it is continually trying to escape. At best, language is a bothersome necessity, for its function in pornography is to set going a series of non-verbal images, of fantasies, and if it could achieve this without the mediation of words it would. Such considerations help us to understand certain of the special qualities of pornographic prose. The prose of a typical pornographic novel consists almost entirely of clichés, dead and dying phrases, and stereotypical formulas; it is also heavily adjectival. These phrases and formulas are often interchangeable, and by and large they are interchangeable without any loss of meaning. They tend to function as non-specific abstractions, and can all be filled with the same general content. Nevertheless, to the extent that they become verbally non-referential, they too express the tendency of pornography to move ideally away from language. Inexorably trapped in words, pornography, like certain kinds of contemporary literature, tries desperately to go beneath and behind language; it vainly tries to reach what language cannot directly express but can only point toward, the primary processes of energy upon which our whole subsequent mental life is built. This effort explains in part why pornography is also the repository of the forbidden, tabooed words. The peculiar power of such words has to do with their primitiveness. They have undergone the least evolution, and retain much of their original force. In our minds, such words are minimally verbal; they present themselves to us as acts; they remain extremely close to those unconscious impulses in which they took their origin and that they continue to express. The language of pornography demonstrates to us that the meaning of this phenomenon is to be found somewhere beyond language—yet we have only language to show us where that is.

Even in its use of metaphor, pornography can be seen to differ from literature. Although the language of pornography is highly metaphoric, its metaphors regularly fail to achieve specific verbal value. Metaphor ordinarily fuses or identifies similar characteristics from disparate objects; its apparent aim, both in literature and in speech, is to increase our command over reality—and the objects in it—by magically exercising our command of the language through which reality is identified and mediated. In pornography, however, the intention of language, including metaphor, is unmetaphoric and literal; it seeks to *de-elaborate* the verbal structure and the distinctions upon which it is built, to move back through language to that part of our minds where all metaphors are literal truths, where everything is possible, and where we were all once supreme. Taking their origins in the same matrix of impulses, pornography and literature tend regularly to move off in opposite directions.

The third way in which pornography is opposed to literature has also been mentioned. Literature is largely concerned with the relations of human beings among themselves; it represents how persons live with each other, and imagines their feelings and emotions as they change; it investigates their motives and demonstrates that these are often complex, obscure, and ambiguous. It proceeds by elaboration, the principal means of this elaboration being the imagination of situations of conflict between persons or within a single person. All of these interests are antagonistic to pornography. Pornography is not interested in persons but in organs. Emotions are an embarrassment to it, and motives are distractions. In pornotopia conflicts do not exist; and if by chance a conflict does occur it is instantly dispelled by the waving of a magic sexual wand. Sex in pornography is sex without the emotions—and this we need not discuss any further: D. H. Lawrence has already done the job.[1]

Finally, something should be said about the historical circumstances of pornography. Although the impulses and fantasies with which pornography deals are transhistorical, pornography itself is a historical phenomenon. It has its origins in the seventeenth century,[2] may be said to come into full meaningful existence in the latter part of

[1] That pornography is almost entirely written by men and for men was demonstrated to me by a reading of one or two of the few works of pornographic fiction known definitely to be written by women. In these stories, there is no focus or concentration upon organs; much more attention is paid to the emotions, and there is a good deal of contemplation, conscious reverie, and self-observation.

I should like, at the close of this discussion, to remind the reader once again that pornotopia does not exist and is not anywhere to be found. It is an ideal type, an instrument to be used for comparison and analysis. None of the works that I have discussed—and none that I have ever read—is actually a pornotopia, though several approach that extreme limit. If the theoretical model which I have constructed is an adequate one, then the reader should be helped in making certain discriminations. It should be possible to apply the idea of pornotopia to concrete, existing works, and to determine in what ways and in how far such works are or are not pornographic. I do not at all mean that this device can be a substitute for critical judgment, but that it can act as an aid to judgment and as one more instrument of analysis.

A concrete illustration may prove useful. In the last few years, much has been written about *Fanny Hill*. Almost every article about this book that I have read seems to me to have been—with the best will in the world—mistaken and misguided. *Fanny Hill* is of course a pornographic novel; it contains, however (as does every other work of pornography), a number of nonpornographic elements, qualities, or attributes—it may even contain these to a more substantial degree than other or subsequent pornographic works of fiction. One does not, it must be emphasized, need a device like pornotopia to arrive at such a judgment; but the device may nevertheless be used in the analysis of that novel, in the effort of demonstrating just how it goes about achieving its pornographic purposes, how it may at certain points be deflected from such purposes, or how in fact other purposes may be included within its larger or overall design.

[2] My own researches and those of David Foxon, referred to in the Introduction, agree in this conclusion. I regret that this is not the place to make a demonstration of these findings, but I refer the reader to Mr. Foxon's essays.

the eighteenth, persists, develops, and flourishes throughout the nineteenth century, and continues on in our own. To ask what caused such a phenomenon to occur is to ask a stupendous question, since the causes of it seem to be inseparable from those vast social processes which brought about the modern world. A few matters may, however, be briefly referred to. The growth of pornography is inseparable from and dependent upon the growth of the novel. Those social forces which acted to contribute to the rise of the novel—and to the growth of its audience—acted analogously in contributing to the development of pornography. Like the novel, pornography is connected with the growth of cities—with an urban society—and with an audience of literate readers rather than listeners or spectators. These considerations are in turn involved with the development of new kinds of experience, in particular with the development of private experience—sociologists call the process "privatization." If the novel is both evidence of and a response to the needs created by the possibilities of increased privacy and private experience, then pornography is a mad parody of the same situation. No experience of reading is more private, more solitary in every possible way.

As an urban, capitalist, industrial, and middle-class world was being created, the sexual character of European society underwent significant modifications. The sexual character or roles attributed to both men and women changed; sexual manners and habits altered; indeed the whole style of sexual life was considerably modified. Among the principal tendencies in this process was a steadily increasing pressure to split sexuality off from the rest of life. By a variety of social means which correspond to the psychological processes of isolation, distancing, denial, and even repression, a separate and insulated sphere in which sexuality was to be confined was brought into existence. Yet even as sexuality was isolated, it continued to develop and change—that is to say, human consciousness of sexuality continued to change and to increase. Indeed that isolation was both the precondition of and the vehicle through which such a development occurred. The growth of pornography was one of the results of these processes —as, in another context, was the development of modern romantic love. Pornography and the history of pornography allow us to see how, on one of its sides, and under the special conditions of isolation and separation, sexuality came to be thought of in European society from the end of the seventeenth to the end of the nineteenth century.

Matters came to a head during the middle and latter decades of the nineteenth century. During that period, pornographic writings were produced and published in unprecedented volume—it became in fact a minor industry. The view of human sexuality as it was represented in the subculture of pornography and the view of sexuality held by the official culture were reversals, mirror images, negative analogues of one another. For every warning against masturbation issued by the official voice of culture, another work of pornography was published; for every cautionary statement against the harmful effects of sexual excess uttered by medical men, pornography represented copulation *in excelsis,* endless orgies, infinite daisy chains of inexhaustibility; for every assertion about the delicacy and frigidity of respectable women made by the official culture, pornography represented legions of maenads, universes of palpitating females; for every effort made by the official culture to minimize the importance of sexuality, pornography cried out—or whispered—that it was the only thing in the world of any importance at all. It is essential for us to notice the similarities even more than the differences between these two groups of attitudes or cultures. In both the same set of anxieties are at work; in both the same obsessive ideas can be made out; and in both sexuality is conceived of at precisely the same degree of consciousness. It was a situation of unbearable contradiction. And it was at this point that the breaking through began.

This breaking through was made in three areas. First and most important was the invention or discovery of modern psychology, most centrally of course in the work of Freud. For the first time in human history it became possible to discuss sexuality in a neutral way; for the first time a diction and a set of analytic concepts or instruments were established through which men could achieve sufficient intellectual distance from their own sexual beliefs and behavior so as to be able to begin to understand them. And it may even be added that for the first time human sexuality achieved a meaning, using the word "meaning" in the sense put to it by philosophy and the social sciences. The work of retrieving human sexuality had begun, but what would be retrieved was in the nature of the case a different thing than what had earlier been set apart.

The second breaking through took place at about the same time. In the work of the great late nineteenth-century and early twentieth-century avant-garde artists, and in particular among the novelists, the entire fabric of modern society came in for attack. The focus of their assault was the sexual life of the bourgeois or middle classes, as those classes and the style of life they conducted had come to be the prevailing social powers. The difficulties, agonies, contradictions, double-dealings, hypocrisies, inequities, guilts, and confusions of the sexual life of the middle classes were for these novelists not only bad in themselves; they were symbolic of general circumstances of injustice, unpleasantness, demoralization, and malaise which for these artists characterized the world they inhabited. They endorsed a freer sexual life as a good in itself; and they depicted the sexual anguish of modern persons and the sexual hypocrisies and contradictions of modern society not merely for the sake of exposure and sensationalism (although there was that too), but in order to outrage and awaken the society which had imposed upon itself such hideous conditions of servitude. Society being what it is, they were often punished for their efforts, but the work of awakening had been furthered, the work of bringing back into the central discourse of civilization that sexual life upon which it is built and through which it is perpetuated.

The third breaking through followed upon the other two, and is still happening. I refer to the general liberalization of sexual life and of social attitudes toward sexuality that is taking place in our time. It seems likely that what we are witnessing today will be as important, momentous, and enduring as that other revolution in sensibility, manners, and attitudes which occurred in England during the latter part of the eighteenth and first part of the nineteenth century. One of the more interesting recent developments in this social drama is that pornography itself is now being openly and legally published. We need not inquire into the motives of those who publish and republish such works —and I feel constrained to add that I would indeed be troubled if I came across my small son studiously conning *Justine*. Nevertheless, this development was inevitable and necessary, and on the whole, so far as we are able to see, benign. It suggests to me, moreover, that we are coming to the end of an era. We are coming to the end of the era in which pornography had a historical meaning and even a historical function. The free publication of all the old pornographic chestnuts does not necessarily indicate to me moral laxness, or fatigue, or deterioration on the part of society. It suggests rather that pornography has lost its old danger, its old power—negative social sanctions and outlawry being always the most reliable indicators of how much a so-

ciety is frightened of anything, how deeply it fears its power, how subversive to its settled order it conceives an idea, or work, or act to be.
(What will happen to sexuality itself if this goes on long enough is a
matter upon which I hesitate to speculate.) As I have said, the impulses and fantasies of pornography are trans-historical—they will
always be with us, they will always exist. Pornography is, after all,
nothing more than a representation of the fantasies of infantile sexual
life, as these fantasies are edited and reorganized in the masturbatory
daydreams of adolescence. Every man who grows up must pass
through such a phase in his existence, and I can see no reason for supposing that our society, in the history of its own life, should not have to
pass through such a phase as well.

24. Pornography, Masturbation, and the Novel

TAYLOR STOEHR

Taylor Stoehr (1931–), author of *Dickens, The Dreamer's Stance*
(1965), teaches at the State University of New York at Buffalo, where
he helped organize a radically new program in Freshman English. He
is presently working on the popular literature of the mid-nineteenth
century in England and America, including works of popular science
and pseudo-science; and it is his knowledge of these that he draws on
for his criticism of Steven Marcus's discussion of pornography in that
period.

At an early point in his "study of sexuality and pornography in mid-
nineteenth-century England" (*The Other Victorians,* Basic Books,
1966) Steven Marcus announces that "psychology is the one mortal
enemy of pornography." After Marcus has had his say and is drawing
conclusions in his final chapter, among them that "we are coming to
the end of the era in which pornography had a historical meaning and

SOURCE: Taylor Stoehr, "Pornography, Masturbation, and the Novel," *Salmagundi* (Fall 1967-Winter 1968), 28–56. Reprinted by permission of the author
and *Salmagundi.*

even a historical function," the reader is constrained to agree, that for Marcus at least, "pornography has lost its old danger, its old power," and that psychology, or one school of psychology, is responsible for this loss.

Although he never says it in so many words, Marcus obviously dislikes pornography. One can sympathize to a certain extent, for the vaults of the "Kinsey" Institute for Sex Research in Bloomington are hardly the ideal surroundings, nor is the job of reading through thousands and thousands of pages the proper mode of enjoying dirty books. Still, it seems something to account for, that Marcus does not quote a single licentious passage for the pure sake of prurience. . . . There is a bit of sniggering, sometimes (but not often) infectious: "This passage teaches us that masturbation was unquestionably at the bottom of all Uriah Heep's troubles," or "In short, he represents Europe as seen through the eye of a penis," or "It is all rather like 'The Solitary Reaper' written in a sewer." But of simple bawdy pleasure, there is none.

The puzzled reader who, with some embarrassment, nonetheless *likes* his pornography, will do well to study the epigraph to *The Other Victorians,* a passage from Freud which gloomily begins, "However strange it may sound, I think the possibility must be considered that something in the nature of the sexual instinct itself is unfavorable to the achievement of absolute gratification . . . ," and which concludes with grim optimism, "This very incapacity . . . becomes the source, however, of the grandest cultural achievements, which are brought to birth by ever greater sublimation of the components of the sexual instinct. For what motive would induce man to put his sexual energy to other uses if by any disposal of it he could obtain fully satisfying pleasure? He would never let go of this pleasure and would make no further progress."

If psychology has finally killed pornography as Marcus hopes, it is Freud's work. "For the first time in human history it became possible to discuss sexuality in a neutral way; for the first time a diction and a set of analytic concepts or instruments were established through which men could achieve sufficient intellectual distance from their own sexual beliefs and behavior so as to be able to begin to understand them." For Marcus this work is a "retrieving of human sexuality," in part a retrieving of it from pornography. Although "the impulses and fantasies of pornography . . . will always be with us, . . . [it is] after all, nothing more than a representation of the fantasies of infantile sexual life, as these fantasies are edited and reorganized in the masturbatory daydreams of adolescence. Every man who grows up must pass through such a phase in his existence, and I can see no reason for supposing that our society, in the history of its own life, should not have to pass through such a phase as well."

Ignoring the obvious inconsistency in the two views of human nature and history presented here, let me move directly to what Marcus' attitude toward sexuality really comes to, stripped of the ameliorating historical consciousness. Speaking of the "truly and literally childish" character of flagellation literature and behavior, at one point Marcus lets slip the following: "For if it is bad enough that we are all imprisoned within our own sexuality, how much worse, how much sadder must it be to be still further confined within this foreshortened, abridged, and parodically grotesque version of it." He might well have been thinking of pornography instead of flagellation, for such is precisely his sense of the relations between actual and pornographic sexuality: "if it is bad enough . . . , how much worse. . . ."

Here is the emotional (*not* "neutral") framework of *The Other Victorians.* The first two-thirds of the book are devoted to Victorian sexuality (bad enough), the last third to Victorian pornography (much worse). Chapters are devoted to official sexual doctrine, as represented in William Acton's *The Functions and Disorders of the Reproductive Organs,* to Henry Spencer Ashbee's incredibly ambitious bibliography of pornography, and to the anonymous eleven-volume sexual autobiography, *My Secret Life* (since brought out in its first public edition by Grove Press). Then there are chapters on pornographic fiction, on flagellation literature, and finally on "pornotopia," that is, the genre (if it is a genre) as genre.

In thus dividing up his book, and distinguishing Victorian sexuality from Victorian pornography, Marcus makes special use of two key terms, "authenticity" and "fantasy." These are indices of value for him, the former signifying plus, the latter minus. The term "inauthentic" is not used, nor is this a phenomenological vocabulary, whatever the title of the book might lead one to expect. Authenticity is what rings true for Marcus, whatever he feels one can trust as accurate to the Victorian facts of life—not, be it emphasized, as *they* understood them, but as Marcus and presumably his reader understand them. Fantasy, contrariwise, is whatever does not ring true, whatever cannot be trusted as more than an obsessive symptom of sexual disorder, interesting only in that light. As it turns out in this scheme, pornography is never authentic (when it seems so, it transcends itself), while other accounts of Victorian lust, as *The Functions and Disorders of the Reproductive Organs* or *My Secret Life,* may sometimes be authentic, though they too are primarily fantasy.

Since authenticity is good and fantasy bad, it follows that pornography is absolutely never "Literature," although it is sometimes "literature" as in "the vast literature of flagellation," and usually fiction. In pornography, according to Marcus, "whenever there is a choice to be made, the pornographic convention or mode [that is, fantasy] triumphs over the literary, and triumphs over its reality and reality itself." No doubt whenever the same choice presents itself in literature, reality triumphs.

Clearly, with distinctions and definitions like these, we are not going to learn very much about authenticity and fantasy, pornography and literature, beyond what we already stubbornly know. Marcus begins by saying that he will "use the word 'pornography' as the general descriptive term for most of the material discussed," but he is soon speaking of it as a "genre." Positive criteria for inclusion as "material discussed" seem, in the preface, to boil down to covert or illegal publication, and as soon as the term shifts from "descriptive" to denotative function, a negative criterion begins to operate, excluding works whose publication was contested or otherwise scandalous because of obscenity or licentiousness IF they happen to be what Marcus calls Literature. This, of course, is precisely the way the Supreme Court views such matters, with what nicely discriminating consequences for the education of public taste we all know. Thus we hear little or nothing of such variously outrageous books as *The Mill on the Floss, Ruth, The Ordeal of Richard Feverel, Griffith Gaunt, Tess, Lesbia Brandon, Esther Waters.* If there is something interesting to be learned from the difference between pornography and literature, as Marcus has the distinction, one would imagine that the borderline cases which barely make it into print would be of some importance. Instead, we get comparisons of Dickens and *My Secret Life,* and a paragraph on *Ulysses* and *Madame Bovary.*

Assuming that pornography, however we define it, does have interesting relations to literature, perhaps even *is* a form of literature, how shall we go about discovering these? Let me offer as an alternative starting-point the sensible remark of Geoffrey Gorer, from his contribution to *Does Pornography Matter?* (London, 1961): "The object of pornography is hallucination. The reader is meant to identify either with the narrator (the 'I' character) or with the general situation to a sufficient extent to produce at least the physical concomitants of sexual excitement; if the work is successful, it should produce orgasm." Marcus cannot help but know this—though he is long in withholding any explicit statement on it. On page 185 he mentions Genet's "masturbatory fantasies," but he has in mind their genesis, not their goal. On page 204 he finally brings the matter into the open, as if too obvious to merit any special recognition: "Pornography, which is a fantasy, regularly tries to extinguish its awareness of that circumstance, for the most obvious reason—a person engaged in an autoerotic fantasy is not aided in his undertaking if he permits himself consciously to reflect upon his state while he is involved in it." The point Marcus is edging into here is, I think, more crucial than he knows; it is, in fact, the missed opportunity of his book, for much as he recognizes the uses of pornography for masturbation fantasies, he never explores the nature and necessities of pornography from this point of view. He spends most of his time isolating a few characteristic fantasies (all he believes exist) and pointing out how "unliterary" they are. Although it is perfectly clear that the underlying and compelling fear of Victorian sexologists, including those Marcus quotes in the first part of his book, is the fear of masturbation; and although it is equally obvious that the pornographic fantasies which are his main concern in the remaining parts of his book are written primarily for masturbators, by masturbators, and are themselves structurally and functionally very much like masturbation; Marcus is curiously uninterested in this significant relationship between the two divisions of his subject. Indeed, when tantalizing evidence of the large correlations offers itself, it goes begging. Marcus states that pornography "is a historical phenomenon . . . [which] begins to exist *significantly* sometime during the middle of the eighteenth century . . . ," but he makes no attempt to correlate this occurrence with the history of masturbation and attitudes toward it, not always what they were in the nineteenth century. At another point, in one of his rare footnotes, he refers us to E. J. Dingwall's *Male Infibulation* (London, 1925) for an "account of the history of mechanical devices used to prevent masturbation. . . ." If Marcus had more than glanced at Dingwall's book, which he calls "slightly eccentric but preternaturally learned and precise," he would know that it is not about the prevention of masturbation at all, but the prevention of intercourse, especially in the cases of actors and athletes of antiquity. This mistake might not be so bad, were it not for the lost connection to be established between the rise of pornography and the first recorded attempts to prevent masturbation. For although Dingwall does not even include the heading in his index, he devotes a few pages to it, where he draws our attention to the earliest suggestions that infibulation might prevent masturbation, in 1786 to be precise.[1] The date is a lovely coincidence, since that year also saw the publication of John Hunter's *Treatise on the Venereal Disease,* the most reasonable and permissive statement on the masturbation question by an English physician (and a very great one) before the twentieth century, thus fixing some probable limits to the rise of concern and the development of Victorian delusions about masturbation that correspond rather remarkably with the rise of pornography. Moreover, since Marcus himself throws out hints regarding the simultaneous and "inseparable" growth of pornography and of the novel, associating these with "the development of private experience—sociologists call the process 'privatization' "—one would expect some revelations, if not about *Moll Flanders* and *Clarissa,* then about *Henry Esmond* or *Bleak House* or *The Ambassadors* or other nineteenth-century variations in the Richardsonian tradition. Is pornography as Marcus says merely a "parody" of the private experiences which such novels render and foster, or—given the changes in attitudes toward masturbation—are there perhaps deeper structural connections than he is willing to admit, on the model of the masturbator's own experience, including his fear and guilt as well as his secret pleasure?

To answer this question we will have to know more than Marcus tells us about the "official" Victorian attitudes toward sexuality, especially masturbation. . . .

As one reads further, the central interests that begins to emerge as underlying such discussions of the claims of will and desire in sexuality, is a concern which engaged nineteenth-century scientists and pseudoscientists alike, namely the mind/body problem, here especially as it complicated what sexologists had noted as the characteristic

[1] Dingwall mentions S. G. Vogel, *Unterricht für Eltern* . . . (Stendal, 1786), and J. C. Jaeger, *Grundriss der Wund-Arzneylkunst in dem altern Zeiten der Romer* (Frankfurt am M., 1789).

relations between lustful thoughts, including those induced by pornography, and lustful acts, including those performed unconsciously, such as wet dreams, and those performed involuntarily, such
as erections and ejaculations. Acton, "considering these phenomena,"
quotes Carpenter on "the very obscure subject of dreams," and ends
up maintaining that "the modified power of control by the will does, I
believe, almost invariably exist in lascivious dreams." Not only can the
will control thought, but even apparently involuntary physiological
events are somewhat susceptible: "not that, after the orgasm itself has
commenced, the will has much power to check the continuation of the
muscular spasms and the ejaculatory efforts of the vesiculae, though
even over these it has, when honestly exerted, no little control, being
able to shorten as well as prolong the ejaculatory act." "But," Acton
concludes ruefully, "to put an entire stop to it, when once commenced,
is apparently impossible."

In Marcus' analysis, these ideas lead to an "anal-economic" theory
of Victorian sexuality. "The sexual hygiene of continence is unmistakably founded on the idea of bowel control, and the connection of this
with the fantasy of semen as money is self-explanatory. . . . [T]he
youth who has learned to control his sphincter should by the same
token be able to constipate his genitals." . . . But however neatly it
all falls into place at this level of analysis, there is something to be
gained from postponing such simplifications until more of the confused Victorian beliefs about the relations of sexuality to will, imagination (fantasy), desire, and other mental activities (especially
memory) have been sorted out. In particular, one wants to know why
the Victorians were so afraid of masturbation and its fantasies, why
they were so anxious to put the realm of fantasy—in masturbation,
reverie, and even dreams—under the tight discipline of the will.

Of course the Victorians understood well enough the masturbatory
use to which pornographic materials were put; what is curious and
perhaps revealing is the connection they saw between lascivious
thoughts and other kinds. The universal hatred of Rousseau among
our authorities was no accident. Not only did he masturbate and *tell*
about it (if not shamelessly, at least brazenly), but he also *thought*
about it. As Marcus says, "however much Acton is for the consciously
willed direction of life, he is unequivocally against turning it inward."
There is much to follow up in this remark. The habit of prying "into
his mental and moral character with a despicably morbid minuteness,"

of which Acton accuses Rousseau, is just the turn of mind that the masturbator is often assumed to possess, as another expert, D. H. Lawrence, has also affirmed in similar language: "The only positive effect of masturbation is that it seems to release a certain mental energy, in some people. But it is mental energy which manifests itself always in the same way, in a vicious circle of analysis and impotent criticism, or else a vicious circle of false and easy sympathy, sentimentalities." Rousseau himself would have accepted much of this description of his own peculiarities. The "mental energy" Lawrence speaks of is, of course, pornographic energy, the "furtive, sneaking, cunning rubbing of an inflamed spot in the imagination." It is the energy which produced not only classics and junk like *The Memoirs of a Woman of Pleasure,* and *The Amatory Experiences of a Surgeon,* and autobiographies like *My Secret Life* and *The Ups and Downs of Life*—but also works like *Julie, Pamela,* and a thousand other novels, variously adapted versions of the materials that feed more explicitly into *Our Lady of the Flowers.* That is to say, in Marcus' terms, it is the energy that creates fantasy rather than that which labors at authenticity. . . .

. . . . .

According to Marcus, pornographic writing, because it is private and self-indulgent, obsessive, fantasizing, and so on, is not literature. It cannot be authentic, because its auto-erotic aims are necessarily hedged in with secrecy and self-deception. While it may produce orgasm, it is never really moving because the true emotions must depend on an "other," and the pornographer is the solipsist par excellence. Like Emerson, the pornographer aspires to be a "transparent eyeball" (substitute "penis"); he yearns for an impossible transcendence— "totality."

Although pleasure is his presumed object, the pornographer has no conception of true pleasure because "the idea of gratification, of an end to pleasure (pleasure being here an endless expression of retentiveness, without release) cannot develop." But all the items in this catalogue of pornography's "mad-parody" of the novel are, in fact, genuinely applicable to the mainstream of fiction from Rousseau and Richardson to Joyce, Kafka, and Genet. If pressed, Marcus might admit as much, so long as he could save Dickens, George Eliot, and a few other Victorian masters from the tradition. I cannot argue the case here, but it seems to me that all the major novelists since Jane Austen (who tried to make the best of Richardson and Fielding) have been in

the Richardsonian camp; and that, indeed, the novel has defined itself
historically in just the terms Marcus uses to condemn pornography.

. . . . .

There is, I grant, something in . . . preference for fantasy over
reality (or better, characters over people) that makes one uneasy. The
sexual interpretation must be that the masturbator prefers his imaginary partners to any actual ones. The possibility that masturbation
might provide more pleasure than ordinary copulation was familiar to
the Victorians. . . .

. . . . .

Implicit in Rousseau . . . is the recognition that the memories he
most desires to retain and transmit are largely fantasy, not a matter of
dates and facts but of feelings and the structures of human relationship
that both excite and represent feelings. In pornography as in masturbation, the same pattern of memory and fantasy feeds into the solitary
imagination, giving expression to deep and often conflicting emotions.
Even more than Rousseau's visions, the usual pornographic and
masturbatory scenes are extremely schematic, having been imagined
so many times and, in the case of pornography, by so many minds that
most of the nuances have rubbed off.

The obsessive impulse in question here is not that which leads to the
writing of history or historical fiction, but rather that which, in combination with other impulses already identified in Rousseau—secrecy,
self-indulgence, self-absorption, willfulness—issues in confession
literature generally, including all those fictional varieties which have
in common the need to ground their "revelations" in supposed or
actual memories, no matter how bare of remembered or invented detail they turn out to be. The excitement of the imagined is, as the Victorian medical authorities understood, much greater for these authors
and their readers than that of actual encounters with life. Memories
themselves are stimulating not as fragments of a loved certitude that
something has happened, but as gritty, irritating uncertainties about
which the secretions of emotional life build layers of fantasy, like a
pearl. Such memories even lose their identity as memory, and become
the bare and abstract fantasies boringly reiterated in the trashiest pornography.

Memory, screened as Rousseau seems almost to recognize, is crucial in the masturbator's fantasy, whether structured as memoir or as
fiction. Perhaps the memories involved are most deeply those of child-

hood (the typical voyeurism of pornography is no doubt, in Freudian terms, peeking at the primal scene), but in literature the content is rarely so important as the medium or mechanism of imagination. Thus many sorts of content may minister to sexual stimulation—as fetish literature strongly proves. Proust has a classic statement of this emphasis:

But none of the feelings which the joys or misfortunes of a "real" person awaken in us can be awakened except through a mental picture of those joys or misfortunes; and the ingenuity of the first novelist lay in his understanding that, as the picture was the one essential element in the complicated structure of our emotions, so that simplification of it which consisted in the suppression, pure and simple, of "real" people would be a decided improvement. . . .

The novelist has brought us to that state, in which, as in all purely mental states, every emotion is multiplied tenfold, into which his book comes to disturb us as might a dream, but a more lucid, and of a more lasting impression, than those which come to us in sleep.

In the process of "recapturing the past" the sorts of "real" things that give pleasure are not potent until disembodied by their pastness. We should compare the similar preference of Rousseau for the non-physical, and the testimony of Acton et al. on the problem of mind and body. The great paradox of masturbation is the ability of the masturbator to excite himself by non-physical means. . . . Thus the Victorian physicians focus on the nocturnal emission (compare Proust's emphasis on dreams) as the most difficult case needing treatment, where the mind alone produces orgasm. These authorities are also fond of enumerating cases of erection and ejaculation brought on by horseback-riding, walking fast, sitting on hard chairs, and the like. What essentially fascinates them is any case of "involuntary emission," the chief symptom of spermatorrhea. One suspects the real meaning—or at least the best metaphor—for all these concerns is the simplest occurrence in sexual life, the erection. The "involuntary" onset of erection might seem particularly puzzling—even frightening to the childish imagination—because, unlike breathing or other similar physiological events, it is not regular or cyclic. Most important, it is ordinarily accompanied by related mental activity, if not volitional then at least causal. In this subject we have already seen the nineteenth-

century sexologists displaying the keenest interest. The enemies of
masturbation and pornography (including Lawrence and Marcus)
quite rightly realize that the battle must be fought against the imagination (fantasy, the pleasure principle), which must be kept strictly
under the control of the will (authenticity, the reality principle) if it is
to be prevented from giving rise to irrevocable physical acts. Pornographers and masturbators, on the other hand, have as their ideal a fantasy so powerful that it results in orgasm without any "physical" stimulation. Here too the will enters in, but not antagonistically: the ideal is,
in fact, "voluntary emission"—orgasm at will.

    . . . Marcus himself has some instructive ideas on the subject else-
where in his book, though he seems not to make the connection here:
"in [pornography] —as in the mind of a child—no distinction is
made between thought and deed, wish and reality, between what ought
to exist, what one wants to exist, and what does in fact exist. It is a
fantasy whose special preconditioning requirement is that it deny, delay, and stave off for as long as possible the recognition that it is a
fantasy. Recognition dispels the dream of omnipotence and returns
one to oneself, alone and palely loitering on the cold hill's side." It is
hard to understand Marcus' objection to pornography in these terms,
since the attempt to bridge the gap "between thought and deed, wish
and reality, . . . what ought to exist . . . and what does in fact
exist," is quite thoroughly established as the great heroic exploit of the
nineteenth century—the central effort of *Daniel Deronda,* Mill's
Autobiography, Alice in Wonderland, of Melville and Tolstoy, of
Emerson and Kierkegaard and Marx, wherever one looks. It was precisely the formulation of Blake and Wordsworth that the loss of the
child's ability to *not* make the distinction was the disastrous beginning
of the modern world. Many Victorians could go no further than to advise that we learn to live with the disjunction, but our own century's
favorite heroes of the past are those who refused to embrace the simple
"fact and fancy" dichotomy of *Hard Times,* a novel Dickens grew beyond. And in particular it was the novelists who plotted the characteristic nineteenth-century solution, the reuniting of "reality" and "fantasy" in fiction itself.

    None of this is especially newsy, nor is the failure of the nineteenth-
century effort, at least in so far as it has led to the modern predicament, likely to be disputed. The point rather is that the pornographer's
contribution, a certain blend of realism and fantasy, memory and de-

sire, is hardly to be dismissed as irrelevant or un-literary or vicious, on *these* grounds, shared with most of the novelists. Moreover, it is an oversimplification to say that the pornographers do not distinguish "between thought and deed, wish and reality." There are degrees of awareness among writers who work in the tradition of Rousseau, but even the most self-conscious and articulate, like Proust, are not in their methodology so far removed from the stupidest retailers of smut, and none are fooled by their own fantasies, nor do their readers imagine that the things described are actually happening—any more than the author or reader of a recipe is fooled into thinking he is eating when his mouth waters at the thought of it.

Presumably one might establish levels or stages of effect on a reader according to how these effects are apparent in his physical condition: heavy breathing, tears, a lump in the throat, smiles, erection, orgasm. To distinguish simply two classes, mental and physical effects, is to fall into the mind/body problem the Victorians were trying to clamber out of, a mistake which I suspect lies behind Marcus' insistence that pornography is not literature, is indeed anti-literary. "There is, on the face of it, nothing illegitimate about a work whose purpose or intention is to arouse its readers sexually. If it is permissible for works of literature to move us to tears, to arouse our passions against injustice, to make us cringe with horror, and to purge us through pity and terror, then it is equally permissible—it lies within the orbit of literature's functions—for works of literature to arouse us sexually." This is Marcus' most generous concession, and he makes it to save *Ulysses* and *Madame Bovary* as literature; but he immediately qualifies: "Literature possesses, however, a multitude of intentions, but pornography possesses only one." What these other intentions are, Marcus is not here obliged to say, but one gathers that, at their "most literary," they are chiefly mental effects, while "pornography falls into the same category as such simpler forms of literary utterance as propaganda and advertising. Its aim is to move us in the direction of action." In fact, as any reader of pornography knows, there are many combinations of purposes to be found in the dirtiest books, even if we limit criteria to the uses they are put to by readers. Moreover, these same readers often use "Literature" for similar purposes. And finally, even limiting the case to those purposes we might think of as sexual, there is still a wide range of effects, from the low level, "soft-core" pornography of the sensibility school (as Paul Krassner says, it "gives you a soft-on"), to the sexualized reverie of Rousseau, the self-conscious and self-indulgent sublimation of Proust, or the anti-sexual sexuality of, say, Kafka and Genet—not to mention the concomitant result, orgasm, which may or may not occur in any of these varieties.

According to Marcus, who does not recognize any of these varieties or degrees, the literary genre to which pornography is most akin is "the utopian fantasy." His catalogue of the paradigmatic features of "pornotopia" includes elements that do indeed appear in some utopian fiction—the isolated setting (castles, islands, etc.), the animated landscape (as in dreams, a body-image, here invariably female), the "abstract" nature of the relations between the characters (and their sexual organs), the "compulsion to repeat," the impatience with the limitations of language, in general the "projective" characteristics of all fantasy—but we do not get a dynamically conceived account of the genre, an analysis of how the parts are necessary to each other and to the whole. To be fair to Marcus' insight we should say that, although pornographic fiction is not like all utopian fantasy, it does share with it the status of sub-genre, both being varieties of the gothic novel.

． ． ． ． ．

The gothic novel has an episodic structure, and as in pornography, the episodes are repetitive. This combination of episode and repetition produces (or represents), in the gothic, an ambivalence toward history: events repeat themselves in succeeding generations, thus undercutting ideas of duration, sequence, temporal cause and effect. The typical formula is the family curse, which is worked out over long periods of time as if in a single moment. Theoretically the novel could continue forever repeating this moment; in fact, the family usually dies out, or is rescued from the curse by the author allowing a symbolic dying-out to occur. In Marcus' example from pornography, *The Lustful Turk,* the symbolic conclusion of the "curse," and the book itself, is the castration of the hero—the end of the generation.

In the most sophisticated cases, the characters must concern themselves with the nature of memory, history, and fate, since these are the terms in which their problem is set. The question of free will plagues either characters or author, generally without resolution. The hero is supposed to be his own victim as well as the victim of his ancestors, and his demons are figments of his imagination "dreamed into" actual existence. In this way, history is "made" by its heroes. Time and space are "inner" and dreamlike, and the plot is not a narrative but a tableau continually re-imagined and re-lived. As in dream, the action is visual, and the meaning hinges on juxtapositions of symbolic content. A characteristic tableau is Oedipal: two men, one with a knife, standing on the threshold of a woman's bedroom, all three related by blood.

Several methods of structural representation are common. The interpolated story provides a convenient way of giving repetition the illusion of progression—as in the "infinite regress" of *Melmoth the Wanderer*. This method is a favorite with pornographers too, as for instance in the recent film "I a Woman." A more revealing technique is the generational chronicle as in Hoffmann, who combines it with the interpolated story (as do Hawthorne and Emily Bronte). In both methods, the heroes of the repeated tableaux nearly always resemble each other, and are frequently doubles. In the generational chronicle, family inheritance accounts for the likeness and also enforces the symbolic point, that the same man (scion) is being afflicted by (is inflicting upon himself) the same recurrent nightmare. Genetically, this is to be explained as the author's own obsession, the characters being projections and fragmentations of the self. Audience reaction would be analyzed similarly.

What is "gained" by this repetition? In some instances it is cathartic, but in the usual case it is merely expressive, a repeated acting-out which does not come to thinking-out. Typically there is a kind of problem posed, but this is a screen for the real intention, namely, to bring repressed matter to the consciousness. The problem is: what would happen next (say, at the threshold of the room)? The answer is usually a given: it is what has already happened, to set the curse going. This throws the answer into the infinite regress. All such "narrative" problems and solutions are a screen, as Kafka discovered, for problems of perception and will (see the climax of *The Castle*, where K falls asleep). For the most sophisticated gothic novelists, the question is not one of what will happen next, but what is real, and what is the author/ hero's responsibility for reality.

One answer to these last questions is implicit in the system of surrogates that the gothic makes use of, different characters standing in for the author/hero in the repeated scenes. Reality, the argument would go, is my dream. It is this wish/fear that the novelist is testing. The very common threat of the "abyss"—a fall into oblivion, as in Poe—seems to be a corollary structure. If the character relaxes his watchfulness, reality will disintegrate. From the genetic point of view, the author must *will* reality (his story) into existence; when he stops exerting his imagination, reality stops too, and then there is nothing. This danger lies behind all gothic terror. Equivalents in pornography are willed sexual play, with the emphasis on control of the foreplay, which may lead either to orgasm (oblivion, courted and feared) or to impotence (symbolically the same loss of power and control). A further twist, in both the gothic and pornography, is the frequent sense that the will is helplessly in the hands of fate (merely the other side of the coin, another symbolic equivalency): thus the awe at the phenomenon of involuntary erection, the fear of loss of control, the ambition of "orgasm at will" (*choosing* oblivion).

In the ordinary novel the end comes when the possibilities of combination given at the beginning have been exhausted. In the gothic, since there is only one possible combination, given in tableau, the end comes only with physical exhaustion pure and simple, or with a leap (as in *The Castle*) outside the realm of the given. In every case, this leap is a *deus ex machina,* since to abandon the given is to admit to being the author, and to refocus attention on what it means to write (imagine, dream). In pornography, the leap is similar, from the world of the projected reality to the author/reader's own body and act of ejaculation. If the end is thus non-literary in one way, it nonetheless says something about literature, a phenomenological comment on the relation of imagination and reality (in Victorian terms, mind and body). This comment is essentially different from that which the endings of other novels suggest, since in most gothic fiction and pornography there is no true plot (only a tableau) and therefore can be no buildup of probabilities for the leap; rather there are continual and equally unsuccessful attempts, suddenly ended by climactic success, through a shift of the attention, a relaxation of the will and watchfulness. The experience of masturbators fantasizing (with or without pornography) is similar. Success is intentional but not part of a predictable sequence. The sequence *is* predictable (repetitive, not really a sequence), but the moment of success (relaxation, orgasm) is not. Of course, in most gothic and pornographic fiction (*as* fiction), the leap never comes at all, or (curiously) is not recognized when it does come. Usually the novel goes on regardless. I confess I do not understand this failure of recognition, but one thing is clear, that the line between fantasy and reality in reading gothic and pornographic fiction is a torn and ragged edge, as compared with the careful knitting-up of loose threads of probability in other genres.

     .   .   .   .   .

Even the realistic convention has as one of its aims *moving* the reader, but the gothic and pornographic modes go further, directly involving the reader less as observer than as participant. To put it another way, the sort of writing Marcus admires as "authentic" is chiefly concerned with *describing,* a matter seemingly of mentioning, naming, referring. Pornography and the gothic—Marcus' "fantasy"—are rather concerned with *creating,* a matter of talking about what does not exist until it *is* talked about (as, for example, Pickwick—a favorite instance of the linguistic philosophers who discuss the subject). Obviously, realistic fiction is, so far as it is fiction at all, also dependent on the creating power of language; the most sophisticated pornographic and gothic fiction, however, tends to shift this power into the center of attention, so that method becomes subject matter. This tendency fits in with the stake these genres have in memory, imagination, and the will. Caught, as they often are, between the referential and the creative theories of language, these authors are struggling toward a synthesis such as that of Proust or Kafka, a kind of "authentic fantasy" to use Marcus' terms.

Before leaving the subject of the relations of pornography and the gothic, I would like to treat one aspect of their conjunction in more detail. I have alluded more than once to the idea or condition of "totality," which Marcus condemns the pornographers for aspiring to. I have also spent a good deal of time discussing the conflict of will and desire as understood by Victorian physicians, and especially as reflected in their belief that lascivious fantasies, waking or dreaming, could be controlled by the will. We have seen how the pornographer similarly attempts to control the imagination by the will, although his ends are quite different—voluntary orgasm rather than continence. Let me now bring these matters together, in order to see what light the theory of the gothic may shed on them.

Victorian authorities on sex point out that masturbation is more exciting (and thus dangerous) than copulation, because the imagination is more powerful a stimulus than the senses themselves. Rousseau and others agree, in their terms, with this priority. It follows, for those who desire the strongest excitement, that even in actual copulation, the imagination and will should be exercised as in masturbation, in the production of fantasy.

Masturbation fantasies are typically visual, and the imagination of pornographers and gothic writers is typically spatial and visual, as the structural principle of the tableau demonstrates. It follows for the case of the "masturbator" who is actually copulating that his greatest pleasures will be voyeuristic—often a matter of adjusting the positions of his partners to his favorite visions. The multiplication of such posturings, by increasing the number of partners, by mirrors, and so on, is also familiar. Masturbating by means of a partner is, then, not simply a matter of having a fantasy, but of regarding an actual, physical and visual, situation as if a fantasy. (Much "normal" sexual intercourse follows this pattern; thus our partners are often more beautiful than familiar, more agitating than soothing; the well-known psychotic extreme is "Romantic Love.")

We have already seen that the power of fantasy largely derives from the attachment of deep feelings to certain "core" memories, as in Rousseau. These memories are the material for the tableaux of the gothic, "family memories," in the form of a curse handed down from generation to generation. Repetition is preferred to novelty in these obsessive fantasies because the emotion attached to the past (structured into the character) does not so much arise from the fantasy as give rise to it. The fantasy expresses the feelings. The reality is brought into existence by the desire for it. Or, to put the matter in terms that confront the Victorian problem of will and imagination, the mind imagines the world necessary to its wishes; and that world then exists.

None of these relations are reciprocal or mutual. They are "one-way," like the infinite regress. In gothic fiction, this is often perceived as fate: how can the hero break the chain of fantasies-growing-into-reality when they arise out of his own deepest wishes (the family curse)? In pornography the equivalent is what Marcus most objects to, the "letch"-ridden hero's return again and again to the "same" keyhole or cunt, the impossibility, as Marcus puts it, of gratification—an end to pleasure. Of course, the point is that there are, in pornography, innumerable ends to pleasure, an infinite series of orgasms. I cannot believe that what Marcus wants is some final orgasm—but then I do not know what else he can mean. In any case, it does seem to me that something of the sort *is* what the pornographer wants—not an end to desire (though perhaps that is implied) but an endless orgasm, the oblivion or loss of self that Freud calls "absolute gratification" and that Marcus calls "totality."

The striving for totality manifests itself in pornography and in gothic fiction in a characteristic way. Given the repetitive structure of these genres, no buildup can grow in the narrative. Yet to achieve totality, each repeated version of the same scene would seem to require some increase of power. Generally this is accomplished by the multiplication (fragmentation) of characters, so that either the descendants of the original hero become more numerous, or if not actually, then symbolically they multiply—in Hoffmann the family breeds in, incestuously, so that each character represents the whole family, while in Hawthorne the ghosts of the dead ancestors hover in the room or the memory. In pornography, familiar bodies from the earlier portions of the novel begin to turn up, or the hero begins to reminisce about old times with new lays. Since the power of the fantasy depends on the accumulation of feelings clinging to a single repeated and remembered scene, the multiplication of characters (each representing an earlier representation of the scene) increases the excitement. In pornographic, gothic, and confessional literature, this multiplication is often symbolically represented by an *affair à trois*—usually two men and a woman, as most commonly in *My Secret Life,* sometimes one man and two women, as in Rousseau's fantasy for *Julie.* The underlying model for such *affaires à trois* is not the triangle,[2] which implies a return of the self and thus a sort of reciprocity (Marcus thinks of the daisy-chain as the appropriate model), but is rather the infinite regress we have recognized as a familiar motif, in which there is no mutual stimulation, only unilateral essentially voyeuristic pleasure. A number of variations occur, but few seem genuinely triangular—mutually pleasurable to all three parties. For example, the author of *My Secret Life* has a particular fondness for intercourse with a woman who has just left another client. Or, frequently in pornography, the narrator describes mounting someone who is mounting someone else. Female narrators, for instance Justine, are often at the other end of the same broken chain, being mounted by two persons at once, an equally unilateral situation from the narrator's point of view.

[2] But compare Rene Girard, *Deceit, Desire, and the Novel,* trans. Yvonne Freccero (Baltimore, 1965).

The symbolic meaning of such an infinite regress is complex. The situation is essentially voyeuristic, as descriptions of such orgies make clear. The excitement comes from watching, either the other or oneself —and this watching is a fantasy, a memory wrapped in sentiment. The other in these cases is representative of *all* the others and thus a convenient means of rendering the central attraction of such fantasy, the accumulation of past feelings and reliving them all at once. This is one reason why pornography generally delays the orgy until late in the book, when there is more to recall. Finally, the fact that the narrator is always at one or the other end (the opposite end is nowhere, hopefully totality) gives the sense of absolute control by the will of the narrator, who typically (as the author of *My Secret Life*) settles the order and duties of those "in line" himself, whose penis is the initial energizing force, all the other organs beating to his time. Sometimes this is thought of as "giving pleasure," but at bottom it is most evidently the desire to control the other, to produce (and watch) an effect, simply to exert the will (with the concomitant fear of relaxing one's watchfulness—that is, orgasm).

Often (perhaps always) the infinite regress scene just described is not only the culminating fantasy of the book (pornography or gothic tale) but also the very fantasy which, in some limited or disguised way lies behind all the previous ones. In gothic fiction that attempts to give the illusion of plot, the action usually amounts to a progressive uncovering of this final scene (for example, at the outset we do not know of what the curse consists, but at the conclusion we discover, in an old manuscript, that it was *this,* and all intermediate scenes have been approximations of it). Furthermore, while the meaning of the scene is rather obviously Oedipal on the surface of it (the threesome equals parents plus child), its deeper meaning seems to me not sexual but metaphysical (or epistemological)—a representation of the relation of self and other. That both pornography and the gothic tradition conceive this relation as unilateral seems not necessarily a failing of those genres (in spite of Marcus' Christian humanist complaints), but rather an indication of the nature of fiction and of the fictive imagination— the subject of the most sophisticated gothic novels. Ultimately gothic and pornographic fictions drive the reader back out of fantasy, however much they may seduce him to it in the meantime, for the effects of terror or orgasm, especially the latter, most obviously take place in the world of everyday reality, unreal and total and absolute as they may seem in that world. That they also take place in private, in the absence of others, is less significant than it may seem—for the orgasm, as other bodily experiences, is always a private experience no matter how its achievement is managed.

The gothic and pornographic writers, in one degree or another, are concerned with the brute fact that man is trapped in his own skin, and the fantasies of these genres explore the possibilities of escaping the prison of the senses, through the agency of the imagination. The failure of the genres is not in their refusal to recognize or allow for the other, but in their inability to reach it (at the opposite end of the infinite regress) despite every effort to believe that they will or do. This failure is given in the nature of the attempt. I would point again to *The Castle*, where K most nearly approaches his goal when he allows himself to recede furthest from it, to give up the striving of the wakeful will. (Compare Aphorism 23: "There is a goal, but no way; what we call the way is only wavering.") This is the "leap" I spoke of earlier, which is the only delivery there is from the infinite regress. It is not something which the hero can accomplish as an exploit, or the author as a tour de force; it is achieved only by "letting up," by an act of faith that the other is there, and need not be proved or attained. (This was the very sensible advice many Victorian physicians gave to victims of impotence.) The pornographer and the gothic novelist attempt to be the voice of God, to say the *logos* that brings the other into being; but the other is the voice of God, which must be listened to, not created. These are not the limits of pornography, but the limits of literature, and of all saying, which cannot call into being an answering voice. Our words make a world, but that world passes with those words. It is willful exercise, dependent on the continual exertion of the mind. It is the nature of writing, to make something of experience, to give it meaning. Books and libraries are man's determined effort to create meaning and hold it in existence, by force of will. One does not find anything but the elaboration of self in this realm—no matter how admirable—humility, love, prayer, notwithstanding. For the rest, it is well to remember that there are possibilities in life quite beyond literature, and not even to be imitated in it. Such literature as we have been discussing so reminds us.

25. *From* Blues People

LE ROI JONES

LeRoi Jones (1934–   ) began as a poet influenced by Charles Olson
and the Black Mountain Poets in general. In recent years he has
moved away from his former associates, as he has become more and
more conscious of his special role as a black man, and more and more
committed to political activism. Whether in such fiction as *The
System of Dante's Hell* (1966), or in plays like *The Dutchman* (1964),
or even in the kind of speculations on jazz which follow, his political
commitment rather than curiosity or scholarship or even pleasure in
the arts determines his accent and tone.

I am trying in this book, by means of analogy and some attention to
historical example, to establish certain general conclusions about a
particular segment of American society.

   This book should be taken as a strictly *theoretical* endeavor. Theoretical, in that none of the questions it poses can be said to have been
answered definitively or for all time, etc. In fact, the book proposes
more questions than it will answer. The only questions it will properly move to answer have, I think, been answered already within the
patterns of American life. We need only give these patterns serious
scrutiny and draw certain permissible conclusions.

   The Negro as slave is one thing. The Negro as American is quite
another. But the *path* the slave took to "citizenship" is what I want to
look at. And I make my analogy through the slave citizen's music —
through the music that is most closely associated with him: blues and a
later, but parallel development, jazz. And it seems to me that if the
Negro represents, or is symbolic of, something in and about the nature

SOURCE: LeRoi Jones, *Blues People: Negro Music in White America* (New York:
William Morrow and Company, Inc., 1963), pp. ix–xii. Copyright © 1963 by
LeRoi Jones. Reprinted by permission of William Morrow and Company, Inc.

of American culture, this certainly should be revealed by his characteristic music.

In other words, I am saying that if the music of the Negro in America, in all its permutations, is subjected to a socio-anthropological as well as musical scrutiny, something about the essential nature of the Negro's existence in this country ought to be revealed, as well as something about the essential nature of this country, *i.e.,* society as a whole.

Blues had, and still has, a certain *weight* in the psyches of its inventors. What I am proposing is that the alteration or repositioning of this weight in those same psyches indicates changes in the Negro that are manifested externally. I am proposing that the weight of the blues for the slave, the completely disenfranchised individual, differs radically from the weight of that same music in the psyches of most contemporary American Negroes. I mean, we know certain definite things about the lives of the Negro slaves. We also, with even more certainty, know things about the lives of the contemporary American Negroes. The one peculiar referent to the drastic change in the Negro from slavery to "citizenship" is his music.

There are definite *stages* in the Negro's transmutation from African to American: or, at least, there are certain very apparent changes in the Negro's reactions to America from the time of his first importation as slave until the present that can, I think, be seen—and again, I insist that these changes are most graphic in his music. I have tried to scrutinize each one of these stages as closely as I could, with a musical as well as a sociological and anthropological emphasis.

If we take 1619, twelve years after the settling of Jamestown in 1607, as the date of the first importation of Negroes into this country to *stay* (not to be merely brought here for a time to do odd jobs, etc., and then be bumped off, as was very often the case), we have a good point in history to move from. First, we know that West Africans, who are the peoples most modern scholarship has cited as contributing almost 85 per cent of the slaves finally brought to the United States, did not sing blues. Undoubtedly, none of the African prisoners broke out into *St. James Infirmary* the minute the first of them was herded off the ship. We also know that the first African slaves, when they worked in those fields, if they sang or shouted at all, sang or shouted in some pure African dialect (either from the parent Bantu or Sudanic, with maybe even the Hamitic as a subbase, which would include Coptic, Berber, or

Cushitic). But there are no records of 12-bar, AAB songs in those languages—at least none that would show a direct interest in social and
agricultural problems in the Southern U.S. (although, it should be
noted here . . . [that] the most salient characteristic of African, or at
least West African, music is a type of song in which there is a leader
and a chorus; the leading lines of the song sung by a single voice, the
leader's, alternating with a refrain sung by the chorus). It is easy
enough to see the definite analogy between a kind of song in which there
is a simple A-B response and a kind of song that could be developed
out of it to be sung by one person, where the first line of the song is
repeated twice (leader), followed by a third line (chorus), sometimes
rhymed but usually dissimilar, and always a direct comment on the
first two lines. And then we know of the patois-type languages and
the other half-African languages that sprang up throughout the
South, which must, after a time, have been what those various
laments, chants, stories, etc., were told and sung in.

But what I am most anxious about here is the American Negro.
When did he emerge? Out of what strange incunabula did the peculiar
heritage and attitudes of the American Negro arise? I suppose it is
technically correct to call any African who was brought here and had
no chance of ever leaving, from that very minute when his residence
and his life had been changed irrevocably, an American Negro. But it
is imperative that we realize that the first slaves did not believe they
would be here forever. Or even if they did, they thought of themselves
as merely *captives*. This, America, was a foreign land. These people
were foreigners, they spoke in a language which was not colonial
American; and the only Western customs or mores of which they had
any idea at all were that every morning at a certain time certain work
had to be done and that they would probably be asked to do it.

And the point I want to make most evident here is that I cite the
beginning of blues as one beginning of American Negroes. Or, let me
say, the reaction and subsequent relation of the Negro's experience in
this country in *his* English is one beginning of the Negro's *conscious*
appearance on the American scene. If you are taken to Mongolia as a
slave and work there seventy-five years and learn twenty words of
Mongolian and live in a small house from which you leave only to
work, I don't think we can call you a Mongolian. It is only when you
begin to accept the idea that you *are* part of that country that you can

be said to be a permanent resident. I mean, that until the time when you have sufficient ideas about this new country to begin making some lasting *moral* generalizations about it—relating your experience, in some lasting form, *in the language* of that country, with whatever subtleties and obliqueness you bring to it—you are merely a transient. There were no formal stories about the Negro's existence in America passed down in any pure African tongue. The stories, myths, moral examples, etc., given in African were *about* Africa. When America became important enough to the African to be passed on, in those *formal* renditions, to the young, those renditions were in some kind of Afro-American language. And finally, when a man looked up in some anonymous field and shouted, "Oh, Ahm tired a dis mess,/Oh, yes, Ahm so tired a dis mess," you can be sure he was an American.

26. The Dance of the Long-Legged Fly:
On Tom Wolfe's Poise

RICHARD HOGGART

Richard Hoggart (1918–   ) is the author of *The Uses of Literacy* (1957), an extremely acute and influential study of English working-class culture in the nineteenth and twentieth centuries; and is presently the Director of the Centre for the Study of Contemporary Culture at the University of Birmingham. He is one of the pioneers in his own country of an approach to literature which puts it in the context of the popular arts and general culture, rather than separating it out for special consideration. Mr. Hoggart functions not only as a professor but also as an adviser and consultant to theater groups, television and radio producers, and, indeed, has come to serve as a sort of unofficial Minister of Culture for the United Kingdom.

SOURCE: Richard Hoggart, *Speaking to Each Other,* a forthcoming collection of Mr. Hoggart's essays to be published by Chatto & Windus, Ltd., London. This essay originally appeared in *Encounter,* August, 1966. Copyright © 1969 by Richard Hoggart. Reprinted by permission of *Encounter* and the author.

Tom Wolfe appeals so widely and powerfully not just because he is fascinated by the phenomena he describes; so are many other reporters of "the contemporary scene." He appeals not simply because he occasionally jumps outside the massive detail and makes a sharp critical remark about it; others are more effectively critical. Nor does he appeal chiefly because he has considerable verbal talent, though that goes a long way towards explaining the immediacy of his attraction and his great "readability." The real cause of his enormous success is his poise.

Almost all the essays in *The Kandy-Kolored Tangerine-Flake Streamline Baby* are in fact about not poise itself but the search for poise today, chiefly among young people. Mr. Wolfe calls it "style" or more often, "form." The kinds of teen-ager he writes about are "absolutely maniacal about form," "serious as always about form." To have realized this is Wolfe's main insight, the thread which holds most of his essays together and gives them their overall energy. It is not, of course, a new insight and others have probed it more.

A paper by Marshall McLuhan, delivered to a conference called *Vision 63* at Southern Illinois University in October 1965, gives a useful pointer. Young people today, says McLuhan, are "data processors" on a large scale. They have to work hard and constantly at (a) processing all the fluid data (offered attitudes and styles) which their technological, electronic, mass-communication, consumers' society throws at them, and (b) matching that against the more ordered, classified, scheduled outlook which the classroom, the older, established environment, offers. So they become bewildered,

baffled because of this extraordinary gap between these two worlds. . . . To grow up is to be absurd [McLuhan is explicitly echoing Paul Goodman here] because we live in two worlds, and neither one of them inclines us to grow up. Our youngsters today are mainly confronted with the problem of just growing up—that is our new work—and it is total. That is why it is not a job; it is a role.

The links in all that are not clear and the meaning of "growing up" is ambiguous. But McLuhan is certainly saying that young people settle, not for ends and purposes (which imply movement out and from), but for balance on the spot, for overall openness and knowingness, for poise. Towards the end of his paper McLuhan quotes a young architect friend speaking about "his generation": "We are not goal-oriented, we just want to know what is going on." McLuhan adds: "The young today reject goals—they want roles—R-O-L-E-S—that is, involvement."

This situation is neither as new nor as total as McLuhan implies. He knows this well enough, though I am not sure that Tom Wolfe does. Still, what McLuhan says there bears directly on both Wolfe's subject-matter and—a different and more important question—on his success. On his subject-matter because, as I have said, he has realised that the search for poise is the impulse behind much in the behaviour of young people in commercial mass-societies, the urge to find a stance before all the free-floating and un-ordered offerings, a stance which accepts without going under; but which rejects the calls of the old, goal-oriented world (the "sclerotic" world of adults, to use one of Wolfe's favourite words), since to do that would involve making choices of value, rejections. It would be inaccurate to call this the wish to stand upright in Emerson's sense or "vertical" in Auden's, since both of those speak from the old world, the world which could talk about the need to immerse in the *"destructive* element"—and that adjective summons up a moral order.

Tom Wolfe's success is ensured because in describing the search for poise, he also exhibits one kind of poise. He says, by all the breathy implications of his confident prose, "Look, it can be done." And in doing so he appeals not just to teen-agers, probably few of whom read him, but to a wider range of people who may not be young but who feel a similar difficulty in making sense of mass society. Wolfe's peculiar hold comes from his apparently sure possession of what looks like a possible stance. He has learned a style for the despair, though the style is often self-deluding and the despair not really faced. But that in itself is part of the point, part of the attraction, part of what is being said.

The assurance, the panache, is the most immediately striking quality. Mr. Wolfe has it partly because he knows his material so well, but also because he knows his readers *don't* know it. Like the Fat Boy he is out to make his readers' flesh creep, with conducted tours to "the teen-age netherworld." And because his readers don't know that world he can get away with murder. Dwight Macdonald has documented the inaccuracy of Wolfe's reportage. This was apropos a description of *The New Yorker*'s editorial methods. One would have had doubts even without Macdonald's circumstantial analysis. Clearly Mr. Wolfe is a painstaking and tireless leech of a reporter. But he sometimes claims to know so much about what goes on inside that he sounds like an omniscient fictional narrator, the invisible man, the fly on the ceiling. Presumably he feels driven to this because everything has to be hep, to be souped up, lest dullness supervene. Look at this small but typical instance: "one has only to list the male stars of the past 20 years [he lists them] . . . and already the mind is overpowered by an awesome montage of swung fists, bent teeth, curled lips, popping neck veins and gurglings." Well—not quite, though one sees the tiny point. Practically every *aperçu* (and some are shrewd) has to be driven home with a vivid metaphor; and often the vividness of the metaphor seems to have counted for more than its truth. Or it is used to inflate the experience. A youth from Lafayette, Indiana, who was bitten with the bug to "customise" cars went off to California where that activity is at its most advanced. ("What you have is something like sculpture in the era of Benvenuto Cellini," says Mr. Wolfe.) Then he came home with his own customised car:

I like to conjecture about his parents. I don't know anything about them, really. All I know is, *I* would have had a hell of a lump in my throat if I had seen Ronny coming up to the front door in his tangerine-flake car, bursting so flush and vertical with triumph that no one would ever think of him as a child of the red sulk—Ronny, all the way back from California with his grail.

Sometimes Wolfe's hectic knowingness becomes a parody even of itself:

O, dear, sweet Harry, with your French gangster-movie bangs, your Ski-Shop turtleneck sweater and your Army-Navy Store blue denim shirt over it, with your Bloomsbury corduroy pants you saw in the *Manchester Guardian* airmail edition and sent away for and your sly intellectual pigeon-toed libido roaming in Greenwich village . . .

We are forced to think that Mr. Wolfe is less fussy about accuracy than about making sure that his prose is always swinging. To complain about this is not niggling and can't be brushed aside by the claim that nevertheless the general "feel" of the descriptions is right. It points to some of the more difficult disciplines in different styles of writing and, since Mr. Wolfe talks a great deal about the strains of "creating art objects," he ought to think about these disciplines more. Documentary has its limits just as fiction has, and can't pinch from fiction without harming both. Mr. Wolfe, one suspects, gives the glossy finish to his pieces by telling more than he could possibly know from his documentary position—and so does violence to his material and his human subjects. His essay on Harrison, the original publisher of *Confidential* (now in the shade) is full of interesting detail. But by some extraordinarily fortunate chance, on the day Mr. Wolfe is interviewing the anxious Harrison in a restaurant, Walter Winchell comes in, is hailed by Harrison and cuts him:

Suddenly Harrison's eyes are fixed on the door. There, by God, in the door is Walter Winchell. Winchell has on his snap-brim police reporter's hat, circa 1924, and an overcoat with the collar turned up. He's scanning the room, like Wild Bill Hickock entering the Crazy Legs Saloon. Harrison gives him a big smile and a huge wave. "There's Walter!" he says.

Winchell gives an abrupt wave with his left hand, keeps his lips set like bowstrings and walks off to the opposite end of Lindy's . . .

By and by Harrison, Reggie and I got up to leave and at the door Harrison says to the maitre d':

"Where's Walter?"

"He left a little while ago," the maitre d' says.

"He was with his granddaughter," Harrison says.

"Oh, was that who that was," the maitre d' says.

"Yeah," says Harrison, "It was his granddaughter. I didn't want to disturb them."

It all comes too pat, like a movie-cliché. It sounds like a betrayal of the relation Tom Wolfe had established with Harrison for the purposes of the interview; it uses him. And for that matter it takes liberties with Winchell.

Still, Mr. Wolfe does know a great deal. He has not only been there; he has looked too. He has noted the curious social rituals of limousine-chauffeurs, waiting for their owners to come out of the opera in New York City; or the ways of New Jersey teen-agers heading for the Manhattan discotheques:

They headed off up Front Street if it was, say, Plainfield, and caught the Somerset Line bus at the stop across the street from the Public Service building around 7.30 p.m. Their bouffant heads would be bouncing up and down like dandelions until the bus hit the Turnpike and those crazy blue lights out there on the toothpaste factories started streaming by. They went through the Lincoln Tunnel, up the spiral ramps into the Port Authority Terminal and disembarked at some platform with an incredible number like 155. One hundred and fifty-five bus platforms; this was New York.

He has listened to the jerky, groping-for-contact, gesturing style of contemporary teen-age talk, the dialogue of "You know . . . sort of . . . like . . . kind of . . . I mean . . ." He has thought a little about the inner meanings of teen-age display. He knows it cannot be explained only in terms of deliberate commercial manipulation but comes from a more complicated interplay. To describe it all he has devised a style which gives his readers the feeling that at last they are really in the thick of it, immersed in it all and yet still riding. He is, to repeat, a talented writer; not only a processor—a clever drawer-upon layers of contemporary curiosities and responses—but occasionally more than that. He can show talent in what he would probably call "the old sclerotic literary sense" of the word. It is on the whole a single-shot, metaphoric talent. He can (and this is only one of many instances) speak about the "secret needle-toothed fury" of a toy poodle and a Yorkshire terrier barking at each other. He can make nicely grotesque juxtapositions, especially about cultural pretensions. The President's wife attends the re-opening of the Museum of Modern Art:

In a few minutes she will address them all, in a drawl that sounds like it came by mail order from Pine Bluff, concerning God, Immortality and Inspiration through Art for the free peoples.

Such gifts being recognised, you still have to separate fairly obvious devices from more symptomatic elements. Recurrent devices include the casual, *in medias res* openings ("One thing that struck my mind, for some reason, was . . ."; "All right, Charlotte, you gorgeous . . ."; "It is a very odd, nice, fey thing . . ."; "Please do not get the idea . . ."); and the saturation-bombing openings ("pastel cars, aqua green, aqua blue, aqua beige, aqua buff, aqua dawn, aqua dusk . . ."; "Hai-ai-ai-ai-ai-ai-ai-ai-ai- . . ."). Then there are strings of "in" phrases like "Whatever became of . . .", and favourite unusual words such as "infarcted" and "epopt." Once he has found a word or verbal device he likes Mr. Wolfe uses it relentlessly—it becomes a trade-mark: the sun "explodes" off windscreens I don't know how many times, and "sclerotic" is always with us.

His style is to quite a large extent a montage of other men's styles. His great catalogues of proper names recall his namesake, Thomas Wolfe. Hemingway has helped with the use of the continuous present, and with "and" used as the link between flat successive clauses. Scott Fitzgerald has taught him something about catching the breathless syncopation of scenes from fashionable life:

Goldie and the Gingerbreads are on a stand at one end of the studio, all electric, electric guitars, electric bass, drums, loudspeakers, and a couple of spotlights exploding off the gold lamé. *Baby baby baby where did our love go.* The music suddenly fills up the room like a giant egg slicer. Sally Kirkland, Jr., a young actress, is out on the studio floor in a leopard print dress with her vast mane flying, doing the frug with Jerry Schatzberg . . .

From Graham Greene he presumably got the three-tier dying fall to end a paragraph ("takes him by the hand and heads for home, the white brick tower, the tacky Louis chaises and the gathering good news"). *Finnegans Wake* makes a small contribution, and there are strong similarities to Aldous Huxley. Huxley likes to penetrate glossy social surfaces by a sudden, brutal anatomical reference. Off with these lendings; back to the poor, bare, forked animal. Wolfe uses this device until it sounds like a trick or tic. The text is scattered with sudden shock references to the ischium and the ilial crest, glutei maximi, trapezii, gemelli, latissimae dorsae. But, to finish with echoes, guess how many you can pick up in this very clever confection. It is Sunday in New York City:

Anne would make scrambled eggs, plain scrambled eggs, but it was a feast. It was incredible. She would bring out a couple of those little smoked fish with golden skin and some smoked oysters that always came in a little can with ornate lettering and royal colours and flourishes and some Kissebrot bread and black cherry preserves, and then the coffee. They had about a million cups of coffee apiece, until the warmth seemed to seep through your whole viscera. And then cigarettes. The cigarettes were like some soothing incense. The radiator was always making a hissing sound and then a clunk. The sun was shining in and the fire escapes and effluvia ducts were just silhouettes out there someplace. George would tear off another slice of Kissebrot and pile on some black cherry preserves and drink some more coffee and have another cigarette, and Anne crossed her legs under the terrycloth bathrobe and crossed her arms and drew on her cigarette, and that was the way it went.

All these echoes have their uses, as short-cuts to the dominant moods. The most revealing is the use of details, of the names of things. Some contemporary English observers like detail too (e.g., Nell Dunn) but it doesn't sound the same. Some English writers have long liked to list particulars and name prices: Virginia Woolf attacked them when she attacked Arnold Bennett. But again it is not the same. I think Virginia Woolf was wrong about Arnold Bennett; for him the poetry was in the particulars. For many Americans—and certainly for Tom Wolfe—the poetry *is* the particulars. The daftest passage in this book is Wolfe's reference to Wordsworth's inventories: "his glorious delicatessen owner's love of minute inventory would overwhelm him." Nothing could be farther from the inner meaning of Wordsworth's naming of the names; but it might do for Tom Wolfe himself.

The American love of detail is different from ours, and goes far back and deep into American experience. It has to do with the continuing sense of the need—the imperative, the challenge—to confront the mass and variety and reality of brute experience; it has to do with the need to make sense of the shapeless, amorphous massiveness of democratic existence; it has to do (as David Lodge also pointed out in writing about Tom Wolfe) with the Redskin/Paleface polarity. For all his cracks about "an ancient, aristocratic aesthetic," Tom Wolfe is substantially a Paleface pretending to be a Redskin, fascinated and slightly appalled at his own daring but always dragged back to the wild, wild scene. Wolfe's exposure to this situation is not quite the same as that of his 19th-century American predecessors. It has a particularly mid-20th-century nervous edge. He dives into the mass, rolls in it, shows he isn't afraid of it, comes up with handfuls, arranges it into sharp, sure little structures. "Murray the K, the D.J. and M.C., O.K.?, comes out from the wings, doing a kind of twist soft shoe, wiggling around, a stocky chap, thirty-eight years old, wearing Italian pants and a Sun Valley snow lodge sweater and a Stingy Brim straw hat. Murray the K! Girls throw balls of paper at him, and as they arc onto the stage, the stage lights explode off them and they look like falling balls of flame."

There is a sort of nervous exhilaration in watching him do it. He is making order out of that "bafflement"; he's dancing above Niagara on a tightrope. And so he speaks to more than American experience today, though probably especially to that. It is essential to get all the names spinning, not to pin them down but so that the reader can feel "involved" in "what's going on," in Marshall McLuhan's phrases. Somehow if you name it you will get a meaning out of it. No: that's the wrong way to put it; somehow, the meaning *is* the thing itself.

Contributing to the total mixture—laced through all the devices, the echoes, the expected big gestures, the naming of the names—is a more personal characteristic which, so far as I know, has not been remarked on before. Wolfe is a very sensual writer, a very sexual writer. Of course, he flogs his inventions to death, here as elsewhere; but you can still tell that a sharp nerve is being stroked. Well may he cry: "Ah, sweet little cigarette-ad. blonde!" He is deeply responsive to the nymphets, the "flaming little buds" as he so often calls them, to the half-exposed globes of their buttocks, their high tight breasts and their "little cupcake bottoms":

Elsewhere, Las Vegas' beautiful little high-school buds in their buttocks-décolletage stretch pants are back on the foam-rubber upholstery of luxury broughams peeling off the entire chick ensemble long enough to establish the highest venereal-disease rate among high-school students anywhere north of the yaws-rotting shanty jungles of the Eighth Parallel.

In getting the right poise this is probably the trickiest element. But a good ambiguous adverb can usually hold the scales between an older man's sexuality and the need to be a sympathetic but detached reporter. A group of girls are waiting to get a famous D.J.'s autograph:

One of them is squeezed into a pair of short shorts that come up to about her ilial crest. Coming down over her left breast she has a row of buttons. The top one says, "We love the Beatles" [and so on down to one button whose motto is only roughly penciled in]. But so what? The letters are big, and her little mary poppins tremble honestly.

That final adverb just, but only just, preserves the poise. But it does so by being intellectually dishonest, through sentimentality.

Yet the most important ingredient in the whole cocktail—if it is to serve its readers in the way they need—is not the fact that Tom Wolfe loves the material. It's that he also hates it. And that he usually manages to hold these two moods in suspension. It is particularly important to be clear here. I am not pointing to the large, self-conscious, critical gestures, the constant use of *OK* intellectual names and notions (Weber, alienation, Apollonian v. Dionysian, symbolic logic). Almost all of this is rubbish, as are the frequent historical vistas ("The

Emperor Commodus . . . the Earl of Chesterfield . . . Phil Spec-
tor"). No more than top dressing; Mr. Wolfe has no real critical distance. His dislike, when it comes out, comes out hard and the boat is
only just saved from capsizing. He can, of course, make routine gestures of rejection in the usual form ("It is as if there were a communal
fear that someone, somewhere in Las Vegas, was going to be left with a
totally vacant minute on his hands"). But he really embodies the rejection when he looks close:

> . . . he was wearing a striped polo shirt with a hip Hollywood solid-color
> collar, and she had on Capri pants, and hooked across their wrinkly old faces
> they both had rimless, wraparound French sun-glasses of the sort young-
> punk heroes in *Nouvelle vague* movies wear, and it was impossible to give
> any earnest contemplation to a word they said. They seemed to have the great
> shiny popeyes of a praying mantis.

He pins Mick Jagger in action with a horrified accuracy:

> . . . this boy has exceptional lips. He has two peculiarly gross and extraor-
> dinary red lips. They hang off his face like giblets. Slowly his eyes pour over
> the flaming bud horde soft as Karo syrup and then close and then the lips
> start spreading into the most languid, most confidential, the wettest, most
> labial, most concupiscent grin imaginable. Nirvana! The buds start shriek-
> ing, pawing towards the stage.

He has an exact eye for nastiness: vicious whores, brutish cab-
drivers. Most of all, he hates and fears the thought of ageing. I gave up
counting the number of contemptuous references to the old or unvirile;
they include "bad hair and reedy faces," "ageing mastoids," "ratty
people with ratty hair and corroded thoracic boxes," "crusty old
arteriosclerotic bastards" . . . all of them "shuffling their shanks."
He may not fully see the skull beneath the skin but he notes and can't
forget that after 40 "the packing under the skin begins to dry up,
wither away." For a 33-year-old this seems a pretty desperate holding-
on to youth; there's still a lot of twilight to get through.

Almost predictably, the strongest reactions are roused against
women once sexually attractive but now ageing. This is more than setting the young against the old, one generation against its predecessor;
it's the old, old elemental retching at the ephemerality of sexual allure,
and nausea at its last gestures. The sexual disgust flares again and
again:

Mrs. Janson fades up the street with her rusting gams and her three Welsh corgies.

Convalescing dowagers taking the rays with lap robes from the old La Salle sedan days over their atrophying shanks.

So gorgeous Charlotte twists around in the chair with her alabaster legs and lamb-chop shanks still crossed and locked together in hard, slippery, glistening skins of nylon and silk . . .

Mr. Wolfe could be a religious recluse at 40. But he might have to fight harder than he has fought so far to save himself from being the pop-purveyor to the New Manichees.

One could go on, isolating the elements which help to make this elaborate balance. Just one more item, and then to move on. The most effective essays (effective in their own terms) are very cunningly structured, and the best is "The Last American Hero," which is about stock-car racing in North Carolina and stock-car culture in general. Souped-up, breathless, detailed, it races along and does seem to get close to the feel of the things it describes. Wolfe weaves into it too a sense of its significance as a symbol of traditional tensions between North and South, as an instance of the collapse of lower-middle-class cultural models, as a contemporary form of Southern States' rhetorical-heroic (echoes of Robert Penn Warren here), and so on. It is all smoothly and energetically done. He has a well-developed sense of when to bring in a new theme, when to alter shutter-opening and speed, when to vary pressure—a well-developed sense, that is, of how to do all these things *so that the poise is maintained.*

So I come back for the last time to the question of poise, to the meaning of this apparent grappling with the swirling phenomena of mass society. In intellectual circles the discussion about the larger issues, in the U.S. and elsewhere, often becomes an argument between the defenders of the old "high culture" and the welcomers of the new. Among contemporary American commentators—though these placings are bound to be too unqualified—you would find, say, Dwight Macdonald and Hannah Arendt on one side and Edward Shils and Patrick Hazard on the other. In Britain you could just as easily and roughly place names on each side.

Where Tom Wolfe and his poise fit in can be made clearer by reference again to the distinction between representative and symptomatic literature. Roughly, symptomatic literature is a symptom of its time, a specimen. Properly regarded, it tells you something about (usually something nasty about) the quality of life in a society. Representative literature examines and explores these conditions and is thus, in a difficult but important sense, outside them. I am not altogether happy with "representative" as the second term. It could appear to mean "representing the state of things" and so seem almost synonymous with "symptomatic." We need a word which suggests "exploratory . . . analytic . . . critical." But probably it is safe to assume that the contrast in meaning between the two terms is sufficiently known.

It would be easy to settle for saying that Tom Wolfe is both representative and symptomatic on the grounds that, though he usually immerses himself in the material, he occasionally floats free. But though his criticisms may sometimes be sharp and brilliant they are, in total effect, local. He never drives them home, never stays with them so long that they hurt. His apparent representativeness is really only an aspect of his symptomatic character. What is at bottom being offered is not a position from without but a poise from within. The most apt epigram—only a little too strong—is in the essay on Harrison of *Confidential*. "Okay, it was bogus. . . . But by God the whole thing had style." Such a poise is not juxtaposition; you do not reach it by being enthusiastic in one paragraph and sombrely critical in the next. It's more subtle than that. You have to keep all doors open, yet never fully go through any one. Acceptance must always keep at the back of the mind the idea of—not the acted fact of—rejection. Rejection must not close any doors—never quite close any doors—on the pleasures of acceptance. The delicate, iridescent film must never be quite broken, though it can be made to bend; that film is, verbally, the play of tone within a narrow range; and, intellectually, the play of perceptions, which may be sharp but not so sharp as to break the skin. We are left feeling that we have never realised how glittering, how interesting in itself, the surface is until that long-legged fly danced on it.

This is why Mr. Wolfe is more symptomatic than representative, though very sophisticatedly symptomatic. His style is the symptom of an important characteristic of modern mass communications. When this period's cultural history comes to be written one chapter ought to have the heading: "It ain't what you do; it's the way that you do it." Mr. Wolfe's medium, his stylistic poise, is more important than his message, his manner more than his matter. His spiritual sister is Baby

Jane Holzer, the subject of one of his essays: "She does not attempt to come on sexy. Her excitement is something else. It is almost pure excitement. It is the excitement of the New Style." We are back once again with Marshall McLuhan, for whom the medium is the message. The way of doing it is the thing being done. Wolfe's book illustrates both the degree of truth in this dictum and the awful shortcomings of the position it describes (shortcomings McLuhan has so far been reluctant to examine).

In Russia the authorities fear that to expose their people to the open, multitudinous play of messages in a "free" consumers' society would be to risk making them dissent (i.e., in search of other goals). So Russian teen-agers are not required to be "data processors" on anything approaching the Western scale. You can see this in the different set of their faces (whether they are accepters or rejectors of the status quo) and in their much less fluid style and gestures. But if Marshall McLuhan is right—and Tom Wolfe's success seems to support him —the Russian authorities are mistaken. The best way to keep their people from seeking alternative goals would be to flood them with "data," to offer them the chance to become anxious only about "form," so that they come to believe that goals are out and poise in. Then they might keep on playing roles endlessly, and harmlessly— with no political effect. But by God they'd have style!

27. The Situation Today

KINGSLEY AMIS

Kingsley Amis (1922–   ) has been a spectacularly successful novelist, with the popular audience throughout his career and with the critics at its beginning, especially just after the publication of his hilarious first novel, *Lucky Jim* (1958). He has always been interested in pop literature, writing the long study of science fiction from which

SOURCE: Kingsley Amis, *New Maps of Hell* (New York: Harcourt, Brace & World, Inc., 1960), pp. 42–63. Copyright © 1960 by Kingsley Amis. Reprinted by permission of Harcourt, Brace & World, Inc.

the following selection comes, in addition to a book on James Bond; and most recently, he has attempted to continue the adventures of 007, after the death of his original author.

The next part of the story, covering the early years of modern science fiction, depends for documentation upon sources difficult of access, for there cannot be many files of forty-year-old magazines outside private hands. The canon at this point tends to resemble those name-dropping catalogues, part acknowledgements, part bibliography, that I seem to remember coming up with some frequency in works of Middle English Literature. However, in April, 1911, a story called "Ralph 124C 41 + : a romance of the year 2660" began to appear serially in a magazine called *Modern Electrics*. The author, a certain Hugo Gernsback, was also founder-editor of the magazine. Gernsback occupies a position in science fiction analogous to that of George Lewis in jazz, or perhaps, to be scholarly, that of Jelly Roll Morton, who likewise is no more than a name to most people, though Gernsback's has been commemorated in the name of the Oscar of the science-fiction world, the trophy known as the Hugo. At any rate, "Ralph 124C 41 + " concerns the technological marvels invented or demonstrated by the ridiculously resourceful eponymous hero, whose plus-sign represents membership of a sort of scientific Order of Merit, and who starts off by burning up from three thousand miles away an avalanche that threatens the heroine in her native Switzerland. After some trouble with a pair of rival suitors, one human, the other Martian, Ralph restores the dead girl to life by a complicated deep-freeze and blood-transfusion technique. Other wonders include the hypnobioscope, a second anticipation of Huxley's hypnopaedia, and three-dimensional colour television, a term which Gernsback is credited, if that is the word, with having invented. Various successors to "Ralph 124" & so on began to appear, chiefly in magazines supposedly devoted to popular-science articles, but it was not until 1926 that Gernsback was able to found the first journal exclusively dedicated to science fiction, *Amazing Stories,* which is still with us. At this time and for some years afterwards, science fiction continued to be overshadowed, as regards bulk and circulation, by work in two adjacent fields.

The more important of these is fantasy, which I tried to differentiate in the previous section. *Weird Tales,* the first magazine of modern fantasy, was founded three years earlier than *Amazing Stories,* and I need do no more than allude to the existence—somewhere in the background—of Algernon Blackwood, Lord Dunsany, and Cabell's *Jurgen.* The most representative writer of the *Weird Tales* school was H. P. Lovecraft, much of whose work is horror fiction of the kind popular in England, at any rate, in the '20's and '30's. Some of Lovecraft's stories, "The Dunwich Horror," for instance, achieve a memorable nastiness; one or two, like "The Rats in the Walls," cross the boundary into the field of the ghost story, or are so anthologised, and a piece called "The Colour out of Space" occasionally finds its way into science-fiction collections, chiefly I imagine on account of its title. Lovecraft's intrinsic importance is small, but he does give that impression of being much more than ripe for psychoanalysis which pervades much fantasy and early science fiction, and the difficulty of categorising some of his work faithfully reflects the confusion of a period when non-realistic writing was in the throes of internal fission.

The other adjacent field competing with science fiction is conveniently described as space-opera, justly recalling the horse-opera which, under a skin of molecular thinness, it so much resembles. In space-opera, Mars takes the place of Arizona with a few physical alterations, the hero totes a blaster instead of a six-gun, bad men are replaced by bad aliens looking just like bad men with green skins and perhaps a perfunctory sixth digit, and Indians turn up in the revised form of what are technically known as bug-eyed monsters, a phrase often abbreviated to BEMs under the psychobiological law that terms frequently used will undergo shortening. Some commentators are opposed to the BEM, and adopt a characteristic self-righteousness in rapping poor Wells over the knuckles for having started the fashion with his Martians. This attitude seems justified if the BEM is a mere surrealist orangutan, rushing off into the Venusian swamp with the heroine in his tentacles, but menace is in itself a legitimate effect, and I have read many a good BEM story. A. E. van Vogt's *Voyage of the Space Beagle,* for instance, moves well for sixty thousand words simply by introducing a succession of BEMs, each nastier than the one before.

Actually, BEMs are not a *sine qua non* of space-opera, and early examples often fill up with stuff lifted from the historical novel, or if you like the parry-and-thrust opera, things like princesses and palace guards and ancient codes of honour. Later space-opera fills up from

the 'tec yarn, with galactic hoodlums, alien dope-runners, etc. The
kind of setup I have been describing is plainly an important ancestor
and collateral of much contemporary fare as seen in comic books and
strips aimed at those of immature age or inclination, and it even
afflicts the occasional story in the serious science-fiction magazines.
Moreover, space-opera with a full complement of BEMs and a small
staff of mad scientists attended by scantily clad daughters constitutes,
I should guess, the main brand-image of science fiction in the minds of
the less *au-courant* trend-hounds, those who haven't yet caught on to
how frightfully significant it all is. To go back in the other direction:
the ancestral figure in the development of space-opera is clearly Rider
Haggard, who in a book like *She* provided elements that needed only
to be shifted to Mars and eked out with a BEM or two to get the whole
new show on the road. Edgar Rice Burroughs performed this very feat
in 1912 with *Under the Moons of Mars,* later republished as *A Princess of Mars,* and in the next quarter of a century or so more than a
dozen successors flowed from his dreadfully fluent pen. The degree of
scientific interest here can be gauged from the way Burroughs shows
his contempt for all interplanetary devices, from waterspouts to gravity insulators: the hero, trapped in a cave by a band of Apaches, simply
finds himself on Mars, and at once enough starts happening in the way
of green men for the more technical questions to be quietly dropped.
Burroughs' most celebrated and profitable creation, Tarzan, is, incidentally, a more complicated person than the continuing spate of films
about him would suggest. Far from being a mere rescuer of lost way-
farers and converser with animals, he meets several adventures stem-
ming even more directly from Rider Haggard, *Tarzan and the Lost
Empire* or *Tarzan and the City of Gold,* for instance, which represent
a kind of terrestrial space-opera,[1] and at least once, in *Tarzan at the
Earth's Core,* we retrace the steps of Verne, though with a less dignified
gait.

[1] This is not a totally unfair label for a whole mode of writing located somewhere
on the borders of science fiction: the tale of the lost race or undiscovered human
tribe. Although most of the less accessible parts of the world have been ransacked
to provide habitation for these isolates—from Atlantis and Mu to Tibet and the
Grand Canyon, from the polar regions to the bowels of the earth—it is rare to
find anything beyond an "adventure" interest emerging. Lord Lytton's *The Coming Race* (1870) and Joseph O'Neill's *Land Under England* (1935), which occur
somewhere near the beginning and end of the period in which the theme was popular, are relatively isolated examples of its use for didactic and admonitory purposes—purposes recognisably characteristic of serious science fiction.

During the 1930's, science fiction established itself, separating with a slowly increasing decisiveness from fantasy and space-opera, advancing in bulk and popularity (most of the time there were at least half a dozen pulps running), but remaining firmly at a humble level of literary endeavour. Some stories leaned heavily on the scientific element, echoing Verne in their reliance on technology, or gadgetry, occasionally far outdoing him both in degree of theoretical complication and in unreadability. For the most part, however, vulgarisations of the early Wells held the field, setting up a pseudo-scientific base for a tale of wonder and terror. I can remember one that fused Lucian with "The Flowering of the Strange Orchid," featuring a plant growth whose upper half was the upper half of a large and fierce young lady. Another introduced a disguised alien leading a supposed mineralogical expedition to a remote underground chamber, where his friends awaited a hasty breakfast of human flesh before setting off to conquer the world. Although disposing of much lethal machinery, they never got their breakfast and expired in a shower of sparks. (I seem to recall that that one was rather well written, though I was only about twelve at the time.) Then there was the one about the scientist, not actually mad, but sternly denounced by his colleagues as irresponsible, who created life in the laboratory. The life was a sort of rubbery jellyfish that engulfed things, not at all unlike the Blob recently on view at our theatres —it was soon frozen into submission with dry-ice extinguishers. This early version was far tougher and at one stage successfully engulfed H.M.S. *Invincible,* on manoeuvres at the time in the North Atlantic. Finally, during its traditional task of attacking Manhattan Island, its creator managed to destroy it at the price of personal engulfment. As far as I know none of these pieces has ever been reprinted, but those of the same period which have show a similar lack of subtlety and an almost incredible ignorance of, or indifference to, elementary literary pitfalls. Here is an extract from a story called "The Monster from Nowhere," published in 1935. One of the characters is telling his friends about an unpleasant experience on the Maratan Plateau:

"We all looked then. And we saw . . . huge, amorphous blobs of jet black, which seemed to be of the earth, yet not quite of it. Sometimes these ever-changing fragments were suspended in air, with no visible support. At other times they seemed to rest naturally enough on solid ground. But ever and ever again—they changed!

"Afire with curiosity, we went to the open spot. It was a mistake."

"A mistake?" I said.

"Yes. Fletcher lost his life—killed by his own curiosity. I need not tell you how he died. It was, you must believe me, horrible. Out of nowhere, one of the jet blobs appeared before him . . . then around him . . . then—he was gone!"

"Gone!" exclaimed Ki. "You mean—dead?"

"I mean gone! One second he was there. The next, both he and the *thing* which had snatched him had disappeared into thin air.

"Toland and I fled, panic-stricken, back to camp. We told Gainelle what we had seen. Gainelle, a crack shot and a gallant sportsman, was incredulous; perhaps even dubious. . . ."

But whichever he was it did him no good, I'm afraid; a *thing* gets him as well. The point about this story, however (and there are plenty of others which prolong their flights of ineptitude nearly as far), is that it is not just a matter of *things:* their origin and the reason for their strange habits are explained quite conscientiously, though in the same repulsive style. "The Monster from Nowhere" is a good instance of the interesting idea badly set out, a very common phenomenon in science fiction even today, and I might remark here that nothing differentiates the addict from the inquirer more than the readiness of the former, and the understandable reluctance of the latter, to finish a story of this kind. Even I myself feel I should have read a little more really unreadable stuff in preparation for this investigation.

The present era in science fiction opened quite suddenly round about 1940; there were five magazines in 1938, thirteen in 1939, and twenty-two in 1941. (These of course were American; Britain had two publications of this sort at the time.) This expansion of outlet virtually coincided with the arrival of a large group of new writers in the field, among them many of the best-known names of today. Sensationalism began to diminish, some degree of literacy made its appearance, and the admonitory utopia, virtually the leading form of contemporary science fiction, came into being again after something like twenty years. The mode had not come of age—it has yet to do that—but at least its crawling days were over. Why this happened when it did, or at all, I am not sure. I cannot feel, for example, that World War II had much to do with it. The sudden increase in the number of magazines can perhaps be explained in part by the tendency of people who dislike the thought or the actuality of military service to grab at a gaudily covered pulp on a newsstand, but the stuff inside would be too full of conflict and unpleasantly possible weapons of war, I should have thought, to provide much of an escape: the funnies, true-life romances, or straight pornography would surely be better. As regards the emergence of the new and better writers, I can just suggest that while in 1930 you were quite likely to be a crank or a hack if you wrote science fiction, by 1940 you could be a normal young man with a career to start, you were a member of the first generation who had grown up with the medium already in existence. More simply, few things are much good to begin with, and the inferiority of early Elizabethan drama is not what makes Shakespeare's appearance remarkable.

Contemporary science fiction has not, I need hardly say, finally and everywhere turned its back on BEMs or stylistic imbecility. Let me tell you about a short work called "Legacy of Terror" in the November, 1958, issue of *Amazing Stories*. Holly Kendall, a six-foot-tall siren in "abbreviated shorts and light cotton sweater," is driving through the Vermont wastes on her way to tidy up at the experimental laboratory of her recently deceased father, in life a "tall, gentle man" with "soft voice and distant eyes." Encountering en route an ant as tall as herself, Holly retreats in panic, more or less into the arms of a young man:

He wasn't handsome, but you couldn't help being attracted to his wide, boyish grin, or being respectful to the steady, penetrating gaze of his deep brown eyes. He was tanned, and the grin he gave her flashed white against his skin.

"I do believe you," he said. "My name's Bryce Cooper; I've been looking for these big bugs for the past month. This is about as close as I came."

"You—you're looking for them?"

"That's right. I'm an associate professor at the university; English Lit's my racket, but I got me a degree in entomology, too. So when I picked up reports of king-sized spiders and stuff in the vicinity . . ." etc.

Very little later in the same scene, Bryce proposes marriage to Holly, mentioning that he earns $5,120 a year. Access to her father's journal leads Holly to the conclusion that the old man had been working on how to get souls to transmigrate during life, that the ant had got to its present size through having the soul of a horse or something injected into it, and that Bryce, alongside his increasingly amorous behaviour, is actually her own father making free with Bryce's body. An "unholy glitter" rapidly comes into the eyes of the composite male ("Mad? An interesting conclusion, Hollyhocks"), he decides to kill the girl to ensure her silence and is stung to death in the nick of time by the king-sized bumblebee. Finally, when Holly tries to burn her father's journal, the parish priest prevents her, explaining "gently" that the professor's work must be carried on, for all understanding leads to God.

From this wealth of analysable material—only the detail about entomology perhaps banishes the suspicion that some fearsome cynic is responsible—very little needs to be singled out, not even the incest motif, the obtrusion of which bears witness rather to the author's naïveté, I feel, than to anything sinister in him or his readers or our culture. Before leaving this bumper number of *Amazing Stories,*[2] I will just mention that it also contains a story called "Mission: Murder!", of which the moral is that terrorism and summary execution are justified if the enemy is dangerous and unpleasant enough—evidence of a political attitude notably rare in contemporary science fiction. The same issue carries a new adventure of Johnny Mayhem, a slightly less incredible version of Superman, and a sensible, vigorously written, apparently well-informed article attacking some of the policies of the Atomic Energy Commission.

This co-presence of the adult with the stupidly or nastily adolescent is highly characteristic of the modern science-fiction magazines, of which we might now make a general inspection. Their number and circulation continues to fluctuate with surprising sharpness—there was a notable drop, I am told, immediately after the launching of the first

[2] Its cover would delight any cultural diagnostician of pretension with its triad of horror (the king-sized ant, here blown up to emperor size), greed (Holly's Cadillac), and lust (Holly). The cover of a recent number of *Super-Science Fiction* simplifies matters further by depicting a space-girl, even more generously shaped than Holly, on the point of engulfment by a tentacled Thing, an event uncommemorated in any of the stories inside. In fairness to *Amazing Stories,* I might add here that it is a model of refinement compared with some of the stuff in this "Third Monster Issue!" of *Super-Science Fiction.* Passing over "Monsters That Once Were Men" and "birth of a Monster," I draw attention to "The Horror in the Attic"—"it was a hideous, horrible THING on a gruesome errand." The errand consists of frightening to death the lover of a fifteen-year-old girl and then of eating the girl alive:

The creature held her tightly. With one massive paw it ripped away her clothing, tossing the tattered garments to the floor, exposing her firm white breasts, her soft woman's body. Close up, she could see the creature's teeth—hideous yellow fangs, [etc. etc.].

Before giving way to panic at such a cultural manifestation, one would do well to remember that vampires, werewolves, and such were behaving exactly like that over a hundred years ago, fulfilling the same function of putting into acceptable form interests that realistic fiction could not accommodate: Sheridan Le Fanu's "Carmilla," with its blatantly lesbian theme, is the most famous example.

Russian sputnik—but the present tendency [3] is clearly one of expansion, with twenty or more titles coming out monthly or, occasionally, bi-monthly. In the current year we can expect something between one hundred and fifty and two hundred complete novels and collections of short stories, of which only about half will be paperbacks. A tendency for established publishers to open a science-fiction list can also be detected, and there are two paperback houses turning out nothing else. It seems that, despite regular jeremiads from editors and authors, the medium is not yet in disrepair. If I now go on to concentrate for a moment on the magazines, it is because they afford a far more catholic view of the field, and far more clues to the nature of its readership, than do anthologies or individual volumes. These, in any case, regularly derive something like sixty per cent of their material from the magazines. The physical aspect of the latter is uniformly repellent, far more so than could be excused by any talk of the technical exigencies of pulp publication. Crude sensationalism vies with crude whimsy on the covers, and although wit occasionally makes an appearance—a recent one had a pirate boarding a space-craft with a slide rule between his teeth—many a potential recruit to the medium must have been lost without having to stretch out a hand. It is hard to believe that anything likely to interest a grown man could lie under a cover-picture of a multi-armed alien Santa Claus, or within a journal called *Fantastic Universe* or *Astounding Science Fiction,* but I hope to establish that these natural suspicions are often unjustified. They would not be much lulled, admittedly, by a quick look through the interior of any given issue, which offers advertisements of the Rosicrucians and of Royal Jelly ("it's the secret of prolonged life"), of firms offering computer construction kits—125 computers with Geniac, only $19.95, or 150 small ones with Brainiac for only $17.95; [4] more appalling art-work;

---

[3] Since this was written there has been another drop, viewed in the relevant circles with wonderfully spontaneous concern. Voluble anxiety about its own commercial future has always been a demerit of the science-fiction industry, one which may be expected to disappear if the medium attains respectability.

[4] The cheaper and nastier magazines offer material that is more sinister (or more absurd). Here, though presumably not only here, you are given the chance of mail-ordering for $1.00 the Exploding Army Hand Grenade (Exact Replica):

Here's real battle authenticity. This menacing hand grenade looks and works just like a real one. All you do is pull the pin, wait 4 seconds, throw the grenade, and watch the fun as it explodes automatically. It's completely harmless, but the explosion it makes can be heard for a block. Really scatters the gang when you throw this baby in their midst. It sure looks and sounds real, [etc. etc.] .

and silly editorial epigraphs: "Hunted by the living and haunted by the dead . . . Blaine had to do a lot better than merely look alive to stay alive in this grim world!"—this prefixed to an exceptionally able and original story. If the stage of actually beginning to read is attained, the material will be found to include a novella of perhaps fifteen thousand words, three or four short stories of between three and eight thousand words each, sometimes an instalment of a three- or four-part serial running up to fifteen thousand (failing that, another novella or a couple of shorts), editorial matter often marked by a hectoring, opinionated tone, readers' letters covering a staggering range of IQs, a book-review section conducted with intelligence and a much greater readiness to be nasty than one finds, say, in the Sunday *Times,* in some cases a popular-science article on atomic physics, sea serpents, telepathy, or the evaporation of the Caspian Sea, and an interesting department in which are tabulated the results of the readers' voting on the stories in the previous issue—these are arranged in order of popularity and, in at least one case, the author receiving the most votes regularly gets a cash bonus from the publisher. While there is a lot of reason for calling the devotees of science fiction uncritical, there is no doubt that in what must often be an ill-instructed way they are far more concerned about the merit of the stories they read than, for instance, the people who buy women's magazines. I shall return to this point in a moment.

To offer a full-dress division of contemporary science fiction into thematic categories would be laborious and out of proportion to its critical usefulness; here instead is a brief gallop through the fiction contents of a representative recent magazine. The October, 1958, *Astounding Science Fiction,* then, kicks off with a story by Clifford D. Simak, who has been writing the stuff for twenty-five years. In the present instance, a small country trader discovers a short-cut from his house into another world and sets up a bartering arrangement with its

---

If your interests differ slightly, what about a "Stuffed" Girl's Head for only $2.98?

Blondes, redheads and brunettes for every man to boast of his conquests . . . the first realistic likeness of the exciting women who play an important part in every man's life . . . and one of the nicest qualities is that they don't talk back! Accurately modelled to three-quarters life-size and molded of skin-textured pliable plastic, these heads are so life-like they almost breathe. Saucy, glittering eyes, full sensuous mouth and liquid satin complexion, combined with radiant hair colors give astonishing realism to these rare and unique Trophies. Blonds [sic]*, red head or brunette mounted on a genuine mahogany plaque is complete and ready to hang on the wall for excitement and conversation.*

inhabitants. The main cruxes are (a) that the arrangement will not work without the intervention of the trader's dull-witted and despised neighbour, who turns out to be telepathic; and (b) that out of sympathy for the neighbour, and feeling that his own house ought to remain his, the trader insists that no outsiders, from the local Chamber of Commerce to the United Nations, shall be allowed to interfere. Thus the rights of the individual are—perhaps rather dully—upheld against the forces of convention and authority. The next story, "The Yellow Pill," by another established writer, presumptively introduces a psychiatrist in New York trying to cure a patient of the delusion that both of them are actually aboard a space-ship in flight. After some exchanges, in which each party systematically explains the other's world in terms of his own, the supposed psychiatrist swallows the yellow pill, an anti-delusion compound which works by amplifying sense-data, and finds himself on board a space-ship. Meanwhile, the other man has acquired the psychiatrical delusion, imagines himself cured of the space-ship delusion, and walks out of the door, which unfortunately leads into empty space instead of the outer office. This is mainly an ingenious little puzzle-thriller, but it also grapples—perhaps rather dully—with an aspect of solipsism. "Big Sword," by a newer author, shows us a distant planet harbouring an intelligent telepathic race of minute size but with some powers of self-defence. When the human expedition is about to destroy a colony of these creatures, out of inadvertence rather than malice, it is left to a small boy to strike up communication with the aliens and persuade his elders to offer them assistance instead of casual harm. Outwardly, the story falls into a familiar category, the biological puzzle (the aliens have a partly vegetable life-cycle that defeats understanding for some time), but again something is clearly being said—not so dully this time—about the rights of the insignificant and the outlandish. There is some sexual interest here, but minor and highly respectable. There is some too in the next story, ". . . . And Check the Oil," even more minor and hardly less respectable; the rest of it is an inconclusive but not illiterate space-filler about some amiable visiting aliens who run out of food. Finally, "False Image" shows alien and man agreeing to overlook the differences of appearance and habit that repel or frighten each of them and so coming to an understanding.

You will have to take my word for it that none of these five stories is offensive in style, since extracts demonstrating inoffensiveness make for wearisome reading. Anyway, there are no degrees in entomology or wide, boyish grins here. Nor, you will have noticed, are there any king-sized spiders or BEMs of any sort. All four of the alien races introduced are friendly creatures, raising difficulties in communication only. In three out of five cases—a representative proportion, probably—there is recognisable moral concern of a sort: I am not interested for the moment in just what sort, merely in noting its presence. I could, of course, go on to note other shared characteristics, such as the comparatively minor role played by science, pseudo-science, technology, gadgetry, sex, but I think I have said enough about the October *Astounding* and the November *Amazing* to have evoked the experience of reading a science-fiction magazine in all its multifariousness and majesty. I have only to add the practical tip that, in addition to *Astounding,* the other periodicals of pretension are *Galaxy Science Fiction* and *The Magazine of Fantasy and Science Fiction,* before rounding off this section with a brief note on other outlets.

Anthologies of short stories, virtually all reprinted from magazines, form a strikingly high proportion, something like a quarter, of total publication in volume form, another quarter being formed by individual collections of shorts or novellas, most of which will also have appeared earlier in magazines. Of the remaining half, the novels, a large minority will be originals, but probably the bulk can again be traced back to the magazines, either in serial or in rudimentary form. It will be seen firstly that science fiction is to a great extent a short-story form, another point for later consideration, secondly that the magazines are a decisive source. A third deduction might be that people like reading stories twice over, or are unaware of doing so, but in fact the number of magazines makes it impossible to catch more than a few of the good stories as they come out, unless one is doing so full-time. A footnote on distribution is that science-fiction stories are spreading into general magazines, including *Playboy, Harper's, Esquire, McCall's, Good Housekeeping,* the *Reporter,* and the *Saturday Evening Post.* Science fiction has also appeared in *Ellery Queen's Mystery Magazine, Cats,* and *PEN* (The Public Employees' News).

A survey of readership can start with a figure or two: *Galaxy* sells about 125,000 an issue in the United States, plus editions in England, France, Belgium, Switzerland, Germany, Italy, Finland, and Sweden, in the appropriate languages. The Swedes are reported to be particularly keen, which recalls the fact that they are also the most jazz-conscious nation in Europe. *Astounding* has its foreign editions and sells something like 100,000 an issue in America, 35,000 in England, with subscribers in Africa, the Near East, Russia, and China. *Amazing,* which seems to circulate only in English, has an American sale of 50,000. Taking into account the tendency whereby those who read science fiction at all will read *Astounding,* and presupposing a good deal of swapping between enthusiasts, one comes up with a total science-fiction readership in the United States of something approaching half a million. Numbering about three-tenths of one per cent of the population, this is far from being a mass audience, a conclusion supported by the qualities of the material. Without making extravagant claims, one can suggest that the characteristics attributable to a mass medium—expensiveness, avoidance of the obscure or heterodox, reassuring-ness, anonymity—do not appear in a considerable quantity of contemporary science fiction, and I remind you that *Galaxy,* which rarely utilises BEMs or salacity, sells two and a half times as well as *Amazing,* in which they appear less rarely. I might just momentarily expand the point about anonymity by asserting that the best-known science-fiction writers are the reverse of anonymous or interchangeable: they are more likely to be annoyingly idiosyncratic. Moreover, readers' letters in the magazines often show a genuinely critical attitude, however crude its bases and arguments, and acquaintance with the whole body of a given author's work is commonly appealed to, implying some sort of power to make distinctions. Science-fiction readers are addicts, but they are active addicts, positive enthusiasts who are conscious, often all too conscious, of being a specialised minority, highly vocal, and given to banding together in fan clubs.

These clubs are a fascinating feature of American—and British—society, and a full account of them would demand an article to itself. A compressed account would have to start with the foundation of the first clubs in the early '30's and go straight on to the situation today, with groups in a score of major cities and dozens of others: the regional breakdown seems to show that interest is strong in the Midwest and on the West Coast, not so strong in New England and Texas. Many clubs will meet weekly, have a hierarchy of officials, hold organised discussions, and mimeograph or even print a magazine. These fan magazines, or fanzines, appear and disappear at a great rate, but there are pretty sure to be forty or fifty different titles in the current year, with critical, fictional, and gossippy contents. The nomenclature of the field

is not reassuring—one fan club is called "The Elves', Gnomes' and
Little Men's Science Fiction, Chowder and Marching Society," one of
the national federations is "The Little Monsters of America"—but
the evidence of energy and serious interest is overwhelming. Every
year there are regional conferences and a three-day world convention.
There are perhaps twenty fan clubs in Great Britain; I don't know
about the Continent. Politically, the clubs are inclined to be progressive, especially on racial questions, and thus reflect a feature of the
medium itself: many stories allegorise the theme of discrimination,
some treat it directly. At one stage, an immoderate degree of radicalism was attained when a Communist group from Brooklyn, baulked in
their attempt to win over the national convention, formed an association for the Political Advancement of Science Fiction—a short-lived
organisation, I imagine. I will add as a footnote that apparently fantasy fans are content to march under the banner of their science-fiction
friends, who far exceed them in number. However, there must be
many who make no distinction between the two forms, and there is
evidence that the name "fantasy" carries some kind of unwelcome
connotation. Anthony Boucher, when acting as co-editor of *The
Magazine of Fantasy and Science Fiction,* reported that "our readers
do not prefer science fiction to fantasy, but they think they do," adding
that the magazine sold more copies when it carried a science-fiction
cover (men in space suits) than when it had a fantasy cover (lepre-
chauns). These facts would strengthen the hand of those who claim
that, without being essentially escapist itself, science fiction is often
used as a means of escape by its addicts.

Apart from being likely to belong to a fan club, what sort of person
reads science fiction? Information about this is profuse, both in bulk
and in self-contradiction. A gingerly attempt to reconcile a number of
sources gives something like this. Males greatly predominate over females—the proportions given vary between fifteen to one and five to
one. The disparity is probably on the decrease. As regards age, the
average would come somewhere in the later twenties, with a sprinkling
of schoolchildren and a number of veteran fans like the present writer.
As for occupation, not unnaturally there is a pronounced technological
or scientific bias, with engineers, chemists, research workers, and so
on accounting for perhaps forty per cent of readers, though the editor
of *Astounding* says that "nearly all" of his readers are "technically
trained and employed." Other groups mentioned as numerically im-

portant are the non-scientific professions, college students, and the armed forces. As a counter-illustration of occupational diversity, I will just mention an anecdote of de Camp's which tells how a science-fiction writer, happening to visit a New Orleans bordello, found his works so popular with the staff that he was asked to consider himself their guest for the evening. To speculate about the motives and attitudes of readers is precarious, but for what it may be worth I will quote what a number of leading writers have to say about this. Science-fiction readers are "the curious who are looking for stimulation or sensation"; "people with technical training who want fictionalised shop-talk and teen-agers who find glamour and excitement in science"; "ten percent mental juveniles who still like fairy stories, ninety percent chronic nosey-parkers who like having their imaginations stimulated"; "misfits in society, often subversive misfits"; "idealistic, forward-looking, well-read, interested in the arts." Except for the last of these, I detect a welcome lack of reverence here, but on the whole the writers and editors would, I think, echo the boast of the editor of *Astounding* that the medium reaches a large minority of a highly creative and in-fluential section of the nation—the younger technologists. However one regards technologists, there is no doubt that they are important, and since I regard science fiction as a humanising rather than a brutal-ising force, its circulation among these people strikes me as a hopeful sign.

What sort of person writes science fiction? He—it is "she" once in about fifty times—very seldom depends wholly on the writing of science fiction for his living. The financial rewards are such as to demand either a fantastic output or resignation to modest living standards. Secondary occupations adopted are often concerned with science—teaching and research—or with fiction—sometimes detective stories and/or Westerns, sometimes "general," as they say. A scrutiny of their work and of their own utterances suggests that most of the writers and editors treat their calling with great, sometimes excessive, seriousness. Their claims for the medium often strike a missionary note: science fiction is "the last refuge of iconoclasm in American lit-erature"; it exists "to afford objectivity to the reader, for better con-sideration of himself and his species"; its function is "to modify the natural conservatism of the creature"; "it helps mankind to be hum-ble." Occasionally, a legitimate pride in a specialised calling unites with an equally understandable desire to see science fiction treated respectfully and produces wild hyperbole. Thus, Reginald Bretnor, an established author and critic, seems to think that science fiction is a much broader field than the whole of the rest of literature; Robert A. Heinlein, an excellent writer, says the stuff "is much more realistic than is most historical and contemporary-scene fiction and is superior to them both," it is "the most difficult of all prose forms," it is "the only form of fiction which stands even a chance of interpreting the spirit of our times." Here one is reminded of the modernist jazz musician claiming that what he plays is superior in subtlety to serious music as well as being more difficult to perform. But to feel that what one is doing is the most important thing in the world is not necessarily undignified, and indeed is perhaps more rather than less likely to lead to good work being done. I have no objection if the science-fiction writer is sometimes a serious and dedicated kind of person.

He would certainly unloose a disapproving frown at my next topic, science fiction on film, television, and radio. The obstacles to successful translation are formidable enough, perhaps resembling, as one commentator sees it, those of converting into the terms of *Life* the values and interests of a class periodical like *The Saturday Review*. In the visual media the effects have got to be lavish: it is no use trying to produce a convincing BEM by fiddling around with slow-motion process shots of newts, and I remember a fearful effort called *The Man from Planet X* in which they made do with just one alien, whose frequent reminders that a lot of his friends from Planet X should be turning up any moment produced only very moderate consternation. Lavishness is costly, and cost must be certain of being recovered; with few exceptions only the most blatant menaces have got on to the screen. With a sad lack of inventiveness, most of the animal kingdom has been successively blown up to giantism and launched against the world: we have had king-sized wasps, ants, spiders, squids, sea-snails, lizards, beetles, birds, and pterodactyls, all doing their best to bring mankind to its knees. *The War of the Worlds,* with excellent Martians and some attempt to set up a logical alien technology, was probably the best of the menace series, if only because it provided a really formidable menace, one that couldn't be polished off with a few rounds of rifle fire. Nowadays, it appears that the boom in science-fiction films has passed—I couldn't find a single one to go to in New York the other day—and without having explored more than a fraction of the possibilities.[5] The same applies to television: my own survey, which took a long time and was very horrible to do, shows that of five hundred programme-hours studied, only six and one-half, or one and three-tenths per cent, could possibly be classed as science fiction, compared with four and three-tenths per cent of mystery and detective and nearly six per cent of Westerns. Radio is often spoken of as the most promising of the three media for science fiction, but, for my own part, that promise has yet to be honoured: I was spoilt, perhaps, by sitting through *Journey into Space,* an interminable saga on the B.B.C., and by having made rather a mess of a play of my own which was done on the Third Programme, the first science fiction they ever attempted and doubtless the last as well. Noises are good fun all right, but I do not much care for having things "left to my imagination," and the most blood-curdling roars will curdle a good deal less blood, I take it, than the jerkiest king-sized spider on the screen.

From the foregoing hasty and subjective sketch one could at any rate deduce, I think, that on the whole, attempts to present science fiction through mass outlets have failed, though not irretrievably so. It remains only to sum up by considering what use the written medium serves or might serve. I cannot see much justice in the commentators' repeated claim that it sugars the pill of a scientific education: most of the science is wrong anyway, and its amount is such that one might as well be reading Westerns in the hope of finding out about ranching methods. Nor is the medium valuable simply as prophecy: science fiction must in its very profusion seem occasionally to have guessed right, and to have guessed wrong invalidates nothing. Its most important use, I submit, is a means of dramatising social inquiry, as providing a fictional mode in which cultural tendencies can be isolated and judged. To be sure, it does this only at its most ambitious, and then it is often vulgarly presumptuous; but many a trend-hound would be surprised and perhaps mortified to discover how many of his cherished insights are common ground in science fiction. Any Martian survey team would be well advised to read a sample of the stuff before reporting on Terran civilisation.

[5] The reported sale to the movies of Christopher's *No Blade of Grass* and Arthur C. Clarke's *Childhood's End,* both of them serious and non-sensationalist efforts, perhaps portends a return to the charge in a less frivolous frame of mind.

28. Along the Midway of Mass Culture

MILTON KLONSKY

Milton Klonsky has published poetry and essays in such journals as *Partisan Review* and *Hudson Review* and has taught English literature at Columbia University, but has never collected his work in book form. He is chiefly interesting as a spokesman for the generation of writers who, in New York City, were already moving during the earliest fifties in directions later to be called "beat" and "hip." Other members of that group were Chandler Brossard, Anatole Broyard, and Seymour Krim, in whose autobiographical book, *Confessions of a One-Eyed Cannoneer*, Mr. Klonsky is portrayed as a kind of model and guide.

A tourist snapshot of Hell, or the entrance of Hell: Coney Island on a hot Sunday during the summer with millions of people stretched naked on the sand, or wallowing, stumbling and falling over one another in the surf. The beaches are so jammed they can occupy only as much space as their bodies. Against the walls of the apartment houses or in the courtyards of the huge Baths facing the ocean, the echoes of all their millions of little voices are reflected back and compounded into a stunning roar—the "strange tongues. . . . words of pain, voices deep and hoarse and sounds of hands" which Dante heard in the outer ring of the Inferno, where the outcasts of Hell turn "in the air forever dyed, as sand when it eddies in a whirlwind." These are the great swarm of humanity who lived their lives "without blame and without praise, but were for themselves," and so were spewed out by both God and the devil.

The masses were put in their place—outside—and socially restricted by Dante even from his Infernal freakshow. In the plays of Shakespeare as well, though he himself was a plebeian, the appearance

SOURCE: *Partisan Review*, XVI (April, 1949), 348–65. Copyright 1949 by *Partisan Review*. Reprinted by permission of author and publisher.

off-stage of the mob, that "beast with many heads," could evoke imagery of profound nausea. When the mass man was given an individual role, it was either as a clown or the butt of ridicule. And yet the revulsion of both poets, deep as it was, merely reflected the universal prejudice of their own ages. The culture of the Renaissance could allow the dignity of Man only in the abstract, or in great individuals, but never in the whole lump.

It is, then, more an historical than a literary problem to account for the gradual leavening and rise of this lump in time—from the domestic tragedy of the seventeenth and eighteenth century, to the pastoral sentimentalism of Grey and Crabbe; from the poor-but-proud "a man's a man for a' that" defiance of Burns and Wordsworth, to the celebration of the "divine average" by Whitman; and from the depiction of low-life in the novels of Dickens up to the psychological casing of debased urban and rural types in Dreiser and Faulkner. By the nineteenth century, this social leavening process had gone so far that Tolstoy, in an attack on the new French symbolist poetry, could even question the sanctity of Art itself and prefer "Uncle Tom's Cabin" to Shakespeare and Russian folksongs to Beethoven (although he himself knew better), solely because they appealed to a greater mass of people.

The Coney Island culture is, of course, a phenomenon of the twentieth century.

> *The age demanded an image*
> *Of its accelerated grimace,*

as Ezra Pound said, which it was quick to find. Comic strips, pulp fiction, movies, radio serials, commercial jazz and the rest are a direct result of modern technology and public education. Whether we choose to dignify these products by the name of Art is a semantic problem— what is central is that they usurp the functions of traditional art in setting the styles, the manners, the images, the standards and the goals of life for millions, almost as though they were the organs of an unofficial state religion. And in its scope, this sub-culture is wide enough to include the millionaire and the dime-store clerk, the president of the United States and the Negro sharecropper, the old and the young, in a truly classless and democratic consonance of spirit.

Whitman imagined that the new forms to be developed by a democratic art would be a further revelation of the old, and could be exposed merely by stripping off the outer layers of decayed sensibility.

But even the form of the novel, which had been the chief literary vehicle of the middle class since its inception, now, in the hands of such
writers as Proust or Joyce or Kafka has become as highbrow and aloof
as any other genre.

   The hope persists that, somehow, in the fullness of time, either
through the Grace of a revolutionary state or, gradually, through the
dissemination of Great Books, the values of advanced art can be sifted
down to the mass. But this is a pathetic consolation, Whitman's
booster optimism turned rancid. It may have some validity in the case
of *kitsch* art exemplified in best-selling novels, jukebox adaptations of
Tchaikovsky, choral works like "Ballad for Americans" or "Freedom
Train," modern dancing in Broadway musicals, etc., that petty-
bourgeois "uplift" by which Americans punish themselves for really
preferring Moon Mullins. (And, incidentally, the type of culture fos-
tered in the Soviet Union today by fiat of its most authoritative critics.)
The base forms of mass art have autonomous values and a parallel
momentum of their own. Moreover, their pervasive power is such, like
the political slogans of authoritarian states, that any influence is most
likely in the reverse direction. Neither the bohemian ghetto nor the
university provide a hiding place.

   When comic strips, jazz, pulp fiction and the rest are not intellectually snubbed, they are regarded as the bastard products of modern
civilization, mere artifacts like juke boxes and slot machines, without
any cultural ancestry or tradition. Their lineaments of descent, however, are unmistakable. Just as the leading forms of bourgeois art were
derived from medieval sources—the novel from feudal *gestes* and romances, the drama from miracle and morality plays performed in the
market place, etc.—so these new upstart genres are grounded in
middle-class culture of the past. To trace even one of them back to its
origins, the comic strip for example, reveals certain early characteristics that apply to all.

2

During the first half of the eighteenth century in England, a period
which saw the consolidation of British mercantile power and the establishment of the Protestant ascendancy, there was a new security of person and a freedom of opinion that was shared by all but the lowest
classes. That vertical chain or ladder of Being on which feudalism had

based its cosmology and its hierarchical social relations was about to be tipped over on its horizontal axis by a levelling of class values. The *canaille* were now citizens with a stake in Parliament and even an interest in the arts. Common Sense—that great virtue of the average —was elevated to a rank as high as all the others. God himself, turning the screws of an erector set universe constructed according to the rational blueprint of Newton and Leibnitz, could have no patience with any monkish hyperdulia or aesthetic faradiddle.

The five great comic novelists of England, Smollett, Fielding, Stern, Richardson and Defoe, as well as the cockney artist Hogarth, appeared at this time almost in a group. All of them had an intimate connection with early journalism, sharing its time-sense as a series of discrete moments, each without self-possession, as well as its notion of the "concrete" as residing in the particular entity or event sensorily observed. The scenes and actions of Smollett's novels, especially, frequently resemble detached anecdotes taken from a newspaper or magazine of the period. With their tortuous plots unwinding upon the spool of a foregone conclusion; their crude characterizations drawn almost to the point of caricature; and their uncertain structure wavering between the narrative and the informal essay (just as the journals of the time wavered between reporting and editorializing); yet with everything drawn in bright color, full of slapstick vigor and spiked with climaxes—these early novels could hardly hope to compete for literary esteem with poetry or drama. On the other hand, by their rootedness in the common daily life they had immense appeal, and achieved an audience for literature greater than any before.

During the same period, this new mass audience was shared by the cartoon art of William Hogarth and his successors. And in the fusion of the two—the early English novel of Smollett and Fielding and Hogarth's drawings—the style of the comic strip was conceived.

Hogarth's declared purpose in his little-known book, *The Analysis of Beauty,* was "to treat (his) subjects as a dramatic writer." What he did achieve for the first time in "The Rake's Progress," "Marriage a la Mode," "The Harlot's Progress," and his other cartoon series, was, in effect, a translation of novelistic situations and character types into pictures. (Of course the medieval paintings and stained-glass windows illustrating Bible stories and the lives of the Saints for the laity preceded Hogarth; but these had a religious rather than a social perspective, as, also, miracle and morality plays compared with Elizabethan drama.) Hogarth's ambition was not to methodize nature, but to see her in all her literalness and materiality—to strip the Quattrocento ideal of any mysticism and reduce it to a physical average. In his work, the knobs, twists and bulges of flesh of ordinary mankind superseded the perfect forms of Venus and Apollo. Yet as he came to understand later on, the concept of the Average was an ideal as abstract as the concept of the Beautiful.

Hogarth served to widen the split between "high" and "low" art, reflected during the eighteenth century by the more academic dispute between the Ancients and the Moderns. For those artists surrounding the official court painter Joshua Reynolds, and for the "connoisseurs." so called, who admired the Italian schools exclusively, he could never restrain his contempt. There was, unmistakably, the bray of the true philistine horselaugh in the way Hogarth ridiculed the claims to "divine inspiration" and the *"Je ne sais quoi"* or Grace, of these artists. His own compositions were often cramped with detail and unbalanced; and his line was coarse, enclosing rather than revealing form, so that his pictures actually improve when they are reduced in size for publication. All his immense inventive genius was restricted by default to the depiction of a literary subject matter:—caricatures of London daily life, both high and low, as seen from the inside.

But since satire and caricature were the dominant modes of art in the eighteenth century, Hogarth was eminently fitted for his age. The social order of England at that time had such stable foundations (or thought it had), that the distortions of view in Hogarth's pictures, like the crazy-mirror expansions and contractions in Swift's *Gulliver's Travels* or Pope's *Rape of the Lock* could easily be refocused and adjusted to the norm. The artist's "slant" was his point of view. Hogarth even posited a standard "line of beauty," the serpentine line or spiral, which was for him the secret grace of the Greek and Italian styles; but, when this spiral twist was flattened or bulged or distorted in any way, it emerged in the shape of caricature. The deviant, the non-average, was also the freakish that could provoke either laughter or disgust, according to the intent of the artist. And, as his pictures show, the wit of connecting "improper" forms in caricature was equal to the wit of connecting "improper" ideas and images in satire.

With this, the general theory underlying the comics was about complete. Hogarth's successors and imitators gradually abandoned his moralistic tone as well as his hopeless battle with the "connoisseurs."

His cartoon art was endowed to the daily newspaper rather than to the museum. The development of illustration and caricature by Rowландson, Cruikshank, Gilray, Seymour and the rest coincided with the growth of modern journalism in Europe and America. By the time Outcalt's "Yellow Kid" appeared in the New York *World* in 1896— generally considered the first of its kind—an embryo comic strip art was already gestating which, upon the consolidation of mass newspapers and syndicates by Pulitzer and Hearst, emerged at last full-grown in the way we know.

3

Those visionary figments—Mutt and Jeff, Smilin' Jack, Blondie, Dick Tracy, Daisy Mae, The Gumps, Popeye, Moon Mullins—every day, exposed in their boxes of light and jails of purposeless energy, they glow in the minds of millions. The services they perform and the needs they fulfill are real. Like the newspapers themselves, the comic strips re-enact a vast and solemn American ritual—The Strip Tease of Time. With each issue, suspense is aroused and discharged in a little climax without relief, anticipating only another climax tomorrow and tomorrow, until, just before the final black-out, time's overwhelming secret is almost but never revealed and always hidden again. As the goal or reward of a culture founded on materialism is the very activity taken to reach it, so the comic strip leads to no final revelation and exhausts itself in immediacy. Its rigid daily pattern is repeated in an overall timeless and shapeless continuum.

And not only the comic strip, but also jazz, soap opera, the movies, pulp fiction have this one great structural principle (or lack of principle) in common. As a consequence, any criticism of the mass arts based on the authority of traditional art is baffled from the start. From the standpoint of organic form, the various genres of mass culture seem closer to artifacts than to art.

To attempt a formal definition of the comic strip, therefore, would be a contradiction in terms, since the very concept of form in art entails unity of time and space and action. Its form—as for the movies, pulp fiction, jazz and the rest—is really formula, whose prescription never varies. Jazz, whether hip or commercial, from blues to be-bop, must serve out its time constricted behind the thirty-two bars of the average record; although, during a performance, it can be extended indefinitely by the addition of new choruses or longer rides. As for the movies, the conventions of plot and character are always so rigid that the circular continuum of feature to newsreel to double feature can be breached at any point without loss. No wrench is suffered during this transition by the audience, which arrives and departs in the same darkness. And in soap opera and serialized pulp fiction, the comic strip device of the strip tease in time is used to provide suspense and direction in a plot going nowhere. But since the strip tease can never be pared down to its essence, these are never formally completed but, rather, discontinued or exhausted.

Moving always on the surface of appearance, it is impossible for any of the mass arts to plunge beneath this surface and into a depth of meaning, symbolic or anagogic, which form alone provides.[1] For this reason, the casts of characters in comic strips, like the stock types in pulp fiction and the stars of Hollywood, who always play themselves in whatever roles they are cast, are mere concretions of characteristics, animated types or "humours" rather than persons. All these characters are self-contained, hermetically sealed by the formula from any growth or change. Once set in motion, they can go on and on for years in a kind of somnambule inviolability.

The most successful and famous comics often survive their authors, and, in rare cases, even the newspapers where they first appeared. It takes a major change in the American *ethos* to effect even a slight alteration in their formulae. But when, after many years, one of these strips recasts its characters and plot, or expires, that is an event as significant as a style of dress or slang going out of fashion. The cocky, sadistic, tough-talking "Yellow Kid" of the 1890's—from whose name, incidentally, the term "yellow journalism" is derived—has been superseded by the still more violent, sophisticated and sensational comics of our own time, just as the old-fashioned demagogy of Pulitzer and Hearst has been streamlined by their successors. In modern comic books and newspaper strips, read by all classes and age-groups with equal fervor, there is such great emphasis on mayhem,

[1] The symbolic devices of certain movies, such as the white gulls in *Potemkin* intended to express freedom, or the Freudian emblems in other "art" films (described by Arnold Hauser in his article "Can 'Movies' Be Profound?" in *Partisan Review,* January 1948), are of a different order from those in painting and literature. They should be regarded instead as cues calculated to arouse a definite response from the audience, as, e.g., a dog howling to evoke foreboding, or a baby gurgling to evoke maternal sympathy.

arson, murder and pathological sex as to necessitate laws for the protection of public morality. "Krazy Kat," "Happy Hooligan," "Mutt and Jeff" and "The Katzenjammer Kids" were products of a more genteel era that has passed away. Sometimes, however, a comic strip remains embalmed in the juices of another time, unable to renew itself, yet too valuable a property to be abandoned. "Maggie and Jiggs," for example, a strip burlesquing the social *gaffes* and foibles of the immigrant *nouveau riche,* has lost much of its point now that the upper and middle classes have learned to forget their manners. In any event, none of the really important old-timers are ever forgotten. Their names and typical wisecracks color the daily speech, and their faded pictures merge gradually into the family album of American life where they are preserved.

For it is the great indistinction of both the mass arts and contemporary life that they reflect one another so closely, feature by feature, it is almost impossible to tell the image from its source. Both collaborate to form a common myth, that vague gray area of the "collective unconscious," where psychoanalysis and sociology overlap one another. The fictive heroes of this myth are the archetypes to which the masses try to conform, and the dies from which they stamp their own behavior. Consider the style of the city gangster, in all his synthetic moods, from the brash hood to the smooth operator; the style of the strong and silent Western cowboy; the style of the country Gable and the hick siren; the style of the Cynical reporter on a metropolitan newspaper; the style of the Woman-with-a-past and her fallen sister, the Whore-with-a-heart-of-gold; and the characters that kids throughout the U.S. assume when they play at War or Cops and Robbers or Cowboys and Indians—all are derived, to a greater or lesser degree, from the classic types of the movies, pulp fiction and comic strips. But with this demurrer—the spell cast by these mythical images would be broken, their charm unwound, without the simple faith of the masses.[2]

As the power of the religious and artistic value has shrunken, the mass arts have taken over. The collapse of Puritanism, for example, has opened a vacuum in the interior lives of millions—the secret

[2] During the war, the type of Rover Boy beach charger and fire fighter celebrated by Hollywood was an open scandal in every camp, but too shocking and too ludicrous to be taken seriously, almost like the war itself. And, for another example, those great lovers of the silent screen, Valentino, Theda Bara, John Gilbert, et al., seem to be playing in a farce when they are shown today.

world of the daydream and the forbidden wish—which is now filled
almost entirely by the sexual codes, styles of courtship, and erotic
images derived from the mass arts. Even the comic strips exhibit
women as lush as those of the beer and cigarette ads; while some like
"The Gumps" and "Winnie Winkle," where sex was once a minor display, have had to be revamped to satisfy their public. (The formulas of
new strips concerned with aviation, such as "Terry and the Pirates" or
"Smilin' Jack," place equal emphasis on sex—new evidence, perhaps, for Freud's theory of the dream symbolism of flying.) In Hollywood, an elaborate and knowing technique has been developed,
known in the trade as the "continental touch," in order to keep within
the bounds of propriety, and for an audience quick to take a hint. As a
result, the provinces today are as cultivated as the large cities.

Romantic and confessional pulp fiction, the most lurid as well as the
tender adolescent varieties, employ the same conventions as Hollywood but affect a kind of mincing virtue which is all their own. Under
all the romantic persiflage, however, there is a bond of understanding
between author and reader not to take it all too seriously. Love is a
bedtime story, but sex is real and earnest. Neverthelesss, the readers of
A Girl Can Dream by Phyllis Pool, *Appointment with Love* by Clinton
Dangerfield, *Banished to Paradise* by Blake Reed, etc., shop girls,
school girls, stenographers, housewives in their millions demand to see
themselves as heroines of romance along with the queens and grand-
dames of the past. Romantic love has been democratized in these
magazines and sold on every newsstand. The ads on the back pages,
however, are a pathetic commentary and as real as a dirty joke—ads
for Loans, Cures for Stammering, Foot Powder for tired feet, Reduce!
Pictures of your favorite Hollywood stars, Stop B.O., and so on.

The moonshine of these romances derives from the movies, from
Hollywood, where the stars like gods and goddesses of a new Olympus
merely play at being human. Their love affairs among themselves and,
sometimes, with favored mortals outside the movies, recounted years
later around every American fireside, bar and soda fountain are already part of our national folklore. The stock characters of romantic
pulp—and of Western, Detective, Sport and Horror stories as well
—are only copies of these larger-than-life originals in Hollywood.
There the daydream is given a local habitation and a name.

Accordingly, what was at first joined only as a metaphor—the
Hollywood constellation and the Pantheon of ancient Greece—now

present certain real points of contact. The stars of Hollywood can be conceived as archetypes existing apart from us, in a preternatural dimension of their own, for the images on the screen are ikons rather than photographic representations of real persons. In this sense, Clark Gable and Lana Turner are merely actors who represent CLARK GABLE and LANA TURNER. These great shadow-gods, entering our lives in all the guises of Zeus—the Swan, the Bull, and the Shower of Gold— and their goddesses, with their smooth, lovely faces unlined by any trace of anxiety or intelligence, together living, loving and dying but always rising again on other screens in other films, immortal and grand, what have they in common with our own petty cares and interests or even, for that matter, with the lives of the actors who portray them? The archetypes persist under many transmogrifications even when the actors who originally portrayed them are dead. Their cosmetic masks are forever renewed. Yet the gossip columns and picture magazines where the stars are worshipped, and the press agents who are their priests, all conspire to identify these ideal images with the physical beings of actors and actresses. And for the millions who surrender themselves and surrogate their passion to these images in playdreams or (with their eyes closed), even in the very act of love, they are more real than the bodies they are possessed by or they themselves possess.

The star system undoubtedly is the most original invention of the movies—in a synecdochal sense, it contains and *is* the movies. European film studios, which have been unable to develop a comparable system of their own, seem to lack the glamor and enchantment of Hollywood. American movies are preferred by the masses even in foreign countries; and this despite the handicap of a strange language and the fact that, from the standpoint of theater art, French and English films are often superior. An actor in foreign films, whether from the Comédie Française or from the Abbey Theater, is merely an actor, but Betty Grable in America is a star. Hollywood can ingest directors, writers, technicians and actors into its thearchy, "the finest that money can buy," with the same divine and imperious appetite with which the Olympians must have devoured the local deities of Greece. It is only after elaborate rites of beatification by press agents, gossip columnists and movie magazines, however, and the further proof of their box-office magic, that the taint of Europe and mortality can be washed away. In this manner, after changes of name, personality, and appearance, some of the highest stars have ascended in Hollywood. American actors, however, whose features might stamp them as minority racial types, are condemned to roles of a sinister and/or sophisticated kind.

The Italians suffer mainly from this prejudice. Jewish film stars are frequently able to "pass" without special observance; but, in the parts of Jews, they are restricted to standardized *schmaltz* characterizations, unctuous, self-conscious, and embarrassed by a fulsome desire to please. On the other hand, it is almost impossible for a Negro to play a romantic or heroic part in the movies. Even the best Negro players are invariably shown as domestic servants or musical clowns or the butts of ridicule—the same roles, incidentally, which were bestowed on the lower classes in Elizabethan drama. What motivates these restrictions is as much political as it is financial. For the collective daydream of Hollywood is as jealous and exclusive as the individual's; and the rise of a new romantic star from a minority race or nationality signifies a rise in social rank for the whole group.

As it has developed, the mythopoeic power of the movies, inherent in its very method, has given it a quasi-religious status and a structure that differs radically from any other literary or theatrical genre. As the anecdote is the concrete substance of the short story and novel; gossip of the drama; soliloquy of the modern poem; so the daydream, with its moving images beamed inside the mind, is the concrete substance and focal point of the movies. The movie theater itself is like a working model, or templet, of a huge mind. While the brilliant hypnotic screen converges all light and movement in the darkness, a simple faith on the part of the audience ("the camera never lies") suspends any disbelief in the projected reality of what it sees—for both the private darkness within and the public darkness of the theater are illuminated at once by the same image. What a machine for the cretinization of the masses! The deadpan with which the camera records its pictures is like the reassuring legal prose of Kafka's dream narratives, whereby, keeping a straight face, the most incredible characters and events are detailed with such a consistently monotonous gravity of emphasis that the fantastic can be taken at its face value. Conversely, the matter-of-fact events shown in the newsreels of Senators speaking, flood waters rising in Iowa, famines in China, etc., are somehow transformed to the same illusory plane as the feature production itself. The shadows of the movies flicker between the black and white world of positive fact and the chrome world of fantasy, unreeling both on a single beam of light.

But this spooky lighting effect is a device of ritual much older than the movies:—

> *Darkness in churches congregates the sight;*
> *Devotion strays in open daring light,*

as a poet observed in the seventeenth century. The silver screen, the hush, the darkness—it *is* a kind of secret Mass where all who attend partake of the Host in common; and, to project along this line into the near future, the movies may yet find in television a comparable Reformation, in which the individual will be left to face his own screen alone.

Whatever style television may ultimately compose for itself is now hidden in a primal chaos of all styles, a super-Vaudeville large enough to include the movies, sports events, grand opera and news events all on the same bill. The earliest films, in turn, were little more than photographic imitations of stage plays or circus tricks, agitated dumbshows, until the camera learned to move and to participate in the action. But from this discovery emerged the great motif of The Chase, a motif which is dominant in Chaplin's early comedies, Westerns, cops and robbers melodramas, cartoons, etc., and, in one way or another, figures in almost every kind of film. The Chase was not only a fulfillment of style, but, even more, created a ritual form out of a mass psychological need. In the spellbound attention with which a newsreel audience watches a football player running and twisting down a broken field away from hands that clutch at him from all sides, there is, under all the excitement and tension, a release from the common nightmare of being pursued by someone or something with the pursuer gaining closer and closer. It is almost as though time itself were the pursuer, that "cinematic" time (to use Bergson's appropriate metaphor), conceived as an absolute, free and mathematical essence with an existence of its own. What better place for the apotheosis of our "cinematic" time than in the movies?

The name of Benjamin Franklin glows on the marquee, appearing as The First American. For his many indigenous qualities, but, especially, for having made a fetish of time, which is money, everyman's commodity, the stuff of life, Franklin was recognized by Europe as the representative type of a different *ethos*. During his lifetime, of course, the main outlines of this ethos were still obscure. But by now the American fetishism of time has exposed itself through many nerves of anxiety—e.g., the obsessive dread of losing one's youth or virility, the dread of growing older without "having lived" (Rip Van Winkle), the dread of missing one's chance or "golden opportunity," etc. It is no contradiction, however, that Progress is conceived to be as steady, ir-resistible and cumulative a process as the ticking of a clock. The new *must* be better, for the same reason that the go-getter *must* come out ahead—or else something is radically wrong. The comic strip "Moon Mullins" provides a negative sort of testimony for this credo—Moon, a character in the old picaresque tradition, never does any work, sleeps too much, chases after women, wastes his money and never thinks of tomorrow. But to balance Moon, at the other end of the evolutionary scale there is "Buck Rogers," "Flash Gordon," and, of course, "Super-man," Tarzan's city bred and more neurotic cousin, who can hear a dripping faucet miles away.

Now the most remarkable fulfillment of these notions of time and progress in the mass arts is, certainly, science-fiction (so-called), whose lineage goes back to Lucian, Kepler, Donne and Swift; yet, paradoxically, this literary tradition has been crossed with the still more ancient ghost story, to produce something essentially different from either and peculiar to our own times, a scientific demonology. The faith of the masses in scientific progress, which has largely super-seded faith in Biblical revelation, can call up its own superstitions of the possible as terrifying as those of the occult. In *Astounding Stories, Wonder Stories, Amazing Stories* and the like, the demons and devils that once haunted mankind have been driven thousands of light years away into the interstellar regions where anything goes. But this is where the paradox unfolds itself—for, to the superstitious mind, the farthest movements of the stars and the innermost movements of the soul (exemplified by the pseudo-science of astrology), are the two poles of one axis.

One of the most original writers of Gothic science-fiction, H. P. Lovecraft (whose paranoid tales of the pre-creation race of Chthulu are in many ways reminiscent of the old Kabbalistic legend of the Breaking of the Vessels), was so possessed by sub-conscious demons that, like W. B. Yeats in *A Vision,* he even invented an elaborate list of Chthulu tracts and incunabula to buttress his stories. Their names could be recited at a black Mass:—1) The Micronomicon of the Mad Arab, Abdul Alhazred; 2) Pnakotic manuscripts; 3) R'lyeh text; 4) Book of Dzyan; 5) Seven Cryptical Books of Hsan; 6) Dhol Chants. In his public life, Lovecraft was a respected citizen of Providence, R.I. and, like many of his profession, declared himself to be an orthodox "mechanical materialist."

The bulk of the science-fiction stories published in pulp magazines —in distinction from the more sophisticated varieties—have, by now, evolved a set of conventions so widely accepted that their fantastic plots can be told straight, without any literary sleight-of-hand, like the tales of ghosts in the Middle Ages. The casts of characters in these stories are cut from the same pattern as Western or Romantic pulp: there is the hero himself (who is the usual daydream hero), an evil scientist (who could be a cattle rustler or suave nightclub operator as well), and, inevitably, a good scientist and his beautiful daughter. Formula proscribes form. And neither space ships, ray blasters, time machines or all the rest of their Gothic furniture can raise them above the level of pulp fiction.

For any of the mass arts, questions of aesthetic value are supererogatory. But the uncertain cultural status of science-fiction, ranging as it does from high to low, presents a problem in criticism that applies to all: namely, whether a transvaluation of the mass arts can be effected, while still maintaining their democratic base, so as to make them serve as vehicles of advanced art. What this really entails is that both halves of our schizoid culture be joined and made whole by an act of the artistic will. In the past, of course, folk songs and country dances were formally developed in the symphonies of Beethoven and Schubert, and the old popular ballads recast in the poems of Wordsworth and Coleridge. Yet the poetry and music of the Romantic era was no more available to the broad mass of people then, than it is now; and, in any case, the natural forms of ballads, folk songs and country dances were derived from the same organic principles as traditional art, which are essentially opposed to the technological art products of our own time. To attempt to anneal the two, therefore, even if it were socially possible, would result in an aesthetic hippogriff, a prodigy as strange as any Shakespearean marriage of the Phoenix and the Turtle.

Those experiments of Stravinsky and Gershwin, while appearing to offer a structural synthesis, are really a hangover of late Romantic "program music"—(the equivalent of *collage* in painting)—in which bird calls, cannon shots, cow bells, train whistles, etc., were sounded off to counterfeit reality. These works may be musically successful notwithstanding, but jazz has its own ways and its own means.

By a reciprocal process, when jazz bands strain to achieve a larger statement by imitating symphonic forms, as in Duke Ellington's suite *Ebony Concerto,* the result is foredoomed to be a humorless parody of both. The movies, infected by the same notions, tend to produce elephantine spectacles or mere photographed versions of stage plays; and comic strips, likewise, when they abandon their cartoon style for devices of chiaroscuro and realistic drawing, resemble the *kitsch* illustrations in *Good Housekeeping* or *The Saturday Evening Post.* Limits and rules, even for the mass arts, define themselves by an excess of their own ends.

So then, to recapitulate what has been assumed all along: the base forms of popular culture have an autonomous system of values indifferent to the standards of artistic criticism, and a career separate from that of traditional Western art. As a corollary to the "cinematic" time sense which they embody, all are committed by formula to the appearance of things presented by immediate sensation. And since, by definition, it is impossible for them to evaluate experience by means of form, the glass they hold up to modern life is a mirror that focuses certain aspects sharply but reflects nothing in depth. It is this two-dimensionality that makes them seem closer to artifacts than to art.

4

Along the midway of our Coney Island culture is jazz or ragtime or blues or swing or be-bop, of many names but one homoousian substance. The nature of jazz music has not been treated in any detail so far, and yet, in a sense, it may be considered a prototype of all the mass arts. For in no other are ideas and feelings presented for their immediate effect at the very moment of conception, nor are the restrictions of formula so exacting and necessary. Only the 2-4-2-4 structure and the 32 set bars of jazz can control the vagaries of improvisation. Consequently, these crude arrangements of popular tunes, stamped out as though by a machine to fit the time of a dance or the length of a record, are in contrast to highly complex rhythms and elaborately figured variations of theme. Many jazzmen, who may be virtuosos on their own instruments, are yet unable to read even the simplest musical score.

Jazz arrangements are usually devised beforehand by the band leader-entrepreneur, but the performance itself is a corporate activity in which the inspiration of each musician is pooled. The American system of checks and balances in a free enterprise system has no better working model. Those jam sessions where musicians get together after hours to play for their own satisfaction constitute an open market for the mutual exchange of ideas. Any new "riff" or "break" of value becomes the property of anyone present and is quickly passed on—one reason why the most original innovations in jazz are often anonymous. As ideas catch and connect, an altogether new style of playing, such as be-bop, can suddenly emerge as though it were "in the air" all the time, the air the trumpet or saxophone man blows through his mouthpiece.

European mimicry of American jazz, especially the French with their quaint Hot Clubs, can never quite approximate its tone. Their very aesthetic seriousness is un-American and gives them away. The brass toughness and disreputable history of jazz (whose origins among the Negroes in the South can be traced to slave plantations, gambling boats on the Mississippi, the dives and cathouses of old New Orleans and Memphis, up to the seamier clip-joints along Fifty-Second Street and in the Harlem ghetto, where it is now enshrined (not to mention its sinister association with drugs and late hours), all this has flattered even the most prosaic Local 802 hipster with a kind of Villon-esque underworld glamour. Among the coteries that surround jazz, a distinctive jabberwocky composed of carnival slang, thieves' argot and Harlem jive has been cultivated, in order to separate the hipsters from the squares.

But at this point certain further distinctions ought to be made. Black jazz, the only chaste and true variety, is but a narrow band at the extreme end of the Tin Pan Alley spectrum, the rest of which ranges from the mixed pied-piper outfits of Benny Goodman or Woody Herman, all the way around to the huge all-white orchestras of Tommy Dorsey, Glen Gray, and Harry James. For these last, the commercial bands that blare on the radio and in the movies, jazz improvisation is ruled out altogether, and every number is rehearsed and mechanically regulated to the smallest crotchet. Yet it is mainly the loudest and most vulgar which are most popular throughout the U.S., perhaps for that reason; while the best colored jazzmen, from whose work all the others are derived, are kept waiting in the kitchen of American success. In Hollywood's recurrent jazz operas, Negro musicians are rushed in and out as discreetly as waiters. By some absurd double irony, however, the great majority of the Negro population penned in the Northern and Midwestern ghettos actually prefer bleached imitations of commercial jazz or even the white varieties themselves—driven by the same levelling pressure of the Boss culture that makes them straighten their hair or value lighter colored women as more sexually desirable; as, for whites of second-class nationalities, it compels many to change their names, their manners, their religions, or even their faces.

But the absorption of Negro jazz by the Leviathan is only one sign of its power. For the American mass culture is also an imperial culture, whose authority is as great abroad as it is at home. It is no exaggeration to state that it occupies a comparable relation to its ethos as Protestantism once held for the British Empire, or the classic Pantheon for ancient Greece and Rome. The base forms of mass culture are capable of undercutting the most rooted traditions of art and religion in Europe, not by any competition of values—they are aesthetically neutral—but because, on the broadest social level, these traditions are already exhausted. The Soviet Union, which would like to fill this vacuum with its own imperial prescriptions, carries on a steady, virulent offensive against American movies, comics and jazz.

In its present setup, however, mass culture is not necessarily confined within the matrix of contemporary society, for it can operate with equal or even greater efficiency under a totalitarian as under a democratic system. Its nature is so closely bound to technology that no one can predict what new shapes and genres it may yet evolve. The real artist behind American culture is Vulcan himself, the great artificer surpassing all his old devices year after year. The invention of television, for example, has at once confined movies, comics, spectator sports and even newspapers within the scope of a single screen and enlarged their view enormously. And there is always a new ride or a new sideshow down the midway.

In contrast, the traditional arts of Europe are gradually freezing into a museum culture, with the trophies of the past hung side by side with those of the present. It has even been suggested seriously, by Malraux and others, that reproductions of the greatest art works in Paris and other capital cities be circulated around remote areas—a sort of French "Freedom Train" for artistic documents—as though this funereal exhibition could substitute for the creative energies of a living art. After the first World War, such piety toward past values would have seemed a ridiculous excess; but Dadaism and Surrealism could afford to paint the moustache on Mona Lisa only because these values were still viable.

Of course, works of art of a high order, equal to the best of the past, can still be produced, though increasingly rarified, professional and aloof. For the tradition begun with the Renaissance is ending. As the advanced arts have surpassed themselves in the refinement of sensibility even to the point of nullity—the blank page of Mallarmé and the empty canvas of Mondrian—so the mass arts have become more violently sensational and garish. Following parallel directions, both lead to an equal exhaustion. The humanistic and scientific tradition of the Renaissance, of which American mass culture is the ultimate product, has strained itself over the centuries to lay those eggs slowly hatching under the deserts of New Mexico.

29. *From* The Great Comic Book Heroes

JULES FEIFFER

Jules Feiffer (1929–   ) is best known as a cartoonist who, beginning with occasional satirical drawings in the *Village Voice,* has ended up with a nationally syndicated comic strip. He is, however, a satirical novelist and playwright as well; and a political activist—much in evidence on the TV screen during the ill-fated 1968 Democratic Convention in Chicago. He confesses in the piece which follows his early love for the comic books which helped make the imagination of many in his generation.

Introduction

1

Comic books, World War II, the depression, and I all got going at roughly the same time. I was eight. *Detective Comics* was on the

SOURCE: Jules Feiffer, *The Great Comic Book Heroes* (New York: The Dial Press, Inc., 1965), pp. 11–17, 18–21, 185–89. Copyright © 1965 by The Dial Press. Reprinted by permission of the publisher.

stands, Hitler was in Spain, and the middle class (by whose employment record we gauge depressions) was, after short gains, again out of
work. I mention these items in tandem, not only to give color to the
period, but as a sly historic survey to those in our own time who, of the
items cited, only know of comic books.

Eight was a bad age for me. Only a year earlier I had won a gold
medal in the John Wanamaker Art Contest for a crayon drawing on
oak tag paper of Tom Mix jailing an outlaw. So at seven I was a winner
—and didn't know how to handle it. Not that triumph isn't at any age
hard to handle, but the younger you are the more of a shock it is to
learn that it simply doesn't change anything. Grownups still wielded
all the power, still could not be talked back to, still were always right
however many times they contradicted themselves. By eight I had become a politician of the grownup, indexing his mysterious ways and
hiding underground my lust for getting even until I was old enough,
big enough, and important enough to make a bid for it. That bid was to
come by way of a career (I knew I'd never grow big enough to beat up
everybody; my hope was to, somehow, get to own everything and fire
everybody). The career I chose, the only one that seemed to fit the
skills I was then sure of—a mild reading ability mixed with a mild
drawing ability—was comics.

So I came to the field with more serious intent than my opiate-
minded contemporaries. While they, in those pre-super days, were eating up *Cosmo, Phantom of Disguise; Speed Saunders;* and *Bart Regan,
Spy,* I was counting how many frames there were to a page, how many
pages there were to a story—learning how to form, for my own use,
phrases like: @X #?/; marking for future reference which comic
book hero was swiped from which radio hero: Buck Marshall from
Tom Mix; the Crimson Avenger from the Green Hornet—

There were, at the time, striking similarities between radio and
comic books. The heroes were the same (often with the same names:
Don Winslow, Mandrake, Tom Mix—); the villains were the same:
oriental spies, primordial monsters, cattle rustlers—but the experience was different. As an apprentice pro I found comic books the more
tangible outlet for fantasy. One could put something down on paper
—hard-lined panels and balloons, done the way the big boys did it.
Far more satisfying than the radio serial game: that of making up programs at night in bed, getting the voices right, the footsteps and door
slams right, the rumbling organ background right—and doing it all in

soft enough undertones so as to escape being caught by that grownup reading Lanny Budd in the next room who at any moment might give his spirit shattering cry: *"For the last time stop talking to yourself and go to sleep!"* Radio was too damn public.

My interest in comics began on the most sophisticated of levels, the daily newspaper strip, and thereafter proceeded downhill. My father used to come home after work, when there was work, with two papers: the *New York Times* (a total loss), and the *World-Telegram.* The *Telegram* had *Joe Jinks* (later called *Dynamite Dunn*), *Our Boarding House, Out Our Way, Little Mary Mixup, Alley Oop*—and my favorite at the time: *Wash Tubbs,* whose soldier of fortune hero, Captain Easy, set a standard whose high point in one field was Pat Ryan and, in another, any role Clark Gable ever played.

For awhile the *Telegram* ran an anemic four-page color supplement that came out on Saturdays—an embarrassing day for color supplements. They so obviously belonged to Sunday. So except for the loss of Captain Easy, I felt no real grief when my father abandoned the *Telegram* to follow his hero, Heywood Broun to the *New York Evening Post.* The *Post* had *Dixie Dugan, The Bungle Family, Dinky Dinkerton, Secret Agent 6⅞, Nancy* (then called *Fritzi-Ritz*), and that masterpiece of sentimental naturalism: *Abbie an' Slats.* I studied that strip —its Sturges-like characters, its Saroyanesque plots, its uniquely cadenced dialogue. No strip other than Will Eisner's *Spirit* rivalled it in structure. No strip, except Caniff's *Terry,* rivalled it in atmosphere.

There were, of course, good strips, *very* good ones in those papers that my father did not let into the house. The *Hearst* papers. The *Daily News.* Cartoons from the outlawed press were not to be seen on weekdays, but on Sundays, one casually dropped in on Hearst-oriented homes (never very clean, as I remember), and read *Puck, The Comic Weekly,* skipping quickly over *Bringing Up Father* to pounce succulently on page two: *Jungle Jim* and *Flash Gordon.* Too beautiful to be believed. When *Prince Valiant* began a few years later, I burned with the temptation of the damned: I begged my father to sell out to Hearst. He never did. My Hearst friends and I drifted apart. My cause lost its urgency; my attention switched to *Terry and the Pirates*—in the *Daily News*—more hated in my house than even Hearst. Why, I must have wondered in kind, was it my lot to be a Capulet when the best strips were Montagues?

It should have been a relief, then, when the first regularly scheduled comic book came out. It was called *Famous Funnies* and, in sixty-four pages of color, minutely reprinted many of my favorites in the enemy camp. Instead, my reaction was that of a movie purist when first confronted with sound: this was not the way it was done. Greatness in order to remain great must stay true to its form. This new form, so jumbled together, so erratically edited and badly colored, was demeaning to that art—basic black and white and four panels across —that I was determined to make my life's work. I read them, yes I read them: *Famous Funnies* first, then *Popular Comics,* then *King* —but with always a sense of being cheated. I was not getting top performance for my dime.

Not until March, 1937, when the first issue of *Detective Comics* came out. Original material had previously been used in comic books, but almost all of it was in the shape and style of then existing newspaper strips.[1] *Detective Comics* was the first of the originals to be devoted to a single theme—crime fighting. And it looked different. Crime was fought in larger panels, fewer to a page. Most stories were complete in that issue (no more of the accursed: "to be continued . . ."). And a lot less shilly shallying before getting down to the action. A strange new world: unfamiliar heroes, unfamiliar drawing styles (if style is the word)—and written (if written is the word), in language not very different from that of a primer:

In every large city there are G-Men. In every large seaport there are G-Men known as Harbor Police. 'Speed' Cyril Saunders is a special operative in a unit of the river patrol.

So began story one, issue one of *Detective Comics.*

The typical comic book circa 1937–38 measured about 7¼ by 10¼, averaged sixty-four pages in length, was glisteningly processed in four colors on the cover and flatly and indifferently colored on the inside, if colored at all. (For in the early days some stories were still in black and white; others in tones of sickly red on one page, sickly blue on another, so that it was quite possible for a character to have a white

[1] *The Funnies* in 1929; *Detective Dan* in 1933; *New Fun* in 1935. The single unique stroke in the pre-*Detective Comics* days was the creation, by Sheldon Mayer, of the humor strip, *Scribbly*—an underrated, often brilliantly wild cartoon about a boy cartoonist with whom, needless to say, I identified like mad. I regret that it is not within the province of this book to give Mayer or *Scribbly* the space both of them deserve.

face and blue clothing for the first two pages of a story and a pink face and red clothing for the rest.) They didn't have the class of the daily strips but, to me, this enhanced their value. The daily strips, by their sleek professionalism held an aloof quality which comic books, being not quite professional, easily avoided. They were closer to home, more comfortable to live with, less like grownups.

The heroes were mostly detectives of one kind or another; or soldiers of fortune; here and there, even a magician. Whatever they were, they were tall, but not too tall—space limitations, you see; they were dark (blonde heroes were an exception, possibly because most movie heroes were dark; possibly because it was a chance for the artist to stick in a blob of black and call it hair. The blonde heroes, in every case, were curlyhaired. The dark heroes, when full color came in, turned blue); they were handsome—well, symbolically handsome. The world of comics was a form of visual shorthand, so that the average hero need not have been handsome in fact, so long as his face was held to the required arrangement of lines that readers had been taught to be the accepted sign of handsome: sharp, slanting eyebrows, thick at the ends, thinning out toward the nose, of which in three-quarter view there was hardly any—just a small V placed slightly above the mouth, casting the faintest knick of a shadow. One never saw a nose full view. There was never a full view. They were too hard to draw. Eyes were usually ball-less, two thin slits. Mouths were always thick, quick single lines—never double. Mouths for some reason, were rarely shown open. Dialogue, theoretically, was spoken from the nose. Heroes' faces were square-jawed; in some cases, all-jawed. Often there was a cleft in the chin. Most heroes, whatever magazine they came from, looked like members of one of two families: Pat Ryan's or Flash Gordon's. Except for the magicians, all of whom looked like Mandrake. The three mythic archetypes.

That first *Detective Comics,* aside from its ground-breaking role, is memorable for the debut of Creig Flessel, not then a good illustrator, but within the first half-dozen issues, to become one of the best in the business—a master of the suspense cover. And another debut: that of Jerry Siegel and Joe Shuster, then in their pre-*Superman* days, weighing in with a slam-bang, hell for leather cross between Victor McLaglen and Captain Easy (with a Flash Gordon jaw), appropriately named *Slam Bradley,* because slamming was what he did most of the time. Always, of course, against bad guys—and always having a wonderful time. It was this action-filled rawness, this world of lusty hoodlumism, of Saturday movie serials seven days a week that made the new comic books, from their first day of publication, the principal reading matter in my life. That, plus the pragmatic insight that here in a field where they hardly knew how to draw at all, I could make my earliest gains.

I studied styles. There was Tom Hickey who lettered with disconcerting open W's; who used an awful lot of dialogue ("printing," was the hated word for it in my neighborhood) to tell a painfully slow-moving story, full of heroes named Ian. Too thin-blooded. Too English.

There was Will Ely, a Caniff gone wrong, whose Pat Ryanish heroes lay flat on the paper, the shadows on their clothing more imposing than they were. The villains were usually bald with a few MacArthurish strands of hair—burly butcher boys smelling of sweat. In a fair fight they could easily take the hero—and often did, the first couple of times. Never in the end. But by that time I no longer cared. If the bad guy won every fight save the last, I had my doubts.

There was Fred Guardineer whose career was magicians—he drew more than anybody, all of them looking like Mandrake. Top hat, tails, flossy tie, mustache, glassy eyes. Each magician was equipped with an enormous brown servant not named Lothar. Guardineer's magicians, whatever they were called, wherever they were published, cast their spells by speaking backwards. "SKCOR KAERB NWOD LLAW!" Zatara would cry and rocks, rising from nowhere, would break down that wall. A fine point: could anybody speaking backwards have Zatara's magic—a villain for instance? The metaphysics shaky, the drawing style stiff, I gave up on Fred Guardineer.

The problem in pre-super days was that, with few exceptions, heroes were not very interesting. And by any realistic appraisal, certainly no match for the villains who were bigger, stronger, smarter (as who wasn't?), and, even worse, were notorious scene stealers. Who cared about Speed Saunders, Larry Steele, Bruce Nelson, et al. when there were oriental villains around? Tong warriors lurking in shadows, with trident beards, pointy fingernails, and skin the color of ripe lemons. With narrow, missile-like eyes slantingly aimed at the nose; a nose aged and curdled with corrupt wisdom, shrivelled in high expectancy of the coming tortures on the next page. How they toyed with those drab ofay heroes: trap set, trap sprung, into the pit, up comes the water, down comes the pendulum, out from the side come the walls.

Through an unconvincing mixture of dumb-luck and general science 1, the hero escaped, just barely; caught and beat up the villain: that wizened ancient who, in toe to toe combat was, of course, no match for the younger man. And readers were supposed to cheer? Hardly! The following month it all happened again. Same hero, different oriental, slight variance in the torture.

Villains, whatever fate befell them in the obligatory last panel, were infinitely better equipped than those silly, hapless heroes. Not only comics, but life taught us that. Those of us raised in ghetto neighborhoods were being asked to believe that crime didn't pay? Tell that to the butcher! Nice guys finished last; landlords, first. Villains by their simple appointment to the role were miles ahead. It was not to be believed that any ordinary human could combat them. More was required. Someone with a call. When *Superman* at last appeared, he brought with him the deep satisfaction of all underground truths: our reaction was less, "How original!" than, "But, of course!"

2

Leaping over skyscrapers, running faster than an express train, springing great distances and heights, lifting and smashing tremendous weights, possessing an impenetrable skin—these are the amazing attributes which Superman, savior of the helpless and oppressed, avails himself of as he battles the forces of evil and injustice.

Superman, *Action Comics*, August 1939

The advent of the super-hero was a bizarre comeuppance for the American dream. Horatio Alger could no longer make it on his own. He needed "Shazam!" Here was fantasy with a cynically realistic base: once the odds were appraised honestly it was apparent you had to be super to get on in this world.

The particular brilliance of Superman lay not only in the fact that he was the first of the super-heroes,[2] but in the concept of his alter ego. What made Superman different from the legion of imitators to follow was not that when he took off his clothes he could beat up everybody —they all did that. What made Superman extraordinary was his point of origin: Clark Kent.

Remember, Kent was not Superman's true identity as Bruce Wayne was the Batman's or (on radio) Lamont Cranston, the Shadow's. Just

[2] *Action Comics*, June 1938.

the opposite. Clark Kent was the fiction. Previous heroes, the Shadow, the Green Hornet, The Lone Ranger were not only more vulnerable, they were fakes. I don't mean to criticize, it's just a statement of fact. The Shadow had to cloud men's minds to be in business. The Green Hornet had to go through the fetishist fol-de-rol of donning costume, floppy hat, black mask, gas gun, menacing automobile, and insect sound effects before he was even ready to go out in the street. The Lone Ranger needed an accoutremental white horse, an Indian, and an establishing cry of Hi-Yo Silver to separate him from all those other masked men running around the West in days of yesteryear.

But Superman had only to wake up in the morning to be Superman. In his case, Clark Kent was the put on. The fellow with the eyeglasses and the acne and the walk girls laughed at wasn't real, didn't exist, was a sacrificial disguise, an act of discreet martyrdom. *Had they but known!*

And for what purpose? Did Superman become Clark Kent in order to lead a normal life, have friends, be known as a nice guy, meet girls? Hardly. There's too much of the hair shirt in the role, too much devotion to the imprimatur of impotence—an insight, perhaps, into the fantasy life of the Man of Steel. Superman as a secret masochist? Field for study there. For if it was otherwise, if the point, the only point, was to lead a "normal life," why not a more typical identity? How can one be a cowardly star reporter, subject to fainting spells in time of crisis, and not expect to raise serious questions?

The truth may be that Kent existed not for the purposes of the story but the reader. He is Superman's opinion of the rest of us, a pointed caricature of what we, the noncriminal element, were really like. His fake identity was our real one. That's why we loved him so. For if that wasn't really us; if there were no Clark Kents, only lots of glasses and cheap suits which, when removed, revealed all of us in our true identities—what a hell of an improved world it would have been!

In drawing style, both in figure and costume, Superman was a simplified parody of Flash Gordon. But if Alex Raymond was the Dior for Superman, Joe Shuster set the fashion from then on. Everybody else's super-costumes were copies from his shop. Shuster represented the best of old-style comic book drawing. His work was direct, unprettied —crude and vigorous; as easy to read as a diagram. No creamy lines, no glossy illustrative effects, no touch of that bloodless prefabrication that passes for professionalism these days. Slickness, thank God, was beyond his means. He could not draw well, but he drew single-mindedly—no one could ghost that style. It was the man. When assistants began "improving" the appearance of the strip it promptly went downhill. It looked like it was being drawn in a bank.

But, oh, those early drawings! Superman running up the sides of dams, leaping over anything that stood in his way (no one drew sky-scrapers like Shuster. Impressionistic shafts, Superman poised over them, his leaping leg tucked under his ass, his landing leg tautly pointed earthward), cleaning and jerking two-ton get-away cars and pounding them into the sides of cliffs—and all this done lightly, un-portentiously, still with that early Slam Bradley exuberance. What matter that the stories quickly lost interest; that once you've made a man super you've plotted him out of believable conflicts; that even super-villains, super-mad scientists and, yes, super-orientals were dull and lifeless next to the overwhelming image of that which Clark Kent became when he took off his clothes. So what if the stories were boring, the villains blah? This was the Superman Show—a touring road company backing up a great star. Everything was a stage wait until he came on. Then it was all worth-while.

Besides, for the alert reader there were other fields of interest. It seems that among Lois Lane, Clark Kent, and Superman there existed a schizoid and chaste *ménage à trois.* Clark Kent loved but felt abashed with Lois Lane; Superman saved Lois Lane when she was in trouble, found her a pest the rest of the time. Since Superman and Clark Kent were the same person this behavior demands explanation. It can't be that Kent wanted Lois to respect him for himself, since himself was Superman. Then, it appears, he wanted Lois to respect him for his fake self, to love him when he acted the coward, to be there when he pretended he needed her. She never was—so, of course, he loved her. A typical American romance. Superman never needed her, never needed anybody—in any event, Lois chased *him*—so, of course, he didn't love her. He had contempt for her. Another typical American romance.

Love is really the pursuit of a desired object, not pursuit by it. Once you've caught the object there is no longer any reason to love it, to have it hanging around. There must be other desirable objects out there, somewhere. So Clark Kent acted as the control for Superman. What Kent wanted was just that which Superman didn't want to be bothered with. Kent wanted Lois, Superman didn't: thus marking the difference

between a sissy and a man. A sissy wanted girls who scorned him; a
man scorned girls who wanted him. Our cultural opposite of the man
who didn't make out with women has never been the man who did—
but rather, the man who could if he wanted to, but still didn't. The
ideal of masculine strength, whether Gary Cooper's, Lil Abner's, or
Superman's, was for one to be so virile and handsome, to be in such a
position of strength that he need never go near girls. Except to help
them. And then get the hell out. Real rapport was not for women. It
was for villains. That's why they got hit so hard.

Afterword

1

> *"Respect for parents, the moral code, and for honorable behavior,
> shall be fostered.*
> *"Policemen, judges, government officials and respected institutions
> shall never be presented in such a way as to create disrespect for es-
> tablished authority.*
> *"In every instance good shall triumph over evil and the criminal
> punished for his misdeeds."*
>
> From The Code of the Comics Magazine
> Association of America

In the years since Dr. Wertham and his supporters launched their
attacks, comic books have toned down considerably, almost antisepti-
cally. Publishers in fear of their lives wrote a code, set up a review
board, and volunteered themselves into censorship rather than have it
imposed from the outside. Dr. Wertham scorns self-regulation as misleading. Old time fans scorn it as having brought on the death of comic
books as they once knew and loved them: for surprisingly, there *are*
old comic book fans. A small army of them. Men in their thirties and
early forties wearing school ties and tweeds, teaching in universities,
writing ad copy, writing for chic-magazines, writing novels—who
continue to be addicts; who save old comic books, buy them, trade
them, and will, many of them, pay up to fifty dollars for the first issues
of *Superman* or *Batman;* who publish and mail to each other mimeo-
graphed "fanzines"—strange little publications deifying what is
looked back on as "the golden age of comic books." Ruined by Wertham. Ruined by growing up.

So Dr. Wertham is wrong in his contention, quoted earlier, that no one matures remembering the things.

His other charges against comic books: that they were participating factors in juvenile delinquency and, in some cases, juvenile suicide, that they inspired experiments, *à la* Superman, in free-fall flight which could only end badly, that they were, in general, a corrupting influence, glorifying crime and depravity can only, in all fairness, be answered: "But of course. Why else read them?"

Comic books, first of all, are junk.[3] To accuse them of being what they are is to make no accusation at all: there is no such thing as *uncorrupt* junk or *moral* junk or *educational* junk—though attempts at the latter have, from time to time, been foisted on us. But education is not the purpose of junk (which is one reason why *True Comics* and *Classic Comics* and other half-hearted attempts to bring reality or literature into the field invariably looked embarrassing). Junk is there to entertain on the basest, most compromised of levels. It finds the lowest fantasmal common denominator and proceeds from there. Its choice of tone is dependent on its choice of audience, so that women's magazines will make a pretense at veneer scorned by movie-fan magazines, but both are, unarguably, junk. If not to their publishers, certainly to a good many of their readers who, when challenged, will say defiantly: "I know it's junk, but I like it." Which is the whole point about junk. It is there to be nothing else but liked. Junk is a second-class citizen of the arts; a status of which we and it are constantly aware. There are certain inherent privileges in second-class citizenship. Irresponsibility is one. Not being taken seriously is another. Junk, like the drunk at the wedding, can get away with doing or saying anything because, by its very appearance, it is already in disgrace. It has no one's respect to lose; no image to endanger. Its values are the least middle class of all the mass media. That's why it is needed so.

The success of the best junk lies in its ability to come close, but not too close; to titillate without touching us. To arouse without giving satisfaction. Junk is a tease; and in the years when the most we need is teasing we cherish it—in later years when teasing no longer satisfies we graduate—hopefully, into better things or haplessly, into pathetic, and sometimes violent attempts to make the teasing come true.

It is this antisocial side of junk that Dr. Wertham scorns in his at-

[3] There are a few exceptions, but nonjunk comic books don't, as a rule, last very long.

tack on comic books. What he dismisses—perhaps, because the case was made badly—is the more positive side of junk. (The entire debate on comic books was, in my opinion, poorly handled. The attack was strident and spotty; the defense, smug and spotty—proving, perhaps, that even when grownups correctly verbalize a point about children, they manage to miss it: so that a child expert can talk about how important fantasies of aggression are for children, thereby destroying forever the value of fantasies of aggression. Once a child is told: "Go on, darling. I'm watching. Fantasize," he no longer has a reason.) Still, there is a positive side to comic books that more than makes up for their much publicized antisocial influence. That is: their *underground* antisocial influence.

2

Adults have their defense against time: it is called "responsibility," and once one assumes it he can form his life into a set of routines which will account for all those hours when he is fresh, and justifies escape during all those hours when he is stale or tired. It is not size or age or childishness that separates children from adults. It is "responsibility." Adults come in all sizes, ages, and differing varieties of childishness, but as long as they have "responsibility" we recognize, often by the light gone out of their eyes, that they are what we call grownup. When grownups cope with "responsibility" for enough number of years they are retired from it. They are given, in exchange, a "leisure problem." They sit around with their "leisure problem" and try to figure out what to do with it. Sometimes they go crazy. Sometimes they get other jobs. Sometimes it gets too much for them and they die. They have been handed an undetermined future of nonresponsible time and they don't know what to do about it.

And that is precisely the way it is with children. Time is the ever-present factor in their lives. It passes slowly or fast, always against their best interests: good time is over in a minute; bad time takes forever. Short on "responsibility," they are confronted with a "leisure problem." That infamous question: "What am I going to do with myself?" correctly rephrased should read: "What am I going to do to get away from myself?"

And then, dear God, there's school! Nobody really knows why he's going to school. Even if one likes it, it is still, in the best light, an authoritarian restriction of freedom: where one has to obey and be subservient to people not even his parents. Where one has to learn concurrently, book rules and social rules, few of which are taught in a way to broaden horizons. So books become enemies and society becomes a hostile force that one had best put off encountering until the last moment possible.

Children, hungry for reasons, are seldom given convincing ones. They are bombarded with hard work, labelled education—not seen therefore as child labor. They rise for school at the same time or earlier than their fathers, start work without office chatter, go till noon without coffee breaks, have waxed milk for lunch instead of dry martinis, then back at the desk till three o'clock. Facing greater threats and riskier decisions than their fathers have had to meet since *their* day in school.

And always at someone else's convenience. Someone else dictates when to rise, what's to be good for breakfast, what's to be learned in school, what's to be good for lunch, what're to be play hours, what're to be homework hours, what's to be delicious for dinner and what's to be, suddenly, bedtime. This goes on until summer—when there is, once again, a "leisure problem." "What," the child asks, "am I going to do with myself?" Millions of things, as it turns out, but no sooner have they been discovered than it is time to go back to school.

It should come as no surprise then, that within this shifting hodgepodge of external pressures, a child, simply to save his sanity, must go underground. Have a place to hide where he cannot be got at by grownups. A place that implies, if only obliquely, that *they're* not so much; that *they* don't know everything; that *they* can't fly the way some people can, or let bullets bounce harmlessly off their chests, or beat up whomever picks on them, or—oh, joy of joys!—even become invisible! A no-man's land. A relief zone. And the basic sustenance for this relief was, in my day, comic books.

With them we were able to roam free, disguised in costume, committing the greatest of feats—and the worst of sins. And, in every instance, getting away with them. For a little while, at least, it was our show. For a little while, at least, we were the bosses. Psychically renewed, we could then return above ground and put up with another couple of days of victimization. Comic books were our booze.

Just as in earlier days for other children it was pulps, and *Nick Carter,* and penny dreadfuls—all junk in their own right, but less disapproved of latterly because they were less violent. But, predictably, as the ante on violence rose in the culture, so too did it rise in the junk.

3

Comic books, which had few public (as opposed to professional) defenders in the days that Dr. Wertham was attacking them, are now looked back on by an increasing number of my generation as samples of our youthful innocence instead of our youthful corruption. A sign, perhaps, of the potency of that corruption. A corruption—a lie, really —that put us in charge, however temporarily, of the world in which we lived; and gave us the means, however arbitrary, of defining right from wrong, good from bad, hero from villain. It is something for which old fans can understandably pine—almost as if having become overly conscious of the imposition of junk on our adult values: on our architecture, our highways, our advertising, our mass media, our politics—and even in the air we breathe, flying black chunks of it—we have staged a retreat to a better remembered brand of junk. A junk that knew its place was underground where it had no power and thus only titillated, rather than above ground where it truly has power— and thus, only depresses.

Part Four

The Discovery of High Culture

The essayist must finally learn to comment not only on raw experience and on popular attempts through "ritual" and "myth" to come to terms with it; he must also be able to reflect on works of the same order as the essay itself: on high art, which is to say, on man's subtlest and loveliest means of ordering and understanding his life. In one sense, the crown and climax of the essay is literary criticism.

It is necessary to distinguish literary criticism proper, which is a branch of the essay, from literary *theory,* which is a branch of philosophy or semantics, and newspaper book-reviewing, which is (most often) a branch of advertising. It is not hard to tell the real article. When the self-declared critic speaks in the humane voice of the essayist, when his ability to judge is attested to by the style in which he asserts it, he has a right to the title he claims. When, on the other hand, he pretends to speak in the authoritative jargon of the expert (it is a great temptation in the world of technicians) or lets himself lapse into the hearty vagueness of the ad-writer, he must be regarded with distrust.

Our age has frequently been called an "age of criticism," and there is real justice in such a label. If we produce an incredible quantity of printed material which boasts that it is criticism (with how much warrant is another matter), that is because we stand in *need* of criticism as

no age has before us. Pledged as we are to the ideal of universal literacy, and plagued as we are by the fact of the popular arts which discourage the development of reading skills, we are caught in a trap
from which we look about desperately for "literary experts" to deliver
us.

The student who has had trouble understanding some of these
essays and has found his classroom time devoted merely to *helping
him read,* will have found himself in a typical situation. More and
more, even so-called courses in literature on the college level become
courses in what should properly be called "The Higher Remedial
Reading." Indeed, it would be futile and hypocritical to devote them to
anything else.

On the other hand, such pedagogy, no matter how necessary, must
not be confused with the real job of the literary critic who provides
delight as well as wisdom. Yet the task of the critic has become one of
mediation analogous to that of the classroom teacher. Between the
writer who has despaired of his audience and the reader who has
despaired of art he intervenes with an art that dares never forget the
reader. Forbidden to descend to the dull level of mass persuasion, he
must yet persuade those happy enough in darkness and passivity before TV to make the effort necessary to read Homer or Shakespeare or
William Faulkner; even though that reading dooms them to a lifetime
of unhappiness before certain staple items of popular art.

With patience and modesty (and the tact that belongs only to art),
the critic must translate much that seems at first obscure, make allur-
ing much that seems unsympathetic, relate to the reader's world much
that seems alien and forbidding. At the same time, he must expose
much that seems clear as merely shallow, much that seems entertaining as dull, much that seems closest to the reader's world as remote
from all reality. All this he must do out of a love for excellence and
beauty, and in a style which guarantees that he himself is at home in
the world into which he is inviting the reader. This is the job which the
modern situation imposes upon critics; and those represented in this
collection are chosen from among the essayists who seem best to have
responded to the challenge.

There are two basic types of criticism, general and particular: a type
which deals with the broader problems of art and the artist, and a type
devoted to the analysis and evaluation of single works of art or the
lifework of a single artist. This section begins with a full-scale debate

between Henry James and Robert Louis Stevenson which is still topical and has to have special interest for the reader who comes to it after a consideration of the popular arts. The novel, as we know it, the kind of literature most of us read when we read anything at all, is in a certain sense the first literary product of mass culture. Certainly, it is the first new genre developed to meet the new possibilities opened up by the printing press, the spread of literacy and the institution of circulating libraries.

In France, the issues raised here had been fought out by the middle of the nineteenth century, but they were still unresolved in England and America when this debate was joined. What was at stake was nothing less than the question of whether the novel should continue to be regarded as a pleasant entertainment (one of the "popular arts"), redeemed by attaching sound morals to its conclusion, or whether it might be considered, in some cases at least, "high art," on the same level as epic or verse tragedy. James's position carried the day for the critics—but the mass of readers remained (and remain) pledged to the beliefs he attacks. This division helps to explain the deeper division of the novel's audience and of the novel itself into highbrow, lowbrow and middlebrow: a situation which finds a minority who read, say, James Joyce's *Ulysses* and look down on the larger group who read *The Robe* and in turn despise the still larger group who read Mickey Spillane.

It is well for the student to realize from the start the *polemical* nature of criticism at its liveliest. Though there may be somewhere absolute standards of good and bad in books (this hope, at least, sustains the critic), no one at any given moment knows them absolutely; and so critic combats critic until time brings in the verdict in favor of one or neither. The essays on individual writers and works which follow the debate on the novel are arranged to show the kind of fruitful disagreement, the passionate commitment to standards which underlie the critical enterprise. Lawrence defining a new Cooper for the twentieth century or Olson a new Melville, along with Melville himself properly recognizing Hawthorne for the first time, will give the reader a sense of the insecurity of literary judgments and of the necessity for making them all the same, if one cares about literature.

The reader will notice further that in some instances it is a matter of a European critic confronting an American (as in the case of Wyndham Lewis versus Randall Jarrell on Walt Whitman), and that some of the same issues are raised through and around literary texts as were posed over more general cultural questions in Part II. The authors discussed are, however, all Americans who lived in the nineteenth century: Cooper, Melville, Hawthorne, Twain and Whitman—writers whom the student is likely to have encountered even before getting to college. Some of them, indeed, may seem to the student only children's writers, because in addition to their art they possess great mythopoeic powers (sharing this quality with the popular arts) and can therefore reach minds not yet able to apprehend their form. Surely, Natty Bumppo, as Lawrence points out, lives in our minds the independent life of a great myth. In no case, however, have writers been included who are valid and moving only for the young.

The critics cover a wider range in time as well as space; not only do they come from France and England as well as America, but they range in period from Melville, who was born in 1819, to Jarrell, whose birthdate is 1914. All of the critics are imaginative writers, not essayists alone but poets or novelists or both: that is, readers (and the critic is finally the ideal reader always ideally prepared to talk about what he has read) who respond not primarily as experts on this or that, not as technicians or journalists, but as *men* pledged more than most to being articulate. For better or worse, the best critics writing in English have been largely those whose first fame rests on achievements in the creative arts outside the essay.

30. The Art of Fiction

H E N R Y   J A M E S

Henry James (1843–1916) is chiefly remarkable—aside from his books—for what did *not* happen to him. He had, from the beginning, no permanent home, moving from America to England to the Continent even as a child; he received, therefore, no formal education. His father—an extraordinarily free spirit for his time—taught him what he himself knew, which was to pursue freedom. He never

Source: *Partial Portraits* (London and New York: Macmillan and Co., 1888).

married or had children or participated in the great social events of his time, escaping the Civil War, for instance, because, it is alleged, of some mysterious "wound." Toward the end of his life, James made for the first time a political commitment, giving up his American citizenship and with it the freedom of the expatriate, to become a citizen of England where he had long resided. But his major continuing commitment was to the art of fiction, never abandoned except for brief, unfortunate flirtations with the drama. He left behind him an immense bulk of work, novels, novellas, short stories, criticism—and, even more importantly, the notion, new and profoundly disturbing in the English-speaking world, that the novel could and should be a work of art.

I should not have fixed so comprehensive a title to these few remarks, necessarily wanting in any completeness upon a subject the full consideration of which would carry us far, did I not seem to discover a pretext for my temerity in the interesting pamphlet lately published under this name by Mr. Walter Besant. Mr. Besant's lecture at the Royal Institution—the original form of his pamphlet—appears to indicate that many persons are interested in the art of fiction, and are not indifferent to such remarks as those who practise it may attempt to make about it. I am therefore anxious not to lose the benefit of this favourable association, and to edge in a few words under cover of the attention which Mr. Besant is sure to have excited. There is something very encouraging in his having put into form certain of his ideas on the mystery of story-telling.

It is a proof of life and curiosity—curiosity on the part of the brotherhood of novelists as well as on the part of their readers. Only a short time ago it might have been supposed that the English novel was not what the French call *discutable*. It had no air of having a theory, a conviction, a consciousness of itself behind it—of being the expression of an artistic faith, the result of choice and comparison. I do not say it was necessarily the worse for that: it would take much more courage than I possess to intimate that the form of the novel as Dickens and Thackeray (for instance) saw it had any taint of incompleteness. It was, however, *naïf* (if I may help myself out with another French word); and evidently if it be destined to suffer in any way for having lost its *naïveté* it has now an idea of making sure of the corresponding advantages. During the period I have alluded to there was a comfortable, good-humoured feeling abroad that a novel is a novel, as

a pudding is a pudding, and that our only business with it could be to
swallow it. But within a year or two, for some reason or other, there
have been signs of returning animation—the era of discussion would
appear to have been to a certain extent opened. Art lives upon discussion, upon experiment, upon curiosity, upon variety of attempt, upon
the exchange of views and the comparison of standpoints; and there is
a presumption that those times when no one has anything particular to
say about it, and has no reason to give for practice or preference,
though they may be times of honour, are not times of development—
are times, possibly, even a little of dulness. The successful application
of any art is a delightful spectacle, but the theory too is interesting; and
though there is a great deal of the latter without the former I suspect
there has never been a genuine success that has not had a latent core of
conviction. Discussion, suggestion, formulation, these things are ferti-
lising when they are frank and sincere. Mr. Besant has set an excellent
example in saying what he thinks, for his part, about the way in which
fiction should be written, as well as about the way in which it should be
published; for his view of the "art," carried on into an appendix,
covers that too. Other labourers in the same field will doubtless take
up the argument, they will give it the light of their experience, and the
effect will surely be to make our interest in the novel a little more what
it had for some time threatened to fail to be—a serious, active, inquiring interest, under protection of which this delightful study may,
in moments of confidence, venture to say a little more what it thinks of
itself.

It must take itself seriously for the public to take it so. The old
superstition about fiction being "wicked" has doubtless died out in
England; but the spirit of it lingers in a certain oblique regard directed
toward any story which does not more or less admit that it is only a
joke. Even the most jocular novel feels in some degree the weight of
the proscription that was formerly directed against literary levity: the
jocularity does not always succeed in passing for orthodoxy. It is still
expected, though perhaps people are ashamed to say it, that a production which is after all only a "make-believe" (for what else is a "story"?)
shall be in some degree apologetic—shall renounce the pretension
of attempting really to represent life. This, of course, any sensible,
wide-awake story declines to do, for it quickly perceives that the tolerance granted to it on such a condition is only an attempt to stifle it
disguised in the form of generosity. The old evangelical hostility to the

novel, which was as explicit as it was narrow, and which regarded it as little less favourable to our immortal part than a stage-play, was in reality far less insulting. The only reason for the existence of a novel is that it does attempt to represent life. When it relinquishes this attempt, the same attempt that we see on the canvas of the painter, it will have arrived at a very strange pass. It is not expected of the picture that it will make itself humble in order to be forgiven; and the analogy between the art of the painter and the art of the novelist is, so far as I am able to see, complete. Their inspiration is the same, their process (allowing for the different quality of the vehicle) is the same, their success is the same. They may learn from each other, they may explain and sustain each other. Their cause is the same, and the honour of one is the honour of another. The Mahometans think a picture an unholy thing, but it is a long time since any Christian did, and it is therefore the more odd that in the Christian mind the traces (dissimulated though they may be) of a suspicion of the sister art should linger to this day. The only effectual way to lay it to rest is to emphasise the analogy to which I just alluded—to insist on the fact that as the picture is reality, so the novel is history. That is the only general description (which does it justice) that we may give of the novel. But history also is allowed to represent life; it is not, any more than painting, expected to apologise. The subject-matter of fiction is stored up likewise in documents and records, and if it will not give itself away, as they say in California, it must speak with assurance, with the tone of the historian. Certain accomplished novelists have a habit of giving themselves away which must often bring tears to the eyes of people who take their fiction seriously. I was lately struck, in reading over many pages of Anthony Trollope, with his want of discretion in this particular. In a digression, a parenthesis or an aside, he concedes to the reader that he and this trusting friend are only "making believe." He admits that the events he narrates have not really happened, and that he can give his narrative any turn the reader may like best. Such a betrayal of a sacred office seems to me, I confess, a terrible crime; it is what I mean by the attitude of apology, and it shocks me every whit as much in Trollope as it would have shocked me in Gibbon or Macaulay. It implies that the novelist is less occupied in looking for the truth (the truth, of course I mean, that he assumes, the premises that we must grant him, whatever they may be) than the historian, and in doing so it deprives him at a stroke of all his standing-room. To represent and illustrate the past, the actions of men, is the task of either writer, and the only difference that I can see is, in proportion as he succeeds, to the honour of the novelist, consisting as it does in his having more difficulty in collecting his evidence, which is so far from being purely literary. It seems to me to give him a great character, the fact that he has at once so much in common with the philosopher and the painter; this double analogy is a magnificent heritage.

It is of all this evidently that Mr. Besant is full when he insists upon the fact that fiction is one of the *fine* arts, deserving in its turn of all the honours and emoluments that have hitherto been reserved for the successful profession of music, poetry, painting, architecture. It is impossible to insist too much on so important a truth, and the place that Mr. Besant demands for the work of the novelist may be represented, a trifle less abstractly, by saying that he demands not only that it shall be reputed artistic, but that it shall be reputed very artistic indeed. It is excellent that he should have struck this note, for his doing so indicates that there was need of it, that his proposition may be to many people a novelty. One rubs one's eyes at the thought; but the rest of Mr. Besant's essay confirms the revelation. I suspect in truth that it would be possible to confirm it still further, and that one would not be far wrong in saying that in addition to the people to whom it has never occurred that a novel ought to be artistic, there are a great many others who, if this principle were urged upon them, would be filled with an indefinable mistrust. They would find it difficult to explain their repugnance, but it would operate strongly to put them on their guard. "Art," in our Protestant communities, where so many things have got so strangely twisted about, is supposed in certain circles to have some vague injurious effect upon those who make it an important consideration, who let it weigh in the balance. It is assumed to be opposed in some mysterious manner to morality, to amusement, to instruction. When it is embodied in the work of the painter (the sculptor is another affair!) you know what it is: it stands there before you, in the honesty of pink and green and a gilt frame; you can see the worst of it at a glance, and you can be on your guard. But when it is introduced into literature it becomes more insidious—there is danger of its hurting you before you know it. Literature should be either instructive or amusing, and there is in many minds an impression that these artistic preoccupations, the search for form, contribute to neither end, interfere indeed with both. They are too frivolous to be edifying, and too serious to be diverting; and they are moreover priggish and paradoxical and superfluous. That, I think, represents the manner in which the latent thought of many people who read novels as an exercise in skipping would explain itself if it were to become articulate. They would argue, of course, that a novel ought to be "good," but they would interpret this term in a fashion of their own, which indeed would vary considerably from one critic to another. One would say that being good means representing virtuous and aspiring characters placed in prominent positions; another would say that it depends on a "happy ending," on a distribution at the last of prizes, pensions, husbands, wives, babies, millions, appended paragraphs, and cheerful remarks. Another still would say that it means being full of incident and movement, so that we shall wish to jump ahead, to see who was the mysterious stranger, and if the stolen will was ever found, and shall not be distracted from this pleasure by a tiresome analysis or "description." But they would all agree that the "artistic" idea would spoil some of their fun. One would hold it accountable for all the description, another would see it revealed in the absence of sympathy. Its hostility to a happy ending would be evident, and it might even in some cases render any ending at all impossible. The "ending" of a novel is, for many persons, like that of a good dinner, a course of dessert and ices, and the artist in fiction is regarded as a sort of meddlesome doctor who forbids agreeable aftertastes. It is therefore true that this conception of Mr. Besant's of the novel as a superior form encounters not only a negative but a positive indifference. It matters little that as a work of art it should really be as little or as much of its essence to supply happy endings, sympathetic characters, and an objective tone, as if it were a work of mechanics: the association of ideas, however incongruous, might easily be too much for it if an eloquent voice were not sometimes raised to call attention to the fact that it is at once as free and as serious a branch of literature as any other.

Certainly this might sometimes be doubted in presence of enormous number of works of fiction that appeal to the credulity of our generation, for it might easily seem that there could be no great character in a commodity so quickly and easily produced. It must be admitted that good novels are much compromised by bad ones, and that the field at large suffers discredit from overcrowding. I think, however, that this injury is only superficial, and that the superabundance of written fiction proves nothing against the principle itself. It has been vulgarised,

like all other kinds of literature, like everything else to-day, and it has
proved more than some kinds accessible to vulgarisation. But there is
as much difference as there ever was between a good novel and a bad
one: the bad is swept with all the daubed canvases and spoiled marble
into some unvisited limbo, or infinite rubbish-yard beneath the back-
windows of the world, and the good subsists and emits its light and
stimulates our desire for perfection. As I shall take the liberty of making but a single criticism of Mr. Besant, whose tone is so full of love of
his art, I may as well have done with it at once. He seems to me to
mistake in attempting to say so definitely beforehand what sort of an
affair the good novel will be. To indicate the danger of such an error as
that has been the purpose of these few pages; to suggest that certain
traditions on the subject, applied *a priori,* have already had much to
answer for, and that the good health of an art which undertakes so immediately to reproduce life must demand that it be perfectly free. It
lives upon exercise, and the very meaning of exercise is freedom. The
only obligation to which in advance we may hold a novel, without in-
curring the accusation of being arbitrary, is that it be interesting. That
general responsibility rests upon it, but it is the only one I can think of.
The ways in which it is at liberty to accomplish this result (of interesting us) strike me as innumerable, and such as can only suffer from
being marked out or fenced in by prescription. They are as various as
the temperament of man, and they are successful in proportion as they
reveal a particular mind, different from others. A novel is in its broadest definition a personal, a direct impression of life: that, to begin with,
constitutes its value, which is greater or less according to the intensity
of the impression. But there will be no intensity at all, and therefore no
value, unless there is freedom to feel and say. The tracing of a line to
be followed, of a tone to be taken, of a form to be filled out, is a limitation of that freedom and a suppression of the very thing that we are
most curious about. The form, it seems to me, is to be appreciated after
the fact; then the author's choice has been made, his standard has been
indicated; then we can follow lines and directions and compare tones
and resemblances. Then in a word we can enjoy one of the most charming of pleasures, we can estimate quality, we can apply the test of execution. The execution belongs to the author alone; it is what is most
personal to him, and we measure him by that. The advantage, the luxury, as well as the torment and responsibility of the novelist, is that
there is no limit to what he may attempt as an executant—no limit to

his possible experiments, efforts, discoveries, successes. Here it is especially that he works, step by step, like his brother of the brush, of whom we may always say that he has painted his picture in a manner best known to himself. His manner is his secret, not necessarily a jealous one. He cannot disclose it as a general thing if he would; he would be at a loss to teach it to others. I say this with a due recollection of having insisted on the community of method of the artist who paints a picture and the artist who writes a novel. The painter *is* able to teach the rudiments of his practice, and it is possible, from the study of good work (granted the aptitude), both to learn how to paint and to learn how to write. Yet it remains true, without injury to the *rapprochement,* that the literary artist would be obliged to say to his pupil much more than the other, "Ah, well, you must do it as you can!" It is a question of degree, a matter of delicacy. If there are exact sciences, there are also exact arts, and the grammar of painting is so much more definite that it makes the difference.

I ought to add, however, that if Mr. Besant says at the beginning of his essay that the "laws of fiction may be laid down and taught with as much precision and exactness as the laws of harmony, perspective, and proportion" he mitigates what might appear to be an extravagance by applying his remark to "general" laws, and by expressing most of these rules in a manner with which it would certainly be unaccommodating to disagree. That the novelist must write from his experience, that his "characters must be real and such as might be met with in actual life"; that "a young lady brought up in a quiet country village should avoid descriptions of garrison life," and "a writer whose friends and personal experiences belong to the lower middle-class should carefully avoid introducing his characters into society"; that one should enter one's notes in a commonplace book; that one's figures should be clear in outline; that making them clear by some trick of speech or of carriage is a bad method, and "describing them at length" is a worse one; that English Fiction should have a "conscious moral purpose"; that "it is almost impossible to estimate too highly the value of careful workmanship—that is, of style"; that "the most important point of all is the story," that "the story is everything": these are principles with most of which it is surely impossible not to sympathise. That remark about the lower middle-class writer and his knowing his place is perhaps rather chilling; but for the rest I should find it difficult to dissent from any one of these recommendations. At the same time, I should

find it difficult positively to assent to them, with the exception, perhaps, of the injunction as to entering one's notes in a commonplace
book. They scarcely seem to me to have the quality that Mr. Besant
attributes to the rules of the novelist—the "precision and exactness"
of "the laws of harmony, perspective, and proportion." They are suggestive, they are even inspiring, but they are not exact, though they are
doubtless as much so as the case admits of: which is a proof of that
liberty of interpretation for which I just contended. For the value of
these different injunctions—so beautiful and so vague—is wholly in
the meaning one attaches to them. The characters, the situation, which
strike one as real will be those that touch and interest one most, but the
measure of reality is very difficult to fix. The reality of Don Quixote or
of Mr. Micawber is a very delicate shade; it is a reality so coloured by
the author's vision that, vivid as it may be, one would hesitate to propose it as a model: one would expose one's self to some very embarrassing questions on the part of a pupil. It goes without saying that you
will not write a good novel unless you possess the sense of reality; but
it will be difficult to give you a recipe for calling that sense into being.
Humanity is immense, and reality has a myriad forms, the most one
can affirm is that some of the flowers of fiction have the odour of it, and
others have not; as for telling you in advance how your nosegay should
be composed, that is another affair. It is equally excellent and inconclusive to say that one must write from experience; to our supposititious
aspirant such a declaration might savour of mockery. What kind of
experience is intended, and where does it begin and end? Experience
is never limited, and it is never complete; it is an immense sensibility, a
kind of huge spider-web of the finest silken threads suspended in the
chamber of consciousness, and catching every air-borne particle in its
tissue. It is the very atmosphere of the mind; and when the mind is
imaginative—much more when it happens to be that of a man of
genius—it takes to itself the faintest hints of life, it converts the very
pulses of the air into revelations. The young lady living in a village has
only to be a damsel upon whom nothing is lost to make it quite unfair
(as it seems to me) to declare to her that she shall have nothing to say
about the military. Greater miracles have been seen than that, imagination assisting, she should speak the truth about some of these gentlemen. I remember an English novelist, a woman of genius, telling me
that she was much commended for the impression she had managed to
give in one of her tales of the nature and way of life of the French

Protestant youth. She had been asked where she learned so much about this recondite being, she had been congratulated on her peculiar opportunities. These opportunities consisted in her having once, in Paris, as she ascended a staircase, passed an open door where, in the household of a *pasteur,* some of the young Protestants were seated at table round a finished meal. The glimpse made a picture; it lasted only a moment, but that moment was experience. She had got her direct personal impression, and she turned out her type. She knew what youth was, and what Protestantism; she also had the advantage of having seen what it was to be French, so that she converted these ideas into a concrete image and produced a reality. Above all, however, she was blessed with the faculty which when you give it an inch takes an ell, and which for the artist is a much greater source of strength than any accident of residence or of place in the social scale. The power to guess the unseen from the seen, to trace the implication of things, to judge the whole piece by the pattern, the condition of feeling life in general so completely that you are well on your way to knowing any particular corner of it—this cluster of gifts may almost be said to constitute experience, and they occur in country and in town, and in the most differing stages of education. If experience consists of impressions, it may be said that impressions *are* experience, just as (have we not seen it?) they are the very air we breathe. Therefore, if I should certainly say to a novice, "Write from experience and from experience only," I should feel that this was rather a tantalising monition if I were not careful immediately to add, "Try to be one of the people on whom nothing is lost!"

I am far from intending by this to minimise the importance of exactness—of truth of detail. One can speak best from one's own taste, and I may therefore venture to say that the air of reality (solidity of specification) seems to me to be the supreme virtue of a novel—the merit on which all its other merits (including that conscious moral purpose of which Mr. Besant speaks) helplessly and submissively depend. If it be not there they are all as nothing, and if these be there, they owe their effect to the success with which the author has produced the illusion of life. The cultivation of this success, the study of this exquisite process, form, to my taste, the beginning and the end of the art of the novelist. They are his inspiration, his despair, his reward, his torment, his delight. It is here in very truth that he competes with life; it is here that he competes with his brother the painter in his attempt to render the look of things, the look that conveys their meaning, to catch the colour, the relief, the expression, the surface, the substance of the human spectacle. It is in regard to this that Mr. Besant is well inspired when he bids him take notes. He cannot possibly take too many, he cannot possibly take enough. All life solicits him, and to "render" the simplest surface, to produce the most momentary illusion, is a very complicated business. His case would be easier, and the rule would be more exact, if Mr. Besant had been able to tell him what notes to take. But this, I fear, he can never learn in any manual; it is the business of his life. He has to take a great many in order to select a few, he has to work them up as he can, and even the guides and philosophers who might have most to say to him must leave him alone when it comes to the application of precepts, as we leave the painter in communion with his palette. That his characters "must be clear in outline" as Mr. Besant says—he feels that down to his boots; but how he shall make them so is a secret between his good angel and himself. It would be absurdly simple if he could be taught that a great deal of "description" would make them so, or that on the contrary the absence of description and the cultivation of dialogue, or the absence of dialogue and the multiplication of "incident," would rescue him from his difficulties. Nothing, for instance, is more possible than that he be of a turn of mind for which this odd, literal opposition of description and dialogue, incident and description, has little meaning and light. People often talk of these things as if they had a kind of internecine distinctness, instead of melting into each other at every breath, and being intimately associated parts of one general effort of expression. I cannot imagine composition existing in a series of blocks, nor conceive, in any novel worth discussing at all, of a passage of description that is not in its intention narrative, a passage of dialogue that is not in its intention descriptive, a touch of truth of any sort that does not partake of the nature of incident, or an incident that derives its interest from any other source than the general and only source of the success of a work of art—that of being illustrative. A novel is a living thing, all one and continuous, like any other organism, and in proportion as it lives will it be found, I think, that in each of the parts there is something of each of the other parts. The critic who over the close texture of a finished work shall pretend to trace a geography of items will mark some frontiers as artificial, I fear, as any that have been known to history. There is an old-fashioned distinction between the novel of character and the novel of incident which must have cost many a smile to the intending fabulist who was keen about his work. It appears to me as little to the point as the equally celebrated distinction between the novel and the romance —to answer as little to any reality. There are bad novels and good novels, as there are bad pictures and good pictures; but that is the only distinction in which I see any meaning, and I can as little imagine speaking of a novel of character as I can imagine speaking of a picture of character. When one says picture one says of character, when one says novel one says of incident, and the terms may be transposed at will. What is character but the determination of incident? What is incident but the illustration of character? What is either a picture or a novel that is not of character? What else do we seek in it and find in it? It is an incident for a woman to stand up with her hand resting on a table and look at you in a certain way; or if it be not an incident I think it will be hard to say what it is. At the same time it is an expression of character. If you say you don't see it (character in *that—allons donc!*), this is exactly what the artist who has reasons of his own for thinking he does see it undertakes to show you. When a young man makes up his mind that he has not faith enough after all to enter the Church as he intended, that is an incident, though you may not hurry to the end of the chapter to see whether perhaps he doesn't change once more. I do not say that these are extraordinary or startling incidents. I do not pretend to estimate the degree of interest proceeding from them, for this will depend upon the skill of the painter. It sounds almost puerile to say that some incidents are intrinsically much more important than others, and I need not take this precaution after having professed my sympathy for the major ones in remarking that the only classification of the novel that I can understand is into that which has life and that which has it not.

The novel and the romance, the novel of incident and that of character—these clumsy separations appear to me to have been made by critics and readers for their own convenience, and to help them out of some of their occasional predicaments, but to have little reality or interest for the producer, from whose point of view it is of course that we are attempting to consider the art of fiction. The case is the same with another shadowy category which Mr. Besant apparently is disposed to set up—that of the "modern English novel"; unless indeed it be that in this matter he has fallen into an accidental confusion of standpoints. It is not quite clear whether he intends the remarks in which he alludes to it to be didactic or historical. It is as difficult to suppose a person intending to write a modern English as to suppose him writing an ancient English novel: that is a label which begs the question. One writes the novel, one paints the picture, of one's language and of one's time, and calling it modern English will not, alas! make the difficult task any easier. No more, unfortunately, will calling this or that work of one's fellow-artist a romance—unless it be, of course, simply for the pleasantness of the thing, as for instance when Hawthorne gave this heading to his story of *Blithedale*. The French, who have brought the theory of fiction to remarkable completeness, have but one name for the novel, and have not attempted smaller things in it, that I can see, for that. I can think of no obligation to which the "romancer" would not be held equally with the novelist; the standard of execution is equally high for each. Of course it is of execution that we are talking—that being the only point of a novel that is open to contention. This is perhaps too often lost sight of, only to produce interminable confusions and cross-purposes. We must grant the artist his subject, his idea, his *donnée:* our criticism is applied only to what he makes of it. Naturally I do not mean that we are bound to like it or find it interesting: in case we do not our course is perfectly simple—to let it alone. We may believe that of a certain idea even the most sincere novelist can make nothing at all, and the event may perfectly justify our belief; but the failure will have been a failure to execute, and it is in the execution that the fatal weakness is recorded. If we pretend to respect the artist at all, we must allow him his freedom of choice, in the face, in particular cases, of innumerable presumptions that the choice will not fructify. Art derives a considerable part of its beneficial exercise from flying in the face of presumptions, and some of the most interesting experiments of which it is capable are hidden in the bosom of common things. Gustave Flaubert has written a story about the devotion of a servant-girl to a parrot, and the production, highly finished as it is, cannot on the whole be called a success. We are perfectly free to find it flat, but I think it might have been interesting; and I, for my part, am extremely glad he should have written it; it is a contribution to our knowledge of what can be done—or what cannot. Ivan Turgeniéff has written a tale about a deaf and dumb serf and a lap-dog, and the thing is touching, loving, a little masterpiece. He struck the note of life where Gustave Flaubert missed it—he flew in the face of a presumption and achieved a victory.

Nothing, of course, will ever take the place of the good old fashion of "liking" a work of art or not liking it: the most improved criticism will not abolish that primitive, that ultimate test. I mention this to guard myself from the accusation of intimating that the idea, the subject, of a novel or a picture, does not matter. It matters, to my sense, in the highest degree, and if I might put up a prayer it would be that artists should select none but the richest. Some, as I have already hastened to admit, are much more remunerative than others, and it would be a world happily arranged in which persons intending to treat them should be exempt from confusions and mistakes. This fortunate condition will arrive only, I fear, on the same day that critics become purged from error. Meanwhile, I repeat, we do not judge the artist with fairness unless we say to him, "Oh, I grant you your starting-point, because if I did not I should seem to prescribe to you, and heaven forbid I should take that responsibility. If I pretend to tell you what you must not take, you will call upon me to tell you then what you must take; in which case I shall be prettily caught. Moreover, it isn't till I have accepted your data that I can begin to measure you. I have the standard, the pitch; I have no right to tamper with your flute and then criticise your music. Of course I may not care for your idea at all; I may think it silly, or stale, or unclean; in which case I wash my hands of you altogether. I may content myself with believing that you will not have succeeded in being interesting, but I shall, of course, not attempt to demonstrate it, and you will be as indifferent to me as I am to you. I needn't remind you that there are all sorts of tastes: who can know it better? Some people, for excellent reasons, don't like to read about carpenters; others, for reasons even better, don't like to read about courtesans. Many object to Americans. Others (I believe they are mainly editors and publishers) won't look at Italians. Some readers don't like quiet subjects; others don't like bustling ones. Some enjoy a complete illusion, others the consciousness of large concessions. They choose their novels accordingly, and if they don't care about your idea they won't *a fortiori,* care about your treatment."

So that it comes back very quickly, as I have said, to the liking: in spite of M. Zola, who reasons less powerfully than he represents, and who will not reconcile himself to this absoluteness of taste, thinking that there are certain things that people ought to like, and that they can be made to like. I am quite at a loss to imagine anything (at any rate in this matter of fiction) that people ought to like or to dislike. Selection will be sure to take care of itself, for it has a constant motive behind it. That motive is simply experience. As people feel life, so they will feel the art that is most closely related to it. This closeness of relation is what we should never forget in talking of the effort of the novel. Many people speak of it as a factitious, artificial form, a product of ingenuity, the business of which it is to alter and arrange the things that surround us, to translate them into conventional, traditional moulds. This, however, is a view of the matter which carries us but a very short way, condemns the art to an external repetition of a few familiar *clichés,* cuts short its development, and leads us straight up to a dead wall. Catching the very note and trick, the strange irregular rhythm of life, that is the attempt whose strenuous force keeps Fiction upon her feet. In proportion as in what she offers us we see life *without* rearrangement do we feel that we are touching the truth; in proportion as we see it *with* rearrangement do we feel that we are being put off with a substitute, a compromise and convention. It is not uncommon to hear an extraordinary assurance of remark in regard to this matter of rearranging, which is often spoken of as if it were the last word of art. Mr. Besant seems to me in danger of falling into the great error with his rather unguarded talk about "selection." Art is essentially selection, but it is a selection whose main care is to be typical, to be inclusive. For many people art means rose-colored windowpanes, and selection means picking a bouquet for Mrs. Grundy. They will tell you glibly that artistic considerations have nothing to do with the disagreeable, with the ugly; they will rattle off shallow commonplaces about the province of art and the limits of art till you are moved to some wonder in return as to the province and the limits of ignorance. It appears to me that no one can ever have made a seriously artistic attempt without becoming conscious of an immense increase—a kind of revelation —of freedom. One perceives in that case—by the light of a heavenly ray—that the province of art is all life, all feeling, all observation, all vision. As Mr. Besant so justly intimates, it is all experience. That is a sufficient answer to those who maintain that it must not touch the sad things of life, who stick into its divine unconscious bosom little prohibitory inscriptions on the end of sticks, such as we see in public gardens—"It is forbidden to walk on the grass; it is forbidden to touch the flowers; it is not allowed to introduce dogs or to remain after dark; it is requested to keep to the right." The young aspirant in the line of fiction whom we continue to imagine will do nothing without taste, for in that case his freedom would be of little use to him; but the first advantage of his taste will be to reveal to him the absurdity of the little sticks and tickets. If he have taste, I must add, of course he will have ingenuity, and my disrespectful reference to that quality just now was not meant to imply that it is useless in fiction. But it is only a secondary aid; the first is a capacity for receiving straight impressions.

Mr. Besant has some remarks on the question of "the story" which I shall not attempt to criticise, though they seem to me to contain a singular ambiguity, because I do not think I understand them. I cannot see what is meant by talking as if there were a part of a novel which is the story and part of it which for mystical reasons is not—unless indeed the distinction be made in a sense in which it is difficult to suppose that any one should attempt to convey anything. "The story," if it represents anything, represents the subject, the idea, the *donnée* of the novel; and there is surely no "school"—Mr. Besant speaks of a school —which urges that a novel should be all treatment and no subject. There must assuredly be something to treat; every school is intimately conscious of that. This sense of the story being the idea, the starting-point, of the novel, is the only one that I see in which it can be spoken of as something different from its organic whole; and since in proportion as the work is successful the idea permeates and penetrates it, informs and animates it, so that every word and every punctuation-point contribute directly to the expression, in that proportion do we lose our sense of the story being a blade which may be drawn more or less out of its sheath. The story and the novel, the idea and the form, are the needle and thread, and I never heard of a guild of tailors who recommended the use of the thread without the needle, or the needle without the thread. Mr. Besant is not the only critic who may be observed to have spoken as if there were certain things in life which constitute stories, and certain others which do not. I find the same odd implication in an entertaining article in the *Pall Mall Gazette,* devoted, as it happens, to Mr. Besant's lecture. "The story is the thing!" says this graceful writer, as if with a tone of opposition to some other idea. I should think it was, as every painter who, as the time for "sending in" his picture looms in the distance, finds himself still in quest of a subject —as every belated artist not fixed about his theme will heartily agree. There are some subjects which speak to us and others which do not, but he would be a clever man who should undertake to give a rule— an *index expurgatorius*—by which the story and the no-story should be known apart. It is impossible (to me at least) to imagine any such rule which shall not be altogether arbitrary. The writer in the *Pall Mall* opposes the delightful (as I suppose) novel of *Margot la Balafrée* to certain tales in which "Bostonian nymphs" appear to have "rejected English dukes for psychological reasons." I am not acquainted with the romance just designated, and can scarcely forgive the *Pall Mall* critic for not mentioning the name of the author, but the title appears to refer to a lady who may have received a scar in some heroic adventure. I am inconsolable at not being acquainted with this episode, but am utterly at a loss to see why it is a story when the rejection (or acceptance) of a duke is not, and why a reason, psychological or other, is not a subject when a cicatrix is. They are all particles of the multitudinous life with which the novel deals, and surely no dogma which pretends to make it lawful to touch the one and unlawful to touch the other will stand for a moment on its feet. It is the special picture that must stand or fall, according as it seem to possess truth or to lack it. Mr. Besant does not, to my sense, light up the subject by intimating that a story must, under penalty of not being a story, consist of "adventures." Why of adventures more than of green spectacles? He mentions a category of impossible things, and among them he places "fiction without adventure." Why without adventure, more than without matrimony, or celibacy, or parturition, or cholera, or hydropathy, or Jansenism? This seems to me to bring the novel back to the hapless little *rôle* of being an artificial, ingenious thing—bring it down from its large, free character of an immense and exquisite correspondence with life. And what is adventure when it comes to that, and by what sign is the listening pupil to recognize it? It is an adventure—an immense one—for me to write this little article; and for a Bostonian nymph to reject an English duke is an adventure only less stirring, I should say, than for an English duke to be rejected by a Bostonian nymph. I see dramas within dramas in that, and innumerable points of view. A psychological reason is, to my imagination, an object adorably pictorial; to catch the tint of its complexion—I feel as if that idea might inspire one to Titianesque efforts. There are few things more exciting to me, in short, than a psychological reason, and yet, I protest, the novel seems to me the most magnificent form of art. I have just been reading, at the same time, the delightful story of *Treasure Island,* by Mr. Robert Louis Stevenson, and, in a manner less consecutive, the last tale from M. Edmond de Goncourt, which is entitled *Chérie.* One of these works treats of murders, mysteries, islands of dreadful renown, hairbreadth escapes, miraculous coincidences and buried doubloons. The other treats of a little French girl who lived in a fine house in Paris, and died of wounded sensibility because no one would marry her. I call *Treasure Island* delightful, because it appears to me to have succeeded wonderfully in what it attempts; and I venture to bestow no epithet upon *Chérie,* which strikes me as having failed deplorably in what it attempts—that is in tracing the development of the moral consciousness of a child. But one of these productions strikes me as exactly as much of a novel as the other, and as having a "story" quite as much. The moral consciousness of a child is as much a part of life as the islands of the Spanish Main, and the one sort of geography seems to me to have those "surprises" of which Mr. Besant speaks quite as much as the other. For myself (since it comes back in the last resort as I say, to the preference of the individual), the picture of the child's experience has the advantage that I can at successive steps (an immense luxury, near to the "sensual pleasure" of which Mr. Besant's critic in the *Pall Mall* speaks) say Yes or No, as it may be, to what the artist puts before me. I have been a child in fact, but I have been on a quest for a buried treasure only in supposition, and it is a simple accident that with M. De Goncourt I should have for the most part to say No. With George Eliot, when she painted that country with a far other intelligence, I always said Yes.

The most interesting part of Mr. Besant's lecture is unfortunately the briefest passage—his very cursory allusion to the "conscious moral purpose" of the novel. Here again it is not very clear whether he be recording a fact or laying down a principle; it is a great pity that in the latter case he should not have developed his idea. This branch of the subject is of immense importance, and Mr. Besant's few words point to considerations of the widest reach, not to be lightly disposed of. He will have treated the art of fiction but superficially who is not prepared to go every inch of the way that these considerations will carry him. It is for this reason that at the beginning of these remarks I was careful to notify the reader that my reflections on so large a theme have no pretention to be exhaustive. Like Mr. Besant, I have left the question of the morality of the novel till the last, and at the last I find I have used up my space. It is a question surrounded with difficulties, as witness the very first that meets us, in the form of a definite question, on the threshold. Vagueness, in such a discussion, is fatal, and what is the meaning of your morality and your conscious moral purpose? Will you not define your terms and explain how (a novel being a picture) a picture can be either moral or immoral? You wish to paint a moral picture or carve a moral statue: will you not tell us how you would set about it? We are discussing the Art of Fiction; questions of art are questions (in the widest sense) of execution; questions of morality are quite another affair, and will you not let us see how it is that you find it so easy to mix them up? These things are so clear to Mr. Besant that he has deduced from them a law which he sees embodied in English Fiction, and which is "a truly admirable thing and a great cause for congratulation." It is a great cause for congratulation indeed when such thorny problems become as smooth as silk. I may add that in so far as Mr. Besant perceives that in point of fact English Fiction has addressed itself preponderantly to these delicate questions he will appear to many people to have made a vain discovery. They will have been positively struck, on the contrary, with the moral timidity of the usual English novelist; with his (or with her) aversion to face the difficulties with which on every side the treatment of reality bristles. He is apt to be extremely shy (whereas the picture that Mr. Besant draws is a picture of boldness), and the sign of his work, for the most part, is a cautious silence on certain subjects. In the English novel (by which of course I mean the American as well), more than in any other, there is a traditional difference between that which people know and that which they agree to admit that they know, that which they see and that which they speak of, that which they feel to be a part of life, and that which they allow to enter into literature. There is the great difference, in short, between what they talk of in conversation and what they talk of in print. The essence of moral energy is to survey the whole field, and I should directly reverse Mr. Besant's remark and say not that the English novel has a purpose, but that it has a diffidence. To what degree a purpose in a work of art is a source of corruption I shall not attempt to inquire; the one that seems to me least dangerous is the purpose of making a perfect work. As for our novel, I may say lastly on this score that as we find it in England today it strikes me as addressed in a large degree to "young people," and that this in itself constitutes a presumption that it will be rather shy. There are certain things which it is generally agreed not to discuss, not even to mention, before young people. That is very well, but the absence of discussion is not a symptom of the moral passion. The purpose of the English novel—"a truly admirable thing, and a great cause for congratulation"—strikes me therefore as rather negative.

There is one point at which the moral sense and the artistic sense lie very near together; that is in the light of the very obvious truth that the deepest quality of a work of art will always be the quality of the mind of the producer. In proportion as that intelligence is fine will the novel, the picture, the statue partake of the substance of beauty and truth. To be constituted of such elements is, to my vision, to have purpose enough. No good novel will ever proceed from a superficial mind; that seems to me an axiom which, for the artist in fiction, will cover all needful moral ground: if the youthful aspirant take it to heart it will illuminate for him many of the mysteries of "purpose." There are many other useful things that might be said to him, but I have come to the end of my article, and can only touch them as I pass. The critic in the *Pall Mall Gazette,* whom I have already quoted, draws attention to the danger, in speaking of the art of fiction, of generalising. The danger that he has in mind is rather, I imagine, that of particularising, for there are some comprehensive remarks which, in addition to those embodied in Mr. Besant's suggestive lecture, might without fear of misleading him be addressed to the ingenuous student. I should remind him first of the magnificence of the form that is open to him, which offers to sight so few restrictions and such innumerable opportunities. The other arts, in comparison, appear confined and hampered; the various conditions under which they are exercised are so rigid and definite. But the only condition that I can think of attaching to the composition of the novel is, as I have already said, that it be sincere. This freedom is a splendid privilege, and the first lesson of the young novelist is to learn to be worthy of it. "Enjoy it as it deserves," I should say to him; "take possession of it, explore it to its utmost extent, publish it, rejoice in it. All life belongs to you, and do not listen either to those who would shut you up into corners of it and tell you that it is only here and there that art inhabits, or to those who would persuade you that this heavenly messenger wings her way outside of life altogether, breathing a superfine air, and turning away her head from the truth of things. There is no impression of life, no manner of seeing it and feeling it, to which the plan of the novelist may not offer a place; you have only to remember that talents so dissimilar as those of Alexandre Dumas and Jane Austen, Charles Dickens and Gustave Flaubert have worked in this field with equal glory. Do not think too much about optimism and pessimism; try and catch the colour of life itself. In France today we see a prodigious effort (that of Emile Zola, to whose solid and serious work no explorer of the capacity of the novel can allude without respect), we see an extraordinary effort, vitiated by a spirit of pessimism on a narrow basis. M. Zola is magnificent, but he strikes an English reader as ignorant; he has an air of working in the dark; if he had as much light as energy, his results would be of the highest value. As for the aberrations of a shallow optimism, the ground (of English fiction especially) is strewn with their brittle particles as with broken glass. If you must indulge in conclusions, let them have the taste of a wide knowledge. Remember that your first duty is to be as complete as possible—to make as perfect a work. Be generous and delicate and pursue the prize."

31. A Humble Remonstrance

R OBERT L OUIS S TEVENSON

Robert Louis Stevenson (1850–1894) was born in Scotland and died in Samoa, pausing briefly in his westward journeying to acquire a wife in the United States. He thus reversed the spiritual pilgrimage of Henry James—their paths actually crossing in England, where they became good friends despite the incompatibility of their books and lives. Stevenson's father, unlike James's, taught him to distrust art, and even when he devoted himself to it, he could never quite convince himself that it was a proper pursuit of maturity. "To play with paper, like a child," he ironically described the writer's task. Fortunately, however, Stevenson had a taste for being a child; and though he never begot a son of his own, he acquired one along with his wife, writing for him *Treasure Island*—a masterpiece by mistake, which is to say, a great mythological book produced in an age which only permitted mythology in the nursery.

SOURCE: Robert Louis Stevenson, *Memories and Portraits* (Boston: Small, Maynard & Co., 1907), pp. 240–62.

We have recently enjoyed a quite peculiar pleasure: hearing, in some detail, the opinions, about the art they practise, of Mr. Walter Besant and Mr. Henry James; two men certainly of very different calibre: Mr. James so precise of outline, so cunning of fence, so scrupulous of finish, and Mr. Besant so genial, so friendly, with so persuasive and humorous a vein of whim: Mr. James the very type of the deliberate artist, Mr. Besant the impersonation of good nature. That such doctors should differ will excite no great surprise; but one point in which they seem to agree fills me, I confess, with wonder. For they are both content to talk about the "art of fiction;" and Mr. Besant, waxing exceedingly bold, goes on to oppose this so-called "art of fiction" to the "art of poetry." By the art of poetry he can mean nothing but the art of verse, an art of handicraft, and only comparable with the art of prose. For that heat and height of sane emotion which we agree to call by the name of poetry, is but a libertine and vagrant quality; present, at times, in any art, more often absent from them all; too seldom present in the prose novel, too frequently absent from the ode and epic. Fiction is in the same case; it is no substantive art, but an element which enters largely into all the arts but architecture. Homer, Wordsworth, Phidias, Hogarth, and Salvini, all deal in fiction; and yet I do not suppose that either Hogarth or Salvini, to mention but these two, entered in any degree into the scope of Mr. Besant's interesting lecture or Mr. James's charming essay. The art of fiction, then, regarded as a definition, is both too ample and too scanty. Let me suggest another; let me suggest that what both Mr. James and Mr. Besant had in view was neither more nor less than the art of narrative.

But Mr. Besant is anxious to speak solely of "the modern English novel," the stay and bread-winner of Mr. Mudie; and in the author of the most pleasing novel on that roll, *All Sorts and Conditions of Men,* the desire is natural enough. I can conceive then, that he would hasten to propose two additions, and read thus: the art of *fictitious* narrative *in prose.*

Now the fact of the existence of the modern English novel is not to be denied; materially, with its three volumes, leaded type, and gilded lettering, it is easily distinguishable from other forms of literature; but to talk at all fruitfully of any branch of art, it is needful to build our definitions on some more fundamental ground than binding. Why, then, are we to add "in prose"? *The Odyssey* appears to me the best of romances; *The Lady of the Lake* to stand high in the second order; and Chaucer's tales and prologues to contain more of the matter and art of the modern English novel than the whole treasury of Mr. Mudie. Whether a narrative be written in blank verse or the Spenserian stanza, in the long period of Gibbon or the chipped phrase of Charles Reade, the principles of the art of narrative must be equally observed. The choice of a noble and swelling style in prose affects the problem of narration in the same way, if not to the same degree, as the choice of measured verse; for both imply a closer synthesis of events, a higher key of dialogue, and a more picked and stately strain of words. If you are to refuse *Don Juan,* it is hard to see why you should include *Zanoni* or (to bracket works of very different value) *The Scarlet Letter;* and by what discrimination are you to open your doors to *The Pilgrim's Progress* and close them on *The Faery Queen?* To bring things closer home, I will here propound to Mr. Besant a conundrum. A narrative called *Paradise Lost* was written in English verse by one John Milton; what was it then? It was next translated by Chateaubriand into French prose; and what was it then? Lastly, the French translation was, by some inspired compatriot of George Gilfillan (and of mine) turned bodily into an English novel; and, in the name of clearness, what was it then?

But, once more, why should we add "fictitious"? The reason why is obvious. The reason why not, if something more recondite, does not want for weight. The art of narrative, in fact, is the same, whether it is applied to the selection and illustration of a real series of events or of an imaginary series. Boswell's *Life of Johnson* (a work of cunning and inimitable art) owes its success to the same technical manoeuvres as (let us say) *Tom Jones:* the clear conception of certain characters of man, the choice and presentation of certain incidents out of a great number that offered, and the invention (yes, invention) and preservation of a certain key in dialogue. In which these things are done with the more art—in which with the greater air of nature—readers will differently judge. Boswell's is, indeed, a very special case, and almost a generic; but it is not only in Boswell, it is in every biography with any salt of life, it is in every history where events and men, rather than ideas, are presented—in Tacitus, in Carlyle, in Michelet, in Macaulay—that the novelist will find many of his own methods most conspicuously and adroitly handled. He will find besides that he, who is free—who has the right to invent or steal a missing incident, who has the right, more precious still, of wholesale omission—is frequently defeated, and, with all his advantages, leaves a less strong impression of reality and passion. Mr. James utters his mind with a becoming fervour on the sanctity of truth to the novelist; on a more careful examination truth will seem a word of very debateable propriety, not only for the labours of the novelist, but for those of the historian. No art—to use the daring phrase of Mr. James—can successfully "compete with life;" and the art that seeks to do so is condemned to perish *montibus aviis*. Life goes before us, infinite in complication; attended by the most various and surprising meteors; appealing at once to the eye, to the ear, to the mind—the seat of wonder, to the touch—so thrillingly delicate, and to the belly—so imperious when starved. It combines and employs in its manifestation the method and material, not of one art only, but of all the arts. Music is but an arbitrary trifling with a few of life's majestic chords; painting is but a shadow of its pageantry of light and colour; literature does but drily indicate that wealth of incident, of moral obligation, of virtue, vice, action, rapture and agony, with which it teems. To "compete with life," whose sun we cannot look upon, whose passions and diseases waste and slay us—to compete with the flavour of wine, the beauty of the dawn, the scorching of fire, the bitterness of death and separation—here is, indeed, a projected escalade of heaven; here are, indeed, labours for a Hercules in a dress coat, armed with a pen and a dictionary to depict the passions, armed with a tube of superior flake-white to paint the portrait of the insufferable sun. No art is true in this sense: none can "compete with life": not even history, built indeed of indisputable facts, but these facts robbed of their vivacity and sting; so that even when we read of the sack of a city or the fall of an empire, we are surprised, and justly commend the author's talent, if our pulse be quickened. And mark, for a last differentia, that this quickening of the pulse is, in almost every case, purely agreeable; that these phantom reproductions of experience, even at their most acute, convey decided pleasure; while experience itself, in the cockpit of life, can torture and slay.

What, then, is the object, what the method, of an art, and what the source of its power? The whole secret is that no art does "compete with life." Man's one method, whether he reasons or creates, is to half-shut his eyes against the dazzle and confusion of reality. The arts, like arithmetic and geometry, turn away their eyes from the gross, coloured and mobile nature at our feet, and regard instead a certain figmentary abstraction. Geometry will tell us of a circle, a thing never seen in nature; asked about a green circle or an iron circle, it lays its hand upon its mouth. So with the arts. Painting, ruefully comparing sunshine and flake-white, gives up truth of colour, as it had already given up relief and movement; and instead of vying with nature, arranges a scheme of harmonious tints. Literature, above all in its most typical mood, the mood of narrative, similarly flees the direct challenge and pursues instead an independent and creative aim. So far as it imitates at all, it imitates not life but speech: not the facts of human destiny, but the emphasis and the suppressions with which the human actor tells of them. The real art that dealt with life directly was that of the first men who told their stories round the savage camp-fire. Our art is occupied, and bound to be occupied, not so much in making stories true as in making them typical; not so much in capturing the lineaments of each fact, as in marshalling all of them towards a common end. For the welter of impressions, all forcible but all discreet, which life presents, it substitutes a certain artificial series of impressions, all indeed most feebly represented, but all aiming at the same effect, all eloquent of the same idea, all chiming together like consonant notes in music or like the graduated tints in a good picture. From all its chapters, from all its pages, from all its sentences, the well-written novel echoes and re-echoes its one creative and controlling thought; to this must every incident and character contribute; the style must have been pitched in unison with this; and if there is anywhere a word that looks another way, the book would be stronger, clearer, and (I had almost said) fuller without it. Life is monstrous, infinite, illogical, abrupt and poignant; a work of art, in comparison, is neat, finite, self-contained, rational, flowing and emasculate. Life imposes by brute energy, like inarticulate thunder; art catches the ear, among the far louder noises of experience, like an air artificially made by a discreet musician. A proposition of geometry does not compete with life; and a proposition of geometry is a fair and luminous parallel for a work of art. Both are reasonable, both untrue to the crude fact; both inhere in nature, neither represents it. The novel, which is a work of art, exists, not by its resemblances to life, which are forced and material, as a shoe must still consist of leather, but by its immeasurable difference from life, which is designed and significant, and is both the method and the meaning of the work.

The life of man is not the subject of novels, but the inexhaustible magazine from which subjects are to be selected; the name of these is legion; and with each new subject—for here again I must differ by the whole width of heaven from Mr. James—the true artist will vary his method and change the point of attack. That which was in one case an excellence, will become a defect in another; what was the making of one book, will in the next be impertinent or dull. First each novel, and then each class of novels, exists by and for itself. I will take, for instance, three main classes, which are fairly distinct: first, the novel of adventure, which appeals to certain almost sensual and quite illogical tendencies in man; second, the novel of character, which appeals to our intellectual appreciation of man's foibles and mingled and inconstant motives; and third, the dramatic novel, which deals with the same stuff as the serious theatre, and appeals to our emotional nature and moral judgment.

And first for the novel of adventure. Mr. James refers, with singular generosity of praise, to a little book about a quest for hidden treasure; but he lets fall, by the way, some rather startling words. In this book he misses what he calls the "immense luxury" of being able to quarrel with his author. The luxury, to most of us, is to lay by our judgment, to be submerged by the tale as by a billow, and only to awake, and begin to distinguish and find fault, when the piece is over and the volume laid aside. Still more remarkable is Mr. James's reason. He cannot criticise the author, as he goes, "because," says he, comparing it with another work, "I have been a child, but I have never been on a quest for buried treasure." Here is, indeed, a wilful paradox; for if he has never been on a quest for buried treasure, it can be demonstrated that he has never been a child. There never was a child (unless Master James) but has hunted gold, and been a pirate, and a military commander, and a bandit of the mountains; but has fought, and suffered shipwreck and prison, and imbrued its little hands in gore, and gallantly retrieved the lost battle, and triumphantly protected innocence and beauty. Elsewhere in his essay Mr. James has protested with excellent reason against too narrow a conception of experience; for the born artist, he contends, the "faintest hints of life" are converted into revelations; and it will be found true, I believe, in a majority of cases, that the artist writes with more gusto and effect of those things which he has only wished to do, than of those which he has done. Desire is a wonderful telescope, and Pisgah the best observatory. Now, while it is true that neither Mr. James nor the author of the work in question has ever, in the fleshly sense, gone questing after gold, it is probable that both have ardently desired and fondly imagined the details of such a life in youthful day-dreams; and the author, counting upon that, and well aware (cunning and low-minded man!) that this class of interest, having been frequently treated, finds a readily accessible and beaten road to the sympathies of the reader, addressed himself throughout to the building up and circumstantiation of this boyish dream. Character to the boy is a sealed book; for him, a pirate is a beard, a pair of wide trousers and a liberal complement of pistols. The author, for the sake of circumstantiation and because he was himself more or less grown up, admitted character, within certain limits, into his design; but only within certain limits. Had the same puppets figured in a scheme of another sort, they had been drawn to very different purpose; for in this elmentary novel of adventure, the characters need to be presented with but one class of qualities—the warlike and formidable. So as they appear insidious in deceit and fatal in the combat, they have served their end. Danger is the matter with which this class of novel deals; fear, the passion with which it idly trifles; and the characters are portrayed only so far as they realise the sense of danger and provoke the sympathy of fear. To add more traits, to be too clever, to start the hare of moral or intellectual interest while we are running the fox of material interest, is not to enrich but to stultify your tale. The stupid reader will only be offended, and the clever reader lose the scent.

The novel of character has this difference from all others: that it requires no coherency of plot, and for this reason, as in the case of *Gil Blas,* it is sometimes called the novel of adventure. It turns on the humours of the persons represented; these are, to be sure, embodied in incidents, but the incidents themselves, being tributary, need not march in a progression; and the characters may be statically shown. As they enter, so they may go out; they must be consistent, but they need not grow. Here Mr. James will recognise the note of much of his own work: he treats, for the most part, the statics of character, studying it at rest or only gently moved; and, with his usual delicate and just artistic instinct, he avoids those stronger passions which would deform the attitudes he loves to study, and change his sitters from the humorists of ordinary life to the brute forces and bare types of more emotional moments. In his recent *Author of Beltraffio,* so just on conception, so nimble and neat in workmanship, strong passion is indeed employed; but observe that it is not displayed. Even in the heroine the working of the passion is suppressed; and the great struggle, the true tragedy, the *scène-à-faire,* passes unseen behind the panels of a locked door. The delectable invention of the young visitor is introduced, consciously or not, to this end: that Mr. James, true to his method, might avoid the scene of passion. I trust no reader will suppose me guilty of undervaluing this little masterpiece. I mean merely that it belongs to one marked class of novel, and that it would have been very differently conceived and treated had it belonged to that other marked class, of which I now proceed to speak.

I take pleasure in calling the dramatic novel by that name, because it enables me to point out by the way a strange and peculiarly English misconception. It is sometimes supposed that the drama consists of incident. It consists of passion, which gives the actor his opportunity; and that passion must progressively increase, or the actor, as the piece proceeded, would be unable to carry the audience from a lower to a higher pitch of interest and emotion. A good serious play must therefore be founded on one of the passionate *cruces* of life, where duty and inclination come nobly to the grapple; and the same is true of what I call, for that reason, the dramatic novel. I will instance a few worthy specimens, all of our own day and a language; Meredith's *Rhoda Fleming,* that wonderful and painful book, long out of print, and hunted for at bookstalls like an Aldine; Hardy's *Pair of Blue Eyes;* and two of Charles Reade's, *Griffith Gaunt* and *The Double Marriage,* originally called *White Lies,* and founded (by an accident quaintly favourable to my nomenclature) on a play by Maquet, the partner of the great Dumas. In this kind of novel the closed door of *The Author of Beltraffio* must be broken open; passion must appear upon the scene and utter its last word; passion is the be-all and the end-all, the plot and the solution, the protagonist and the *deus ex machina* in one. The characters may come anyhow upon the stage: we do not care; the point is, that, before they leave it, they shall become transfigured and raised out of themselves by passion. It may be part of the design to draw them with detail; to depict a full-length character, and then behold it melt and change in the furnace of emotion. But there is no obligation of the sort; nice portraiture is not required; and we are content to accept mere abstract types, so they be strongly and sincerely moved. A novel of this class may be even great, and yet contain no individual figure; it may be great, because it displays the workings of the perturbed heart and the impersonal utterance of passion; and with an artist of the second class it is, indeed, even more likely to be great, when the issue has thus been narrowed and the whole force of the writer's mind directed to passion alone. Cleverness again, which has its fair field in the novel of character, is debarred all entry upon this more solemn theatre. A far-fetched motive, an ingenious evasion of the issue, a witty instead of a passionate turn, offend us like an insincerity. All should be plain, all straightforward to the end. Hence it is that, in *Rhoda Fleming,* Mrs. Lovel raises such resentment in the reader; her motives are too flimsy, her ways are too equivocal, for the weight and strength of her surroundings. Hence the hot indignation of the reader when Balzac, after having begun the *Duchesse de Langeais* in terms of strong if somewhat swollen passion, cuts the knot by the derangement of the hero's clock. Such personages and incidents belong to the novel of character; they are out of place in the high society of the passions; when the passions are introduced in art at their full height, we look to see them, not baffled and impotently striving, as in life, but towering above circumstance and acting substitutes for fate.

And here I can imagine Mr. James, with his lucid sense, to intervene. To much of what I have said he would apparently demur; in much he would, somewhat impatiently, acquiesce. It may be true; but it is not what he desired to say or to hear said. He spoke of the finished picture and its worth when done; I, of the brushes, the palette, and the north light. He uttered his views in the tone and for the ear of good society; I, with the emphasis and technicalities of the obtrusive student. But the point, I may reply, is not merely to amuse the public, but to offer helpful advice to the young writer. And the young writer will not so much be helped by genial pictures of what an art may aspire to at its highest, as by a true idea of what it must be on the lowest terms. The best that we can say to him is this: Let him choose a motive, whether of character or passion; carefully construct his plot so that every incident is an illustration of the motive, and every property employed shall bear to it a near relation of congruity or contrast; avoid a sub-plot, unless, as sometimes in Shakespeare, the sub-plot be a reversion or complement of the main intrigue; suffer not his style to flag below the level of the argument; pitch the key of conversation, not with any thought of how men talk in parlours, but with a single eye to the degree of passion he may be called on to express; and allow neither himself in the narrative nor any character in the course of the dialogue, to utter one sentence that is not part and parcel of the business of the story or the discussion of the problem involved. Let him not regret if this shortens his book; it will be better so; for to add irrelevant matter is not to lengthen but to bury. Let him not mind if he miss a thousand qualities, so that he keeps unflaggingly in pursuit of the one he has chosen. Let him not care particularly if he miss the tone of conversation, the pungent material detail of the day's manners, the reproduction of the atmosphere and the environment. These elements are not essential: a novel may be excellent, and yet have none of them; a passion or a character is so much the better depicted as it rises clearer from material circumstance. In this age of the particular, let him remember the ages of the abstract, the great books of the past, the brave men that lived before Shakespeare and before Balzac. And as the root of the whole matter, let him bear in mind that his novel is not a transcript of life, to be judged by its exactitude; but a simplification of some side or point of life, to stand or fall by its significant simplicity. For although, in great men, working upon great motives, what we observe and admire is often their complexity, yet underneath appearances the truth remains unchanged: that simplification was their method, and that simplicity is their excellence. . . .

32. Hawthorne and His Mosses

HERMAN MELVILLE

Herman Melville (1819–1891) is best known, of course, for *Moby-Dick,* a novel not universally appreciated in its own day but now celebrated as one of the very greatest American books. His discovery of Hawthorne and his consequent brief friendship with him was one of the decisive events in the development of Melville's own career. The essay reprinted here was written in the first flush of that discovery and represents a classic statement of the problems of the American novelist as well as providing an eminent example of the recognition of one talent by another.

A papered chamber in a fine old farm-house, a mile from any other dwelling, and dipped to the eaves in foliage—surrounded by moun-

SOURCE: *Literary World,* August 17 and 24, 1850.

tains, old woods, and Indian ponds, this, surely, is the place to write of Hawthorne. Some charm is in this northern air, for love and duty seem both impelling to the task. A man of deep and noble nature has seized me in this seclusion. His wild, witch-voice rings through me; or, in softer cadences, I seem to hear it in the songs of the hill-side birds that sing in the larch trees at my window.

Would that all excellent books were foundlings, without father or mother, that so it might be we could glorify them, without including their ostensible authors! Nor would any true man take exception to this; least of all, he who writes, "When the Artist rises high enough to achieve the Beautiful, the symbol by which he makes it perceptible to mortal senses becomes of little value in his eyes, while his spirit possesses itself in the enjoyment of the reality."

But more than this. I know not what would be the right name to put on the title-page of an excellent book; but this I feel, that the names of all fine authors are fictitious ones, far more so than that of Junius; simply standing, as they do, for the mystical, ever-eluding spirit of all beauty, which ubiquitously possesses men of genius. Purely imaginative as this fancy may appear, it nevertheless seems to receive some warranty from the fact, that on a personal interview no great author has ever come up to the idea of his reader. But that dust of which our bodies are composed, how can it fitly express the nobler intelligences among us? With reverence be it spoken, that not even in the case of one deemed more than man, not even in our Saviour, did his visible frame betoken anything of the augustness of the nature within. Else, how could those Jewish eye-witnesses fail to see heaven in his glance!

It is curious how a man may travel along a country road, and yet miss the grandest or sweetest of prospects by reason of an intervening hedge, so like all other hedges, as in no way to hint of the wide landscape beyond. So has it been with me concerning the enchanting landscape in the soul of this Hawthorne, this most excellent Man of Mosses. His "Old Manse" has been written now four years, but I never read it till a day or two since. I had seen it in the book-stores—heard of it often—even had it recommended to me by a tasteful friend, as a rare, quiet book, perhaps too deserving of popularity to be popular. But there are so many books called "excellent," and so much unpopular merit, that amid the thick stir of other things, the hint of my tasteful friend was disregarded; and for four years the Mosses on the Old Manse never refreshed me with their perennial green. It may be, however, that all this while the book, like wine, was only improving in flavor and body. At any rate, it so chanced that this long procrastination eventuated in a happy result. At breakfast the other day, a mountain girl, a cousin of mine, who for the last two weeks has every morning helped me to strawberries and raspberries, which, like the roses and pearls in the fairy tale, seemed to fall into the saucer from those strawberry-beds, her cheeks—this delightful creature, this charming Cherry says to me—"I see you spend your mornings in the hay-mow; and yesterday I found there 'Dwight's Travels in New England.' Now I have something far better than that, something more congenial to our summer on these hills. Take these raspberries, and then I will give you some moss." "Moss!" said I. "Yes, and you must take it to the barn with you, and good-bye to 'Dwight.' "

With that she left me, and soon returned with a volume, verdantly bound, and garnished with a curious frontispiece in green; nothing less than a fragment of real moss, cunningly pressed to a fly-leaf. "Why, this," said I, spilling my raspberries, "this is the 'Mosses from an Old Manse.' " "Yes," said cousin Cherry, "yes, it is that flowery Hawthorne." "Hawthorne and Mosses," said I, "nor more; it is morning; it is July in the country; and I am off for the barn."

Stretched on that new mown clover, the hill-side breeze blowing over me through the wide barn-door, and soothed by the hum of the bees in the meadows around, how magically stole over me this Mossy Man! and how amply, how bountifully, did he redeem that delicious promise to his guests in the Old Manse, of whom it is written— "Others could give them pleasure, or amusement, or instruction— these could be picked up anywhere—but it was for me to give them rest. Rest, in a life of trouble! What better could be done for weary and world-worn spirits? What better could be done for anybody, who came within our magic circle, than to throw the spell of a magic spirit over him?" So all that day, half-buried in the new clover, I watched this Hawthorne's "Assyrian dawn, and Paphian sunset and moonrise, from the summit of our Eastern Hill."

The soft ravishments of the man spun me round about in a web of dreams, and when the book was closed, when the spell was over, this wizard "dismissed me with but misty reminiscences, as if I had been dreaming of him."

What a wild moonlight of contemplative humor bathes that Old Manse! the rich and rare distilment of a spicy and slowly-oozing heart.

No rollicking rudeness, no gross fun fed on fat dinners, and bred in the lees of wine,—but a humor so spiritually gentle, so high, so deep, and yet so richly relishable, that it were hardly inappropriate in an angel. It is the very religion of mirth; for nothing so human but it may be advanced to that. The orchard of the Old Manse seems the visible type of the fine mind that has described it—those twisted and contorted old trees, "that stretch out their crooked branches, and take such hold of the imagination, that we remember them as humorists and odd-fellows." And then, as surrounded by these grotesque forms, and hushed in the noon-day repose of this Hawthorne's spell, how aptly might the still fall of his ruddy thoughts into your soul be symbolized by "the thump of a great apple, in the stillest afternoon, falling without a breath of wind, from the mere necessity of perfect ripeness!" For no less ripe than ruddy are the apples of the thoughts and fancies in this sweet Man of Mosses—

"Buds and Bird-voices"—

What a delicious thing is that! "Will the world ever be so decayed, that Spring may not renew its greenness?" And the "Fire-Worship." Was ever the hearth so glorified into an altar before? The mere title of that piece is better than any common work in fifty folio volumes. How exquisite is this:—"Nor did it lessen the charm of his soft, familiar courtesy and helpfulness, that the mighty spirit, were opportunity offered him, would run riot through the peaceful house, wrap its inmates in his terrible embrace, and leave nothing of them save their whitened bones. This possibility of mad destruction only made his domestic kindness the more beautiful and touching. It was so sweet of him, being endowed with such power, to dwell, day after day, and one long, lonesome night after another, on the dusky hearth, only now and then betraying his wild nature, by thrusting his red tongue out of the chimney-top! True, he had done much mischief in the world, and was pretty certain to do more, but his warm heart atoned for all; He was kindly to the race of man."

But he has still other apples, not quite so ruddy, though full as ripe; —apples, that have been left to wither on the tree, after the pleasant autumn gathering is past. The sketch of "The Old Apple-Dealer" is conceived in the subtlest spirit of sadness; he whose "subdued and nerveless boyhood prefigured his abortive prime, which, likewise, con-

tained within itself the prophecy and image of his lean and torpid age."
Such touches as are in this piece cannot proceed from any common
heart. They argue such a depth of tenderness, such a boundless sympathy with all forms of being, such an omnipresent love, that we must
need say that this Hawthorne is here almost alone in his generation,—
at least, in the artistic manifestation of these things. Still more. Such
touches as these,—and many, very many similar ones, all through his
chapters—furnish clues whereby we enter a little way into the intricate, profound heart where they originated. And we see that suffering,
some time or other and in some shape or other,—this only can enable
any man to depict it in others. All over him, Hawthorne's melancholy
rests like an Indian-summer, which, though bathing a whole country in
one softness, still reveals the distinctive hue of every towering hill and
each far-winding vale.

But it is the least part of genius that attracts admiration. Where
Hawthorne is known, he seems to be deemed a pleasant writer, with a
pleasant style,—a sequestered, harmless man, from whom any deep
and weighty thing would hardly be anticipated—a man who means
no meanings. But there is no man, in whom humor and love, like
mountain peaks, soar to such a rapt height as to receive the irradia-
tions of the upper skies,—there is no man in whom humor and love
are developed in that high form called genius; no such man can exist
without also possessing, as the indispensable complement of these, a
great, deep intellect, which drops down into the universe like a plummet. Or, love and humor are only the eyes through which such an intellect views this world. The great beauty in such a mind is but the
product of its strength. What, to all readers, can be more charming
than the piece entitled "Monsieur du Miroir"; and to a reader at all
capable of fully fathoming it, what, at the same time, can possess more
mystical depth of meaning?—yes, there he sits and looks at me,—
this "shape of mystery," this "identical Monsieur du Miroir." "Methinks I should tremble now, were his wizard power of gliding through
all impediments in search of me, to place him suddenly before my
eyes."

How profound, nay appalling, is the moral evolved by the "Earth's
Holocaust"; where—beginning with the hollow follies and affecta-
tions of the world,—all vanities and empty theories and forms are,
one after another, and by an admirably graduated, growing compre-

hensiveness, thrown into the allegorical fire, till, at length, nothing is left but the all-engendering heart of man; which remaining still unconsumed, the great conflagration is naught.

Of a piece with this, is the "Intelligence Office," a wondrous symbolizing of the secret workings in men's souls. There are other sketches still more charged with ponderous import.

"The Christmas Banquet," and "The Bosom Serpent," would be fine subjects for a curious and elaborate analysis, touching the conjectural parts of the mind that produced them. For spite of all the Indian-summer sunlight on the hither side of Hawthorne's soul, the other side—like the dark half of the physical sphere—is shrouded in a blackness, ten times black. But this darkness but gives more effect to the ever-moving dawn, that for ever advances through it, and circumnavigates his world. Whether Hawthorne has simply availed himself of this mystical blackness as a means to the wondrous effects he makes it to produce in his lights and shades; or whether there really lurks in him, perhaps unknown to himself, a touch of Puritanic gloom, —this, I cannot altogether tell. Certain it is, however, that this great power of blackness in him derives its force from its appeal to that Calvinistic sense of Innate Depravity and Original Sin, from whose visitations, in some shape or other, no deeply thinking mind is always and wholly free. For, in certain moods, no man can weigh this world without throwing in something, somehow like Original Sin, to strike the uneven balance. At all events, perhaps no writer has ever wielded this terrific thought with greater terror than this same harmless Hawthorne. Still more: this black conceit pervades him through and through. You may be witched by his sunlight,—transported by the bright gildings in the skies he builds over you; but there is the blackness of darkness beyond; and even his bright gildings but fringe and play upon the edges of thunder-clouds. He himself must often have smiled at its absurd misconception of him. He is immeasurably deeper than the plummet of the mere critic. For it is not the brain that can test such a man; it is only the heart. You cannot come to know greatness by inspecting it; there is no glimpse to be caught of it, except by intuition; you need not ring it, you but touch it, and you find it is gold.

Now, it is that blackness in Hawthorne, of which I have spoken, that so fixes and fascinates me. It may be, nevertheless, that it is too largely developed in him. Perhaps he does not give us a ray of his light for every shade of his dark. But however this may be, this blackness it is that furnishes the infinite obscure of his back-ground,—that back-ground, against which Shakspeare plays his grandest conceits, the things that have made Shakspeare his loftiest but most circumscribed renown, as the profoundest of thinkers. For by philosophers Shakspeare is not adored as the great man of tragedy and comedy,—"Off with his head; so much for Buckingham!" This sort of rant, interlined by another hand, brings down the house,—those mistaken souls, who dream of Shakspeare as a mere man of Richard-the-Third humps and Macbeth daggers. But it is those deep far-away things in him; those occasional flashings-forth of the intuitive Truth in him; those short, quick probings at the very axis of reality;—these are the things that make Shakspeare, Shakspeare. Through the mouths of the dark characters of Hamlet, Timon, Lear, and Iago, he craftily says, or sometimes insinuates the things which we feel to be so terrifically true, that it were all but madness for any good man, in his own proper character, to utter, or even hint of them. Tormented into desperation, Lear, the frantic king, tears off the mask, and speaks the same madness of vital truth. But, as I before said, it is the least part of genius that attracts admiration. And so, much of the blind, unbridled admiration that has been heaped upon Shakspeare, has been lavished upon the least part of him. And few of his endless commentators and critics seem to have remembered, or even perceived, that the immediate products of a great mind are not so great as that undeveloped and sometimes undevelopable yet dimly-discernible greatness, to which those immediate products are but infallible indices. In Shakspeare's tomb lies infinitely more than Shakspeare ever wrote. And if I magnify Shakspeare, it is not so much for what he did not do, or refrained from doing. For in this world of lies, Truth is forced to fly like a scared white doe in the woodlands; and only by cunning glimpses will she reveal herself, as in Shakspeare and other masters of the great Art of Telling the Truth,— even though it be covertly and by snatches.

But if this view of the all-popular Shakspeare be seldom taken by his readers, and if very few who extol him have ever read him deeply, or perhaps, only have seen him on the tricky stage (which alone made, and is still making him his mere mob renown)—if few men have time, or patience, or palate, for the spiritual truth as it is in that great genius; —it is then no matter of surprise, that in a contemporaneous age, Nathaniel Hawthorne is a man as yet almost utterly mistaken among men. Here, and there, in some quiet arm-chair in the noisy town, or some deep nook among the noiseless mountains, he may be appreciated for something of what he is. But unlike Shakspeare, who was forced to the contrary course by circumstances, Hawthorne (either from simple disinclination, or else from inaptitude) refrains from all the popularizing noise and show of broad farce and blood-besmeared tragedy; content with the still, rich utterance of a great intellect in repose, and which sends few thoughts into circulation, except they be arterialized at his large warm lungs, and expanded in his honest heart.

Nor need you fix upon that blackness in him, if it suit you not. Nor, indeed, will all readers discern it; for it is, mostly, insinuated to those who may best understand it, and account for it; it is not obtruded upon every one alike.

Some may start to read Shakspeare and Hawthorne on the same page. They may say, that if an illustration were needed, a lesser light might have sufficed to elucidate this Hawthorne, this small man of yesterday. But I am not willingly one of those who, as touching Shakspeare at least, exemplify the maxim of Rochefoucauld, that "we exalt the reputation of some, in order to depress that of others;" who, to teach all noble-souled aspirants that there is no hope for them, pronounce Shakspeare absolutely unapproachable. But Shakspeare has been approached. There are minds that have gone as far as Shakspeare into the universe. And hardly a mortal man, who, at some time or other, has not felt as great thoughts in him as any you will find in Hamlet. We must not inferentially malign mankind for the sake of any one man, whoever he may be. This is too cheap a purchase of contentment for conscious mediocrity to make. Besides, this absolute and unconditional adoration of Shakspeare has grown to be a part of our Anglo-Saxon superstitions. The Thirty-Nine Articles are now Forty. Intolerance has come to exist in this matter. You must believe in Shakspeare's unapproachability, or quit the country. But what sort of a belief is this for an American, a man who is bound to carry republican progressiveness into Literature as well as into Life? Believe me, my friends, that men, not very much inferior to Shakspeare, are this day being born on the banks of the Ohio. And the day will come when you shall say, Who reads a book by an Englishman that is a modern? The great mistake seems to be, that even with those Americans who look forward to the coming of a great literary genius among us, they somehow fancy he will come in the costume of Queen Elizabeth's day; be a writer of dramas founded upon old English history or the tales of Boccaccio.

Whereas, great geniuses are parts of the times, they themselves are the times, and possess a correspondent coloring. It is of a piece with the Jews, who, while their Shiloh was meekly walking in their streets, were still praying for his magnificent coming; looking for him in a chariot, who was already among them on an ass. Nor must we forget that, in his own lifetime, Shakspeare was not Shakspeare, but only Master William Shakspeare of the shrewd, thriving business firm of Condell, Shakspeare & Co., proprietors of the Globe Theatre in London; and by a courtly author, of the name of Chettle, was looked at as an "upstart crow," beautified "with other birds' feathers." For, mark it well, imitation is often the first charge brought against real originality. Why this is so, there is not space to set forth here. You must have plenty of searoom to tell the Truth in; especially when it seems to have an aspect of newness, as America did in 1492, though it then was just as old, and perhaps older than Asia, only those sagacious philosophers, the common sailors, had never seen it before, swearing it was all water and moonshine there.

Now I do not say that Nathaniel of Salem is a greater than William of Avon, or as great. But the difference between the two men is by no means immeasurable. Not a very great deal more, and Nathaniel were verily William.

This, too, I mean, that if Shakspeare has not been equalled, give the world time, and he is sure to be surpassed, in one hemisphere or the other. Nor will it at all do to say, that the world is getting grey and grizzled now, and has lost that fresh charm which she wore of old, and by virtue of which the great poets of past times made themselves what we esteem them to be. Not so. The world is as young to-day as when it was created; and this Vermont morning dew is as wet to my feet, as Eden's dew to Adam's. Nor has nature been all over ransacked by our progenitors, so that no new charms and mysteries remain for this latter generation to find. Far from it. The trillionth part has not yet been said; and all that has been said, but multiplies the avenues to what remains to be said. It is not so much paucity as superabundance of material that seems to incapacitate modern authors.

Let America, then, prize and cherish her writers; yea, let her glorify them. They are not so many in number as to exhaust her good-will. And while she has good kith and kin of her own, to take to her bosom, let her not lavish her embraces upon the household of an alien. For believe it or not, England, after all, is in many things as alien to us.

China has more bonds of real love for us than she. But even were there no strong literary individualities among us, as there are some dozens at least, nevertheless, let America first praise mediocrity even, in her own children, before she praises (for everywhere, merit demands acknowledgement from every one) the best excellence in the children of any other land. Let her own authors, I say, have the priority of appreciation. I was much pleased with a hot-headed Carolina cousin of mine, who once said, —"If there were no other American to stand by, in literature, why, then, I would stand by Pop Emmons and his 'Fredoniad,' and till a better epic came along, swear it was not very far behind the Iliad." Take away the words, and in spirit he was sound.

Not that American genius needs patronage in order to expand. For that explosive sort of stuff will expand though screwed up in a vice, and burst it, though it were triple steel. It is for the nation's sake, and not for her authors' sake, that I would have America be heedful of the increasing greatness among her writers. For how great the shame, if other nations should be before her, in crowning her heroes of the pen! But this is almost the case now. American authors have received more just and discriminating praise (however loftily and ridiculously given, in certain cases) even from some Englishmen, than from their own countrymen. There are hardly five critics in America; and several of them are asleep. As for patronage, it is the American author who now patronizes his country, and not his country him. And if at times some among them appeal to the people for more recognition, it is not always with selfish motives, but patriotic ones.

It is true, that few of them as yet have evinced that decided originality which merits great praise. But that graceful writer, who perhaps of all Americans has received the most plaudits from his own country for his productions, —that very popular and amiable writer, however good and self-reliant in many things, perhaps owes his chief reputation to the self-acknowledged imitation of a foreign model, and to the studied avoidance of all topics but smooth ones. But it is better to fail in originality than to succeed in imitation. He who has never failed somewhere, that man cannot be great. Failure is the true test of greatness. And if it be said, that continual success is a proof that a man wisely knows his powers, —it is only to be added, that, in that case, he knows them to be small. Let us believe it, then, once for all, that there is no hope for us in these smooth, pleasing writers that know their powers. Without malice, but to speak the plain fact, they but furnish

an appendix to Goldsmith, and other English authors. And we want no
American Goldsmiths: nay, we want no American Miltons. It were
the vilest thing you could say of a true American author, that he were
an American Tompkins. Call him an American and have done, for you
cannot say a nobler thing of him. But it is not meant that all American
writers should studiously cleave to nationality in their writings; only
this, no American writer should write like an Englishman or a Frenchman; let him write like a man, for then he will be sure to write like an
American. Let us away with this leaven of literary flunkeyism towards
England. If either must play the flunkey in this thing, let England do it,
not us. While we are rapidly preparing for that political supremacy
among the nations which prophetically awaits us at the close of the
present century, in a literary point of view, we are deplorably unprepared for it; and we seem studious to remain so. Hitherto, reasons
might have existed why this should be; but no good reason exists now.
And all that is requisite to amendment in this matter, is simply this:
that while freely acknowledging all excellence everywhere, we should
refrain from unduly lauding foreign writers, and, at the same time,
duly recognize meritorious writers that are our own;—those writers
who breathe that unshackled, democratic spirit of Christianity in all
things, which now takes the practical lead in this world, though at the
same time led by ourselves—us Americans. Let us boldly condemn
all imitation, though it comes to us graceful and fragrant as the morning; and foster all originality, though at first it be crabbed and ugly as
our own pine knots. And if any of our authors fail, or seem to fail,
then, in the words of my enthusiastic Carolina cousin, let us clap him
on the shoulder, and back him against all Europe for his second round.
The truth is, that in one point of view, this matter of a national literature has come to such a pass with us, that in some sense we must turn
bullies, else the day is lost, or superiority so far beyond us, that we can
hardly say it will ever be ours.

And now, my countrymen, as an excellent author of your own flesh
and blood,—an unimitating, and, perhaps, in his way, an inimitable
man—whom better can I commend to you, in the first place, than
Nathaniel Hawthorne. He is one of the new, and far better generation
of your writers. The smell of your beeches and hemlocks is upon him;
your own broad prairies are in his soul; and as you travel away inland
into his deep and noble nature, you will hear the far roar of his Niagara. Give not over to future generations the glad duty of acknowledg-

ing him for what he is. Take that joy to yourself, in your own generation; and so shall he feel those grateful impulses on him, that may possibly prompt him to the full flower of some still greater achievement in
your eyes. And by confessing him you thereby confess others; you
brace the whole brotherhood. For genius, all over the world, stands
hand in hand, and one shock of recognition runs the whole circle
round.

In treating of Hawthorne, or rather of Hawthorne in his writings
(for I never saw the man; and in the chances of a quiet plantation life,
remote from his haunts, perhaps never shall); in treating of his works,
I say, I have thus far omitted all mention of his "Twice Told Tales,"
and "Scarlet Letter." Both are excellent, but full of such manifold,
strange, and diffusive beauties, that time would all but fail to point the
half of them out. But there are things in those two books, which, had
they been written in England a century ago, Nathaniel Hawthorne had
utterly displaced many of the bright names we now revere on authority. But I am content to leave Hawthorne to himself, and to the infallible finding of posterity; and however great may be the praise I have
bestowed upon him, I feel that in so doing I have served and honored
myself and him. For, at bottom, great excellence is praise enough to
itself; but the feeling of a sincere and appreciative love and admiration
towards it, this is relieved by utterance; and warm, honest praise ever
leaves a pleasant flavor in the mouth; and it is an honorable thing to
confess to what is honorable in others.

But I cannot leave my subject yet. No man can ever read a fine
author, and relish him to his very bones while he reads, without subse-
quently fancying to himself some ideal image of the man and his mind.
And if you rightly look for it, you will almost always find that the
author himself has somewhere furnished you with his own picture. For
poets (whether in prose or verse), being painters of nature, are like
their brethren of the pencil, the true portrait-painters, who, in the
multitude of likenesses to be sketched, do not invariably omit their
own; and in all high instances, they paint them without any vanity,
though at times with a lurking something, that would take several
pages to properly define.

I submit it, then, to those best acquainted with the man personally,
whether the following is not Nathaniel Hawthorne;—and to himself,
whether something involved in it does not express the temper of his
mind,—that lasting temper of all true, candid men—a seeker, not a
finder yet: —

"A man now entered, in neglected attire, with the aspect of a thinker, but somewhat too rough-hewn and brawny for a scholar. His face was full of sturdy vigor, with some finer and keener attribute beneath; though harsh at first, it was tempered with the glow of a large, warm heart, which had force enough to heat his powerful intellect through and through. He advanced to the Intelligencer, and looked at him with a glance of such stern sincerity, that perhaps few secrets were beyond its scope.

" 'I seek for Truth,' said he."

Twenty-four hours have elapsed since writing the foregoing. I have just returned from the hay-mow, charged more and more with love and admiration of Hawthorne. For I have just been gleaning through the Mosses, picking up many things here and there that had previously escaped me. And I found that but to glean after this man, is better than to be in at the harvest of others. To be frank (though, perhaps, rather foolish) not-withstanding what I wrote yesterday of these Mosses, I had not then culled them all; but had, nevertheless, been sufficiently sensible of the subtle essence in them, as to write as I did. To what infinite height of loving wonder and admiration I may yet be borne, when by repeatedly banqueting on these Mosses I shall have thoroughly incorporated their whole stuff into my being,—that, I cannot tell. But already I feel that this Hawthorne has dropped germinous seeds into my soul. He expands and deepens down, the more I contemplate him; and further and further, shoots his strong New England roots in the hot soil of my Southern soul.

By careful reference to the "Table of Contents," I now find that I have gone through all the sketches; but that when I yesterday wrote, I had not at all read two particular pieces, to which I now desire to call special attention,—"A Select Party," and "Young Goodman Brown." Here, be it said to all those whom this poor fugitive scrawl of mine may tempt to the perusal of the "Mosses," that they must on no account suffer themselves to be trifled with, disappointed, or deceived by the triviality of many of the titles to these sketches. For in more than one instance, the title utterly belies the piece. It is as if rustic demijohns containing the very best and costliest of Fakernian and Tokay, were labelled "Cider," "Perry," and "Elder-berry wine." The truth seems to be, that like many other geniuses, this Man of Mosses, takes great delight in hoodwinking the world,—at least, with respect to himself. Personally, I doubt not that he rather prefers to be generally esteemed but a so-so sort of author; being willing to reserve the thorough and acute appreciation of what he is, to that party most qualified to judge —that is, to himself. Besides, at the bottom of their natures, men like Hawthorne, in many things, deem the plaudits of the public such strong presumptive evidence of mediocrity in the object of them, that it would in some degree render doubtful of their own powers, did they hear much and vociferous braying concerning them in the public pastures. True, I have been braying myself (if you please to be witty enough to have it so), but then I claim to be the first that has so brayed in this particular matter; and therefore, while pleading guilty to the charge, still claim all the merit due to originality.

But with whatever motive, playful or profound, Nathaniel Hawthorne has chosen to entitle his pieces in the manner he has, it is certain that some of them are directly calculated to deceive—egregiously deceive, the superficial skimmer of pages. To be downright and candid once more, let me cheerfully say, that two of these titles did dolefully dupe no less an eagle-eyed reader than myself; and that, too, after I had been impressed with a sense of the great depth and breadth of this American man. "Who in the name of thunder" (as the country-people say in this neighborhood), "who in the name of thunder, would anticipate any marvel in a piece entitled 'Young Goodman Brown'?" You would of course suppose that it was a simple little tale, intended as a supplement to "Goody Two Shoes." Whereas, it is deep as Dante; nor can you finish it, without addressing the author in his own words —"It is yours to penetrate, in every bosom, the deep mystery of sin." And with Goodman, too, in allegorical pursuit of his Puritan wife, you cry out in your anguish:

" 'Faith!' shouted Goodman Brown, in a voice of agony and desperation; and the echoes of the forest mocked him, crying,—'Faith! Faith!' as if bewildered wretches were seeking her all through the wilderness."

Now this same piece, entitled "Young Goodman Brown," is one of the two that I had not all read yesterday; and I allude to it now, because it is, in itself, such a strong positive illustration of that blackness in Hawthorne, which I had assumed from the mere occasional shadows of it, as revealed in several of the other sketches. But had I previously perused "Young Goodman Brown," I should have been at no pains to draw the conclusion, which I came to at a time when I was ignorant that the book contained one such direct and unqualified manifestation of it.

The other piece of the two referred to, is entitled "A Select Party," which, in my first simplicity upon originally taking hold of the book, I fancied must treat of some pumpkin-pie party in old Salem, or some chowder-party on Cape Cod. Whereas, by all the gods of Peedee, it is the sweetest and sublimest thing that has been written since Spenser wrote. Nay, there is nothing in Spenser that surpasses it, perhaps nothing that equals it. And the test is this: read any canto in "The Faery Queen," and then read "A Select Party" and decide which pleases you the most,—that is, if you are qualified to judge. Do not be frightened at this; for when Spenser was alive, he was thought of very much as Hawthorne is now,—was generally accounted just such a "gentle" harmless man. It may be, that to common eyes, the sublimity of Hawthorne seems lost in his sweetness,—as perhaps in that same "Select Party" of his; for whom he has builded so august a dome of sunset clouds, and served them on richer plate than Belshazzar's when he banqueted his lords in Babylon.

But my chief business now, is to point out a particular page in this piece, having reference to an honored guest, who under the name of "The Master Genius," but in the guise, "of a young man of poor attire, with no insignia of rank or acknowledged eminence," is introduced to the man of Fancy, who is the giver of the feast. Now, the page having reference to this "Master Genius," so happily expresses much of what I yesterday wrote, touching the coming of the literary Shiloh of America, that I cannot but be charmed by the coincidence; especially, when it shows such a parity of ideas, at least in this one point, between a man like Hawthorne and a man like me.

And here, let me throw out another conceit of mine touching this American Shiloh, or "Master Genius," as Hawthorne calls him. May it not be, that this commanding mind has not been, is not, and never will be, individually developed in any one man? And would it, indeed, appear so unreasonable to suppose, that this great fulness and overflowing may be, or may be destined to be, shared by a plurality of men of genius? Surely, to take the very greatest example on record, Shakspeare cannot be regarded as in himself the concretion of all the genius of his time; nor as so immeasurably beyond Marlow, Webster, Ford, Beaumont, Jonson, that those great men can be said to share none of his power? For one, I conceive that there were dramatists in Elizabeth's day, between whom and Shakspeare the distance was by no means great. Let any one, hitherto little acquainted with those neglected old authors, for the first time read them thoroughly, or even read Charles Lamb's Specimens of them, and he will be amazed at the wondrous ability of those Anaks of men, and shocked at this renewed example of the fact, that Fortune has more to do with fame than merit, —though, without merit, lasting fame there can be none.

Nevertheless, it would argue too ill of my country were this maxim to hold good concerning Nathaniel Hawthorne, a man, who already, in some few minds, has shed "such a light, as never illuminates the earth save when a great heart burns as the household fire of a grand intellect."

The words are his,—in the "Select Party"; and they are a magnificent setting to a coincident sentiment of my own, but ramblingly expressed yesterday, in reference to himself. Gainsay it who will, as I now write, I am Posterity speaking by proxy—and after times will make it more than good, when I declare, that the American, who up to the present day has evinced, in literature, the largest brain with the largest heart, that man is Nathaniel Hawthorne. Moreover, that whatever Nathaniel Hawthorne may hereafter write, "The Mosses from an Old Manse" will be ultimately accounted his masterpiece. For there is a sure, though a secret sign in some works which proves the culmination of the powers (only the developable ones, however) that produced them. But I am by no means desirous of the glory of a prophet. I pray Heaven that Hawthorne may *yet* prove me an impostor in this prediction. Especially, as I somehow cling to the strange fancy, that, in all men, hiddenly reside certain wondrous, occult properties—as in some plants and minerals—which by some happy but very rare accident (as bronze was discovered by the melting of the iron and brass at the burning of Corinth) may chance to be called forth here on earth; not entirely waiting for their better discovery in the more congenial, blessed atmosphere of heaven.

Once more—for it is hard to be finite upon an infinite subject, and all subjects are infinite. By some people this entire scrawl of mine may be esteemed altogether, inasmuch "as years ago" (they may say) "we found out the rich and rare stuff in this Hawthorne, whom you now parade forth, as if only *yourself* were the discoverer of this Portuguese diamond in our literature." But even granting all this—and adding to it, the assumption that the books of Hawthorne have sold by the five thousand,—what does that signify? They should be sold by the hundred thousand; and read by the million; and admired by every one who is capable of admiration.

33. Was Walt Whitman the Father of the American Baby?

WYNDHAM LEWIS

Wyndham Lewis (1882–1957) is one of the embattled figures of recent literature. A painter, a novelist, a critic of art and life, he sustained with almost brutal vigor immensely unpopular opinions. Two
subjects which concerned him always were contemporary art and
contemporary culture, and of the latter he felt America to be the
clearest example. He returns again and again to our country and our
writers, choosing Whitman as a special butt (in *Paleface* from which
this essay is taken), a symbol of tendencies which develop via Sherwood Anderson and Ernest Hemingway into a kind of literature
which he especially despises.

It is a widely-held notion in Europe that the American is a kind of
baby-man: that the American is not adult, that he remains all his life a
child. And that is of course one of the things that Mr. Mencken's criticism suggests. Mr. Sherwood Anderson says, 'Most American men
never pass the age of seventeen.' This would equally well describe
most men everywhere: but when the typical educated European thinks
of the inhabitant of the United States he thinks of something childish,
super-young, undeveloped, excitable and helpless. He thinks of him
(and of the American Woman equally) as a creature of 'crazes' and
impulses, who when not 'crazy about' this is 'crazy about' that; a half-
cocked, foolishly-eager, snob of every idea that can get itself adver-
tised and describe itself as novel and 'stimulating' (the last invariably-
used adjective suggesting some radical impotence in the public): but
generally and to sum up all the rest, as substantially prone to an ever-
deepening juvenility, ever more of which merely receptive quality is

SOURCE: Wyndham Lewis, *Paleface: The Philosophy of the 'Melting Pot'* (London:
Chatto & Windus, Ltd., 1929), pp. 140–42. Reprinted by permission of Mrs.
Wyndham Lewis.

willed for itself by this spoilt-child of fortune—for that is precisely what it wishes to be, an irresponsible child, sheltered from the rough embarrassments, fatigues and battles of the surrounding universe. It would indeed not at all surprise this type of European if the entire American Nation, pressing on back into the rosy lands of self-deceiving childhood and breathless illusion, vanished, one fine day, into the womb out of which it came.

That this cannot, in reality, describe the great mass of the population of America I need not say, nor is that my view, or that of the better-informed European. But it is still a widely-held opinion. So, if European opinion ever reached and touched America, it would not lessen the 'inferiority complex' being manufactured for it on the home-soil. So to the older White countries America cannot look for help in the analysis of its 'complex.' For them America is a baby, the baby of Europe and—after a hundred and fifty years—a peculiarly infantile one, making on all-fours for the womb of its origin.

Was Walt Whitman the Father of the American Baby?

Although I know, as I have said, that the whole of America is not a gigantic baby, tied to the apron-strings of some 'cosmic' Mama, nevertheless it really does seem that the American mind is today more infantile than it was in the days of Edgar Allan Poe, for instance. The Virginians and New Englanders of that day it would have entered nobody's head to accuse, even, of this peculiar infantilism. The American mind was at that time, no doubt, much abused by the enemies or rivals of the master-state of the New World, but that state was governed and represented by adult Europeans at a few removes tempered in the sternest roman traditions of English enterprise. So it does seem that America, as it has grown older, has grown younger and younger, in the sense that there is a patch or streak in the mind of the American aggregate that gives some colour to the more recent European myth of the American Baby.

If we take this patch, or this tendency, and if we isolate it, and so form an entire Baby, and proceed to call that 'America' (which is what has happened, I believe, in the case of the European belief I am here discussing), then who was responsible for that particular child? For, as it did not exist a century ago, it must have made its appearance in the interim.

Walt Whitman was, I feel sure, the father of the American Baby, looked at in that light. Walt showed all those enthusiastic expansive habits that we associate with the Baby. He rolled about naked in the Atlantic surf, uttering 'barbaric yawps,' as he called them, in an ecstasy of primitive exhibitionism. He was prone to 'cosmic' raptures. A freudian analyst specializing in inversion or perversion would have said, observing his behavior over a suitable period, that he was certainly the victim of a psychical 'fixation,' which incessantly referred him back to the periods of earliest childhood. He was a great big heavy old youngster, of a perfect freudian type, with the worst kind of 'enthusiasm' in the Greek sense of that word. He was also, it should be remembered, the epic ancestor of the now celebrated American 'fairy.'

Walt Whitman, as the father of the American Baby, is a hint, only, to the American analyst of these questions, and I of course may be wrong in stressing that particular figure. But he does seem to fit so wonderfully the requirements of the case: so I at all events recommended him in that capacity.

The Healthy Attitude of the American to His 'Babylon'

When I visited New York I found the pictorial effects exceedingly curious and beautiful. This was not a view in any way shared by the more intelligent New Yorkers, I was glad and surprised to find. They, who lived in the place, and understood the motives of the builders and their masters, regarded it as so much vulgar and childish display. The 'Down-town' towers and cathedrals produced nothing but a contemptuous and rather bitter mirth in them. For me it was purely the satisfactions of the eye that made me like it. In every other way I was in agreement with them. For towards everything, and all the people, that are behind the creation of these 'swinging gardens of Babylon,' I feel about as they do.

Strange as it was to find this disillusioned and hostile attitude on the part of the intelligent educated men, it was far stranger to find it as well amongst the workmen and average of the community. Far from boasting of their city, they seemed to take very little interest in it, except occasionally to remark that they did not like New York, and that one of these days—I should see—it 'would all blow up,' since Nature did not approve of such structures as were to be found there, and Nature would have the last word!

These traces of Nature-worship are reminiscent of Whitman, it is true. It was the good side of Whitman—the very ancient gospel that was the matrix of his own, but which he was not able to incarnate, and only succeeded in making exaggerated and ridiculous.

34. Some Lines from Whitman

RANDALL JARRELL

Randall Jarrell (1914–1966) was a poet, novelist, critic and teacher, who died tragically at the peak of his career. He is especially noted for his refusal to accept any idea merely because it is fashionable and for his extravagant and bitter wit. His unerring taste in poetry, his ability always to find the truly excellent lines and passages of the poet he is discussing, are illustrated with special aptness here. It is by no means easy to give in so short a space so complete an idea of a poet as vast and various as Whitman.

Whitman, Dickinson, and Melville seem to me the best poets of the 19th Century here in America. Melville's poetry has been grotesquely underestimated, but of course it is only in the last four or five years that it has been much read; in the long run, in spite of the awkwardness and amateurishness of so much of it, it will surely be thought well of. (In the short run it will probably be thought entirely too well of. Melville is a great poet only in the prose of *Moby Dick*.) Dickinson's poetry has been thoroughly read, and well though undifferentiatingly loved—after a few decades or centuries almost everybody will be able to see through Dickinson to her poems. But something odd has happened to the living changing part of Whitman's reputation: nowadays it is people who are not particularly interested in poetry, people who say that they read a poem for what it says, not for how it says it,

SOURCE: Randall Jarrell, *Poetry and the Age* (New York: Alfred A. Knopf, Inc., 1953), pp. 112–32. Copyright 1953 by Randall Jarrell. Reprinted by permission of Alfred A. Knopf, Inc.

who admire Whitman most. Whitman is often written about, either approvingly or disapprovingly, as if he were the Thomas Wolfe of 19th Century democracy, the hero of a De Mille movie about Walt Whitman. (People even talk about a war in which Walt Whitman and Henry James chose up sides, to begin with, and in which you and I will go on fighting till the day we die.) All this sort of thing, and all the bad poetry that there of course is in Whitman—for any poet has written enough bad poetry to scare away anybody—has helped to scare away from Whitman most "serious readers of modern poetry." They do not talk of his poems, as a rule, with any real liking or knowledge. Serious readers, people who are ashamed of not knowing all Hopkins by heart, are not at all ashamed to say, "I don't really know Whitman very well." This may harm Whitman in your eyes, they know, but that is a chance that poets have to take. Yet "their" Hopkins, that good critic and great poet, wrote about Whitman, after seeing five or six of his poems in a newspaper review: "I may as well say what I should not otherwise have said, that I always knew in my heart Walt Whitman's mind to be more like my own than any other man's living. As he is a very great scoundrel this is not a very pleasant confession." And Henry James, the leader of "their" side in that awful imaginary war of which I spoke, once read Whitman to Edith Wharton (much as Mozart used to imitate, on the piano, the organ) with such power and solemnity that both sat shaken and silent; it was after this reading that James expressed his regret at Whitman's "too extensive acquaintance with the foreign languages." Almost all the most "original and advanced" poets and critics and readers of the last part of the 19th Century thought Whitman as original and advanced as themselves, in manner as well as in matter. Can Whitman really be a sort of Thomas Wolfe or Carl Sandburg or Robinson Jeffers or Henry Miller—or a sort of Balzac of poetry, whose every part is crude but whose whole is somehow good? He is not, nor could he be; a poem, like Pope's spider, "lives along the line," and all the dead lines in the world will not make one live poem. As Blake says, "all sublimity is founded on minute discrimination," and it is in these "minute particulars" of Blake's that any poem has its primary existence.

To show Whitman for what he is one does not need to praise or explain or argue, one needs simply to quote. He himself said, "I and mine do not convince by arguments, similes, rhymes, / We convince by our presence." Even a few of his phrases are enough to show us that

Whitman was no sweeping rhetorician, but a poet of the greatest and oddest delicacy and originality and sensitivity, so far as words are concerned. This is, after all, the poet who said, "Blind loving wrestling touch, sheath'd hooded sharp-tooth'd touch"; who said, "Smartly attired, countenance smiling, form upright, death under the breast-bones, hell under the skull-bones"; who said, "Agonies are one of my changes of garments"; who saw grass as the "flag of my disposition," saw "the sharp-peak'd farmhouse, with its scallop'd scum and slender shoots from the gutters," heard a plane's "wild ascending lisp," and saw and heard how at the amputation "what is removed drops horribly in a pail." This is the poet for whom the sea was "howler and scooper of storms," reaching out to us with "crooked inviting fingers"; who went "leaping chasms with a pike-pointed staff, clinging to topples of brittle and blue"; who, a runaway slave, saw how "my gore dribs, thinn'd with the ooze of my skin"; who went "lithographing Kronos . . . buying drafts of Osiris"; who stared out at the "little plentiful mannikins skipping around in collars and tail'd coats,/ I am aware who they are, (they are positively not worms or fleas)." For he is, at his best, beautifully witty: he says gravely, "I find I incorporate gneiss, coals, long-threaded moss, fruits, grain, esculent roots,/ And am stucco'd with quadrupeds and birds all over"; and of these quadrupeds and birds "not one is respectable or unhappy over the whole earth." He calls advice: "Unscrew the locks from the doors! Unscrew the doors from their jambs!" He publishes the results of research: "Having pried through the strata, analyz'd to a hair, counsel'd with doctors and calculated close,/ I find no sweeter fat than sticks to my own bones." Everybody remembers how he told the Muse to "cross out please those immensely overpaid accounts,/ That matter of Troy and Achilles' wrath, and Aeneas', Odysseus' wanderings," but his account of the arrival of the "illustrious emigre" here in the New World is even better: "Bluff'd not a bit by drainpipe, gasometer, artificial fertilizers,/ Smiling and pleas'd with palpable intent to stay,/ She's here, install'd amid the kitchenware." Or he sees, like another Breughel, "the mechanic's wife with the babe at her nipple interceding for every person born,/ Three scythes at harvest whizzing in a row from three lusty angels with shirts bagg'd out at their waists,/ The snag-toothed hostler with red hair redeeming sins past and to come"—the passage has enough wit not only (in Johnson's phrase) to keep it sweet, but enough to make it believable. He says:

> I project my hat, sit shame-faced, and beg.
> Enough! Enough! Enough!
> Somehow I have been stunn'd. Stand back!
> Give me a little time beyond my cuff'd head,
>   slumbers, dreams, gaping,
> I discover myself on the verge of a usual mistake.

There is in such changes of tone as these the essence of wit. And Whitman is even more far-fetched than he is witty; he can say about Doubters, in the most improbable and explosive of juxtapositions: "I know every one of you, I know the sea of torment, doubt, despair and unbelief. / How the flukes splash! How they contort rapid as lightning, with splashes and spouts of blood!" Who else would have said about God: "As the hugging and loving bed-fellow sleeps at my side through the night, and withdraws at the break of day with stealthy tread, / Leaving me baskets cover'd with white towels, swelling the house with their plenty"?—the Psalmist himself, his cup running over, would have looked at Whitman with dazzled eyes. (Whitman was persuaded by friends to hide the fact that it was God he was talking about.) He says, "Flaunt of the sunshine I need not your bask—lie over!" This unusual employment of verbs is usual enough in participle-loving Whitman, who also asks you to "look in my face while I snuff the sidle of evening," or tells you, "I effuse my flesh in eddies, and drift it in lacy jags." Here are some typical beginnings of poems: "City of orgies, walks, and joys. . . . Not heaving from my ribb'd breast only. . . . O take my hand Walt Whitman! Such gliding wonders! Such sights and sounds! Such join'd unended links. . . ." He says to the objects of the world, "You have waited, you always wait, you dumb, beautiful ministers"; sees "the sun and stars that float in the open air, / The apple-shaped earth"; says, "O suns—O grass of graves—O perpetual transfers and promotions, / If you do not say anything how can I say anything?" Not many poets have written better, in queerer and more convincing and more individual language, about the world's *gliding wonders:* the phrase seems particularly right for Whitman. He speaks of those "circling rivers the breath," of the "savage old mother incessantly crying, / To the boy's soul's questions sullenly timing, some drown'd secret hissing"—ends a poem, once, "We have voided all but freedom and our own joy." How can one quote enough? If the reader thinks that all this is like Thomas Wolfe he *is* Thomas Wolfe; nothing else could explain it. Poetry like this is as far as possible from the work of any ordinary rhetorician, whose phrases cascade over us like suds of the oldest and most-advertised detergent.

The interesting thing about Whitman's worst language (for, just as few poets have ever written better, few poets have ever written worse) is how unusually absurd, how really ingeniously bad, such language is. I will quote none of the most famous examples; but even a line like *O culpable! I acknowledge. I exposé!* is not anything that you and I could do—only a man with the most extraordinary feel for language, or none whatsoever, could have cooked up Whitman's worst messes. For instance: what other man in all the history of this planet would have said, "I am a habitan of Vienna"? (One has an immediate vision of him as a sort of French-Canadian halfbreed to whom the Viennese are offering, with trepidation, through the bars of a zoological garden, little mounds of whipped cream.) And *enclaircise*—why, it's as bad as *explicate!* We are right to resent his having made up his own horrors, instead of sticking to the ones that we ourselves employ. But when Whitman says, "I dote on myself, there is that lot of me and all so luscious," we should realize that we are not the only ones who are amused. And the queerly bad and the merely queer and the queerly good will often change into one another without warning: "Hefts of the moving world, at innocent gambols silently rising, freshly exuding,/ Scooting obliquely high and low"—not good, but *queer!*—suddenly becomes, "Something I cannot see puts up libidinous prongs,/Seas of bright juice suffuse heaven," and it is sunrise.

But it is not in individual lines and phrases, but in passages of some length, that Whitman is at his best. In the following quotation Whitman has something difficult to express, something that there are many formulas, all bad, for expressing; he expresses it with complete success, in language of the most dazzling originality:

The orchestra whirls me wider than Uranus flies,
It wrenches such ardors from me I did not know I possess'd them,
It sails me, I dab with bare feet, they are lick'd by the indolent waves,
I am cut by bitter and angry hail, I lose my breath,
Steep'd amid honey'd morphine, my windpipe throttled in fakes of death,
At length let up again to feel the puzzle of puzzles,
And that we call Being.

One hardly knows what to point at—everything works. But *wrenches* and *did not know I possess'd them;* the incredible *it sails me, I dab*

with bare feet; lick'd by the indolent; steep'd amid honey'd morphine;
my windpipe throttled in fakes of death—no wonder Crane admired
Whitman! This originality, as absolute in its way as that of Berlioz'
orchestration, is often at Whitman's command:

I am a dance—play up there! the fit is whirling me fast!

I am the ever-laughing—it is new moon and twilight,
I see the hiding of coucuers, I see nimble ghosts whichever way I look,
Cache and cache again deep in the ground and sea, and where it is neither
  ground nor sea.
Well do they do their jobs those journeymen divine,
Only from me can they hide nothing, and would not if they could,
I reckon I am their boss and they make me a pet besides,
And surround me and lead me and run ahead when I walk,
To lift their sunning covers to signify me with stretch'd arms, and resume the
  way;
Onward we move, a gay gang of blackguards! with mirth-shouting music and
  wild-flapping penants of joy!

If you did not believe Hopkins' remark about Whitman, that *gay gang*
of blackguards ought to shake you. Whitman shares Hopkins' passion
for "dappled" effects, but he slides in and out of them with ambiguous
swiftness. And he has at his command a language of the calmest and
most prosaic reality, one that seems to do no more than present:

The little one sleeps in its cradle.
I lift the gauze and look a long time, and silently brush away flies with my
  hand.

The youngster and the red-faced girl turn aside up the bushy hill,
I peeringly view them from the top.

The suicide sprawls on the bloody floor of the bedroom.
I witness the corpse with its dabbled hair, I note where the pistol has fallen.

It is like magic: that is, something has been done to us without our
knowing how it was done; but if we look at the lines again we see the
gauze, silently, youngster, red-faced, bushy, peeringly, dabbled—not
that this is all we see. "Present! present!" said James; these are presented, put down side by side to form a little "view of life," from the

cradle to the last bloody floor of the bedroom. Very often the things presented form nothing but a list:

The pure contralto sings in the organ loft,
The carpenter dresses his plank, the tongue of his foreplane whistles its wild ascending lisp,
The married and unmarried children ride home to their Thanksgiving dinner,
The pilot seizes the king-pin, he heaves down with a strong arm,
The mate stands braced in the whale-boat, lance and harpoon are ready,
The duck-shooter walks by silent and cautious stretches,
The deacons are ordained with cross'd hands at the altar,
The spinning-girl retreats and advances to the hum of the big wheel,
The farmer stops by the bars as he walks on a First-day loafe and looks at the oats and rye.
The lunatic is carried at last to the asylum a confirm'd case,
(He will never sleep any more as he did in the cot in his mother's bedroom;)
The jour printer with gray head and gaunt jaws works at his case,
He turns his quid of tobacco while his eyes blur with the manuscript,
The malform'd limbs are tied to the surgeon's table,
What is removed drops horribly in a pail. . . .

It is only a list—but what a list! And how delicately, in what different ways—likeness and opposition and continuation and climax and anticlimax—the transitions are managed, whenever Whitman wants to manage them. Notice them in the next quotation, another "mere list":

The bride unrumples her white dress, the minute-hand of the clock moves slowly,
The opium-eater reclines with rigid head and just-open'd lips,
The prostitute draggles her shawl, her bonnet bobs on her tipsy and pimpled neck. . . .

The first line is joined to the third by *unrumples* and *draggles, white dress* and *shawl;* the second to the third by *rigid head, bobs, tipsy, neck;* the first to the second by *slowly, just-open'd,* and the slowing-down of time in both states. And occasionally one of these lists is metamorphosed into something we have no name for; the man who would call the next quotation a mere list—anybody will feel this—would boil his babies up for soap:

Ever the hard unsunk ground,
Ever the eaters and drinkers, ever the upward and downward sun,
Ever myself and my neighbors, refreshing, wicked, real,
Ever the old inexplicable query, ever that thorned thumb, that breath of
    itches and thirsts,
Ever the vexer's hoot! hoot! till we find where the sly one hides and bring him
    forth,
Ever the sobbing liquid of life,
Ever the bandage under the chin, ever the trestles of death.

Sometimes Whitman will take what would generally be considered
an unpromising subject (in this case, a woman peeping at men in bathing naked) and treat it with such tenderness and subtlety and understanding that we are ashamed of ourselves for having thought it unpromising, and murmur that Chekhov himself couldn't have treated it
better:

Twenty-eight young men bathe by the shore,
Twenty-eight young men and all so friendly,
Twenty-eight years of womanly life and all so lonesome.

She owns the fine house by the rise of the bank,
She hides handsome and richly drest aft the blinds of the window.
Which of the young men does she like the best?
Ah the homeliest of them is beautiful to her.

Where are you off to, lady? for I see you,
You splash in the water there, yet stay stock still in your room.

Dancing and laughing along the beach came the twenty-ninth bather,
The rest did not see her, but she saw them and loved them.

The beards of the young men glistened with wet, it ran from their long hair,
Little streams pass'd all over their bodies.

An unseen hand also pass'd over their bodies,
It descended tremblingly from their temples and ribs.

The young men float on their backs, their white bellies bulge to the sun, they
    do not ask who seizes fast to them,
They do not know who puffs and declines with pendant and bending arch,
They do not know whom they souse with spray.

And in the same poem (that "Song of Myself" in which one finds half his best work) the writer can say of a sea-fight:

Stretched and still lies the midnight,
Two great hulls motionless on the breast of the darkness,
Our vessel riddled and slowly sinking, preparations to pass to the one we have
conquer'd,
The captain on the quarter-deck coldly giving his orders through a counte-
nance white as a sheet,
Near the corpse of the child that serv'd in the cabin,
The dead face of an old salt with long white hair and carefully curl'd whisk-
ers,
The flames spite of all that can be done flickering aloft and below,
The husky voices of the two or three offices yet fit for duty,
Formless stacks of bodies and bodies by themselves, dabs of flesh upon the
masts and spars,
Cut of cordage, dangle of rigging, slight shock of the soothe of waves,
Black and impassive guns, litter of powder-parcels, strong scent,
A few large stars overhead, silent and mournful shining,
Delicate snuffs of sea-breeze, smells of sedgy grass and fields by the shore,
death-messages given in charge to survivors,
The hiss of the surgeon's knife, the gnawing teeth of his saw,
Wheeze, cluck, swash of falling blood, short wild scream, and long, dull,
tapering groan,
These so, these irretrievable.

There are faults in this passage, and they *do not matter:* the serious truth, the complete realization of these last lines make us remember that few poets have shown more of the tears of things, and the joy of things, and of the reality beneath either tears or joy. Even Whitman's most general or political statements often are good: everybody knows his "When liberty goes out of place it is not the first to go, nor the sec-ond or third to go,/ It waits for all the rest to go, it is the last"; these sentences about the United States just before the Civil War may be less familiar:

Are those really Congressmen? are those the great Judges? is that the Presi-
dent?
Then I will sleep awhile yet, for I see that these States sleep, for reasons;
(With gathering murk, with muttering thunder and lambent shoots we all
duly awake,
South, North, East, West, inland and seaboard, we will surely awake.)

How well, with what firmness and dignity and command, Whitman
does such passages! And Whitman's doubts that he has done them or
anything else well—ah, there is nothing he does better:

The best I had done seemed to me blank and suspicious,
My great thoughts as I supposed them, were they not in reality meagre?
I am he who knew what it was to be evil,
I too knitted the old knot of contrariety . . .
Saw many I loved in the street or ferry-boat or public assembly, yet never told
 them a word,
Lived the same life with the rest, the same old laughing, gnawing, sleeping,
Played the part that still looks back on the actor and actress,
The same old role, the role that is what we make it . . .

Whitman says once that the "look of the bay mare shames silliness
out of me." This is true—sometimes it is true; but more often the silliness and affectation and cant and exaggeration are there shamelessly, the Old Adam that was in Whitman from the beginning and the
awful new one that he created to keep it company. But as he says, "I
know perfectly well my own egotism, / Know my omnivorous lines and
must not write any less." He says over and over that there are in him
good and bad, wise and foolish, anything at all and its antonym, and he
is telling the truth; there is in him almost everything in the world, so
that one responds to him, willingly or unwillingly, almost as one does
to the world, that world which makes the hairs of one's flesh stand up,
which seems both evil beyond any rejection and wonderful beyond any
acceptance. We cannot help seeing that there is something absurd
about any judgment we make of its whole—for there is no "point of
view" at which we can stand to make the judgment, and the moral
categories that mean most to us seem no more to apply to its whole
than our spatial or temporal or causal categories seem to apply to its
beginning or its end. (But we need no arguments to make our judgments seem absurd—we feel their absurdity without argument.) In some like sense Whitman is a world, a waste with, here and
there, systems blazing at random out of the darkness. Only an innocent
and rigidly methodical mind will reject it for this disorganization, particularly since there are in it, here and there, little systems as beautifully and astonishingly organized as the rings and satellites of Saturn:

I understand the large hearts of heroes,
The courage of present times and all times,

How the skipper saw the crowded and rudderless wreck of the steam-ship,
    and Death chasing it up and down the storm,
How he knuckled tight and gave not back an inch, and was faithful of days
    and faithful of nights,
And chalked in large letters on a board, Be of good cheer, we will not desert
    you;
How he follow'd with them and tack'd with them three days and would not
    give it up,
How he saved the drifting company at last,
How the lank loose-gown'd women looked when boated from the side of their
    prepared graves,
How the silent old-faced infants and the lifted sick, and the sharp-lipp'd un-
    shaved men;
All this I swallow, it tastes good, I like it well, it becomes mine,
I am the man, I suffered, I was there.

In the last lines of this quotation Whitman has reached—as great
writers always reach—a point at which criticism seems not only unnecessary but absurd: these lines are so good that even admiration
feels like insolence, and one is ashamed of anything that one can find
to say about them. How anyone can dismiss or accept patronizingly the
man who wrote them, I do not understand.

    The enormous and apparent advantage of form, of omission and se-
lection, of the highest degree of organization, are accompanied by important disadvantages—and there are far greater works than *Leaves
of Grass* to make us realize this. But if we compare Whitman with that
very beautiful poet Alfred Tennyson, the most skillful of all Whitman's contemporaries, we are at once aware of how limiting Tennyson's forms have been, of how much Tennyson has had to leave out,
even in those discursive poems where he is trying to put everything in.
Whitman's poems *represent* his world and himself much more satisfactorily than Tennyson's do his. In the past a few poets have both formed
and represented, each in the highest degree; but in modern times what
controlling, organizing, selecting poet has created a world with as
much in it as Whitman's, a world that so plainly *is* the world? Of all
modern poets he has, quantitatively speaking, "the most comprehensive soul"—and, qualitatively, a most comprehensive and compre-
hending one, with charities and concessions and qualifications that are
rare in any time.

    "Do I contradict myself? Very well then I contradict myself," wrote

Whitman, as everybody remembers, and this is not naive, or something he got from Emerson, or a complacent pose. When you organize
one of the contradictory elements out of your work of art, you are getting rid not just of it, but of the contradiction of which it was a part;
and it is the contradictions in works of art which make them able to
represent to us—as logical and methodical generalizations cannot
—our world and ourselves, which are also full of contradictions. In
Whitman we do not get the controlled, compressed, seemingly con-
cordant contradictions of the great lyric poets, of a poem like, say,
Hardy's *During Wind and Rain;* Whitman's contradictions are sometimes announced openly, but are more often scattered at random
throughout the poems. For instance: Whitman specializes in ways of
saying that there is in some sense (a very Hegelian one, generally) no
evil—he says a hundred times that evil is not Real; but he also specializes in making lists of the evil of the world, lists of an unarguable
reality. After his minister has recounted "the rounded catalogue divine complete," Whitman comes home and puts down what has been
left out: "the countless (nineteen-twentieths) low and evil, crude and
savage . . . the barren soil, the evil men, the slag and hideous rot."
He ends another such catalogue with the plain unexcusing "All these
—all meanness and agony without end I sitting look out upon,/ See,
hear, and am silent." Whitman offered himself to everybody, and said
brilliantly and at length what a good thing he was offering:

Sure as the most certain sure, plumb in the uprights, well entretied, braced in
      the beams,
Stout as a horse, affectionate, haughty, electrical,
I and this mystery here we stand.

Just for oddness, characteristicalness, differentness, what more could
you ask in a letter of recommendation? (Whitman sounds as if he were
recommending a house—haunted, but what foundations!) But after a
few pages he is oddly different:

Apart from the pulling and hauling stands what I am,
Stands amused, complacent, compassionating, idle, unitary,
Looks down, is erect, or bends an arm on an impalpable certain rest
Looking with side curved head curious what will come next,
Both in and out of the game and watching and wondering at it.

Tamburlaine is already beginning to sound like Hamlet: the employer
feels uneasily, *Why, I might as well hire myself.* . . . And, a few
pages later, Whitman puts down in ordinary-sized type, in the middle
of the page, this warning to any *new person drawn toward me:*

Do you think I am trusty and faithful?
Do you see no further than this facade, this smooth and tolerant manner of
   me?
Do you suppose yourself advancing on real ground toward a real heroic man?
Have you no thought O dreamer that it may be all maya, illusion?

Having wonderful dreams, telling wonderful lies, was a temptation
Whitman could never resist; but telling the truth was a temptation he
could never resist, either. When you buy him you know what you are
buying. And only an innocent and solemn and systematic mind will
condemn him for his contradictions: Whitman's catalogues of evils
represent realities, and his denials of their reality represent other realities, of feeling and intuition and desire. If he is faithless to logic, to
Reality As It Is—whatever that is—he is faithful to the feel of
things, to reality as it seems; this is all that a poet has to be faithful to,
and philosophers even have been known to leave logic and Reality for
it.
   Whitman is more coordinate and parallel than anybody, is *the* poet
of parallel present participles, of twenty verbs joined by a single subject: all this helps to give his work its feeling of raw hypnotic reality, of
being that world which also streams over us joined only by *ands,* until
we supply the subordinating conjunctions; and since as children we see
the *ands* and not the *becauses,* this method helps to give Whitman
some of the freshness of childhood. How inexhaustibly *interesting* the
world is in Whitman! Arnold all his life kept wishing that we could see
the world "with a plainness as near, as flashing" as that with which
Moses and Rebekah and the Argonauts saw it. He asked with elegiac
nostalgia, "Who can see the green earth any more / As she was by the
sources of Time?"—and all the time there was somebody alive who
saw it so, as plain and near and flashing, and with a kind of calm, pastoral, biblical dignity and elegance as well, sometimes. The *thereness*
and *suchness* of the world are incarnate in Whitman as they are in few
other writers.
   They might have put on his tombstone WALT WHITMAN: HE
HAD HIS NERVE. He is the rashest, the most inexplicable and un-

likely—the most impossible, one wants to say—of poets. He some-how *is* in a class by himself, so that one compares him with other poets about as readily as one compares *Alice* with other books. (Even his free verse has a completely different effect from anybody else's.) Who would think of comparing him with Tennyson or Browning or Arnold or Baudelaire?—it is Homer, or the sagas, or something far away and long ago, that comes to one's mind only to be dismissed; for sometimes Whitman *is* epic, just as *Moby Dick* is, and it surprises us to be able to use truthfully this word that we have misused so many times. Whitman *is* grand, and elevated, and comprehensive, and real with an astonish-ing reality, and many other things—the critic points at his qualities in despair and wonder, all method failing, and simply calls them by their names. And the range of these qualities is the most extraordinary thing of all. We can surely say about him, "He was a man, take him for all in all. I shall not look upon his like again"—and wish that people had seen this and not tried to be his like: one Whitman is miracle enough, and when he comes again it will be the end of the world.

I have said so little about Whitman's faults because they are so plain: baby critics who have barely learned to complain of the lack of ambiguity in *Peter Rabbit* can tell you all that is wrong with *Leaves of Grass*. But a good many of my readers must have felt that it is ridicu-lous to write an essay about the obvious fact that Whitman is a great poet. It is ridiculous—just as, in 1851, it would have been ridiculous for anyone to write an essay about the obvious fact that Pope was no "classic of our prose" but a great poet. Critics have to spend half their time reiterating whatever ridiculously obvious things their age or the critics of their age have found it necessary to forget: they say despair-ingly, at parties, that Wordsworth is a great poet, and *won't* bore you, and tell Mr. Leavis that Milton is a great poet whose deposition *hasn't* been accomplished with astonishing ease by a few words from Eliot and Pound. . . . There is something essentially ridiculous about critics, anyway: what is good is good without our saying so, and be-neath all our majesty we know this.

Let me finish by mentioning another quality of Whitman's—a quality, delightful to me, that I have said nothing of. If some day a tourist notices, among the ruins of New York City, a copy of *Leaves of Grass,* and stops and picks it up and reads some lines in it, she will be able to say to herself: "How very American! If he and his country had not existed, it would have been impossible to imagine them."

35. Huck and Oliver

W. H. AUDEN

W. H. Auden, who was born in England and educated at Oxford, left
Europe just before World War II to join the "rootless" peoples of
America. Though a citizen of the United States, he has continued to
spend part of every year in Europe—and thus enjoys the special advantage of standing between two worlds. His essay on *Huckleberry
Finn* represents (in addition to his critical acuteness) his double point
of view and his desire to mediate between England and America. (For
additional material on Auden, see the headnote to Selection 22,
"The Guilty Vicarage.")

About six months ago I re-read *Huckleberry Finn,* by Mark Twain, for
the first time since I was a boy, and I was trying when I read it to put
myself back in the position of what it would seem like to re-read the
book without knowing the United States very well. Because *Huckleberry Finn* is one of those books which is a key book for understanding
the United States; just as I think one could take other books, English
books—shall I say *Oliver Twist?*—as corresponding pictures of a
British attitude.

Two Attitudes Towards Nature

When you read *Huckleberry Finn,* the first thing maybe that strikes
somebody who comes from England about it is the difference in nature
and in the attitude towards nature. You will find the Mississippi, and
nature generally, very big, very formidable, very inhuman. When
Oliver goes to stay in the country with Mrs. Maylie, Dickens writes:

> Who can describe the pleasure and delight and peace of mind and tran-
> quillity the sickly boy felt in the balmy air, and among the green hills and
> rich woods of an inland village?

SOURCE: *The Listener,* L (October 1, 1953), 540–41. Reprinted by permission of
Curtis Brown, Ltd.

All very human, very comforting. Huck describes how he gets lost in a fog on the Mississippi, and he writes as follows:

I was floating along, of course, four or five miles an hour; but you don't ever think of that. No, you *feel* like you are laying dead still on the water; and if a little glimpse of a snag slips by, you don't think to yourself how fast *you're* going, but you catch your breath and think, my! how that snag's tearing along. If you think it ain't dismal and lonesome out in a fog that way, by yourself, in the night, you try it once—you'll see.

One of the great differences between Europe in general and America is in the attitude towards nature. To us over here, perhaps, nature is always, in a sense, the mother or the wife: something with which you enter into a semi-personal relation. In the United States, nature is something much more savage; it is much more like—shall we say? —St. George and the dragon. Nature is the dragon, against which St. George proves his manhood. The trouble about that, of course, is that if you succeed in conquering the dragon, there is nothing you can do with the dragon except enslave it, so that there is always the danger with a wild and difficult climate of alternating, if you like, between respecting it as an enemy and exploiting it as a slave.

The second thing that will strike any European reader in reading *Huckleberry Finn* is the amazing stoicism of this little boy. Here he is, with a father who is a greater and more horrible monster than almost any I can think of in fiction, who very properly gets murdered later. He runs into every kind of danger; he observes a blood feud in which there is a terrible massacre, and he cannot even bear, as he writes afterwards, to think exactly what happened. Yet, in spite of all these things, which one would expect to reduce a small child either into becoming a criminal or a trembling nervous wreck, Huck takes them as Acts of God which pass away, and yet one side of this stoicism is an attitude towards time in which the immediate present is accepted as the immediate present; there is no reason to suppose that the future will be the same, and therefore it does not, perhaps, have to affect the future in the same kind of way as it does here.

Then, more interestingly, the European reader is puzzled by the nature of the moral decision that Huck takes. Here Huck is with his runaway slave, Jim, and he decides that he is not going to give Jim up, he is going to try to get him into safety. When I first read *Huckleberry Finn* as a boy, I took Huck's decision as being a sudden realisation, although he had grown up in a slave-owning community, that slavery was wrong. Therefore I completely failed to understand one of the most wonderful passages in the book, where Huck wrestles with his conscience. Here are two phrases. He says:

> I was trying to make my mouth *say* I would do the right thing and the clean thing, and go and write to that nigger's owner and tell where he was; but deep down inside I knowed it was a lie, and He knowed it. You can't pray a lie—I found that out.

He decides that he will save Jim. He says:

> I will go to work and steal Jim out of slavery again; and if I could think up anything worse, I would do that, too; because as long as I was in, and in for good, I might as well go the whole hog.

When I first read the book I took this to be abolitionist satire on Mark Twain's part. It is not that at all. What Huck does is a pure act of moral improvisation. What he decides tells him nothing about what he should do on other occasions, or what other people should do on other occasions; and here we come to a very profound difference between American and European culture. I believe that all Europeans, whatever their political opinions, whatever their religious creed, do believe in a doctrine of natural law of some kind. That is to say there are certain things about human nature, and about man as a historical creature, not only as a natural creature, which are eternally true. If a man is a conservative, he thinks that law has already been discovered. If he is a revolutionary he thinks he has just discovered it; nobody knew anything in the past, but now it is known. If he is a liberal, he thinks we know something about it and we shall gradually know more. But neither the conservative, nor the revolutionary, nor the liberal has really any doubt that a natural law exists.

It is very hard for an American to believe that there is anything in human nature that will not change. Americans are often called, and sometimes even believe themselves to be, liberal optimists who think that the world is gradually getting better and better. I do not really believe that is true, and I think the evidence of their literature is against it. One should say, rather, that deep down inside they think that all things pass: the evils we know will disappear, but so will the goods.

For that very reason you might say that America is a country of amateurs. Here is Huck who makes an essentially amateur moral decision. The distinction between an amateur and a professional, of course, is not necessarily a matter of learning; an amateur might be a very learned person, but his knowledge would be, so to speak, the result of his own choice of reading and chance. *Vice versa,* a professional is not necessarily unoriginal, but he will always tend to check his results against the past and with his colleagues. The word "intellectual" in Europe has always meant, basically, the person who knew what the law was, in whatever sphere, whether it was religion, medicine, or what have you. There has always been a distrust in the States of the person who claimed in advance to know what the law was. Naturally, in any country where people are faced with situations which are really new, the amateur often is right where the professional is wrong; we sometimes use the phrase "professional caution," and that sometimes applies when situations are quite different. On the other hand, the amateur tends, necessarily, to think in terms of immediate problems and to demand immediate solutions, because if you believe that everything is going to be completely different the day after tomorrow, it is no good trying to think about that.

A Sad Book

A third thing, coupled with that, is that on reading *Huckleberry Finn* most Europeans will find the book emotionally very sad. Oliver Twist has been through all kinds of adventures; he has met people who have become his friends, and you feel they are going to be his friends for life. Huck has had a relationship with Jim much more intense than any that Oliver has known, and yet, at the end of the book, you know that they are going to part and never see each other again. There hangs over the book a kind of sadness, as if freedom and love were incompatible. At the end of the book Oliver the orphan is adopted by Mr. Brownlow, and that is really the summit of his daydream—to be accepted into a loving home. Almost the last paragraph of *Oliver Twist* runs:

Mr. Brownlow went on, from day to day, filling the mind of his adopted child with stories of knowledge . . . becoming attached to him, more and more, as his nature developed itself, and showed the thriving seeds of all he wished him to become. . . .

How does Huck end:

> I reckon I got to light out for the Territory ahead of the rest, because Aunt
> Sally she's going to adopt me and sivilise me, and I can't stand it. I been there
> before.

In that way, of course, he is like a character in *Oliver Twist*—the
Artful Dodger. But in the case of the Artful Dodger, Dickens shows us
this charming young man as nevertheless corrupt, and over him hangs
always the shadow of the gallows; he is not the natural hero, as Huck is
in *Huckleberry Finn*.

In addition to the attitude towards nature, the attitude towards natural law, there are two more things one might take up briefly; the attitude towards time, and the attitude towards money. Imagine two
events in history (a) followed by (b), which in some way are analogous.
The danger to the European will be to think of them as identical, so
that if I know what to do over (a), I shall know exactly what to do with
(b). The danger in America will be to see no relation between these
things at all, so that any knowledge I have about (a) will not help me to
understand (b). The European fails to see the element of novelty; the
American fails to see the element of repetition. You may remember
that both Oliver and Huck come into some money. In Oliver's case it is
money that is his by right of legal inheritance. In Huck's case, it is pure
luck. He and Tom Sawyer found a robber's cache. The money came to
them only because it could not be restored to its rightful owners. The
money, therefore, is not something that you ever think of inheriting by
right.

One might put it this way: in Europe, money represents power—
that is to say, freedom from having to do what other people want you
to do, and freedom to do what you yourself want to do; so that in a
sense all Europeans feel they would like to have as much money themselves as possible, and other people to have as little as possible.

In the States, money, which is thought of as something you extract
in your battle with the dragon of nature, represents a proof of your
manhood. The important thing is not to have money, but to have made
it. Once you have made it you can perfectly well give it all away. There
are advantages and disadvantages on both sides. The disadvantage in
Europe is a tendency towards avarice and meanness; the danger in
America is anxiety because, since this quantitative thing of money is
regarded as a proof of your manhood, and to make a little more of it

would make you even more manly, it becomes difficult to know where to stop. This ties up with something that always annoys me: when I see Europeans accusing Americans of being materialists. The real truth about Americans is they do not care about matter enough. What is shocking is waste; just as what shocks Americans in Europe is avarice.

I have mentioned a few of these things because we live in a time when it has never been so important that America and Great Britain should understand each other. Many misunderstandings arise, not over concrete points, but over a failure to recognise certain presuppositions or attitudes which we all make, according to our upbringing, in such a way that we cannot imagine anybody taking any other one. When those are understood, it is much more possible to help each other's strong points and weaknesses by exchanging them to our mutual profit.

In so far as that can be done, and I am sufficiently much of a liberal optimist to believe it can, the alliance between the States and Great Britain can become a real and genuine and mutually self-critical thing, instead of the rather precarious relationship forced by circumstances which it seems to be at present.—*From an extempore recording made during a visit to this country and broadcast in the Third Programme.*

36. Shakespeare, or the Discovery of *Moby-Dick*

CHARLES OLSON

Charles Olson (1910–   ) is an important poet in his own right, but even more significant as the founder and spiritual father of a group of poets who have recently moved to the center of the American scene in poetry. His followers are known as the Black Mountain Poets after an

SOURCE: Charles Olson, *Call Me Ishmael* (San Francisco: City Lights Books, 1947), pp. 35–58, 64–73. Copyright 1947 by Charles Olson. Reprinted by permission of City Lights Books.

experimental college of which he was Dean for several years. More recently he has taught at the State University of New York at Buffalo, but has again withdrawn to his home in Gloucester, Massachusetts, to write and hold court. His book on Melville, *Call Me Ishmael* (1947), from which the following is excerpted, has had a broader appeal than his other scattered critical pieces, and even perhaps than his poetry.

Which is the best of Shakespeare's plays? I mean in what mood and with what accompaniment do you like the sea best?

KEATS, *Letter to Jane Reynolds*
Sept. 14, 1817

Moby-Dick was two books written between February, 1850 and August, 1851.

The first book did not contain Ahab.

It may not, except incidentally, have contained Moby-Dick.

On the 7th of August, 1850, the editor Evert Duyckinck reported to his brother:

Melville has a new book mostly done, a romantic, fanciful & most literal & most enjoyable presentment of the Whale Fishery—something quite new.

It is not surprising that Melville turned to whaling in February, 1850, on his return from a trip to England to sell his previous book, *White-Jacket*. It was the last of the materials his sea experience offered him.

He had used his adventures among the South Sea islands in *Typee* (1846) and *Omoo* (1847). He had gone further in the vast archipelago of *Mardi,* written in 1847 and 1848, to map the outlines of his vision of life. The books of 1849, *Redburn* and *White-Jacket,* he had based on his experiences aboard a merchant ship and a man-of-war. The whaling voyage in the *Acushnet* was left.

There is no evidence that Melville had decided on the subject before he started to write in February. On the contrary. Melville's reading is a gauge of him, at all points of his life. He was a skald, and knew how to appropriate the work of others. He read to write. Highborn stealth, Edward Dahlberg calls originality, the act of a cutpurse Autolycus who makes his thefts as invisible as possible. Melville's books batten on other men's books. Yet he bought no books on whaling among the many volumes purchased in England on his trip and soon after his return Putnam's the publishers were picking up in London for him such things as Thomas Beale's *The Natural History of the Sperm Whale*.

He went at it as he had his last two books, "two jobs," as he called *Redburn* and *White-Jacket* in a letter to his father-in-law, "which I have done for money—being forced to it, as other men are to sawing wood." He had a family to support.

By May it was half done. So he told Richard Henry Dana in a letter on the 1st, the only other information of the first Moby-Dick which has survived. The book was giving Melville trouble. Referring to it as "the 'whaling voyage,' " he writes:

It will be a strange sort of a book, I fear; blubber is blubber you know; tho you may get oil out of it, the poetry runs as hard as sap from a frozen maple tree;—& to cook the thing up, one must needs throw in a little fancy, which from the nature of the thing, must be ungainly as the gambols of the whales themselves. Yet I mean to give the truth of the thing, spite of this.

That's the record of Moby-Dick No. 1, as it stands. There is nothing on why, in the summer of 1850, Melville changed his conception of the work and, on something "mostly done" on August 7th, spent another full year until, in August, 1851, he had created what we know as *Moby-Dick or, The Whale.*

"Dollars damn me." Melville had the bitter thing of men of originality, the struggle between money and me. It was on him, hard, in the spring of 1850. He says as much in the Dana letter: "I write these books of mine almost entirely for 'lucre'—by the job, as a woodsawyer saws wood," repeating on Moby-Dick what he had said about *Redburn* and *White-Jacket*.

He knew the cost if he let his imagination loose. He had taken his head once, with *Mardi*. In this new work on whaling he felt obliged, as he had, after *Mardi,* with *Redburn* and *White-Jacket,* "to refrain from writing the kind of book I would wish to."

He would give the truth of the thing, spite of this, yes. His head was lifted to Dana as it was to his father-in-law seven months earlier. He did his work clean. *Exs: Redburn* and *White-Jacket*. "In writing these two books I have not repressed myself much—so far as *they* are concerned; but have spoken pretty much as I feel."

There was only one thing in the spring of 1850 which he did not feel he could afford to do: "So far as I am individually concerned, & independent of my pocket, it is my earnest desire to write those sort of books which are said to 'fail.' "

In the end, in *Moby-Dick,* he did. Within three months he took his head again. Why?

Through May he continued to try to do a quick book for the market: "all my books are botches." Into June he fought his materials: "blubber is blubber." Then something happened. What, Melville tells:

I somehow cling to the strange fancy, that, in all men hiddenly reside certain wondrous, occult properties—as in some plants and minerals—which by some happy but very rare accident (as bronze was discovered by the melting of the iron and brass at the burning of Corinth) may chance to be called forth here on earth.

When? Melville is his own tell-tale: he wrote these words in July, 1850. They occur in an article he did for Duyckinck's magazine. He gave it the title HAWTHORNE AND HIS MOSSES, WRITTEN BY A VIRGINIAN SPENDING A JULY IN VERMONT.

The subject is Hawthorne, Shakespeare and Herman Melville. It is a document of Melville's rights and perceptions, his declaration of the freedom of a man to fail. Within a matter of days after it was written (July 18 ff.), Melville had abandoned the account of the Whale Fishery and gambled it and himself with Ahab and the White Whale.

The *Mosses* piece is a deep and lovely thing. The spirit is asweep, as in the book to come. The confusion of May is gone. Melville is charged again. *Moby-Dick* is already shadowed in the excitement over genius, and America as a subject for genius. You can feel Ahab in the making, Ahab of "the globular brain and ponderous heart," so much does Melville concern himself with the distinction between the head and the heart in Hawthorne and Shakespeare. You can see the prose stepping off.

The germinous seeds Hawthorne has dropped in Melville's July soil begin to grow: Bulkington, the secret member of the crew in *Moby-Dick,* is here, hidden, in what Melville quotes as Hawthorne's self-portrait—the "seeker," rough-hewn and brawny, of large, warm heart and powerful intellect.

Above all, in the ferment, Shakespeare, the cause. The passages on him—the manner in which he is introduced, the detail with which he is used, the intensity—tell the story of what had happened. Melville had read him again. His copy of THE PLAYS survives. He had bought it in Boston in February, 1849. He described it then to Duyckinck:

It is an edition in glorious great type, every letter whereof is a soldier, & the top of every 't' like a musket barrel.

I am mad to think how minute a cause has prevented me hitherto from reading Shakespeare. But until now any copy that was come-at-able to me happened to be a vile small print unendurable to my eyes which are tender as young sperms.

But chancing to fall in with this glorious edition, I now exult over it, page after page.

The set exists, seven volumes, with passages marked, and comments in Melville's hand. The significant thing is the rough notes for the composition of *Moby-Dick* on the fly-leaf of the last volume. These notes involve Ahab, Pip, Bulkington, Ishmael, and are the key to Melville's intention with these characters. They thus relate not to what we know of the Moby-Dick that Melville had been working on up to July but to *Moby-Dick* as he came to conceive it at this time.

Joined to the passages on Shakespeare in the *Mosses* piece, the notes in the Shakespeare set verify what *Moby-Dick* proves: Melville and Shakespeare had made a Corinth and out of the burning came *Moby-Dick,* bronze.

American Shiloh

Shakespeare emerged from the first rush of Melville's reading a Messiah: as he put it in the *Mosses* piece in 1850, a "Shiloh"; as he put it to Duyckinck in 1849, "full of sermons-on-the-mount, and gentle, aye, almost as Jesus." Melville had a way of ascribing divinity to truth-tellers, Solomon, Shakespeare, Hawthorne, or Jesus.

He next limited Shakespeare. He advanced a criticism in his second letter to Duyckinck in 1849 which is central to all his later published passages on the poet. It keeps him this side idolatry. It arises from what Melville takes to be an "American" advantage:

I would to God Shakespeare had lived later, & promenaded in Broadway. Not that I might have had the pleasure of leaving my card for him at the Astor, or made merry with him over a bowl of the fine Duyckinck punch; but that the muzzle which all men wore on their souls in the Elizabethan day, might not have intercepted Shakespeare's free articulations, for I hold it a verity, that even Shakespeare was not a frank man to the uttermost. And, indeed, who in this intolerant universe is, or can be? But the Declaration of Independence makes a difference.

In the *Mosses* piece, a year and a half later, he gives it tone:

In Shakespeare's tomb lies infinitely more than Shakespeare ever wrote. And if I magnify Shakespeare, it is not so much for what he did do as for what he did not do, or refrained from doing.
For in this world of lies, Truth is forced to fly like a scared white doe in the woodlands; and only by cunning glimpses will she reveal herself, as in Shakespeare and other masters of the great Art of Telling the Truth,—even though it be covertly and by snatches.

In his copy of the PLAYS, when Shakespeare muzzles truth-speakers, Melville is quick to mark the line or incident. In *Antony and Cleopatra* he puts a check beside Enobarbus' blunt answer to Antony's correction of his speech: "That truth should be silent I had almost forgot."

In *Lear* he underscores the Fool's answer to Lear's angry threat of the whip: "Truth's a dog must to kennel; he must be whipp'd out, when Lady the brach may stand by th' fire and stink." The very language of Melville in the *Mosses* thing is heard from the Fool's mouth.

As an artist Melville chafed at representation. His work up to *Moby-Dick* was a progress toward the concrete and after *Moby-Dick* a breaking away. He had to fight himself to give truth dramatic location. Shakespeare's dramatic significance was not lost upon him, but he would have been, as he says, "more content with the still, rich utterance of a great intellect in repose." Melville's demand uncovers a flaw in himself.

Fortunately—for *Moby-Dick*—the big truth was not sermons-on-the-mount. Melville found these in *Measure for Measure*. It is, rather

those deep far-away things in him; those occasional flashings-forth of the intuitive Truth in him; those short, quick probings at the very axis of reality; —these are the things that make Shakespeare, Shakespeare.

Such reality is in the mouths of the "dark" characters, Hamlet, Timon, Lear and Iago, where the drama Melville could learn from, lay. For blackness fixed and fascinated Melville. Through such dark men Shakespeare

craftily says, or sometimes insinuates the things which we feel to be so terrifically true, that it were all but madness for any good man, in his own proper character, to utter or even hint of them!

It is this side of Shakespeare that Melville fastens on. Madness, villainy and evil are called up out of the plays as though Melville's pencil were a wand of black magic. To use Swinburne's comment on *Lear,* it is not the light of revelation but the darkness of it that Melville finds most profound in Shakespeare. He was to write in *Moby-Dick:*

Though in many of its aspects the visible world seems formed in love, the invisible spheres were formed in fright.

Man, to Man

Shakespeare reflects Melville's disillusion in the treacherous world. In *The Tempest,* when Miranda cries out "O brave new world!", Melville encircles Prospero's answer " 'Tis new to thee," and writes this note at the bottom of the page:

Consider the character of the persons concerning whom Miranda says this —then Prospero's quiet words in comment—how terrible! In *Timon* itself there is nothing like it.

Shakespeare frequently expresses disillusion through friendship and its falling off. The theme has many variations. Melville misses none of them. Caesar and Antony on the fickleness of the people to their rulers, in *Antony and Cleopatra.* Achilles and Ulysses on the people's faithlessness to their heroes, in *Troilus and Cressida.* Henry V and Richard II on treachery within the councils of the state. Melville pulls it out of the tragedies: in *Lear,* when the Fool sings how fathers who bear bags draw forth love and those who wear rags lose love; and in *Hamlet,* the lines of the Player King:

> For who not needs, shall never lack a friend
> And who in want a hollow friend doth try,
> Directly seasons him his enemy.

To betray a friend was to make—for Melville as for Richard—a second fall of cursed man. Shakespeare gives the theme its great counterpoint in *Timon*. In that play the whole issue of idealism is objectified through friendship. When his friends fail him Timon's love turns to hate. His world—and with it the play—wrenches into halves as the earth with one lunge tore off from a sun.

Melville took a more personal possession of the tragedy of Timon than of any of the other dark men. In *Lear* he found ingratitude, but what gave *Timon* its special intensity was that Timon was undone by friends, not daughters.

Melville makes little out of the love of man and woman. It is the friendship of men which is love. That is why Hawthorne was so important to him, to whom he wrote his best letters and to whom he dedicated *Moby-Dick*. That is why he never forgot Jack Chase, the handsome sailor he worked under in the Pacific, to whom he dedicated his last book, *Billy Budd*.

Melville had the Greek sense of men's love. Or the Roman's, as Shakespeare gives it in *Coriolanus*. In that play the only place Melville heavily marks is the long passage in which Coriolanus and Aufidius meet and embrace. They are captains, with the soldier's sense of comrade. Melville's is the seaman's, of a shipmate. Aufidius speaks the same passionate images of friendship Melville uses to convey the depth of feeling between Ishmael and Queequeg in *Moby-Dick*. Ishmael and Queequeg are as "married" as Aufidius feels toward Coriolanus:

> that I see thee here
> Thou noble thing, more dances my rapt heart
> Than when I first my wedded mistress saw
> Bestride my threshold.

Like Timon Melville found only disappointment. He lost Jack Chase, and Hawthorne, shyest grape, hid from him. In a poem of his later years Melville wrote:

> To have known him, to have loved him
> After loneness long
> And then to be estranged in life
> And neither in the wrong
> Ease me, a little ease, my song!

Timon is mocked with glory, as his faithful Steward says, lives, as Melville notes, but in a dream of friendship. Melville uses the blasted hero as a symbol throughout his books, sometimes in Plutarch's convention as a misanthrope, often as another Ishmael of solitude, most significantly—in *Pierre*—as disillusion itself, man undone by goodness. It is the subject of *Pierre* and the lesson of *The Confidence Man*.

Melville's feeling for the play is summarized by a line he underscores in it, the Stranger's observation on the hypocrisy of Timon's friends:

> Why, this is the world's soul.

Lear *and* Moby-Dick

It was *Lear* that had the deep creative impact. In *Moby-Dick* the use is pervasive. That its use is also the most implicit of any play serves merely to enforce a law of the imagination, for what has stirred Melville's own most is heaved out, like Cordelia's heart, with most tardiness.

In the Hawthorne-Mosses article it is to Lear's speeches that Melville points to prove Shakespeare's insinuations of "the things we feel to be so terrifically true:"

Tormented into desperation, Lear, the frantic king, tears off the mask, and speaks the same madness of vital truth.

His copy of the play is marked more heavily than any of the others but *Antony and Cleopatra*. Of the characters the Fool and Edmund receive the attention. I have said Melville found his own words in the Fool's mouth when the Fool cries, "Truth's a dog must to kennel." He found them in such other speeches of that boy, as

Nay, an thou canst not smile as the wind sits, thou'lt catch cold shortly.

For Melville sees the Fool as the Shakespeare he would have liked more of, not one who refrained from hinting what he knew.

Melville is terrified by Edmund who took his fierce quality in the lusty stealth of nature and who, in his evil, leagued with that world whose thick rotundity Lear would strike flat. The sources of this man's evil, and his qualities, attract the writer who is likewise drawn to Goneril, to Iago—and who himself creates a Jackson in *Redburn* and a Claggart in *Billy Budd.*

It is the positive qualities in the depraved: Edmund's courage, and his power of attracting love. When Edmund outfaces Albany's challenge, denies he is a traitor, and insists he will firmly prove his truth and honor, Melville writes this footnote:

> The infernal nature has a valor often denied to innocence.

When Edmund is dying he fails to revoke his order for the death of Lear and Cordelia, only looks upon the bodies of Goneril and Regan and consoles himself: "Yet Edmund was belov'd!" This Melville heavily checks. It is a twisting ambiguity like one of his own—Evil beloved.

Melville is dumb with horror at the close, blood-stop double meaning of Shakespeare's language in the scene of the blinding of Gloucester. His comment is an exclamation: "Terrific!" When Regan calls Gloucester "Ingrateful fox!" Melville writes:

> Here's a touch Shakespearean—*Regan* talks of *ingratitude!*

First causes were Melville's peculiar preoccupation. He concentrates on an Edmund, a Regan—and the world of *Lear,* which is almost generated by such creatures, lies directly behind the creation of an Ahab, a Fedallah and the White, lovely, monstrous Whale.

Melville found answers in the darkness of *Lear.* Not in the weak goodness of an Albany who thinks to exclude evil from good by a remark as neat and corrective as Eliphaz in the Book of Job:

> Wisdom and goodness to the vile seem vile;
> Filths savor but themselves.

The ambiguities do not resolve themselves by such "right-mindedness." Albany is a Starbuck.

Melville turned rather to men who suffered as Job suffered—to Lear and Edgar and Gloucester. Judged by his markings upon the scene in which Edgar discovers, with a hot burst in his heart, his father's blindness, Melville perceived what suggests itself as a symbol so inherent to the play as to leave one amazed it has not been more often observed—that to lose the eye and capacity to see, to lose the physical organ, "vile jelly," is to gain spiritual sight.

The crucifixion in *Lear* is not of the limbs on a cross-beam, but of the eyes put out, the eyes of pride too sharp for feeling. Lear himself in the storm scene senses it, but Gloucester blind speaks it: "I stumbled when I saw."

Lear's words:

> Poor naked wretches, wheresoe'er you are,
> That bide the pelting of this pitiless storm,
> How shall your houseless heads and unfed sides,
> Your loop'd and window'd raggedness, defend you
> From seasons such as these? O, I have ta'en
> Too little care of this! Take physic, pomp;
> Expose thyself to feel what wretches feel,
> That thou mayst shake the superflux to them
> And show the heavens more just.

Gloucester's words came later, Act IV, Sc. 1. It is the purgatorial dispensation of the whole play. Gloucester, who aches to have his son Edgar back—

> Might I but live to *see thee in my touch*,
> I'ld say I had eyes again!

—has his wish and does not know it. He does not know, because he cannot see, that Edgar is already there beside him in the disguise of Tom o' Bedlam. Gloucester takes him for the poor, mad beggar he says he is. He seconds Lear thus:

> Here, take this purse, thou whom the heavens' plagues
> Have humbled to all strokes. That I am wretched
> Makes thee the happier. Heavens, deal so still!
> Let the superfluous and lust-dieted man,
> That slaves your ordinance, <u>that will not see</u>
> <u>Because he does not feel</u>, feel your pow'r quickly;
> So distribution should undo excess,
> And each man have enough.

The underscore is Melville's.

What moves Melville is the stricken goodness of a Lear, a Gloucester, an Edgar, who in suffering feel and thus probe more closely to the truth. Melville is to put Ahab through this humbling.

Shakespeare drew *Lear* out of what Melville called "the infinite obscure of his background." It was most kin to Melville. He uses it as an immediate obscure around his own world of *Moby-Dick*. And he leaves Ishmael at the end to tell the tale of Ahab's tragedy as Kent remained to speak these last words of Lear:

> Vex not his ghost. O, let him pass! He hates him
> That would upon the rack of this tough world
> Stretch him out longer.

A Moby-Dick *Manuscript*

It is beautifully right to find what I take to be rough notes for *Moby-Dick* in the Shakespeare set itself. They are written in Melville's hand, in pencil, upon the last fly-leaf of the last volume, the one containing *Lear, Othello* and *Hamlet*. I transcribe them as they stand:

> Ego non baptizo te in nomine Patris et
> Filii et Spiritus Sancti—sed in nomine
> Diaboli.—madness is undefinable—
> It & right reason extremes of one,
> —not the (black art) Goetic but Theurgic magic—
> seeks converse with the Intelligence, Power, the
> Angel.

The Latin is a longer form of what Melville told Hawthorne to be the secret motto of *Moby-Dick*. In the novel Ahab howls it as an inverted benediction upon the harpoon he has tempered in savage blood:

Ego non baptizo te in nomine patris, sed in nomine diaboli.

I do not baptize thee in the name of the father, but in the name of the devil.

The change in the wording from the notes to the novel is of extreme significance. It is not for economy of phrase. The removal of Christ and the Holy Ghost—Filii et Spiritus Sancti—is a mechanical act mirroring the imaginative. Of necessity, from Ahab's world, both Christ and the Holy Ghost are absent. Ahab moves and has his being in a world to which They and what They import are inimical: remember, Ahab fought a deadly scrimmage with a Spaniard before the altar at Santa, and spat into the silver calabash. The conflict in Ahab's world is abrupt, more that between Satan and Jehovah, of the old dispensation than the new. It is the outward symbol of the inner truth that the name of Christ is uttered but once in the book and then it is torn from Starbuck, the only possible man to use it, at a moment of anguish, the night before the fatal third day of the chase.

Ahab is Conjur Man. He invokes his own evil world. He himself uses black magic to achieve his vengeful ends. With the very words "in nomine diaboli" he believes he utters a Spell and performs a Rite of such magic.

The Ahab-world is closer to *Macbeth* than to *Lear*. In it the supernatural is accepted. Fedallah appears as freely as the Weird Sisters. Before Ahab's first entrance he has reached that identification with evil to which Macbeth out of fear evolves within the play itself. The agents of evil give both Ahab and Macbeth a false security through the same device, the unfulfillable prophecy. Ahab's tense and nervous speech is like Macbeth's, rather than Lear's. Both Macbeth and Ahab share a common hell of wicked, sleep-bursting dreams. They both endure the torture of isolation from humanity. The correspondence of these two evil worlds is precise. In either the divine has little place. Melville intended certain exclusions, and Christ and the Holy Ghost were two of them. Ahab, alas, could not even baptize in the name of the Father. He could only do it in the name of the Devil.

That is the Ahab-world, and it is wicked. Melville meant exactly what he wrote to Hawthorne when the book was consummated:

I have written a wicked book, and feel as spotless as the lamb.

Melville's "wicked book" is the drama of Ahab, his hot hate for the White Whale, and his vengeful pursuit of it from the moment the ship plunges like fate into the Atlantic. It is that action, not the complete novel *Moby-Dick*. The *Moby-Dick* universe contains more, something different. Perhaps the difference is the reason why Melville felt "spotless as the lamb." The rough notes in the Shakespeare embrace it.

"Madness is undefinable." Two plays from which the thought could have sprung are in the volume in which it is written down: *Lear* and *Hamlet*. Of the modes of madness in *Lear*—the King's, the Fool's— which is definable? But we need not rest on supposition as to what

Melville drew of madness from *Hamlet,* or from *Lear: Moby-Dick* includes both Ahab and Pip. Melville forces his analysis of Ahab's
mania to incredible distances, only himself to admit that "Ahab's
larger, darker, deeper part remains unhinted." Pip's is a more fathom-
able idiocy: "his shipmates called him mad." Melville challenges the
description, refuses to leave Pip's madness dark and unhinted, declares: "So man's insanity is heaven's sense."

   The emphasis in this declaration is the key to resolve apparent difficulties in the last sentence of the notes in the Shakespeare volume:

It & right reason extremes of one,—not the (black art) Goetic but Theurgic
magic—seeks converse with the Intelligence, Power, the Angel.

I take "it" to refer to the "madness" of the previous sentence. "Right
reason," less familiar to the 20th century, meant more to the last, for in
the Kant-Coleridge terminology "right reason" described the highest
range of the intelligence and stood in contrast to "understanding."
Melville had used the phrase in *Mardi.* What he did with it there discloses what meaning it had for him when he used it in these cryptic
notes for the composition of *Moby-Dick. Mardi:*

Right reason, and Alma (Christ), are the same; else Alma, not reason, would
we reject. The Master's great command is Love; and here do all things wise,
and all things good, unite. Love is all in all. The more we love, the more we
know; and so reversed.

Now, returning to the notes, if the phrase "not the (black art) Goetic
but Theurgic magic" is recognized as parenthetical, the sentence has
some clarity: "madness" and its apparent opposite "right reason" are
the two extremes of one way or attempt or urge to reach "the Intelligence, Power, the Angel" or, quite simply, God.

   The adjectives of the parenthesis bear this reading out. "Goetic"
might seem to derive from Goethe and thus *Faust,* but its source is the
Greek "goetos," meaning variously trickster, juggler and, as here,
magician. (Plato called literature "Goeteia.") Wherever Melville
picked up the word he means it, as he says, for the "black art."
"Theurgic," in sharp contrast, is an accurate term for a kind of occult
art of the Neoplatonists in which, through self-purification and sacred

rites, the aid of the divine was evoked. In thus opposing "Goetic" and "Theurgic" Melville is using a distinction as old as Chaldea between black and white magic, the one of demons, the other of saints and angels, one evil, the other benevolent. For white or "Theurgic" magic, like "madness" and "right reason," seeks God, while the "black art Goetic" invokes only the devil.

Now go to *Moby-Dick*. In the Ahab-world there is no place for "converse with the Intelligence, Power, the Angel." Ahab cannot seek it, for understood between him and Fedallah is a compact as binding as Faust's with Mephistopheles. Melville's assumption is that though both Ahab and Faust may be seekers after truth, a league with evil closes the door to truth. Ahab's art, so long as his hate survives, is black. He does not seek true converse.

"Madness," on the contrary, does, and Pip is mad, possessed of an insanity which is "heaven's sense." When the little Negro almost drowned, his soul went down to wondrous depths and there he "saw God's foot upon the treadle of the loom, and spoke it." Through that accident Pip, of all the crew, becomes "prelusive of the eternal time" and thus achieves the converse Ahab has denied himself by his blasphemy. The chapter on THE DOUBLOON dramatizes the attempts on the part of the chief active characters to reach truth. In that place Starbuck, in his "mere unaided virtue," is revealed to have no abiding faith: he retreats before "Truth," fearing to lose his "righteousness." . . . Stubb's jollity and Flask's clod-like stupidity blunt the spiritual. . . . The Manxman has mere superstition, Queequeg mere curiosity. . . . Fedallah worships the doubloon evilly. . . . Ahab sees the gold coin solipsistically: "three peaks as proud as Lucifer" and all named "Ahab!" Pip alone, of all, has true prescience: he names the doubloon the "navel" of the ship—"Truth" its life.

"Right reason" is the other way to God. It is the way of man's sanity, the pure forging of his intelligence in the smithy of life. To understand what use Melville made of it in *Moby-Dick* two characters, both inactive to the plot, have to be brought forth.

Bulkington is the man who corresponds to "right reason." Melville describes him once early in the book when he enters the Spouter Inn. "Six feet in height, with noble shoulders, and a chest like a cofferdam." In the deep shadows of his eyes "floated some reminiscences that did not seem to give him much joy." In the LEE SHORE chapter Bulkington is explicitly excluded from the action of the book, but not before Melville has, in ambiguities, divulged his significance as symbol. Bulkington is Man who, by "deep, earnest thinking" puts out to sea, scorning the land, convinced that "in landlessness alone resides the highest truth, shoreless, indefinite as God."

The rest of the *Pequod's* voyage Bulkington remains a "sleeping-partner" to the action. He is the secret member of the crew, below deck' always, like the music under the earth in *Antony and Cleopatra,* strange. He is the crew's heart, the sign of their paternity, the human thing. And by that human thing alone can they reach their apotheosis.

There remains Ishmael. Melville framed Ahab's action, and the parts Pip, Bulkington and the rest of the crew played in the action, within a narrative told by Ishmael. Too long in criticism of the novel Ishmael has been confused with Herman Melville himself. Ishmael is fictive, imagined, as are Ahab, Pip and Bulkington, not so completely perhaps, for the very reason that he is so like his creator. But he is not his creator only: he is a chorus through whom Ahab's tragedy is seen, by whom what is black and what is white magic is made clear. Like the Catskill eagle Ishmael is able to dive down into the blackest gorges and soar out to the light again.

He is passive and detached, the observer, and thus his separate and dramatic existence is not so easily felt. But unless his choric function is recognized some of the vision of the book is lost. When he alone survived the wreck of the *Pequod,* he remained, after the shroud of the sea rolled on, to tell more than Ahab's wicked story. Ahab's self-created world, in essence privative, a thing of blasphemies and black magic, has its offset. Ahab has to dominate over a world where the humanities may also flower and man (the crew) by Pip's or Bulkington's way reach God. By this use of Ishmael Melville achieved a struggle and a catharsis which he intended, to feel "spotless as the lamb."

Ishmael has that cleansing ubiquity of the chorus in all drama, back to the Greeks. It is interesting that, in the same place where the notes for *Moby-Dick* are written in his Shakespeare, Melville jots down: "Eschylus Tragedies." Ishmael alone hears Father Mapple's sermon out. He alone saw Bulkington, and understood him. It was Ishmael who learned the secrets of Ahab's blasphemies from the prophet of the fog, Elijah. He recognized Pip's God-sight, and moaned for him. He cries forth the glory of the crew's humanity. Ishmael tells *their* story and *their* tragedy as well as Ahab's, and thus creates the *Moby-Dick* universe in which the Ahab-world is, by the necessity of life—or the Declaration of Independence—*included.*

.　.　.　.　.

Shakespeare, Concluded

Melville was no naïve democrat. He recognized the persistence of the "great man" and faced, in 1850, what we have faced in the 20th century. At the time of the rise of the common man Melville wrote a tragedy out of the rise, and the fall, of uncommon Ahab.

In the old days of the Mediterranean and Europe it was the flaw of a king which brought tragedy to men. A calamity was that which "unwar strook the regnes that been proude." When fate was feudal, and a great man fell, his human property, the people, paid.

A whaleship reminded Melville of two things: (1) democracy had not rid itself of overlords; (2) the common man, however free, leans on a leader, the leader, however dedicated, leans on a straw. He pitched his tragedy right there.

America, 1850 was his GIVEN:

> "a poor old whale-hunter" the great man;
> fate, the chase of the Sperm whale, plot (economics
>   is the administration of scarce resources);
> the crew the commons, the Captain over them;

EQUALS:

      tragedy.

For a consideration of dominance in man, read by all means the chapter in *Moby-Dick* called THE SPECKSYNDER, concerning emperors and kings, the forms and usages of the sea:

through these forms that certain sultanism of Ahab's brain became incarnate in an irresistible dictatorship.

For be a man's intellectual superiority what it will, it can never assume the practical, available supremacy over other men, without the aid of some sort of external arts and entrenchments, always, in themselves, more or less paltry and base.

Nor will the tragic dramatist who would depict mortal indomitableness in its fullest sweep and direct swing, ever forget a hint, incidentally so important in his art, as the one now alluded to.

More, much more.

Melville saw his creative problem clearly:

> He had a prose world, a NEW.
> But it was "tragedie," old.
> Shakespeare gave him a bag of tricks.
>
> The Q.E.D.: *Moby-Dick*.

The shape of *Moby-Dick,* like the meaning of its action, has roots deep in THE PLAYS. Melville studied Shakespeare's craft. For example, *characterization*. In at least three places Melville analyzes *Hamlet*. There are two in *Pierre*. One enlarges upon the only note he writes in his copy of the play: "the great Montaignism of Hamlet." The third and most interesting passage is in *The Confidence Man*. There Melville makes a distinction between the making of "odd" and the creation of "original" characters in literature. Of the latter he allows only three: Milton's Satan, Quixote, and Hamlet. The original character is

like a revolving Drummond light, raying away from itself all round it— everything is lit by it, everything starts up to it (mark how it is with Hamlet).

Melville likens the effect to "that which in Genesis attends upon the beginning of things." In the creation of Ahab Melville made the best use of that lesson he knew how.

Structure, likewise. *Moby-Dick* has a rise and fall like the movement of an Elizabethan tragedy. The first twenty-two chapters, in which Ishmael as chorus narrates the preparations for the voyage, are precedent to the action and prepare for it. Chapter XXIII is an interlude, THE LEE SHORE; Bulkington, because he is "right reason," is excluded from the tragedy. With the next chapter the book's drama begins. The first act ends in the QUARTER-DECK chapter, the first precipitation of action, which brings together for the first time Ahab, the crew, and the purpose of the voyage—the chase of the White Whale. All the descriptions of the characters, all the forebodings, all the hints are brought to their first manifestation.

Another interlude follows: Ishmael expands upon MOBY-DICK and THE WHITENESS OF THE WHALE.

Merely to summarize what follows, the book then moves up to the meeting with the *Jeroboam* and her mad prophet *Gabriel* (chp. LXXI) and, after that, in a third swell, into the visit of Ahab to the *Samuel Enderby* to see her captain who had lost his arm as Ahab his leg to Moby-Dick (chp. C). The pitch of the action is the storm scene, THE CANDLES. From that point on Ahab comes to repose, fifth act, in his fate.

In this final movement Moby-Dick appears, for the first time. It is a mistake to think of the Whale as antagonist in the usual dramatic sense. (In democracy the antagonisms are wide.) The demonisms are dispersed, and Moby-Dick but the more assailable mass of them. In fact the actual physical whale finally present in *Moby-Dick* is more comparable to death's function in Elizabethan tragedy: when the white thing is encountered first, he is in no flurry, but quietly gliding through the sea, "a mighty mildness of repose in swiftness."

Obviously *Moby-Dick* is a novel and not a play. It contains creations impossible to any stage—a ship the *Pequod,* whales, Leviathan, the vast sea. In the making of most of his books Melville used similar things. In *Moby-Dick* he integrated them as he never had before nor was to again.

The whaling matter is stowed away as he did not manage the ethnology of *Typee* nor was to, the parables of *The Confidence Man.* While the book is getting under way—that is, in the first forty-eight chapters—Melville allows only four "scientific" chapters on whaling to appear. Likewise as the book sweeps to its tragic close in the last thirty chapters, Melville rules out all such exposition. The body of the book supports the bulk of the matter on the Sperm whale—"scientific or poetic." Melville carefully controls these chapters, skillfully breaking them up: the eight different vessels the *Pequod* meets as she moves across the oceans slip in and cut between the considerations of cetology. Actually and deliberately the whaling chapters brake the advance of the plot. Van Wyck Brooks called them "ballast."

Stage directions appear throughout. *Soliloquies,* too. There is a significant use of the special Elizabethan soliloquy to the skull in Ahab's mutterings to the Sperm whale's head in THE SPHINX (chp. LXX). One of the subtlest *supernatural effects,* the "low laugh from the hold" in the QUARTER-DECK scene, echoes Shakespeare's use of the Ghost below ground in *Hamlet.*

Properties are used for precise theater effect. Ahab smashes his quadrant as Richard his mirror. Of them the Doubloon is the most important. Once Ahab has nailed the coin to the mast it becomes FOCUS. The imagery, the thought, the characters, the events precedent and to come, are centered on it. It is there, midstage, Volpone, gold.

Of the soliloquies Ahab's show the presence of *Elizabethan speech* most. The cadences and acclivities of Melville's prose change. Melville characterized Ahab's language as "nervous, lofty." In the soliloquies it is jagged like that of a Shakespeare hero whose speech like his heart often cracks in the agony of fourth and fifth act.

The long ease and sea swell of Ishmael's narrative prose contrasts this short, rent language of Ahab. The opposition of cadence is part of the counterpoint of the book. It adumbrates the part the two characters play, Ishmael the passive, Ahab the active. More than that, it arises from and returns, contrapunto, to the whole concept of the book revealed by the notes in Melville's copy of Shakespeare—the choric Ishmael can, like the Catskill eagle, find the light, but Ahab, whose only magic is Goetic, remains dark. The contrast in prose repeats the theme of calm and tempest which runs through the novel. Without exception action rises out of calm, whether it is the first chase of a whale, the appearance of the Spirit Spout, the storm, or the final chase of Moby-Dick precipitously following upon THE SYMPHONY.

As the strongest literary force Shakespeare caused Melville to approach tragedy in terms of the drama. As the strongest social force America caused him to approach tragedy in terms of democracy.

It was not difficult for Melville to reconcile the two. Because of his perception of America: Ahab.

It has to do with size, and how you value it. You can approach BIG America and spread yourself like a pancake, sing her stretch as Whitman did, be puffed up as we are over PRODUCTION. It's easy. THE AMERICAN WAY. Soft. Turns out paper cups, lies flat on the brush. N.G.

Or recognize that our power is simply QUANTITY. Without considering purpose. Easy too. That is, so long as we continue to be INGENIOUS about machines, and have the resources.

Or you can take an attitude, the creative vantage. See her as OBJECT in MOTION, something to be shaped, for use. It involves a first act of physics. You can observe POTENTIAL and VELOCITY separately, have to, to measure THE THING. You get approximate results. They are usable enough if you include the Uncertainty Principle, Heisenberg's law that you learn the speed at the cost of exact knowledge of the energy and the energy at the loss of exact knowledge of the speed.

Melville did his job. He calculated, and cast Ahab. BIG, first of all. ENERGY, next. PURPOSE: lordship over nature. SPEED: of the brain. DIRECTION: vengeance. COST: the people, the Crew.

Ahab is the FACT, the Crew the IDEA. The Crew is where what America stands for got into *Moby-Dick*. They're what we imagine democracy to be. They're Melville's addition to tragedy as he took it from Shakespeare. He had to do more with the people than offstage shouts in a *Julius Caesar*. This was the difference a Declaration of Independence made. In his copy of the play Melville writes the note

TAMMANY HALL

in heavy strokes beside Casca's description of the Roman rabble before Caesar:

If the tag-rag people did not clap him and hiss him, according as he pleas'd and displeas'd them, as they use to do the players in the theatre, I am no true man.

Melville thought he had more searoom to tell the truth. He was writing in a country where an Andrew Jackson could, as he put it, be "hurled higher than a throne." A political system called "democracy" had led men to think they were "free" of aristocracy. The fact of the matter is Melville couldn't help but give the "people" a larger part because in the life around him they played a larger part. He put it this way:

this august dignity I treat of, is not the dignity of kings and robes, but that abounding dignity which has no robed investiture.

Thou shalt see it shining in the arm that wields a pick and drives a spike; that democratic dignity which, on all hands, radiates without end from God; Himself! The great God absolute! The center and circumference of all democracy! His omnipresence, our divine equality!

If, then, to meanest mariners, and renegades and castaways, I shall hereafter ascribe high qualities, though dark; weave round them tragic graces; if even the most mournful, perchance the most abased, among them all, shall at times lift himself to the exalted mounts; if I shall touch that workman's arm with some ethereal light; if I shall spread a rainbow over his disastrous set of sun; then against all mortal critics bear me out in it, thou just Spirit of Equality, which hast spread one royal mantle of humanity over all my kind!

Remember Bulkington.

To MAGNIFY is the mark of *Moby-Dick*. As with workers, castaways, so with the scope and space of the sea, the prose, the Whale, the Ship and, OVER ALL, the Captain. It is the technical act compelled by the American fact. Cubits of tragic stature. Put it this way. Three forces operated to bring about the dimensions of *Moby-Dick:* Melville, a man of MYTH, antemosaic; an experience of SPACE, its power and price, America; and ancient magnitudes of TRAGEDY, Shakespeare.

It is necessary now to consider *Antony and Cleopatra,* the play Melville pencilled most heavily. Rome was the World, and Shakespeare gives his people and the action imperial size. His hero and heroine love as Venus and Mars, as planets might.

> His legs bestrid the ocean; his rear'd arm
> Crested the world.

So Cleopatra dreamed of Antony. Melville marked her words. He marked Antony's joyful greeting to Cleopatra after he has beaten Caesar back to his camp:

> O thou day o' th' world!

And Cleopatra's cry of grief when Antony dies:

> The crown o' th' earth doth melt.

Antony and Cleopatra is an East. It is built as Pyramids were built. There is space here, and objects big enough to contest space. These are men and women who live life large. The problems are the same but they work themselves out on a stage as wide as ocean.

When Enobarbus comments on Antony's flight from Actium in pursuit of Cleopatra, we are precisely within the problems of *Moby-Dick:*

> To be furious
> Is to be frighted out of fear, and in that mood

> The dove will peck the estridge. I see still
> A diminution in our captain's brain
> Restores his heart. When valour preys on reason
> It eats the sword it fights with.

In exactly what way Ahab, furious and without fear, retained the instrument of his reason as a lance to fight the White Whale is a central concern of Melville's in *Moby-Dick*. In his Captain there was a diminution in his heart.

From whaling, which America had made distinctly a part of her industrial empire, he took this "poor old whale-hunter," as he called him, this man of "Nantucket grimness and shagginess." Out of such stuff he had to make his tragic hero, his original. He faced his difficulties. He knew he was denied "the outward majestical trappings and housings" that Shakespeare had for his Antony, his Lear and his Macbeth. Melville wrote:

Oh, Ahab! what shall be grand in thee, must needs be plucked at from the skies, and dived for in the deep, and featured in the unbodied air!

He made him "a khan of the plank, and a king of the sea, and a great lord of leviathans." For the American has the Roman feeling about the world. It is his, to dispose of. He strides it, with possession of it. His property. Has he not conquered it with his machines? He bends its resources to his will. The pax of legions? the Americanization of the world. Who else is lord?

Melville isolates Ahab in "a Grand-Lama-like exclusiveness." He is captain of the *Pequod* because of "that certain sultanism of his brain." He is proud and morbid, willful, vengeful. He wears a "hollow crown," not Richard's. It is the Iron Crown of Lombardy which Napoleon wore. Its jagged edge, formed from a nail of the Crucifixion, galls him. He worships fire and swears to strike the sun.

OVER ALL, hate—huge and fixed upon the imperceptible. Not man but all the hidden forces that terrorize man is assailed by the American Timon. That HATE, extra-human, involves his Crew, and Moby-Dick drags them to their death as well as Ahab to his, a collapse of a hero through solipsism which brings down a world.

At the end of the book, in the heart of the White Whale's destruction, the Crew and Pip and Bulkington and Ahab lie down together.

> All scatt'red in the bottom of the sea.

37. Fenimore Cooper's Leatherstocking Novels

D. H. LAWRENCE

Here, in a startlingly prophetic voice, Lawrence contrasts the mythical wish-fulfillment of Cooper's *Leatherstocking Novels* with his perception of the reality behind the American ideals of democracy, freedom, and individualism, and finds that at the heart of both myth and reality there is something in common.

In his Leatherstocking books, Fenimore is off on another track. He is no longer concerned with social white Americans that buzz with pins through them, buzz loudly against every mortal thing except the pin itself. The pin of the Great Ideal.

One gets irritated with Cooper because he never for once snarls at the Great Ideal Pin which transfixes him. No, indeed. Rather he tries to push it through the very heart of the Continent.

But I have loved the Leatherstocking books so dearly. Wish-fulfilment!

Anyhow, one is not supposed to take LOVE seriously, in these books. Eve Effingham, impaled on the social pin, conscious all the time of her own ego and of nothing else, suddenly fluttering in throes of love: no, it makes me sick. LOVE is never LOVE until it has a pin pushed through it and becomes an IDEAL. The ego, turning on a pin, is wildly IN LOVE, always. Because that's the thing to be.

Cooper was a GENTLEMAN, in the worst sense of the word. In the Nineteenth Century sense of the word. A correct, clock-work man.

Not altogether, of course.

The great national Grouch was grinding inside him. Probably he called it COSMIC URGE. Americans usually do: in capital letters.

Best stick to National Grouch. The great American grouch.

SOURCE: D. H. Lawrence, *Studies in Classic American Literature* (New York: Thomas Seltzer, 1923), pp. 67–92. Copyright 1923, 1951 by Frieda Lawrence. Reprinted by permission of The Viking Press, Inc.

Cooper had it, gentleman that he was. That is why he flitted round Europe so uneasily. Of course, in Europe he could be, and was, a gentleman to his heart's content.

"In short," he says in one of his letters, "we were at table two counts, one monsignore, an English Lord, an Ambassador, and my humble self."

Were we really!

How nice it must have been to know that one self, at least, was humble.

And he felt the democratic American tomahawk wheeling over his uncomfortable scalp all the time.

The great American grouch.

Two monsters loomed on Cooper's horizon.

Mrs. Cooper	*My Work*
My Work	*My Wife*
My Wife	*My Work*

The Dear Children
My Work!!!

There you have the essential keyboard of Cooper's soul.

If there is one thing that annoys me more than a business man and his BUSINESS, it is an artist, a writer, painter, musician, and MY WORK. When an artist says MY WORK, the flesh goes tired on my bones. When he says MY WIFE, I want to hit him.

Cooper grizzled about his work. Oh, heaven, he cared so much whether it was good or bad, and what the French thought, and what Mr. Snippy Knowall said, and how Mrs. Cooper took it. The pin, the pin!

But he was truly an artist: then an American: then a gentleman.

And the grouch grouched inside him, through all.

They seem to have been specially fertile in imagining themselves "under the wigwam," do these Americans, just when their knees were comfortably under the mahogany, in Paris, along with the knees of

> *4 Counts*
> *2 Cardinals*
> *1 Milord*
> *5 Cocottes*
> *1 Humble self*

You bet, though, that when the cocottes were being raffled off, Fenimore went home to his WIFE.

WISH FULFILMENT		ACTUALITY
The Wigwam	vs.	*My Hotel*
Chingachgook	vs.	*My Wife*
Natty Bumppo	vs.	*My Humble Self*

Fenimore, lying in his Louis Quatorze hotel in Paris, passionately musing about Natty Bumppo and the pathless forest, and mixing his imagination with the Cupids and Butterflies on the painted ceiling, while Mrs. Cooper was struggling with her latest gown in the next room, and the déjeuner was with the Countess at eleven. . . .

Men live by lies.

In actuality, Fenimore loved the genteel continent of Europe, and waited gasping for the newspapers to praise his WORK.

In another actuality he loved the tomahawking continent of America, and imagined himself Natty Bumppo.

His actual desire was to be: *Monsieur Fenimore Cooper, le grand écrivain américain.*

His innermost wish was to be: Natty Bumppo.

Now Natty and Fenimore, arm-in-arm, are an odd couple.

You can see Fenimore: blue coat, silver buttons, silver-and-diamond buckle shoes, ruffles.

You see Natty Bumppo: a grizzled, uncouth old renegade, with gaps in his old teeth and a drop on the end of his nose.

But Natty was Fenimore's great wish: his wish-fulfilment.

"It was a matter of course," says Mrs. Cooper, "that he should dwell on the better traits of the picture rather than on the coarser and more revolting, though more common points. Like West, he could see Apollo in the young Mohawk."

The coarser and more revolting, though more common points.

You see now why he depended so absolutely on MY WIFE. She had to look things in the face for him. The coarser and more revolting, and certainly more common points, she had to see.

He himself did so love seeing pretty-pretty, with the thrill of a red scalp now and then.

Fenimore, in his imagination, wanted to be Natty Bumppo, who, I am sure, belched after he had eaten his dinner. At the same time Mr.

Cooper was nothing if not a gentleman. So he decided to stay in France and have it all his own way.

In France, Natty would not belch after eating, and Chingachgook could be all the Apollo he liked.

As if ever any Indian was like Apollo. The Indians, with their curious female quality, their archaic figures, with high shoulders and deep, archaic waists, like a sort of woman! And their natural devilishness, their natural insidiousness.

But men see what they want to see: especially if they look from a long distance, across the ocean, for example.

Yet the Leatherstocking books are lovely. Lovely half-lies.

They form a sort of American Odyssey, with Natty Bumppo for Odysseus.

Only, in the original Odyssey, there is plenty of devil, Circes and swine and all. And Ithacus is devil enough to outwit the devils. But Natty is a saint with a gun, and the Indians are gentlemen through and through, though they may take an occasional scalp.

There are five Leatherstocking novels: a *decrescendo* of reality, and a crescendo of beauty.

1. *Pioneers:* A raw frontier-village on Lake Champlain, at the end of the eighteenth century. Must be a picture of Cooper's home, as he knew it when a boy. A very lovely book. Natty Bumppo an old man, an old hunter half civilized.

2. *The Last of the Mohicans:* A historical fight between the British and the French, with Indians on both sides, at a Fort by Lake Champlain. Romantic flight of the British general's two daughters, conducted by the scout, Natty, who is in the prime of life; romantic death of the last of the Delawares.

3. *The Prairie:* A wagon of some huge, sinister Kentuckians trekking west into the unbroken prairie. Prairie Indians, and Natty, an old, old man; he dies seated on a chair on the Rocky Mountains, looking east.

4. *The Pathfinder:* The Great Lakes. Natty, a man of about thirty-five, makes an abortive proposal to a bouncing damsel, daughter of the Sergeant at the Fort.

5. *Deerslayer:* Natty and Hurry Harry, both quite young, are hunting

in the virgin wild. They meet two white women. Lake Champlain again.

These are the five Leatherstocking books: Natty Bumppo being Leatherstocking, Pathfinder, Deerslayer, according to his ages.

Now let me put aside my impatience at the unreality of this vision, and accept it as a wish-fulfilment vision, a kind of yearning myth. Because it seems to me that the things in Cooper that make one so savage, when one compares them with actuality, are perhaps, when one considers them as presentations of a deep subjective desire, real in their way, and almost prophetic.

The passionate love for America, for the soil of America, for example. As I say, it is perhaps easier to love America passionately, when you look at it through the wrong end of the telescope, across all the Atlantic water, as Cooper did so often, than when you are right there. When you are actually *in* America, America hurts, because it has a powerful disintegrative influence upon the white psyche. It is full of grinning, unappeased aboriginal demons, too, ghosts, and it persecutes the white men, like some Eumenides, until the white men give up their absolute whiteness. America is tense with latent violence and resistance. The very common sense of white Americans has a tinge of helplessness in it, and deep fear of what might be if they were not commonsensical.

Yet one day the demons of America must be placated, the ghosts must be appeased, the Spirit of Place atoned for. Then the true passionate love for American Soil will appear. As yet, there is too much menace in the landscape.

But probably, one day America will be as beautiful in actuality as it is in Cooper. Not yet, however. When the factories have fallen down again.

And again, this perpetual blood-brother theme of the Leatherstocking novels, Natty and Chingachgook, the Great Serpent. At present it is a sheer myth. The Red Man and the White Man are not bloodbrothers: even when they are most friendly. When they are most friendly, it is as a rule the one betraying his race-spirit to the other. In the white man—rather high-brow—who "loves" the Indian, one feels the white man betraying his own race. There is something unproud, underhand in it. Renegade. The same with the Americanised Indian who believes absolutely in the white mode. It is a betrayal. Renegade again.

In the actual flesh, it seems to me the white man and the red man cause a feeling of oppression, the one to the other, no matter what the good will. The red life flows in a different direction from the white life. You can't make two streams that flow in opposite directions meet and mingle soothingly.

Certainly, if Cooper had had to spend his whole life in the backwoods, side by side with a Noble Red Brother, he would have screamed with the oppression of suffocation. He had to have Mrs. Cooper, a straight strong pillar of society, to hang on to. And he had to have the culture of France to turn back to, or he would just have been stifled. The Noble Red Brother would have smothered him and driven him mad.

So that the Natty and Chingachgook myth must remain a myth. It is a wish-fulfilment, an evasion of actuality. As we have said before, the folds of the Great Serpent would have been heavy, very heavy, too heavy, on any white man. Unless the white man were a true renegade, hating himself and his own race-spirit, as sometimes happens.

It seems there can be no fusion in the flesh. But the spirit can change. The white man's spirit can never become as the red man's spirit. It doesn't want to. But it can cease to be the opposite and the negative of the red man's spirit. It can open out a new great area of consciousness, in which there is room for the red spirit too.

To open out a new wide area of consciousness means to slough the old consciousness. The old consciousness has beome a tight-fitting prison to us, in which we are going rotten.

You can't have a new, easy skin before you have sloughed the old, tight skin.

You can't.

And you just can't, so you may as well leave off pretending.

Now the essential history of the people of the United States seems to me just this: At the Renaissance the old consciousness was becoming a little tight. Europe sloughed her last skin, and started a new, final phase.

But some Europeans recoiled from the last final phase. They wouldn't enter the *cul de sac* of post-Renaissance, "liberal" Europe. They came to America.

They came to America for two reasons:

1. To slough the old European consciousness completely.
2. To grow a new skin underneath, a new form. This second is a hidden process.

The two processes go on, of course, simultaneously. The slow forming of the new skin underneath is the slow sloughing of the old skin. And sometimes this immortal serpent feels very happy, feeling a new golden glow of a strangely-patterned skin envelop him: and sometimes he feels very sick, as if his very entrails were being torn out of him, as he wrenches once more at his old skin, to get out of it.

Out! Out! he cries, in all kinds of euphemisms.

He's got to have his new skin on him before ever he can get out.

And he's got to get out before his new skin can ever be his own skin.

So there he is, a torn, divided monster.

The true American, who writhes and writhes like a snake that is long in sloughing.

Sometimes snakes can't slough. They can't burst their old skin. Then they go sick and die inside the old skin, and nobody ever sees the new pattern.

It needs a real desperate recklessness to burst your old skin at last. You simply don't care what happens to you, if you rip yourself in two, so long as you do get out.

It also needs a real belief in the new skin. Otherwise you are likely never to make the effort. Then you gradually sicken and go rotten and die in the old skin.

Now Fenimore stayed very safe inside the old skin: a gentleman, almost a European, as proper as proper can be. And, safe inside the old skin, he *imagined* the gorgeous American pattern of a new skin.

He hated democracy. So he evaded it, and had a nice dream of something beyond democracy. But he belonged to democracy all the while.

Evasion!—Yet even that doesn't make the dream worthless.

Democracy in America was never the same as Liberty in Europe. In Europe Liberty was a great life-throb. But in America Democracy was always something anti-life. The greatest democrats, like Abraham Lincoln, had always a sacrificial, self-murdering note in their voices. American Democracy was a form of self-murder, always. Or of murdering somebody else.

Necessarily. It was a *pis aller*. It was the *pis aller* to European Liberty. It was a cruel form of sloughing. Men murdered themselves into this democracy. Democracy is the utter hardening of the old skin, the old form, the old psyche. It hardens till it is tight and fixed and inorganic. Then it *must* burst, like a chrysalis shell. And out must come the soft grub, or the soft damp butterfly of the American-at-last.

America has gone the *pis aller* of her democracy. Now she must slough even that, chiefly that, indeed.

What did Cooper dream beyond democracy? Why, in his immortal friendship of Chingachgook and Natty Bumppo he dreamed the nucleus of a new society. That is, he dreamed a new human relationship. A stark, stripped human relationship of two men, deeper than the deeps of sex. Deeper than property, deeper than fatherhood, deeper than marriage, deeper than love. So deep that it is loveless. The stark, loveless, wordless unison of two men who have come to the bottom of themselves. This is the new nucleus of a new society, the clue to a new world-epoch. It asks for a great and cruel sloughing first of all. Then it finds a great release into a new world, a new moral, a new landscape.

Natty and the Great Serpent are neither equals nor unequals. Each obeys the other when the moment arrives. And each is stark and dumb in the other's presence, starkly himself, without illusion created. Each is just the crude pillar of a man, the crude living column of his own manhood. And each knows the godhead of this crude column of manhood. A new relationship.

The Leatherstocking novels create the myth of this new relation. And they go backwards, from old age to golden youth. That is the true myth of America. She starts old, old, wrinkled and writhing in an old skin. And there is a gradual sloughing of the old skin, towards a new youth. It is the myth of America.

You start with actuality. *Pioneers* is no doubt Cooperstown, when Cooperstown was in the stage of inception: a village of one wild street of log cabins under the forest hills by Lake Champlain: a village of crude, wild frontiersmen, reacting against civilization.

Towards this frontier-village in the winter time, a negro slave drives a sledge through the mountains, over deep snow. In the sledge sits a fair damsel, Miss Temple, with her handsome pioneer father, Judge Temple. They hear a shot in the trees. It is the old hunter and backwoodsman, Natty Bumppo, long and lean and uncouth, with a long rifle and gaps in his teeth.

Judge Temple is "squire" of the village, and he has a ridiculous,

commodious "hall" for his residence. It is still the old English form.
Miss Temple is a pattern young lady, like Eve Effingham: in fact, she
gets a young and very genteel but impoverished Effingham for a husband. The old world holding its own on the edge of the wild. A bit
tiresomely too, with rather more prunes and prisms than one can digest. Too romantic.

Against the "hall" and the gentry, the real frontiers-folk, the rebels.
The two groups meet at the village inn, and at the frozen church, and
at the Christmas sports, and on the ice of the lake, and at the great
pigeon shoot. It is a beautiful, resplendent picture of life. Fenimore
puts in only the glamour.

Perhaps my taste is childish, but these scenes in *Pioneers* seem to
me marvellously beautiful. The raw village street, with woodfires
blinking through the unglazed window-chinks, on a winter's night.
The inn, with the rough woodsman and the drunken Indian John; the
church, with the snowy congregation crowding to the fire. Then the
lavish abundance of Christmas cheer, and turkey-shooting in the
snow. Spring coming, forests all green, maple-sugar taken from the
trees: and clouds of pigeons flying from the south, myriads of pigeons,
shot in heaps; and night-fishing on the teeming, virgin lake; and deer-
hunting.

Pictures! Some of the loveliest, most glamorous pictures in all literature.

Alas, without the cruel iron of reality. It is all real enough. Except
that one realizes that Fenimore was writing from a safe distance,
where he would idealize and have his wish-fulfilment.

Because, when one comes to America, one finds that there is always
a certain slightly devilish resistance in the American landscape, and a
certain slightly bitter resistance in the white man's heart. Hawthorne
gives this. But Cooper glosses it over.

The American landscape has never been at one with the white man.
Never. And white men have probably never felt so bitter anywhere, as
here in America, where the very landscape, in its very beauty, seems a
bit devilish and grinning, opposed to us.

Cooper, however, glosses over this resistance, which in actuality can
never quite be glossed over. He *wants* the landscape to be at one with
him. So he goes away to Europe and sees it as such. It is a sort of vision.

And, nevertheless, the oneing will surely take place—some day.

The myth is the story of Natty. The old, lean hunter and backwoodsman lives with his friend, the grey-haired Indian John, an old Delaware chief, in a hut within reach of the village. The Delaware is christianized and bears the Christian name of John. He is tribeless and lost. He humiliates his grey hairs in drunkenness, and dies, thankful to be dead, in a forest fire, passing back to the fire whence he derived.

And this is Chingachgook, the splendid Great Serpent of the later novels.

No doubt Cooper, as a boy, knew both Natty and the Indian John. No doubt they fired his imagination even then. When he is a man, crystallized in society and sheltering behind the safe pillar of Mrs. Cooper, these two old fellows become a myth to his soul. He traces himself to a new youth in them.

As for the story: Judge Temple has just been instrumental in passing the wise game laws. But Natty has lived by his gun all his life in the wild woods, and simply childishly cannot understand how he can be poaching on the Judge's land among the pine trees. He shoots a deer in the close season. The Judge is all sympathy, but the law *must* be enforced. Bewildered Natty, an old man of seventy, is put in stocks and in prison. They release him as soon as possible. But the thing was done.

The letter killeth.

Natty's last connexion with his own race is broken. John, the Indian, is dead. The old hunter disappears, lonely and severed, into the forest, away, away from his race.

In the new epoch that is coming, there will be no letter of the Law.

Chronologically, *The Last of the Mohicans* follows *Pioneers*. But in the myth, *The Prairie* comes next.

Cooper of course knew his own America. He travelled west and saw the prairies, and camped with the Indians of the prairie.

The Prairie, like *Pioneers,* bears a good deal the stamp of actuality. It is a strange, splendid book, full of sense of doom. The figures of the great Kentuckian men, with their wolf-women, loom colossal on the vast prairie, as they camp with their wagons. These are different pioneers from Judge Temple. Lurid, brutal, tinged with the sinisterness of crime; these are the gaunt white men who push west, push on and on against the natural opposition of the continent. On towards a doom. Great wings of vengeful doom seem spread over the west, grim against the intruder. You feel them again in Frank Norris' novel, *The Octopus*. While in the West of Bret Harte there is a very devil in the air, and beneath him are sentimental self-conscious people being wicked and goody by evasion.

In *The Prairie* there is a shadow of violence and dark cruelty flickering in the air. It is the aboriginal demon hovering over the core of the continent. It hovers still, and the dread is still there.

Into such a prairie enters the huge figure of Ishmael, ponderous, pariah-like Ishmael and his huge sons and his were-wolf wife. With their wagons they roll on from the frontiers of Kentucky, like Cyclops into the savage wilderness. Day after day they seem to force their way into oblivion. But their force of penetration ebbs. They are brought to a stop. They recoil in the throes of murder and entrench themselves in isolation on a hillock in the midst of the prairie. There they hold out like demi-gods against the elements and the subtle Indian.

The pioneering brute invasion of the West, crime-tinged!

And into this setting, as a sort of minister of peace, enters the old, old hunter Natty, and his suave, horse-riding Sioux Indians. But he seems like a shadow.

The hills rise softly west, to the Rockies. There seems a new peace: or is it only suspense, abstraction, waiting? Is it only a sort of beyond?

Natty lives in these hills, in a village of the suave, horse-riding Sioux. They revere him as an old wise father.

In these hills he dies, sitting in his chair and looking far east, to the forest and great sweet waters, whence he came. He dies gently, in physical peace with the land and the Indians. He is an old, old man.

Cooper could see no further than the foothills where Natty died, beyond the prairie.

The other novels bring us back east.

The Last of the Mohicans is divided between real historical narrative and true "romance." For myself, I prefer the romance. It has a myth meaning, whereas the narrative is chiefly record.

For the first time we get actual women: the dark, handsome Cora and her frail sister, the White Lily. The good old division, the dark sensual woman and the clinging, submissive little blonde, who is so "pure."

These sisters are fugitives through the forest, under the protection of a Major Heyward, a young American officer and Englishman. He is just a "white" man, very good and brave and generous, etc., but limited, most definitely *borné*. He would probably love Cora, if he dared, but he finds it safer to adore the clinging White Lily of a younger sister.

This trio is escorted by Natty, now Leatherstocking, a hunter and scout in the prime of life, accompanied by his inseparable friend Chingachgook, and the Delaware's beautiful son—Adonis rather than Apollo—Uncas, the last of the Mohicans.

There is also a "wicked" Indian, Magua, handsome and injured incarnation of evil.

Cora is the scarlet flower of womanhood, fierce, passionate offspring of some mysterious union between the British officer and a Creole woman in the West Indies. Cora loves Uncas, Uncas loves Cora. But Magua also desires Cora, violently desires her. A lurid little circle of sensual fire. So Fenimore kills them all off, Cora, Uncas, and Magua, and leaves the White Lily to carry on the race. She will breed plenty of white children to Major Heyward. These tiresome "lilies that fester," of our day.

Evidently Cooper—or the artist in him—has decided that there can be no blood-mixing of the two races, white and red. He kills 'em off.

Beyond all this heart-beating stand the figures of Natty and Chingachgook: the two childless, womanless men, of opposite races. They are the abiding thing. Each of them is alone, and final in his race. And they stand side by side, stark, abstract, beyond emotion, yet eternally together. All the other loves seem frivolous. This is the new great thing, the clue, the inception of a new humanity.

And Natty, what sort of a white man is he? Why, he is a man with a gun. He is a killer, a slayer. Patient and gentle as he is, he is a slayer. Self-effacing, self-forgetting, still he is a killer.

Twice, in the book, he brings an enemy down hurtling in death through the air, downwards. Once it is the beautiful, wicked Magua—shot from a height, and hurtling down ghastly through space, into death.

This is Natty, the white forerunner. A killer. As in *Deerslayer,* he shoots the bird that flies in the high, high sky, so that the bird falls out of the invisible into the visible, dead, he symbolizes himself. He will bring the bird of the spirit out of the high air. He is the stoic American killer of the old great life. But he kills, as he says, only to live.

Pathfinder takes us to the Great Lakes, and the glamour and beauty of sailing the great sweet waters. Natty is now called Pathfinder. He is about thirty-five years old, and he falls in love. The damsel is Mabel Dunham, daughter of Sergeant Dunham of the Fort garrison. She is blonde and in all things admirable. No doubt Mrs. Cooper was very much like Mabel.

And Pathfinder doesn't marry her. She won't have him. She wisely prefers a more comfortable Jasper. So Natty goes off to grouch, and to end by thanking his stars. When he had got right clear, and sat by the campfire with Chingachgook, in the forest, didn't he just thank his stars! A lucky escape!

Men of an uncertain age are liable to these infatuations. They aren't always lucky enough to be rejected.

Whatever would poor Mabel have done, had she been Mrs. Bumppo?

Natty had no business marrying. His mission was elsewhere.

The most fascinating Leatherstocking book is the last, *Deerslayer*. Natty is now a fresh youth, called Deerslayer. But the kind of silent prim youth who is never quite young, but reserves himself for different things.

It is a gem of a book. Or a bit of perfect paste. And myself, I like a bit of perfect paste in a perfect setting, so long as I am not fooled by pretence of reality. And the setting of *Deerslayer could* not be more exquisite. Lake Champlain again.

Of course it never rains: it is never cold and muddy and dreary: no one has wet feet or toothache: no one ever feels filthy, when they can't wash for a week. God knows what the women would really have looked like, for they fled through the wilds without soap, comb, or towel. They breakfasted off a chunk of meat, or nothing, lunched the same, and supped the same.

Yet at every moment they are elegant, perfect ladies, in correct toilet.

Which isn't quite fair. You need only go camping for a week, and you'll see.

But it is a myth, not a realistic tale. Read it as a lovely myth. Lake Glimmerglass.

Deerslayer, the youth with the long rifle, is found in the woods with a big, handsome, blonde-bearded backwoodsman called Hurry Harry. Deerslayer seems to have been born under a hemlock tree out of a pine-cone: a young man of the woods. He is silent, simple, philosophic, moralistic, and an unerring shot. His simplicity is the simplicity of age rather than of youth. He is race-old. All his reactions and impulses are fixed, static. Almost he is sexless, so race-old. Yet intelligent, hardy, dauntless.

Hurry Harry is a big blusterer, just the opposite of Deerslayer. Deerslayer keeps the centre of his own consciousness steady and un-perturbed. Hurry Harry is one of those floundering people who bluster from one emotion to another, very self-conscious, without any centre to them.

These two young men are making their way to a lovely, smallish lake, Lake Glimmerglass. On this water the Hutter family has estab-lished itself. Old Hutter, it is suggested, has a criminal, coarse, buc-caneering past, and is a sort of fugitive from justice. But he is a good enough father to his two grown-up girls. The family lives in a log hut "castle," built on piles in the water, and the old man has also con-structed an "ark," a sort of house-boat, in which he can take his daugh-ters when he goes on his rounds to trap the beaver.

The two girls are the inevitable dark and light. Judith, dark, fear-less, passionate, a little lurid with sin, is the scarlet-and-black blos-som. Hetty, the younger, blonde, frail and innocent, is the white lily again. But alas, the lily has begun to fester. She is slightly imbecile.

The two hunters arrive at the lake among the woods just as war has been declared. The Hutters are unaware of the fact. And hostile Indi-ans are on the lake already. So, the story of thrills and perils.

Thomas Hardy's inevitable division of women into dark and fair, sinful and innocent, sensual and pure, is Cooper's division too. It is indicative of the desire in the man. He wants sensuality and sin, and he wants purity and "innocence." If the innocence goes a little rotten, slightly imbecile, bad luck!

Hurry Harry, of course, like a handsome impetuous meat-fly, at once wants Judith, the lurid poppy-blossom. Judith rejects him with scorn.

Judith, the sensual woman, at once wants the quiet, reserved, un-mastered Deerslayer. She wants to master him. And Deerslayer is half tempted, but never more than half. He is not going to be mastered. A philosophic old soul, he does not give much for the temptations of sex. Probably he dies virgin.

And he is right of it. Rather than be dragged into a false heat of deliberate sensuality, he will remain alone. His soul is alone, for ever alone. So he will preserve his integrity, and remain alone in the flesh. It is a stoicism which is honest and fearless, and from which Deerslayer never lapses, except when, approaching middle age, he proposes to the buxom Mabel.

He lets his consciousness penetrate in loneliness into the new continent. His contacts are not human. He wrestles with the spirits of the forest and the American wild, as a hermit wrestles with God and Satan. His one meeting is with Chingachgook, and this meeting is silent, reserved, across an unpassable distance.

Hetty, the White Lily, being imbecile, although full of vaporous religion and the dear, good God, "who governs all things by his providence," is hopelessly infatuated with Hurry Harry. Being innocence gone imbecile, like Dostoevsky's Idiot, she longs to give herself to the handsome meat-fly. Of course he doesn't want her.

And so nothing happens: in that direction. Deerslayer goes off to meet Chingachgook, and help him woo an Indian maid. Vicarious.

It is the miserable story of the collapse of the white psyche. The white man's mind and soul are divided between these two things: innocence and lust, the Spirit and Sensuality. Sensuality always carries a stigma, and is therefore more deeply desired, or lusted after. But spirituality alone gives the sense of uplift, exaltation, and "winged life", with the inevitable reaction into sin and spite. So the white man is divided against himself. He plays off one side of himself against the other side, till it is really a tale told by an idiot, and nauseating.

Against this, one is forced to admire the stark, enduring figure of Deerslayer. He is neither spiritual nor sensual. He is a moralizer, but he always tries to moralize from actual experience, not from theory. He says: "Hurt nothing unless you're forced to." Yet he gets his deepest thrill of gratification, perhaps, when he puts a bullet through the heart of a beautiful buck, as it stoops to drink at the lake. Or when he brings the invisible bird fluttering down in death, out of the high blue. "Hurt nothing unless you're forced to." And yet he lives by death, by killing the wild things of the air and earth.

It's not good enough.

But you have there the myth of the essential white America. All the other stuff, the love, the democracy, the floundering into lust, is a sort of by-play. The essential American soul is hard, isolate, stoic, and a killer. It has never yet melted.

Of course, the soul often breaks down into disintegration, and you have lurid sin and Judith, imbecile innocence lusting, in Hetty, and bluster, bragging, and self-conscious strength, in Harry. But these are the disintegration products.

What true myth concerns itself with is not the disintegration product. True myth concerns itself centrally with the onward adventure of the integral soul. And this, for America, is Deerslayer. A man who turns his back on white society. A man who keeps his moral integrity hard and intact. An isolate, almost selfless, stoic, enduring man, who lives by death, by killing, but who is pure white.

This is the very intrinsic-most American. He is at the core of all the other flux and fluff. And when *this* man breaks from his static isolation, and makes a new move, then look out, something will be happening.

Part Five

The Discovery of the Future

Since the middle of the fifties, a new subject has been opened up for the essay, the "Future," which until that point had been the exclusive province of the popular arts: comic strips and comic books and science fiction, in which such subtopics as the exploration of outer space, time travel, the invention of humanoid machines, and, most terribly, the End of Man had been suggested in flat images shadowing forth deep myths. But suddenly the Future as prefigured in such works is upon us. It is what we live now rather than foresee in times to come; and therefore its impact on all of us, not only on our environment but also on our changing innermost selves, has come to seem assimilable to the traditional form of the essay, the traditional art of the essayist.

Indeed, all but one of the writers represented in this section practiced the essay on quite other subjects before the Future swam into their view: Norman O. Brown writing on Greek literature; Marshall McLuhan on Shakespeare and James Joyce and Gerard Manley Hopkins; Paul Goodman on Kafka and the writings of Sigmund Freud; Norman Mailer on Jewish mysticism, boxing and the state of his own soul; Leslie Fiedler on Simone Weil and comic books and Huck Finn. Only Buckminster Fuller (who is actually older than any of the rest) has never been concerned with any other subject; and it remains a problem whether, in fact, he ever was a proper writer, or is now. Not only was he trained as an engineer, but he has always considered himself primarily a technologist, tinkerer, inventor; and though he has long stumped up and down this country talking and talking and talking, sometimes at inordinate length, he has never been inclined to make books or submit his speeches for publication.

Not the printed page is Fuller's medium, but the tape—an electronic ear rather than a mechanical eye his preferred register; and, indeed, the "essay" reproduced here is from a book never written down at all, only transcribed from tapes—one hopes by an electric typewriter keyed to a computer. As a matter of fact, the only human hand involved in the whole process of producing Fuller's selection was the editor's, who has cut and trimmed the present text to a kind of scale and coherence that suits the shape of the collection and (hopefully) does not falsify Bucky Fuller too much. It is, however, not Fuller alone who raises the question of whether in dealing with the Discovery of the Future, the essay does not itself become radically transformed.

Fiedler and Goodman and Mailer still work pretty much inside the old limits of the form, despite occasional mantic or dithyrambic outbursts and some signs of impatience with conventional diction; but McLuhan (who is to go much further along these lines than the present selection indicates) and Brown are already in the process of blowing up order and syntax, diction and unity, even predication itself, as traditionally defined and considered essential to the essay. And perhaps in a world in which politics has become what Mailer suggests in his description of J.F.K. as first President of the Future; in which technology has totally transformed itself along with the rest of the world, as Fuller contends; in which education must alter its very essence or perish, as Paul Goodman argues; in which conventional reading skills have become as irrelevant as McLuhan understands them to be; in which the very nature of man is mutating, as Leslie Fiedler describes—perhaps it is high time to be through with the essay, and to begin with something else.

But what to call that something else as already practiced by McLuhan and especially Brown, and as adumbrated in the pioneering genre invented by Lawrence and carried on by Olson in selections reproduced elsewhere in this collection? Prophecy? Poetry? Nonsense? Speaking with tongues? Plotless science fiction? These are honorifics or pejoratives, not definitions; and none of them quite works for a form of prose or meta-prose whose aim is to reproduce in words the very idea of the feeling self, the very feel of the thinking self—and only through that sense of the self, feeling or thinking or meditating or in ecstasy, the world. But was it not precisely for this use of language that Montaigne found for the first time an adequate name? Was it not this —the form we have only thought we destroyed, renewing, re-inventing it—that he called, what we might as well call it still, even in our present Future—the Essay?

38. *From* Love's Body

NORMAN O. BROWN

Norman O. Brown (1913–   ) was trained in Classics at the University of Wisconsin, and his earliest published work consists of a translation of Hesiod and a rather conventional study of ancient literature called *Hermes the Thief.* His real impact on the mind of the age begins, however, with *Life Against Death* (1959), a long, speculative essay in which his discovery of Freud enables him to move beyond Karl Marx, who was apparently his first guru; and his mystical impulses take him to a place neither could have imagined. Of all the ideas developed in that book, it is perhaps the notion that "polymorphous perverse" rather than "genital" love should be the goal of adults in our society which made the greatest impact. But though his theories were already unconventional at that point, his style remained quite traditional. In *Love's Body* (1966), he finally found a new voice for his new point of view—oracular, anti-syntactical, flirting with silence, and depending on metaphor rather than analysis to make his points.

Originally everything was body, ONE BODY (Novalis); or Freud: "Originally the ego includes everything, later it detaches from itself the external world. The ego-feeling we are aware of now is thus only a shrunken vestige of a far more extensive feeling—a feeling which embraced the universe and expressed an inseparable connection of the ego with the external world." The possibilities adumbrated in infancy are to be taken as normative: as in Wordsworth's "Ode": before shades of the prison house close in; before we shrink up into the fallen condition which is normal adulthood.

> Novalis, *Hymne,* "Wenigewissen das Geheimniss der Liebe," *Geistliche Lieder.* S. Freud, *Civilization and Its Discontents,* trans. J. Riviere (London, 1930), 13.

> Man is the dwarf of himself. Once he was permeated and dissolved by spirit. He filled nature with his overflowing currents. Out from him sprang the sun and moon; from man, the sun; from woman, the moon. The laws of his mind, the periods of his actions externized themselves into day and night, into the year and the seasons. But, having made for himself this huge shell, his waters retired; he no longer fills the veins and veinlets; he is shrunk to a drop. He sees, that the structure still fits him, but fits him colossally. Say, rather, once it fitted him, now it corresponds to him from far and on high.

> Emerson, *Nature,* ch. VIII.

Psychoanalysis can be used to uncover the principle of union, or communion, buried beneath the surface separations, the surface declarations of independence, the surface signs of private property. Psychoanalysis also discloses the pathology of the process whereby the normal sense of being a self separate from the external world was constructed. Contrary to what is taken for granted in the lunatic state called normalcy or common sense, the distinction between self and external world is not an immutable fact, but an artificial construction. It is a boundary line; like all boundaries not natural but conventional; like all boundaries, based on love and hate.

The distinction between self and not-self is made by the childish decision to claim all that the ego likes as "mine," and to repudiate all that the ego dislikes as "not-mine." It is as simple as that; but here is Freud's more formal description: "The objects presenting themselves, in so far as they are sources of pleasure, are absorbed by the ego into itself, 'introjected' (according to an expression coined by Ferenczi);

while, on the other hand, the ego thrusts forth upon the external world whatever within itself gives rise to pain (the mechanism of projection)." "Thus at the very beginning, the external world, objects, and that which was hated were one and the same thing. When later on an object manifests itself as a source of pleasure, it becomes loved, but also incorporated into the ego."

S. Freud, "Instincts and their Vicissitudes," *Collected Papers*, IV, 78, 79; cf. "Negation," *Collected Papers*, V, 183; *Civilization and Its Discontents*, 12.

Here is the fall: the distinction between "good" and "bad," between "mine" and "thine," between "me" and "thee" (or "it"), come all together—boundaries between persons; boundaries between properties; and the polarity of love and hate.

The boundary line between self and external world bears no relation to reality; the distinction between ego and world is made by spitting out part of the inside, and swallowing in part of the outside. On this Freudian insight Melanie Klein and her followers have built. "Owing to these mechanisms [of introjection and projection] the infant's object can be defined as what is inside or outside his own body, but even while outside, it is still part of himself and refers to himself, since 'outside' results from being ejected, 'spat out': thus the body boundaries are blurred. This might also be put the other way round: because the object outside the body is 'spat out,' and still relates to the infant's body, there is no sharp distinction between his body and what is outside."

P. Heimann, "Certain Functions of Introjection and Projection in Early Infancy," in J. Riviere, ed., *Developments in Psycho-Analysis* (London, 1952), 143.

The net-effect of the establishment of the boundary between self and external world is inside-out and outside-in; confusion. The erection of the boundary does not alter the fact that there is, in reality, no boundary. The net-effect is illusion, self-deception; the big lie. Or alienation. "Le premier mythe du dehors et du dedans: l'aliénation se fond sur ces deux termes." Where Freud and Marx meet.

J. Hyppolite, "Commentaire parlé sur la Verneinung de Freud," in *La Psychanalyse*, I (1955), 35.
Cf. G. Bachelard, *La Poétique de l'espace*, (Paris, 1958), 192.

The soul (self) we call our own is an illusion. The real psychoana-
lytical contribution to "ego-psychology" is the revelation that the ego
is a bit of the outside world swallowed, introjected; or rather a bit of
the outside world that we insist on pretending we have swallowed. The
nucleus of one's own self is the incorporated other.

The super-ego is your father in you; your father introjected; your
father swallowed. In his most sophisticated description of super-ego
formation Freud says: "A portion of the external world has, at least
partially, been given up as an object and instead, by means of identification, taken into the ego—that is, has become an integral part of the
internal world."

> S. Freud, *An Outline of Psychoanalysis,* trans. J. Strachey (London,
> 1949), 77.

Melanie Klein has shown the same kind of origin for the ego. The
ego "is based on object libido reinvested in the body"; the self is a substitute for the lost other, a substitute which pretends to be the lost
other; so that we may embrace ourselves thinking we embrace our
mother. Our identity is always a case of mistaken identity. The ego is
our mother in us. It originally "embraced the universe and expressed
an inseparable connection of the ego with the external world," because
originally the whole world is the mother and the mother is the whole
world. It originates in the dual unity of mother and child; mother and
child, these two, as one. Its present structure, its illusory separate and
substantial identity results from the desire to perpetuate that original
union with the mother, by the device of pretending to have swallowed
her, i.e., to have incorporated her into oneself. The shadow of the lost
object becomes the nucleus of the ego; a shade, a spectre.

> G. Roheim, *War, Crime and the Covenant* (Monticello, N.Y., 1945), 142.

Possessive introjection is the basis of the ego; the soul is something
that we can call our own. "The ambitions of the Id, while that was the
sole governing force, were towards *being* the thing at the other side of
whatever relationship it established. When the Ego takes control of
the Id's impulses, it directs them towards *having*." The possessive
orientation originates in what Freud calls instinctual ambivalence,

i.e., the split between "good" and "bad," love and hatred, Eros and Thanatos. The aim of the possessive orientation is to keep the loved object entire and intact: to separate and keep the good, to separate and expel the bad. An either/or or undialectical attitude. What we desire to possess we fear to lose; it is a source of anxiety and we are ambivalent toward it, hate as well as love.

> B. Brophy, *Black Ship to Hell* (New York, 1962), 56.
> Cf. M. Klein and J. Riviere, *Love, Hate and Reparation* (New York, 1964), 96–98.

I am what is mine. Personality is the original personal property. As the great philosopher of private property says, "By property I must be understood here, as in other places, to mean that property which men have in their persons as well as goods." Here is the psychological root of private property. Every man has a "property" in his own person. "Man (by being master of himself, and proprietor of his own person, and the actions or labour of it) had still in himself the great foundation of property." The boundaries of our property are extended by mixing our persons with things, and this is the essence of the labor process: "Whatsoever, then, he removes out of the state that Nature hath provided and left it in, he hath mixed his labour with it, and joined to it something that is his own, and thereby makes it his property."

> J. Locke, *Two Treatises of Civil Government*, Everyman edition (London and New York, n.d.), 130, 138, 206.

"Cain means 'ownership.' Ownership was the originator of the earthly city." The crucial bit of property is neither nature (land) nor natural produce, nor factories nor manufactured products, but persons, our own persons. Free persons, whether in the state of nature or in civil society, are those who own their own persons. It is because we own our own persons that we are entitled to appropriate things that, through labor, become part of our personality or personalty. The defense of personal liberty is identical with the defense of property. There is a part of Karl Marx which attempts to base communism on Lockean premises. The Marxian proletariat is propertyless; they do not own themselves; they sell their labor (themselves) and are therefore not free, but wage-slaves; they are not persons. The case against the notion of private property is based on the notion of person: but they are the same notion. Hobbes says a person is either his own or another's. This dilemma is escaped only by those willing to discard personality.

> Augustine, *De Civitate Dei*, XV, 17.
> Cf. T. Hobbes, *Leviathan*, Everyman edition (New York, 1950), 133.

The existence of the "let's pretend" boundary does not prevent the continuance of the real traffic across it. Projection and introjection, the process whereby the self as distinct from the other is constituted, is not past history, an event in childhood, but a present process of continuous creation. The dualism of self and external world is built up by a constant process of reciprocal exchange between the two. The self as a stable substance enduring through time, an identity, is maintained by constantly absorbing good parts (or people) from the outside world and expelling bad parts from the inner world. "There is a continual 'unconscious' wandering of other personalities into ourselves."

> P. Schilder, *The Image and Appearance of the Human Body* (London, 1935), 252.
> Cf. Klein, *The Psychoanalysis of Children* (New York, 1960), 203–204, 217, 246–249. R. E. Money-Kyrle, *Psychoanalysis and Politics* (New York, 1951), 51.

Every person, then, is many persons; a multitude made into one person; a corporate body; incorporated, a corporation. A "corporation sole"; everyman a parson-person. The unity of the person is as real, or unreal, as the unity of the corporation.

We tend to think of any one individual in isolation; it is a convenient fiction. We may isolate him physically, as in the analytic room; in two minutes we find that he has brought his world in with him, and that even before he set eyes on the analyst, he had developed inside himself an elaborate relation with him. There is no such thing as a single human being, pure and simple, unmixed with other human beings. Each personality is a world in himself, a company of many. That self, that life of one's own, which is in fact so precious though so casually taken for granted, is a composite structure which has been and is being formed and built up since the day of our birth out of countless never-ending influences and exchanges between ourselves and others. . . . These other persons are in fact therefore parts of ourselves. And we ourselves similarly have and have had effects and influences, intended or not, on all others who have an emotional relation to us, have loved or hated us. We are members one of another.

J. Riviere, "The Unconscious Phantasy of an Inner World Reflected in Examples from Literature," in M. Klein, ed., *New Directions in Psychoanalysis* (New York, 1957), 358–359.
Cf. F. W. Maitland, "The Corporation Sole," *The Collected Papers of Frederick William Maitland* III, ed. H. A. L. Fisher (Cambridge, 1911), 214.

Separation (on the outside) is repression (on the inside): "The ego is incapable of splitting the object [or splitting with the object] without a corresponding split taking place within the ego." The declaration of independence from the mother (country) is a claim to be one's own mother; it splits the self into mother and child.

M. Klein, "Notes on Some Schizoid Mechanisms," in J. Riviere, ed., *Developments in Psycho-Analysis*, 298.

Separation (on the outside) is repression (on the inside). The boundary between the self and the external world is the model for the boundary between the ego and the id. The essence of repression, says Freud, is to treat an inner stimulus as if it were an outer one; casting it out (projection). The external world and inner id are both foreign territory—the same foreign territory.

Cf. S. Freud, "The Two Principles in Mental Functioning," 15n.

And all the boundaries, the false fronts or frontiers—between ego and external world, between ego and super-ego, between ego and id—are fortified. The walls are fortified, with "defense-mechanisms," and "character armor." "The natural man is self-centered, or ego-centric; everything he regards as real he also regards as outside himself; everything he takes 'in' immediately becomes unreal and 'spectral.' He tries to become an armored crustacean alert for attack or defense; the price of selfishness is eternal vigilance. This kind of Argus-eyed tenseness proceeds from the sealed prison of consciousness which Blake calls 'opaque.' "

N. Frye, *Fearful Symmetry*, (Princeton, 1947), 348–349.

Separateness, then, is the fall—the fall into division, the original lie. Separation is secrecy, hiding from one another, the private parts or property. Ownership is hiding; separation is repression. It is a private corporation. The right to privacy: something secret and shameful, which is one's own. "We hide in secret. I will build thee a Labyrinth where we may remain for ever alone." "The striving for the right to have secrets from which the parents are excluded is one of the most powerful factors in the formation of the ego." The plague of darkness is a symbol of the opaque Selfhood: "For while they thought they were unseen in their secret sins, they were sundered one from another by a dark curtain of forgetfulness, stricken with terrible awe, and sore troubled by spectral forms."

W. Blake, *Night* I, 28; cf. 21–27. V. Tausk, "On the Origin of the 'Influencing Machine' in Schizophrenia," *Psychoanalytic Quarterly,* II (1933), 535. Wisdom of Solomon XVII, 3.
Cf. G. Roheim, *Riddle of the Sphinx; or, Human Origins* (London, 1934), p. 153. Frye, *Fearful Symmetry*, 133–134.

The self being made by projection and introjection, to have a self is to have enemies, and to be a self is to be at war (the war of every man against every man). To abolish war, therefore, is to abolish the self; and the war to end war is total war; to have no more enemies, or self.

The conclusion of the whole matter is, break down the boundaries, the walls. Down with defense mechanisms, character-armor; disarmament. Ephesians II, 14: For he is our peace, who hath made both one, and hath broken down the middle wall of partition between us.

To give up boundaries is to give up the reality-principle. The reality-principle, the light by which psychoanalysis has set its course, is a false boundary drawn between inside and outside; subject and object; real and imaginary; physical and mental. It gives us the divided world, the split or schizoid world—the "two principles of mental functioning" —in which psychoanalysis is stuck. Psychoanalysis begins on the side of imperialism, or enlightenment, invading the heart of darkness, carrying bright shafts of daylight (*lucida tela diei*), carrying the Bible and flag of the reality-principle. Psychoanalysis ends in the recognition of the reality-principle as Lucifer, the prince of darkness, the prince of this world, the governing principle, the ruler of the darkness of this world. The reality-principle is the prince of darkness; its function is to *scotomize,* to spread darkness; to make walls of thick darkness, walls of separation and concealment. Psychoanalysis ends here: Freud remained officially faithful to the principle whose pretensions he finally exposed. Really to go beyond Freud means to go beyond the reality-principle. And really to go beyond the pleasure-principle is to go beyond the reality-principle; for Freud himself showed that these two are one.

The reality-principle is an unreal boundary drawn between real and imaginary. Psychoanalysis itself has shown that "There is a most surprising characteristic of unconscious (repressed) processes to which every investigator accustoms himself only by exercising great control; it results from their entire disregard of the reality-test; thought-reality is placed on an equality with external reality, wishes with fulfillment and occurrence." "What determines the symptoms is the reality not of experience but of thought."

> Freud, "The Two Principles in Mental Functioning," 20; *Totem and Taboo,* trans. J. Strachey (New York, 1962), 86.

"Animism, magic and omnipotence of thought"—the child, the savage and the neurotic are right. "The omnipotence of thoughts, the over-valuation of mental processes as compared with reality, is seen to have unrestricted play in the emotional life of neurotic patients. . . . This behaviour as well as the superstitions which he practises in ordinary life, reveals his resemblance to the savages, who believe they can alter the external world by mere thinking." But the lesson of psychoanalysis is that "we have to give up that prejudice in favor of external reality, that underestimation of internal reality, which is the attitude of the ego in ordinary civilized life to-day." That "advance," that "adaptation to reality," which consists in the child's learning to distinguish between the wish and the deed, between external facts and his feelings about them has to be undone, or overcome. "Mental Things are alone Real."

> Freud, *Totem and Taboo,* 87. S. Isaacs, "The Nature and Function of Phantasy," in J. Riviere, ed., *Developments in Psycho-Analysis,* 82. W. Blake, *A Vision of the Last Judgement,* 617.

The real world, which is not the world of the reality-principle, is the world where thoughts are omnipotent, where no distinction is drawn between wish and deed. As in the New Testament: "Ye have heard that it was said by them of old time, Thou shalt not commit adultery: But I say unto you, That whosoever looketh on a woman to lust after her hath committed adultery with her already in his heart." Or Freud: "It is a matter of indifference who actually committed the crime; psychology is only concerned to know who desired it emotionally and who welcomed it when it was done. And for that reason all of the brothers [of the family Karamazov; or of the human family] are equally guilty."

> Matthew V, 27–28. Freud, "Dostoevsky and Parricide," *Collected Papers*, V, 236.

The outcome, then, of Freud or of Dostoevsky, is a radical rejection of government of the reality-principle. Freud sees the collision between psychoanalysis and our penal institutions: "It is not psychology that deserves to be laughed at, but the procedure of judicial inquiry." Reik, in a moment of apocalyptic optimism, declares that "The enormous importance attached by criminal justice to the deed as such derives from a cultural phase which is approaching its end." A social order based on the reality-principle, a social order which draws a distinction between the wish and the deed, between the criminal and the righteous, is still a kingdom of darkness. It is only as long as a distinction is made between real and imaginary murders that real murders are worth committing: as long as the universal guilt is denied, there is a need to resort to individual crime, as a form of confession, and a request for punishment. The strength of sin is the law. Heraclitus said, the law is a wall.

> Freud, "Dostoevsky and Parricide," 236. T. Reik, *The Compulsion to Confess* (New York, 1959), 155. I Corinthians XV, 56.

Psychoanalysis manages to salvage its allegiance to the (false) reality-principle by its use of the word *fantasy* to describe the contents of the unconscious ("unconscious fantasies"). It is in the unconscious that "we are members one of another," "we incorporate each other." As long as we accept the reality-principle, the reality of the boundary between inside and outside, we do not "really" incorporate each other. It is then in fantasy that we "project" or "introject"; it is then purely mental, and mental means not real; the unconscious then contains not the hidden reality of human nature but some (aberrant) fancies, or fantasies. But the unconscious is the true psychic reality. The language of psychoanalysis becomes self-contradictory: "Phantasy has real effects, not only on the inner world of the mind, but also on the external world of the subject's bodily development and behaviour." "When contrasted with external and bodily realities, the phantasy, like other mental activities, is a figment, since it cannot be touched or handled or seen; yet it is real in the experience of the subject."

Isaacs, "The Nature and Function of Phantasy," 99.
Cf. Klein, "Notes on Some Schizoid Mechanisms," 298.

"Fantasy" is not real; is mental; is inside. The psychoanalytic model of two principles of mental functioning still adheres to the Lockean and Cartesian notion of human experience as consisting of mental events, inside the mind, and distinct from external, material, reality. Freud says, "With the introduction of the reality-principle one mode of thought-activity was split off; it was kept free from reality-testing and remained subordinated to the pleasure-principle alone. This is the act of phantasy-making." Reality-testing grows out of fantasy-making —"it is now a question whether something which is present in the ego as an image can also be rediscovered in reality." And in the final "reality-ego"—that is to say, the separate self of private property— "Once more it will be seen, the question is one of *external* and *internal*. What is not real, what is merely imagined or subjective, is only *internal;* while on the other hand what is real is also present externally." Then the basic stock in trade of the mind is images, fantasies, obtained by the power of the mind to revive the image of former perceptions, i.e., to hallucinate, as in dreams. The nucleus of mental life is then a spectral double of the external world, on the model of the dream; a world of images; a mental, an imaginary internal subjective unreal world, which may or may not reflect (correspond to) the bodily real external and material world.

Freud, "The Two Principles in Mental Functioning," 16–17; "Negation," 183.

In rejecting the split world of the reality-principle—"Two Horn'd Reasoning, Cloven Fiction"—Blake said "Mental Things are alone Real; what is call'd Corporeal, Nobody Knows of its Dwelling Place."

There is, then, after all a sense in which the body is not real; but the body that is not real is the false body of the separate self, the reality-ego. That false body we must cast off; in order to begin the Odyssey of consciousness in quest of its own true body.

Blake, *The Gates of Paradise,* 770; *A Vision of the Last Judgement,* 617.

The fallacy in the false body is Whitehead's Fallacy of Simple Location; which is the notion that "material can be said to be *here* in space and *here* in time, or *here* in space-time, in a perfectly definite sense which does not require for its explanation any reference to other regions of space-time." The fallacy of Simple Location is to accept the boundary as real: to accept as real that separateness which the reality-principle takes to be the essence of a body or a thing, the essence of the body as thing.

A. N. Whitehead, *Science and the Modern World,* (Cambridge, 1928), 62; cf. 72.

The reality-principle says, if *here,* then not *there;* if inside, then not outside. The alternative to dualism is dialectics; that is to say, love—

> Two distincts, division none:
> Number there in love was slain.

Whitehead says the reality is unification: reality is events (not things), which are prehensive unifications; gathering diversities together in a unity; not simply *here,* or *there,* but a gathering of here and there (subject and object) into a unity.

Shakespeare, "The Phoenix and the Turtle."
Cf. Whitehead, *Science and the Modern World,* 86–92.

Reality is not things (dead matter, or heavy stuff), in simple location. Reality is energy, or instinct; Eros and Thanatos, "the 'prehensive' and 'separative' characters of space time"; one sea of energy: "In the analogy with Spinoza, his one substance is for me the one underlying activity of realization individualizing itself in an interlocking plurality of modes." One substance, the id or It.

Whitehead, *Science and the Modern World,* 80, 87.

The human body is not a thing or substance, given, but a continuous creation (Nietzsche: *beständige Schöpfung*). The human body is an energy system, Schilder's postural model, which is never a complete structure; never static; is in perpetual inner self-construction and self-destruction; we destroy in order to make it new. Destroy this temple, and in three days I will raise it up.

> Cf. Schilder, *The Image and Appearance of the Human Body*, 15–16, 166, 193, 241, 287. John II, 19.

Reality does not consist of substances, solidly and stolidly each in its own place; but in events, activity; activity which crosses the boundary; action at a distance. Whitehead finds his paradigm in a text from Francis Bacon: "It is certain that all bodies whatsoever, though they have no sense, yet they have perception. . . . And this perception is sometimes at a distance, as well as upon the touch; as when the loadstone draweth iron: or flame naphtha of Babylon, a great distance off." Compare Nietzsche: "Man kann Druck und Stoss selber nicht 'erklären,' man wird die *actio in distans* nicht los."

> Whitehead, *Science and the Modern World*, 52, 86. F. Nietzsche, *Aus dem Nachlass der Achtzigerjahre, Werke* III (Munich, 1956), 455.

The "postural model" of the body consists of "lines of energy," "Psychic streams," Freud's "libidinal cathexes," which are, like electricity, action at a distance; flux, influx, reflux; connecting different erogenous points in the body (the psychosexual organizations); and connecting one body with other bodies. "The space in and around the postural model is not the space of physics. The body-image incorporates objects or spreads itself in space." "In an individual's own postural image many postural images of others are melted together." "We could describe the relation between the body-images of different persons under the metaphor of a magnetic field with stream-lines going in all directions." A Magnetic field, of action at a distance; or a magical field; "magic action is an action which influences the body-image irrespective of the actual distance in space." In magic action there is a space connection between the most distant things—

> For head with foot hath private amity,
> And both with moons and tides.

Herbert, "Man." P. Schilder, *The Image and Appearance of the Human Body* (London, 1935), 213, 216, 234, 236; cf. 16, 137, 241, 252.

The processes of identification and incorporation known to psychoanalysis conform to Lévy-Bruhl's pattern of mystical (magical) participation in primitive mentality; "The opposition between the one and the many, the same and another, etc., does not impose upon this mentality the necessity of affirming one of these terms if the other be denied." "Identification" is participation; self and notself identified; an extrasensory link between self and notself. Identification is action at a distance; or *telepathy;* the center of Freud's interest in the "Occult." If body, corporeal substance, is taken to be in Simple Location (as Freud took it to be) then the question of telepathy is whether thoughts or spiritual beings can exist with no ascertainable connection with a corporeal body. But Freud himself said, that "by inserting the unconscious between the physical and what has been regarded as the mental, psychoanalysis has prepared the way for the acceptance of such processes as telepathy." The question is not the existence of disembodied spirit, but the modalities of bodily action at a distance.

Lévy-Bruhl, cited in Shilder, *The Image and Appearance of the Human Body,* 274. S. Freud, *New Introductory Lectures,* trans. W. J. H. Sprott (London, 1949), 75–76.
Cf. E. Jones, *The Life and Work of Sigmund Freud* (New York, 1957), III, 402. O. Barfield, *Saving the Appearances,* (London, 1957), 32–34.

The hidden psychic reality contained in the unconscious does not consist of fantasies, but of action at a distance, psychic streams, projects, in a direction: germs of movement; seeds of living thought. These seeds are Freud's "unconscious ideas," which are concrete ideas; that is to say ideas of things, and not simply of the words, or images inside the mind corresponding to the things outside. Concrete ideas are cathexes of things: "The Unconscious contains the thing-cathexes of objects, the first and true object-cathexes"; the original telepathy.

Freud, "The Unconscious," *Collected Papers,* IV, 134.

The "thing-cathexes of the objects, the first and true object-cathexes"; "a proto-mental system in which physical and mental activity is undifferentiated." A kind of body-thinking, "at first without visual or other plastic images"; "unconscious knowledge," carried in deeper centers of the body than head or eye; a knowledge not derived from the senses, extrasensory; sub-sensible or super-sensible. For example, that unconscious knowledge about sexual intercourse between parents attributed by psychoanalysis to babes in arms. "The world of thought at those levels is quite alien to our own, so that it is quite impossible to reproduce them in words as one seems to perceive them in analysis. Let us consider, for instance, what a demand we are making on anyone who has not been able to convince himself of the fact in an analysis, if we ask him to believe that a small child becomes like his mother because he thinks he has eaten her up, and that, if he thinks he is being tormented or 'poisoned' by this internal mother, he can in some circumstances spit her out again. The details of this kind of 'body-thinking' of which we have a glimpse in analysis and which is bound up with ideas of incorporation must perpetually evade any exact comprehension."

S. Isaacs, "The Nature and Function of Phantasy," in J. Riviere, ed., *Developments in Psycho-Analysis* (London, 1952), 92.
Cf. M. Klein, "Criminal Tendencies in Normal Children," *Contributions to Psycho-Analysis* (London, 1950), 188. O. Fenichel, "Further Light upon the Pre-oedipal Phase in Girls," *Collected Papers* I (New York, 1953), 242. W. R. Bion, "Group Dynamics: A Re-view," in M. Klein, ed., *New Directions in Psychoanalysis* (New York, 1957), 449. M. Klein, *The Psychoanalysis of Children* (New York, 1960), 296–297.

In the deepest level of the unconscious we find not fantasies, but telepathy. That is to say, the deepest and still unconscious level of our being is not modeled on the dream; in which fission, duplication, is the basic mechanism; in which we withdraw from the world into a second world of (visual) images, projected.

Reuben slept on Penmaenmawr and Levi slept on Snowdon.
Their eyes, their ears, nostrils and tongues roll outward, they behold
What is within now seen without.

To overcome the dualism would be to awake out of sleep; to arise from the dead.

Blake, *Night* II, 52–54.
Cf. Schilder, *Image and Appearance of the Human Body,* 51–52, 60. Roheim, *Gates of the Dream* (New York, 1953), 20, 58, 116. Ephesians V, 14; Romans XIII, 11.

It is not schizophrenia but normality that is split-minded; in schizophrenia the false boundaries are disintegrating. "From pathology we have come to know a large number of states in which the boundary lines between ego and outside world become uncertain." Schizophrenics are suffering from the truth. " 'Every one knows' the patient's thoughts: a regression to a stage before the first lie." Schizophrenia testifies to "experiences in which the discrimination between the consciousness of self and the consciousness of the object was entirely suspended, the ego being no longer distinct from the object; the subject no longer distinct from the object; the self and the world were fused in an inseparable total complex." Schizophrenic thought is "adualistic"; lack of ego-boundaries makes it impossible to set limits to the process of identification with the environment. The schizophrenic world is one of mystical participation; an "indescribable extension of inner sense"; "uncanny feelings of reference"; occult psychosomatic influences and powers; currents of electricity, or sexual attraction—action at a distance.

> Freud, *Civilization and Its Discontents,* 11. Tausk, "The 'Influencing Machine' in Schizophrenia," 535. A. Storch, *Primitive Archaic Forms of Inner Experiences and Thought in Schizophrenia,* trans. C. Willard (New York and Washington, 1924), 31, 61, 62.
> Cf. M. A. Sèchehaye, *A New Psychotherapy in Schizophrenia* (New York, 1956), 134. Roheim, *Magic and Schizophrenia* (New York, 1955), 101.

"The patient connects herself with everybody." "You and I, are we not the same? . . . Sometimes I cannot tell myself from other people. . . . It seemed to me as though I no longer existed in my own person alone, as though I were one with the all." In a patient called Julie, "all perception seemed to threaten confusion with the object. 'That's the rain. I could be the rain.' 'That chair—that wall. I could be that wall. It's a terrible thing for a girl to be a wall.' "

> Storch, *Primitive Archaic Forms,* 27–28. R. D. Laing, *The Divided Self: A Study of Sanity and Madness* (London, 1960), 217.
> Cf. Schilder, *Image and Appearance of the Human Body,* 215. Roheim, *Magic and Schizophrenia,* 101, 115.

Definitions are boundaries; schizophrenics pass beyond the reality-principle into a world of symbolic connections: "all things lost their definite boundaries, became iridescent with many-colored significances." Schizophrenics pass beyond ordinary language (the language of the reality-principle) into a truer, more symbolic language: "I'm thousands. I'm an in-divide-you-all. I'm a no un (i.e., nun, no-un, no one)." The language of *Finnegans Wake*. James Joyce and his daughter, crazy Lucia, these two are one. The god is Dionysus, the mad truth.

Storch, *Primitive Archaic Forms*, 62. Laing, *Divided Self*, 223.
Cf. Sèchehaye, *A New Psychotherapy for Schizophrenia*, 135–150. Ellmann, *James Joyce*, 692, 692n. Roheim, *Magic and Schizophrenia*, 94, 108.

The mad truth: the boundary between sanity and insanity is a false one. The proper outcome of psychoanalysis is the abolition of the boundary, the healing of the split, the integration of the human race. The proper posture is to listen to and learn from lunatics, as in former times—"We cannot deny them a measure of that awe with which madmen were regarded by people of ancient times." The insane do not share "the normal prejudice in favor of external reality." The "normal prejudice in favor of external reality" can be sustained only by ejecting (projecting) these dissidents from the human race; scotomizing them, keeping them out of sight, in asylums; insulating the so-called reality-principle from all evidence to the contrary.

Freud, *New Introductory Lectures*, 80.
Cf. Storch, *Primitive Archaic Forms*, 97.

Dionysus, the mad god, breaks down the boundaries; releases the prisoners; abolishes repression; and abolishes the *principium individuationis,* substituting for it the unity of man and the unity of man with nature. In this age of schizophrenia, with the atom, the individual self, the boundaries disintegrating, there is, for those who would save our souls, the ego-psychologists, "the Problem of Identity." But the breakdown is to be made into a breakthrough; as Conrad said, in the destructive element immerse. The soul that we can call our own is not a real one. The solution to the problem of identity is, get lost. Or as it says in the New Testament: "He that findeth his own psyche shall lose it, and he that loseth his psyche for my sake shall find it."

Matthew X, 39.

39. Education Automation

R. BUCKMINSTER FULLER

R. Buckminster Fuller (1895–   ), "Bucky" Fuller as he is known to everyone who knows of him at all, was educated at Harvard and the United States Naval Academy, and has worked in industry for most of his adult life—except for a term of service in the United States Navy. A practicing technologist and an inventor (most famously of the geodesic dome), he has scorned the narrow point of view typical of his profession, and has pondered the implications of technology in our culture. More prophet than teacher, more orator than writer, he has made disciples from the lecture platform, until in 1962 the Southern Illinois University Press published some of his speeches and occasional essays in book form. Since then other books have appeared, but he continues to influence more through the spoken than the written word.

I have talked to you about solving problems by design competence instead of by political reform. It is possible to get one-to-one correspondence of action and reaction without political revolution, warfare, and reform. I find it possible today with very short electromagnetic waves to make small reflectors by which modulated signals can be beamed. After World War II, we began to beam our TV messages from city to city. One reason television didn't get going before World War II was because of the difficulty in distributing signals over long distances from central sources on long waves or mildly short waves. We were working on coaxial cables between cities, but during the war we found new short ranges of electromagnetic frequencies. We worked practically with very much higher frequencies, very much shorter wave lengths. We found that we could beam these short waves from city to city. Television programs are brought into the small city now by beam

SOURCE: R. Buckminster Fuller, *Education Automation: Freeing the Scholar to Return to His Studies* (Carbondale: Southern Illinois University Press, 1962), pp. 545–62. Copyright © 1962 by Southern Illinois University Press. Reprinted by permission of publisher.

from a few big cities and then *re-broadcast* locally to the home sets. That is the existing TV distribution pattern. My invention finds it is now possible to utilize the local TV masts in any community in a new way. Going up to, say, two hundred, three hundred, or four hundred feet and looking down on a community you see the houses individually in the middle of their respective land plots. Therefore, with a few high masts having a number of tiny Retrometer light-beams, lasers, or other radiation reflectors, each beam aimed accurately at a specific house, the entire community could be directly "hooked up" by beams, instead of being broadcast to. This means a great energy saving, for less than 1 per cent of the omnidirectionally *broadcast* pattern ever hits a receiving antenna. The beaming makes for very sharp, clear, frequency-modulated signals.

In the beaming system, you also have a reflector at the house that picks up the signal. It corresponds directly to the one on the mast and is aimed right back to the specific beaming cup on the mast from which it is receiving. This means that with beam casting you are able to send individual messages to each of those houses. There is a direct, fixed, wireless connection, an actual direct linkage to individuals; and it works in both directions. Therefore, the receiving individual can beam back, "I don't like it." He may and can say "yes" or "no." This "yes" or "no" is the basis of a binary mathematical system, and immediately brings in the "language" of the modern electronic computers. With two-way TV, constant referendum of democracy will be manifest, and democracy will become the most practical form of industrial and space-age government by all people, for all people.

It will be possible not only for an individual to say, "I don't like it," on his two-way TV but he can also beam-dial (without having to know mathematics), "I want number so and so." It is also possible with this kind of two-way TV linkage with individuals' homes to send out many different programs simultaneously; in fact, as many as there are two-way beamed-up receiving sets and programs. It would be possible to have large central storages of documentaries—great libraries. A child could call for a special program information locally over the TV set.

With two-way TV we will develop selecting dials for the children which will not be primarily an alphabetical but a visual *species* and *chronological category* selecting device with secondary alphabetical subdivisions. The child will be able to call up any kind of information he wants about any subject and get his latest authoritative TV documentary, the production of which I have already described to you. The answers to his questions and probings will be *the best information* that man has available up to that minute in history.

All this will bring a profound change in education. We will stop training individuals to be "teachers," when all that most young girl "education" students really want to know is how they are going to earn a living in case they don't get married. Much of the educational system today is aimed at answering: "How am I going to survive? How am I going to get a job? I must earn a living." That is the priority item under which we are working all the time—the idea of *having to earn a living*. That problem of "how are we going to earn a living?" is going to go out the historical window, forever, in the next decade, and education is going to be disembarrassed of the unseen "practical" priority bogeyman. Education will then be concerned primarily with exploring to discover not only more about the universe and its history but about what the universe is trying to do, about why man is part of it, and about how can, and may, man best function in universal evolution.

Automation is with us. There is no question about it. Automation was inevitable to intellect. Intellect was found to differentiate out experience continually and to articulate and develop new tools to do physically repeated tasks. Man is now no longer *essential* as a worker in the fabulously complex industrial equation. Marx's *worker* is soon to become utterly obsolete. Automation is coming in Russia just as it is here. The word *worker* describing man as a muscle-and-reflex machine will not have its current 1961 meaning a decade hence. Therefore, if man is no longer essential as a worker we ask: "How can he live? How does he acquire the money or credits with which to purchase what he needs or what he wants that is available beyond immediate needs?" At the present time we are making all kinds of economic pretenses at covering up this overwhelming automation problem because we don't realize adequately the larger significance of the truly fundamental change that is taking place in respect to man-in-universe. As automation advanced man began to create secondary or nonproductive jobs to make himself look busy so that he could rationalize a necessity for himself by virtue of which he could "earn" his living. Take all of our bankers, for example. They are all fixtures; these men don't have anything to do that a counting machine couldn't do; a punch button box would suffice. They have no basic banking authority whatsoever today. They do not loan you their own wealth. They loan you your own wealth. But man has a sense of vanity and has to invent these things that make him look important.

I am trying to keep at the realities with you. Approximately total automation is coming. Men will be essential to the industrial equation but not as workers. People are going to be utterly essential as consumers—what I call *regenerative consumers,* however, not just swill pails. . . . .

Every time we educate a man, we as educators have a regenerative experience, and we ought to learn from that experience how to do it much better the next time. The more educated our population the more effective it becomes as an integral of regenerative consumer individuals. We are going to have to invest in our whole population to accelerate its consumer regeneration. We are going to be completely unemployed as muscle-working machines. *We as economic society are going to have to pay our whole population to go to school and pay it to stay at school.* That is, we are going to have to put our whole population into the educational process and get *everybody* realistically literate in many directions. Quite clearly, *the new political word* is going to be *investment.* It is not going to be *dole,* or socialism, or the idea of people hanging around in bread lines. The new popular *regenerative investment* idea is actually that of making people more familiar with the patterns of the universe, that is, with what man has learned about the universe to date, and that of getting everybody inter-communicative at ever higher levels of literacy. People are then going to stay in the education process. They are going to populate ever increasing numbers of research laboratories and universities.

As we now disemploy men as muscle and reflex machines, the one area where employment is gaining abnormally fast is the research and development area. Research and development are a part of the educational process itself. We are going to have to invest in our people and make available to them participation in the great educational process of research and development in order to learn more. When we learn more, we are able to do more with our given opportunities. We can relate federally paid-for education as a high return, mutual benefit investment. When we plant a seed and give it the opportunity to grow, its fruits pay us back many fold. Man is going to "improve" rapidly in the same way by new federally underwritten educational "seeding" by new tools and processes.

Our educational processes are in fact the upcoming major world industry. This is *it;* this is the essence of today's educational facilities meeting. You are caught in that new educational upward draughting process. The cost of education will be funded regeneratively right out of earnings of the technology, the industrial equation, because we can only afford to reinvest continually in humanity's ability to go back and turn out a better job. As a result of the new educational processes our consuming costs will be progressively lower as we also gain ever higher performance per units of invested resources, which means that our wealth actually will be increasing at all times rather than "exhausted by spending." It is the "capability" wealth that really counts. It is very good that there is an international competitive system now operating, otherwise men would tend to stagnate, particularly in large group undertakings. They would otherwise be afraid to venture in this great intellectual integrity regeneration.

I would say, then, that you are faced with a future in which education is going to be number one amongst the great world industries, within which will flourish an educational machine technology that will provide tools such as the individually selected and articulated two-way TV and an intercontinentally networked, documentaries call-up system, operative over any home two-way TV set. . . .

I think that all the patterns I have been giving you are going to unfold rapidly and that primarily the individual is going to *study* at home. That is in elementary, high school, and college years. Not until his graduate work days begin will he take residence on campus. I am quite sure that the students of all ages will keep on going to "school houses" to get *social experiences*—or to be "baby-sat." We will probably keep the schools open in the evening because of the growing need for babysitters. Real education, however, will be something to which individuals will discipline themselves spontaneously under the stimulus of their own ticker-tapes—their individually unique chromosomes. Everyone has his own chromosomal pattern. No two persons have the same appetite at the same time. There is no reason why they should. There is no reason why everyone should be interested in the geography of Venezuela on the same day and hour unless there is some "news" event there, such as a revolution. However, most of us are going to be interested in the geography of Venezuela at some time —our own time—but not all on the same day. *Simultaneous curricula are obsolete.* We must make *all* the information immediately available over the two-way TV's ready for the different individual human chromosomal ticker-tapes to call for it.

There are two more things I would like to talk about if we have the time. I am a comprehensive designer—that is, I try to organize all the data and challenges and problems in such a manner that they may be solved by inanimate technology, as I mentioned to you earlier, rather than by organization reforms. Therefore, when I talk about educational problems, I am interested in how these can be satisfied by some kind of physical apparatus along the lines of the trend requirements I have been outlining to you. The kind of equipment that would be involved would be such as the two-way TV and the Geoscope and also what I call *automated education facilities*. We know about teaching machines, etc., today, and much of this is sound. In our consideration of equipment we must also include the environment-controlling structures which will house the computer-integrated equipment and activities.

I am going to give you one more "big" introductory concept that may shed considerable light on these problems and may lead to acquisition of logical apparatus of solution. C. P. Snow, the writer, has a great following today. He writes about "two worlds." His two worlds are the literary world and the scientific world. In the literary world, man writes the books that people can understand with least effort. They seem to be good romance books because they seem to fit many lives. Science writes in ways that require complete dedication of effort to comprehend. Snow says the dichotomy between the two worlds began approximately two centuries ago with the inception of the industrial revolution. In England it is as yet evident that the popular writers of a century ago and since were not helped by the scientist. The scientist tended to be preoccupied, obscure, and not interested in the literary man's needs. A pertinent fact that Snow does not mention is that the important scientific events were often withheld from the public because of their unique military advantages. The scientist's information began to be the grist of the industrial technology. The scientist was intimately tied up with industry, even though he didn't look upon his personal work in terms of economics. The scientist was aloof to the ultimate fact that industry was the user of the information that he was able to gather.

The literary man, not understanding either science or its technology, developed an animosity toward industrialization. Snow points out for us that in America this dichotomy was in evidence, for instance, in Emerson and Thoreau who were antipathetic to industrialization. As I grew up at the turn of the century I saw that society looked on industrialization as something noisy, smoky, and full of so-called "artificialities." (In my viewpoint, there is no meaning to the word "artificial." Man can only do what nature permits him to do. Man does not invent anything. He makes discoveries of principles operative in nature and often finds ways of generalizing those principles and reapplying them in surprise directions. That is called invention. But he does not do anything artificial. Nature has to permit it, and if nature permits it, it is natural. There is naught which is unnatural.)

The literary and popular concept of industrialization grew out of erroneous definitions and terms. The static viewpoint was seemingly supported by the Newtonian statement that "a body persists in *a state of rest* (or in a line of motion) except as affected by other bodies." Primarily the norm was "at rest" and changes were therefore abnormal and undesirable. Changes were exploited from time to time only because of military advantage or because men could make large amounts of money out of the changes and not because of any social voting that the changes were constructively desirable. The literati just didn't try to understand change, and they stayed apart from science and abhorred the changes. Snow says the gulf between the scientist and the literati is now so great that the chasm is no longer spannable. He feels there has now developed an irreparable dichotomy between literary and scientific man. I do not agree with him as you shall learn.

Alfred North Whitehead came to Harvard University early in this twentieth century from the great universities of England. He said that one of the things that was very noticeable at Harvard was that this great private school was initiating a new kind of pattern. It was beginning to build and staff the great graduate schools. The graduate schools dealt in specializations. In England the special preoccupations could be taken up within the general university. There were no special schools. Whitehead said that the American populus applauded the high specialization, and Whitehead saw that this pattern was being followed by the other leading private schools, colleges, and universities.

Of course, the public schools and public universities immediately followed suit, taking on the graduate school patterns, because the political representatives of the public saw that their constituents would want the state school to incorporate these educational advances of the rich man's private schools. So specialization in graduate schools also became the "thing."

Whitehead said this meant that we deliberately sorted out the students, sieved them, picked out the bright ones, and persuaded the brights to stay in the university and to go on to the graduate school. This meant that we began to make specialists out of our bright ones. The bright ones within their own special category of their special school went on to develop further special nuances within their special areas. This all worked toward expertism and hybridism in the educational pursuits. It meant that the bright ones would learn much about their special subject. The public thought this to be desirable, because people like the idea of an "all-star" team. They thought that if we took groups of all-stars and put them together our commonwealth would surely prosper.

Whitehead said, "So far so good, and everybody is applauding." But he then said that the educational hybridism would mean that these men who were of high intellectual capabilities would have very high intellectual integrity. As men of high intellectual integrity they would quickly discover that they were making great progress in highly specialized areas of inquiry and thus also they would know how little any other man outside of their own field could possibly understand of what was going on inside their own and inside any one field other than their respective specializations. Therefore, no specialist of integrity would think of going into some other expert's field and making quick assumptions as to the significance of that unfamiliar work. This would be considered preposterous. There would thus develop an increasing tendency to break down generalized communications and comprehensive prospecting between these experts. Certainly, they would not tend to join together and say: "I see I am developing this and you are developing that; if we associated them thus and so, such and such would be the economic consequences; therefore, let us do so by employing our credit as scientists with the banks in order to fund our undertakings." These men, Whitehead said, would do just the opposite and would become more and more subjective, growing into purer and purer scientists, to whom no banker would think of lending money on the basis of intellectual integrity alone. The scientists went in just the opposite direction of applied science. The more expert they were the less they would think of searching into the concept of how society might enjoy the fruits of their discoveries.

Whitehead pointed out that this system tended to break down the communication between the men of high intellectual capability in all special fields. Inasmuch as society wanted exploitation of the gains of their "all-star" teams, it meant that someone other than the prime intellects had to integrate and exploit their capabilities and their findings.

Then Whitehead said—which came as quite a surprise—inasmuch as we have deliberately sorted out the bright ones from the dull ones, we have inadvertently created a class of dull ones. Just as in mining, we have a big pile of tailings, and no one thinks much about tailings because they are interested only in the high-grade, quick-cash ore and the net metal that is taken out of the latter. He said that inasmuch as the "bright ones" are not going to be able to realize, integrate, and exploit their own potentials we will have to leave it to the not-so-brights to put things together. This is what I have termed "Whitehead's dilemma."

I have developed "Whitehead's dilemma" a little further than he could go at that time. I find that there is a second grade of men who get passing marks, but are not selected to be specialists, who, however, though not "gleaming bright" have a dull polish and are good healthy fellows who play good football and are liked by everybody. These second grade "clean ones" become the first choice for executives in business, which does integrate potentials of demand and supply. Then as corporation executives these not-quite-so-brights take on the pure scientist experts and cultivate them like special hybrid egg-laying hens in special houses. The corporations take on the task of putting appropriate specializations together to exploit the synergetic advantages thus accruing. The businessman becomes the integrator of the bright ones' capabilities. The business executive himself, however, tends to be a specialist of a less fine order. Pretty soon, he will say, for instance: "I am in the automobile business and don't know anything about stockings; so I am just going to stick to my automobiles." He might also say: "I find that an automobile won't run across an open field. Therefore it is only half of the invention—automotive transportation. The *highway* itself is a large part of the invention—high speed highway transportation." Automobiling is schematically like a monkey wrench—the ratchet half is the "highway," and the thumbscrew-adjustable traveling jaw is the "automobile." The automobile is literally geared by its tire-treads to the road. So the business executive might say: "An automobile company could not possibly afford to build the highways —it is a very difficult political matter; you have to have costly condemnation proceedings and so forth to get a highway through; it is all so expensive that our company would never make a profit if we took the responsibility of providing highways. All we can produce is automobiles. To get the show going, however, we will have a little auto race track over here, and we will have automobile shows in many big cities and at county and state fairs. We will get people very excited about the way our automobile can go and how fascinating it looks." Thus it went, and the people began to envision personal use and enjoyment of the automobile "if only they had a highway." What the auto executive did was to excite the people into demanding highways for the cars.

We next come down to a duller class of not-so-brights—much duller—who didn't even go to college. This much duller class is that of the politicians. The politicians saw that the people in general wanted automobiles and wanted to "joy ride"; so they immediately voted for highways to get the peoples' votes for themselves.

Thus, a much bigger geographical pattern of the automobile emerged than the domain of the factory and the auto executive's specialized territory. The bigger pattern was the total highway system —state, interstate, and federal. We also find that generally speaking *the geographically larger the physical task to be done, the duller the conceptual brain that is brought to bear* upon the integration of the scientific discoveries and their technically realized applications. Finally we get to international affairs, and you know what is happening today. The most highly polished of the dullest class, scientifically and intellectually speaking, may wear their striped pants very beautifully and be charming fellows, but they have not produced any mutually-acceptable, constructive, world peace generating ideas. They traffic successfully only in peoples' troubles and emergency compromises. One of the great mistakes that society has been demonstrating in our last century has been that of leaving the most important problems to the men who are bankrupt in creative thinking ability.

World War I marked the end of the old great masters of the water-ocean earth commerce. These were the world "bankers" who were the not-too-dull businessmen who had high courage and co-ordination and who developed successful world-pattern cartels and trusts quite transcendentally to any one nation's anti-trust laws or to any one nation's popular knowledge, advantaged by men's world-around preoccupations with their own respective domestic affairs. These old masters kept the world peoples in complete ignorance of their world planning and let it be thought that the latter was the consequence of their appointed local politicians' deliberations.

At Harvard just before World War I —and this was the time when I was having my little troubles there—the dilemma Whitehead was talking about was developing in a very interesting way. What Whitehead didn't ask was how Harvard could afford those graduate schools. The fact is that neither Harvard nor any other university has ever operated at a profit. Certainly, schools, colleges, and universities don't have surplus earnings accruing which they can reinvest. Establishing graduate schools wasn't something private colleges could do on their own. The explanation is that the graduate schools were *given* to Harvard and the other leading private universities.

The next interesting question is *who gave* them the graduate *specialty* schools? Well, the people who gave Harvard the schools were primarily the partners of J. P. Morgan and Company or they were men who were founders or presidents of companies whose boards were run by J. P. Morgan. J. P. Morgan or his partners were at that time on the boards of nearly every important, powerful company in America. Morgan or his associates were also partners in the great unseen syndicate of world commerce mastery up to World War I. . . .

Since World War I, the old masters have been extinct. Because they operated always in secret, they of course didn't announce their own demise. As they died secretly they inadvertently left many accepted patterns, such as, for instance, the "head men" on the world thrones and the university patterns which Whitehead described. As the new problems brought about by the old masters' demise arose, everybody began to turn to the local political head men and new head men who arose easily, pushing over the old who no longer had the support of the now defunct invisible masters. . . .

As a consequence, since 1918 world men speaking always under their conditioned reflex concepts of static geographical "nations" have been challenging the local political heads with the responsibility of getting them out of their troubles. Then suddenly, realistic "head men" haven't the slightest idea how to solve such problems. These were problems that only their old masters could solve. Nobody could have been duller in *world* stratagems than the political leaders of the world's many separate nations. Ruthless, tough bluffing became the new winning technique, but it was implemented by the politicians' exploitation of their respective hybrid, economic slaves, the scientific specialists.

In respect to "Whitehead's dilemma" everybody today tends to believe that specialization is the best way to earn a living, by establishing one's own special monopoly at some strategic point in the specialization network. As a consequence of comprehensively undertaken specialization we have today a general lack of comprehensive thinking. The specialist is therefore, in effect, a slave to the economic system in which he happens to function. The concept of inevitable specialization by the brightest has become approximately *absolute* in today's social-economic reflexing. The fixation is false and is soon to be altered. . . .

At the World Affairs Conference in Colorado this last week, they brought Ludwig Von Bertalanffy together with me on five panels. Ludwig Von Bertalanffy is a great biologist. He is in the front ranks of the "academy." As a great scientist in biology, he discovered that there were comprehensive system behaviors in nature unpredicted by the behaviors of the systems' components, a phenomenon known to scientists as synergy. Von Bertalanffy, along with other mathematicians who had discovered synergy in the theories of games and so forth, began to discover that there were complex patterns which could never be apprehended, understood, operated on, or dealt with if we approached them only in terms of their separate elements; that is, *literally* in an *elementary* manner. Our whole educational process, all the way up from the elementary school, is one of taking the child who has an innate comprehensive coordinate capability (not only to teach itself to walk but to be interested in the *heavens*) and give him differentiated parts—elements to work with. The prime patrons of the planetariums and the like are the children, because they are spontaneously interested in the universe, that is, in the comprehensive rather than in the specialty—the elements. We get them to school, and we say forget the universe, and we give them A, B, and C. We go toward the very opposite of comprehensiveness. We go to the specialization right away. We render the children more and more specialized from elementary school onwards. Ludwig Von Bertalanffy began to find that nature, as biology, did not tend toward hybridism or more limited specialization by itself. Nature reverted toward generalism. Nature tended to work toward broader adaptation, ergo, more comprehensive capabilities. As a consequence, Dr. Von Bertalanffy was the scientist who developed an expression you are quite familiar with today— General Systems Theory. Von Bertalanffy employs his General Systems Theory subjectively. He agreed with me that my *comprehensive anticipatory design science* is an objective employment of systems theory and that I had discovered the same phenomenon that he had discovered through completely different circumstances.

If we apply General Systems Theory to the analysis of our total world problem, today we obtain an excellent view of the techno-scientific, industrial theatre and the *socio-economic drama* in which our swiftly evolving educational processes are going to function and we can see far more clearly what the roles therein may be of the kinds of new educational developments which I have been describing to you. We will also be able to comprehend better the problems that were insurmountable to the old "world masters" and how the coming universities may now solve them under the newer circumstances. . . .

What I now propose is that all the universities around the world be encouraged to invest the next ten years in a continuing problem of *how to make the total world's resources, which now serve only 43 per cent, serve 100 per cent of humanity through competent complex design science.*

The general theory of education at present starts students off with elementary components and gradually increases the size of the complex of components with which the student will be concerned. The scheme is to go from the particular toward the whole but never to reach the whole. . . .

I think that one of the most important events of the educational revolution is the present realization that we are going to discover that the child is born comprehensively competent and co-ordinate and that it is capable of treating with large quantities of data and families of variables right from the start.

When parents make babies they don't know what they are making. They don't know how to make what they make. All they do is "press a button." Ours and our babies' brains have a quadrillion times a quadrillion atoms already operative in coordinate patterning operation utterly transcendental to our conscious control. A quadrillion times a quadrillion atoms operative subconsciously in most extraordinary coordination make it possible, for example, for me to be communicating with you. We don't have anything consciously to do with the fundamentals of our communicating capability. Nor do we have anything to do consciously with pushing a million hairs out of our heads at preferred rates, colors, and shapes. We don't know how to consciously coordinate our heart beating and our breathing. We don't know at all how we charge energies back into the various glands of our systems. We really don't know what is going on at all, but we do co-ordinate it all subconsciously. What we do have in the brain is an extraordinary, orderly pattern manipulating capability to deal with that quadrillion times a quadrillion invisible atoms. This is all born into the child. The parent doesn't consciously put it there. Men may take no credit for the fundamentals of their relative success upon earth.

I will say that it is very clear to me that when a child stands up, breathing and co-ordinating all these complex patterns by himself and gets his own balance and starts drinking in the patterns of cosmos and earth he is apparently spontaneously interested in co-ordinating the total information—the total stimulation. He craves to understand— to comprehend. That is why he asks his myriad questions.

I am quite confident we are going to find ways of helping the child to co-ordinate his spontaneous comprehension of the *whole* instead of becoming a specialist without losing any of the advantages gained by yesterday's exclusive specialization. With general comprehension there will also come an entirely new way of looking at our mutual problems around the earth. We will not be easily influenced by ignorant persuasion and propaganda, such as pronouncements that "we are against this man and that man," and so forth. We are going to look at our problems quite differently than we do now. There will be a co-ordinated comprehensive continuation of development of the child in appreciation of the subconsciously co-ordinate design of humans not forcing them into prolonged special focus, yet accomplishing with automated tools and instruments far greater probing than was accomplished by the utter specialist while conserving the comprehensive comprehension of the significance to society of the increasing flow of discovered data.

Next, let us think carefully and daringly of the equipment we will need and that we won't need for the large, new research establishments for students staying longer and longer at the university, as the new major industry of mankind. At M.I.T., for instance, where I visited as lecturer for eight years, there are rooms full of special and expensive apparatus which everyone thought would put M.I.T. at the top of the heap. Room after room of this equipment is now obsolete —at best these collections of machinery make a dull museum. . . .

I would counsel you in your deliberation regarding getting campuses ready now to get general comprehensive environment controls that are suitable to all-purposes like a circus. A circus is a transformable environment. You get an enclosure against "weather" that you can put up in a hurry, within which you can put up all kinds of apparatus—high trapezes, platforms, rings, nets, etc. You can knock it down in a few minutes. That is the way the modern laboratory goes. In laboratories you can get the generalized pipette or whatever it is, the crucible and the furnace. You can put the right things together very fast, rig them up, get through the experiment, knock it down. It's one clean space again. You want clean spaces. The circus concept is very important for you. I would get buildings where it is possible for many to meet. On the Carbondale campus you have succeeded in getting some good auditoriums—but we need more auditoriums and more auditoriums time and time again. We want places where there is just a beautiful blank floor and beautiful blank walls upon which to cast our pictures or apply crayons. You don't have to put any "architecture" there at all. You don't have to build any sculptured architecture—use the ephemeral. Work from the visible to the invisible very rapidly.

I would not waste dollars on great, heavy, stone masonry and any kind of Georgian architecture, and I would forget all the old architecture and even the curricula patterns of any schools before this moment. You might better consider putting up one big one-half-mile-diameter geodesic dome over your whole campus and thereafter subdivide off local areas temporarily for various activities.

Anything that is static, forget it. Work entirely toward the dynamic. Get yourself the tools and ways of enclosing enormous amounts of space, and make it possible for large numbers of human beings to come together under more preferred conditions than have ever before come together. Then give them large clear spaces so that their privacy results from having sufficient distance between people or groups of people. Get over the ideas of partitions. Partitions are like socialism. They came out of living and working in fortresses where there wasn't enough room to go around, so they put up partitions—really making cells. Partitions simply say you shall not pass. That's all they do. They are improvised to make that which is fundamentally inadequate work "after a fashion."

There are four kinds of privacy: if I can't touch you, we're *tactilely* private; if I can't smell you, we are *olfactorily* private; if I can't hear you, we're *aurally* private; and if I can't see you, we are *visually* private. Just a little space will take care of the first three. For the fourth —since we can see a great distance—all we need are delicate occulting membranes, possibly rose bushes or soap bubbles or smoke screens.

40. Blondie

MARSHALL MCLUHAN

Marshall McLuhan (1911–   ) has taught all his adult life in universities, chiefly at St. Michael's College in the University of Toronto, though presently he is the Schweitzer Professor at Fordham University. Basically conservative in his views, a resolute Roman Catholic, for instance, and a follower since student days of the Southern Agrarians, he has come to seem revolutionary for suggesting that we are through with the Gutenberg skills of reading and writing (which is to say, the skills highly prized in Protestant society); and are, thanks to

SOURCE: Marshall McLuhan, *The Mechanical Bride* (New York: Vanguard Press, Inc., 1951), pp. 68–69. Copyright 1951 by Herbert Marshall McLuhan. Reprinted by permission of Vanguard Press, Inc.

electronic media, entering an age when men will be moved once more by archetypal images, and the true community (the "global village") will replace the soulless industrial city. Mr. McLuhan has developed his ideas in a magazine called *Explorations* (1953–1959), which he edited in collaboration with Edmund Carpenter; and, spectacularly, in a series of books, *The Gutenberg Galaxy* (1962), *Understanding Media* (1964), and (with Quentin Fiore) *The Medium is the Massage* (1967)—the last a comic and graphic version, as it were, of what he had proffered more seriously and in words earlier.

Putting up with Father?

Why is that shrill, frantic, seedy, saggy little guy so popular?

Why those piratical raids on the icebox?

Is Dagwood the American backbone?

Why is Blondie so crisp, cute, and bossily assured?

It is not without point that Chic Young's strip is now misnamed and that popular use has long since changed its title to "Dagwood." This is because Blondie herself is of no interest. She is a married woman. It is only the sufferings, the morose stupidities, and the indignities of her husband, Dagwood Bumstead, which matter. These make up the diary of a nobody.

Blondie is cute. She started out as a Tillie the Toiler, a frisky coke-ad girl, supposed to be universally desirable because twice-bathed, powdered, patted, deodorized, and depilatorized. But the moment this little love-goddess is married, she is of little interest to anybody but to the advertisers and to her children. And to them she is conscience, the urgent voice of striving and aspiration. To them she apportions affection as reward for meritorious effort. She has "poise and confidence," know-how, and drive. Dagwood is a supernumerary tooth with weak hams and a cuckold hair-do. Blondie is trim, pert, resourceful. Dagwood is seedy, saggy, bewildered, and weakly dependent. Blondie lives for her children, who are respectful toward her and contemptuous of Dagwood. Dagwood is "living and partly living" in hope of a little quiet, a little privacy, and a wee bit of mothering affection from Blondie and his son, Alexander. He is an apologetic intruder into a hygienic, and, save for himself, a well-ordered dormitory. His attempts to eke out some sort of existence in the bathroom or on the sofa (face to the wall) are always promptly challenged. He is a joke which his children thoroughly understand. He has failed, but Alexander will succeed.

Dagwood expresses the frustration of the suburban commuters of our time. His lack of self-respect is due partly to his ignoble tasks, partly to his failure to be hep to success doctrines. His detestation of his job is plain in the postponement of the morning departure till there comes the crescendo of despair and the turbulent take-off. Rising and departure are traumatic experiences for him, involving self-violence. His swashbuckling, midnight forays to the icebox, whence he returns covered with mayonnaise and the gore of catsup, is a wordless charade of self-pity and Mitty-Mouse rebellion. Promiscuous gormandizing as a basic dramatic symbol of the abused and the insecure has long been understood.

The number of suburban-marriage strips and radio programs is increasing. Each has the same theme—model mother saddled with a sad sack and a dope. We are confronted on a large scale with what Wyndham Lewis has described as mothering-wedlock. Each evening the male tends to assume the little-boy role, not only in the hope of reducing the frightening tensions which still attach to his vestigial father role but also to excuse himself from the burden of being a downtown quarterback by day.

It is part of the success of Chic Young's entertaining strip that he glorifies Dagwood quite as much as he glorifies Blondie, the industrial girl. And this, it would seem, is the measure of his inferiority to Al Capp, who refuses to glorify the inglorious. Capp is conscious of what standards he employs; Young is much less so. It was likewise part of Charlie Chaplin's career and fame that he dramatized with wit and genius the pathos of the little man of an industrial world. Chaplin saved himself from the worst effects of his syrupy sentiment by assimilating his little-man-what-now figure to that of the traditional clown. By that means he maintained a taproot reaching down to the deeper terrors and desires of the heart. And by the same taproot and by means of intelligent insight Kafka, Rouault, and Picasso have raised this combination of clown and citizen to levels of tragic intensity.

Chic Young's timidity appears simply in his exploiting, rather than exploring, a popular image of domesticity. In the same way, however, can be seen the failure of many serious American artists and writers to employ the rich materials of popular art. Serious American artists equally pursue not the serious but the genteel by working from the

outside, with only the themes and manners of European art and literature. They appear to lack any conviction that the probing of native tradition can bring them into the main current of traditional human experience. When it comes to art, they have the immigrant humility. Perhaps it is part of our willingness to believe that we are "different" from
the rest of mankind because we wish to believe that we are better. If
that Pollyanna fixation is the root of the trouble, it can scarcely last
much longer. Meantime it is the function of the critic to direct serious,
controversial attention to the layers of human significance beneath the
most banal and evasive features of native tradition and experience.

To put Young's amiable strip in terms of cold anthropological categories, Dagwood is second generation. His father (first generation)
made good because he was compelled to do so to justify his rejection of
his European father. (Blondie was originally introduced as the elder
Bumstead's stenographer.) But Dagwood doesn't feel the same inner
tensions. His very desire to belong passively and comfortably in a
country in which his father was only a new arrival robs him of his success drive. But Blondie sees and admires the pattern of competitive
striving which Dagwood neglects and, rigid with the social cocksure-
ness of the schoolmarm, she points out the arduous path to her children, who are soon to leave the monotonous flats along which
Dagwood is idling.

All of which is to say that we are still riding a psychological escalator which seems to raise us above the perennial human problems that
will begin to confront the "fourth generation." The present, or "third,"
generation is once again success-ridden, like the first generation, but it
has exhausted the obvious frontiers, leaving its children free to get out
of the squirrel cage of success obsession. But has not that interim
mechanism of immigrant adjustment served its function? If allowed to
continue its operations, would it not prove an instrument of unnecessary mental torture and social perversion?

In short, the prospect of soon reaching, at least for a time, the end of
success obsession may prove to be a serious crisis which for many will
look like the end of "the American way of life." But Chic Young's strip
seems to be assured of survival into a world which will be as alien to it
as it already is to McManus's Jiggs. Those who grew up with Dagwood
will, like those who grew up with Jiggs, insist on growing old with him.
For many millions on this continent Jiggs and Dagwood are fixed
points of geniality, beacons of orientation, amid flux and stress. They

represent a new kind of entertainment, a sort of magically recurrent daily ritual which now exerts on the spontaneous popular feelings a rhythmic reassurance that does substitute service, as it were, for the old popular experience of the recurrence of the seasons.

Perhaps that is why "the strip must go on" even when authors die. It also suggests a reason for the strange indifference the public has always felt toward the authors of these strips. Even frequent mention of the name of the author does little to disturb his anonymity. Their creations have been caught up in the gentler ebb and flow of habitual existence, serving a very different function from equally popular art forms like the sports page and detective fiction.

41. The New Mutants

LESLIE FIEDLER

Leslie Fiedler has always been interested in the myths which operate at the points where art and society interfuse: the myth of race, of the generations, of Left and Right, and so on. It is, of course, the myths of the generations—especially of the young—which intrigue us now, and the essay which follows has had the ambiguous honor of being quoted in sociology texts and an official report of a Senate subcommittee.

A realization that the legitimate functions of literature are bewilderingly, almost inexhaustibly various has always exhilarated poets and dismayed critics. And critics, therefore, have sought age after age to legislate limits to literature—legitimizing certain of its functions and disavowing others—in hope of insuring to themselves the exhilaration of which they have felt unjustly deprived, and providing for poets the dismay which the critics at least have thought good for them.

Such shifting and exclusive emphasis is not, however, purely the

SOURCE: *Partisan Review*, XXXII (Fall, 1965), 505–25. Copyright © 1965 by *Partisan Review*. Reprinted by permission of the author and publisher.

product of critical malice, or even of critical principle. Somehow every period is, to begin with, especially aware of certain functions of literature and especially oblivious to others: endowed with a special sensitivity and a complementary obtuseness, which, indeed, give to that period its characteristic flavor and feel. So, for instance, the Augustan Era is marked by sensitivity in regard to the uses of diction, obtuseness in regard to those of imagery.

What the peculiar obtuseness of the present age may be I find it difficult to say (being its victim as well as its recorder), perhaps toward the didactic or certain modes of the sentimental. I am reasonably sure, however, that our period is acutely aware of the sense in which literature if not invents, at least collaborates in the invention of time. The beginnings of that awareness go back certainly to the beginnings of the Renaissance, to Humanism as a self-conscious movement; though a critical development occurred toward the end of the eighteenth century with the dawning of the Age of Revolution. And we may have reached a second critical point right now.

At any rate, we have long been aware (in the last decades uncomfortably aware) that a chief function of literature is to express and in part to create not only theories of time but also attitudes toward time. Such attitudes constitute, however, a politics as well as an esthetics; or, more properly perhaps, a necessary mythological substratum of politics—as, in fact, the conventional terms reactionary, conservative, revolutionary indicate: all involving stances toward the past.

It is with the past, then, that we must start, since the invention of the past seems to have preceded that of the present and the future; and since we are gathered in a university at whose heart stands a library —the latter, like the former, a visible monument to the theory that a chief responsibility of literature is to preserve and perpetuate the past. Few universities are explicitly (and none with any real degree of confidence) dedicated to this venerable goal any longer. The Great Books idea (which once transformed the University of Chicago and lives on now in provincial study groups) was perhaps its last desperate expression. Yet the shaky continuing existence of the universities and the building of new college libraries (with matching Federal funds) remind us not only of that tradition but of the literature created in its name: the neo-epic, for instance, all the way from Dante to Milton; and even the frantically nostalgic Historical Romance, out of the counting house by Sir Walter Scott.

Obviously, however, literature has a contemporary as well as a traditional function. That is to say, it may be dedicated to illuminating the present and the meaning of the present, which is, after all, no more given than the past. Certainly the modern or bourgeois novel was thus contemporary in the hands of its great inventors, Richardson, Fielding, Smollett and Sterne; and it became contemporary again—with, as it were, a sigh of relief—when Flaubert, having plunged deep into the Historical Romance, emerged once more into the present of Emma Bovary. But the second function of the novel tends to transform itself into a third: a revolutionary or prophetic or futurist function; and it is with the latter that I am here concerned.

Especially important for our own time is the sense in which literature first conceived the possibility of the future (rather than an End of Time or an Eternal Return, an Apocalypse or Second Coming); and then furnished that future in joyous or terrified anticipation, thus preparing all of us to inhabit it. Men have dreamed and even written down utopias from ancient times; but such utopias were at first typically allegories rather than projections: nonexistent models against which to measure the real world, exploitations of the impossible (as the traditional name declares) rather than explorations or anticipations or programs of the possible. And, in any event, only recently have such works occupied a position anywhere near the center of literature.

Indeed, the movement of futurist literature from the periphery to the center of culture provides a clue to certain essential meanings of our times and of the art which best reflects it. If we make a brief excursion from the lofty reaches of High Art to the humbler levels of Pop Culture—where radical transformations in literature are reflected in simplified form—the extent and nature of the futurist revolution will become immediately evident. Certainly, we have seen in recent years the purveyors of Pop Culture transfer their energies from the Western and the Dracula-type thriller (last heirs of the Romantic and Gothic concern with the past) to the Detective Story especially in its hard-boiled form (final vulgarization of the realists' dedication to the present) to Science Fiction (a new genre based on hints in E. A. Poe and committed to "extrapolating" the future). This development is based in part on the tendency to rapid exhaustion inherent in popular forms; but in part reflects a growing sense of the irrelevance of the past and even of the present to 1965. Surely, there has never been a moment in which the most naïve as well as the most sophisticated have been so acutely aware of how the past threatens momentarily to disappear from the present, which itself seems on the verge of disappearing into the future.

And this awareness functions, therefore, on the level of art as well as entertainment, persuading quite serious writers to emulate the modes of Science Fiction. The novel is most amenable to this sort of adaptation, whose traces we can find in writers as various as William Golding and Anthony Burgess, William Burroughs and Kurt Vonnegut, Jr., Harry Matthews and John Barth—to all of whom young readers tend to respond with a sympathy they do not feel even toward such forerunners of the mode (still more allegorical than prophetic) as Aldous Huxley, H. G. Wells and George Orwell. But the influence of Science Fiction can be discerned in poetry as well, and even in the polemical essays of such polymath prophets as Wilhelm Reich, Buckminster Fuller, Marshall McLuhan, perhaps also Norman O. Brown. Indeed, in Fuller the prophetic–Science-Fiction view of man is always at the point of fragmenting into verse:

> *men are known as being six feet tall*
> *because that is their tactile limit;*
> *they are not known by how far we can hear them,*
> *e.g., as a one-half mile man*
> *and only to dogs are men known*
> *by their gigantic olfactoral dimensions. . . .*

I am not now interested in analyzing, however, the diction and imagery which have passed from Science Fiction into post-Modernist literature, but rather in coming to terms with the prophetic content common to both: with the myth rather than the modes of Science Fiction. But that myth is quite simply the myth of the end of man, of the transcendence or transformation of the human—a vision quite different from that of the extinction of our species by the Bomb, which seems stereotype rather than archetype and consequently the source of editorials rather than poems. More fruitful artistically is the prospect of the radical transformation (under the impact of advanced technology and the transfer of traditional human functions to machines) of *homo sapiens* into something else: the emergence—to use the language of Science Fiction itself—of "mutants" among us.

A simpleminded prevision of this event is to be found in Arthur C. Clarke's *Childhood's End,* at the conclusion of which the mutated offspring of parents much like us are about to take off under their own power into outer space. Mr. Clarke believes that he is talking about a time still to come because he takes metaphor for fact; though simply translating "outer space" into "inner space" reveals to us that what he is up to is less prediction than description; since the post-human future is now, and if not we, at least our children, are what it would be comfortable to pretend we still only foresee. But what, in fact, are they: these mutants who are likely to sit before us in class, or across from us at the dinner table, or who stare at us with hostility from street corners as we pass?

Beatniks or hipsters, layabouts and drop-outs we are likely to call them with corresponding hostility—or more elegantly, but still without sympathy, passive onlookers, abstentionists, spiritual catatonics. There resides in all of these terms an element of truth, at least about the relationship of the young to what we have defined as the tradition, the world we have made for them; and if we turn to the books in which they see their own destiny best represented (*The Clockwork Orange,* say, or *On the Road* or *Temple of Gold*), we will find nothing to contradict that truth. Nor will we find anything to expand it, since the young and their laureates avoid on principle the kind of definition (even of themselves) for which we necessarily seek.

Let us begin then with the negative definition our own hostility suggests, since this is all that is available to us, and say that the "mutants" in our midst are non-participants in the past (though our wisdom assures us this is impossible), drop-outs from history. The withdrawal from school, so typical of their generation and so inscrutable to ours, is best understood as a lived symbol of their rejection of the notion of cultural continuity and progress, which our graded educational system represents in institutional form. It is not merely a matter of their rejecting what happens to have happened just before them, as the young do, after all, in every age; but of their attempting to disavow the very idea of the past, of their seeking to avoid recapitulating it step by step—up to the point of graduation into the present.

Specifically, the tradition from which they strive to disengage is the tradition of the human, as the West (understanding the West to extend from the United States to Russia) has defined it, Humanism itself, both in its bourgeois and Marxist forms; and more especially, the cult of reason—that dream of Socrates, redreamed by the Renaissance and surviving all travesties down to only yesterday. To be sure, there have

long been anti-rational forces at work in the West, including primitive
Christianity itself; but the very notion of literary culture is a product of
Humanism, as the early Christians knew (setting fire to libraries), so
that the Church in order to sponsor poets had first to come to terms
with reason itself by way of Aquinas and Aristotle.

Only with Dada was the notion of an anti-rational anti-literature
born; and Dada became Surrealism, i.e., submitted to the influence of
those last neo-Humanists, those desperate Socratic Cabalists, Freud
and Marx—dedicated respectively to contriving a rationale of violence and a rationale of impulse. The new irrationalists, however,
deny all the apostles of reason, Freud as well as Socrates; and if they
seem to exempt Marx, this is because they know less about him, have
heard him evoked less often by the teachers they are driven to deny.
Not only do they reject the Socratic adage that the unexamined life is
not worth living, since for them precisely the unexamined life is the
only one worth enduring at all. But they also abjure the Freudian one:
"Where id was, ego shall be," since for them the true rallying cry is,
"Let id prevail over ego, impulse over order," or—in negative terms
—"Freud is a fink!"

The first time I heard this irreverent charge from the mouth of a
student some five or six years ago (I who had grown up thinking of
Freud as a revolutionary, a pioneer), I knew that I was already in the
future; though I did not yet suspect that there would be no room in that
future for the university system to which I had devoted my life.
Kerouac might have told me so, or Ginsberg, or even so polite and genteel a spokesman for youth as J. D. Salinger, but I was too aware of
what was wrong with such writers (their faults more readily apparent
to my taste than their virtues) to be sensitive to the truths they told. It
took, therefore, certain public events to illuminate (for me) the literature which might have illuminated them.

I am thinking, of course, of the recent demonstrations at Berkeley
and elsewhere, whose ostensible causes were civil rights or freedom of
speech or Vietnam, but whose not so secret slogan was all the time:
The Professor is a Fink! And what an array of bad anti-academic
novels, I cannot help reminding myself, written by disgruntled professors, created the mythology out of which that slogan grew. Each generation of students is invented by the generation of teachers just before
them; but how different they are in dream and fact—as different as
self-hatred and its reflection in another. How different the professors

in Jeremy Larner's *Drive, He Said* from those even in Randall Jarrell's *Pictures from an Institution* or Mary McCarthy's *Groves of Academe.*

To be sure, many motives operated to set the students in action, some of them imagined in no book, however good or bad. Many of the thousands who resisted or shouted on campuses did so in the name of naïve or disingenuous or even nostalgic politics (be careful what you wish for in your middle age, or your children will parody it forthwith!); and sheer ennui doubtless played a role along with a justified rage against the hypocrisies of academic life. Universities have long rivaled the churches in their devotion to institutionalizing hypocrisy; and more recently they have outstripped television itself (which most professors affect to despise even more than they despise organized religion) in the institutionalization of boredom.

But what the students were protesting in large part, I have come to believe, was the very notion of man which the universities sought to impose upon them: that bourgeois-Protestant version of Humanism, with its view of man as justified by rationality, work, duty, vocation, maturity, success; and its concomitant understanding of childhood and adolescence as a temporarily privileged time of preparation for assuming those burdens. The new irrationalists, however, are prepared to advocate prolonging adolescence to the grave, and are ready to dispense with school as an outlived excuse for leisure. To them work is as obsolete as reason, a vestige (already dispensible for large numbers) of an economically marginal, pre-automated world; and the obsolescence of the two adds up to the obsolescence of everything our society understands by maturity.

Nor is it in the name of an older more valid Humanistic view of man that the new irrationalists would reject the WASP version; Rabelais is as alien to them as Benjamin Franklin. Disinterested scholarship, reflection, the life of reason, a respect for tradition stir (however dimly and confusedly) chiefly their contempt; and the Abbey of Theleme would seem as sterile to them as Robinson Crusoe's Island. To the classroom, the library, the laboratory, the office conference and the meeting of scholars, they prefer the demonstration, the sit-in, the riot: the mindless unity of an impassioned crowd (with guitars beating out the rhythm in the background), whose immediate cause is felt rather than thought out, whose ultimate cause is itself. In light of this, the Teach-in, often ill understood because of an emphasis on its declared political ends, can be seen as implicitly a parody and mockery of the real classroom: related to the actual business of the university, to real teaching only as the Demonstration Trial (of Dimitrov, of the Soviet Doctors, of Eichmann) to real justice or Demonstration Voting (for one party or a token two) to real suffrage.

At least, since Berkeley (or perhaps since Martin Luther King provided students with new paradigms for action) the choice has been extended beyond what the earlier laureates of the new youth could imagine in the novel: the nervous breakdown at home rather than the return to "sanity" and school, which was the best Salinger could invent for Franny and Holden; or Kerouac's way out for his "saintly" vagrants, that "road" from nowhere to noplace with homemade gurus at the way stations. The structure of those fictional vaudevilles between hard covers that currently please the young (*Catch 22, V., A Mother's Kisses*), suggest in their brutality and discontinuity, their politics of mockery something of the spirit of the student demonstrations; but only Jeremy Larner, as far as I know, has dealt explicitly with the abandonment of the classroom in favor of the dionysiac pack, the turning from *polis* to *thiasos,* from forms of social organization traditionally thought of as male to the sort of passionate community attributed by the ancients to females out of control.

Conventional slogans in favor of "Good Works" (pious emendations of existing social structures, or extensions of accepted "rights" to excluded groups) though they provide the motive power of such protests are irrelevant to their form and their final significance. They become their essential selves, i.e., genuine new forms of rebellion, when the demonstrators hoist (as they did in the final stages of the Berkeley protests) the sort of slogan which embarrasses not only fellow-travelers but even the bureaucrats who direct the initial stages of the revolt: at the University of California, the single four-letter word no family newspaper would reprint, though no member of a family who could read was likely not to know it.

It is possible to argue on the basis of the political facts themselves that the word "fuck" entered the whole scene accidentally (there were only four students behind the "Dirty Speech Movement," only fifteen hundred kids could be persuaded to demonstrate for it, etc., etc.). But the prophetic literature which anticipates the movement indicates otherwise, suggesting that the logic of their illogical course eventually sets the young against language itself, against the very counters of logical discourse. They seek an anti-language of protest as inevitably as they seek anti-poems and anti-novels, end with the ultimate anti-word, which the demonstrators at Berkeley disingenuously claimed stood for FREEDOM UNDER CLARK KERR.

Esthetics, however, had already anticipated politics in this regard; porno-poetry preceding and preparing the way for what Lewis Feuer has aptly called porno-politics. Already in 1963, in an essay entitled *"Phi Upsilon Kappa,"* the young poet Michael McClure was writing: "Gregory Corso has asked me to join with him in a project to free the word FUCK from its chains and strictures. I leap to make some new freedom. . . ." And McClure's own "Fuck Ode" is a product of this collaboration, as the very name of Ed Saunders' journal, *Fuck You,* is the creation of an analogous impulse. The aging critics of the young who have dealt with the Berkeley demonstrations in such journals as *Commentary* and the *New Leader* do not, however, read either Saunders' porno-pacifist magazine or *Kulchur,* in which McClure's manifesto was first printed—the age barrier separating readership in the United States more effectively than class, political affiliation or anything else.

Their sense of porno-esthetics is likely to come from deserters from their own camp, chiefly Norman Mailer, and especially his recent *An American Dream,* which represents the entry of anti-language (extending the tentative explorations of "The Time of Her Time") into the world of the middle-aged, both on the level of mass culture and that of yesterday's ex-Marxist, post-Freudian avant-garde. Characteristically enough, Mailer's book has occasioned in the latter quarters reviews as irrelevant, incoherent, misleading and fundamentally scared as the most philistine responses to the Berkeley demonstrations, Philip Rahv and Stanley Edgar Hyman providing two egregious examples. Yet elsewhere (in sectors held by those more at ease with their own conservatism, i.e., without defunct radicalism to uphold) the most obscene forays of the young are being met with a disheartening kind of tolerance and even an attempt to adapt them to the conditions of commodity art.

But precisely here, of course, a disconcerting irony is involved; for after a while, there will be no Rahvs and Hymans left to shock—anti-language becoming mere language with repeated use and in the face of acceptance; so that all sense of exhilaration will be lost along with the possibility of offense. What to do then except to choose silence, since raising the ante of violence is ultimately self-defeating; and the way of obscenity in any case leads as naturally to silence as to further excess? Moreover, to the talkative heirs of Socrates, silence is the one offense that never wears out, the radicalism that can never become fashionable; which is why, after the obscene slogan has been hauled down, a blank placard is raised in its place.

There are difficulties, to be sure, when one attempts to move from the politics of silence to an analogous sort of poetry. The opposite number to the silent picketer would be the silent poet, which is a contradiction in terms; yet there are these days non-singers of (perhaps) great talent who shrug off the temptation to song with the muttered comment, "Creativity is out." Some, however, make literature of a kind precisely at the point of maximum tension between the tug toward silence and the pull toward publication. Music is a better language really for saying what one would prefer not to say at all—and all the way from certain sorts of sufficiently cool jazz to Rock'n'Roll (with its minimal lyrics that defy understanding on a first hearing), music is the preferred art of the irrationalists.

But some varieties of skinny poetry seem apt, too (as practised, say, by Robert Creeley after the example of W. C. Williams), since their lines are three parts silence to one part speech:

> *My lady*
> *fair with*
> *soft*
> *arms, what*
> *can I say to*
> *you—words, words* . . .

And, of course, fiction aspiring to become Pop Art, say, *An American Dream* (with the experiments of Hemingway and Nathanael West behind it), works approximately as well, since clichés are almost as inaudible as silence itself. The point is not to shout, not to insist, but to hang cool, to baffle all mothers, cultural and spiritual as well as actual.

When the Town Council in Venice, California, was about to close down a particularly notorious beatnik cafe, a lady asked to testify before them, presumably to clinch the case against the offenders. What she reported, however, was that each day as she walked by the café and looked in its windows, she saw the unsavory types who inhabited it "just standing there, looking—nonchalant." And, in a way, her improbable adjective does describe a crime against her world; for non-chaleur ("cool," the futurists themselves would prefer to call it) is the essence of their life-style as well as of the literary styles to which they respond: the offensive style of those who are not so much *for* anything in particular, as "with it" in general.

But such an attitude is as remote from traditional "alienation," with its profound longing to end disconnection, as it is from ordinary forms of allegiance, with their desperate resolve not to admit disconnection. The new young celebrate disconnection—accept it as one of the necessary consequences of the industrial system which has delivered them from work and duty, of that welfare state which makes disengagement the last possible virtue, whether it call itself Capitalist, Socialist or Communist. "Detachment" is the traditional name for the stance the futurists assume; but "detachment" carries with it irrelevant religious, even specifically Christian overtones. The post-modernists are surely in some sense "mystics," religious at least in a way they do not ordinarily know how to confess, but they are not Christians.

Indeed, they regard Christianity, quite as the Black Muslim (with whom they have certain affinities) do, as a white ideology: merely one more method—along with Humanism, technology, Marxism—of imposing "White" or Western values on the colored rest of the world. To the new barbarian, however, that would-be post-Humanist (who is in most cases the white offspring of Christian forebears) his whiteness is likely to seem if not a stigma and symbol of shame, at least the outward sign of his exclusion from all that his Christian Humanist ancestors rejected in themselves and projected mythologically upon the colored man. For such reasons, his religion, when it becomes explicit, claims to be derived from Tibet or Japan or the ceremonies of the Plains Indians, or is composed out of the non-Christian submythology that has grown up among Negro jazz musicians and in the civil rights movement. When the new barbarian speaks of "soul," for instance, he means not "soul" as in Heaven, but as in "soul music" or even "soul food."

It is all part of the attempt of the generation under twenty-five, not exclusively in its most sensitive members but especially in them, to become Negro, even as they attempt to become poor or pre-rational. About this particular form of psychic assimilation I have written sufficiently in the past (summing up what I had been long saying in chapters seven and eight of *Waiting for the End*), neglecting only the sense in which what starts as a specifically American movement becomes an

international one, spreading to the *yé-yé* girls of France or the working-
class entertainers of Liverpool with astonishing swiftness and ease.

What interests me more particularly right now is a parallel assimila-
tionist attempt, which may, indeed, be more parochial and is certainly
most marked at the moment in the Anglo-Saxon world, i.e., in those
cultural communities most totally committed to bourgeois-Protestant
values and surest that they are unequivocally "white." I am thinking of
the effort of young men in England and the United States to assimilate
into themselves (or even to assimilate themselves into) that otherness,
that sum total of rejected psychic elements which the middle-class
heirs of the Renaissance have identified with "woman." To become
new men, these children of the future seem to feel, they must not only
become more Black than White but more female than male. And it is
natural that the need to make such an adjustment be felt with especial
acuteness in post-Protestant highly industrialized societies, where the
functions regarded as specifically male for some three hundred years
tend most rapidly to become obsolete.

Surely, in America, machines already perform better than humans a
large number of those aggressive-productive activities which our ancestors considered man's special province, even his *raison d'être*. Not
only has the male's prerogative of making things and money (which is
to say, of working) been preempted, but also his time-honored privilege of dealing out death by hand, which until quite recently was regarded as a supreme mark of masculine valor. While it seems theoretically possible, even in the heart of Anglo-Saxondom, to imagine a
leisurely, pacific male, in fact the losses in secondary functions sustained by men appear to have shaken their faith in their primary masculine function as well, in their ability to achieve the conquest (as the
traditional metaphor has it) of women. Earlier, advances in technology had detached the wooing and winning of women from the begetting of children; and though the invention of the condom had at least
left the decision to inhibit fatherhood in the power of males, its replacement by the "loop" and the "pill" has placed paternity at the mercy
of the whims of women.

Writers of fiction and verse registered the technological obsolescence of masculinity long before it was felt even by the representative minority who give to the present younger generation its character
and significance. And literary critics have talked a good deal during
the past couple of decades about the conversion of the literary hero

into the non-hero or the anti-hero; but they have in general failed to notice his simultaneous conversion into the non- or anti-male. Yet ever since Hemingway at least, certain male protagonists of American literature have not only fled rather than sought out combat but have also fled rather than sought out women. From Jake Barnes to Holden Caulfield they have continued to run from the threat of female sexuality; and, indeed, there are models for such evasion in our classic books, where heroes still eager for the fight (Natty Bumppo comes to mind) are already shy of wives and sweethearts and mothers.

It is not absolutely required that the anti-male anti-hero be impotent or homosexual or both (though this helps, as we remember remembering Walt Whitman), merely that he be more seduced than seducing, more passive than active. Consider, for instance, the oddly "womanish" Herzog of Bellow's best seller, that Jewish Emma Bovary with a Ph.D., whose chief flaw is physical vanity and a taste for fancy clothes. Bellow, however, is more interested in summing up the past than in evoking the future; and *Herzog* therefore seems an end rather than a beginning, the product of nostalgia (remember when there were real Jews once, and the "Jewish Novel" had not yet been discovered!) rather than prophecy. No, the post-humanist, post-male, post-white, post-heroic world is a post-Jewish world by the same token, anti-Semitism as inextricably woven into it as into the movement for Negro rights; and its scriptural books are necessarily *goyish,* not least of all William Burroughs' *The Naked Lunch.*

Burroughs is the chief prophet of the post-male post-heroic world; and it is his emulators who move into the center of the relevant literary scene, for *The Naked Lunch* (the later novels are less successful, less exciting but relevant still) is more than it seems: no mere essay in heroin-hallucinated homosexual pornography—but a nightmare anticipation (in Science Fiction form) of post-Humanist sexuality. Here, as in Alexander Trocchi, John Rechy, Harry Matthews (even an occasional Jew like Allen Ginsberg, who has begun by inscribing properly anti-Jewish obscenities on the walls of the world), are clues to the new attitudes toward sex that will continue to inform our improbable novels of passion and our even more improbable love songs.

The young to whom I have been referring, the mythologically representative minority (who, by a process that infuriates the mythologically inert majority out of which they come, "stand for" their times), live in a community in which what used to be called the "Sexual Revo-

lution," the Freudian-Laurentian revolt of their grandparents and
parents, has triumphed as imperfectly and unsatisfactorily as all revo-
lutions always triumph. They confront, therefore, the necessity of de-
termining not only what meanings "love" can have in their new world,
but—even more disturbingly—what significance, if any, "male"
and "female" now possess. For a while, they (or at least their literary
spokesmen recruited from the generation just before them) seemed
content to celebrate a kind of *reductio* or *exaltatio ad absurdum* of
their parents' once revolutionary sexual goals: The Reichian-inspired
Cult of the Orgasm.

Young men and women eager to be delivered of traditional ideolo-
gies of love find especially congenial the belief that not union or relationship (much less offspring) but physical release is the end of the
sexual act; and that, therefore, it is a matter of indifference with whom
or by what method ones pursues the therapeutic climax, so long as that
climax is total and repeated frequently. And Wilhelm Reich happily
detaches this belief from the vestiges of Freudian rationalism, setting
it instead in a context of Science Fiction and witchcraft; but his emphasis upon "full genitality," upon growing up and away from infantile pleasures, strikes the young as a disguised plea for the "maturity"
they have learned to despise. In a time when the duties associated with
adulthood promise to become irrelevant, there seems little reason for
denying oneself the joys of babyhood—even if these are associated
with such regressive fantasies as escaping it all in the arms of little
sister (in the Gospel according to J. D. Salinger) or flirting with the
possibility of getting into bed with papa (in the Gospel according to
Norman Mailer).

Only Norman O. Brown in *Life Against Death* has come to terms on
the level of theory with the aspiration to take the final evolutionary
leap and cast off adulthood completely, at least in the area of sex. His
post-Freudian program for pan-sexual, non-orgasmic love rejects "full
genitality" in favor of a species of indiscriminate bundling, a dream of
unlimited sub-coital intimacy which Brown calls (in his vocabulary the
term is an honorific) "polymorphous perverse." And here finally is an
essential clue to the nature of the second sexual revolution, the post-
sexual revolution, first evoked in literature by Brother Antoninus
more than a decade ago, in a verse prayer addressed somewhat im-
probably to the Christian God:

Annul in me my manhood, Lord, and make
Me woman sexed and weak . . .
                    Make me then
Girl-hearted, virgin-souled, woman-docile, maiden-meek . . .

Despite the accents of this invocation, however, what is at work is not essentially a homosexual revolt or even a rebellion against women, though its advocates seek to wrest from women their ancient privileges of receiving the Holy Ghost and pleasuring men; and though the attitudes of the movement can be adapted to the anti-female bias of, say, Edward Albee. If in *Who's Afraid of Virginia Woolf?* Albee can portray the relationship of two homosexuals (one in drag) as the model of contemporary marriage, this must be because contemporary marriage has in fact turned into something much like that parody. And it is true that what survives of bourgeois marriage and the bourgeois family is a target which the new barbarians join the old homosexuals in reviling, seeking to replace Mom, Pop and the kids with a neo-Whitmanian gaggle of giggling *camerados*. Such groups are, in fact, whether gathered in coffee houses, university cafeterias or around the literature tables on campuses, the peace-time equivalents, as it were, to the demonstrating crowd. But even their program of displacing Dick-Jane-Spot-Baby, etc., the WASP family of grade school primers, is not the fundamental motive of the post-sexual revolution.

What is at stake from Burroughs to Bellow, Ginsberg to Albee, Salinger to Gregory Corso is a more personal transformation: a radical metamorphosis of the Western male—utterly unforeseen in the decades before us, but visible now in every high school and college classroom, as well as on the paperback racks in airports and supermarkets. All around us, young males are beginning to retrieve for themselves the cavalier role once piously and class-consciously surrendered to women: *that of being beautiful and being loved.* Here once more the example to the Negro—the feckless and adorned Negro male with the blood of Cavaliers in his veins—has served as a model. And what else is left to young men, in any case, after the devaluation of the grim duties they had arrogated to themselves in place of the pursuit of loveliness?

All of us who are middle-aged and were Marxists, which is to say, who once numbered ourselves among the last assured Puritans, have surely noticed in ourselves a vestigial roundhead rage at the new hair

styles of the advanced or—if you please—delinquent young. Watching young men titivate their locks (the comb, the pocket mirror and the
bobby pin having replaced the jackknife, catcher's mitt and brass
knuckles), we feel the same baffled resentment that stirs in us when we
realize that they have rejected work. A job and unequivocal maleness
—these are two sides of the same Calvinist coin, which in the future
buys nothing.

Few of us, however, have really understood how the Beatle hair-do
is part of a syndrome, of which high heels, jeans tight over the buttocks, etc., are other aspects, symptomatic of a larger retreat from
masculine aggressiveness to female allure—in literature and the arts
to the style called "camp." And fewer still have realized how that style,
though the invention of homosexuals, is now the possession of basically heterosexual males as well, a strategy in their campaign to establish a new relationship not only with women but with their own masculinity. In the course of that campaign, they have embraced certain
kinds of gesture and garb, certain accents and tones traditionally associated with females or female impersonators; which is why we have
been observing recently (in life as well as fiction and verse) young
boys, quite unequivocally male, playing all the traditional roles of
women: the vamp, the coquette, the whore, the icy tease, the pure
young virgin.

Not only oldsters, who had envisioned and despaired of quite another future, are bewildered by this turn of events, but young girls, too,
seem scarcely to know what is happening—looking on with that new,
schizoid stare which itself has become a hallmark of our times. And
the crop-headed jocks, those crew-cut athletes who represent an obsolescent masculine style based on quite other values, have tended to
strike back blindly; beating the hell out of some poor kid whose hair is
too long or whose pants are too tight—quite as they once beat up
young Communists for revealing that their politics had become obsolete. Even heterosexual writers, however, have been slow to catch up,
the revolution in sensibility running ahead of that in expression; and
they have perforce permitted homosexuals to speak for them (Burroughs and Genet and Baldwin and Ginsberg and Albee and a score of
others), even to invent the forms in which the future will have to speak.

The revolt against masculinity is not limited, however, to simple
matters of coiffure and costume, visible even to athletes; or to the
adaptation of certain campy styles and modes to new uses. There is

also a sense in which two large social movements that have set the young in motion and furnished images of action for their books—movements as important in their own right as porno-politics and the pursuit of the polymorphous perverse—are connected analogically to the abdication from traditional maleness. The first of these is non-violent or passive resistance, so oddly come back to the land of its inventor, that icy Thoreau who dreamed a love which ". . . has not much human blood in it, but consists with a certain disregard for men and their erections. . . ."

The civil rights movement, however, in which nonviolence has found a home, has been hospitable not only to the sort of post-humanist I have been describing; so that at a demonstration (Selma, Alabama will do as an example) the true hippie will be found side by side with backwoods Baptists, nuns on a spiritual spree, boy bureaucrats practicing to take power, resurrected socialists, Unitarians in search of a God, and just plain tourists, gathered, as once at the Battle of Bull Run, to see the fun. For each of these, nonviolence will have a different sort of fundamental meaning—as a tactic, a camouflage, a passing fad, a pious gesture—but for each in part, and for the post-humanist especially, it will signify the possibility of heroism without aggression, effective action without guilt.

There have always been two contradictory American ideals: to be the occasion of maximum violence, and to remain absolutely innocent. Once, however, these were thought hopelessly incompatible for males (except, perhaps, as embodied in works of art), reserved strictly for women: the spouse of the wife-beater, for instance, or the victim of rape. But males have now assumed these classic roles; and just as a particularly beleaguered wife occasionally slipped over the dividing line into violence, so do the new passive protestors—leaving us to confront (or resign to the courts) such homey female questions as: *Did Mario Savio really bite that cop in the leg as he sagged limply toward the ground?*

The second social movement is the drug cult, more widespread among youth, from its squarest limits to its most beat, than anyone seems prepared to admit in public; and at its beat limit at least inextricably involved with the civil rights movement, as the recent arrests of Peter DeLissovoy and Susan Ryerson revealed even to the ordinary newspaper reader. "Police said that most of the recipients [of marijuana] were college students," the U.P. story runs. "They quoted Miss

Ryerson and DeLissovoy as saying that many of the letter packets were sent to civil rights workers." Only fiction and verse, however, has dealt with the conjunction of homosexuality, drugs and civil rights, eschewing the general piety of the press which has been unwilling to compromise "good works" on behalf of the Negro by associating it with the deep radicalism of a way of life based on the ritual consumption of "pot."

The widespread use of such hallucinogens as peyote, marijuana, the "mexican mushroom," LSD, etc., as well as pep pills, goof balls, airplane glue, certain kinds of cough syrups and even, though in many fewer cases, heroin, is not merely a matter of a changing taste in stimulants but of the programmatic espousal of an anti-puritanical mode of existence—hedonistic and detached—one more strategy in the war on time and work. But it is also (to pursue my analogy once more) an attempt to arrogate to the male certain traditional privileges of the female. What could be more womanly, as Elémire Zolla was already pointing out some years ago, than permitting the penetration of the body by a foreign object which not only stirs delight but even (possibly) creates new life?

In any case, with drugs we have come to the crux of the futurist revolt, the hinge of everything else, as the young tell us over and over in their writing. When the movement was first finding a voice, Allen Ginsberg set this aspect of it in proper context in an immensely comic, utterly serious poem called "America," in which "pot" is associated with earlier forms of rebellion, a commitment to catatonia, and a rejection of conventional male potency:

America I used to be a communist when I was a kid I'm not sorry.
I smoke marijuana every chance I get.
I sit in my house for days on end and stare at the roses in the closet.
When   I   go   to   Chinatown   I . . . never   get   laid . . .

Similarly, Michael McClure reveals in his essay, *"Phi Upsilon Kappa,"* that before penetrating the "cavern of Anglo-Saxon," whence he emerged with the slogan of the ultimate Berkeley demonstrators, he had been on mescalin. "I have emerged from a dark night of the soul; I entered it by Peyote." And by now, drug-taking has become as standard a feature of the literature of the young as oral-genital lovemaking. I flip open the first issue of yet another ephemeral San Francisco little magazine quite at random and read: "I tie up and the main pipe [the ante-cobital vein, for the clinically inclined] swells like a prideful beggar beneath the skin. Just before I get on it is always the worst." Worse than the experience, however, is its literary rendering; and the badness of such confessional fiction, flawed by the sentimentality of those who desire to live "like a cunning vegetable," is a badness we older readers find it only too easy to perceive, as our sons and daughters find it only too easy to overlook. Yet precisely here the age and the mode define themselves; for not in the master but in the hacks new forms are established, new lines drawn.

Here, at any rate, is where the young lose us in literature as well as life, since here they pass over into real revolt, i.e., what we really cannot abide, hard as we try. The mother who has sent her son to private schools and on to Harvard to keep him out of classrooms overcrowded with poor Negroes, rejoices when he sets out for Mississippi with his comrades in SNCC, but shudders when he turns on with LSD; just as the ex-Marxist father, who has earlier proved radicalism impossible, rejoices to see his son stand up, piously and pompously, for CORE or SDS, but trembles to hear him quote Alpert and Leary or praise Burroughs. Just as certainly as liberalism is the LSD of the aging, LSD is the radicalism of the young.

If whiskey long served as an appropriate symbolic excess for those who chafed against Puritan restraint without finally challenging it— temporarily releasing them to socially harmful aggression and (hopefully) sexual self-indulgence, the new popular drugs provide an excess quite as satisfactorily symbolic to the post-Puritans—releasing them from sanity to madness by destroying in them the inner restrictive order which has somehow survived the dissolution of the outer. It is finally insanity, then, that the futurists learn to admire and emulate, quite as they learn to pursue vision instead of learning, hallucination rather than logic. The schizophrenic replaces the sage as their ideal, their new culture hero, figured forth as a giant schizoid Indian (his madness modeled in part on the author's own experiences with LSD) in Ken Kesey's *One Flew Over the Cuckoo's Nest*.

The hippier young are not alone, however, in their taste for the insane; we live in a time when readers in general respond sympathetically to madness in literature wherever it is found, in established writers as well as in those trying to establish new modes. Surely it is not the lucidity and logic of Robert Lowell or Theodore Roethke or John Berryman which we admire, but their flirtation with incoherence and disorder. And certainly it is Mailer at his most nearly psychotic, Mailer the creature rather than the master of his fantasies who moves us to admiration; while in the case of Saul Bellow, we endure the theoretical optimism and acceptance for the sake of the delightful melancholia, the fertile paranoia which he cannot disavow any more than the talent at whose root they lie. Even essayists and analysts recommend themselves to us these days by a certain redemptive nuttiness; at any rate, we do not love, say, Marshall McLuhan less because he continually risks sounding like the body-fluids man in *Dr. Strangelove.*

We have, moreover, recently been witnessing the development of a new form of social psychiatry [1] (a psychiatry of the future already anticipated by the literature of the future) which considers some varieties of "schizophrenia" not diseases to be cured but forays into an unknown psychic world: random penetrations by bewildered internal cosmonauts of a realm that it will be the task of the next generations to explore. And if the accounts which the returning schizophrenics give (the argument of the apologists runs) of the "places" they have been are fantastic and garbled, surely they are no more so than, for example, Columbus' reports of the world he had claimed for Spain, a world bounded—according to his newly drawn maps—by Cathay on the north and Paradise on the south.

In any case, poets and junkies have been suggesting to us that the new world appropriate to the new men of the latter twentieth century is to be discovered only by the conquest of inner space: by an adventure of the spirit, an extension of psychic possibility, of which the flights into outer space—moonshots and expeditions to Mars—are precisely such unwitting metaphors and analogues as the voyages of exploration were of the earlier breakthrough into the Renaissance, from whose consequences the young seek now so desperately to escape. The laureate of that new conquest is William Burroughs; and it is fitting that the final word be his:

"This war will be won in the air. In the Silent Air with Image Rays. You were a pilot remember? Tracer bullets cutting the right wing you were free in space a few seconds before in blue space between eyes. Go back to Silence. Keep Silence. Keep Silence. K.S. K.S. . . . From Silence re-write the message that is you. You are the message I send to The Enemy. My Silent Message."
The Naked Astronauts were free in space. . . .

[1] Described in an article in the *New Left Review* of November–December, 1964, by R. D. Laing, who advocates "ex-patients helping future patients go mad."

42. *From* Growing Up Absurd

PAUL GOODMAN

Paul Goodman (1911–   ) has written novels, short stories and poems, as well as articles and books that speculate about city planning, politics, depth psychology and the nature of literature. He has been a teacher and a lay analyst, but is primarily a social reformer with a commitment to anarchism and a belief in non-violent resistance. Recently he has concerned himself more and more exclusively with the role, status and psychological health of the young in an industrial society, speaking most cogently on these subjects in *Growing Up Absurd* (1960).

"Human Nature" and the Organized System

1

Growing up as a human being, a "human nature" assimilates a culture, just as other animals grow up in strength and habits in the environments that are for them, and that complete their natures. Present-day sociologists and anthropologists don't talk much about this process, and not in this way. Among the most competent writers, there is not much mention of "human nature." Their diffidence makes scientific sense, for everything we observe, and even more important, our way of observing it, is already culture and a pattern of culture. What is the sense of mentioning "human nature" if we can never observe it? The old-fashioned naïve thought, that primitive races or children are more natural, is discounted. And the classical anthropological question, What is Man?—"how like an angel, this quintessence of dust!"—is not now asked by anthropologists. Instead, they commence with a chapter on Physical Anthropology and then forget the whole topic and go on to Culture.

On this view, growing up is sometimes treated as if it were acculturation, the process of giving up one culture for another, the way a tribe of Indians takes on the culture of the whites: so the wild Babies give up their "individualistic" mores and ideology, e.g., selfishness or magic thinking or omnipotence, and join the tribe of Society; they are "socialized." More frequently, however, the matter is left vague: we start with a *tabula rasa* and end up with "socialized" and cultured. ("Becoming cultured" and "being adjusted to the social group" are taken almost as synonymous.) Either way, it follows that you can teach people anything; you can adapt them to anything if you use the right techniques of "socializing" or "communicating." The essence of "human nature" is to be pretty indefinitely malleable. "Man," as C. Wright Mills suggests, is what suits a particular type of society in a particular historical stage.

This fateful idea, invented from time to time by philosophers, seems finally to be empirically evident in the most recent decades. For instance, in our highly organized system of machine production and its corresponding social relations, the practice is, by "vocational guidance," to fit people wherever they are needed in the productive system; and whenever the products of the system need to be used up, the practice is, by advertising, to get people to consume them. This works. There is a man for every job and not many are left over, and the shelves are almost always cleared. Again, in the highly organized political industrial systems of Germany, Russia, and now China, it has been possible in a short time to condition great masses to perform as desired. Social scientists observe that these are the facts, and they also devise theories and techniques to produce more facts like them, for the social scientists too are part of the highly organized systems.

2

Astonishingly different, however, is the opinion of experts who deal with human facts in a more raw, less highly processed, state. Those who have to cope with people in small groups rather than statistically, attending to *them* rather than to some systematic goal—parents and teachers, physicians and psychotherapists, policemen and wardens of jails, shop foremen and grievance committees—these experts are likely to hold stubbornly that there is a "human nature." You can't teach people some things or change them in some ways, and if you persist, you're in for trouble. Contrariwise, if you *don't* provide them with certain things, they'll fill the gaps with eccentric substitutes.

This is immediately evident when something goes wrong; for instance, when a child can't learn to read because he has not yet developed the muscular accommodation of his eyes; if you persist, he withdraws or becomes tricky. Such a case is clear-cut (it is "physical"). But the more important cases have the following form: the child *does* take on the cultural habit, e.g., early toilet training, and indeed the whole corresponding pattern of culture, but there is a diminishing of force, grace, discrimination, intellect, feeling, in specific behaviors or even in his total behavior. He may become too obedient and lacking in initiative, or impractically careful and squeamish; he may develop "psychosomatic" ailments like constipation. Let me give an instance even earlier in life: an infant nurtured in an institution without a particular nurse attending him during the first six months, does not seem to develop abnormally; but if during the end of the first year and for some time thereafter he is not given personal care, he will later be in some ways emotionally cold and unreachable—either some function has failed to develop, or he has already blocked it out as too frustrated and painful. In such examples, the loss of force, grace, and feeling seems to be evidence that somehow the acquired cultural habits do not draw on unimpeded outgoing energy, they are against the grain, they do not fit the child's needs or appetites; *therefore* they have been ill adapted and not assimilated.

That is, on this view we do not need to be able to say what "human nature" *is* in order to be able to say that some training is "against human nature" and you persist in it at peril. Teachers and psychologists who deal practically with growing up and the blocks to growing up may never mention the word "human nature" (indeed, they are better off without too many a priori ideas), but they cling stubbornly to the presumption that at every stage there is a developing potentiality *not* yet cultured, and yet not blank, and that makes possible the taking on of culture. We must draw "it" out, offer "it" opportunities, not violate "it" except for unavoidable reasons. What "it" is, is not definite. It is what, when appealed to in the right circumstances, gives behavior that has force, grace, discrimination, intellect, feeling. This vagueness is of course quite sufficient for education, for education is an art. A good teacher feels his way, looking for response.

3

The concept of "human nature" has had a varied political history in modern times. If we trace it, we can see the present disagreement developing.

In the eighteenth century, the Age of Reason and the early Romantic Movement, the emphasis was on *"human* nature," referring to man's naturally sympathetic sentiments, his communicative faculties, and unalienable dignity. (Immanuel Kant immortally thought up a philosophy to make these cohere.) Now this human nature was powerfully enlisted in revolutionary struggles against courts and classes, poverty and humiliation, and it began to invent progressive education. Human nature unmistakably demanded liberty, equality, and fraternity—and every man a philosopher and poet.

As an heir of the French Revolution, Karl Marx kept much of this concept. Sympathy recurred as solidarity. Dignity and intellect were perhaps still in the future. But he found an important new essential: man is a maker, he must use his productive nature or be miserable. This too involved a revolutionary program, to give back to man his tools.

During the course of the nineteenth century, however, "human nature" came to be associated with conservative and even reactionary politics. The later Romantics were historical minded and found man naturally traditional and not to be uprooted. A few decades later, narrow interpretations of Darwin were being used to support capitalist enterprise; and racial and somatic theories were used to advance imperial and elite interests. (The emphasis was now on *"nature"*; the humanity became dubious.) It was during this later period that the social scientists began to be diffident about "human nature"; for, politically, they wanted fundamental social changes, different from those indicated by the "natural" theory of the survival of the fittest; and, scientifically, it was evident that many anthropological facts were being called natural which were overwhelmingly cultural. Most of the social scientists began to lay all their stress on political organization, to bring about reform. Nevertheless, scientifically trained anarchists like Kropotkin insisted that "human nature"—which had now become mutual-aiding, knightly, and craftsmanlike—was still on the side of revolution.

In our own century, especially since the Twenties and Thirties, the social scientists have found another reason for diffidence: it seems to them that "human nature" implies "not social" and refers to something prior to society, belonging to an isolated individual. They have felt that too much importance has been assigned to Individual Psychology (they were reacting to Freud) and this has stood in the way of organizing people for political reform. It is on this view, finally, that growing up is now interpreted as a process of socializing some rather indefinite kind of animal, and "socializing" is used as a synonym for teaching him the culture.

4

Let us now proceed more carefully, for we are approaching our present plight. *Is* "being socialized," no matter what the society, the same as growing up and assimilating human culture? The society to which one is socialized would have to be a remarkably finished product.

There are here three distinct concepts, which sometimes seem the same but sometimes very different: (1) society as the relations of human social animals, (2) the human culture carried by society, and (3) a particular society, like ours, formed by its pattern of culture and institutions, and to which its members are socialized or adjusted.

In ordinary, static circumstances, and especially when a dominant system in a society is riding high (as the organized system is with us), socializing to that society seems to provide all valuable culture. But *as soon as we think of a fundamental social change,* we begin to say that people are being adjusted, "socialized," to a very limited kind of human society; and our notion of "human culture" at once broadens out to include ancient, exotic, and even primitive models as superior to the conventional standards (as, e.g., our disaffected groups lay store by the Japanese or the Samoans and Trobriand Islanders). Then at once "human nature" is again invoked to prove the necessity of change, for "human nature" has been thwarted or insulted by the dominant system. "Man" can no *longer* be defined as what suits the dominant system, when the dominant system apparently does not suit men.

I think many social scientists have been making an error in logic. Certainly only society is the carrier of culture (it is not inborn). But it does not follow that socialized and cultured are synonymous. What follows, rather, is that, since culture is so overwhelmingly evident in observing mankind, social properties must be of the essence of original "human nature," and indeed that the "isolated individual" is a product of culture.

This, of course, was just the line that Freud really took. Far from having an Individual Psychology, he tended to exaggerate the social nature of the baby by reading into it pre-formed traits of his own society. From the earliest infancy, imitation and emulation, love, striving to communicate, rivalry, exclusiveness and jealousy, punishment, introjected authority, identification, growing up on a model, finding safety in conforming—these were among the conflicting elementary functions of the "human nature" that must grow into culture. And Freud, with magnificent originality, tried to show that by their very conflict they made it possible to assimilate culture; only such a social animal could become cultured. Every step of education was the resolution of a difficult social conflict. As might have been expected, from this hectic theory of human nature were drawn the most various political implications. Some, in the interests of community and sex reform, have wanted fundamental social changes, like Ferenczi and Reich. Others, to save religion, have been ultratraditionalist, like Jung or Laforgue. The run of orthodox psychoanalytic practice has been quietist, as the social scientists claimed. But the most surprising implication has been drawn by the social scientists themselves, when they finally got around to making use of modern psychology: they have found in it techniques for harmoniously belonging to the organized system of society!

A curious thing has occurred. Unlike the majority of their predecessors for a century and a half, most of our contemporary social scientists are not interested in fundamental social change. To them, we have apparently reached the summit of institutional progress, and it only remains for the sociologists and applied-anthropologists to mop up the corners and iron out the kinks. Social scientists are not attracted to the conflictful core of Freud's theory of human nature; a more optimistic theory, like Reich's, is paid no attention at all. But they have hit on the theory I mentioned at the beginning: that you can adapt people to anything, if you use the right techniques. Our social scientists have become so accustomed to the highly organized and by-and-large smoothly running society that they have begun to think that "social animal" means "harmoniously belonging." They do not like to think that fighting and dissenting are proper social functions, nor that rebelling or initiating fundamental change is a social function. Rather, if something does not run smoothly, they say it has been improperly socialized; there has been a failure in communication. The animal part is rarely mentioned at all; if it proves annoying, it too has been inadequately socialized.

5

Nevertheless, we see groups of boys and young men disaffected from the dominant society. The young men are Angry and Beat. The boys are Juvenile Delinquents. These groups are not small, and they will grow larger. Certainly they are suffering. Demonstrably they are not getting enough out of our wealth and civilization. They are not growing up to full capacity. They are failing to assimilate much of the culture. As was predictable, most of the authorities and all of the public spokesmen explain it by saying there has been a failure of socialization. They say that background conditions have interrupted socialization and must be improved. And, not enough effort has been made to guarantee belonging, there must be better bait or punishment.

But perhaps there has *not* been a failure of communication. Perhaps the social message has been communicated clearly to the young men and is unacceptable.

In this book I shall therefore take the opposite tack and ask, "Socialization to what? to what dominant society and available culture?" And if this question is asked, we must at once ask the other question, "Is the harmonious organization to which the young are inadequately socialized, perhaps against human nature, or not worthy of human nature, and *therefore* there is difficulty in growing up?" If this is so, the disaffection of the young is profound and it will not be finally remediable by better techniques of socializing. Instead, there will have to be changes in our society and its culture, so as to meet the appetites and capacities of human nature, in order to grow up.

This brings me to another proposition about growing up, and perhaps the main theme of this book. *Growth, like any ongoing function, requires adequate objects in the environment* to meet the needs and capacities of the growing child, boy, youth, and young man, until he can better choose and make his own environment. It is not a "psychological" question of poor influences and bad attitudes, but an objective question of real opportunities for worthwhile experience. It makes no difference whether the growth is normal or distorted, only real objects will finish the experience. (Even in the psychotherapy of adults one finds that many a stubborn symptom vanishes if there is a real change in the vocational and sexual opportunities, so that the symptom is no longer needed.) It is here that the theory of belonging and socializing breaks down miserably. For it can be shown—I intend to show— that with all the harmonious belonging and all the tidying up of background conditions that you please, our abundant society is at present simply deficient in many of the most elementary objective opportunities and worth-while goals that could make growing up possible. It is lacking in enough man's work. It is lacking in honest public speech, and people are not taken seriously. It is lacking in the opportunity to be useful. It thwarts aptitude and creates stupidity. It corrupts ingenuous patriotism. It corrupts the fine arts. It shackles science. It dampens animal ardor. It discourages the religious convictions of Justification and Vocation and it dims the sense that there is a Creation. It has no Honor. It has no Community.

Just look at that list. There is nothing in it that is surprising, in either the small letters or the capitals. I have nothing subtle or novel to say in this book; these are the things that *everybody* knows. And nevertheless the Governor of New York says, "We must give these young men a sense of belonging."

Thwarted, or starved, in the important objects proper to young capacities, the boys and young men naturally find or invent deviant objects for themselves; this is the beautiful shaping power of our human nature. Their choices and inventions are rarely charming, usually stupid, and often disastrous; we cannot expect average kids to deviate with genius. But on the other hand, the young men who conform to the dominant society become for the most part apathetic, disappointed, cynical, and wasted.

(I say the "young men and boys" rather than the "young people" because the problems I want to discuss in this book belong primarily, in our society, to the boys: how to be useful and make something of oneself. A girl does not *have* to, she is not expected to, "make something" of herself. Her career does not have to be self-justifying, for she will have children, which is absolutely self-justifying, like any other natural or creative act. With this background, it is less important, for instance, what job an average young woman works at till she is married. The quest for the glamour job is given at least a little substance by its relation to a "better" marriage. Correspondingly, our "youth troubles" are boys' troubles—female delinquency is sexual: "incorrigibility" and unmarried pregnancy. Yet as every woman knows, these problems are intensely interesting to women, for if the boys do not grow to be men, where shall the women find men? If the husband is running the rat race of the organized system, there is not much father for the children.)

6

This essay is on "Youth Problems." But the reader will find, perhaps to his surprise, that I shall make little distinction in value between talking about middle-class youths being groomed for ten-thousand-dollar "slots" in business and Madison Avenue, or underprivileged hoodlums fatalistically hurrying to a reformatory; or between hard-working young fathers and idle Beats with beards. For the salient thing is the sameness among them, the waste of humanity. In our society, bright lively children, with the potentiality for knowledge, noble ideals, honest effort, and some kind of worth-while achievement, are transformed into useless and cynical bipeds, or decent young men trapped or early resigned, whether in or out of the organized system. My purpose is a simple one: to show how it is desperately hard these days for an average child to grow up to be a man, for our present organized system of society does not want men. They are not safe. They do not suit.

Our public officials are now much concerned about the "waste of human resources." Dr. Conant, the former president of Harvard, has surveyed the high schools. But our officials are not serious, and Dr. Conant's report is superficial. For the big causes of stupidity, of lack of initiative and lack of honorable incentive, are glaring; yet they do not intend to notice or remedy these big causes. (This very avoidance of the real issues on the part of our public officials is, indeed, one of the big causes.) Our society cannot have it both ways: to maintain a conformist and ignoble system *and* to have skillful and spirited men to man that system with.

7

It is not my purpose in this essay to outline a better world. But I think it requires no deep wisdom or astonishing imagination to know what we need. . . . The prevalent sentiment that it is infinitely impractical to follow the suggestions of common reason, is not sound. If it is impractical, it is because some people don't want to, and the rest of us don't want to enough.

For instance, there is a persistent presumption among our liberal statesmen that the old radical-liberal program has been importantly achieved, and that therefore there is no familiar major proposal practical to remedy admittedly crying ills. This is a false presumption. Throughout the nineteenth and twentieth centuries, the radical-liberal program was continually compromised, curtailed, sometimes realized in form without content, sometimes swept under the rug and heard of no more. I shall later list more than twenty fundamental liberal demands that have gone unfulfilled which would still be live and salutary issues today if anybody wanted to push them. This has occurred, and keeps occurring, by the mutual accommodation of both "liberals" and "conservatives" in the interests of creating our present coalition of semimonopolies, trade unions, government, Madison Avenue, etc. (including a large bloc of outlaw gangsters); thriving on maximum profits and full employment; but without regard for utility, quality, rational productivity, personal freedom, independent enterprise, human scale, manly vocation, or genuine culture. It is in this accommodation that our politicians survive, but it does not make for statesmanship. Even so mild a critic as Henry Steele Commager, in the *New York Times,* judges that we have had only three reputable statesmen in fifty years, the last of whom died fifteen years ago. While one may not agree with his number and examples, there is no doubt that we have been living in a political limbo.

Naturally this unnatural system has generated its own troubles, whether we think of the unlivable communities, the collapse of public ethics, or the problems of youth. I shall try to show in this essay that these ills are by no means inherent in modern technological or ecological conditions, nor in the American Constitution as such. But they have followed precisely from the betrayal and neglect of the old radical-liberal program and other changes proposed to keep up with the advancing technology, the growth of population, and the revolution in morals. Important reforms did not occur when they were ripe, and we have inherited the consequences: a wilderness of unfinished situations, unequal developments and inconsistent standards, as well as new business. And now, sometimes the remedy must be stoically to go back and carry *through* the old programs (as we are having to do with racial integration), e.g., finally to insist on stringent master-planning of cities and conserving of resources, or on really limiting monopolies. Sometimes we must make changes to catch up—e.g., to make the laws more consistent with the sexual revolution, or to make the expenditure on public goods more commensurate with the geometrically increasing complications of a more crowded population. And sometimes, finally, we have to invent really new devices—e.g., how to make the industrial technology humanly important for its workmen, how to use leisure nobly, or even how, in a rich society, to be decently poor if one so chooses.

This book is not about these great subjects. But they hover in the background of the great subject that it is about. For it is impossible for the average boy to grow up and use the remarkable capacities that are in every boy, unless the world is for him and makes sense. And a society makes sense when it understands that its chief wealth *is* these capacities.

Jobs

1

It's hard to grow up when there isn't enough man's work. There is "nearly full employment" (with highly significant exceptions), but there get to be fewer jobs that are necessary or unquestionably useful; that require energy and draw on some of one's best capacities; and that can be done keeping one's honor and dignity. In explaining the widespread troubles of adolescents and young men, this simple objective factor is not much mentioned. Let us here insist on it.

By "man's work" I mean a very simple idea, so simple that it is clearer to ingenuous boys than to most adults. To produce necessary food and shelter is man's work. During most of economic history most men have done this drudging work, secure that it was justified and worthy of a man to do it, though often feeling that the social conditions under which they did it were *not* worthy of a man, thinking, "It's better to die than to live so hard"—but they worked on. When the environment is forbidding, as in the Swiss Alps or the Aran Islands, we regard such work with poetic awe. In emergencies it is heroic, as when the bakers of Paris maintained the supply of bread during the French Revolution, or the milkman did not miss a day's delivery when the bombs recently tore up London.

At present there is little such subsistence work. In *Communitas* my brother and I guess that one-tenth of our economy is devoted to it; it is more likely one-twentieth. Production of food is actively discouraged.

Farmers are not wanted and the young men go elsewhere. (The farm population is now less than 15 per cent of the total population.) Building, on the contrary, is immensely needed. New York City needs 65,000 new units a year, and is getting, net, 16,000. One would think that ambitious boys would flock to this work. But here we find that building, too, is discouraged. In a great city, for the lasty twenty years hundreds of thousands have been ill housed, yet we do not see science, industry, and labor enthusiastically enlisted in finding the quick solution to a definite problem. The promoters are interested in long-term investments, the real estate men in speculation, the city planners in votes and graft. The building craftsmen cannily see to it that their own numbers remain few, their methods antiquated, and their rewards high. None of these people is much interested in providing shelter, and nobody is at all interested in providing new manly jobs.

Once we turn away from the absolutely necessary subsistence jobs, however, we find that an enormous proportion of our production is not even unquestionably useful. Everybody knows and also feels this, and there has recently been a flood of books about our surfeit of honey, our insolent chariots, the follies of exurban ranch houses, our hucksters and our synthetic demand. Many acute things are said about this useless production and advertising, but not much about the workmen producing it and their frame of mind; and nothing at all, so far as I have noticed, about the plight of a young fellow looking for a manly occupation. The eloquent critics of the American way of life have themselves been so seduced by it that they think only in terms of selling commodities and point out that the goods are valueless; but they fail to see that people are being wasted and their skills insulted. (To give an analogy, in the many gleeful onslaughts on the Popular Culture that have appeared in recent years, there has been little thought of the plight of the honest artist cut off from his audience and sometimes, in public arts such as theater and architecture, from his medium.)

What is strange about it? American society has tried so hard and so ably to defend the practice and theory of production for profit and not primarily for use that now it has succeeded in making its jobs and products profitable and useless.

2

Consider a likely useful job. A youth who is alert and willing but not "verbally intelligent"—perhaps he has quit high school at the eleventh grade (the median), as soon as he legally could—chooses for auto mechanic. That's a good job, familiar to him, he often watched them as a kid. It's careful and dirty at the same time. In a small garage its's sociable; one can talk to the customers (girls). You please people in trouble by fixing their cars, and a man is proud to see rolling out on its own the car that limped in behind the tow truck. The pay is as good as the next fellow's, who is respected.

So our young man takes this first-rate job. But what when he then learns that the cars have a built-in obsolescence, that the manufacturers do not want them to be repaired or repairable? They have lobbied a law that requires them to provide spare parts for only five years (it used to be ten). Repairing the new cars is often a matter of cosmetics, not mechanics; and the repairs are pointlessly expensive—a tail fin might cost $150. The insurance rates therefore double and treble on old and new cars both. Gone are the days of keeping the jalopies in good shape, the artist-work of a proud mechanic. But everybody is paying for foolishness, for in fact the new models are only trivially superior; the whole thing is a sell.

It is hard for the young man now to maintain his feelings of justification, sociability, serviceability. It is not surprising if he quickly becomes cynical and time-serving, interested in a fast buck. And so, on the notorious *Reader's Digest* test, the investigators (coming in with a disconnected coil wire) found that 63 per cent of mechanics charged for repairs they didn't make, and lucky if they didn't also take out the new fuel pump and replace it with a used one (65 per cent of radio repair shops, but *only* 49 per cent of watch repairmen "lied, overcharged, or gave false diagnoses").

There is an hypothesis that an important predisposition to juvenile delinquency is the combination of low verbal intelligence with high manual intelligence, delinquency giving a way of self-expression where other avenues are blocked by lack of schooling. A lad so endowed might well apply himself to the useful trade of mechanic.

3

Most manual jobs do not lend themselves so readily to knowing the facts and fraudulently taking advantage oneself. In factory jobs the workman is likely to be ignorant of what goes on, since he performs a small operation on a big machine that he does not understand. Even so, there is evidence that he has the same disbelief in the enterprise as a whole, with a resulting attitude of profound indifference.

Semiskilled factory operatives are the largest category of workmen. (I am leafing through the U. S. Department of Labor's *Occupational Outlook Handbook,* 1957.) Big companies have tried the devices of applied anthropology to enhance the loyalty of these men to the firm, but apparently the effort is hopeless, for it is found that a thumping majority of the men don't care about the job or the firm; they couldn't care less and you can't make them care more. But this is *not* because of wages, hours, or working conditions, or management. On the contrary, tests that show the men's indifference to the company show also their (unaware) admiration for the way the company has designed and manages the plant; it is their very model of style, efficiency, and correct behavior. (Robert Dubin, for the U. S. Public Health Service.) Maybe if the men understood more, they would admire less. The union and the grievance committee take care of wages, hours, and conditions; these are the things the workmen themselves fought for and won. (Something was missing in that victory, and we have inherited the failure as well as the success.) The conclusion must be that workmen are indifferent to the job because of its intrinsic nature: it does not enlist worth-while capacities, it is not "interesting"; it is not his, he is not "in" on it; the product is not really useful. And indeed, research directly on the subject, by Frederick Herzberg on Motivation to Work, shows that it is defects in the intrinsic aspects of the job that make workmen "unhappy." A survey of the literature (in Herzberg's *Job Attitudes*) shows that Interest is second in importance only to Security, whereas Wages, Conditions, Socializing, Hours, Ease, and Benefits are far less important. But foremen, significantly enough, think that the most important thing to the workman is his wages. (The investigators do not seem to inquire about the usefulness of the job—as if a primary purpose of *working* at a job were not that it is good *for* something!) My guess is that a large factor in "Security" is the resigned reaction to not being able to take into account whether the work of one's hands is useful for anything; for in a normal life situation, if what we do is useful, we feel secure about being needed. The other largest factor in "Security" is, I think, the sense of being needed for one's unique contribution, and this is measured in these tests by the primary importance the workers assign to being "in" on things and to "work done being appreciated." (Table prepared by Labor Relations Institute of New York.)

Limited as they are, what a remarkable insight such studies give us, that men want to do valuable work and work that is somehow theirs! But they are thwarted.

Is not this the "waste of our human resources"?

The case is that by the "sole-prerogative" clause in union contracts the employer has the sole right to determine what is to be produced, how it is to be produced, what plants are to be built and where, what kinds of machinery are to be installed, when workers are to be hired and laid off, and how production operations are to be rationalized. (Frank Marquart.) There is *none* of this that is inevitable in running a machine economy; but *if* these are the circumstances, it is not surprising that the factory operatives' actual code has absolutely nothing to do with useful service or increasing production, but is notoriously devoted to "interpersonal relations"; (1) don't turn out too much work; (2) don't turn out too little work; (3) don't squeal on a fellow worker; (4) don't act like a big-shot. This is how to belong.

4

Let us go on to the Occupational Outlook of those who are verbally bright. Among this group, simply because they cannot help asking more general questions—e.g., about utility—the problem of finding man's work is harder, and their disillusion is more poignant.

> *He explained to her why it was hard to find a satisfactory job of work to do. He had liked working with the power drill, testing the rocky envelope of the shore, but then the employers asked him to take a great oath of loyalty.*
>
> *"What!" cried Rosalind. "Do you have scruples about telling a convenient fib?"*
>
> *"No, I don't. But I felt uneasy about the sanity of the director asking me to swear to opinions on such complicated questions when my job was digging with a power drill. I can't work with a man who might suddenly have a wild fit."*
>
> *. . . "Why don't you get a job driving one of the big trucks along here?"*
>
> *"I don't like what's in the boxes," said Horatio sadly. "It could just as well drop in the river—and I'd make mistakes and drop it there."*
>
> *"Is it bad stuff?"*
>
> *"No, just useless. It takes the heart out of me to work at something useless*

*and I begin to make mistakes. I don't mind putting profits in somebody's
pocket—but the job also has to be useful for something."*
     . . . *"Why don't you go to the woods and be a lumberjack?"*
"No! they chop down the trees just to print off the New York Times!"
                                                    (*The Empire City,* III, i, 3.)

The more intelligent worker's "indifference" is likely to appear more
nakedly as profound resignation, and his cynicism may sharpen to out-
right racketeering.

"Teaching," says the *Handbook,* "is the largest of the professions."
So suppose our now verbally bright young man chooses for teacher, in
the high school system or, by exception, in the elementary schools if he
understands that the elementary grades are the vitally important ones
and require the most ability to teach well (and of course they have less
prestige). Teaching is necessary and useful work; it is real and creative, for it directly confronts an important subject matter, the children themselves; it is obviously self-justifying; and it is ennobled by
the arts and sciences. Those who practice teaching do not for the most
part succumb to cynicism or indifference—the children are too immediate and real for the teachers to become callous—but, most of the
school systems being what they are, can teachers fail to come to suffer
first despair and then deep resignation? Resignation occurs psychologically as follows: frustrated in essential action, they nevertheless cannot quit in anger, because the task is necessary; so the anger turns inward and is felt as resignation. (Naturally, the resigned teacher may
then put on a happy face and keep very busy.)

For the job is carried on under impossible conditions of overcrowding and saving public money. *Not* that there is not enough social
wealth, but first things are not put first. Also, the school system has
spurious aims. It soon becomes clear that the underlying aims are to
relieve the home and keep the kids quiet; or, suddenly, the aim is to
produce physicists. Timid supervisors, bigoted clerics, and ignorant
school boards forbid real teaching. The emotional release and sexual
expression of the children are taboo. A commercially debauched popular culture makes learning disesteemed. The academic curriculum is
mangled by the demands of reactionaries, liberals, and demented warriors. Progressive methods are emasculated. Attention to each case is
out of the question, and all the children—the bright, the average, and
the dull—are systematically retarded one way or another, while the
teacher's hands are tied. Naturally the pay is low—for the work is

hard, useful, and of public concern, all three of which qualities tend to bring lower pay. It is alleged that the low pay is why there is a shortage of teachers and why the best do not choose the profession. My guess is that the best avoid it because of the certainty of miseducating. Nor are the best *wanted* by the system, for they are not safe. Bertrand Russell was rejected by New York's City College and would not have been accepted in a New York grade school.

5

Next, what happens to the verbally bright who have no zeal for a serviceable profession and who have no particular scientific or artistic bent? For the most part they make up the tribes of salesmanship, entertainment, business management, promotion, and advertising. Here of course there is no question of utility or honor to begin with, so an ingenuous boy will not look here for a manly career. Nevertheless, though we can pass by the sufferings of these well-paid callings, much publicized by their own writers, they are important to our theme because of the model they present to the growing boy.

Consider the men and women in TV advertisements, demonstrating the product and singing the jingle. They are clowns and mannequins, in grimace, speech, and action. And again, what I want to call attention to in this advertising is not the economic problem of synthetic demand, and not the cultural problem of Popular Culture, but the human problem that these are human beings working as clowns; that the writers and designers of it are human beings thinking like idiots; and the broadcasters and underwriters know and abet what goes on—

> *Juicily glubbily*
> Blubber *is dubbily*
> *delicious and nutritious*
> *—eat it, Kitty, it's good.*

Alternately, they are liars, confidence men, smooth talkers, obsequious, insolent, etc., etc.

The popular-cultural content of the advertisements is somewhat neutralized by *Mad* magazine, the bible of the twelve-year-olds who can read. But far more influential and hard to counteract is the *fact* that the workmen and the patrons of this enterprise are human beings. (Highly approved, too.) They are not good models for a boy looking for a manly job that is useful and necessary, requiring human energy and capacity, and that can be done with honor and dignity. They are a good sign that not many such jobs will be available.

The popular estimation is rather different. Consider the following: "As one possible aid, I suggested to the Senate subcommittee that they alert celebrities and leaders in the fields of sports, movies, theater and television to the help they can offer by getting close to these [delinquent] kids. By giving them positive 'heroes' they know and can talk to, instead of the misguided image of trouble-making buddies, they could aid greatly in guiding these normal aspirations for fame and status into wholesome progressive channels." (Jackie Robinson, who was formerly on the Connecticut Parole Board.) Or again: when a mass cross-section of Oklahoma high school juniors and seniors was asked which living person they would like to be, the boys named Pat Boone, Ricky Nelson, and President Eisenhower; the girls chose Debbie Reynolds, Elizabeth Taylor, and Natalie Wood.

The rigged Quiz shows, which created a scandal in 1959, were a remarkably pure distillate of our American cookery. We start with the brute facts that (a) in our abundant expanding economy it is necessary to give money away to increase spending, production, and profits; and (b) that this money must not be used for useful public goods in taxes, but must be plowed back as "business expenses," even though there is a shameful shortage of schools, housing, etc. Yet when the TV people at first tried simply to give the money away for nothing (for having heard of George Washington), there was a great Calvinistic outcry that this was demoralizing (we may gamble on the horses only to improve the breed). So they hit on the notion of a real contest with prizes. But then, of course, they could not resist making the show itself profitable, and competitive in the (also rigged) ratings with other shows, so the experts in the entertainment-commodity manufactured phony contests. And to cap the climax of fraudulence, the hero of the phony contests proceeded to persuade himself, so he says, that his behavior was educational!

The behavior of the networks was correspondingly typical. These business organizations claim the loyalty of their employees, but at the first breath of trouble they were ruthless and disloyal to their employees. (Even McCarthy was loyal to his gang.) They want to maximize profits and yet be absolutely safe from any risk. Consider their claim that they knew nothing about the fraud. But if they watched the shows that they were broadcasting, they could not *possibly,* as professionals, not have known the facts, for there were obvious type-casting, acting, plot, etc. If they are not professionals, they are incompetent. But if they don't watch what they broadcast, then they are utterly irresponsible and on what grounds do they have the franchises to the channels? We may offer them the choice: that they are liars or incompetent or irresponsible.

The later direction of the investigation seems to me more important, the inquiry into the bribed disk-jockeying; for this deals directly with our crucial economic problem of synthesized demand, made taste, debauching the public and preventing the emergence and formation of natural taste. In such circumstances there cannot possibly be an American culture; we are doomed to nausea and barbarism. And *then* these baboons have the effrontery to declare that they give the people what the people demand and that they are not responsible for the level of the movies, the music, the plays, the books!

Finally, in leafing through the *Occupational Outlook Handbook*, we notice that the armed forces employ a large number. Here our young man can become involved in a world-wide demented enterprise, with personnel and activities corresponding.

6

Thus, on the simple criteria of unquestioned utility, employing human capacities, and honor, there are not enough worthy jobs in our economy for average boys and adolescents to grow up toward. There are of course thousands of jobs that are worthy and self-justifying, and thousands that can be made so by stubborn integrity, especially if one can work as an independent. Extraordinary intelligence or special talent, also, can often carve out a place for itself—conversely, their usual corruption and waste are all the more sickening. But by and large our economic society is *not* geared for the cultivation of its young or the attainment of important goals that they can work toward.

This is evident from the usual kind of vocational guidance, which consists of measuring the boy and finding some place in the economy where he can be fitted; chopping him down to make him fit; or neglecting him if they can't find his slot. Personnel directors do not much try to scrutinize the economy in order to find some activity that is a real opportunity for the boy, and then to create an opportunity if they can't find one. To do this would be an horrendous task; I am not sure it could be done if we wanted to do it. But the question is whether anything less makes sense if we mean to speak seriously about the troubles of the young men.

Surely by now, however, many readers are objecting that this entire argument is pointless because people in *fact* don't think of their jobs in this way at all. *Nobody* asks if a job is useful or honorable (within the limits of business ethics). A man gets a job that pays well, or well enough, that has prestige, and good conditions, or at least tolerable conditions. I agree with these objections as to the fact. (I hope we are wrong.) But *the question is what it means to grow up into such a fact as: "During my productive years I will spend eight hours a day doing what is no good."*

7

Yet, economically and vocationally, a very large population of the young people are in a plight more drastic than anything so far mentioned. In our society as it is, there are not enough worthy jobs. But if our society, being as it is, were run more efficiently and soberly, for a majority there would soon not be any jobs at all. There is at present nearly full employment and there may be for some years, yet a vast number of young people are rationally unemployable, useless. This paradox is essential to explain their present temper.

Our society, which is not geared to the cultivation of its young, *is* geared to a profitable expanding production, a so-called high standard of living of mediocre value, and the maintenance of nearly full employment. Politically, the chief of these is full employment. In a crisis, when profitable production is temporarily curtailed, government spending increases and jobs are manufactured. In "normalcy"—a condition of slow boom—the easy credit, installment buying, and artificially induced demand for useless goods create jobs for all and good profits for some.

Now, back in the Thirties, when the New Deal attempted by hook or crook to put people back to work and give them money to revive the shattered economy, there was an outcry of moral indignation from the conservatives that many of the jobs were "boondoggling," useless made-work. It was insisted, and rightly, that such work was demoralizing to the workers themselves. It is a question of a word, but a candid critic might certainly say that many of the jobs in our present "normal" production are useless made-work. The tail fins and built-in obsolescence might be called boondoggling. The $64,000 Question and the busy hum of Madison Avenue might certainly be called boondoggling. Certain tax-dodge Foundations are boondoggling. What of business lunches and expense accounts? fringe benefits? the comic categories of occupation in the building trades? the extra stagehands and musicians of the theater crafts? These jolly devices to put money back to work no doubt have a demoralizing effect on somebody or other (certainly on me, they make me green with envy), but where is the moral indignation from Top Management?

Suppose we would cut out the boondoggling and gear our society to a more sensible abundance, with efficient production of quality goods, distribution in a natural market, counterinflation and sober credit. At once the work week would be cut to, say, twenty hours instead of forty. (Important People have already mentioned the figure thirty.) Or alternately, half the labor force would be unemployed. Suppose too—and how can we not suppose it?—that the automatic machines are used generally, rather than just to get rid of badly organized unskilled labor. The unemployment will be still more drastic.

(To give the most striking example: in steel, the annual increase in productivity is 4 per cent, the plants work at 50 per cent of capacity, and the companies can break even and stop producing at *less than 30 per cent* of capacity. These are the conditions that forced the steel strike, as desperate self-protection.—Estes Kefauver, quoting Gardiner Means and Fred Gardner.)

Everybody knows this, nobody wants to talk about it much, for we don't know how to cope with it. The effect is that we are living a kind of lie. Long ago, labor leaders used to fight for the shorter work week, but now they don't, because they're pretty sure they don't want it. Indeed, when hours are reduced, the tendency is to get a second, part-time, job and raise the standard of living, *because* the job is meaningless and one must have something; but the standard of living is pretty meaningless, too. Nor is this strange atmosphere a new thing. For at least a generation the maximum sensible use of our productivity could have thrown a vast population out of work, or relieved everybody of a lot of useless work, depending on how you take it. (Consider with how little cutback of useful civilian production the economy produced the war goods and maintained an Army, economically unemployed.) The plain truth is that at present very many of us are useless, not needed, rationally unemployable. It is in this paradoxical atmosphere that young persons grow up. It looks busy and expansive, but it is rationally at a stalemate.

8

These considerations apply to all ages and classes; but it is of course among poor youth (and the aged) that they show up first and worst. They are the most unemployable. For a long time our society has not been geared to the cultivation of the young. In our country 42 per cent have graduated from high school (predicted census, 1960); less than 8 per cent have graduated from college. The high school trend for at least the near future is not much different: there will be a high proportion of drop-outs before the twelfth grade; but *markedly more* of the rest will go on to college; that is, the stratification will harden. Now the schooling in neither the high schools nor the colleges is much good — if it were better more kids would stick to it; yet at present, if we made a list we should find that a large proportion of the dwindling number of unquestionably useful or self-justifying jobs, in the humane professions and the arts and sciences, require education; and in the future, there is no doubt that the more educated will have the jobs, in running an efficient, highly technical economy and an administrative society placing a premium on verbal skills.

(Between 1947 and 1957, professional and technical workers increased 61 per cent, clerical workers 23 per cent, but factory operatives only 4 ½ per cent and laborers 4 per cent.—Census.)

For the uneducated there will be no jobs at all. This is humanly most unfortunate, for presumably those who have learned something in schools, and have the knack of surviving the boredom of those schools, could also make something of idleness; whereas the uneducated are useless at leisure too. It takes application, a fine sense of value, and a powerful community-spirit for a people to have serious leisure, and this has not been the genius of the Americans.

From this point of view we can sympathetically understand the pathos of our American school policy, which otherwise seems so inexplicable; at great expense compelling kids to go to school who do not want to and who will not profit by it. There are of course unpedagogic motives, like relieving the home, controlling delinquency, and keeping kids from competing for jobs. But there is also this desperately earnest pedagogic motive, of preparing the kids to take *some* part in a democratic society that does not need them. Otherwise, what will become of them, if they don't know anything?

Compulsory public education spread universally during the nineteenth century to provide the reading, writing, and arithmetic necessary to build a modern industrial economy. With the overmaturity of the economy, the teachers are struggling to preserve the elementary system when the economy no longer requires it and is stingy about paying for it. The demand is for scientists and technicians, the 15 per cent of the "academically talented." "For a vast majority [in the high schools]," says Dr. Conant in *The Child, the Parent, and the State,* "the vocational courses are the vital core of the program. They represent something related directly to the ambitions of the boys and girls." But somehow, far more than half of these quit. How is that?

9

Let us sum up again. The majority of young people are faced with the following alternative: Either society is a benevolently frivolous racket in which they'll manage to boondoggle, though less profitably than the more privileged; or society is serious (and they hope still benevolent enough to support them), but they are useless and hopelessly out. Such thoughts do not encourage productive life. Naturally young people are more sanguine and look for man's work, but few find it. Some settle for a "good job"; most settle for a lousy job; a few, but an increasing number, don't settle.

I often ask, "What do you want to work at? If you have the chance. When you get out of school, college, the service, etc."

Some answer right off and tell their definite plans and projects, highly approved by Papa. I'm pleased for them, but it's a bit boring, because they are such squares.

Quite a few will, with prompting, come out with astounding stereotyped, conceited fantasies, such as becoming a movie actor when they are "discovered"—"like Marlon Brando, but in my own way."

Very rarely somebody will, maybe defiantly and defensively, maybe diffidently but proudly, make you know that he knows very well what he is going to do; it is something great; and he is indeed already doing it, which is the real test.

The usual answer, perhaps the normal answer, is "I don't know," meaning, "I'm looking; I haven't found the right thing; it's discouraging but not hopeless."

But the terrible answer is, "Nothing." The young man doesn't want to do anything.

—I remember talking to half a dozen young fellows at Van Wagner's Beach outside of Hamilton, Ontario; and all of them had this one thing to say: "Nothing." They didn't believe that what to work at was the kind of thing one *wanted*. They rather expected that two or three of them would work for the electric company in town, but they couldn't care less. I turned away from the conversation abruptly because of the uncontrollable burning tears in my eyes and constriction in my chest. Not feeling sorry for them, but tears of frank dismay for the waste of our humanity (they were nice kids). And it is out of that incident that many years later I am writing this book.

43. The Third Presidential Paper—The Existential Hero: Superman Comes to the Supermarket

NORMAN MAILER

Norman Mailer (1923–   ) is perhaps better known as a novelist than anything else. Certainly, he first made his reputation with *The Naked and the Dead* (1948) and (with a ten-year dry spell) has continued to write fiction ever since, his latest novel being *Why Are We in Vietnam?* (1967). But he has also written poetry and drama, has ventured into film-making, and is a first-class journalist on the subjects of boxing and politics in general. In this latter field he has now forged a new style and almost a new genre—that of the documentary essay—in *Armies of the Night,* on the October, 1967, march on the Pentagon, and in *Miami and the Siege of Chicago.* What distinguishes him as an essayist is his unwillingness ever to sacrifice his personal voice to a quest for objectivity or authority.

SOURCE: Norman Mailer, *The Presidential Papers* (New York: G. P. Putnam's Sons, 1963), pp. 25–57. Copyright © 1960, 1961, 1962, 1963 by Norman Mailer. Reprinted by permission of G. P. Putnam's Sons.

Not too much need be said for this piece; it is possible it can stand by itself. But perhaps its title should have been "Filling the Holes in No Man's Land."

American politics is rarely interesting for its men, its ideas, or the style of its movements. It is usually more fascinating in its gaps, its absences, its uninvaded territories. We have used up our frontier, but the psychological frontier talked about in this piece is still alive with untouched possibilities and dire unhappy all-but-lost opportunities. In European politics the spaces are filled—the average politician, like the average European, knows what is possible and what is impossible for him. Their politics is like close trench warfare. But in America, one knows such close combat only for the more banal political activities. The play of political ideas is flaccid here in America because opposing armies never meet. The Right, the Center, and what there is of the Left have set up encampments on separate hills, they face one another across valleys, they send out small patrols to their front and vast communiqués to their rear. No Man's Land predominates. It is a situation which calls for guerrilla raiders. Any army which would dare to enter the valley in force might not only determine a few new political formations, but indeed could create more politics itself, even as the guerrilla raids of the Negro Left and Negro Right, the Freedom Riders and the Black Muslims, have discovered much of the secret nature of the American reality for us.

I wonder if I make myself clear. Conventional politics has had so little to do with the real subterranean life of America that none of us know much about the real—which is to say the potential—*historic nature of America. That lies buried under apathy, platitudes, Rightist encomiums for the FBI, programmatic welfare from the liberal Center, and furious pips of protest from the Peace Movement's Left. The mass of Americans are not felt as a political reality. No one has any idea of how they would react to radically new sense. It is only when their heart-land, their no man's land, their valley is invaded, that one discovers the reality. In Birmingham during the days of this writing, the jails are filled with Negro children, 2000 of them. The militancy of the Negroes in Birmingham is startling, so too is the stubbornness of the Southern white, so too and unbelievable is the procrastination of the Kennedy administration. Three new realities have been discovered. The potential Left and potential Right of America are more vigorous than one would have expected and the Center is more irreso-*

lute. An existential political act, the drive by Southern Negroes, led by Martin Luther King, to end segregation in restaurants in Birmingham, an act which is existential precisely because its end is unknown, has succeeded en route in discovering more of the American reality to us.

If a public speaker in a small Midwestern town were to say, "J. Edgar Hoover has done more harm to the freedoms of America than Joseph Stalin," the act would be existential. Depending on the occasion and the town, he would be manhandled physically or secretly applauded. But he would create a new reality which would displace the old psychological reality that such a remark could not be made, even as for example the old Southern psychological reality that you couldn't get two Negroes to do anything together, let alone two thousand has now been destroyed by a new and more accurate psychological reality: you can get two thousand Negroes to work in cooperation. The new psychological realities are closer to history and so closer to sanity and they exist because, and only because, the event has taken place.

It was Kennedy's potentiality to excite such activity which interested me most; that he was young, that he was physically handsome, and that his wife was attractive were not trifling accidental details but, rather, new major political facts. I knew if he became President, it would be an existential event: he would touch depths in American life which were uncharted. Regardless of his politics, and even then one could expect his politics would be as conventional as his personality was unconventional, indeed one could expect his politics to be pushed toward conventionality precisely to counteract his essential unconventionality, one knew nonetheless that regardless of his overt politics, America's tortured psychotic search for security would finally be torn loose from the feverish ghosts of its old generals, its MacArthurs and Eisenhowers—ghosts which Nixon could cling to—and we as a nation would finally be loose again in the historic seas of a national psyche which was willy-nilly and at last, again, adventurous. And that, I thought, that was the hope for America. So I swallowed my doubts, my disquiets, and my certain distastes for Kennedy's dullness of mind and prefabricated politics, and did my best to write a piece which would help him to get elected.

For once let us try to think about a political convention without losing ourselves in housing projects of fact and issue. Politics has its virtues, all too many of them—it would not rank with baseball as a topic of conversation if it did not satisfy a great many things—but one can suspect that its secret appeal is close to nicotine. Smoking cigarettes insulates one from one's life, one does not feel as much, often happily so, and politics quarantines one from history; most of the people who nourish themselves in the political life are in the game not to make history but to be diverted from the history which is being made.

If that Democratic Convention which has now receded behind the brow of the Summer of 1960 is only half-remembered in the excitements of moving toward the election, it may be exactly the time to consider it again, because the mountain of facts which concealed its features last July has been blown away in the winds of High Television, and the man-in-the-street (that peculiar political term which refers to the quixotic voter who will pull the lever for some reason so salient as: "I had a brown-nose lieutenant once with Nixon's looks," or "that Kennedy must have false teeth"), the not so easily estimated man-in-the-street has forgotten most of what happened and could no more tell you who Kennedy was fighting against than you or I could place a bet on who was leading the American League in batting during the month of June.

So to try to talk about what happened is easier now than in the days of the convention, one does not have to put everything in—an act of writing which calls for a bulldozer rather than a pen—one can try to make one's little point and dress it with a ribbon or two of metaphor. All to the good. Because mysteries are irritated by facts, and the 1960 Democratic Convention began as one mystery and ended as another.

Since mystery is an emotion which is repugnant to a political animal (why else lead a life of bad banquet dinners, cigar smoke, camp chairs, foul breath, and excruciatingly dull jargon if not to avoid the echoes of what is not known), the psychic separation between what was happening on the floor, in the caucus rooms, in the headquarters, and what was happening in parallel to the history of the nation was mystery enough to drown the proceedings in gloom. It was on the one hand a dull convention, one of the less interesting by general agreement, relieved by local bits of color, given two half hours of excitement by two demonstrations for Stevenson, buoyed up by the class of the Kennedy machine, turned by the surprise of Johnson's nomination as vice-president, but, all the same, dull, depressed in its over-all tone, the big fiestas subdued, the gossip flat, no real air of excitement, just moments —or as they say in bullfighting—details. Yet it was also, one could argue—and one may argue this yet—it was also one of the most important conventions in America's history, it could prove conceivably to be the most important. The man it nominated was unlike any politician who had ever run for President in the history of the land, and if elected he would come to power in a year when America was in danger of drifting into a profound decline.

A Descriptive of the Delegates: Sons and Daughters of the Republic in a Legitimate Panic; Small-time Practitioners of Small-town Political Judo in the Big Town and the Big Time

Depression obviously has its several roots: it is the doubtful protection which comes from not recognizing failure, it is the psychic burden of exhaustion, and it is also, and very often, that discipline of the will or the ego which enables one to continue working when one's unadmitted emotion is panic. And panic it was I think which sat as the largest single sentiment in the breast of the collective delegates as they came to convene in Los Angeles. Delegates are not the noblest sons and daughters of the Republic; a man of taste, arrived from Mars, would take one look at a convention floor and leave forever, convinced he had seen one of the drearier squats of Hell. If one still smells the faint living echo of a carnival wine, the pepper of a bullfight, the rag, drag, and panoply of a jousting tourney, it is all swallowed and regurgitated by the senses into the fouler cud of a death gas one must rid oneself of —a cigar-smoking, stale-aired, slack-jawed, butt-littered, foul, bleak, hard-working, bureaucratic death gas of language and faces ("Yes, those *faces*," says the man from Mars: lawyers, judges, ward heelers, *mafiosos,* Southern goons and grandees, grand old ladies, trade unionists and finks), of pompous words and long pauses which lay like a leaden pain over fever, the fever that one is in, over, or is it that one is just behind history? A legitimate panic for a delegate. America is a nation of experts without roots; we are always creating tacticians who are blind to strategy and strategists who cannot take a step, and when the culture has finished its work the institutions handcuff the infirmity. A delegate is a man who picks a candidate for the largest office in the land, a President who must live with problems whose borders are in ethics, metaphysics, and now ontology; the delegate is prepared for this office of selection by emptying wastebaskets, toting garbage and saying yes at the right time for twenty years in the small political machine of some small or large town; his reward, one of them anyway, is that he arrives at an invitation to the convention. An expert on local catch-as-catch-can, a small-time, often mediocre practitioner of small-town political judo, he comes to the big city with nine-tenths of his mind made up, he will follow the orders of the boss who brought him. Yet of course it is not altogether so mean as that: his opinion is listened to—the boss will consider what he has to say as one interesting factor among five hundred, and what is most important to the delegate, he has the illusion of partial freedom. He can, unless he is severely honest with himself—and if he is, why sweat out the low levels of a political machine?—he can have the illusion that he has helped to choose the candidate, he can even worry most sincerely about his choice, flirt with defection from the boss, work out his own small political gains by the road of loyalty or the way of hard bargain. But even if he is there for no more than the ride, his vote a certainty in the mind of the political boss, able to be thrown here or switched there as the boss decides, still in some peculiar sense he is reality to the boss, the delegate is the great American public, the bar he owns or the law practice, the piece of the union he represents, or the real-estate office, is a part of the political landscape which the boss uses as his own image of how the votes will go, and if the people will like the candidate. And if the boss is depressed by what he sees, if the candidate does not feel right to him, if he has a dull intimation that the candidate is not his sort (as, let us say, Harry Truman was his sort, or Symington might be his sort, or Lyndon Johnson), then vote for him the boss will if he must; he cannot be caught on the wrong side, but he does not feel the pleasure of a personal choice. Which is the center of the panic. Because if the boss is depressed, the delegate is doubly depressed, and the emotional fact is that Kennedy is not in focus, not in the old political focus, he is not comfortable; in fact it is a mystery to the boss how Kennedy got to where he is, not a mystery in its structures; Kennedy is rolling in money, Kennedy got the votes in primaries, and, most of all, Kennedy has a jewel of a political machine. It is as good as a crack Notre Dame team, all discipline and savvy and go-go-go, sound, drilled, never dull, quick as a knife, full of the salt of hipper-dipper, a beautiful machine; the boss could adore it if only a sensible candidate were driving it, a Truman, even a Stevenson, please God a Northern Lyndon Johnson, but it is run by a man who looks young enough to be coach of the

Freshman team, and that is not comfortable at all. The boss knows political machines, he knows issues, farm parity, Forand health bill, Landrum-Griffin, but this is not all so adequate after all to revolutionaries in Cuba who look like beatniks, competitions in missiles, Negroes looting whites in the Congo, intricacies of nuclear fallout, and NAACP men one does well to call Sir. It is all out of hand, everything important is off the center, foreign affairs is now the lick of the heat, and senators are candidates instead of governors, a disaster to the old family style of political measure where a political boss knows his governor and knows who his governor knows. So the boss is depressed, profoundly depressed. He comes to this convention resigned to nominating a man he does not understand, or let us say that, so far as he understands the candidate who is to be nominated, he is not happy about the secrets of his appeal, not so far as he divines these secrets; they seem to have too little to do with politics and all too much to do with the private madnesses of the nation which had thousands—or was it hundreds of thousands—of people demonstrating in the long night before Chessman was killed, and a movie star, the greatest, Marlon the Brando out in the night with them. Yes, this candidate for all his record, his good, sound, conventional liberal record has a patina of that other life, the second American life, the long electric night with the fires of neon leading down the highway to the murmur of jazz.

An Apparent Digression: A Vivid View of the
"City of Lost Angels"; The Democrats Defined;
A Pentagon of Traveling Salesmen;
Some Pointed Portraits of the Politicians

"I was seeing Pershing Square, Los Angeles, now for the first time . . . the nervous fruithustlers darting in and out of the shadows, fugitives from Times Square, Market Street SF, the French Quarter—masculine hustlers looking for lonely fruits to score from, anything from the legendary $20 to a pad at night and breakfast in the morning and whatever you can clinch or clip; and the heat in their holy cop uniforms, holy because of the Almighty Stick and the Almightier Vagrancy Law; the scattered junkies, the small-time pushers, the queens, the sad panhandlers, the lonely, exiled nymphs haunting the entrance to the men's head, the fruits with the hungry eyes and the jingling coins; the tough teen-age chicks—'dittybops'—making it with the lost hustlers . . . all amid the incongruous piped music and the flowers—

*twin fountains gushing rainbow colored: the world of Lonely America
squeezed into Pershing Square, of the Cities of Terrible Night, downtown
now trapped in the City of lost Angels . . . and the trees hang over it all like
some type of apathetic fate."*

—JOHN RECHY: *Big Table 3*

Seeing Los Angeles after ten years away, one realizes all over again
that America is an unhappy contract between the East (that Faustian
thrust of a most determined human will which reaches up and out
above the eye into the skyscrapers of New York) and those flat lands of
compromise and mediocre self-expression, those endless half-pretty
repetitive small towns of the Middle and the West, whose spirit is forever horizontal and whose marrow comes to rendezvous in the pastel
monotonies of Los Angeles architecture.

So far as America has a history, one can see it in the severe heights
of New York City, in the glare from the Pittsburgh mills, by the color
in the brick of Louisburg Square, along the knotted greedy façades of
the small mansion on Chicago's North Side, in Natchez' antebellum
homes, the wrought-iron balconies off Bourbon Street, a captain's
house in Nantucket, by the curve of Commercial Street in Province-
town. One can make a list; it is probably finite. What culture we have
made and what history has collected to it can be found in those few
hard examples of an architecture which came to its artistic term, was
born, lived and so collected some history about it. Not all the roots of
American life are uprooted, but almost all, and the spirit of the super-
market, that homogenous extension of stainless surfaces and psycho-
analyzed people, packaged commodities and ranch homes, interchangeable, geographically unrecognizable, that essence of the new
postwar SuperAmerica is found nowhere so perfectly as in Los Angeles' ubiquitous acres. One gets the impression that people come to
Los Angeles in order to divorce themselves from the past, here to live
or try to live in the rootless pleasure world of an adult child. One
knows that if the cities of the world were destroyed by a new war, the
architecture of the rebuilding would create a landscape which looked,
subject to specifications of climate, exactly and entirely like the San
Fernando Valley.

It is not that Los Angeles is altogether hideous, it is even by degrees
pleasant, but for an Easterner there is never any salt in the wind; it is
like Mexican cooking without chile, or Chinese egg rolls missing their

mustard; as one travels through the endless repetitions of that city which is the capital of suburbia with its milky pinks, its washed-out oranges, its tainted lime-yellows of pastel on one pretty little architectural monstrosity after another, the colors not intense enough, the styles never pure, and never sufficiently impure to collide on the eye, one conceives the people who live here—they have come out to express themselves, Los Angeles is the home of self-expression, but the artists are middle-class and middling-minded; no passions will calcify here for years in the gloom to be revealed a decade later as the tessellations of a hard and fertile work, no, it is all open, promiscuous, borrowed, half bought, a city without iron, eschewing wood, a kingdom of stucco, the playground for mass men—one has the feeling it was built by television sets giving orders to men. And in this land of the pretty-pretty, the virility is in the barbarisms, the vulgarities, it is in the huge billboards, the screamers of the neon lighting, the shouting farm-utensil colors of the gas stations and the monster drugstores, it is in the swing of the sports cars, hot rods, convertibles, Los Angeles is a city to drive in, the boulevards are wide, the traffic is nervous and fast, the radio stations play bouncing, blooping, rippling tunes, one digs the pop in a pop tune, no one of character would make love by it but the sound· is good for swinging a car, electronic guitars and Hawaiian harps.

So this is the town the Democrats came to, and with their unerring instinct (after being with them a week, one thinks of this party as a crazy, half-rich family, loaded with poor cousins, traveling always in caravans with Cadillacs and Okie Fords, Lincolns and quarter-horse mules, putting up every night in tents to hear the chamber quartet of Great Cousin Eleanor invaded by the Texas-twanging steel-stringing geetarists of Bubber Lyndon, carrying its own mean high-school principal, Doc Symington, chided for its manners by good Uncle Adlai, told the route of march by Navigator Jack, cut off every six months from the rich will of Uncle Jim Farley, never listening to the mechanic of the caravan, Bald Sam Rayburn, who assures them they'll all break down unless Cousin Bubber gets the concession on the garage; it's the Snopes family married to Henry James, with the labor unions thrown in like a Yankee dollar, and yet it's true, in tranquility one recollects them with affection, their instinct is good, crazy family good) and this instinct now led the caravan to pick the Biltmore Hotel in downtown Los Angeles for their family get-together and reunion.

The Biltmore is one of the ugliest hotels in the world. Patterned after the flat roofs of an Italian Renaissance palace, it is eighty-eight times as large, and one-millionth as valuable to the continuation of man, and it would be intolerable if it were not for the presence of Pershing Square, that square block of park with cactus and palm trees, the three-hundred-and-sixty-five-day-a-year convention of every junkie, pot-head, pusher, queen (but you have read that good writing already). For years Pershing Square has been one of the three or four places in America famous to homosexuals, famous not for its posh, the chic is round-heeled here, but because it is one of the avatars of the good old masturbatory sex, dirty with the crusted sugars of smut, dirty rooming houses around the corner where the score is made, dirty book and photograph stores down the street, old-fashioned out-of-the-Thirties burlesque houses, cruising bars, jukeboxes, movie houses; Pershing Square is the town plaza for all those lonely, respectable, small-town homosexuals who lead a family life, make children, and have the Philbrick psychology (How I Joined the Communist Party and Led Three Lives). Yes, it is the open-air convention hall for the small-town inverts who live like spies, and it sits in the center of Los Angeles, facing the Biltmore, that hotel which is a mausoleum, that Pentagon of traveling salesmen the Party chose to house the headquarters of the Convention.

So here came that family, cursed before it began by the thundering absence of Great-Uncle Truman, the delegates dispersed over a run of thirty miles and twenty-seven hotels: the Olympian Motor Hotel, the Ambassador, the Beverly Wilshire, the Santa Ynez Inn (where rumor has it the delegates from Louisiana had some midnight swim), the Mayan, the Commodore, the Mayfair, the Sheraton-West, the Huntington-Sheraton, the Green, the Hayward, the Gates, the Figueroa, the Statler Hilton, the Hollywood Knickerbocker—does one have to be a collector to list such names?—beauties all, with that up-from-the-farm Los Angeles décor, plate-glass windows, patio and terrace, foam-rubber mattress, pastel paints, all of them pretty as an ad in full-page color, all but the Biltmore where everybody gathered every day—the newsmen, the TV, radio, magazine, and foreign newspapermen, the delegates, the politicos, the tourists, the campaign managers, the runners, the flunkies, the cousins and aunts, the wives, the grandfathers, the eight-year-old girls, and the twenty-eight-year-old girls in the Kennedy costumes, red and white and blue, the Symingteeners, the Johnson Ladies, the Stevenson Ladies, everybody—and

for three days before the convention and four days into it, everybody
collected at the Biltmore, in the lobby, in the grill, in the Biltmore
Bowl, in the elevators, along the corridors, three hundred deep always
outside the Kennedy suite, milling everywhere, every dark-carpeted
grey-brown hall of the hotel, but it was in the Gallery of the Biltmore
where one first felt the mood which pervaded all proceedings until the
convention was almost over, that heavy, thick, witless depression
which was to dominate every move as the delegates wandered and
gawked and paraded and set for a spell, there in the Gallery of the
Biltmore, that huge depressing alley with its inimitable hotel color,
that faded depth of chiaroscuro which unhappily has no depth, that
brown which is not a brown, that grey which has no pearl in it, that
color which can be described only as hotel-color because the beiges,
the tans, the walnuts, the mahoganies, the dull blood rugs, the moan-
ing yellows, the sick greens, the greys and all those dumb browns
merge into that lack of color which is an over-large hotel at convention
time, with all the small-towners wearing their set, starched faces, that
look they get at carnival, all fever and suspicion, and proud to be there,
eddying slowly back and forth in that high block-long tunnel of a room
with its arched ceiling and square recesses filling every rib of the arch
with art work, escutcheons and blazons and other art, pictures I think,
I cannot even remember, there was such a hill of cigar smoke the eye
had to travel on its way to the ceiling, and at one end there was
galvanized-pipe scaffolding and workmen repairing some part of the
ceiling, one of them touching up one of the endless squares of painted
plaster in the arch, and another worker, passing by, yelled up to the
one who was working on the ceiling: "Hey, Michelangelo!"

Later, of course, it began to emerge and there were portraits one
could keep, Symington, dogged at a press conference, declaring with
no conviction that he knew he had a good chance to win, the disappointment eating at his good looks so that he came off hard-faced,
mean, and yet slack—a desperate dullness came off the best of his
intentions. There was Johnson who had compromised too many contradictions and now the contradictions were in his face: when he
smiled the corners of his mouth squeezed gloom; when he was pious,
his eyes twinkled irony; when he spoke in a righteous tone, he looked
corrupt; when he jested, the ham in his jowls looked to quiver. He was
not convincing. He was a Southern politician, a Texas Democrat, a
liberal Eisenhower; he would do no harm, he would do no good, he

would react to the machine, good fellow, nice friend—the Russians would understand him better than his own.

Stevenson had the patina. He came into the room and the room was different, not stronger perhaps (which is why ultimately he did not win), but warmer. One knew why some adored him; he did not look like other people, not with press lights on his flesh; he looked like a lover, the simple truth, he had the sweet happiness of an adolescent who has just been given his first major kiss. And so he glowed, and one was reminded of Chaplin, not because they were the least alike in features, but because Charlie Chaplin was luminous when one met him and Stevenson had something of that light.

There was Eleanor Roosevelt, fine, precise, hand-worked like ivory. Her voice was almost attractive as she explained in the firm, sad tones of the first lady in this small town why she could not admit Mr. Kennedy, who was no doubt a gentleman, into her political house. One had the impression of a lady who was finally becoming a woman, which is to say that she was just a little bitchy about it all; nice bitchy, charming, it had a touch of art to it, but it made one wonder if she were not now satisfying the last passion of them all, which was to become physically attractive, for she was better-looking than she had ever been as she spurned the possibilities of a young suitor.

Jim Farley. Huge. Cold as a bishop. The hell he would consign you to was cold as ice.

Bobby Kennedy, that archetype Bobby Kennedy, looked like a West Point cadet, or, better, one of those unreconstructed Irishmen from Kirkland House one always used to have to face in the line in Harvard house football games. "Hello," you would say to the ones who looked like him as you lined up for the scrimmage after the kickoff, and his type would nod and look away, one rock glint of recognition your due for living across the hall from one another all through Freshman year, and then bang, as the ball was passed back, you'd get a bony king-hell knee in the crotch. He was the kind of man never to put on the gloves with if you wanted to do some social boxing, because after two minutes it would be a war, and ego-bastards last long in a war.

Carmine DeSapio and Kenneth Galbraith on the same part of the convention floor. DeSapio is bigger than one expects, keen and florid, great big smoked glasses, a suntan like Mantan—he is the kind of heavyweight Italian who could get by with a name like Romeo—and Galbraith is tall-tall, as actors say, six foot six it could be, terribly thin, enormously attentive, exquisitely polite, birdlike, he is sensitive to the stirring of reeds in a wind over the next hill. "Our grey eminence," whispered the intelligent observer next to me.

Bob Wagner, the mayor of New York, a little man, plump, groomed, blank. He had the blank, pomaded, slightly worried look of the first barber in a good barbershop, the kind who would go to the track on his day off and wear a green transparent stone in a gold ring.

And then there was Kennedy, the edge of the mystery. But a sketch will no longer suffice.

Perspective from the Biltmore Balcony: The
Colorful Arrival of the Hero with the Orange-
brown Suntan and Amazingly White Teeth;
Revelation of the Two Rivers Political Theory

". . . it can be said with a fair amount of certainty that the essence of his political attractiveness is his extraordinary political intelligence. He has a mind quite unlike that of any other Democrat of this century. It is not literary, metaphysical and moral, as Adlai Stevenson's is. Kennedy is articulate and often witty, but he does not seek verbal polish. No one can doubt the seriousness of his concern with the most serious political matters, but one feels that whereas Mr. Stevenson's political views derive from a view of life that holds politics to be a mere fraction of existence, Senator Kennedy's primary interest is in politics. The easy way in which he disposes of the question of Church and State—as if he felt that any reasonable man could quite easily resolve any possible conflict of loyalties—suggests that the organization of society is the one thing that really engages his interest."

—RICHARD ROVERE: *The New Yorker*, July 23, 1960

The afternoon he arrived at the convention from the airport, there was of course a large crowd on the street outside the Biltmore, and the best way to get a view was to get up on an outdoor balcony of the Biltmore, two flights above the street, and look down on the event. One waited thirty minutes, and then a honking of horns as wild as the getaway after an Italian wedding sounded around the corner, and the Kennedy cortege came into sight, circled Pershing Square, the men in the open and leading convertibles sitting backwards to look at their leader, and finally came to a halt in a space cleared for them by the police in the crowd. The television cameras were out, and a Kennedy band was playing some circus music. One saw him immediately. He had the deep orange-brown suntan of a ski instructor, and when he smiled at the crowd his teeth were amazingly white and clearly visible at a distance of fifty yards. For one moment he saluted Pershing Square, and Pershing Square saluted him back, the prince and the beggars of glamour staring at one another across a city street, one of those very special moments in the underground history of the world, and then with a quick move he was out of the car and by choice headed into the crowd instead of the lane cleared for him into the hotel by the police, so that he made his way inside surrounded by a mob, and one expected at any moment to see him lifted to its shoulders like a matador being carried back to the city after a triumph in the plaza. All the while the band kept playing the campaign tunes, sashaying circus music, and one had a moment of clarity, intense as a *déjà vu,* for the scene which had taken place had been glimpsed before in a dozen musical comedies; it was the scene where the hero, the matinee idol, the movie star comes to the palace to claim the princess, or what is the same, and more to our soil, the football hero, the campus king, arrives at the dean's home surrounded by a court of open-singing students to plead with the dean for his daughter's kiss and permission to put on the big musical that night. And suddenly I saw the convention, it came into focus for me, and I understood the mood of depression which had lain over the convention, because finally it was simple: the Democrats were going to nominate a man who, no matter how serious his political dedication might be, was indisputably and willy-nilly going to be seen as a great box-office actor, and the consequences of that were staggering and not at all easy to calculate.

Since the First World War Americans have been leading a double life, and our history has moved on two rivers, one visible, the other underground; there has been the history of politics which is concrete, factual, practical and unbelievably dull if not for the consequences of the actions of some of these men; and there is a subterranean river of untapped, ferocious, lonely and romantic desires, that concentration of ecstasy and violence which is the dream life of the nation.

The twentieth century may yet be seen as that era when civilized man and underprivileged man were melted together into mass man, the iron and steel of the nineteenth century giving way to electronic circuits which communicated their messages into men, the unmistakable tendency of the new century seeming to be the creation of men as interchangeable as commodities, their extremes of personality singed out of existence by the psychic fields of force the communicators would impose. This loss of personality was a catastrophe to the future of the imagination, but billions of people might first benefit from it by having enough to eat—one did not know—and there remained citadels of resistance in Europe where the culture was deep and roots were visible in the architecture of the past.

Nowhere, as in America, however, was this fall from individual man to mass man felt so acutely, for America was at once the first and most prolific creator of mass communications, and the most rootless of countries, since almost no American could lay claim to the line of a family which had not once at least severed its roots by migrating here. But, if rootless, it was then the most vulnerable of countries to its own homogenization. Yet America was also the country in which the dynamic myth of the Renaissance—that every man was potentially extraordinary—knew its most passionate persistence. Simply, America was the land where people still believed in heroes: George Washington; Billy the Kid; Lincoln, Jefferson; Mark Twain, Jack London, Hemingway; Joe Louis, Dempsey, Gentleman Jim; America believed in athletes, rum-runners, aviators; even lovers, by the time Valentino died. It was a country which had grown by the leap of one hero past another—is there a county in all of our ground which does not have its legendary figure? And when the West was filled, the expansion turned inward, became part of an agitated, overexcited, superheated dream life. The film studios threw up their searchlights as the frontier was finally sealed, and the romantic possibilities of the old conquest of land turned into a vertical myth, trapped within the skull, of a new kind of heroic life, each choosing his own archetype of a neo-renaissance man, be it Barrymore, Cagney, Flynn, Bogart, Brando or Sinatra, but it was almost as if there were no peace unless one could fight well, kill well (if always with honor), love well and love many, be cool, be daring, be dashing, be wild, be wily, be resourceful, be a brave gun. And this myth, that each of us was born to be free, to wander, to have adventure and to grow on the waves of the violent, the perfumed, and the unexpected, had a force which could not be tamed no matter how the nation's regulators—politicians, medicos, policemen, professors, priests, rabbis, ministers, *idéologues,* psychoanalysts, builders, executives and endless communicators—would brick-in the modern life with hygiene upon sanity, and middle-brow homily over platitude; the myth would not die. Indeed a quarter of the nation's business must have depended upon its existence. But it stayed alive for more than that—it was as if the message in the labyrinth of the genes would insist that violence was locked with creativity, and adventure was the secret of love.

Once, in the Second World War and in the year or two which followed, the underground river returned to earth, and the life of the nation was intense, of the present, electric; as a lady said, "That was the time when we gave parties which changed people's lives." The Forties was a decade when the speed with which one's own events occurred seemed as rapid as the history of the battlefields, and for the mass of people in America a forced march into a new jungle of emotion was the result. The surprises, the failures, and the dangers of that life must have terrified some nerve of awareness in the power and the mass, for, as if stricken by the orgiastic vistas the myth had carried up from underground, the retreat to a more conservative existence was disorderly, the fear of communism spread like an irrational hail of boils. To anyone who could see, the excessive hysteria of the Red wave was no preparation to face an enemy, but rather a terror of the national self: free-loving, lust-looting, atheistic, implacable—absurdity beyond absurdity to label communism so, for the moral products of Stalinism had been Victorian sex and a ponderous machine of material theology.

Forced underground again, deep beneath all *Reader's Digest* hospital dressings of Mental Health in Your Community, the myth continued to flow, fed by television and the film. The fissure in the national psyche widened to the danger point. The last large appearance of the myth was the vote which tricked the polls and gave Harry Truman his victory in '48. That was the last. Came the Korean War, the shadow of the H-bomb, and we were ready for the General. Uncle Harry gave way to Father, and security, regularity, order, and the life of no imagination were the command of the day. If one had any doubt of this, there was Joe McCarthy with his built-in treason detector, furnished by God, and the damage was done. In the totalitarian wind of those days, anyone who worked in Government formed the habit of being not too original, and many a mind atrophied from disuse and private shame. At the summit there was benevolence without leadership, regularity without vision, security without safety, rhetoric without life. The ship drifted on, that enormous warship of the United States, led by a

Secretary of State whose cells were seceding to cancer, and as the world became more fantastic—Africa turning itself upside down, while some new kind of machine man was being made in China—two events occurred which stunned the confidence of America into a new night: the Russians put up their Sputnik, and Civil Rights—that reluctant gift to the American Negro, granted for its effect on foreign affairs—spewed into real life at Little Rock. The national Ego was in shock: the Russians were now in some ways our technological superiors, and we had an internal problem of subject populations equal conceivably in its difficulty to the Soviet and its satellites. The fatherly calm of the General began to seem like the uxorious mellifluences of the undertaker.

Underneath it all was a larger problem. The life of politics and the life of myth had diverged too far, and the energies of the people one knew everywhere had slowed down. Twenty years ago a post-Depression generation had gone to war and formed a lively, grousing, by times inefficient, carousing, pleasure-seeking, not altogether inadequate army. It did part of what it was supposed to do, and many, out of combat, picked up a kind of private life on the fly, and had their good time despite the yaws of the military system. But today in America the generation which respected the code of the myth was Beat, a horde of half-begotten Christs with scraggly beards, heroes none, saints all, weak before the strong, empty conformisms of the authority. The sanction for finding one's growth was no longer one's flag, one's career, one's sex, one's adventure, not even one's booze. Among the best in this newest of the generations, the myth had found its voice in marijuana, and the joke of the underground was that when the Russians came over they could never dare to occupy us for long because America was too Hip. Gallows humor. The poorer truth might be that America was too Beat, the instinct of the nation so separated from its public mind that apathy, schizophrenia, and private beatitudes might be the pride of the welcoming committee any underground could offer.

Yes, the life of politics and the life of the myth had diverged too far. There was nothing to return them to one another, no common danger, no cause, no desire, and, most essentially, no hero. It was a hero America needed, a hero central to his time, a man whose personality might suggest contradictions and mysteries which could reach into the alienated circuits of the underground, because only a hero can capture the secret imagination of a people, and so be good for the vitality of his nation; a hero embodies the fantasy and so allows each private mind the liberty to consider its fantasy and find a way to grow. Each mind can become more conscious of its desire and waste less strength in hiding from itself. Roosevelt was such a hero, and Churchill, Lenin and De Gaulle; even Hitler, to take the most odious example of this thesis, was a hero, the hero-as-monster, embodying what had become the monstrous fantasy of a people, but the horror upon which the radical mind and liberal temperament foundered was that he gave outlet to the energies of the Germans and so presented the twentieth century with an index of how horrible had become the secret heart of its desire. Roosevelt is of course a happier example of the hero; from his paralytic leg to the royal elegance of his geniality he seemed to contain the country within himself; everyone from the meanest starving cripple to an ambitious young man could expand into the optimism of an improving future because the man offered an unspoken promise of a future which would be rich. The sexual and the sex-starved, the poor, the hard-working and the imaginative well-to-do could see themselves in the President, could believe him to be like themselves. So a large part of the country was able to discover its energies because not as much was wasted in feeling that the country was a poisonous nutrient which stifled the day.

Too simple? No doubt. One tries to construct a simple model. The thesis is after all not so mysterious; it would merely nudge the notion that a hero embodies his time and is not so very much better than his time, but he is larger than life and so is capable of giving direction to the time, able to encourage a nation to discover the deepest colors of its character. At bottom the concept of the hero is antagonistic to impersonal social progress, to the belief that social ills can be solved by social legislating, for it sees a country as all-but-trapped in its character until it has a hero who reveals the character of the country to itself. The implication is that without such a hero the nation turns sluggish. Truman for example was not such a hero, he was not sufficiently larger than life, he inspired familiarity without excitement, he was a character but his proportions came from soap opera: Uncle Harry, full of salty common-sense and small-minded certainty, a storekeeping uncle.

Whereas Eisenhower has been the anti-Hero, the regulator. Nations do not necessarily and inevitably seek for heroes. In periods of dull anxiety, one is more likely to look for security than a dramatic confrontation, and Eisenhower could stand as a hero only for that large number of Americans who were most proud of their lack of imagination. In American life, the unspoken war of the century has taken place between the city and the small town: the city which is dynamic, orgiastic, unsettling, explosive and accelerating to the psyche; the small town which is rooted, narrow, cautious and planted in the life-logic of the family. The need of the city is to accelerate growth; the pride of the small town is to retard it. But since America has been passing through a period of enormous expansion since the war, the double-four years of Dwight Eisenhower could not retard the expansion, it could only denude it of color, character, and the development of novelty. The small-town mind is rooted—it is rooted in the small town —and when it attempts to direct history the results are disastrously colorless because the instrument of world power which is used by the small-town mind is the committee. Committees do not create, they merely proliferate, and the incredible dullness wreaked upon the American landscape in Eisenhower's eight years has been the triumph of the corporation. A tasteless, sexless, odorless sanctity in architecture, manners, modes, styles has been the result. Eisenhower embodied half the needs of the nation, the needs of the timid, the petri-fied, the sanctimonious, and the sluggish. What was even worse, he did not divide the nation as a hero might (with a dramatic dialogue as the result); he merely excluded one part of the nation from the other. The result was an alienation of the best minds and bravest impulses from the faltering history which was made. America's need in those years was to take an existential turn, to walk into the nightmare, to face into that terrible logic of history which demanded that the country and its people must become more extraordinary and more adventurous, or else perish, since the only alternative was to offer a false security in the power and the panacea of organized religion, family, and the FBI, a totalitarianization of the psyche by the stultifying techniques of the mass media which would seep into everyone's most private associations and so leave the country powerless against the Russians even if the denouement were to take fifty years, for in a competition between totalitarianisms the first maxim of the prizefight manager would doubtless apply: "Hungry fighters win fights."

*The Hipster as Presidential Candidate: Thoughts
on a Public Man's Eighteenth-Century Wife;
Face-to-Face with the Hero; Significance of a
Personal Note, or the Meaning of His Having
Read an Author's Novel*

Some part of these thoughts must have been in one's mind at the moment there was that first glimpse of Kennedy entering the Biltmore Hotel; and in the days which followed, the first mystery—the profound air of depression which hung over the convention—gave way to a second mystery which can be answered only by history. The depression of the delegates was understandable: no one had too much doubt that Kennedy would be nominated, but if elected he would be not only the youngest President ever to be chosen by voters, he would be the most conventionally attractive young man ever to sit in the White House, and his wife—some would claim it—might be the most beautiful first lady in our history. Of necessity the myth would emerge once more, because America's politics would now be also America's favorite movie, America's first soap opera, America's bestseller. One thinks of the talents of writers like Taylor Caldwell or Frank Yerby, or is it rather *The Fountainhead* which would contain such a fleshing of the romantic prescription? Or is it indeed one's own work which is called into question? "Well, there's your first hipster," says a writer one knows at the convention, "Sergius O'Shaugnessy born rich," and the temptation is to nod, for it could be true, a war hero, and the heroism is bona-fide, even exceptional, a man who has lived with death, who, crippled in the back, took on an operation which would kill him or restore him to power, who chose to marry a lady whose face might be too imaginative for the taste of a democracy which likes its first ladies to be executives of home-management, a man who courts political suicide by choosing to go all out for a nomination four, eight, or twelve years before his political elders think he is ready, a man who announces a week prior to the convention that the young are better fitted to direct history than the old. Yes, it captures the attention. This is no routine candidate calling every shot by safety's routine book. ("Yes," Nixon said, naturally but terribly tired an hour after his nomination, the TV cameras and lights and micro-

phones bringing out a sweat of fatigue on his face, the words coming
very slowly from the tired brain, somber, modest, sober, slow, slow
enough so that one could touch emphatically the cautions behind each
word, "Yes, I want to say," said Nixon, "that whatever abilities I have,
I got from my mother." A tired pause . . . dull moment of warning,
". . . and my father." The connection now made, the rest comes easy,
". . . and my school and my church." Such men are capable of anything.)

One had the opportunity to study Kennedy a bit in the days that
followed. His style in the press conferences was interesting. Not terribly popular with the reporters (too much a contemporary, and yet too
difficult to understand, he received nothing like the rounds of applause
given to Eleanor Roosevelt, Stevenson, Humphrey, or even Johnson),
he carried himself nonetheless with a cool grace which seemed indifferent to applause, his manner somehow similar to the poise of a fine
boxer, quick with his hands, neat in his timing, and two feet away from
his corner when the bell ended the round. There was a good lithe wit to
his responses, a dry Harvard wit, a keen sense of proportion in disposing of difficult questions—invariably he gave enough of an answer to
be formally satisfactory without ever opening himself to a new question which might go further than the first. Asked by a reporter, "Are
you for Adlai as vice-president?" the grin came forth and the voice
turned very dry, "No, I cannot say we have considered *Adlai* as a vice-
president." Yet there was an elusive detachment to everything he did.
One did not have the feeling of a man present in the room with all his
weight and all his mind. Johnson gave you all of himself, he was a political animal, he breathed like an animal, sweated like one, you knew
his mind was entirely absorbed with the compendium of political fact
and maneuver; Kennedy seemed at times like a young professor whose
manner was adequate for the classroom, but whose mind was off in
some intricacy of the Ph.D. thesis he was writing. Perhaps one can give
a sense of the discrepancy by saying that he was like an actor who had
been cast as the candidate, a good actor, but not a great one—you
were aware all the time that the role was one thing and the man another—they did not coincide, the actor seemed a touch too aloof (as,
let us say, Gregory Peck is usually too aloof) to become the part. Yet
one had little sense of whether to value this elusiveness, or to beware
of it. One could be witnessing the fortitude of a superior sensitivity or
the detachment of a man who was not quite real to himself. And his

voice gave no clue. When Johnson spoke, one could separate what was fraudulent from what was felt, he would have been satisfying as an actor the way Broderick Crawford or Paul Douglas are satisfying; one saw into his emotions, or at least had the illusion that one did. Kennedy's voice, however, was only a fair voice, too reedy, near to strident, it had the metallic snap of a cricket in it somewhere, it was more impersonal than the man, and so became the least-impressive quality in a face, a body, a selection of language, and a style of movement which made up a better-than-decent presentation, better than one had expected.

With all of that, it would not do to pass over the quality in Kennedy which is most difficult to describe. And in fact some touches should be added to this hint of a portrait, for later (after the convention), one had a short session alone with him, and the next day, another. As one had suspected in advance the interviews were not altogether satisfactory, they hardly could have been. A man running for President is altogether different from a man elected President: the hazards of the campaign make it impossible for a candidate to be as interesting as he might like to be (assuming he has such a desire). One kept advancing the argument that this campaign would be a contest of personalities, and Kennedy kept returning the discussion to politics. After a while one recognized this was an inevitable caution for him. So there would be not too much point to reconstructing the dialogue since Kennedy is hardly inarticulate about his political attitudes and there will be a library vault of text devoted to it in the newspapers. What struck me most about the interview was a passing remark whose importance was invisible on the scale of politics, but was altogether meaningful to my particular competence. As we sat down for the first time, Kennedy smiled nicely and said that he had read my books. One muttered one's pleasure. "Yes," he said, "I've read . . ." and then there was a short pause which did not last long enough to be embarrassing in which it was yet obvious no title came instantly to his mind, an omission one was not ready to mind altogether since a man in such a position must be obliged to carry a hundred thousand facts and names in his head, but the hesitation lasted no longer than three seconds or four, and then he said, "I've read *The Deer Park* and . . . the others," which startled me for it was the first time in a hundred similar situations, talking to someone whose knowledge of my work was casual, that the sentence did not come out, "I've read *The Naked and the Dead* . . .

and the others." If one is to take the worst and assume that Kennedy was briefed for this interview (which is most doubtful), it still speaks well for the striking instincts of his advisers.

What was retained later is an impression of Kennedy's manners which were excellent, even artful, better than the formal good manners of Choate and Harvard, almost as if what was creative in the man had been given to the manners. In a room with one or two people, his voice improved, became low-pitched, even pleasant—it seemed obvious that in all these years he had never become a natural public speaker and so his voice was constricted in public, the symptom of all orators who are ambitious, throttled, and determined.

His personal quality had a subtle, not quite describable intensity, a suggestion of dry pent heat perhaps, his eyes large, the pupils grey, the whites prominent, almost shocking, his most forceful feature: he had the eyes of a mountaineer. His appearance changed with his mood, strikingly so, and this made him always more interesting than what he was saying. He would seem at one moment older than his age, forty-eight or fifty, a tall, slim, sunburned professor with a pleasant weathered face, not even particularly handsome; five minutes later, talking to a press conference on his lawn, three microphones before him, a television camera turning, his appearance would have gone through a metamorphosis, he would look again like a movie star, his coloring vivid, his manner rich, his gestures strong and quick, alive with that concentration of vitality a successful actor always seems to radiate. Kennedy had a dozen faces. Although they were not at all similar as people, the quality was reminiscent of someone like Brando whose expression rarely changes, but whose appearance seems to shift from one person into another as the minutes go by, and one bothers with this comparison because, like Brando, Kennedy's most characteristic quality is the remote and private air of a man who has traversed some lonely terrain of experience, of loss and gain, of nearness to death, which leaves him isolated from the mass of others.

The next day while they waited in vain for rescuers, the wrecked half of the boat turned over in the water and they saw that it would soon sink. The group decided to swim to a small island three miles away. There were other islands bigger and nearer, but the Navy officers knew that they were occupied by the Japanese. On one island, only one mile to the south, they could see a Japanese camp. McMahon, the engineer whose legs were disabled by burns, was unable to swim. Despite his own painfully crippled back, Kennedy swam the three miles with a breast stroke, towing behind him by a life-belt strap that he held between his teeth the helpless McMahon . . . it took Kennedy and the suffering engineer five hours to reach the island.

The quotation is from a book which has for its dedicated unilateral title, *The Remarkable Kennedys,* but the prose is by one of the best of the war reporters, the former *Yank* editor, Joe McCarthy, and so presumably may be trusted in such details as this. Physical bravery does not of course guarantee a man's abilities in the White House —all too often men with physical courage are disappointing in their moral imagination—but the heroism here is remarkable for its tenacity. The above is merely one episode in a continuing saga which went on for five days in and out of the water, and left Kennedy at one point "miraculously saved from drowning (in a storm) by a group of Solomon Island natives who suddenly came up beside him in a large dugout canoe." Afterward, his back still injured (that precise back injury which was to put him on crutches eleven years later, and have him search for "spinal-fusion surgery" despite a warning that his chances of living through the operation were "extremely limited") afterward, he asked to go back on duty and became so bold in the attacks he made with his PT boat "that the crew didn't like to go out with him because he took so many chances."

It is the wisdom of a man who senses death within him and gambles that he can cure it by risking his life. It is the therapy of the instinct, and who is so wise as to call it irrational? Before he went into the Navy, Kennedy had been ailing. Washed out of Freshman year at Princeton by a prolonged trough of yellow jaundice, sick for a year at Harvard, weak already in the back from an injury at football, his trials suggest the self-hatred of a man whose resentment and ambition are too large for his body. Not everyone can discharge their furies on an analyst's couch, for some angers can be relaxed only by winning power, some rages are sufficiently monumental to demand that one try to become a hero or else fall back into that death which is already within the cells. But if one succeeds, the energy aroused can be exceptional. Talking to a man who had been with Kennedy in Hyannis Port the week before the convention, I heard that he was in a state of deep fatigue.

"Well, he didn't look tired at the convention," one commented.

"Oh, he had three days of rest. Three days of rest for him is like six months for us."

One thinks of that three-mile swim with the belt in his mouth and McMahon holding it behind him. There are pestilences which sit in the mouth and rot the teeth—in those five hours how much of the psyche must have been remade, for to give vent to the bite in one's jaws and yet use that rage to save a life: it is not so very many men who have the apocalyptic sense that heroism is the First Doctor.

If one had a profound criticism of Kennedy it was that his public mind was too conventional, but that seemed to matter less than the fact of such a man in office because the law of political life had become so dreary that only a conventional mind could win an election. Indeed there could be no politics which gave warmth to one's body until the country had recovered its imagination, its pioneer lust for the unexpected and incalculable. It was the changes that might come afterward on which one could put one's hope. With such a man in office the myth of the nation would again be engaged, and the fact that he was Catholic would shiver a first existential vibration of consciousness into the mind of the White Protestant. For the first time in our history, the Protestant would have the pain and creative luxury of feeling himself in some tiny degree part of a minority, and that was an experience which might be incommensurable in its value to the best of them.

A Vignette of Adlai Stevenson; The Speeches:
What Happened When the Teleprompter
Jammed: How U.S. Senator Eugene McCarthy
Played the Matador. An Observation
on the Name Fitzgerald

As yet we have said hardly a word about Stevenson. And his actions must remain a puzzle unless one dares a speculation about his motive, or was it his need?

So far as the people at the convention had affection for anyone, it was Stevenson, so far as they were able to generate any spontaneous enthusiasm, their cheers were again for Stevenson. Yet it was obvious he never had much chance because so soon as a chance would present itself he seemed quick to dissipate the opportunity. The day before the nominations, he entered the Sports Arena to take his seat as a delegate —the demonstration was spontaneous, noisy and prolonged; it was quieted only by Governor Collins' invitation for Stevenson to speak to the delegates. In obedience perhaps to the scruple that a candidate must not appear before the convention until nominations are done, Stevenson said no more than: "I am grateful for this tumultuous and

moving welcome. After getting in and out of the Biltmore Hotel and
this hall, I have decided I know whom you are going to nominate. It
will be the last survivor." This dry reminder of the ruthlessness of politics broke the roar of excitement for his presence. The applause as he
left the platform was like the dying fall-and-moan of a baseball crowd
when a home run curves foul. The next day, a New York columnist
talking about it said bitterly, "If he'd only gone through the motions, if
he had just said that now he wanted to run, that he would work hard,
and he hoped the delegates would vote for him. Instead he made that
lame joke." One wonders. It seems almost as if he did not wish to win
unless victory came despite himself, and then was overwhelming.
There are men who are not heroes because they are too good for their
time, and it is natural that defeats leave them bitter, tired, and doubtful of their right to make new history. If Stevenson had campaigned for
a year before the convention, it is possible that he could have stopped
Kennedy. At the least, the convention would have been enormously
more exciting, and the nominations might have gone through half-a-
dozen ballots before a winner was hammered into shape. But then
Stevenson might also have shortened his life. One had the impression
of a tired man who (for a politician) was sickened unduly by compromise. A year of maneuvering, broken promises, and detestable partners might have gutted him for the election campaign. If elected, it
might have ruined him as a President. There is the possibility that he
sensed his situation exactly this way, and knew that if he were to run
for president, win and make a good one, he would first have to be restored, as one can indeed be restored, by an exceptional demonstration
of love—love, in this case, meaning that the Party had a profound
desire to keep him as their leader. The emotional truth of a last-minute
victory for Stevenson over the Kennedy machine might have given him
new energy; it would certainly have given him new faith in a country
and a party whose good motives he was possibly beginning to doubt.
Perhaps the fault he saw with his candidacy was that he attracted only
the nicest people to himself and there were not enough of them. (One
of the private amusements of the convention was to divine some of the
qualities of the candidates by the style of the young women who put on
hats and clothing and politicked in the colors of one presidential gent
or another. Of course, half of them must have been hired models, but
someone did the hiring and so it was fair to look for a common denominator. The Johnson girls tended to be plump, pie-faced, dumb sexy

Southern; the Symingteeners seemed a touch mulish, stubborn, good-looking pluggers; the Kennedy ladies were the handsomest; healthy, attractive, tough, a little spoiled—they looked like the kind of girls who had gotten all the dances in high school and/or worked for a year as an airline hostess before marrying well. But the Stevenson girls looked to be doing it for no money; they were good sorts, slightly horsy-faced, one had the impression they played field hockey in college.) It was indeed the pure, the saintly, the clean-living, the pacifistic, the vegetarian who seemed most for Stevenson, and the less humorous in the Kennedy camp were heard to remark bitterly that Stevenson had nothing going for him but a bunch of Goddamn Beatniks. This might even have had its sour truth. The demonstrations outside the Sports Arena for Stevenson seemed to have more than a fair proportion of tall, emaciated young men with thin, wry beards and three-string guitars accompanied (again in undue proportion) by a contingent of ascetic, face-washed young Beat ladies in sweaters and dungarees. Not to mention all the Holden Caulfields one could see from here to the horizon. But of course it is unfair to limit it so, for the Democratic gentry were also committed half en masse for Stevenson, as well as a considerable number of movie stars, Shelley Winters for one: after the convention she remarked sweetly, "Tell me something nice about Kennedy so I can get excited about him."

What was properly astonishing was the way this horde of political half-breeds and amateurs came within distance of turning the convention from its preconceived purpose, and managed at the least to bring the only hour of thoroughgoing excitement the convention could offer.

But then nominating day was the best day of the week and enough happened to suggest that a convention out of control would be a spectacle as extraordinary in the American scale of spectator values as a close seventh game in the World Series or a tied fourth quarter in a professional-football championship. A political convention is after all not a meeting of a corporation's board of directors; it is a fiesta, a carnival, a pig-rooting, horse-snorting, band-playing, voice-screaming medieval get-together of greed, practical lust, compromised idealism, career-advancement, meeting, feud, vendetta, conciliation, of rabble-rousers, fist fights (as it used to be), embraces, drunks (again as it used to be) and collective rivers of animal sweat. It is a reminder that no matter how the country might pretend it has grown up and become tidy in its manners, bodiless in its legislative language, hygienic in its separation of high politics from private life, that the roots still come grubby from the soil, and that politics in America is still different from politics anywhere else because the politics has arisen out of the immediate needs, ambitions, and cupidities of the people, that our politics still smell of the bedroom and the kitchen, rather than having descended to us from the chill punctilio of aristocratic negotiation.

So. The Sports Arena was new, too pretty of course, tasteless in its design—it was somehow pleasing that the acoustics were so bad for one did not wish the architects well; there had been so little imagination in their design, and this arena would have none of the harsh grandeur of Madison Square Garden when it was aged by spectators' phlegm and feet over the next twenty years. Still it had some atmosphere; seen from the streets, with the spectators moving to the ticket gates, the bands playing, the green hot-shot special editions of the Los Angeles newspapers being hawked by the newsboys, there was a touch of the air of promise that precedes a bullfight, not something so good as the approach to the Plaza Mexico, but good, let us say, like the entrance into El Toreo of Mexico City, another architectural monstrosity, also with seats painted, as I remember, in rose-pink, and dark, milky sky-blue.

Inside, it was also different this nominating day. On Monday and Tuesday the air had been desultory, no one listened to the speakers, and everybody milled from one easy chatting conversation to another —it had been like a tepid Kaffeeklatsch for fifteen thousand people. But today there was a whip of anticipation in the air, the seats on the floor were filled, the press section was working, and in the gallery people were sitting in the aisles.

Sam Rayburn had just finished nominating Johnson as one came in, and the rebel yells went up, delegates started filing out of their seats and climbing over seats, and a pullulating dance of bodies and bands began to snake through the aisles, the posters jogging and whirling in time to the music. The dun color of the floor (faces, suits, seats and floor boards), so monotonous the first two days, now lit up with life as if an iridescent caterpillar had emerged from a fold of wet leaves. It was more vivid than one had expected, it was right, it felt finally like a convention, and from up close when one got down to the floor (where your presence was illegal and so consummated by sneaking in one time as demonstrators were going out, and again by slipping a five-dollar bill to a guard) the nearness to the demonstrators took on high color, that electric vividness one feels on the side lines of a football game when it is necessary to duck back as the ballcarrier goes by, his face tortured in the concentration of the moment, the thwomp of his tackle as acute as if one had been hit oneself.

That was the way the demonstrators looked on the floor. Nearly all had the rapt, private look of a passion or a tension which would finally be worked off by one's limbs, three hundred football players, everything from seedy delegates with jowl-sweating shivers to livid models, paid for their work that day, but stomping out their beat on the floor with the hypnotic adulatory grimaces of ladies who had lived for Lyndon these last ten years.

Then from the funereal rostrum, whose color was not so rich as mahogany nor so dead as a cigar, came the last of the requests for the delegates to take their seats. The seconding speeches began, one minute each; they ran for three and four, the minor-league speakers running on the longest as if the electric antenna of television was the lure of the Sirens, leading them out. Bored cheers applauded their concluding Götterdämmerungen and the nominations were open again. A favorite son, a modest demonstration, five seconding speeches, tedium.

Next was Kennedy's occasion. Governor Freeman of Minnesota made the speech. On the second or third sentence his television prompter jammed, an accident. Few could be aware of it at the moment; the speech seemed merely flat and surprisingly void of bravura. He was obviously no giant of extempore. Then the demonstration. Well-run, bigger than Johnson's, jazzier, the caliber of the costumes and decorations better chosen: the placards were broad enough, "Let's Back Jack," the floats were garish, particularly a papier-mâché or plastic balloon of Kennedy's head, six feet in diameter, which had nonetheless the slightly shrunken, over-red, rubbery look of a toy for practical jokers in one of those sleazy off—Times Square magic-and-gimmick stores; the band was suitably corny; and yet one had the impression this demonstration had been designed by some hands-to-hip interior decorator who said, "Oh, joy, let's have fun, let's make this *true* beer hall."

Besides, the personnel had something of the Kennedy *élan,* those paper hats designed to look like straw boaters with Kennedy's face on the crown, and small photographs of him on the ribbon, those hats which had come to symbolize the crack speed of the Kennedy team, that Madison Avenue cachet which one finds in bars like P. J. Clarke's, the elegance always giving its subtle echo of the Twenties so that the raccoon coats seem more numerous than their real count, and the colored waistcoats are measured by the charm they would have drawn from Scott Fitzgerald's eye. But there, it occurred to one for the first time that Kennedy's middle name was just that, Fitzgerald, and the tone of his crack lieutenants, the unstated style, was true to Scott. The legend of Fitzgerald had an army at last, formed around the self-image in the mind of every superior Madison Avenue opportunist that he was hard, he was young, he was In, his conversation was lean as wit, and if the work was not always scrupulous, well the style could aspire. If there came a good day . . . he could meet the occasion.

The Kennedy snake dance ran its thirty lively minutes, cheered its seconding speeches, and sat back. They were so sure of winning, there had been so many victories before this one, and this one had been scouted and managed so well, that hysteria could hardly be the mood. Besides, everyone was waiting for the Stevenson barrage which should be at least diverting. But now came a long tedium. Favorite sons were nominated, fat mayors shook their hips, seconders told the word to constituents back in Ponderwaygot County, treacly demonstrations tried to hold the floor, and the afternoon went by; Symington's hour came and went, a good demonstration, good as Johnson's (for good cause—they had pooled their demonstrators). More favorite sons, Governor Docking of Kansas declared "a genius" by one of his lady speakers in a tense go-back-to-religion voice. The hours went by, two, three, four hours, it seemed forever before they would get to Stevenson. It was evening when Senator Eugene McCarthy of Minnesota got up to nominate him.

The gallery was ready, the floor was responsive, the demonstrators were milling like bulls in their pen waiting for the *toril* to fly open—it would have been hard not to wake the crowd up, not to make a good speech. McCarthy made a great one. Great it was by the measure of convention oratory, and he held the crowd like a matador, timing their *oles!*, building them up, easing them back, correcting any sag in attention, gathering their emotion, discharging it, creating new emotion on the wave of the last, driving his passes tighter and tighter as he readied for the kill. "Do not reject this man who made us all proud to be called Democrats, do not leave this prophet without honor in his own party." One had not heard a speech like this since 1948 when Vito Marcantonio's voice, his harsh, shrill, bitter, street urchin's voice screeched through the loud-speakers at Yankee Stadium and lashed seventy thousand people into an uproar.

"There was only one man who said let's talk sense to the American

people," McCarthy went on, his muleta furled for the *naturales*.
"There was only one man who said let's talk sense to the American
people," he repeated. "He said the promise of America is the promise
of greatness. This was his call to greatness. . . . Do not forget this
man. . . . Ladies and Gentlemen, I present to you not the favorite
son of one state, but the favorite son of the fifty states, the favorite son
of every country he has visited, the favorite son of every country which
has not seen him but is secretly thrilled by his name." Bedlam. The
kill. "Ladies and Gentlemen, I present to you Adlai Stevenson of Illinois." Ears and tail. Hooves and bull. A roar went up like the roar one
heard the day Bobby Thomson hit his home run at the Polo Grounds
and the Giants won the pennant from the Dodgers in the third playoff
game of the 1951 season. The demonstration cascaded onto the floor,
the gallery came to its feet, the Sports Arena sounded like the inside of
a marching drum. A tidal pulse of hysteria, exaltation, defiance, exhilaration, anger and roaring desire flooded over the floor. The cry which
had gone up on McCarthy's last sentence had not paused for breath in
five minutes, and troop after troop of demonstrators jammed the floor
(the Stevenson people to be scolded the next day for having collected
floor passes and sent them out to bring in new demonstrators) and still
the sound mounted. One felt the convention coming apart. There was a
Kennedy girl in the seat in front of me, the Kennedy hat on her head, a
dimpled healthy brunette; she had sat silently through McCarthy's
speech, but now, like a woman paying her respects to the power of natural thrust, she took off her hat and began to clap herself. I saw a
writer I knew in the next aisle; he had spent a year studying the Kennedy machine in order to write a book on how a nomination is won. If
Stevenson stampeded the convention, his work was lost. Like a reporter at a mine cave-in I inquired the present view of the widow.
"Who can think," was the answer, half frantic, half elated, "just watch
it, that's all." I found a cool one, a New York reporter, who smiled in
rueful respect. "It's the biggest demonstration I've seen since Wendell
Willkie's in 1940," he said, and added, "God, if Stevenson takes it, I
can wire my wife and move the family on to Hawaii."

"I don't get it."

"Well, every story I wrote said it was locked up for Kennedy."

Still it went on, twenty minutes, thirty minutes, the chairman could
hardly be heard, the demonstrators refused to leave. The lights were
turned out, giving a sudden theatrical shift to the sense of a crowded

church at midnight, and a new roar went up, louder, more passionate than anything heard before. It was the voice, it was the passion, if one insisted to call it that, of everything in America which was defeated, idealistic, innocent, alienated, outside and Beat, it was the potential voice of a new third of the nation whose psyche was ill from cultural malnutrition, it was powerful, it was extraordinary, it was larger than the decent, humorous, finicky, half-noble man who had called it forth, it was a cry from the Thirties when Time was simple, it was a resentment of the slick technique, the oiled gears, and the superior generals of Fitzgerald's Army; but it was also—and for this reason one could not admire it altogether, except with one's excitement—it was also the plea of the bewildered who hunger for simplicity again, it was the adolescent counterpart of the boss's depression before the unpredictable dynamic of Kennedy as President, it was the return to the sentimental dream of Roosevelt rather than the approaching nightmare of history's oncoming night, and it was inspired by a terror of the future as much as a revulsion of the present.

Fitz's Army held; after the demonstration was finally down, the convention languished for ninety minutes while Meyner and others were nominated, a fatal lapse of time because Stevenson had perhaps a chance to stop Kennedy if the voting had begun on the echo of the last cry for him, but in an hour and a half depression crept in again and emotions spent, the delegates who had wavered were rounded into line. When the vote was taken, Stevenson had made no gains. The brunette who had taken off her hat was wearing it again, and she clapped and squealed when Wyoming delivered the duke and Kennedy was in. The air was sheepish, like the mood of a suburban couple who forgive each other for cutting in and out of somebody else's automobile while the country club dance is on. Again, tonight, no miracle would occur. In the morning the papers would be moderate in their description of Stevenson's last charge.

Exercise Questions

PART ONE: *The Discovery of the Self*

1. Of Presumption, MICHEL DE MONTAIGNE (pp. 5–33)

1. In what way is the title of this essay especially appropriate to all autobiographical essays?
2. How would you describe the tone of this piece? the attitudes which determine the tone?
3. What is the function of the numerous allusions to history and past literature? Are such allusions any longer viable in the essay?
4. What are the virtues Montaigne is willing to grant himself? What strategy is involved in his beginning with his weaknesses and then passing on to his strengths?
5. What are Montaigne's chief objections to "our absurd educational system"? What would he desire in its place? How would he judge the system under which you have been educated?

2. The Crack-Up, F. SCOTT FITZGERALD (pp. 33–38)

1. Do these comments seem to you merely jottings in a journal or do they finally add up to something like a true essay? Where is their unity to be found?
2. What attitude toward the self is revealed here? what attitude toward humanity in general? Does the bleakness of that attitude seem to be the product of a particular personality, a particular age—or

do you find in it some applicability to the human situation always?

3. Does Fitzgerald seem to you to get bogged down in feeling sorry for himself or is he able to rise above his own predicament to a large philosophical point of view?

4. Try to show how the metaphor of a "crack-up" is developed throughout this passage.

3. The Revolver in the Corner Cupboard, GRAHAM GREENE (pp. 39–43)

1. What is the particular kind of love that is being examined and commented on in this essay? What seems to be the author's attitude toward that kind of love at the moment of writing this piece? What possible connection does he allude to between this kind of feeling and a religious one?

2. What is the writer's attitude toward the self he was at the time of the events he is describing?

3. For all its extravagant features, does the experience described here seem to you quite peculiar or one with more general application to other lives in other places?

4. What tricks of style does the author use to heighten the emotional effect and to give a certain portentousness of tone to his prose?

5. In what ways does this piece resemble a story as much as an essay?

4. A Visit to Grandpa's, DYLAN THOMAS (pp. 43–48)

1. What role is played in this essay by the recurrent descriptions of dreams?

2. How are the tone and feeling influenced by the persistent use of unusual metaphors? Which metaphors seem to you especially apt and striking? Why?

3. Does it seem to you useful to think of this prose as "poetic"? What do you mean when you use such a term? Compare its feeling and effects with such conversational prose styles as Gertrude Stein's.

4. With whom are we supposed to sympathize and whom believe at

the end, Grandpa or his neighbors? How does Thomas determine our attitudes in this regard?

5. What is revealed of the narrator's changing self in this account of his grandfather?

5. Stranger in the Village, JAMES BALDWIN (pp. 49–60)

1. What notions about the relationship of Europe and America emerge from this essay?
2. What notions about the special relationship of the American Negro to Europe are suggested?
3. In what way does his European experience illuminate for Baldwin his situation at home in the United States?
4. What special problems lie in the way of a Negro's attempts to discover himself? Would this apply equally to other minorities?
5. How does Baldwin keep his piece from becoming merely an editorial on the "Negro Question"? How does he personalize and humanize it?

6. *From* The Autobiography of Alice B. Toklas, GERTRUDE STEIN (pp. 61–68)

1. Do you have the sense that what is being said in this essay about Hemingway, for instance, is quite literally true?
2. Check what Hemingway has to say about Gertrude Stein in *Death in the Afternoon* and see what feelings underlie their estimates of each other.
3. What seem to you to be the motives behind the descriptions of people in this essay? Do such motives seem to you compatible with the production of literature? Is there any motive which cannot produce literature?
4. What image of Gertrude Stein and her world emerges from her images of other people?
5. What gives special vividness and force to her prose?
6. What is the point of pretending that this is the autobiography of her companion rather than herself?

PART TWO: *The Discovery of Place*

7. Soirée in Hollywood, HENRY MILLER (pp. 72–81)

1. What do you make of the offhand style, or rather non-style, of this essay? What is the point of the simple, rather monotonous sentences, the slang ("old geezer"), the clichés of conversation ("three sheets to the wind") and the rather commonplace similes ("running around like a wet hen")? What feeling are they trying to communicate? What assurance are they aimed at giving the reader?

2. How do President McKinley and Mr. Smith's new boarding house manage to get into the middle of a dinner-table conversation in Hollywood? What is the effect of introducing them without transition?

3. Do you find the reported conversation of the author with the drunken "old geezer" funny? What is Miller trying to do in his responses to this pathetic character?

4. Why is the friend of the writer, Alred Perlès, mentioned as the essay approaches its conclusion? What standard or set of values is Perlès apparently intended to represent?

5. Shortly after the Marquis de Sade looked out of the windows of the Bastille in the scene Miller evokes, the French Revolution began. Why does such a scene with such an aftermath seem especially relevant to Miller in Hollywood?

8. Princeton, JOHN PEALE BISHOP (pp. 81–91)

1. What role does irony play in this essay? Quote some examples demonstrating Bishop's ability to imply a meaning quite different from the one he seems to be stating.

2. Does the constant play of irony over the subject matter make it difficult to tell what the author's final attitude is toward the issues he raises? What in fact *is* it? How can you be sure?

3. Tom D'Invilliers is actually Bishop himself. The name is one given his fictional prototype by Scott Fitzgerald in the novel quoted in the essay. What is the point of the literary reference implicit in calling himself by this fictional name?

4. In what sense can a university be considered a home place, that is, the place through or against which a man defines himself? Does one get out of this essay not only a sense of Princeton, but of the Princeton man, of a particular Princeton man called John Peale Bishop? Could a large, co-educational, State University be dealt with in the same way? Explain.

5. Does the whole essay prepare us for the final sentence; or does that sentence seem merely a wisecrack, an epigrammatic and pleasantly humorous way of bringing things to a close?

9. Audubon's Happy Land, KATHERINE ANNE PORTER (pp. 91–99)

1. What do you take to be the meaning of the phrase near the opening of this essay: "unfold almost at once into grace and goodness"? What two meanings are commonly attached to the word "grace"? Do both seem relevant here? How?

2. Why is Audubon so frequently mentioned in this piece? Is it sufficient explanation merely to point out that he lived in St. Francisville? What is the link between him and St. Francis? between both and the "grace and goodness" alluded to above?

3. Why is the possible discovery of oil mentioned as a threat? What assumptions about the Good Life underlie the author's attitudes on this subject?

10. The Hustlers, NELSON ALGREN (pp. 99–103)

1. Compare the use of slang and ordinary speech, the deliberate grammatical laxness in Algren's essay, with similar devices in Miller's.

2. In what sense can this prose piece be called a poem? What effect is gained by juxtaposing such passages as "waters restlessly, with every motion, slipping out of used colors for new" and "they were out to make a fast buck off whoever was standing nearest . . ."?

3. What sort of man are we presumably to imagine speaking these words, striking these attitudes?

4. What is Algren's attitude toward reform? toward Chicago? toward our present social system? Can you find any connection between these attitudes and the writer's handling of grammar and prose style?

11. The Open Street, ALFRED KAZIN (pp. 104–11)

1. Why does Kazin use the words "rage" "tenderness" and "regret" to set the tone of this essay? What later specific descriptions or memories justify each term? Why does he speak only of the "tenderness" as unexpected?

2. List some characteristic metaphors and similes used to establish the mood of this essay. Point out how each contributes to the final feeling of the piece.

3. What is *new* in the Brownsville to which the essayist returns? How have international affairs touched its life? Do they seem to you to have made any *essential* difference?

4. What does the word "Gentile" really seem to have meant to Kazin in his boyhood? Did it merely describe people who were not Jews? What relationship do *his* Jews have to the stereotype of the Jew as successful, rich, master of his own and other men's fates?

5. What role and meaning do the Negroes and Gypsies have in this essay? How do they help define the world Kazin evokes? What is the significance of the Old Testament and Israel, ancient and modern, in defining that world?

6. Is there any way to defend Kazin's dismay at "the project"? Is this mere sentimentality or something more?

12. St. Paul: Home of the Saints, J. F. POWERS (pp. 112–19)

1. Why does the writer prefix to his essay the quotation from F. C. Miller, Ph.D.? What is his attitude toward Miller? How do you know?
2. Check through the material included by the author in his fairly frequent parentheses. What do you think are their functions?
3. List what you consider to be some typical figures of speech used by this writer. What do they reveal about his attitude to St. Paul? about his approach to life in general?
4. Humor of various sorts is essential to this piece. Is it, then, in any sense serious? How are its incidental jokes compatible with its final intent?
5. Why is the figure of Fitzgerald given so much importance in this essay? (What do you remember about him from the selection included in Part One?) Compare his role in this essay and the author's attitude toward him with the role of Whitman and Kazin's attitude in Kazin's essay.

13. Montana: or The End of Jean Jacques Rousseau, LESLIE FIEDLER (pp. 119–28)

1. Why is Rousseau's name mentioned in the subtitle of this essay? In what sense does Montana represent the "end" of something for which he stands?
2. Does it seem to you plausible that certain cultural conditions can produce certain kinds of faces? Or do you find it easier to believe that the so-called "Montana Face" is the product of the blending of certain racial stocks?
3. Do the reactions of this essayist strike you as the sort of observations possible only to a newcomer in a place, or do they seem to you the kind that might hold up even after years of close acquaintance with the people described? What is the value of any first impressions?
4. How would you describe Mr. Fiedler's style? What sort of effects

does he seem to you to be interested in pursuing? What rhetorical devices does he apparently like to use?

5. What is the function of the long series of allusions to literature, to Goethe and Mark Twain, for instance, and to Romanticism in general? Does there seem to you to be any real point in trying to understand social and political facts in terms of literary concepts?

14. *From* Letters from an American Farmer, HECTOR ST. JEAN DE CRÈVECOEUR (pp. 128–41)

1. This passage is, of course, translated from the French; yet there remain traces of the style and, behind the style, of the personality of the author. How would you describe that style and that personality?

2. With what elements in European society does Crèvecoeur favorably compare certain aspects of life in America? In this somewhat stacked comparison, what does he leave out of his implicit account of European life?

3. How much of what he says depends on his identification of the American with the farmer? How many of his observations remain true of us after several decades of urbanization?

4. As you read the accounts of later European visitors, compare their reactions with his. What is the source of the difference? Does it lie chiefly in later American developments or in certain changes in the society of Europe? Or is it simply a question of personal predilections?

5. What does Crèvecoeur seem to assume to be the fundamental principle of human nature? How much of his estimate of our life depends on this assumption?

6. How do you explain Crèvecoeur's constant shifting from "they" to "we" in speaking of Americans?

15. America Is Not Interesting, MATTHEW ARNOLD (pp. 141–49)

1. What fundamental notions about the nature of a good society underlie Arnold's comments on America?

2. What does he really mean by his key word "interesting"? Does it seem to you to express clearly and unequivocally a reliable criterion for judging societies and cultures?

3. What are the connections and resemblances between English and American society as Arnold understands them? How does he explain the differences of worlds so closely related?

4. What sort of man do you picture behind the opinions expressed? In what ways does he seem to you admirable? in what ways limited?

5. "American artists live chiefly in Europe." Is this true? Has it been true at any other period beside the one to which Arnold refers? If our present situation is notably different in this regard, what has made it so?

16. The Spirit of Place, D. H. LAWRENCE (pp. 149–54)

1. How would you describe the tone of this essay? Does it seem to you that Lawrence's style here resembles more the spoken word or the written word? By what devices does Lawrence give this effect? Why does he go out of his way to be *offensive?* Do you feel he is finally sympathetic or hostile to America?

2. Why does Lawrence seem to find the term "land of the free" especially inapplicable to America? How does he define "freedom"?

3. What role does Caliban play in Shakespeare's *The Tempest?* What makes the allusion to him pertinent here?

4. What does Lawrence mean when he sees the American eagle as a "hen-Eagle"?

5. What is the meaning of the phrase "spirit of place" which gives this essay its title? What, according to Lawrence, is the American "spirit of place"?

6. What does Lawrence mean by "IT"? How does he see the American dilemma in terms of this concept?

17. American Cities, JEAN PAUL SARTRE (pp. 155–65)

1. What does Sartre suggest are the real "homes" of Americans? Does his observation seem to you true?
2. What is the view of a city: of what an ideal city might be or at any rate, of what a European city is, against which Sartre measures our American towns? Explain the phrase "our cities are our shells."
3. What metaphors come almost spontaneously to Sartre's mind as he attempts to describe the cities of America? List a few and see if you can deduce from them the kind of feeling that moves him at the deepest levels.
4. To whom does he seem to be speaking in this essay? to what sort of reader? How can you tell?
5. What is it that Sartre finally comes to like, or at least claims to like, in American cities? How would you define the tone in which he expresses his final measured approval: uneasy? condescending? grudging? wholehearted? What specific items in the text can you quote as evidence?

18. Innocents at Home, JACQUES BARZUN (pp. 165–83)

1. When Jacques Barzun speaks of none of America being "art," what is he assuming "art" to mean? Why does he raise the issue anyhow?
2. Why does Barzun believe there can be no "national" American history? What, according to him, is the consequence of this lack?
3. What particular points in this essay seem directed primarily to the European critics of American culture? Which of the European essayists represented in this collection does he manage to answer?
4. Does Barzun's assurance that here "two generations of schooling . . . create social peace" seem to you to be borne out by the facts as you observe them in your home town or read about them in the daily newspapers?

5. Can it be asserted with any degree of fairness that Barzun's piece is an *editorial* rather than a study or a personal response to the American experience? What rhetorical devices, what tricks of style does he use to make his points?

19. America the Beautiful, MARY MC CARTHY (pp. 184–94)

1. What do you understand the author to mean when she remarks that "there were no good Hollywood movies, no good Broadway plays"? From what critical point of view does she seem to be talking? What standards must one assume she is measuring current productions against?
2. What does Miss McCarthy mean by "conditions" in the phrase: "nearly all the 'sights' in America fall under the head of conditions"?
3. Does it seem to you that this piece really defends America, or undercuts it behind the flimsiest pretext of being a defense? How does it compare as an apology with Barzun's essay?
4. The essential method of Miss McCarthy is the use of paradox. Explain the meaning of the term and collect as many examples as you can from her work. What would you say is the *central* paradox on which her defense turns?

PART THREE: *The Discovery of Popular Culture*

20. A Theory of Mass Culture, DWIGHT MACDONALD (pp. 200–18)

1. Is Macdonald approaching the problems of mass culture from a "scientific" or a "literary" point of view? What do you take to be

the advantages and disadvantages of his method? Which sort of approach would you prefer to read? Why?

2. Why does Macdonald prefer the term "mass culture" to "popular culture"? What is the relation of both these terms to the German word *kitsch?*

3. Why does Macdonald consider the magazine *Life* a typical product of mass culture?

4. What does the switch from "idols of production" to "idols of consumption" have to do with the general phenomenon Macdonald is discussing? What basic changes in society are reflected in this shift?

5. Macdonald's article is chiefly concerned with the mass arts, but he refers briefly, too, to the effects of mass culture on the social sciences. What is his criticism of contemporary sociology?

21. Movie Chronicle: The Westerner, ROBERT WARSHOW (pp. 218–33)

1. What is the relevance of the quoted sonnet from Shakespeare to the major theme of this essay?

2. Why does the writer find such ambitious westerns as *Shane, High Noon,* etc. not "right"? What does he assume a western must do to be true to itself?

3. What does the author feel to be the moral value of the western? What does he think is its aesthetic value?

4. What is the point of the carefully worked out series of comparisons between the western and the gangster movie? Do such comparisons seem to you to shed much light on the subject?

5. What does the writer mean by "honor"? Do you believe his assertion that in our time this value survives chiefly, or perhaps only, in the western?

6. What effect is achieved by writing so gravely, so literarily about a subject generally treated condescendingly or in an offhand manner?

22. The Guilty Vicarage, W. H. AUDEN (pp. 233–44)

1. What view of the nature of a work of art is implicit in Auden's statement that the detective story does not belong to this category?
2. Why is Aristotle referred to early in this piece? With what subject did the earlier Greek writer concern himself, much as Auden concerns himself here with the detective story? What interesting or rewarding comparisons can be made between the subject of his study and that of Auden's?
3. What are the "classic unities" to which Auden refers?
4. What do you make of the constant allusions to religious ideas and concepts? What special light is cast on the detective story when it is associated with theology?
5. Why does Auden call the Quest story (what is it?) the "mirror image" of the detective story?
6. What effect is created by the outline form, the rather dry, analytic tone used by Auden? Does this result in making the subject matter seem dull and respectable? What pleasurable elements (if any) do you find in this essay?

23. *From* The Other Victorians, STEVEN MARCUS (pp. 245–62)

1. What is the difference between pornotopia, as presented in this essay, and a pornographic creation? Can ideal types refer to artistic creations? Is the ideal the formula for a perfect creation? Ought the ideal be mentioned only in reference to abstract cultural phenomena, such as values, interests, art, and creativity in general, rather than the specific manifestations of a culture, such as the novel?
2. What are the differences, according to Marcus, between nonpornographic literature and pornography in regard to intention, form, unities of time and space, setting, emotionality?
3. Does Marcus's suggestion of a computer writing pornographic fic-

tion dismiss the notion of aesthetically as well as sexually satisfying pornography? Is Marcus making any assumptions here?

4. What comparison does the author make between the force of language as used in literature and as used in pornography? Does the use of tabooed words and clichés recall the tabooed act or fantasy more immediately than the more subtle literary devices? (In other words, do you agree that in the workings of the mind, the metaphor may become the literal truth?)

5. Why does the author explicitly point out his lengthy metaphoric parody of the supine woman? Might this offer a clue as to the intent or tone of the whole book?

6. What sort of explanation does the author offer for the rise of pornography? Is it a psychological one? Is it justified? How does he explain the statement, "We are coming to the end of the era in which pornography had a historical meaning and even a historical function"?

7. Marcus offers a psychological description of the writer of pornography. Is it convincing? Might it apply to writers who have occasionally departed from their more usual genres to write pornography? Might it include poets and novelists in general?

24. Pornography, Masturbation, and the Novel, TAYLOR STOEHR (pp. 262–81)

1. What is the author objecting to in Marcus's approach? Is Stoehr's use of references and quotations a remedy or corrective, or do they simply express additional points of view? Does this essay clarify Marcus's in any way?

2. What is the "mind/body problem" as presented in this essay? What does it have to do with sex?

3. Is it valid to make a *moral* distinction between the "authenticity" of sexuality, and the "fantasy" of pornography? Do you then agree with Stoehr or with Marcus or with neither?

4. Discuss the relationship of masturbation to pornography, and possibly to the novel in general—perhaps from the point of view of the "solitary imagination." Consider the relevance of the relationship between memory and fantasy.

5. Rather than considering the pornographic novel to be a subgenre of the utopian novel (as does Marcus), Stoehr considers them both a kind of gothic novel. According to Stoehr's definitions, what are the similarities in technique and content in the utopian and pornographic novel, for example, use of repetition, the question of reality versus dream, the conflict of will and desire.

25. *From* Blues People, LE ROI JONES (pp. 282–85)

1. What do you gather are the differences between the essay used as an introduction, and an essay used as a chapter of a book?
2. Toward what ends does Jones propose studying blues and jazz music? Can this be a valid anthropological or sociological endeavor, that is, as an undertaking in the social sciences that will arrive at new conclusions, truths, or insights?
3. Jones makes distinctions between the African Negro in America and the American Negro. What are they, and are they particularly relevant currently? If so, why?

26. The Dance of the Long-Legged Fly: On Tom Wolfe's Poise, RICHARD HOGGART (pp. 285–97)

1. What, in broad terms, is the author's critical opinion of Tom Wolfe's work? Does it appear consistently the same throughout the essay, or is it progressive? Does this add or detract from the essay?
2. What are some of the techniques Wolfe uses to create his writing style? What does Richard Hoggart say about Wolfe's use of metaphor? How does Hoggart use metaphor?
3. What is meant by "poise" in the essay? How is it related to style? Why does the author call the quote "Okay, it was bogus. . . . But by God the whole thing had style" the most apt epigram for Tom Wolfe's book?
4. Why does the author emphasize the maintenance of a "balance" or of a suspension between two moods in Wolfe's writing? In Hoggart's view, does the suspension ever appear to fail? Do you agree?
5. Do you believe the reader gains a realistic picture of Wolfe from

this essay? Consider the liberal use of quotations from Wolfe and
the author's distance from the American scene, and perhaps the
"argument between defenders of the old 'high culture' and the welcomers of the new."

27. The Situation Today, KINGSLEY AMIS (pp. 297–313)

1. What is the author's tone in the essay? Is it appropriate to the subject? If so, why? What kind of effect do phrases such as "frightfully
   significant" and "dreadfully fluent" have on the tone?

2. Why does the author consider the two excerpts he quotes to have
   repulsive style?

3. What is the evolution of science-fiction writing as Kingsley Amis
   conceives it? To what extent does he find it necessary to define the
   subclassifications of science fiction? Why?

4. What does the author mean by the "admonitory utopia" form of
   contemporary science fiction?

5. Do you agree with the author that the following characteristics are
   attributable to the mass media: expensiveness, avoidance of the obscure or heterodox, reassuringness, anonymity?

6. Do you agree that the short story is a most, if not the most, convenient form for science fiction? Why do you think so?

7. In the second part, the author states his intentions. What are they?
   Are they fulfilled by his method and procedure?

28. Along the Midway of Mass Culture, MILTON
KLONSKY (pp. 314–31)

1. How is traditional art distinguished from mass culture in this
   essay? Is there a clear-cut distinction between art and nonart that
   can be derived from these definitions? Amplify your opinion.

2. What are some characteristics of satire, in both art and literature?
   In what way can satire contribute to the growth of a mass culture?

3. What does Milton Klonsky offer to be the relationship between
   mass culture and American mythology? Do you believe that the

mythology and archetypes are caused by mass culture or that the mass culture merely reflects the mythology inherent in American life or neither of these? Why?

4. How is mass culture a part of American political, economic, and social phenomena?

5. To what extent are the examples given especially relevant to our contemporary world? Does the character of mass culture ever change?

6. How would you describe the author's tone? How does it compare with Kingsley Amis's? On the strength of this essay, would you venture an opinion of Milton Klonsky's view of the masses? If so, what is it?

29. *From* The Great Comic Book Heroes, JULES FEIFFER (pp. 331–44)

1. How do the brief autobiographical references, including the author's personal feelings, contribute to the theme and style of the essay?

2. Are subject matter and style related? Are they separable or not? Would the discussion be more efficacious if they were one or the other?

3. What, in the author's opinion, is the definition and purpose of junk? Are these views applicable only to children or to other or all segments of the population?

4. What is a possible explanation for the current change in the popular attitude toward comic books from samples of youthful corruption to samples of youthful innocence?

PART FOUR: *The Discovery of High Culture*

30. The Art of Fiction, HENRY JAMES (pp. 348–68)

1. What is the significance of the word "art" in the title of this essay? In what way is it connected with James' feeling that discussion of

the novel has at last in his time become possible? In what way is it bound up with his conception of "form"?

2. In what way does James deal with the difficult question of "morality" in fiction? What relationship does he postulate between "morality" and "form"?

3. James is usually regarded as one of the truly great stylists of fiction. Is there any evidence of his skill in the essay before you? Give examples. What would you expect his fictional style to be like?

4. What, according to James, is a novel? What help to us, if any, is such a general definition as he gives? Does it provide us with any real assistance in our attempts to come to terms with the particular novels we read?

5. When James asks of the novel that it be "interesting," is he using the term with the same meaning it had for Matthew Arnold in his essay on America? Does it seem to you useful to apply to either novels or nations a criterion that can be equally applied to both?

31. A Humble Remonstrance, ROBERT LOUIS STEVENSON (pp. 368–77)

1. On what grounds does Stevenson propose to substitute for James' term "the art of fiction" the alternative "the art of narrative"?

2. What is his response to James' plea for "truth" in the novel and to the latter's contention that the novelist must "compete with life"? How does Stevenson move from his objection to James on this score to his own central definition of the function of the novel? Does he use the word "emasculate" of the novel apologetically? scornfully? proudly?

3. Why does Stevenson feel it profitable to divide the novel into various sub-classes? What would James have said to such a device?

4. To what sort of audiences does Stevenson appear to be addressing his remarks? To whom does he accuse James of addressing his? Does his charge seem to you justified?

5. Compare the style and strategy of the two essayists: the rhetoric they use, the kind of organization, the tone. What sort of artist and

on what terms with the popular audience would you judge each to be on the basis of these selections?

32. Hawthorne and His Mosses, HERMAN MELVILLE (pp. 377–92)

1. Both Melville and Hawthorne are, of course, writers themselves; and as such they criticize in a special way, i.e., in light of what they themselves were trying to do in their own work. How does this essay illustrate the special advantages and limitations of the writer-critic?

2. What do you find most striking in Melville's own style? Do you ever feel his self-conscious pursuit of rhythms and effects gets in the way of the critical analysis in which he is engaged? What qualities of his diction clearly distinguish him from writers of our own day?

3. What does Melville mean when he asserts that "the names of all fine writers are fictitious ones"?.

4. What commentary on popular taste is implicit in the phrase "it is the least part of genius that attracts admirers"?

5. Why does Melville believe that readers in his time should make a special point of celebrating the achievement of American writers? In what does he believe the true Americanism of the American author consists?

6. "For genius, all over the world, stands hand in hand, and one shock of recognition runs the whole circle round." Why does the "shock of recognition" take effect in some cases and not in others?

33. Was Walt Whitman the Father of the American Baby?, WYNDHAM LEWIS (pp. 393–96)

1. Why does Lewis propound the notion of the American as a baby, if, as he says, "this cannot, in reality, describe the great mass of the population of America"? Is his disclaimer not quite candid?

2. Do you know the poetry of Whitman? Can you quote passages which would sustain Lewis' description of him? passages which would challenge it?

3. What were Lewis' reactions to New York? Why was he glad to find that New Yorkers did not share his view of their city?

4. What does New York have to do with Whitman? Why do these two passages follow each other? Does Kazin's earlier essay cast any light on this problem?

34. Some Lines from Whitman, RANDALL JARRELL (pp. 396–409)

1. What assumptions about the nature of poetry and of poetic excellence underlie Jarrell's resolve to quote extensively from Whitman in defending him?

2. In what sense does Jarrell use the word "witty" in speaking of Whitman's verse? In what way is Jarrell's own approach "witty"?

3. What point does Jarrell make about the nature of Whitman's badness? about the quality of his failures in language? What do you take Jarrell to mean when he says of one of Whitman's coined words "why, it's as bad as *explicate!*"? What's wrong with "explicate"?

4. What does Jarrell mean when he speaks of Whitman's ability to "present"? Henry James is quoted as advocating such a method in prose. Is "presentation" a quality common to both at their best? more at home in one or the other?

5. What is essentially at issue in this essay is the question of whether there can be literary greatness without a high degree of selection and organization. What conclusion on this subject does Jarrell draw from an examination of Whitman? on what grounds precisely?

6. Does Jarrell anywhere in this essay meet Lewis' thematic and moral criticism of Whitman? Do you believe it possible to make a final judgment of a poet merely on the basis of his technique and his ability to handle language? Do you believe Jarrell is trying to do this?

35. Huck and Oliver, W. H. AUDEN (pp. 410–15)

1. This was delivered orally and *ex tempore*. What do you find in its over-all structure or in the way its sentences are composed which seems to derive from the way in which it was given and which makes it different from written essays?

2. What does Auden mean when he refers to himself as "sufficiently much of a liberal optimist"? How does this influence his point of view in the present essay? How is that point of view further influenced by the fact that Auden is a naturalized American citizen of British birth?

3. What is Auden's understanding of Huck's attitude toward nature? society? Is it plausible?

4. Explain Auden's understanding of the *tone* of the passage in which Huck decides to run away with Jim. How would you describe that tone? What does Auden mean by "moral improvisation" and "amateur moral decision"?

5. What real value does there seem to you to be in the comparison of Huck and Oliver Twist? Huck and the "Artful Dodger"? What is the difference between the American boy and the two English ones? How does Auden understand this to illuminate the differences between American and English national character?

36. Shakespeare, or the Discovery of Moby-Dick, CHARLES OLSON (pp. 415–37)

1. How would you describe Olson's style? Consider the fragmented sentences, the essay's structure.

2. Many essays use a historical analysis to present their ideas. What method of analysis does Charles Olson use? Why do you think he does this?

3. Olson uses many examples to illustrate the meanings of "black madness," "white madness," "right reason," and their relations to God. Explain these terms.

4. What in the author's view is the particular connection (or connections) between the tragedy of *Moby Dick* and American democracy? On the other hand, what is universal about the tragedy?

37. Fenimore Cooper's Leatherstocking Novels, D. H. LAWRENCE (pp. 438–53)

1. How does the style of this essay compare with Charles Olson's style? What are similarities and differences in, for instance, language, method of literary analysis, tone of voice?
2. What picture emerges of the man Cooper? of his wife?
3. How does Lawrence reconcile the picture of the man with the artist, creator of the hero Natty Bumppo?
4. Aside from his specific references to the content of Cooper's novels, what does Lawrence say about America and Americans? American democracy? American myth? American dichotomies?
5. Using Lawrence's examples and commentary, explain why the Leatherstocking novels are called "a decrescendo of reality, and a crescendo of beauty."

PART FIVE: *The Discovery of the Future*

38. *From* Love's Body, NORMAN O. BROWN (pp. 457–73)

1. How are the terms "introjection" and "projection" used in this context?
2. What are some of the perspectives from which a "person" or "self" is identified and defined?
3. What is the purpose of using nonpsychoanalytical concepts such as property and corporation? Is the reason akin to that applied to using a wide variety of reference sources? Comment.
4. Does the presentation suit the subject matter? Why?

5. What is the "reality principle"? Does it conflict with the belief in omnipotent thought? If so, how?

6. What sort of effect do you think Brown is after in splitting the essay up into short paragraphs rather than writing an unbroken continuous discussion? What is the effect of introducing references to other works between such paragraphs? What peculiarities do you find in the actual sentence structure used by Brown? How do these various stylistic devices help to reinforce his meaning?

39. Education Automation, R. BUCKMINSTER FULLER (pp. 474–89)

1. What changes in the purposes of education does Buckminster Fuller propose? How are they affected by great technological advance?

2. What is the separation between the literary and the scientific worlds? How does industrialization enter into the problem?

3. How does the argument describing specialization and its consequences proceed? Is it both logical and justified?

4. What is the value of comprehensive thinking? What example does Fuller offer as an illustration of this?

5. How does architecture reflect and enhance the philosophy that is being offered?

6. This selection from Buckminster Fuller was in fact originally delivered in spoken form. Do you find any evidence of this in the text, and does it seem to you to work for or against more immediate communication?

40. Blondie, MARSHALL MC LUHAN (pp. 489–93)

1. What point is the author making with the essay? What is a possible reason for the essay's inclusion in this section, "The Discovery of the Future," rather than in the "Popular Culture" section?

2. What version of the American myth is depicted by these archetypes of the industrial man and wife?

3. Why does the author feel Dagwood has become the focus of the public's attention? What is the pathos of the citizen-clown?

4. Though *Blondie* itself belongs to an era now gone, there is an attempt on McLuhan's part to prophesy what the children and grandchildren of these old comic-strip characters would be like in the light of recent events. Does his prophecy seem to you accurate or not?

41. The New Mutants, LESLIE FIEDLER (pp. 493–512)

1. How have we arrived at a "politics of silence"? What does this phrase mean?

2. Explain the current generation's antipathy toward the Christian tradition. How does this involve the values of humanism, technology, Marxism, and history?

3. Why is the new generation referred to as new "mutants" and "barbarians"? Is the author being pejorative?

4. How does Fiedler's view of the effects of automation compare with Buckminster Fuller's?

5. What is Fiedler's concept of the antihero antimale? What is the new male role? Where has it come from?

6. Is there anything in Fiedler's concluding remarks concerning insanity that is similar to Brown's exposition (Selection 39)? Discuss.

42. *From* Growing Up Absurd, PAUL GOODMAN (pp. 513–36)

1. What is the primary theme of Goodman's essay? How does it relate to the corruption in the system, the inadequacy of its mechanisms, and the human beings it produces?

2. What is the concept of "useless work"? Is it inherent only in the capitalist economy?

3. What is the distinction between the social human being and his human nature? Why, according to the essay, is it necessary to make

the distinction when referring to a person growing up in a particular culture?

4. Do you believe the author's argument is convincingly presented? Is it because of his logic, his technique, or both?

5. Does the author have an accurate view of the feelings of modern youth? Are his generalizations about them appropriate for the subject discussed? What are the reasons for your opinion?

43. The Third Presidential Paper—The Existential Hero: Superman Comes to the Supermarket, NORMAN MAILER (pp. 536–67)

1. What is the meaning of "existential" as used in this essay? of the "second American life"? of our "underground history"?

2. What method or methods of presentation does Norman Mailer employ? What is the purpose of the digressions? Does the description of Adlai Stevenson at the conclusion of the essay divert from the author's stated intention? Why?

3. Do you feel the essay might move the intellectual community in the direction of Mailer's stated purpose? Does literature have the potentiality to influence in this way, that is, toward action?

4. Is Mailer's use of descriptive detail unusual? Is his use of metaphor unusual? If so, why do you think so?

5. Can the reader glean the author's true political sympathies from this essay? Comment.